Medieval History

General Editors
JOHN BLAIR   HELENA HAMEROW

Gold and Gilt, Pots and Pins

MEDIEVAL HISTORY AND ARCHAEOLOGY

General Editors

John Blair   Helena Hamerow

The volumes in this series bring together archaeological, historical, and visual methods to offer new approaches to aspects of medieval society, economy, and material culture. The series seeks to present and interpret archaeological evidence in ways readily accessible to historians, while providing a historical perspective and context for the material culture of the period.

PREVIOUSLY PUBLISHED IN THIS SERIES

THE ICONOGRAPHY OF EARLY ANGLO-SAXON COINAGE
Anna Gannon

EARLY MEDIEVAL SETTLEMENTS
The Archaeology of Rural Communities in North-West Europe 400–900
Helena Hamerow

GOLD AND GILT, POTS AND PINS

Possessions and People in Medieval Britain

DAVID A. HINTON

OXFORD
UNIVERSITY PRESS

Great Clarendon Street, Oxford OX2 6DP

Oxford University Press is a department of the University of Oxford.
It furthers the University's objective of excellence in research, scholarship,
and education by publishing worldwide in

Oxford New York

Auckland Cape Town Dar es Salaam Hong Kong Karachi
Kuala Lumpur Madrid Melbourne Mexico City Nairobi
New Delhi Shanghai Taipei Toronto

With offices in

Argentina Austria Brazil Chile Czech Republic France Greece
Guatemala Hungary Italy Japan South Korea Poland Portugal
Singapore Switzerland Thailand Turkey Ukraine Vietnam

Published in the United States
by Oxford University Press Inc., New York

© David A. Hinton 2005

The moral rights of the author(s) have been asserted
Database right Oxford University Press (maker)

First published 2005
First published in paperback 2006

All rights reserved. No part of this publication may be reproduced,
stored in a retrieval system, or transmitted, in any form or by any means,
without the prior permission in writing of Oxford University Press,
or as expressly permitted by law, or under terms agreed with the appropriate
reprographics rights organization. Enquiries concerning reproduction
outside the scope of the above should be sent to the Rights Department,
Oxford University Press, at the address above

You must not circulate this book in any other binding or cover
and you must impose this same condition on any acquirer

British Library Cataloguing in Publication Data

Data available

Library of Congress Cataloging in Publication Data

Data available

Typeset by SNP Best-set Typesetter Ltd., Hong Kong
Printed in Great Britain
on acid-free paper by
Biddles Ltd, King's Lynn

ISBN 0-19-926453-8 0-19-992645-X
ISBN 0-19-926454-6 (Pbk.) 978-0-19-9926454-4 (Pbk.)

1 3 5 7 9 10 8 6 4 2

Preface and Acknowledgements

My interest in medieval artefacts began more than forty years ago when I had the good fortune to be accepted by the late Rupert Bruce-Mitford as a temporary assistant in the British Museum. Similar luck led to an appointment at the Ashmolean Museum, Oxford, where I looked after the Alfred Jewel (Hinton 1973). Although it is now thirty years since I left there, I have continued to work on medieval metal objects as opportunities presented themselves (e.g. Hinton 1990, 1996, 2000). This book therefore draws on long experience, though it will be obvious from the Bibliography how much I owe to the work of others; in most cases, the debt is directly proportional to the number of entries (e.g. J. Cherry, J. Graham-Campbell, and L. Webster), but the endnotes reveal how much I have also drawn from a few authors who have written fundamental books (e.g. G. Egan and R. Lightbown). All those who knew her will understand why I feel it appropriate to record here the contribution to studies of medieval material culture made by the late Sue Margeson of Norwich Castle Museum, who was always so generous in sharing her knowledge.

The first draft of the book was written in the second half of 2002 and the first half of 2003, during sabbatical leave; I am grateful to the University of Southampton for allowing me to defer one leave entitlement so that I could work on it for a whole year almost without interruption, and for financial help towards the cost of illustrations.

The book benefits greatly from the drawings of Nick Griffiths, and it has been a pleasure to resume a collaboration that began at Winchester in the mid-1970s. I have also been fortunate to be able to draw on the excellent photographs taken for the Portable Antiquities Scheme for many colour plates, which has enabled me to reproduce images that are less familiar than some. (Similarly, I have tried in the later part of the book when feasible to use documentary examples that have not been quoted by other writers so far as I know.) In selecting pictures, I have found it very difficult to know whether to reproduce images at their actual size, as so many have exquisite detail that deserves detailed enlargement; on the whole, however, I have felt it better to show these things at their real size, even though it may look a little bizarre to see a lead badge looking rather crude at full size when compared to a gold brooch. Some things have had to be reduced, of course, because of the page size, and a few I have decided to enlarge because their detail seemed likely to be lost altogether otherwise.

Copyright permission given for illustrations is acknowledged in the captions, but I have been helped to collect photographs and drawings both by a large number of friends and by people whom I have never met but many of whom I hope that I can now consider friends: Vivien Adams, Kay Ainsworth, John Allan, David Allen, Paul Backhouse, Roger Bland, Thorn Brett, Michael Burden, Louise Bythell, Thomas Cadbury, Bernice Cardy, John Clark, Julie Cochrane, Maggie Cox, Hannah Crowdy, Jan Dunbar, Bruce Eagles, Helen Geake, Mark Hall, Richard Hall, Stephen Harrison, Jill Ivy, Ralph Jackson, David Jennings, Adrian James, Alan Lane, Christopher Loveluck, Arthur MacGregor, Victoria Newton-Davies, Helen Nicholson, Ken Penn, Daniel Pett, Mark Redknap, Paul Robinson, Peter Saunders, Roland Smith, Shovati Smith, Judith Stones, Tracey Walker, Karen Wardley, Leslie Webster, and David Williams. I am also grateful to the publishers of *Anglo-Saxon England*, *Archaeological Journal*, *Britannia*, and *Medieval Archaeology*, of the East Anglian Archaeology and the Hampshire Field Club and Archaeological Society monographs, and of the Council for British Archaeology research report series for permission to reproduce illustrations direct from published work.

The launch of the Oxford University Press's 'Medieval History and Archaeology' series provided the opportunity for this book to appear, and I am grateful to Ruth Parr for commissioning it, to the joint editors John Blair and Helena Hamerow for sanctioning it, to the referees of the proposal for recommending it, to the two anonymous readers (one of whom remains frustratingly unguessed) of the draft for approving it, and to Louisa Lapworth for seeing it through to publication.

Contents

List of Colour Plates   viii
List of Figures   ix

    Introduction   1

1. Adapting to Life Without the Legions   7
2. Expressions of the Elites   39
3. Kings and Christianity   75
4. Alfred *et al.*   108
5. An Epoch of New Dynasties   141
6. Feudal Modes   171
7. Material Culture and Social Display   206
8. The Wars and the Posies   233

    Envoi   260

Endnotes   262
Bibliography   369
Index   429

List of Colour Plates

between pp. 212 and 213

A.1.	Quoit-brooch from Sarre, Kent
A.2.	Equal-arm brooch from Collingbourne Ducis, Wiltshire
B.1.	Composite disc-brooch from Sarre, Kent
B.2.	Composite disc-brooch from Monkton, Kent
B.3.	Sword-pommel from Aldbrough, Yorkshire
B.4.	Pyramid stud from near Bury St Edmunds, Suffolk
B.5.	Seal-ring from near Norwich
C.1.	Smith's tools and scrap from Tattershall Thorpe, Lincolnshire
C.2 and 3.	Gold pendants from *Hamwic*, Southampton
D.	Six brooches from Pentney, Norfolk
E.	Details of the Pentney brooches
F.1 and 2.	Panels from the St Cuthbert stole and maniple
F.3.	Disc from Holberrow Green, Worcestershire
F.4–6.	Finger-rings from South Kyme and West Lindsey, both Lincolnshire, and from Shrewsbury
G.	Jug from Exeter
H.1–3.	Posy-rings from Kirk Deighton, Yorkshire, Alkmonkton, Derbyshire, and North Warnborough, Hampshire
H.4–5.	Iconographic rings from Carisbrooke, Isle of Wight, and Scotton, Lincolnshire
H.6.	Seal-ring from Raglan, Monmouthshire
H.7.	Badge from Chiddingly, East Sussex

List of Figures

1.1.	Late Roman buckle from Stanwick	9
1.2.	Traprain Law hoard	10
1.3.	Patching hoard objects	11
1.4.	Mucking belt-set	14
1.5.	Penannular brooch from Caerwent	17
1.6.	Mould and reconstruction of penannular brooch from Dunadd	19
1.7.	Equal-arm brooch from Collingbourne Ducis	23
1.8.	Great square-headed brooch from Pewsey	24
1.9.	Great square-headed brooch distribution maps	25
1.10.	Button-brooch from Wonston; saucer-brooches from Fairford	26
1.11.	Sword and fittings from Pewsey	30
1.12.	Claw-beaker from Great Chesterford	37
2.1.	Bird-headed penannular brooch moulds from Dunadd	41
2.2.	Annular brooch from Llanbedrgoch	42
2.3.	Pictish silver chain from Whitecleugh	44
2.4.	Norrie's Law hoard	46
2.5.	Motif-piece from Dunadd	47
2.6.	The Hunterston brooch	48
2.7.	Coin-pendants from Faversham	50
2.8.	Balance and weights from Watchfield	52
2.9.	The Snape ring	52
2.10.	Garnets from Tattershall Thorpe	54
2.11.	The Sutton Hoo great gold buckle	55
2.12.	Inlaid iron buckle from Monk Sherborne	56
2.13.	Hanging-bowl from Loveden Hill	59
2.14.	Buckle from Alton	64
2.15.	The Finglesham buckle	66
2.16.	St Cuthbert's cross	68
2.17.	Woman's grave and pendant at Lechlade	69
2.18.	Fittings from Tattershall Thorpe	71
2.19.	Hammers from Tattershall Thorpe	72
2.20.	Tools from Tattershall Thorpe	73
3.1.	*Hamwic* grave and contents	76
3.2.	Finger-ring with inset *solidus* from London	78
3.3.	Composite disc-brooch from Caistor St Edmund	79
3.4.	The St Ninian's Isle hoard	81
3.5.	Seventh-/ninth-century objects	86
3.6.	Ipswich ware and *sceatta* distribution map	90
3.7.	Ipswich-ware sherd	91
3.8.	Inscribed lead plaque from Flixborough	94

3.9.	Other objects from Flixborough	95
3.10.	The Franks Casket	99
3.11.	The Windsor pommel	101
3.12.	The Coppergate helmet	104
3.13.	The Repton cross-shaft	105
4.1.	Two ninth-century royal rings	109
4.2.	The Abingdon sword	111
4.3.	The Fuller brooch	112
4.4.	Strap-end from Cranborne	113
4.5.	Oval brooches from Santon Downham	118
4.6.	Penannular brooch from Orton Scar	121
4.7.	Rings from Red Wharf Bay	122
4.8.	Contents of a man's grave at Ballinaby, Islay	125
4.9.	Contents of a woman's grave at Westness, Rousay	126
4.10.	Four *aestels*	130
4.11.	Objects from late Saxon Winchester	134
4.12.	Anglo-Scandinavian objects from York	137
5.1.	Disc-brooch made or commissioned by Wudeman	144
5.2.	Seal-matrix from Wallingford	146
5.3.	Penannular ring from Oxford	147
5.4.	Mount from Lincoln	148
5.5.	The Skaill hoard	150
5.6.	Object from Pakenham	153
5.7.	Stirrups from Oxford	155
5.8.	Stirrup-mounts and terminals	156
5.9.	The Cheapside hoard	159
5.10.	Spouted pitcher from Oxford	161
5.11.	London shoes	163
5.12.	Knife-scabbard from London	164
5.13.	The St Mary Hill, London, hoard	168
6.1.	Henry I's nightmare	173
6.2.	Spur from Perth	174
6.3.	Romanesque objects from Winchester	176
6.4.	Tripod pitcher from Loughor Castle	177
6.5.	Seal-matrix from Perth	180
6.6.	Stone mould from Perth	181
6.7.	Swivel from Rattray Castle	182
6.8.	Strip and spoon from the Iona hoard	184
6.9.	Aquamanile from Nant Col	186
6.10.	The Lark Hill, Worcester, hoard	189
6.11.	Ring-brooch from York	190
6.12.	Unprovenanced ring-brooch	191
6.13.	The Folkingham brooch	192
6.14.	Pilgrims' badges	194
6.15.	Spangle from Perth	196
6.16.	Rings from Southampton and Llantrithyd	198
6.17.	Horse-harness pendants	202

7.1.	Ring-brooches from the Coventry hoard	207
7.2.	The Canonbie hoard	208
7.3.	Quatrefoil frame-brooch from Rattray Castle	209
7.4.	Secular and shrine badges	210
7.5.	Mirror-case valve from Perth	212
7.6.	Pewter saucer from Southampton	215
7.7.	Ring-brooches from Oxwich Castle and Manchester	219
7.8.	The Dunstable swan	221
7.9.	The Wilton Diptych	225
7.10.	Knife-handle from Perth	230
8.1.	Copper-alloy vessels from Wales	235
8.2.	The Thame hoard finger-rings	239
8.3.	The Fishpool hoard finger-rings	240
8.4.	The Thame ring reverse view	240
8.5.	Jewels from the Fishpool hoard	242
8.6.	Chains and seal-ring from the Fishpool hoard	243
8.7.	Reliquaries from Threave Castle	246
8.8.	Brooch given to New College, Oxford	250
8.9.	Late medieval costume ornaments	252
8.10.	Pilgrims' and family badges	254
8.11.	The Gainsford badge	254

Introduction

The aim of this book is to examine some of the ways in which people in medieval Britain presented themselves. It is primarily about small artefacts, especially jewellery. It says little about costume, although that provided the immediate setting for many of the objects discussed; nor is it a study of buildings, although those provided the backdrop for the people wearing the costume. Nor is it a catalogue. Instead, it considers the reasons for people's decisions to acquire, display, conceal, and discard some of the things that were important to them, and examines how much the wish to acquire, retain, and pass such things on to heirs explains behaviour in the Middle Ages.

The book's approach is chronological, to explore the changes and the reasons for them during the whole of the Middle Ages.[1] It is not restricted to the study of a single group of people, but explores the significance to the whole of society of some of the things available at various times, and the restrictions that limited their acquisition and use. Many of the objects considered and the documents cited relate to the richest or most powerful people, but one of the aims of the book is to consider whether theirs was an example that others invariably sought to follow, or whether at different times different aspirations were expressed, showing social disharmony and disunity.

Because the emphasis of the book is on the artefacts that people used in order to show their affiliations and status,[2] it says little about such things as household items. Locks and keys, for instance, were in most periods primarily functional; important as they are for showing the need for security in medieval buildings, they were rarely made with an eye on what people were going to think of those who turned them—except in the early period, they do not seem to have been regarded as things that served to define their owners' social place or aspirations. Details of weapons, armour, and horse trappings do not get much attention either, since their finer points would have mattered only to a very privileged few. On the other hand, drinking-vessels and tableware are included, because they were very often used in ways that made them visible and a direct reflection of social standing. Kitchenware is rarely mentioned, except when the food and drink prepared or stored in it changed in ways that affected lifestyles in a major way—or, admittedly inconsistently, when its distribution provides substantial evidence of availability, trading patterns, or purchasing power, serving as a model for other products. In the same way, things made for use in churches are usually only mentioned if there is some question of identification, and whether they were not actually secular and personal. Coins are discussed as artefacts that reflect the claims of the kings who issued them, rather than as mechanisms for exchange; once their infiltration into the economy had been effected, less is said of them except to illustrate their availability to different people at different times, as they could be one of the factors restricting medieval developments.

One of the important questions about artefacts is their role in shaping differences between different regions, or in creating integration. To examine this, the book reviews the whole of mainland Britain.[3] A long-standing role of artefact interpretation has been to consider whether there are things so distinctive and so numerous that they must have left their place of origin in the baggage of migrating peoples. Too often this has been assumed too readily, and recent work has stressed that one of the ways in which artefacts are used is to reflect not an actual origin but one claimed by those seeking to establish for themselves an ethnicity based on myth rather than history, let alone biology. This book aims to consider whether some of the ideas developed in the early period can be applied to the later, to understand the motives of people who were not creating an ethnic distinction for themselves, but a group identity based on their social role.

The book has been devised to take advantage of new data that have accumulated over the last thirty years. Archaeological excavations have now taken place in most medieval towns in Britain, and probably in all the major ones. Rural sites of various sorts and sizes have also been investigated.[4] Many reports have been published, and finds from towns like London, York, Norwich, Winchester, Perth, Northampton, Colchester, and Southampton, and from rural sites like Wharram Percy, Cottam, and Westbury, figure prominently in this book as a result. Also welcome are several recent reports of early medieval cemeteries, after a period when too few were appearing. The consequence of all this work is that there is now a much better idea of the range of items available in different places at different times, and a greater potential to infer what they are likely to have meant to those who made, used, wore, observed, and abandoned them.

The second major source of new discoveries in the last thirty years has been information from metal-detector users. However deplorable the activities of a few detectorists, and however dubious the principle that archaeological material should be owned, bought, and sold rather than be in public ownership, recording of items found by those who responsibly and accurately report them is certainly adding to our knowledge; at times, the wrenching of artefacts from their contexts destroys much of the most important information that they could provide, but material recovered from plough-soils is already unstratified.[5]

Another major source of information used in this book has also increased in quantity in the last thirty years, as many newly printed texts of documents and commentaries upon them have been published. Poems, histories, inventories, and expenditure accounts may all contain information about the buying, selling, and use of objects, some more directly than others, but all allow inferences to be drawn about the roles that those objects played. Like artefacts, texts cannot be used without interpretation of their contexts and meanings. A ring with a stated value of 2s. may in fact have been worth a lot less if the figure was given by someone anxious to be compensated for its loss, while one sold for £2 may have been worth a lot less than its buyer knew. Even when a ring is recorded as being a gift, it may have been what would now be regarded as a bribe. Nor can the value of a ring be stated only in monetary terms; a ring may only be worth 2s. in cold metal, but mean much more to an owner for whom it has personal associations. £2 may have been more than something was worth to most purchasers, but for the person who wanted it at that particular time it may have been worth paying the price.

A fourth source of information on the uses of artefacts in the Middle Ages is pictorial. Manuscript illuminations, funeral effigies, monumental brasses, even caricatures doodled in the margins of records of legal proceedings, all present images which have a purpose that has to be understood. Most medieval figures were not representations of actual people as they appeared to their contemporaries, but were idealized or exaggerated images expressing a social role.[6]

The long Bibliography at the end of this book shows the large number of papers on individual objects, and syntheses of some of the material discussed, that have been published in the last twenty years, many of them the work of museum curators.[7] The 1980s also saw a number of notable exhibitions in London, which brought the whole range of medieval artefacts to public attention. After more than a decade, it is excellent to know that the Victoria and Albert Museum is to host the conclusion of the series, broadly covering the time-period discussed in Chapter 8.[8]

Although there are archaeologists who consider that they should study the medieval period as though it was an extension of prehistory, because taking texts into consideration inevitably leads to attempts to answer historians' questions from archaeological data, most take the more balanced view that if a question is worth asking, it is worth answering with the use of all the information that is available, be it material survival or textual statement. This book tries to avoid giving priority to one sort of data over any other, but seeks to examine the most informative. It has also been an intention to keep an approximate balance between the subdivisions of the period. Centuries are a convenient way of creating divisions, provided that they are not regarded as real cultural breaks, and many chapters have been deliberately broken at some time after the start or before the end of a century, to emphasize that point.[9]

More problematical than whether to use texts because they may raise historians' questions is how far to apply questions raised by social anthropologists to medieval studies. The importance of gift-giving as a mechanism for establishing and maintaining social relationships is one concept that has amplified understanding of the Middle Ages, although it was originally recognized in studies of 'chieftain' societies in other parts of the world. Many of those societies seem quite comparable to the early medieval worlds of *Beowulf* and Sutton Hoo. Gift-giving was very important again in the later medieval period, however, by which time very different hierarchical societies had evolved within states that have no such obvious comparability across the globe.[10] Where anthropologists have concentrated on gift-giving between lord and followers or between equals, in the later Middle Ages it could also be between lord and contracted servants.[11] Votive offerings, sacrifices, monumental displays, and bequests can also be seen as a form of giving, but different beliefs mean that gifts to the gods are not necessarily made for the same reasons as those to the Christian God.

Even in the most thoroughly documented society, acceptance of what is appropriate in behaviour or appearance may not get discussed in texts, and may never even be put into words at all. Archaeologists have become increasingly aware that late medieval people created social structures to keep relationships functioning in ways which they may not have fully understood themselves, but which were articulated through their artefacts. One of the central tenets of this book is that even detailed documentary records do not usually explain behaviour; when King Edward I threw his daughter's coronet into the fire on what was perhaps her wedding-day, are we being told of the petulance of an irascible old man during a family quarrel, or did the king choose to destroy his daughter's most prominent expression of status to remind her that he could still break any aspirations that she may have had? Documents provide only part of the total evidence for social roles and meanings. Buildings, for instance, had 'meanings' about status and aspirations, and were constructed to express them even if the intentions were not given written expression, because they reflected 'a common visual code through which one knows how to behave'.[12] The same is true of smaller artefacts.

Various terms are used for codes of behaviour; *mentalité* does not translate very well into English—'mentality' has different overtones; 'mindset' is often used, though 'outlook' is usually satisfactory. *Habitus* was an early medieval word, but used in a wider sense than the modern 'habits', which suggests minor idiosyncrasies. 'Custom' has retained most of the sense in which it would have been understood in the Middle Ages.[13] These are words for things that are accepted, or understood, and may not need to be defined even in volatile periods.

Some medieval writers sought similar definitions to show how a people or a nation could be recognized; Isidore of Seville considered a *gens* to have a distinct body of laws, language, origin, and customs, though he did not set out what he meant by the last; perhaps surprisingly, as he was writing in the seventh century when the Arabs were threatening to overwhelm his Mediterranean world, he did not include religion.[14] Nor did a Norman bishop writing in the twelfth century, who considered the Welsh to be a *natio* because they had their own distinctive 'language, laws, habits, modes of judgements and customs', even though there was no territorial unification, a *regnum*, under a single prince such as had occurred in England; his omission of religion is less surprising, as neither Islam nor heresy was then a major problem in Britain.[15] His omission of 'origins' may have been because he did not think that that was a criterion applicable to a nation, as opposed to a folk, or because by his day large-scale movements and settlements were no longer occurring, though there were still of course a good many migrants—Flemings in south-west Wales a notable example. This is an issue that has been explored particularly by those researching the early Middle Ages, but is no less apposite in studies of the development of nations and states. Artefacts could be used to emphasize a community of interest, but could also deliberately negate it.

In relation to the later Middle Ages, 'closure theory' seems a very appropriate general model, because it argues that a ranked society operates through competing groups which practise different ways of excluding others from power, wealth, work, or land.[16] When kings and aristocrats sought Italian or French jewellery, were they deliberately distancing themselves thereby yet further from those who could not afford what foreign cities could provide? How often did people look at a coin and acknowledge that its inscriptions and images expressed the claims of the ruler who had issued it, and that in using it they were accepting that ruler's more general claim to the right to issue laws and judgements? Since feasting and drinking are a form of social bonding, how important was it that some drank from gold, others from glass, and yet others from pottery?

'Closure theory' is in part a study of restrictions, as one group sought to restrict the opportunities of another. Sometimes restrictions are a reflection of supply, which is particularly true of gold because it was always scarce in the medieval West, although its availability and therefore the extent of its use varied. Kings sought it for their treasuries, their regalia, their plate, their adornment, and their coinage; the aristocracy shared the same aspirations, except usually the last; the Church sought it to make works for the glory of God; merchants sought it for exchange; but did agricultural workers and urban artisans seek it? The answer might seem obvious—and at least from the late twelfth century directly answerable from crime records—but would such people invariably want what kings and nobles wanted, or did they feel that the behaviour of their landlords and employers was not their concern, and that to try to copy them would be inappropriate? In other words, restrictions may be social as well as economic, and it may be false to assume that everyone will seek to emulate those with greater resources.

Restrictions were also caused by the Church. Christian dogma taught that Avarice was one of the seven deadly sins, and that hoarding treasure led to it; Lust was another of the seven that gold and silver could represent.[17] Such teaching was not confined to the niceties of university debate, but was made part of the outlook of medieval people through repeated sermons and images. Just as Anglo-Saxon artefacts of the seventh and eighth centuries may show how Christianity became more than an official religion but permeated everyone's view of their world, so in the later Middle Ages depth of shared belief may be shown by the ubiquity of inscriptions and gems on objects and rings that offered their wearers protection against sudden death and other afflictions. Informal as such things may appear, they are an indication of the mindset of their time, and if it is true that they were falling out of use in the early part of the sixteenth century, they present a way of seeing how some of the changes made during the Reformation could have been acceptable.[18]

Change and the reasons for it are a main focus of debate in medieval studies.[19] The criticism has been levelled at closure theory that it is explanatory and descriptive, but not predictive;[20] it does not give reasons why change occurred, except in terms of shifting balances of power between groups, which merely takes the question one stage further back, to why did the balance alter. That no single causative factor seems adequate on its own—class struggle may be outweighed by demographic factors or commercial development—does not seem a reason for abandoning the attempt to address the issue.[21] It is one of the arguments of this book that artefacts and attitudes towards their acquisition, ownership, and disposal, be it for public display or for personal gratification, have been underestimated as a motivating factor for social change.

1

Adapting to Life Without the Legions
From the End of the Fourth Century to the Mid-Sixth

If gold and silver are a measure of wealth, late Roman Britain was very rich. Hoards of coins, jewellery, and plate buried in the late fourth and early fifth centuries show that their owners' lifestyle was coming to an end as central imperial authority broke down, troops were withdrawn from the island, villas fell into disuse, and towns lost their markets and trade. Raiders threatened by land and sea: Irish from the west, Pictish from the north, Frisian, Saxon, and others from the east; and as civic order broke down, the likelihood of robbery by people living south of Hadrian's Wall grew worse. The hoards' owners were right to worry, and their subsequent failure to retrieve their valuables must testify to many personal catastrophes.

Hoards containing dishes, bowls, and spoons as well as coins and jewellery have been found on the east side of Roman Britain from Canterbury, Kent, in the south to Whorlton, Yorkshire, in the north. Further west, coin-hoards are quite plentiful, although none has any plate. Some contain jewellery, like one found in 1843 at Amesbury, Wiltshire, that included three silver finger-rings; in the same area, another hoard with eight gold coins and one of silver was found in 1990, apparently concealed in a pot around the year 405, to judge from the date of the latest coin. But as with plate so with jewellery, the contrast with the east is still considerable; Thetford, Norfolk, has gold finger-rings as well as ornamental chains, bracelets, and a buckle; Hoxne, Suffolk, has gold bracelets, and again chains, these with elaborate mounts. Some of the craftsmanship shown in these pieces is of a high order, that only well-off patrons could have afforded. The plate suggests displays of tableware by a society that set great store on being able to offer lavish feasts and entertainment.[1]

These late Roman treasures may be giving a slightly false impression of Britain's prosperity. Silver was probably extracted from the same native deposits that yielded lead, so would have been more available than in most parts of the Empire. Some may also have entered Britain from Ireland, where evidence of Roman intervention is accumulating. With exports of precious metal subject to imperial restrictions, there was good reason to hang on to it.

On the other hand, the amount of gold extracted from Dolaucothi in central Wales is unlikely to have been enough to account for all the jewellery at Thetford and Hoxne; the gold coins known as *solidi* were certainly not minted in late Roman Britain, yet more than 500 were in the latter hoard alone. All the silver coins—nearly 15,000 at Hoxne—were minted abroad also.[2]

Much of the goldwork in the Thetford hoard seems unworn, and could be taken as a jeweller's stock but that some of its spoons have inscriptions associating them with a deity, Faunus, so the collection may have been a temple treasure rather than an individual's. Whether the god's cult was still active is a moot point, however; some late Roman objects have Christian motifs, and one large hoard of silver plate found at Water Eaton, Cambridgeshire, could have been specifically for use in the Christian liturgy.[3] Christianity had become the Empire's official religion in the fourth century, but how deeply it had penetrated British society remains controversial.

The jewellery that people were actually wearing in Britain while the imperial administration was withdrawing from it may not be fully represented in hoards; in particular, base-metal ornaments were not valuable enough to be worth storing. Brooches were produced in various different styles, although manufacture of those with brightly coloured enamels made from glass seems to have ceased during, if not before, the fourth century. A few brooches of types used by people living beyond the Empire's frontiers have been found; the 'tutulus', for instance, suggests that there were some Germanic people in the country. Such outsiders cannot be assumed to have been forerunners of any migrations that were to take place during the next two centuries, any more than a man buried at Gloucester with silver buckles and strap-ends that had probably been made in south-east Europe was the advance guard of an invasion of Goths. He may have been one of a troop of soldiers billeted on the late Roman town, but such troops, and any families that they had with them, would mostly have been withdrawn to serve in other parts of the Empire considered to be in even greater need of protection than Britain.[4]

Absent from the late Roman hoards are any examples of the gold 'crossbow-brooch', an imperial badge of authority. Crossbow-brooches were copied in lesser metals—unfinished copper-alloy castings have been found at Wroxeter, Shropshire—but the official ones were presumably not things to be bought and sold, and would not have been seen as part of a normal display of wealth; nor were they things to be used as a pledge, or for hoarding or melting down, however extreme the need. Certain types of belt- or strap-buckle were also associated with imperial authority, originally for soldiers, but subsequently for civilian officers, and some came to be buried with women.[5] They have frames shaped as dolphins or sea-horses, and plates engraved with a range of animals, fishes, birds, and plants, some of which carry recognizably Christian meanings (Fig. 1.1); many were worn with distinctive shapes of strap-end. The only

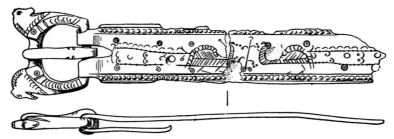

Fig. 1.1. Late Roman buckle from Stanwick, Yorkshire, with animal heads projecting from the frame, and two peacocks incised into the plate—their tails suggesting a craftworker who had never seen one. The birds' flesh supposedly never decayed, so they became a symbol of Christ's promise of eternal life through His incorruptibility. The design should have a plant, a chalice, or a spring-head between the two birds, so that they can peck at it, thus symbolizing Christ as the Fountain of Life feeding God's creation. (Drawing by E. Fry-Stone, reproduced from Hawkes, S. C. and Dunning 1961, 46. Actual size.)

buckle in a hoard is a gold one from Thetford, which has a zoomorphic frame, but a plate with a figure, perhaps Faunus, on it.

A very different sort of hoard was found at Traprain Law hillfort in West Lothian, only about 50 miles north of Hadrian's Wall; its deposition is dated by four silver coins, called *siliquae*, to no earlier than c.395 (Fig. 1.2). Although it contained a few pieces of plate that were still usable, most had been cut up, apparently to make conveniently portable units, like other 'hack-silver' in the hoard. The weights of some of these silver offcuts conform to the Roman pound, or fractions of it, suggesting careful measurement—either as a way of ensuring that everyone in a raiding party received their due share of the loot, or because someone in the south was sending subsidies to a chieftain at Traprain Law to discourage him from attacking the donor. A copper-alloy buckle in the hoard had no economic value, and could have been intended for someone with authority, like the buckles worn further south. In other respects, however, the hoard seems to imply social values very different from those of the plate's original owners; north of the Wall, whole dishes to display at great feasts had to take second place to chunks of raw metal, either to be recast into jewellery or simply to be shown off as justification for boasts of prowess.[6]

Siliquae continued to circulate in Britain at the beginning of the fifth century, but were increasingly likely to be reduced in size by clipping, an illegal practice that proved impossible to control as imperial power waned. Other parts of the Empire continued to obey its law, so a clipped *siliqua* can be taken as one that had knocked around in Britain, and had been interfered with by people who expected the coin still to be accepted at its face value; some continuing respect for authority seems to be shown by the way that the clipping never cut into the emperor's head, and none of the *siliquae* were halved or quartered to allow them to be used as small change.[7] Gold *solidi* seem not to

Fig. 1.2. 'The grandeur that was Rome' becomes the plunder of a raid? Part of the great hoard of silver found within the hillfort at Traprain Law, north of Hadrian's Wall. Although some pieces of plate can still be recognized, most had been squashed or cut up because they were valued for their weight, not their function. At the top right is one of ten flasks; although crushed, it was complete enough to be restored. On the left are two wide-based wine-cups that could also be restored, but bits of stem and bowl show the fate of another three. Next to them is a cylindrical vessel, thought to have been for ointment; the lid does not necessarily belong to it, but was found crushed up with part of a vessel of the same shape. In the middle, the shell-shaped bowl had been folded over, first one side, then the other, but had not been totally flattened, so could be opened out again. It has a central medallion engraved with a Nereid riding the waves on a sea-monster. The hooks on its sides may presage the hanging-bowls of the later Celtic world (Fig. 2.13). (Photograph reproduced by courtesy of the Trustees of the National Museums of Scotland, Edinburgh.)

have been clipped, probably because their value meant that each would have been individually inspected when exchanged, but also perhaps because of a sense of their special status. This distinction seems to have applied in the remarkable recent discovery at Patching, West Sussex, of twenty-three gold and twenty-seven silver coins, two gold rings, and a quantity of scrap silver, including a silver chape from the end of a leather scabbard, and bits of broken

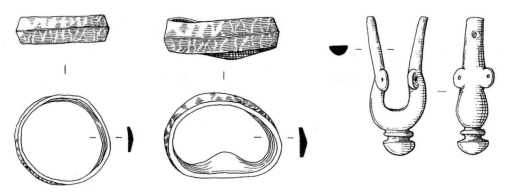

Fig. 1.3. The two gold rings and the silver scabbard-chape from the Patching hoard, deposited after c.461 and found in West Sussex in 1999. (Drawing by Jane Russell reproduced from White, S. *et al.* 1999, 312, by permission of the Worthing Borough Council Museum and Art Gallery. Actual size.)

spoons (Fig. 1.3). The *solidi* show some wear, and two had been bent, but none had been clipped, unlike several of the silver coins. They are of various dates, but the latest were Visigothic, minted in about 461, by which time the earliest were some 160 years old.[8]

Some of the Patching coins are types that circulated in Roman Britain, so they and some of the scrap, such as the spoon fragments, could have formed a late Roman assemblage, to which later additions had been made. The Patching hoard is therefore unlike those from Thetford, Hoxne, and elsewhere, in which none of the coins bear the names of emperors who reigned after the death of Honorius in 423; indeed, none needs to be any later than *c.*411.[9] They could, of course, have been buried long after the legions had withdrawn, but if so, it now has to be explained why fresh coins were not added to them over the years, since whoever owned the Patching hoard had been able to acquire some.

Patching may represent something more akin to the Traprain Law hoard than to any in Roman Britain. Not only do its pieces of silver bullion seem to be deliberate units of a weight system,[10] but the two gold rings may have been intended as coin-substitutes—they were not ornaments, since both are undecorated and uneven, and the larger still has hammer-marks all over it; it is simply a strip of not very pure gold that had been bent and had its ends beaten together (Fig. 1.3). The smaller ring, however, is 98 per cent gold, its metal apparently freshly extracted rather than obtained by melting down coins or jewellery.[11] Presumably it had come from the Visigothic-controlled sources in southern France or north-west Spain[12]—though why it had not been turned into coin at one of the Visigothic mints is unknown. Rings, however, are easier than flat bars to carry round, as they can be tied together or slipped over a rod.

The silver chape at Patching was almost certainly made well after the end of the fourth century, and is further evidence of the hoard's late date; unlike the coins, however, it was not from the continental south, but had probably been made somewhere in modern Germany, though a few others like it have been found elsewhere in England, in graves.[13] The hoard therefore shows a mixed range of sources and contacts. There is no other contemporary Visigothic material in south-east Britain, such as pottery,[14] so the gold may have come not directly from southern France or northern Spain, but by way of the increasingly powerful Franks centred in northern Gaul, conceivably sending subsidies to an ally rather than trading for goods. The second half of the fifth century is recorded in the *Anglo-Saxon Chronicle* as a time of political change in Sussex, and the Patching hoard may reflect these troubles, although its owner's allegiance is not clear from its contents. He—political power was almost invariably expressed in documentary sources as wielded by males in the early Middle Ages—might have been a local leader, either the heir of someone who had taken over authority in the region from whatever structures had operated there during the Roman occupation, or a newcomer challenging for power. People like that needed treasure-stores to enable them to create warbands for protection and raiding, or to buy alliances, perhaps through a marriage and a dowry payment. A hoard like Patching represented success, showing that here was someone whom overseas kings were anxious to cultivate by sending him gifts, or who was able to get gold and silver in return for slaves and other booty won in raids.[15]

Patching is near a large cemetery at Highdown, in which are burials containing objects that, before the hoard was found, had already suggested the possibility of people with a mixture of cultural ideas.[16] In particular, it had a buckle-frame and belt-end, a belt-slide, and a brooch in what is usually called the 'quoit-brooch' style because the frames have openwork centres and a series of concentric rings (Col. pl. A.1), in Highdown's case set within a square panel. The buckles probably owe their origins to the Roman 'official' series,[17] and the style is particularly interesting because it was originally used on formal male costume but was adapted for female use, some of the buckles and all the brooches being found in women's graves. This may be an instance of males showing their social position vicariously, by transferring the expression of their status to their womenfolk, and the brooches may also be part of a long-term trend towards greater signalling of gender difference in the way that people were buried.[18]

If the owners of quoit-brooches felt that the expression of Roman authority, or at least of its memory, mattered, they did not pursue it to the point of including contemporary coins in their graves; yet coins with emperors' heads and inscriptions are the most overt statements of that authority, and Patching now shows that, at least in the Highdown area, a few were available.[19] Because of known practice on the continent, and because the British writer Gildas decried British leaders for making a treaty, *foedus*, with barbarians who agreed to defend the province against raiders in return for land,[20] fourth- and fifth-century objects have long been scrutinized for evidence of shape or decoration that could signify either official imperial issues of military equipment; or copies of such things aimed at people who wanted to be thought entitled to them; or, like the tutulus-brooches, alien costume fittings worn by people either from other parts of the Empire or from beyond its frontiers. That the quoit-brooch style's palmettes, rosettes, and fairly naturalistic animals derive from general late classical sources seems agreed, but the direct sources are not; paired animals, for instance, can be seen as evidence either of continuity from late Roman Britain, exemplified by the Amesbury rings or by images such as peacocks with the Fountain of Life (Fig. 1.1);[21] or of continuing contacts with late Roman Gaul;[22] or of new contacts either with the Franks or with southern Scandinavia. In the fifth century, therefore, such things could be evidence of people whose forebears had lived on the island, though in that case Christian motifs, as on the earlier buckles and strap-ends, might be expected; or of contracted settlers, *foederati*; or of mercenaries, not expected to stay after their period of hire; or of uninvited newcomers who were wresting land away from the natives, using quoit-brooch-style objects to claim a special position for themselves as inheritors of Roman power and thus of its control of land.

The quoit-brooch style was used on a belt-set found in one of Roman London's extramural cemeteries, in a grave that also contained a gilt cross-bow-brooch. In another grave were two tutulus-brooches.[23] Their inclusion within an established cemetery implies that their wearers were as acceptable to London's citizens as had been the Goth to Gloucester's, and the belt-set could well have been given either to an early fifth-century *foederatus* or to a mercenary brought in by its local administrators for the city's defence, rather than to a member of the imperial forces whose troop was subsequently withdrawn from the province. A similar belt-set found at Mucking, Essex (Fig. 1.4), could have belonged to a soldier hired to defend the Thames estuary and the approach to London. The circumstances there were different, however, in that that belt-set was not in a Romano-British cemetery, but in one that was newly established and that subsequently remained in use, probably for the burial of people who lived in a small group of adjacent farmsteads; its owner could have been the leader of a small group of incoming settlers, therefore.[24] Both the London and the Mucking belt-sets were in good enough condition to make it quite possible that those buried with them had also been their only owners. That is not true of everything; a scabbard from a grave at Brighthampton, Oxfordshire, is very worn, particularly the chape at its end,[25] and is much less likely therefore to have been buried with its first owner. Things that started life as a kind of badge for a *foederatus* might have ended up after two or three generations as part of an eclectic assemblage that was a fusion of ideas, a way

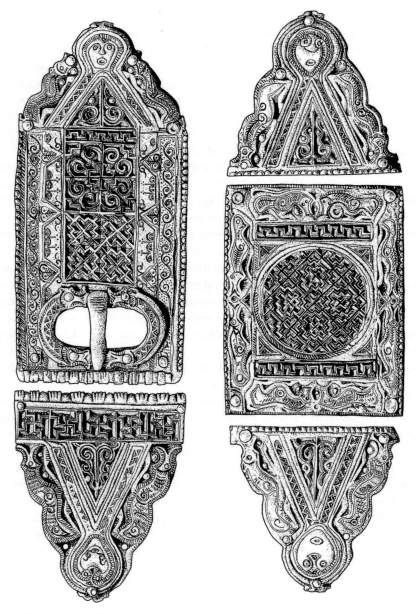

Fig. 1.4. The copper-alloy Mucking belt-set, probably made in the first half of the fifth century, decorated in the late Roman 'chip-carved' style—despite the name, the design was not cut directly into the metal, but was cast in a mould and finished by hand. As well as geometrical patterns, there are 'classical' palmettes in the triangular panels and animals comparable to those on the Sarre quoit-brooch (Col. pl. A.1), but more elongated. The human heads are unusual, and may have led to their appearance on later brooches (e.g. Fig. 1.10). (Reproduced with his permission from a drawing by Peter Inker, published in Inker 2000, 30. Actual size.)

of creating an altogether new identity rather than of stressing differences between groups of old natives and new arrivals.

Two quoit-brooch-style buckle-plates found in different cemeteries in Kent are so similar that manufacture by the same craftsman, or by men sharing tools in a single workshop, seems likely; use of a particular punch can sometimes be identified if it had a distinctive mark, as has been suggested of the stamps on two objects found as far apart as Wiltshire and Kent.[26] The smiths may have worked in established centres, or travelled from place to place with their punches and tools, but no debris from their workshops has yet been found. This raises a problem that applies to most of the metalwork of the early Anglo-Saxon period—how far had something come from its place of manufacture and how many hands had it passed through before it was buried or lost? Some of these quoit-brooch-style pieces may well have been made in Kent, but they are found quite widely across southern Britain, and the number excavated in Gaul is sufficient to indicate that some were made there as well.[27]

Another group of copper-alloy buckles and strap-ends that appears to have late Roman antecedents but which may have been used long into the fifth century seems to concentrate west of the quoit-brooch objects, particularly in Gloucestershire.[28] This is an area in which things were not usually put in graves, so the finds are effectively without context. Different again are various brooches, such as 'cruciforms', mostly but not all in graves, which are also thought to be from the first half of the fifth century and a little later; most of those are from East Anglia and the upper Thames valley, with a couple from Dorset.[29] Their direct antecedents were not made in the Roman provinces but in modern Denmark and north Germany. Not only are they very often found in women's graves, but many are from cremations, a rite practised in those areas; the burning of corpses had ceased to be an accepted practice in late Roman Britain, so its reintroduction strongly supports the old interpretation that whole families were migrating, and in sufficient numbers to have a greater effect on the culture of the areas in which they settled than in other parts of the island. Furnished inhumation burials alone could more plausibly be put down to the disproportionate effect that quite small numbers of migrants might have had on a native population unsettled by the Romans' abandonment, and therefore less likely to insist on retention of their established ways of talking and doing things.[30] Cremations were usually in urns, of shapes and with decoration that also hark back to north Germany and Scandinavia, notably faces and stamped animals, birds, and what look like oared ships.

These regional distributions are not without overlap, but it has been pointed out that there is a broad correlation with the old provinces of Roman Britain, which could indicate that those institutional structures were part of the formation process of cultural regions in the fifth century.[31]

The fifth-century objects are often very well made; the casting of some involved high-quality craftsmanship, as on the Mucking belt-set. The arrangements of some of the animals, plants, human faces, and other elements of the quoit-brooch style may even conform to a set of rules.[32] What seems surprising in view of the quality of the casting and finishing is that precious metal was not used more frequently; a few quoit-brooches and a pair of pendants are in solid silver, three of the Kent brooches being gilded with a thin gold coating (Col. pl. A.1), as are parts of the Brighthampton scabbard. One or two had settings, but those that survive are merely glass pellets. All the others are in copper alloy, occasionally gilded, more often embellished with silver wire or plating, which had sometimes been stripped off before burial. None is in solid gold.[33] The same is true of the western belt fittings, and the cruciform and other brooches. Nor do the furnished graves in the south and east have any silver plate, either whole or chopped into hack-silver. The *Anglo-Saxon Chronicle* for the year 418 states that 'the Romans collected all the treasures which were in Britain, and hid some in the ground, so that no-one could find them afterwards, and took some with them into Gaul', and the archaeological record seems to bear this statement out, even though the *Chronicle* was written many centuries later, drawing on some source no longer identifiable. Even pewter plate is absent from graves.[34]

Glass vessels give a contrasting picture to plate, in that some seem likely still to have been available. Bowls and beakers found in graves in the south-east may have been made in the first half of the fifth century, some perhaps in Kent and some elsewhere, though as with the fifth-century metalwork there is no site evidence for manufacture. Also like the metalwork, the basic technology was retained, probably dependent on waste glass (cullet) collected for recyling because freshly manufactured glass ingots were more difficult if not impossible to import—the raw materials used in making Roman glass would never have been readily transportable to Britain. There are even a few exotic pieces that probably came from the Mediterranean, and their shapes and decoration suggest that they were made there in the fifth century, not that they were already old when buried, heirlooms handed down from Roman Britain. Whatever mechanism had brought gold and coins from southern Gaul into the Patching hoard may also have supplied occasional luxuries, like a narrow-necked flask in a Highdown grave, though mostly it was glasses to drink from, not to store perfumes or spices in, that were sought.[35]

The *Chronicle*'s statement that all the treasure in late Roman Britain was buried or taken to Gaul seems to get further support from excavated sites in Cornwall, Devon, Somerset, Wales, and further north, none of which has yielded a nest-egg like that at Traprain Law. Nor do they have any trace of pewter, which had also been plentiful in late Roman Britain, nor of copper-alloy bowls.[36]

Because these are areas effectively without furnished graves,[37] there is much less recovery of whole objects from them than from the south-east, but by contrast there is plenty of evidence of metalworking, mostly from sites that are likely to have had use by local potentates,[38] who may have succeeded to the powers exercised by the magistrates who had helped to run Roman Britain. Much of the post-Roman metalworking cannot be very precisely dated, but among the discarded waste and accidental losses are examples of copper-alloy 'penannular' brooches, a type that had already had a long history and which takes many forms.[39] Some are large, like one found within the Roman town at Caerwent that has terminals cast in the shape of fairly abstract animals' heads, its findspot justifying a date perhaps back in the fourth century (Fig. 1.5). Various zoomorphic forms have been found elsewhere in Wales, and in

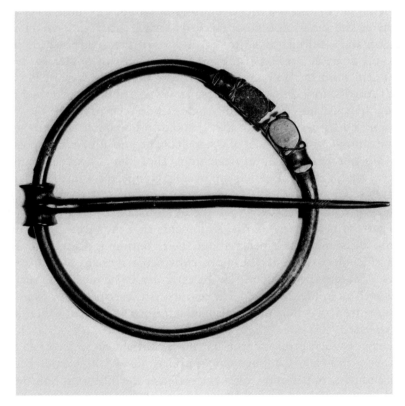

Fig. 1.5. Cast copper-alloy penannular brooch from the Roman town at Caerwent, Monmouthshire, with animal-head terminals, the eyes, and other details picked out in enamel. Although this one may have been made in the fourth century, the type probably continued to be produced well into the fifth. (Photograph reproduced by courtesy of Newport City Council Museums and Heritage Service. Actual size.)

Ireland, but also in England, for instance at Highdown, the Sussex cemetery that also produced quoit-brooch-style objects, and at other places well to the east of where they might be most expected, including one in a Kent cemetery, Bifrons, where it was found in a woman's grave being worn as a bracelet, not as a brooch. Some had red enamel in their terminals, a late Roman tradition, as background to cast relief designs. Iron penannulars were produced inside Wroxeter's town walls, where some could be post-Roman. A fragment in lead found on the hillfort Dinas Powys in south Wales would not have been strong enough for practical use on costume, as it would have distorted when holding folds of cloth together, so must have been made during the manufacture of a mould, either as a 'model' or as a test casting.[40]

Most penannular brooches are smaller than the Caerwent and Highdown examples, and have various terminals such as square panels with simple relief ornament—a raised dot or its opposite, a countersunk circle, for instance. This type, classified as G, may start in the fourth century, but most examples are known from later contexts; they are found in Wales, including Caerwent, this time outside the walls, and most recently during excavations at Hen Gastell in Glamorgan, a hillfort close to an important crossing-point of the River Neath, and at such sites as Cadbury Congresbury in Somerset, possibly a shrine. Further north, finds of moulds show that they were being made at Dunadd, Argyllshire (Fig. 1.6). Others, however, are from furnished graves in what may by this time be labelled 'Anglo-Saxon' cemeteries in the Warwickshire Avon and Upper Thames valleys, and at a few other eastern sites.[41]

The penannular brooches of the late Roman and immediate post-Roman periods are not particularly eye-catching. The animal-headed terminals are neatly executed, and the Type Gs are usually competent, but even if they were finished with a plating of tin or other white metal, as some may have been, they would not have compared with the opulence of the late Roman jewellery in the Thetford and other hoards. Arguments that they were worn by people who wanted to make statements about their continuing Roman or Romano-British/Celtic identity would be more convincing if there were any trace of bracelets or finger-rings, such as were certainly being worn, occasionally in death as well as in life, in the fourth century. An inscription, or even an occasional attempt at a letter, might also be expected if Roman inheritance was being expressed.[42]

There is not much precious metal at these 'British' sites. A couple of scraps of gold were found at Cadbury Congresbury; silver was found to be a tiny element within a copper-alloy ingot excavated at the hillfort at South Cadbury, also in Somerset; Dinas Powys had evidence that both gold and silver were worked, the former trapped in the residues solidified to the sides of clay crucibles; further west, the coastal site at Longbury Bank had a small sheet of very pure silver.[43] The great majority of the material is copper alloy, however. Although Gildas wrote that gold and silver were 'the chains of all royal power',

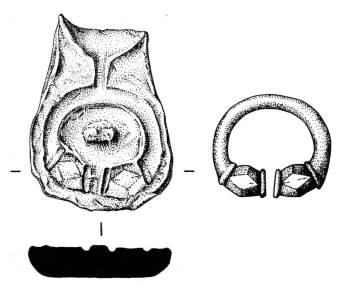

Fig. 1.6. Left: one half of a clay mould for making a Type G small penannular brooch, excavated at the Dunadd hillfort, Argyllshire. Its matching half would have been attached to it, and liquid copper alloy poured into the funnel, or ingate, at the top; after cooling, the brooch would have been removed for hand-finishing. This normally meant that the mould would be broken and discarded, a reason for the large numbers of various kinds found at Dunadd. Right: drawing to show the brooch that would have emerged from the mould. (Drawings by Howard Mason reproduced by permission of Cardiff University from the collections of the National Museums of Scotland, Edinburgh. Actual size.)

as though in his experience ability to acquire and dispense such treasure was an important aspect of social control, actual access to precious metal seems to have been limited—gold was probably not still being extracted from Dolaucothi. Visigothic and Byzantine gold coins, like those at Patching, have not been found at any of the western hillforts; little confidence can be placed in most of the records of stray finds, but those from around Meols, Cheshire, seem acceptable, while three from Exeter or nearby are at least credible, and provide a slight justification of the Greek historian who recorded that the Emperor Justinian was sending money to Britain.[44]

The potentates were certainly within networks that brought them goods from the Mediterranean. Imports of pottery, mostly from the east (Phocaean red-slip wares) and some from the Carthage area (African red-slip), are thought to have begun in the middle of the fifth century, after a hiatus of some fifty years. Quantities are small, which allows them to be interpreted as evidence of no more than an occasional visit by a speculative venturer; or, on the basis that what has entered the archaeological record is only a tiny fraction of the total, of Mediterranean merchants regularly and predictably trading at various landing-places. There they could rely upon meeting a king or his agent, who wanted the wine and olive oil that was transported in pottery amphoras, and spices and tableware.[45] Quantities of finds at two coastal sites, Bantham Bay in south Devon and Meols, a sandy beach near Liverpool, are enough to suggest regularly used landing-places, even perhaps open beach-markets where exchanges were not restricted solely to royalty. Meols, which on the evidence of coins was used as a landing-place from the Iron Age, throughout the Roman period, and on into the early Middle Ages, has yielded a number of penannular brooches and a small pottery flask from Egypt, the latter a reminder that travellers included pilgrims who would have brought some special things back with them.[46]

It is usually assumed that the kings' systems of control would have given them command of supplies of metals sought by Mediterranean merchants—tin from Cornwall and Devon is substantiated by finds of ingots, but lead and possibly silver from Devon, Somerset, north Wales, the Peak District, and Cumberland, and perhaps iron from various different ore deposits, have no such direct evidence, nor is there any from excavations that metals were stored at the potentate sites. Other commodities may have been hides or finished leather—though both would have been susceptible to damage on the return voyage—slaves captured in a king's raids, or hunting-dogs, reflecting another aristocratic activity. As there is no imported pottery from any enclaves of British administration that may have survived in the east, such as the London/St Albans area,[47] this was an exchange system in which they did not take part, at least directly.

That British kings should have wanted to acquire olive oil, despite two generations having passed who may have had no experience of food cooked or soaked in anything but animal fat, is probably even more of an indication that they wanted to affect a Romanized lifestyle than is their anxiety for wine, surely an easier taste to reacquire. Glass vessels were also coming to these sites, some from the Anglo-Saxon parts of the country, like a funnel beaker from Dinas Powys, but others from the continent, as at Longbury Bank.[48] A lord who could serve exotic food and wine in fine vessels at feasts both displayed his success and invited his followers to share in it. The middle of the fifth century may have marked a turning-point, with new efforts to establish dynasties and to use new systems of control, based on fortified power-bases. A similar aspiration is implied by the use of Latin for inscriptions on memorial stones and on a piece of slate found at Tintagel, Cornwall; both also stress the importance of family and lineal descent.[49] The metalworking could indicate that the kings controlled the main craftworkers, but as the evidence is not confined to the residential sites,[50] they may not have had a complete monopoly on penannular brooches and the like. Nevertheless, at least in Wales, the relative lack of metalwork and of anything else of value at farmsteads implies that their occupants could produce enough surplus to pay the food renders demanded of them, but not to acquire things for their own enjoyment or social enhancement.[51]

The Phocaean and African red-slip wares seem to have been imported for about a hundred years; the supply then dried up, not because of any wish on the part of the British elites, but because of events in the Mediterranean and beyond.[52] By that time pottery tableware and perhaps glass from south-western France was entering Britain, some of the former stamped with the Christian *chi-rho*; it reached the same sorts of site as the Mediterranean wares, but in no greater quantity. Although pottery imports are the best indicators of British sites in the early post-Roman period, they are not always found; in the whole of the Severn valley there is only a possible sherd at Wroxeter.[53]

North of Hadrian's Wall, Traprain Law and its hoard show that local chiefs outside the Empire had established power-bases long before those inside it. The contents of that hoard show awareness of Roman culture, but little interest in sharing in it. The absence of imported Mediterranean pottery from such places is not only a factor of geographical distance, but also of there being no enthusiasm for a Roman lifestyle.

Traprain Law seems to have been abandoned by or soon after the end of the fifth century, its role perhaps taken over by the coastal promontory fort at Dunbar, a move that could show increased concern for maritime connections. Dating at the latter is dependent on radiocarbon, however, not on artefacts, so no accompanying change in the material culture can be seen.[54] A very different site, on the western coast, is Whithorn, Galloway, where a Christian community may have been created in the fifth century. The contrast between the two places is visible in the pottery at Whithorn, which includes both the Mediterranean and southern French wares, and small amounts of glass. The only other site in modern Scotland to have yielded any Mediterranean pottery is Iona, also a Christian community—and even there only a single sherd has been found.[55]

In between the two church sites is the hillfort at Dunadd, Argyllshire, which was probably in use by the sixth century. Moulds show that penannular brooches were produced in quantity there (Fig. 1.6), though perhaps in the seventh rather than in the sixth century; there was no gold or silver at the site at that early time, nor certainly at other sites in present-day Scotland. Dunadd was a strongpoint for control of Dàl Riata, a Gaelic kingdom said to have been created by the *Scotti* from Ireland in the sixth century; this is now disputed, not least because some types of object found in Ireland do not occur in Argyll.[56] Away from the ecclesiastical and aristocratic sites, farmsteads in the north had little metalwork. Wood and leather might give a rather different picture, of course, if they had survived, and the drystone structures well to the north of the Forth-Clyde at sites like Birsay that can be dated to the period are certainly substantial enough to deny abject poverty.[57]

Still open to debate for the Anglo-Saxon areas is the ascription of close dates both to objects and to the graves in which many occur, not least because of similar difficulties on the continent. Use of computers to create correspondence analyses and sequences based not only on a grave's contents, but on exactly where within it objects had been placed, gives new ways of adding yet more complexities to such problems. They show not only that practice varied across the country, but that one cemetery's customs could vary from another's even when they were not far apart, and quite possibly one family's from another's even within the same cemetery.[58]

The places where the different objects have been found raise traditional but still important questions about the contacts and origins of the people buried with them. Overlapping chronologically with the cruciform brooches that began to appear quite early in the fifth century are 'equal-arm' brooches that, at their most striking, have openwork ornament with animals, plants, and spirals. Never common, they probably originate in the Elbe–Weser region of north Germany, where they are found in graves from the end of the fourth century.[59] The most westerly in England, at Collingbourne Ducis, Wiltshire (Fig. 1.7 and Col. pl. A.2), is most similar to the most southerly in Germany, and it has been pointed out that both may have been buried, probably in the late fifth or the early sixth century, where they were most admired, not necessarily where they were most commonly worn; their last owners both happened to see them as something rather exotic and worth repairing if damaged, so they do not prove a direct connection between the two areas. More meaningful are comparisons between total assemblages and arrangements of grave-goods, rather than individual and exceptional items. The burial of weapons with males is not particularly 'Germanic', for instance, though there are likenesses between swords and knives.[60]

In the second half of the fifth century further new brooch types appeared. 'Great square-headed' brooches have recently been reappraised and a revised chronology proposed (Figs. 1.8 and 1.9), which sees their earliest variants in England as few but very widespread at the end of the fifth century and early in the sixth, with many more in the Midlands but still with some south of the Thames in the next phase, and then in the later sixth century spreading north beyond the Humber and east into Norfolk and Suffolk, but with none any longer in the Thames valley or further south.[61] They are more or less contemporary with 'saucer-brooches' (Fig. 1.10), which are found in more or less the same areas—until the later sixth century, when the saucers failed to impact on East Anglia, Lincolnshire, and Yorkshire.[62] Is the difference in any way an indication of differences between groups of people—do they conform to differences in the manner of burial, to language and dialect as those are later recorded, or to divisions between the later kingdoms? The last phase of the great square-headed brooches allows them to be seen as 'Anglian', because they are broadly found in the areas that Bede, writing in the eighth century, said had been settled by people from the *Angulus* area of north Germany, explaining names like East Anglia in England. But in their earlier phases these brooches were not confined to the area north of the Thames, so if their

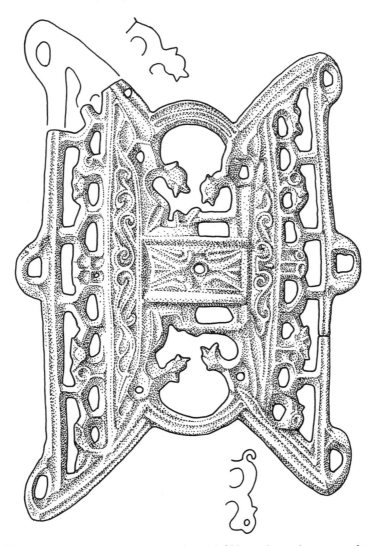

Fig. 1.7. Gilt copper-alloy equal-arm brooch, mid fifth-/early sixth-century, from Collingbourne Ducis, Wiltshire (see also Col. pl. A.2). The decoration includes running friezes of animals, clarified in the outline drawings, perhaps derived from Roman provincial work such as also led to the Mucking belt-set's (Fig. 1.4); the running scrolls can be compared to late Roman palmettes, and the projecting heads to buckle frames (e.g. Fig. 1.1). Although equal-arm brooches were usually worn horizontally and on the centre of the chest as though to hold a shawl, this example was found aligned vertically, as illustrated here, and on a woman's right shoulder. Repairs on the back of the brooch show that it was far from new when buried, and may therefore have been placed in the grave by people who admired and valued it, but did not know how it had originally been meant to function in a territory with which they had never had direct contact. (Drawn by Nick Griffiths from the collections of the Wiltshire Heritage Museum, Devizes. Actual size.)

Fig. 1.8. Gilt copper-alloy great square-headed brooch, from a cemetery at Blacknall Field, Pewsey, Wiltshire. Despite their modern name, these brooches were normally worn with the rectangular plate at a downward angle. Human heads, bearded in the bottom row, are easily recognized on the projections, and masks on the central bar can also be seen without difficulty. Other brooches of this type have heads in the projecting circles (cf. those on the Mucking belt-set, Fig. 1.4, and on saucer- and button-brooches, Fig. 1.10)—how are they to be understood here? Two creatures with long open jaws can be recognized on the sides, but only someone very familiar with the limbs and torsos of Style I animals (cf. Fig. 1.10) would 'see' them in the various panels.

The woman buried with this brooch also had a pair of saucer-brooches (cf. Fig. 1.10), amber beads, and other items including a small wooden pail, something often filled with food and therefore probably associated with feasting. These signs of her high status and thus of that associated with great square-headed brooches generally seems confirmed by the position of her grave next to that of a man buried with a sword (Fig. 1.11). (Drawn by Nick Griffiths from the collections of the Wiltshire Heritage Museum, Devizes. Actual size.)

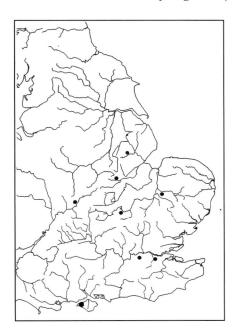
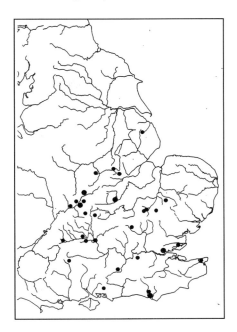
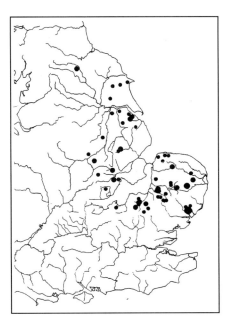

Fig. 1.9. Distributions over time of sixth-century great square-headed brooches, showing how widespread were the earliest (upper left), becoming more frequent (right), but finally confined to areas where they had hardly appeared at first (lower left). (Maps by John Hines reproduced with his permission from Hines 1997, 203–4; one phase omitted.)

Fig. 1.10. Left: one of a pair of saucer-brooches from Fairford, Gloucestershire, also with face-masks, but in these cases surrounded by Style I animal ornament, its 'exploded' features clarified in the drawing alongside; the creatures have recognizable ancestry in late Roman provincial art (cf. Fig. 1.4), but had mutated in Scandinavia. Right: a button-brooch from Wonston, Hampshire, with a face-mask. (Drawn by Nick Griffiths from the original shown to Winchester City Museums in 1996, and from the collections of the Ashmolean Museum, Oxford. Actual sizes.)

distribution has any meaning, it is that 'Anglian' culture only emerged as distinct from 'Saxon' quite a long time after the majority of the migrants are thought to have been on the move.

Some saucer-brooches have geometrical ornament probably derived from late Roman and quoit-brooch styles, providing another example of the transfer of designs from male to female gear. Others have what is known as Style I decoration, which also occurs on great square-headed brooches. This creates complex patterns of strange animals and human masks thought to have emerged from Scandinavia, but much affected by late Roman motifs and brought to England in part at least through Kent. Saucer-brooches are nearly all found a long way from the east coast. Was Style I nevertheless being used to claim ancestral descent from faraway places overseas?[63] Why does Style I occur on brooches worn by women so much more than on sword fittings or shield mounts that would better have asserted male affiliations?[64] How many people would even have stood close enough to the wearer to see them? Why are some of the punch-marks similar to some on pottery urns, but not all?

The complexities of claims to origins can be explored further through another type of square-headed brooch, which has a different terminal shape from the others, but often also has Style I ornament. In Britain, such brooches are found mostly in Kent, and since their parallels are mostly with Jutland, they have been used to argue for the truth of Bede's eighth-century assertion that the people of Kent were of Jutish origin.[65] An early sixth-century solid silver example was excavated in a cemetery at Apple Down in West Sussex, in the grave of a young woman who was also wearing a buckle of Kentish type; she had two saucer-brooches as well, however, which are very rarely found in Kent. Because 'Sussex' derives from 'South Saxons', the Kentish-style objects demand explanation. West Sussex is not far from the Isle of Wight, whose people Bede said were Jutish like those of Kent, as were those on the mainland opposite Wight. Bede may have been explaining a link between Kent and Wight that need not have been a matter of race, but which certainly shows up in some of the objects found in graves on the island. Was that where the girl had come from, taking some of her own things with her when she married someone in west Sussex—and, since saucer-brooches are not known on Wight, had she been given them by her mother-in-law? Or, since there were fly pupae on two of her brooches, showing that there had been sufficient time between her death and funeral for 'flies to have been attracted to the corpse and laid eggs there',[66] could she even have died somewhere a long way from west Sussex, and been brought to Apple Down to be buried in the community in which she had been born, rather than where she had spent her brief married life? Had she gone to be married in the Isle of Wight, or even in Kent, taking with her saucer-brooches that had belonged to her mother, returning with them in death together with a Jutish brooch from her mother-in-law, which thus only entered Sussex after its final owner's death? If the latter is the explanation, then nothing in any grave should automatically be assumed to have had much meaning for those living locally.

In other words, this single grave neatly demonstrates some of the problems in discussing a person's origins, for one object signals in one direction and another in the opposite.[67] The costume in which the woman had been buried might not even have been what she had worn in life, as those who saw to her last rites may have preferred to dress her according to their own customs, which she herself might have rejected. Not only were many brooches old and much worn or repaired when buried, but some were sewn in place, suggesting that they may not have been taken on and off as everyday clothes-fasteners. It cannot even, therefore, be taken for granted that what accompanies someone in a grave had accompanied them in life, or that the number or quality of the objects directly reflected their status or wealth.[68]

Occasionally an object is found which suggests that it was being worn by someone who did not know what it was. Pairs of metal fittings are found in positions indicating that they held sleeve-ends together on costume worn in the Midlands and the north; there are one or two of these wrist-clasps in Kent and Sussex, but there they are single pieces, apparently worn as though they were brooches.[69] Were they spoils of war; or had they originally been brought to Kent by a bride, but not buried with her and perhaps passed on to a daughter? The appropriate way to wear them was subsequently forgotten because Kentish costume did not include wrist-fastenings, but they nevertheless retained some value as heirlooms, a reminder of distant origins. Another example of an object not being used in its original manner is the zoomorphic penannular brooch being worn as a bracelet at Bifrons.[70]

Wrist-clasps are usually seen as one of the ways in which material culture helped to create a sense of 'Anglian' identity in the sixth century north of the Thames. From its distribution south of the Thames, a 'Saxon' brooch type seems to have been a small gilt 'button-brooch', usually with a recognizable human face cast on its surface (Fig. 1.10),[71] masks that also occur in the centres of some of the saucer-brooches[72]—yet those brooches were acceptable in both areas. There are also a few saucer- and rather more button-brooches in east Kent, despite its supposedly being peopled by Jutes—and indeed, having more objects with parallels in Denmark than in the rest of England. But no grave in Kent has objects that are all exclusively 'Jutish'; it is as though some items were accepted and others rejected, as were things from Francia and other parts of the continent, creating an identity that was specific to east Kent itself.[73]

Another example of objects which on their own might suggest close links and assimilation includes the small Type G 'British' penannular brooches found in 'Anglo-Saxon' graves. But many were not being worn on the dead person's costume, as some seem to have been in bags or purses, and they occur with a seemingly miscellaneous assortment of other items, not with things that suggest a strong affinity with the societies in the west and north. One in a cemetery at West Heslerton, North Yorkshire, was with necklaces of amber and glass beads, including four 'gold-in-glass' examples, probably late fifth- or sixth-century Anglo-Saxon.[74] That cemetery had as many as sixteen purse-groups in female graves. The contents of these little bags have been variously interpreted: as random collections of scrap brought together for recycling; as amulets for healing and fortune-telling; and as demonstrations of respect for things from the past.[75] Respect for things that carried the authority of Rome may well be shown by the use of base-metal coins pierced to be worn on necklaces, and unpierced ones in the purse-groups.[76]

The role of women in long-distance social transactions is shown by the possible interpretations of material like the wrist-clasps in Kent and the Jutish square-headed brooch at Apple Down. Objects could travel by a variety of means, and the movers need not always have been male, whether smiths, traders, raiders, or warriors. If the great *Beowulf* poem can be taken as reflecting anything of the values of the sixth century, it shows the importance of aristocratic women in creating alliances and the settling of feuds through marriage—and how they could restart such feuds when their precarious position in an alien society caused them to be abused in some way that their blood family needed to avenge.[77] Women, especially young women, were important as political negotiators or 'peace-weavers', even if they did not wield formal power. Marriages were probably important social events, no less important than funerals, and occasions when gifts would be exchanged, some of which might end up in graves.[78] Furthermore, it may not have been only women of the highest status who married out of their local communities, for there is now evidence of everyday contacts over the sort of distance that could easily have taken a young person more than 50 miles from their birthplace.[79]

This evidence is provided by a seemingly mundane type of pottery, used both for burial urns and domestically, which is distinctive only for one thing: that it happens to contain within its clay a mineral which is found in this country nowhere except in Leicestershire's Forest of Charnwood. Yet this unimpressive pottery has been recognized at sites as far apart as the London basin and central Yorkshire.[80] Communities receiving it cannot have been very self-contained, because surely only regular and routine exchange would have taken this everyday pottery from place to place, not the sort of aristocratic, political, or ritual mechanisms that could account for the travels of prestigious goods. The same is true of whetstones and hones, which are also found both in graves and in occupation sites, some of which were made from stone that outcrops a long way from the findspot.[81]

Partly because traditional explanations seem no longer fully adequate and distributions of object types do not necessarily make patterns that neatly coincide with long-held assumptions derived from Bede and other written sources, alternative meanings are now sought in studies of early Anglo-Saxon objects, taking advantage of their considerable quantity and the precision of their contexts when properly recorded. That the number of objects and the probable scarcity of materials used in making them suggest a society with distinct hierarchies—some people having more access to resources than others—is no longer seen as quite such an obvious deduction. The 'wealthier' might have been heads of households, for instance, rather than local leaders like Sussex's putative Paecca. An increase in the quantities and values of things deposited can be seen as 'social' or 'symbolic' capital, reflecting long-term accumulation of family rather than personal prestige, and perhaps of obligations as well.[82] The age at which people died is one factor that probably affected what was put in their graves, women being most important to a family while they were producing its next generation, and thus, like the young woman at Apple Down, given the most jewellery in death. Infants and children, however, were rarely included in cemeteries with adults, and even more rarely provided with grave-goods, as though they had died before they could become people. Such objects as they were given often seem 'amuletic', to drive off evil spirits.[83]

A spear in a burial need not simply be symbolic of someone who had the right to defend their community; it could be a symbol of their right to take part in violence to avenge personal injury, the theme of the early law codes.[84] The men given shields, or even more rarely swords (Fig. 1.11), were not necessarily the richest; they tend to be people who had died in their fighting prime, when most useful to their communities. Swords may have had overtones that went beyond wealth and status. As 'the work of giants' or of magic smiths, they may have been viewed as something generally less suitable for graves. On

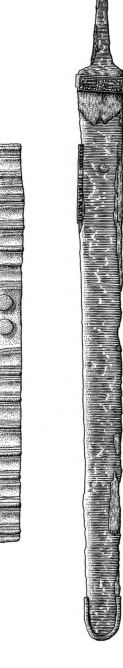
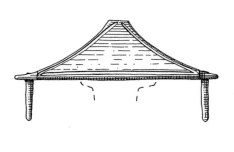

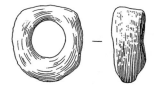

Fig. 1.11. A sword and its fittings from a late fifth-/sixth-century male grave at the Blacknall Field cemetery (cf. Fig. 1.8). It has a copper-alloy triangular pommel of no great distinction apart from a white-metal coating to make it flash in the sun, but the gilded mouth-band of the scabbard is one of the most elaborate known, with a face-mask flanked by Style I animal/bird heads, and spiral ornament in the panel above (cf. Figs. 1.4 and 1.10). The scabbard was edged with copper-alloy strips, of which one length is shown, and had an iron chape at the end; it was made of wood and leather, partly surviving below the mouth-band. The bone bead was probably attached to a short upper guard that has not survived but can be assumed from the nails at the ends of the pommel; bead-rings seem to have been amulets for good fortune in war. The copper-alloy chain may be a union for linking two narrow straps; poems refer to 'peace-bands' holding a sword in its scabbard, so undoing them was a challenge to fight. (Drawn by Nick Griffiths from the collections of the Wiltshire Heritage Museum, Devizes. Sword 1:6, fittings actual size.)

the other hand, fifth-century swords were not usually made of good enough iron to have been reliable in battle; during the sixth century an increasing number of blades was made by 'pattern-welding', creating a composite of straight and twisted rods that has greater ability to absorb blows as well as a more eye-catching surface. An early example at West Heslerton has a wavy, snakelike pattern created by the welding; most have a herringbone effect. Swords may have become special, as gifts from a lord rather than things inherited or acquired by exchange. Their particular significance was sometimes enhanced by a bead or metal ring fitted to their pommels, presumably as an amulet, which was often removed from a sword before burial, suggesting some particular belief.[85]

Most cemeteries have substantial proportions of unfurnished graves, which are not usually in distinct zones but in amongst the furnished graves. So their occupants were probably members of the same household—not necessarily always of the same family, as some might have been slaves or young people being fostered.[86] Objects in inhumation burials usually emphasize the difference between the male and female genders, but that may not mean that in their working lives such differences were strongly maintained. The need for everyone to take part in all farming and household activities is very strong when there are quite small populations working in tight-knit groups. In death the gender difference was re-established, at least for the more important people.[87] If daily tasks were done by whoever was available at the time, iron tools would not have been associated with one gender rather than another, and besides may have been too important to a household's survival to be sacrificed to graves, in which few are found.[88] Knives are not like other iron tools, because they are frequent finds in graves, with both men and women. There is a correlation between the length of a knife and someone's age,[89] which suggests that a new knife was bestowed on people at progressive stages in their lives, making the knife more particular to the individual, an affinity strengthened by its being carried on a belt most of the time.

The near-absence of tools from graves has always cast doubt on the assumption that people were given things that they might need in the afterlife, as though it was like Valhalla.[90] Instead, some parallel spirit world may be envisaged, in which the dead might transmute into invisible presences within the visible and tangible world, capable of causing harm if upset. The dragon that protected its treasure and was killed by Beowulf may be an example, and the Style I human and animal masks another: not whole creatures, but 'exploded' to break up their magical powers.[91] Disposing of tokens with the dead might mean that they would not resent seeing things that they had owned in the human world still being used or worn.

Young people who died in their prime might need more such tokens to appease them. An example may be a young man buried at Carisbrooke on the Isle of Wight around the middle of the sixth century with a gold-plated coin in his mouth, gaming-counters—of ivory except for one in cobalt-blue glass—

an iron knife, four different types of vessel, including a drinking-horn with Style I mounts—but no weapons.[92] Placing a coin in the mouth was a traditional Roman practice to provide the dead with 'Charon's obol', a token to pay for the ferry across the River Styx. This custom may have lingered on the other side of the Channel, so could account for the Wight example;[93] if so, it is another example of the range of possible burial beliefs in the Anglo-Saxon sixth century.

Less likely to be expressions of age or hierarchical standing are bone combs, which are not unusual in graves; nor are tweezers for removing hair and clipping nails. Broken ones in settlement sites show that people paid attention to their personal appearance, and were not merely smartened up for their funerals. Such functional explanations are only part of the story, however, since miniature combs, shears, and tweezers are sometimes found in cremation urns, and must have been specially made to go into them. Objects like these may show that the Anglo-Saxons paid particular attention to clippings removed from human bodies, perhaps attributing magical powers to them.[94]

Other interpretations stress social behaviour. When a death occurs, those who are left have to revise their relationships to each other. Some of the things in graves may therefore be ritualized gifts, symbols that someone is displaying their dependence on or subservience to the dead person, and that that relationship is being continued with the heirs if the gift symbolizes an acceptance that tributes must be given. The objects and the rituals that accompany the burial become a way of claiming inheritance, displaying the right of an heir to dispose of the dead person and thus to take over their role in life. It is sometimes said that the more that is buried, the more such relationships are in doubt and have to be affirmed by lavish display. This may happen when there is competition, for land or other resources, particularly between small groups, whereas when an aristocracy is confident of its inheritance it does not need to demand sacrifices from its people, who are not going to cease to be submissive because their old lord is dead.

Societies in which kin relations dominate will need less display to reaffirm relationships than those in which feckless warbands constantly form, dissolve, and regroup according to the successes and failure of their members. On that basis the sixth century certainly seems more unstable and fluid than the fifth, but such interpretations can be taken too literally; increases in weapons may signal warbands and warfare, or they may have been illustrations of myths about ancestors coming from overseas and fighting to win the land where their descendants now lived—and who were now buried with symbols of their forebears' prowess so that they could claim to be worthy heirs. Some types of object might have been favoured if they could be seen as stressing differences from a competing group who claimed different origins, but so few are clearly exclusive to any identifiable region, except perhaps Kent, that fluidity rather than stability of territories seems likely.[95]

Even though a few brooches were old when buried, there was rapid change in their designs, showing that people were not resistant to new ideas and modes. Much of the jewellery became flashier than the quoit-brooch and other styles had been. The equal-arm brooches showed the way, with eye-catching gilding (Col. pl. A.2). The effect of silver could be achieved by white-metal plating, used even on simple flat disc-brooches with a few 'ring-and-dot' devices countersunk in their faces. Cruciform brooches became more elaborate in their shapes.[96] Saucer-brooches and great square-headed brooches were cast with deep relief ornament, so that they would sparkle whatever angle the light came from. The latter were often further embellished with punch-marks, and much more rarely inlaid with niello, a black sulphide powder heated to form a paste, or enamelled; one or two have glass or garnet settings.[97] The saucer-brooches were sometimes punched, but apparently never inlaid.[98] There are also more beads, made of glass, amber, and sometimes crystal. Gold, however, is notably scarce, except for the small amounts used in gilding. Even silver was not common. The great square-headed brooches seem to have been high-status objects, yet only half-a-dozen of the couple of hundred known are of silver, none of gold.[99]

Some opportunities for display seem not to have been grasped. One new introduction enabled iron to be made more spectacular, either by inlaying it with silver or by overlaying it with silver sheets, on weapons and buckles. Used in various parts of the continent, this technique may have originated in Scandinavia; nevertheless, despite so much evidence of style borrowings from the north, silver on or in iron remained unusual in Britain, even when commonly found on seemingly prestigious objects overseas (cf. Fig. 2.12).[100] It may have been too obviously new and thus too directly associated with alien cultures to be acceptable, unlike objects and styles that developed traditional modes, albeit taking them in new directions.

A little less rare are gold discs, thin enough to have patterns impressed into them, some also being punched or given gold-wire surrounds. Worn as pendants, the earliest of these 'bracteates' are embossed with crowned heads in imitation of imperial coins, like two from Oxfordshire, where they were not from graves but may represent some sort of votive sacrifice deposited in running water, as they must have been too valuable to lose casually.[101] One is the first known post-Roman object on which there are Latin letters, so it is probably not coincidence that another bracteate, from Undley, Suffolk, is the first to have the Germanic script, runes.[102] The bracteates' origins are again in Scandinavia, where they developed into a means of promoting the cult of Woden.[103] A die for making one with a Woden image was found in a grave at Broadstairs, Kent, but the designs on the earlier pendants in England are otherwise mostly in Style I. Again, therefore, they can be seen as Kent's partial acceptance and partial rejection of a Jutish identity. Outside Kent they were more likely to be made in silver, or even copper alloy. Although they were pendants, they may have had a role that went beyond the ornamental and amuletic; their derivation from coins means that they might have been what anthropologists term 'primitive valuables' that can be used as units of assessment.[104]

In the same way, gold coins were beginning to reach England from the continent in the sixth century, as the Carisbrooke grave shows, making people familiar with the concept of fixed values and weighed payments. The coins were not only *solidi*, but their one-third subdivisions, 'thrymsas' (also called *trientes* or 'tremisses'). They are not found in large numbers, and most come from east Kent, where, in contrast to the continent, they are nearly all in graves, often set in mounts to be worn as pendants (Fig. 2.7), so that their date of burial may be long after their minting, itself usually a very uncertain date. The only sixth-century hoard reported anywhere in Britain is of ten thrymsas recorded as found in 1848 in the bed of the River Thames at Kingston, Surrey. Unfortunately, too little is known about it for anything further to be said.[105] Gold was again available in western Europe, principally because of subsidies paid in Byzantine coins; already in the fifth century the Frankish leader Chilperic had received 50,000 *solidi* from the emperor, who was also buying the support of Ostrogoths and others. In their turn the Ostrogoths paid the Franks 150,000 *solidi* in 537. If sums like these had any reality in fact, royal treasuries were awash with gold, where it sat inertly until required for gift-giving to reward loyal supporters and to show largesse, or was released to goldsmiths for turning into jewellery. It presented a constant temptation to challenge for power, so was one of the destabilizing factors in western societies.[106]

Whilst furnished graves provide a plethora of data about deliberately deposited objects, accidentally lost or discarded things are also found in profusion within the backfills of the below-ground hollows of the many 'sunken-featured buildings' that characterize settlements of the fifth century onwards, in which rubbish accumulated when they were abandoned. Much of this residue of everyday activities consists of things that were not usually chosen for burial, such as clay loom-weights. Bits of pottery are common; one distinctive type is low-fired and handmade, with quantities of straw and other farmyard debris, probably from animal dung, mixed in to bind the clay. This 'organic-tempered' pottery is not a late Roman type, but nor is it Germanic. It seems to have been made in the south in the fifth century, spreading northwards well beyond the Thames, but was less universal than the sunken-featured buildings.[107] Like Charnwood Forest ware, it might be used both domestically and for burial, as it is found in many settlements as well as in cemeteries.[108] Indeed, discarded sherds suggest that even decorated vessels were not treated with particular respect, despite the same stamps being used on cremation urns.[109] Where direct comparison has been possible between pots in a settlement with urns from an adjacent cemetery, however, it has appeared that some forms were considered less appropriate for burial than for everyday use.[110]

Charnwood Forest ware must have been made within the small area where the granitic mineral that characterizes it occurs, implying specialist producers, perhaps doing their own distribution. The settlement at West Heslerton, which apparently originated from a Roman shrine and where the cemetery has also been excavated, has been interpreted as having a distinct 'industrial' zone, which could have been supplying manufactured goods to a wide area as well as to its own people and cemetery, perhaps because the shrine had given it a focal role in its region.[111] Most settlements, however, probably concentrated on agriculture and domestic production of basics like textiles, having no particular specialization. West Heslerton is also unlike most in having been used in the fourth century. Even sites which, from their names, might have been expected to have had an origin in the Roman period did not necessarily have one; Walton, the *tun* or 'farmstead' of the *wala*, 'Welsh'/'British', is a frequent name in Anglo-Saxon areas, implying an enclave of indigenes. But excavation within the Walton near Aylesbury in Buckinghamshire had no Roman predecessor below it, though an unstratified late Roman buckle-frame and a quoit-brooch imply some sort of use of the immediate area in the first half of the fifth century. The contents of its backfilled sunken-featured buildings included such 'Anglo-Saxon' objects as a 'small-long' brooch, however.[112]

As well as objects, many of these early post-Roman settlement sites contain evidence of metalworking: blacksmithing predominates because of the slag residues, with smelting slag from preparation of the ores less common.[113] Some scrap metal seems to have been scavenged from Roman sites for recycling, as Roman iron and copper-alloy items have been found in settlements which were not used before the fifth century.[114] Even if some base-metal Roman coins were respected and buried, others may have been intended for the melting-pot,[115] and analyses show a wide range of alloys being used, indicative of eclectic mixing and what has been called a 'scrap economy'.[116] Collections seemingly of scrap iron are another manifestation of it, and may account for the low carbon content of analysed sword-blades. The availability of metals affected jewellery also; the first wrist-clasps, for instance, were often in good-quality silver because it was quite accessible to the smiths working in Norway, but its greater scarcity in Britain meant that designs had to be adapted for copper alloy. Seeming anomalies become comprehensible, such as the use of the same punches on a great square-headed brooch at Linton Heath, Cambridgeshire, as on another pair of brooches in the same grave, made in a different alloy— the smith had to use what metal he could get.[117]

Roman pottery may also have been gathered up occasionally, though the reason is less clear; colour-coated and samian ware were often selected, however, so the hope may have been to scrape off the colours for use as dyes. Whole bases made convenient hard discs, perhaps for gaming-pieces.[118] Glass was also collected, both for bead-making and for recycling into new vessels, with coloured glass being especially sought.[119] Lead and tin are found in small quantities, the former perhaps for soldering rather than turning into pewter.[120]

Just as Charnwood Forest pottery is causing reconsideration of the extent and frequency of the contacts enjoyed by the post-Roman settlements, so too there is increasing evidence from the rubbish-pits that what must have been quite precious things were available and in use, not carefully stored and reserved for special occasions and funerals. At Mucking only six pieces of broken glass escaped recycling, but one was a 'claw' from an elaborate claw-beaker, probably sixth-century (cf. Fig. 1.12).[121] Four broken pieces of claw-beakers, as well as other glass, were excavated at West Stow, Suffolk.[122] At Mucking various brooches had been mislaid, one a saucer-brooch that had not been properly cast, another a Type G penannular; there were also parts of an unused clay mould for making a sixth-century great square-headed brooch.[123]

Direct evidence of brooch manufacture is rare, but enough to suggest that some took place at sites that seem to be ordinary houses and farms with their cemeteries adjacent to them. Presumably they were visited by travelling smiths, since few people would have had the skill,[124] the tools, or the materials, let alone the knowledge of the designs, to make them. Whether scavenging could have yielded enough gold to allow for new brooches to be gilded may be doubted, and it certainly could not have produced the mercury needed to 'fire' the gold into place. The smiths who made the jewellery must have had their own ways of getting at least the latter, which probably came ultimately from north Spain.[125] If the customers travelled, it has to be believed that the pattern on a brooch was so distinctive of a family or other group that even a broken mould was taken home to stop it falling into the wrong hands.[126] But there may also have been smiths who used permanent centres; buildings next to the predominantly cremation cemetery at Spong Hill, Norfolk, contained debris that could well have been a metalworker's, raising the possibility of things regularly made there for putting into the funeral pyres.[127]

In Kent continental coins were used as a gold source by smiths, as is shown by the fragment of a late fifth-century thrymsa with jeweller's rouge on it found close to a small sheet of gold within the walls of Canterbury. These finds show that a goldsmith worked there, though not necessarily on a permanent basis— he may have been an occasional visitor serving patrons who came there on special occasions for royal assemblies.[128] Other early coins in Kent include some in graves at Faversham, a name meaning 'the homestead, *ham*, of the smith(s)', in a cemetery still known as King's Field in the nineteenth century, in which were found what could be unfinished items of jewellery. Glass was probably being made in Kent at least in the sixth century, and permanent glass-houses for that are essential; Faversham is a distinct possibility.[129]

Fig. 1.12. Claw-beaker in light green glass from Great Chesterford, Essex, probably sixth-century and made, perhaps in Kent, by blowing a stemmed beaker on a punty rod, applying extra trails of glass below the rim and above the base, and adding the claws individually. (Photograph reproduced by courtesy of the British Museum, London. This example was selected for illustration in recognition of the contribution to glass studies made by its excavator, Vera I. Evison. Actual size.)

Faversham may provide an example of a place already serving aristocratic and royal patrons by the middle of the sixth century. Otherwise, the settlement sites excavated in the areas with furnished graves are not distinctive enough in the fifth and sixth centuries for separate chieftains' places like the hillforts in the north and west to be recognized. That situation was soon to change.

2

Expressions of the Elites

From the Later Sixth Century to the Later Seventh

Because both Gildas and Bede wrote of mutual antipathy between Britons and Anglo-Saxons, it used to be thought self-evident that their hostility was expressed by the cultural differences that appear so obvious in the formers' Christianity, Celtic speech, hillforts, and unfurnished graves, and the latters' cremations, furnished inhumations, sunken-featured buildings, great square-headed brooches, and the like. Different ideas about the adaptations that had to be made to meet changing circumstances have led to reappraisals of extreme positions about racial exclusiveness, however, and emphasis is now placed on the ways that people created new identities rather than on how they inherited one of two alternative dichotomies.[1] The spread of furnished graves westwards and northwards in the second half of the sixth century could be taken as evidence of further waves of immigrants from the continent, but at least as likely is that existing populations were changing their practices as new conditions developed.

In the west and north, the most visible change in the archaeological record after the middle of the sixth century is the disappearance of Mediterranean imported pottery from hillforts and other sites, replaced by southern French wares, implying that wine and olive oil shipped in wooden casks from the Loire valley and Bordeaux replaced Greek and African supplies sent in clay amphoras. As with the earlier bowls and dishes, the assumption is that much of the pottery was 'associative', sought after because it was seen as appropriate to use at feasts when luxuries were offered by a host. Unlike the earlier imports, however, in the seventh century there were also open-topped jars that seem to have been used as containers, presumably for dry goods as liquids would have slopped out. Some were used for cooking. The French seventh-century pottery, now called E-ware, is a little more often found than are the earlier wares; its absence from South Cadbury is good evidence that that site went out of use c.600, despite its former importance—a sign of the continued instability of the period.[2]

Just as none of the Mediterranean imported pottery had reached places far from the west coast, so too the French wares did not pass inland, or up the English Channel. Imports of glass have a broadly similar distribution, although dating is more difficult. A glassmaking kiln found recently in Bordeaux is further evidence that south-west France is the likely source of fragments found at many of the sites that have E-ware, but the glass may have started to arrive earlier.[3] It does not, however, seem to have been going any further eastwards, though a couple of pieces have been found in the upper Severn valley.[4] This limited distribution seems particularly strange as the south-west of France passed from Visigothic to Frankish control, and the Franks' existing, and expanding, contacts with eastern parts of the island would have removed any political reason for limiting the trade. Southern Gaul had retained much of its Romanized culture, however, to which the British in the north and west may still have aspired, in contrast to the peoples in the east.

Assimilation as well as polarization is also hinted at, however; glass and metal artefacts found in western Britain were not all made either in France or by the British themselves. In the sixth century someone took a 'Saxon' button-brooch to South Cadbury, which seems to have been casually lost there (cf. Fig. 1.10). Deliberately deposited under the metalled track through the main gate, however, along with a formidable iron axe-hammer, was a disc with Style I ornament.[5] The latter is not necessarily an Anglo-Saxon product just because it has Anglo-Saxon ornament, as it is an exceptional object, but despite its stylistic connotations it seems to have been a votive offering at this important British site.[6] Style II (e.g. Col. pls. B.2–4 and C.1–2, and Figs. 2.11 and 2.12), which generally replaced Style I around the end of the sixth century, with sinuous, ribbon-like creatures either on their own or intricately paired, was not found at South Cadbury, but objects with it have been found at other western sites, such as a mount with an elegant, almost abstract, outline of two long-snouted animals at the Cannington cemetery, also in Somerset.[7] Its occurrence there could result from the Wessex kingdom's conquests during the second half of the seventh century, helping to explain a few furnished inhumations in Somerset and Dorset. But conquest is not likely to account for a sixth-century great square-headed brooch fragment at Bath, and certainly not for objects in Anglo-Saxon forms, including some with Style II, at Dinas Powys.[8] Such things might have been brought in as scrap metal for melting down, but there seem rather too many of them still in a recognizable condition for that. The same applies to glass vessels, as 'Germanic' ones were arriving as well as those from south-west France.[9] In the same way, a thin scatter of Anglo-Saxon objects shows contact, if not conquest, in the north-west around the River Mersey and in Cumbria; at least some of the latter were found in graves.[10]

Southern French pottery and imported glass were also getting to sites north of Hadrian's Wall, but here too there is growing evidence of contact with the

Fig. 2.1. Some of the moulds found at Dunadd used for casting bird-headed penannular brooches. The one on the left has very fine interlace cut into the frame—a feature that might be expected to have been engraved freehand into the metal after casting. (Drawing by Howard Mason reproduced by permission of Cardiff University from the collections of the National Museums of Scotland, Edinburgh. Actual size.)

Anglo-Saxon world. Excavations at the Dunadd hillfort produced fragments such as a thin copper-alloy sheet impressed with a Style II creature which are more likely to have come directly from the Anglo-Saxon south than to be local adaptations of Anglo-Saxon designs. Things like that could have been waiting to be melted down for recycling, but a gold and garnet stud that is almost certainly of Anglo-Saxon workmanship looks as if it was something being kept for resetting rather than for breaking up.[11]

Broken moulds show that production of penannular brooches continued at Dunadd; particularly interesting are six for casting some with bird-headed terminals, a design idea derived from the south (Fig. 2.1). Brooches with terminals very similar to those that would have come from the Dunadd moulds have been found in Northumbrian cemeteries in England, such as Sewerby, Yorkshire. They are rather different from the Type G penannulars, as those did not have specifically Germanic design elements.[12] The Sewerby brooch and others like it could have been made in the north for sale in the south, but more likely the Dunadd moulds were copied from Anglo-Saxon work, so that a double borrowing was taking place—the 'Celtic' penannular brooch was having 'Germanic' ornament added to it by the Anglo-Saxons, which the British were then copying. The same thing was probably happening in Wales, as an annular brooch with two confronted birdlike heads with many Anglo-Saxon parallels was found recently at Llanbedrgoch, Anglesey (Fig. 2.2).[13]

The smiths working at Dunadd made things which drew on very eclectic sources, and were not seeking to create a style specific to the emerging kingdom; they were more concerned to show contacts with other elites than to express differences from them. Whoever was ruling, the population may not have changed much.[14] Further south, the Solway Firth came under Anglo-Saxon political control during the seventh century, as did the Cheviot Hills up to the Firth of Forth, but again there may have been little population change.

Fig. 2.2. Cast copper-alloy seventh-century annular brooch, from Llanbedrgoch, Anglesey. Although a complete circle, it is very similar to the penannulars made at Dunadd (Fig. 2.1), but its heads with their curved beaks and angular backs are more similar to seventh-century Anglo-Saxon styles (e.g. Figs. 2.11 and 2.14). Despite these parallels, there is no reason to assume that it was not made in Wales. (Photograph reproduced by courtesy of the National Museums and Galleries of Wales, Cardiff. Actual size, detail enlarged ×3.)

A few Anglo-Saxon objects have been found at sites like Dunbar, where ownership probably switched for a while. Some of the things were valuable, such as the arm of a small gold and garnet cross. Dunbar was another site where various metals were being worked.[15] On the other hand, some sites where metalworking had been practised may have been abandoned as the Anglo-Saxons advanced; the Mote of Mark had been a flourishing centre in Kirkcudbrightshire, but was apparently deserted in the 670s, although its metalworking had shown earlier acceptance of Anglo-Saxon idioms.[16]

It was partly because of such external pressure that some sort of political coalition emerged north of the Firth of Forth, in what came to be known as Pictland,[17] where incised into rock faces are some distinctive designs that also occur on freestanding stone slabs, cave walls, silverware, and even large pebbles. Some are animals and birds, mostly identifiable to species and chosen perhaps for their aggressive qualities, like boars and stags, or for the mysterious way that they appear and disappear with the seasons, like geese.[18] Some symbols are geometrical, others identifiable as objects such as combs and perhaps tableware.[19] Their meanings have been much discussed; one possibility is that they were a statement of defiance against Northumbrian and Irish raiders—and Scandinavian at the end of the eighth century—and a reminder of former triumphs against the Roman Empire.[20] Individual symbols may relate to particular families and kin-groups, and those on rocks or slabs may be territorial markers, though the latter's association with burials presumably means that they were also memorials. Something else must be meant by the grim-looking man at Barflat, Aberdeenshire,[21] who carries a long-shafted axe-hammer reminiscent of the votive deposit at South Cadbury, and is one of the earliest representations anywhere in post-Roman Britain of a full-length figure—earlier metalwork had had human masks, but seems generally to have shunned whole bodies.[22] Even more problematic are the precise dates of these Pictish pieces, and therefore whether they originated before similar designs were used in paintings in illuminated manuscripts such as the Book of Durrow, itself of very uncertain date and origin, though within the seventh century.[23]

Pictish symbols occur on a few pieces of silver, including some remarkably heavy chains which were once thought to be crowns, on the basis of a Celtic poem which has now been shown to be a forgery.[24] The chains have no parallel in the rest of Europe; some have been found well to the south of the heart of Pictland, though still within modern Scotland (Fig. 2.3). Two hoards, one found at Gaulcross, near Banff, Aberdeenshire, the other at Norrie's Law, Fifeshire (Fig. 2.4), also show that plenty of silver was available to the Picts; the latter is estimated to have contained at least 400 ounces.[25] A spoon suggests that much of the metal came from late Roman tableware acquired much earlier, at the time of the Traprain Law hoard, rather than from more recent raids or subsidy payments, as there is no reason to think that such quantities could any longer have been acquired in the south. Both hoards have handpins (Fig. 2.4), a type of object known in Roman Britain but which seems to have been maintained by the Picts and Irish from outside the Empire.[26] One of the Norrie's Law handpins has a Pictish symbol, but there are no symbols on any of the Gaulcross objects, which may therefore be a little earlier in date. Also in the Norrie's Law hoard were two plaques with symbols (Fig. 2.4), and two silver bands with flat terminals, which may also have a Roman ancestry, but in this case in army insignia worn on the chest—they might have been what was in the poet's mind when he wrote in *Y Gododdin* of 'torc-wearing' warriors; the British word derives from the Latin *torquis*, meaning 'twisted'.[27]

The Pictish symbols occur on small stones even as far north as the Orkney islands, which were being drawn not only into Pictish politics but into its culture, with metalworking and possibly bead-making practised at sites like Birsay.[28] The Irish-derived ogam script also reached the Orkneys, at least by the eighth century.[29] It was in use earlier in Dàl Riata, and further south in Wales and the south-west. The Picts may have made adaptations, but they were not isolated from developments elsewhere. They were even making and using copper-alloy hanging-bowls, so called because they have ring-handles from which they could be suspended. The rings were usually held by escutcheon-plates that fitted to the side of the bowls, and a mould for an openwork one has been found at Craig Phadrig, right up in Inverness.[30] Although nearly all the complete hanging-bowls have been found in seventh-century Anglo-Saxon graves, the manufacturing evidence suggests that they were no less sought after in the north (cf. Figs. 2.13 and 3.4).[31] A different type of disc, with enamel and spiral ornament, perhaps from the base of a bowl, was found at Dunadd; it could have been made there, or could be another of the objects brought there

Fig. 2.3. Pictish silver chain, seventh-century or earlier, from Whitecleugh, Lanarkshire. The terminal ring is engraved and has red enamel infill. The designs visible at the break do not seem particularly significant, but the rest of the circumference includes Pictish symbols (cf. Fig. 2.4). (Photograph reproduced by courtesy of the Trustees of the National Museums of Scotland, Edinburgh. About two-thirds actual size.)

for reuse, but—if indeed a base-escutcheon—again shows that the bowls had a wide circulation.[32] A disc with similar 'Celtic' ornament, though again not necessarily from a bowl, was excavated at Clatchard Craig, Fife, another site where broken clay moulds for penannular brooches and other debris show that metalworking was taking place.[33]

At Dunadd and Clatchard Craig fragments of moulds and motif-pieces show that before the end of the seventh century increasingly elaborate penannular brooches were being made, including some with large, flat triangular terminals, on which gold and other panels could be set (Fig. 2.5). Gold filigree wire was used on the most elaborate, which owed much to Anglo-Saxon designs and techniques, without being identical to them. A brooch found at Hunterston, Ayrshire, has Style II animal ornament, but can be differentiated from Anglo-Saxon workmanship (Fig. 2.6). Furthermore, it has insets of amber, which was almost never used on Anglo-Saxon metalwork, despite its popularity for beads. More difficult to determine is whether the brooch was made in Ireland or in Scotland, but the former is hinted at by the frame, which is not actually penannular, as the gap between its terminals is bridged by a large panel with a cross on it, a feature possibly copying a prototype that was a reliquary. The animals on it may look at first glance like Anglo-Saxon *wyrms* (serpents), but their meaning may have shifted to indicate the evil that threatens those who stray from God's protection, which could account for their appearance in illustrations in books like Durrow, a new medium of expression. Or they may be protecting the contents of the reliquary or book on which they appear. Craftworkers in different materials interacted with each other, so manuscripts were also embellished with Celtic spirals, coloured like enamelled hanging-bowl escutcheons or elaborate brooch terminals.[34]

Large penannular brooches are shown on two Pictish relief carvings, both being worn by women, one of whom seems to be leading a hunting party and is thus placed in the highest social rank. These sculptures may be the earliest representations in Britain of unequivocally contemporary secular costume, since the brooches could not have been copied from some classical drawing or carving. Their prominence suggests that they had significance as badges of status, so it is informative about gender roles in Pictish society that women are shown wearing them. Access to the most splendid brooches could have been deliberately restricted by kings in order to maintain the social hierarchy; the moulds at Dunadd were certainly at a site in royal control.[35]

To sustain the craftworkers at Dunadd and elsewhere required considerable resources, not least because they had to be supplied with metals and amber if they were to make things like the Hunterston brooch. Anything from outside a leader's own territory had to be acquired, by booty, tribute, gift, or trade. The E-ware pottery makes the last the most likely; a raider may make off with a barrel of wine, but would be less likely to take away the pottery that had arrived with it, nor would any king of another polity with gold to spare have

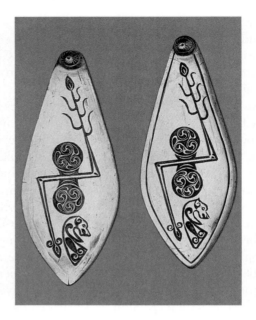

Fig. 2.4. Survivors from the Norrie's Law, Fife, hoard found in 1819 include two silver handpins and two plaques usually attributed to the seventh century—the total weight of the hoard is thought to have been some 25 pounds of silver. The handpins have red enamel and Celtic spirals on the front, and one has a Pictish Z-rod symbol on the back (not shown), like those on the plaques. Spirals occur again on those, within the two circles; at the bottoms are doglike heads and necks, with curves and spirals seen in other Pictish symbols. There are bosses at the tops, but no rivets or other means of attachment on the backs, and the function of the plaques is unknown. (Photographs reproduced by courtesy of the Trustees of the National Museums of Scotland, Edinburgh. Pin actual size (head enlarged × 1.5), plaques actual height 91 mm.)

Fig. 2.5. As well as moulds for casting brooches, Dunadd and other sites have produced examples of motif-pieces, preliminary designs worked out on flat stones or slates—presumably something more usually done on wood, scraps of parchment, wax tablets, or metal (cf. Fig. 3.3). This example is a design using compass-points for the layout of a large flat terminal for a penannular brooch (cf. Fig. 2.6). Although this motif-piece was unstratified, moulds for casting similar designs at Dunadd are from layers dated to the mid-seventh century—which suggests that some of the St Ninian's brooches (Fig. 3.4) were quite old when concealed, if they were indeed hidden during viking raids. (Photograph reproduced by courtesy of the Trustees of the National Museums of Scotland, Edinburgh. Actual size.)

needed to send tribute or subsidies to Dunadd, so far as is known. Gifts and marriage dowries may account for some finds of gold and silver, but people's regular payments to their king of agricultural products such as cattle that could be predicted as annually available, and which could be used in exchanges, would have made trade possible.[36]

By the time that the Hunterston brooch was manufactured Christianity had spread northwards and eastwards from Iona, and the Church probably played a major part in developing agriculture and trade, to support its members and its buildings. The range of crafts practised at churches was similar to that at the secular sites, with the addition of book production, at least at some of them. The Book of Durrow is often now attributed to Iona, where among the excavated evidence for metalworking are moulds for glass studs such as are known in Ireland, and which may have been intended for book covers.[37] Whithorn, another important church site, produced evidence such as a small gold ingot and rod, moulds, crucibles, and what may be iron-smelting as well as smithing debris in a sixth-/seventh-century workshop complex pre-dating the site's passing into Northumbrian control.[38] Waterlogged peat layers at Iona

Fig. 2.6. The Hunterston brooch was probably made towards the end of the seventh or early in the eighth century, perhaps in Ireland, subsequently fell into viking hands and had a runic inscription added to it on the back, and was eventually lost or hidden in Ayrshire, Scotland. Made of gilt silver, it has inset gold panels and amber settings, the latter now mostly decayed. Many of the the gold filigree wires in its panels form Style II ribbon animals, some with interlaced legs, tails, and lappets (coming out of the backs of their heads), others more snake-like; grains of gold are used for eyes and hipjoints. Bird-like heads mark the junctions of the hoop with the terminals, and the curved panels in the four corners of the filling between the terminals can be read as birds' beaks, with amber studs for eyes. Wherever it was originally made, it shows the wide range of cultural contact that typifies 'insular' pre-viking work. (Photograph reproduced by courtesy of the Trustees of the National Museums of Scotland, Edinburgh. Actual size.)

preserved leather and wood, the latter including evidence of oak and ash bowls being turned.[39] This reminder of what is usually missing from the archaeological record is useful, not least in showing one of the alternatives to the use of pottery. Buiston Crannog, Strathclyde, is another site where organic matter survived.

Of all the sites where E-ware from seventh-century France has been excavated, Buiston Crannog is the only one to have produced any evidence that coins were also known, albeit that the pottery was coming from an area where minting was reasonably prolific until the middle of the seventh century. Even so, Buiston Crannog did not yield an actual, solid gold coin, but a forgery of an English thrymsa made by soldering gold on to a copper-alloy flan. A little further south, another plated forgery was found at Yeavering, a Northumbrian palace site.[40] The earlier grave-find at Carisbrooke was also a plated copy. It seems strange that such pieces could have been so deceptive, but all three were beyond the zones where coins were reasonably familiar, and may have been passed off more easily; the jeweller at Canterbury had not been cheated, but he presumably knew what to look for.[41]

As more gold coins have been found, so the view has grown that their numbers are likely to indicate trade, not only subsidies and other forms of gift, compensation payments, or marriage dowries.[42] The thrymsas seem too small to have been very effective as a means of displaying prestige, and most look less elegant than the bigger *solidi*. Nevertheless, many had loops added to them so that they could be worn on necklaces (Fig. 2.7), and this would have taken them out of any incipient currency circulation. Those adapted for costume use are mostly from graves, as are a good many unmounted coins, so they may have had meanings which made them sought after and kept, perhaps in some areas more than others. Distribution is not therefore necessarily an exact guide to where coins were actually most available, and the high proportion found in graves in Kent may be a little misleading as evidence of a preponderance of overseas trade into that kingdom in the later sixth and first half of the seventh centuries; although fewer in number, stray finds in other areas could be an indication of links that may have been just as strong—the five north of the Thames in Essex, for instance, become more significant when viewed against the near absence of furnished burials in that area.[43]

All the same, Kent is associated with the earliest known coin to have an English place-name struck on it, a thrymsa with *Dorovernis Civitas*, the Latin name for Canterbury, on one side, and its maker's name, Eusebius, on the other.[44] Both his name and his skill (or more precisely that of the die-maker—who may have been an anonymous servant) suggest that Eusebius was a Frank, and from his literacy quite probably a cleric. The coin's design also includes a cross, and a bust in imperial style, like those on contemporary Merovingian issues. Its production early in the seventh century can be seen as a step towards

Fig. 2.7. Six Merovingian gold thrymsas dating to the two or three decades after c.590, mounted to be worn as pendants, probably from a single necklace in a woman's grave at Faversham, Kent, though because they were found during railway construction in the nineteenth century their precise context is not known. Coins like these provided the raw material for making gold jewellery in England, as well as being valued in their own right. These examples were minted at different places in modern France. The letters on the one at top left are BODANEX, the moneyer's name; the other legible one, lower right, is another name, FRANCIO. The design on that one is of two figures between a cross, whereas most have an imitation of a classical imperial bust. (Photograph reproduced by courtesy of the British Museum, London. Actual sizes.)

putting King Aethelberht of Kent on a par with continental and Christian rulers—one of whose daughters he had married.[45] The coin may have been his own idea, or that of the newly arrived archbishop, Augustine, who might have commissioned it as a flattering gift for the king. The queen's priest, Liudhard, may have provided some sort of precedent for this, if he had a hand in the production of the coinlike pendant that bears his name, found at one of the churches in Canterbury.[46]

Other uses to which gold coins might be put are shown by two hoards. One was found at Crondall, Hampshire, in 1828, and had probably been concealed in a richly decorated purse; there is no record of its being in a grave.[47] It was made up of ninety-seven thrymsas, three unstruck gold flans, and a gold-plated forgery. The intended number is surely an exact hundred, the forgery being a reject. If the thrymsa was a shilling,[48] that would be precisely the sum required as compensation for the slaying of a freeman if a feud with his family were to be avoided, according to the earliest known English written law code, that of King Aethelberht, promulgated *c*.600.[49] The other hoard was also in a purse, buried in Mound 1 at Sutton Hoo, Suffolk, one of the two ship-burials there; it contained thirty-seven thrymsas and three gold flans, suggesting that forty was an important number, though the two small ingots also in the purse do not weigh enough to be the equivalent of ten coins, to make up a half-hundred.[50] All the thrymsas were from different mints, which could have been deliberate—if picked at random from coins that were freely circulating, some duplication would be expected; some in the Sutton Hoo hoard were from mints that had very small outputs.[51] It could be a compensation payment, a subsidy, or a bribe, but the rather strange composition suggests that it is something more than just a casually collected treasure-store.

Aethelberht's use of writing to give authority to his laws is bound up with his acceptance of Christianity with its veneration for Holy Writ, to be expounded by the educated and revered by all. The laws' contents were not revolutionary, however, and preserve at least some elements of much older systems, modified into the custom current at the time.[52] As well as to shillings, the code refers to a 'lord-ring' payment, which suggests the use of something such as the rings in the fifth-century Patching hoard. The word 'shilling' derives from an old Germanic root *scilja*, 'to cut', which implies slicing gold from a ring or an ingot.[53] The importance of weights for creating and checking coins and other units is attested in England from as early as the middle of the sixth century by the finds of balance-sets, capable of accuracy to 0.2 g, of which one in a box at Watchfield, Oxfordshire, may be the earliest (Fig. 2.8).[54] The Anglo-Saxon thrymsas in the Crondall hoard mostly vary between 1.28 g and 1.33 g, with a few as low as 1.23 g and as high as 1.38 g, suggesting a limited 'tolerance' band either side of a target weight of 1.3 g.[55]

Just as the use of weights pre-dated the earliest production of coins amongst the Anglo-Saxons, so awareness of writing pre-dating their first documents is implied by a gold finger-ring set with a Roman gem found in a ship-burial at Snape, Suffolk, which probably dates to the second half of the sixth century (Fig. 2.9).[56] Because the gem could have been used as a seal, it might have been valued for that association by someone who had no real need for it, but who knew and respected what it was. It also shows an appreciation of Roman objects that goes well beyond the collection of scrap metal and the occasional use of a coin as a pendant. The gold coins with Latin inscriptions and

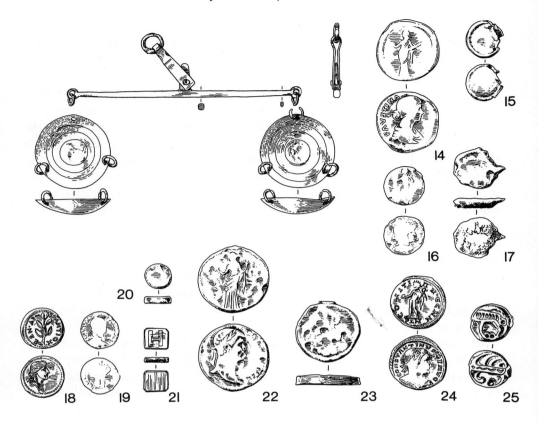

Fig. 2.8. A balance-scales set, probably mid- or late sixth-century, found in a decayed leather case in a cemetery at Watchfield, Oxfordshire. The pans would have hung down from the ends of the balance-beam on chains or thread. Properly adjusted, the balance is accurate to within 0.2 g, and the weights in the set seem to have been carefully graded down from the 18.1 g of the heaviest, no. 22, a Roman second-century *dupondius* coin. In some other sets coins were cut or filed to achieve precision. Here no. 18 is a Greek-inscribed coin from Syria and no. 25 a British first-century BC 'potin'. This eclectic mixture is augmented by two lead discs, nos. 15 and 20, and by a Byzantine weight, no. 21, for one third of a *solidus* (cf. Fig. 3.2). Other sets also have coins and objects that could not have come from a single source—some could have been scavenged from British or Romano-British sites, but not the Byzantine weight, and the Syrian coin would never have circulated in Britain; what lay behind the selection processes remains a mystery. (Drawing by Marion Cox reproduced with the author's permission from Scull 1990, 201. Actual size.)

Fig. 2.9. Gold ring from the ship-burial at Snape, Suffolk, with an antique gem in the bezel showing a standing figure representing *bonus eventus*, a wish for good fortune, though whether that would have been understood in late sixth-century Suffolk is doubtful. Instead, it was respect for the gem's classicism, antiquity, and refinement that would have made it sought. The goldwork is filigree wires and granulation; it is north European, not necessarily Anglo-Saxon, workmanship, and was not new when buried, as it is a little rubbed in places. (Photograph reproduced by courtesy of the British Museum, London. Actual size.)

imperial-style busts continued the trend. A gold ring with a pivoting seal-matrix recently discovered near Norwich may be a little later in date than the Snape ring, but is still remarkably early if it was ever used in England (Col. pl. B.5).[57]

Proximity to the continent rather than any other natural advantages placed Kent in the forefront of contacts with the Franks, whose coins and use of red garnets in jewellery were clearly influential. They were still getting most of their gold from the east, receiving subsidies from the Byzantine emperors of 50,000 *solidi* in the 570s and 30,000 in the 580s, and tribute from the Lombards of 12,000.[58] Garnets also had to be imported (Col. pls. B.1–2, B.4 and C.2, and Fig. 2.10). The flat ones that predominated until about the middle of the seventh century could have come from central East Europe, especially southern Bohemia, though they may have come from further away, in Afghanistan.[59] Shaping them involved highly skilled work; if it could be done with a bow-drill, which gives alternating backward and forward rotation, the craftsmen were not necessarily confined to one place, because the equipment was light and portable, allowing them to travel between patrons and from one royal residence to another. Continuous rotation would have required sophisticated plant that could not be moved, and the smiths would have had to be sedentary. Faversham, the 'homestead of the smiths', might have been a permanent centre, but the range of differently shaped garnets used, for instance at Sutton Hoo, which are not replicated in Kent suggests different makers and more than one centre. A third alternative is that the cutting was so skilled that it was only practised on the continent, perhaps at Cologne or Trier, and that drawings were sent there as templates.[60] The cut stones had to be polished, an operation that requires special sands; if carborundum was essential, it had to come from the island of Naxos in the Greek Cyclades,[61] which would have been another restriction. Nevertheless, to separate the cutting and polishing of the intricate shapes of the garnets from the goldworkers who were to set them into their cells would have created great practical difficulties.

Flat red, blue, and green glass could be cut to shape and used as inlays instead of garnets, but it was very difficult to achieve a pure and long-lasting white. Natural magnesite, which can be found near Faversham, cristobalite, or even powdered chalk mixed into a paste might be used for flat surfaces, but getting it to stay in place was tricky. Ivory was used for occasional bosses, but apparently not for flat inlays. Shells were turned into bosses also (Col. pl. B.2), and slivers were used in a few complex beads; native ones are unsuitable as they are either too soft or too brittle, and those used were from the Red Sea, so they were probably the rarest element in the jewellery in which they appeared, an inverse of modern values. Another good contrast with gold is niello, a black metallic sulphide fused into channels engraved into the gold, particularly well seen in the Sutton Hoo 'great gold buckle' (Fig. 2.11).[62]

Goldworkers not only had to make the cells into which the garnets fitted, but also twisted or beaded filigree wires made either by twisting a plain wire

Fig. 2.10. Highly magnified examples of red garnets of the kind increasingly used during the later sixth until the middle of the seventh century (cf. Col. pls. B.1 and B.2). The two on the left have very smooth curved edges and were probably cut using a wheel; on the right, the garnet appears to have been chipped, leaving much rougher edges. From the smith's grave at Tattershall Thorpe, Lincolnshire, cf. Figs. 2.18 and 2.19. (Photographs reproduced by courtesy of Lincolnshire County Council, City and County Museum. Enlarged ×15.)

or by rolling a grooved file or other tool across one. The wires then had to be manipulated into animal, herringbone, and other patterns, soldered to the gold backplate. Separate grains of gold soldered into place individually or in clusters also required skilled handling; their sizes help to make credible the precision required for the regulation of the alloys and weights of the coins (cf. Fig. 3.11).[63]

Considering all this effort and more, Aethelberht's law code says surprisingly little about material culture, apart from referring to 'property' inside a man's homestead. A 'king's smith' was given prominence and a high value, however, implying craftsmen in royal service who were unfree; such people could have been concentrated at a place like Faversham, to which supplies of food and materials were taken so that workers could concentrate on producing the most delicate objects and the most illustrious weapons. The food could have come from the king's own estates, or have been the 'renders' which his subjects owed him. If he and his entourage did not consume all this produce themselves, surpluses could be redirected—to the Church and for overseas trade, among other things. But other craftsmen were almost certainly free, like Eusebius the moneyer, whose literacy suggests that he was a cleric.[64]

Fig. 2.11. The great gold buckle from the Sutton Hoo ship-burial. The details of various Style II creatures are picked out on it in black niello; the head of one with a hooked beak can be seen above the boss on the buckle-plate, abutting the hind-leg of another whose body interlaces with yet another until eventually ending, at the bigger boss, in a head with open jaws swallowing a smaller animal which is suffering attack from the rear as well. Creatures interlace on the frame and the tongue-plate. (Photograph reproduced by courtesy of the British Museum, London. Slightly smaller than actual size.)

Despite the obvious links of Kent with the Franks in the later sixth and seventh centuries, they should not be exaggerated; there are few examples of inlaid ironwork, for instance (Fig. 2.12), although it was popular among Frankish aristocrats,[65] and many Kentish products do not have Frankish equivalents. The taste for thin gold pendants of Scandinavian origin seen on the bracteates developed into a range of pendant discs, into many of which were set garnets with a distinctive 'keystone' shape, seen on many brooches as well. Also distinctive of Kent were buckles with long triangular plates (Fig. 2.15). Most striking of all are the 'composite' disc-brooches attributed to the first half of the seventh century (Col. pls. B.1 and B.2).[66]

Some Kentish-made pieces are sufficiently distinctive as to be recognizable when found in other areas. Some could have been won in raids or in retaliation—the *Chronicle* records that in 568 two Gewissan kings 'drove Aethelberht in flight into Kent', which implies that he had led a raid out of it, and he may have been so weakened that he had to buy off a counterattack.[67] At other times Kent may have been releasing such things as gifts, sometimes with brides to cement alliances, which may account for a woman buried at Chessell Down on the Isle of Wight, probably near the end of the sixth century,

Fig. 2.12. An iron buckle inlaid with silver wire excavated at Monk Sherborne, Hampshire, not in a grave, but in what seemed to be a rubbish-pit, close to Romano-British buildings, although the object—which was found with a similarly decorated belt-mount, not shown here—dates to the late sixth or seventh century. Inlaid ironwork like this is not common in England, and this example was probably made in Francia. It is particularly interesting to compare its decoration to precious-metal pieces like the Sutton Hoo buckle (Fig. 2.11) or the cloisonné garnets in disc-brooches (Col. pls. B.1 and B.2). Like the former, it has Style II animal ornament, with very clear heads on the tongue-plate and in the outer border of the main plate, which is a double-headed, double-ribbon-bodied creature. Yet despite the care taken over the design, the bosses obscured the creature's heads—the one visible can only be seen because the rivet has come adrift. The step pattern at the top around the tongue-plate could be reproduced in garnets, as could the honeycomb-cell pattern around the top of the frame. (Photograph reproduced by courtesy of the Hampshire County Museums Service. Approximately twice actual size.)

who had distinctive brooches, gold braid that may have come from a veil or shawl, a silver spoon, and other objects. Alternatively, however, she may have been a Wight-born aristocrat whose burial costume and goods were chosen to show off Kentish connections.[68] She could have looked like the sort of bride in her wedding finery envisaged by Bede when he made an analogy with the Church as Christ's bride. Weddings were presumably special occasions, a time for exchanges of gifts as well as dowries, as they were on the continent.[69]

Apart from the ring, no gold has been recovered from the Snape cemetery, let alone garnets. Yet as well as the ship, it had two graves in which dugout log-boats seem to have been used as coffins, one containing a pair of drinking-horns, the other a wide range of objects including a sword, a yew-wood pail, and a horse's head with harness on it.[70] This emphasis on feasting and travel—the ship-burial had in it a glass claw-beaker (cf. Fig. 1.12) and at least one other glass vessel—suggests heightened emphases on the exaltation of successful leaders. Their daring raids and the booty and slaves they won in them might be the reason for the choice of burial-goods and the things that imply travelling, or the principal message may have been their distant origins, proclaimed in stories told to the sound of the lyre or *hearp*, like one found in another of the Snape graves.[71] The Undley bracteate, also from Suffolk, had already shown an image illustrating one foundation-myth—the wolf that suckled the founders of Rome—and a century later the rulers of East Anglia were claiming Julius Caesar amongst their ancestors.[72]

The Snape ship-burial suggests someone of outstanding significance, possibly the leader of a small folk group which rocketed to power and then transferred itself to Sutton Hoo, where the leading family's separation further stressed its social position.[73] Separation of elites became a seventh-century trend, with barrows containing men or women with a rich array of possessions, either isolated or with just a few other burials around them, usually in a prominent position as though to provide a constant reminder of the dead person, like Beowulf's mound in the poem. The choice of burial at a Christian church by Kent's King Aethelberht can be seen as a similar exclusiveness, but achieved in a different way.[74] The isolated barrows are not evenly spread across England, however, so customs continued to vary.[75] There are none known in Kent after the end of the sixth century,[76] and it would be easy to put this down to the early arrival there of Christianity, except that there are also none on the Isle of Wight, which was the last kingdom to be converted, many generations later.

In seventh-century Kent some aristocrats may have sought church burial like King Aethelberht, or at least have wanted to be in new cemeteries close to church centres, like a woman interred with a gold pendant set with garnets forming a cross, found outside Canterbury. It may have been made in the 620s, but had had some wear before being buried, so was perhaps some thirty or more years old by then.[77] Two glass palm-cups, and perhaps a coin, from the same area may also have come from graves, suggesting a cemetery set apart for an elite group who did not quite merit being with their king in Augustine's church, but who wanted nevertheless to associate themselves in some way with Canterbury's emerging importance.[78]

Barrows, new cemeteries, and church burials can all be seen as part of a general European trend towards elites' increasing self-awareness, even while accepting Christianity.[79] Decline in the number of weapon-burials within established cemeteries is another sign of increased social stratification, along with a general trend towards less jewellery in women's graves from the end of the sixth century; not only is there less in quantity, but there is much less variety, the great square-headed, saucer-, and other gilded brooches dying out and not being replaced by new types. Kentish disc-brooches were an exception, adapting their ornament to include Style II animals, but even they seem to have gone out of production by or soon after the middle of the seventh century. Swords remained important, as the decorated fittings on them show (Col. pls. B.3 and B.4), and their blades were all pattern-welded; some jewellery was outstanding, especially necklaces worn by a few women, at least in death, up to the end of the seventh century. These changes suggest elites more concerned to make displays to their social equals and challengers in other territories than to their own people, a process known as peer-polity competition, or interaction, but the sheer variety of what was included in their graves is also an indication that there were no very clear codes to follow.[80]

Many of the richest graves contain hanging-bowls (Fig. 2.13), of which there are so many that, despite the escutcheon moulds found at Craig Phadrig, they are unlikely all to have been made in Scotland—there is no evidence of them in Wales. This is not only because of furnished graves, as some escutcheons are found detached—as at Dunadd—and are sometimes pierced as though to be worn as pendants.[81] The whole ones are in both male and female graves, usually with other objects. At Sutton Hoo, Mound 1 had three of them; the largest has a three-dimensional fish inside, and the ends of the hooks are shaped into animal- or bird-heads that seem to be drinking from whatever the fish was swimming in.[82] That bowl and at least one of the others had been repaired, as though they were respected objects in their own right, since there is no reason to think that new ones were unobtainable, and so much else in that burial was in pristine condition.

The use of glass to make red enamel was long established on penannular brooches, but the range of colours grew, to yellows, blues, greens, and rather murky whites.[83] That native British craftsmen retained their Celtic skills in Anglo-Saxon areas such as East Anglia, although none of their products went into graves until the later sixth century, is one possibility.[84] Alternatively, knowledge of enamelling was retained in the British areas, and craftsmen trained there and in Ireland were prepared to travel widely to find patrons, expanding their repertoire the more that they found their work appreciated—patronage on the scale of Sutton Hoo could have brought together craftsmen with different skills from many different backgrounds. Another technique was to fuse together different-coloured rods into a stick that could be heated, drawn out, and sliced across to produce millefiori; unsurprisingly, this was sparingly used, though it can be seen both in hanging-bowl escutcheons and some of the gold jewellery in Sutton Hoo. The latter was Roman glass—either millefiori slices taken out of old objects into which it was set, or Roman glass melted and used for new rods. The hanging-bowls, however, used new glass.[85]

Expressions of the Elites 59

Fig. 2.13. Hanging-bowl, probably seventh-century, from Loveden Hill, south Lincolnshire, one of at least three from graves in the Anglo-Saxon cemetery there; made of copper-alloy sheet metal, with three enamelled escutcheons holding hooks, and another escutcheon inside at the base. It is reported to have contained a cremation, a burnt glass vessel, and some other offerings, and was found with a sword which had had its blade folded in three, and iron strips thought to have been bindings from a wooden bucket. The holes in the bowl's side result from corrosion, but in the base there is a hole deliberately pierced through from the inside before burial, as also happened to some pottery urns—to 'kill' them? A few other urns have glass insets in their sides, which seems a different concept—to let the occupant see out and be seen? Whatever the motives behind such practices, the Loveden Hill cemetery provides evidence that cremation still occurred in the seventh century, perhaps particularly for some higher-status people, as the accompanying objects show. (Photograph reproduced by courtesy of Lincolnshire County Council, City and County Museum. Slightly under half actual size.)

The function of the hanging-bowls is not defined by their contexts. A few have had traces of edibles inside them,[86] which might seem to confirm their feasting associations, except that crab-apples and onions are not obvious delicacies to have chosen. The discovery of a hanging-bowl in a grave inside a church at Lincoln[87] resurrected older ideas about the possible use of at least some of the bowls in the Christian liturgy rather than in secular feasting; a few escutcheons have cross designs.[88] It is just possible, therefore, that the

Sutton Hoo fish is meant as the early Christian symbol for the Saviour, which may have been known in seventh-century England.[89] The creatures round the rim would then be drinking from the Fountain of Life that is the Word of God, nourishing all His natural world, symbolized in the baptism ceremony.

Whether the final owner of the Sutton Hoo bowl had any notion of such an interpretation cannot be known, but there is certainly Christian imagery in the Mound 1 assemblage. The silver bowls, for instance, all have crosses incised inside them, and could originally have been for use in the Eucharist. The two spoons have even been seen as alluding to baptism, 'Paul' inscribed on the handle of one becoming 'Saul' on the other. Unfortunately for that argument, 'Saul' is probably a western miscopying of the Greek letters for 'Paul'. Even if the silverware was originally made for Christian liturgical use, it may have transmuted into tableware for secular feasting like other things in the grave.[90] The largest of the silver items, the great Byzantine dish, was not with the rest, and may have had a separate function; Bede's story of King Oswald of Northumbria having a silver vessel presumably part of his treasure, cut up to distribute to the poor could reflect the actual practice of kings dividing up such things, though to give to their followers rather than to the needy, in the tradition exemplified by Traprain Law, and perhaps by a piece of high-alloy silver at Longbury Bank.[91] On the continent some salvers had a special fame from association with particular kings, though none survives.[92]

The attraction of exotica from the Byzantine world may not have been their religious meaning, but their association with its surviving imperial tradition.[93] Because the Sutton Hoo silver is effectively unique in western Europe, there is no pattern to help explain its arrival. The only comparable object known from England seems to be a cup cremated in a barrow at Asthall, Oxfordshire, where the barrow's size as well as its contents indicate the burial of someone of great importance.[94]

There is a much clearer trail for some other objects from the east Mediterranean, notably copper-alloy bowls. Again, Sutton Hoo provides an outstanding example, but they are also found in several of the richly furnished isolated graves of the late sixth and early seventh centuries, such as Taplow, Buckinghamshire, and Cuddesdon, Oxfordshire, as well as Asthall. These vessels, misleadingly called 'Coptic', are also found on mainland Europe, particularly in northern Italy and along the Rhine valley, suggesting a route that took them across the Alps to areas where they were sought after, perhaps starting as traded items in the Mediterranean and becoming more likely to be passed from hand to hand as gifts the further north they reached; many were buried, creating a down-the-line distribution as they became rarer. A few are not bowls; a kettle-like ewer at Wheathampstead, Hertfordshire, is the most extraordinary. A censer reputedly found in Glastonbury, Somerset, may have been used as its maker expected, but not within a church building of a kind that he could possibly have envisaged. It raises the possibility that, despite the cessation of Mediterranean pottery supplies, occasional contacts with the British west were maintained in the later sixth and early seventh centuries; alternatively, it reached Glastonbury after Somerset had passed into Anglo-Saxon control towards the end of the seventh century.[95]

Also from the east Mediterranean are sheet-metal pails with incised ornament of hunting scenes and men fighting savage beasts, often with Greek inscriptions as incomprehensible to their final owners as the runic text added to one that was with the late sixth-century young woman found at Chessell Down is to us.[96] Despite coming from the Christian east, the pails seem to have been arriving before Christianity formally reached the areas in which they have been found.[97]

Once only does an explicit Christian symbol appear on any of the English-made objects in Mound 1 at Sutton Hoo, on two gold scabbard-bosses which both have a round-armed cross defined by the selection of lighter garnets.[98] Otherwise the great gold buckle can be opened to reveal a cavity, so it could have been a Christian reliquary, its contents 'guarded' by the interlaced creatures on the outside; the cavity may, however, have been no more than a device to hold the end of a leather belt securely.[99] If Christianity mattered much to the occupant of the mound, surely he would have ordered his own smiths to be a lot more explicit about it. The scabbard-bosses may mean nothing more than awareness that the cross was some sort of protective symbol.

It is the extraordinarily eclectic range of motifs at Sutton Hoo that stands out. The Scandinavian elements, particularly the shield and helmet, and the very idea of burying a ship, have been seen as assertions of northern and therefore pagan origins. The birds on the shield and the musical instrument may represent Woden's eagle, a symbol that perhaps became attributed to him because ultimately it was imperial. Boars on the helmet and the shoulder-clasps, and the stag on the whetstone, may refer to the boldness and courage needed to hunt them, which a king needed to lead his people in war. Visual similarity of images may disguise different meanings dependent on contexts, however—a bird on a Scandinavian shield might not have meant the same as one on an Anglo-Saxon lyre.[100] Imperial allusions seem strong in Sutton Hoo, particularly in the shoulder-clasps, an echo of Roman military epaulettes, and the 'sceptre/whetstone', echoing consular and imperial sceptres.[101] In that case, however, why were the designs on the Greek pails never copied—were the lions and other creatures beyond northern recognition?[102]

Many other suggestions have been made about the whetstone, such as that it ties in with Thor, whose speciality was throwing thunderbolts; the iron axe-hammer has also been linked to him, and to killing sacrifices for ritual feasts.[103] When the probably British hanging-bowls are thrown into the cultural mêlée, it becomes impossible to see one single message, such as rejection of old gods for new.[104]

Other questions that hang over Sutton Hoo result from the loss of information from the other ship-burial, Mound 2, and the evidence from the cremations that some very exotic things went into the pyres, such as a cameo and a bone box from Mound 3.[105] The only fixed point in the dating is derived from the coins in Mound 1, which cannot possibly pre-date 595, but could all have been minted by *c.*613.[106] Some might be later, however, and in any case the hoard might have been assembled some years before its burial, without having had any new coins added to it. Nevertheless, a connection with East Anglia's King Redwald, particularly notorious because Bede was so scandalized by his setting up a pagan altar next to a Christian one, is far from established. Nor can it be taken for granted that the burial was that of a king, since it is not known what, if any, 'regalia' would have distinguished one at this time.[107] The importance of material objects for the display of royal authority is attested very soon afterwards, however, in another passage from Bede where he describes how King Edwin of Northumbria was preceded by a 'type of standard which the Romans call a *tufa* and the English call a *thuf*';[108] this could have been something like the iron 'standard' at Sutton Hoo, but were it not for Bede, the association of that object and kingship might never have been made, and besides, staffs of office may not have been exclusive to kings.[109] Another use of objects to display King Edwin's power was the placing of bronze drinking-cups at springs so that travellers could drink from them; people were too scared of the king to steal them.[110]

Even if royal regalia cannot be clearly identified, some objects like the Roman-style shoulder-clasps and the great gold buckle seem to have more than the significance of great wealth, even though they do not necessarily proclaim kingship. Furthermore, they seem too new to have been heirlooms supporting inheritance claims. The Pictish silver bands that may show similar Roman ancestry are a case in point. Such things may have been understood as having particular status, in the same way that certain brooches may have had, like the large penannulars in Scotland and Ireland. Those have never been found in England, suggesting that they did not carry the same meanings for the Anglo-Saxons. In Kent, however, there are a few square-headed brooches with a disc fixed to the central bow. A gold and garnet brooch of that type was found on the continent at a royal site, Wijnaldum in Friesland, and one is clearly shown being worn by a Scandinavian image of the goddess Freya. There are no representations like that in England, but the wearing of things with very special meanings, not necessarily universally understood, is credible. Even the choice to use Style II animal ornament can be seen as a political statement, as versions of it in Kent may have reflected Frankish connections, whereas in East Anglia its characteristics are different, closer to Scandinavian representations.[111]

Another aspect of Sutton Hoo is that none of the objects from it can be recognized as Kentish. The garnets are in shapes and patterns that cannot be traced directly to influences from Kentish craftsmen. Its Style II animal ornament, as on the great gold buckle, is only remotely like the beasts found in Kent on things like a pommel from Crundale.[112] Mound 1 has drinking-horns, maple cups—but no glass vessels such as were probably being made in Kent,[113] though there was a blue glass cup in Mound 2.[114] None of the coins in the purse was from Kent, though the Eusebius coin suggests that a few were already being minted there.[115]

Deliberate rejection by one king of things supplied by another could have been because they would have implied acceptance of the latter's overlordship, if they had not been won in battle or sent as tribute or bribe. Occasionally such dependence has been suggested, for instance in the case of the man buried under the barrow at Taplow, who had Kentish gold clasps and a buckle, and other items such as drinking-horns and glass vessels that may also have come from Kent. The riverside location of this grave suggests a man who could extract tolls from boats going up and down the Thames, and its contents may show that he was passing some of his profits to Kent, receiving in exchange gifts that enabled him to maintain his local status—except that several of the objects were not new when buried, and are more likely to have been heirlooms than recent acquisitions, so their last owner may himself have had no direct contact with Kent. A man kitted out with a sword and other weapons at Alton, Hampshire, who had a repaired Kentish-style buckle with him, may be another example (Fig. 2.14).[116] Upstream of Taplow in the Thames valley, near Abingdon, a cemetery at Milton had two composite disc-brooches of the sort mostly found in Kent, and which have a close parallel from Faversham; they could attest marriage alliances.[117]

Drinking-horns such as were in the Taplow burial, and earlier at Carisbrooke, probably had the sort of cachet that distinguished a particularly important person, but any that did not have metal mounts would have deteriorated beyond recognition in many cemeteries, however carefully excavated; only the tips of the pair at Snape survived, the rest of them only identifiable as dark stains in the soil, and apart from being in a log-boat the burial had no other particularly distinctive things in it except for 'very fine twill' mineralized on the back of a buckle. None was found at Asthall, but there horns would probably not have survived the original cremation, let alone the way that the burial was eventually excavated. Horns were important enough to be imitated in glass, notably in a fine pair at Rainham, Essex. The Sutton Hoo and Taplow horns were particularly special, not only because of the quality of their metal mounts but because they were made from the horns of aurochs, wild bulls that were outstandingly savage and therefore required outstanding courage to hunt down; they had long been extinct in Britain, so must have come from north of the Rhine or Danube, probably as special gifts.[118]

If allies could be created by gifts like aurochs' horns to men who then controlled their regions in the interests of another king, the condition of both the Taplow and the Alton buckles shows how tenuous and impermanent the

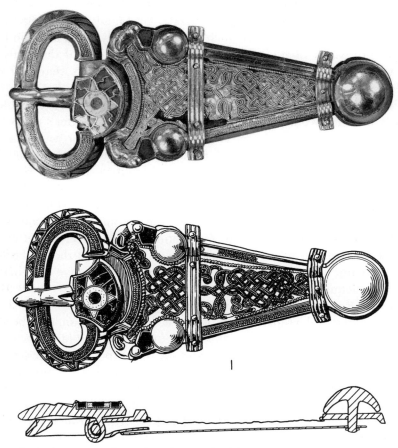

Fig. 2.14. Seventh-century silver-gilt and garnet buckle with gold filigree panels, from Alton, Hampshire, found in a grave with a man who also had with him a sword, a shield, two spears, and at least one drinking-vessel. On the buckle-plate are four plaits of interlaced filigree gold wires in which animal heads are almost hidden. At the sides are two bird heads with hooked beaks and red garnet necks (cf. Fig. 2.6). Red garnets are also used on the base of the buckle's tongue, with a shell forming a ring around a central garnet. The buckle had been damaged, as wire missing from the border shows, and had been repaired by two gold strips rather crudely riveted across the triangular plate. The sword in the same grave, despite its importance as a weapon, had simple copper-alloy hilt fittings. (Drawings from Evison 1988, 94; photograph reproduced by courtesy of the Hampshire County Museums Service. Actual size.)

relationship was, liable to break up if the subsidy flow ceased, or the ally ceased to fear what would happen to him if he did not do what was expected of him. Aethelberht's raid into a neighbouring kingdom (if it actually happened) may have done him more damage by undermining his authority than by any physical injury. In some cases, conspicuous burials containing rich grave-goods which had been well advertised at a lavish funeral may have been a deliberate challenge to an existing authority, showing disrespect to an overlord whose power would then have to be re-established. Placing such a burial near a disputed frontier could create a claim to dominate territory on its other side. Beowulf's barrow was on a headland, so that passers-by at sea could see his barrow and remember his reputation—in other cases, a barrow would remind some who saw it that the grave contained treasures won from them or their forebears, with the implication that the man's heirs challenged them to come and reclaim them.[119]

Although the Christian images at Sutton Hoo need not mean that the burial was of a Christian, equally there was nothing specifically anti-Christian about furnished burial, and being buried in costume jewellery remained quite acceptable throughout the seventh century. The Canterbury pendant is not the only gold and garnet ornament to display a cross. Some composite disc-brooches, particularly those with less gold and perhaps therefore the later ones in the series, have a similar round-armed cross as their principal design element, although it may not always be obvious at first glance (Col. pl. B.2 forms a round-armed cross overlaid by what might be meant as the pointed arms of another).[120] The intention was probably not to conceal the cross, but to force attention upon it; the viewer had to look hard to see it, and that would help to concentrate the mind on its significance. Several pendant gold crosses are known, some laid out using geometrical grids, as were many manuscript paintings.[121]

Pendant crosses were worn on necklaces, either alone or with other ornaments, such as one found in a cemetery at Desborough, Northamptonshire.[122] Necklaces seem to have been especially prominent in seventh-century thinking. Bede relates how the mother of St Hild, abbess of Hartlepool and founder of Whitby, dreamt of finding a 'most precious necklace under her garment ... which spread such a blaze of light that it filled all Britain with its gracious splendour', thus presaging the glorious future of her daughter and no doubt comforting her for having also dreamt, correctly, that her husband had just died of poison while in exile.[123] Bede also knew that jewellery was a temptation to human pride: St Etheldreda, royal founder of Ely Abbey, considered that God 'in His goodness' made her suffer 'a fiery red tumour' where previously as a girl she had worn 'gold and pearls' on 'the unnecessary weight of necklaces', to absolve her from the sin of Pride. In fact she was unlikely to have had pearls, but amber from the Baltic was widely used for beads, and amethysts from the East were evidently highly prized.[124]

Some of the seventh-century objects in Kent could suggest that conversion to Christianity was a slower process than Bede tells, though even he allows that after Aethelberht's death there was an episode of pagan revival in Kent.[125] The most famous evidence is the gilt-bronze Finglesham buckle, on which a distinctly male figure wearing nothing but a horned head-dress and a

Fig. 2.15. The Finglesham buckle; cast copper-alloy, thickly gilded so that it looks like gold, and with gold wires around the bosses. The triangular plate with its three prominent bosses is typical of late sixth-/seventh-century Kent, but the figure holding two spears is probably an image of Woden, so it may be a Swedish piece. The horned headdress is seen on the Sutton Hoo helmet, which has also been attributed to Sweden, but it has appeared on some other metalwork finds in England recently. (Photograph reproduced by courtesy of the British Museum, London. Actual size.)

waist-belt is brandishing a spear in each hand. This spear-dancer is almost certainly a Woden-worshipper, the god who had already been referred to on bracteates (Fig. 2.15).[126] His cult may have been quite strongly established by the seventh century, so it was politic for Christian clerics to transmute the god slowly into a mythical hero, appropriate as an ancestor of the royal family.[127] The horses and horse-gear in several rich graves, such as one of the two Snape log-boat burials and Sutton Hoo's Mound 17, might be allusions to raids and journeys, but also to stallion-worship and sacrifice, later recorded as an aspect of the cult of Woden in Scandinavia.[128] Traditions of the importance of horses and harness in gift-giving are probably preserved in the story of King Oswine's present to Bishop Aidan, and his subsequent donation of them to a beggar.[129]

The kings of Kent began to issue their gold coins at just the time that the ratio of gold to silver in Merovingian coins was falling, part of a general trend which began because less gold was coming into western Europe as Byzantine subsidies dried up. In the 630s King Dagobert was supposed to receive 200,000 *solidi* from the Visigoths, which if they actually arrived may for a time have halted the debasement of the Frankish coins that are assumed to have been the main source of gold supplies into England.[130] If so it was only a temporary check, and the increasing scarcity of gold was presumably a factor in restraining most other English kings from imitating Kent. A small number of gold thrymsas were probably produced for Northumbria, however, a few having been found in York, and a variant in Lincolnshire. The design looks crude, but is based on a recognizable fourth-century Roman type, another indication of the importance of claiming descent and legitimacy from the imperial past.[131] More doubtful is a West Saxon series.[132]

The decline in the gold content of the coins can be seen by comparing the Sutton Hoo thrymsas, most of which are above 80 per cent gold and none less than 70,[133] with the Crondall hoard, in which most are between 50 and 60 per cent.[134] The fall-off was not a uniform process, but would have depended on whatever particular rulers or moneyers had available to them at a particular time, and also presumably on what they thought that they could get away with. The Northumbrian coins have between 50 and 65 per cent gold, so on analogy with Crondall would date to around the 640s, but the northern kingdom may have been able to find enough of the metal for something passable as late as the 670s or 680s, even though others' coins had fallen to much lower percentages before then.[135] For jewellery, the alloys would be even more varied; if a patron was prepared to have an old brooch melted down but had no silver to add to the crucible, an object of purer gold than the contemporary coins would emerge, unless the goldsmith cheated. Overall supply problems seem to be revealed by those composite disc-brooches which have copper-alloy cells, their tops gilded to hide the use of base metal, unless they were simply cheaper but contemporary versions of those that had pure gold. More significant, therefore, may be that the gold panels in them became whiter (Col. pls. B.1 and B.2).[136]

Seemingly parallel with this trend is a diminution in the supply of well-cut and shaped garnets. The Sarre brooch has notably more than the Monkton brooch, which has complicated step patterns round its centre, but otherwise only simple rectangles. Others have even smaller garnets, in rectangles, squares, and triangles. Those shapes could all have been achieved by chipping, not by using the wheel, so it seems that as larger flat garnets became scarcer, the skill to cut them to curves was quickly lost. Further evidence of growing scarcity is that the only English assemblage of a smith's equipment in an Anglo-Saxon grave, at Tattershall Thorpe, Lincolnshire, included a few garnets that he was presumably hoping to reset into some new piece; three were quite well shaped, the others already more crudely chipped down (Fig. 2.10).[137] This collection may have been buried in the 660s. If the flat garnets came from Bohemia, their supply was probably cut off by the Avars,[138] so their decreasing availability and that of gold would have been more or less contemporaneous, but not directly connected.

The last known object to have flat garnets is the cross buried with St Cuthbert on the island of Lindisfarne in 687 (Fig. 2.16). It is almost certainly one that he had worn as a pendant, so it was quite old when he died, and had had to be repaired. At its centre is a roundel that probably came off a Kentish disc-brooch, the sort of reuse that would explain why the Dunadd stud was being kept. The red inlays on St Cuthbert's cross, however, are not arranged like anything known in Kent, and their similarity to the Dunbar cross-arm suggests a craftsman working in Northumbria. Each of the St Cuthbert cross-arms has

Fig. 2.16. The gold and garnet cross found in the tomb of St Cuthbert was presumably his personal property when he died in 687. Its garnets are not arranged like those on Kentish brooches (e.g. Col. pls. B.1 and B.2), and Northumbria may have had differently trained craftsmen working in it. (Photograph reproduced by courtesy of the Dean and Chapter, Durham Cathedral. Actual size.)

twelve inlays, perhaps for the twelve apostles, to concentrate thoughts on God—set in gold, for Bede the symbol of wisdom, which comes from God.[139]

It is difficult to chart declining supplies of gold and garnets with any precision, despite the relative abundance of evidence, for St Cuthbert provides one of the very few fixed dating points. Despite the decline in Byzantine gold supplies, other goods, such as purple amethyst beads, seem if anything to have increased in number, at least as buried objects, and they must have passed through the east Mediterranean.[140] An emerald and two sapphires that have been identified in a 'jewel' from Milton, Kent, must have come from the East, unless they were Roman gems reset.[141] Flat garnets may have become unobtainable, but rounded 'cabochon' garnets seem to have stayed relatively plentiful, including some very large ones; their source may have been Iran or the Black Sea.[142] The Red Sea and Indian Ocean were the source of cowrie shells and of elephant ivory, whether African or Indian,[143] so trade routes were still open.

As well as favouring the elites, the seventh century may have placed a higher value than before on certain people with special skills. There are, for instance, a number of small copper-alloy lidded cylinders, some with small bits of cloth inside. These might well suggest some continuation of unofficial pagan practices associated with divination and healing, hinted at in the Old English 'Charm' poems. Many of the lids have the Christian cross on them, but one appears to show Sigurd, who figures in later Scandinavian sagas. The threads could be Christian relics, and mixed practices and beliefs could well be

Fig. 2.17. The importance of textile production may be shown by this burial of a woman at Lechlade, Gloucestershire, with a very long spearhead, perhaps originally from Kent, that seems likely to have had final use as a weaving batten, used on upright looms to hold the vertical threads apart and then to push down the horizontal threads. A lump of ochre in the same grave could symbolize dyes. Not visible in the excavation photograph is the gold pendant set with small round garnets and filigree gold wires found under the woman's chin, a testimony that she was of more than ordinary importance; she might have been respected for having special textile skills, but more probably the weapon-converted tool was a token of a supervisory role, as would have befitted someone of her age, as she was in her late thirties when she died. The pendant probably dates well into the seventh century (cf. Col. pl. B.3), and has a cross pattern. (Photographs from Boyle *et al.* 1998, 97 and 266 reproduced by courtesy of Oxford Archaeology. Pendant actual size.)

expected under the circumstances of conversion, as indeed the Charms suggest.[144] But a more prosaic interpretation is that the boxes and their contents symbolize the embroidery or weaving skills of their owner (cf. Fig. 2.17).[145] Pairs of shears in leather pouches or specially shaped boxes are another example of tools associated with textile production being carefully buried. It was quite as important to the elite to be able to wear the finest woollen cloth, linen, or even silk as to have a gold brooch.[146]

Not new in the seventh century, but relatively more frequent, are purse-collections; some seem to have contained no more than scraps collected for recycling, but others have strange assemblages that, like the little cylindrical boxes, could have been associated with healing or divination. A few burials with odd little collections are to one side of a cemetery, or even isolated altogether, as though it was thought sensible to keep a 'cunning' person with healing or fortune-telling powers at a distance, like a woman on the extreme edge of a cemetery at Bidford-on-Avon, Warwickshire, and a young man with a crow at Lechlade—fortune-telling by ornithomancy was frequently proscribed. Something of that sort may explain the iron rings, knife-guard, hanging-bowl mounts, and other seemingly miscellaneous items under a woman's body at Orsett, Essex, on a site with only one other grave nearby; both were surrounded by circular ditches, and had probably had low barrows over them, so they were not insubstantial people. They were buried well into the seventh, or even in the early eighth century, by which time Essex had been a Christian kingdom for two or more generations. They could have been people seen as a little different from the norm, to be treated with respect but kept at a distance. The same sense of unease over seemingly magical skills could explain the lonely location of the Tattershall Thorpe smith. He may have had amulets with him as well as his tools, a set of weights, and scrap (Col. pl. C.1, and Figs. 2.10 and 2.18–20). A bell that was in the assemblage may have been one of the things that he was intending to rework, but he might have had to ring it while on his travels; Kent and Wessex laws at the end of the seventh century expressed concern that strangers should make their presence known if they left a recognized path through woods, or they would be assumed to be robbers. There may be more to it than that, however, as the young man with the crow at Lechlade also had a bell with him, as did a child otherwise well provided for, who may have been given it to ward off evil spirits.[147]

The seventh century saw a new weapon form, the single-sided *seax*, that was perhaps used in hunting, an aristocratic sport with which anything associated would certainly have signalled exclusivity (e.g. Figs. 3.1 and 3.13).[148] A fashion for gold pins, often set with small round garnets in the heads, joined by chains from which pendants might be suspended, as in a woman's grave in a barrow at Roundway Down, Wiltshire,[149] was followed in both silver and copper-alloy, with glass or simply cast bosses in the heads, at a few cemeteries such as Winnall Down II, near Winchester, Hampshire.[150] The Roundway Down chains end in gold animal heads that are very like a silver pair at Harford Farm, Norfolk,[151] which is just one example among many of how widespread such things were at elite level, with no obvious differentiation between kingdoms. By the middle of the seventh century, if not by its beginning, the aristocracy throughout England were as similar in their costume as they were in their speech. The difficulty is to know whether this was also true of the lesser

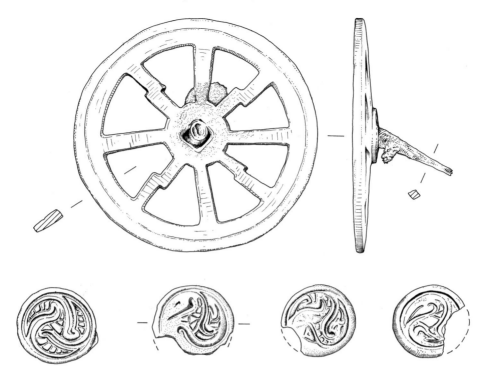

Fig. 2.18. The smith at Tattershall Thorpe had with him objects that had almost certainly not been made in England: the copper-alloy 'wheel', for instance, is a type dated to between c.525 and c.600 found otherwise in the upper Rhine valley, where they were often worn on festoons strung from women's waists. The long iron nail through the centre of this one hints that its last use could have been on a wooden casket. The four scabbard-studs are later in date, c.640–70; they had only previously been found in the Low Countries and northern France when excavated in 1981, but examples have now come also from both Ipswich and Southampton (Fig. 3.1). These things may have been awaiting refitting on something a patron required, but, like other objects in the collection, may have been attributed with magical powers. (Drawings by Dave Watts from the collections of Lincolnshire County Council, City and County Museum. Actual sizes.)

folk, or if the paucity of their representation, as grave-goods diminish in quantity, disguises continuing regional variation.[152]

Because nearly everything in later sixth- and seventh-century graves was deliberately buried, the contents of pits, sunken-featured buildings, and post-holes can be expected to give a more representative idea of what people used in their everyday lives. There may be exceptions even here: the plated-gold coin forgery at the great Northumbrian royal site at Yeavering was found in a post-hole of one of the halls, and although assumed by the excavator to have rolled in, could conceivably have been included deliberately as a good-luck token.[153] Finds from the site were few, but a gold ring from a mount and a silver-inlaid

Fig. 2.19. Three hammers of different weights were among the Tattershall Thorpe smith's tools; traces of their wooden handles survive. The implication of the widening of the ends of their heads is that their main purpose was to beat out sheets of metal (cf. Col. pl. C.1 and Fig. 2.13). (Photograph reproduced by courtesy of Lincolnshire County Council, City and County Museum. Actual sizes.)

iron buckle are other indications of the wealth and status of the site's owners and visitors. The quality of its pottery may not be such as to confirm the sort of feasting rituals implied by the ox skulls found there, but presumably it was for use in the kitchens, not for eating or drinking from in the hall. Another excavated seventh-century site, Cowdery's Down, Hampshire, where a larger building than usual suggests ownership by someone of above-average importance, had nothing amongst the few artefacts recovered to confirm high-status occupation, partly because that status may have meant that its floor was kept cleaner than most.[154] Both halls may have had raised wooden floors, and any-

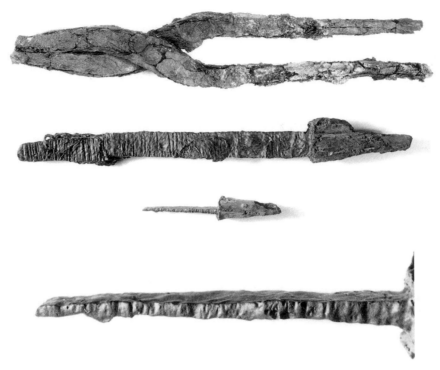

Fig. 2.20. Other tools from Tattershall Thorpe included a well-preserved pair of tongs and three different sizes of file, only two shown here, all with parts of their wooden handles surviving. The enlarged view of the teeth of the smallest file shows that the smith must have been producing some very delicate work. (Photographs reproduced by courtesy of Lincolnshire County Council, City and County Museum. Tongs half size, files actual size, close-up enlarged ×4.)

thing dropped on them would either have been picked up or swept out more easily than from the usual earth-floored buildings.[155]

Sites with sunken-featured buildings continue to provide greater quantities of data. Mucking, for instance, unlike anything recovered from Yeavering or Cowdery's Down, had imported wheel-made pottery coming to it, a reflection of its favoured Thames-side estuary location. Even so, this amounted to only fifteen sherds amongst over 30,000.[156] Of those, only two others showed signs of having been made on a wheel, though not all were simply plain. Surfaces were given some variation by applying slip, by dragging a comblike tool across the surface or by burnishing it, or by laboriously pinching the whole of the outside. The last technique was used mostly on a specific type of bowl, not on 'organic-tempered' vessels of any sort, so the bowls may have been given special treatment because they were to be used at meals. Most of this pottery was locally made, though some types had a wider distribution. Charnwood Forest ware continued to be sent out from Leicestershire during the seventh century, but well before its end was being ousted from sites like Flixborough, North Humberside, where it was replaced by 'Maxey-type' pottery;[157] unfortunately this lacks distinctive minerals in its tempering, and cannot be attributed to a particular manufacturing area. In the same way, textile equipment continues to be found virtually everywhere that there is occupation evidence: from Catterick, Yorkshire, in the north to Bishopstone, Sussex, in the south; and from Collingbourne Ducis, Wiltshire, in the west to Mucking in the east.[158]

Just as Mucking had had some quite valuable things broken and lost in it in the fifth and sixth centuries, so too in the seventh a few luxury items like an amethyst bead and a garnet-headed pin suggest that such objects were not exclusively reserved for burial with an elite.[159] Inland sites also have examples of people 'not without fine things' in seemingly ordinary houses, like a silver-plated iron mount with wood adhering to it, thought to have come off a box, in a building at Puddlehill, Bedfordshire.[160] This find suggests that the boxes and caskets in a range of different woods, now being recognized in many seventh-century graves,[161] were in daily use. The same site also produced a broken Indian Ocean cowrie shell, like those in cemeteries.[162] Whatever significance it might have had as an amulet, this one was not so highly regarded as to have been worth either preserving, or getting rid of as far away as possible, in case it might have the reverse of its original effect after it had had the bad luck to be broken.

The only largely excavated settlement site in Suffolk which was in use contemporaneously with the Sutton Hoo burials is West Stow, where lost objects are enough to suggest that East Anglia's wealth was sufficient to support its kings in the manner to which they wanted to become accustomed. Later sixth- and seventh-century objects there include two discoid silver pins, a silver-gilt buckle-slide, and a silver shield-pendant.[163] In Wessex, too, there are a few objects, despite the less than abundant evidence at Cowdery's Down; Chalton, Hampshire, yielded an enamelled hanging-bowl escutcheon from excavations,[164] and at Swindon, Wiltshire, a gold roundel with a garnet that looks like the centre of a Kentish disc-brooch was found.[165] Even textile equipment may be more than utilitarian; in Collingbourne Ducis one of the pin-beaters was made out of walrus ivory, a material notably rare in Wiltshire.[166]

These objects may be too few and too random to show a pattern, but they suggest a greater access to resources and a wider dissemination of wealth than do the cemeteries, in which grave-goods decreasingly occur. Although traditionally taken as a sign of spreading Christianity and appreciation that there was no need for things to be buried as offerings or tokens, this trend has more recently been seen as the result of the growing division between a few exceptionally rich people and the taxpayers who were increasingly exploited to support them, and so had nothing left over to acquire goods for themselves.[167] At present, the settlement evidence does not seem to justify the new interpretation, but more precision in dating both objects and their loss is needed.

3

Kings and Christianity
From the Late Seventh Century to the Early Ninth

New discoveries play a major part in archaeological research, but coincidence can also have a role. When four copper-alloy scabbard-studs with Style II ornament were excavated in the smith's grave at Tattershall Thorpe in 1981 (Fig. 2.18), they were the first of their kind to have been found in England, despite being well known on the continent, where they are dated to between 640 and 670.[1] Within a couple of years, however, another set turned up, on a scabbard in a cemetery in Buttermarket, Ipswich, Suffolk.[2] Then, in 1999, yet another set was found, in a grave at the new football stadium in Southampton, Hampshire (Fig. 3.1).[3]

These studs adorned scabbards that were not for double-edged swords, but for the single-edged long seax, not a very practical weapon, but one that was probably used in hunting and was therefore redolent of aristocratic practice.[4] At Tattershall Thorpe the studs were not attached to anything, and were presumably going to be shown to a prospective patron with a view to reuse. At Ipswich and Southampton both sets were in cemeteries at what were about to become major trading-places, *Gippeswic* and *Hamwic*. These *wic* sites had continental counterparts and suggest new ways of organizing and systematizing exchanges of goods; others in England were London, *Lundenwic*, and York, *Eoforwic*, both former Roman towns, with the *wics* outside the walls but episcopal churches inside.[5] Neither Ipswich nor Southampton had a major church, so there was no reason for important burials at either unless they were of people involved in the places' emergence as commercial centres. One explanation is that some of the graves were for kings' 'reeves' and their families, royal agents placed to oversee merchants and to ensure that tolls were paid,[6] who were buried slightly away from where the commerce was to take place.

The Southampton cemetery had other signs of an elite presence, such as a woman's grave that contained a gold pendant with garnets and Style II animals in filigree gold wire on it (Col. pl. C.2), which seems likely to be mid- to later seventh-century.[7] A gold and garnet composite disc-brooch excavated in Floral Street, London, was within the *Lundenwic* area, and again implies an elite

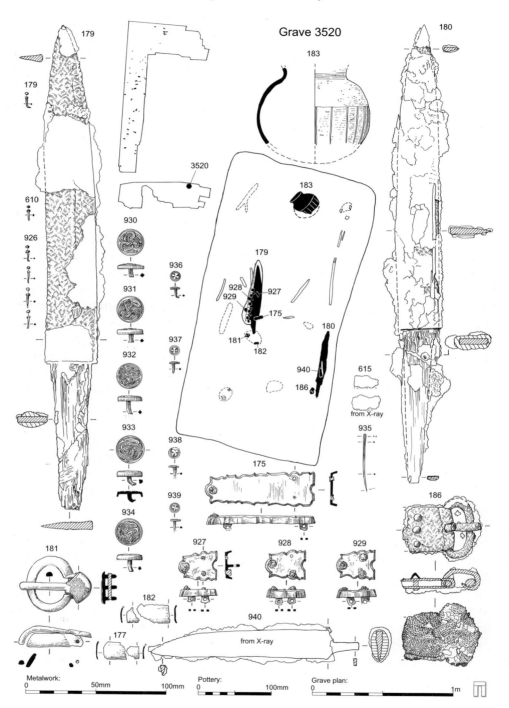

associated with the new trading-places.[8] London's regeneration can be seen starting earlier in the seventh century, with the founding of St Paul's and the minting of thrymsas for King Eadbald of Kent (616–40) with a garbled version of the city's name on them, presumably to reinforce his claim to control it; the disc-brooch was probably from Kent.[9] Among other seventh-century evidence is at least one gold finger-ring, set with a very worn *solidus* of the Emperor Theodosius II (408–50), found some way to the north of the *wic* near Euston Square (Fig. 3.2); two gold earrings cut down from a Byzantine disc, found north-west of the city; another gold finger-ring, less certainly seventh-century but from Garrick Street, much closer to the new trading-centre; and two glass palm-cups from near its edge, at St Martin-in-the-Fields. Clearly there were important people interested in London.[10]

The Floral Street composite disc-brooch is not the only such brooch found recently, the other two both coincidentally having evidence that they were of some age when buried. One was in a woman's grave at Boss Hall, about 3 kilometres from Ipswich and so perhaps not directly associated with the new *wic*; it had been repaired, and was buried with a coin dated within ten years either side of 700, as well as with an older gold coin and other gold pendants, a silver toilet set, and other items.[11] The second, in the Harford Farm cemetery, had also been repaired, probably at a time when flat garnets were no longer available to replace some that had been lost (Fig. 3.3).[12] That brooch has an inscription scratched on the back in runes: 'Luda [or possibly Tudda] repaired the brooch'; Luda is thus the first Anglo-Saxon craftsman whose name is known, because he had enough literacy to use a text to identify himself as an individual.[13]

Fig. 3.1. A single grave with two inhumation burials is unusual, and this one from Southampton is unusual also in its contents, notably the two long, single-edged knives (*seaxes*), which are evidence that both the burials were almost certainly of males, though the preservation of bone was so poor that all that can be said from it is that one was 18 years or older, the other between 25 and 35. Both *seaxes* were in wood-and-leather scabbards, one fitted with two rows of decorative studs and a line of small nails to secure the seam. The copper-alloy buckle at bottom left is a 'shield-on-tongue' type, distinctive but quite widespread in England, unlike the four scabbard-studs which are otherwise known only at Tattershall Thorpe (Fig. 2.19), in Ipswich, and on the continent. At bottom right is an iron buckle with three copper-alloy rivets to hold it to a strap—the mounts have both rivets and loops on the back, which seems unnecessary. On the back of the iron buckle are the mineralized remains of woollen twill, presumably from the clothes that the man was wearing; the shield-on-tongue buckle pin has a small patch on the front, perhaps from a cloak that lay over it. The *seax* on the right had a small knife above it, and a horn handle—the other's was willow or poplar wood. The small pot would have been between the two men's feet; it seems to have been incomplete when it was buried, as its rim and base are both missing. Although glass and suchlike obviously prestigious vessels are quite often in richer graves, a pot like this one is another matter—and unexplained. (Information from contributors to Birbeck and Smith, forthcoming; drawing by Elizabeth James reproduced by courtesy of Wessex Archaeology, Salisbury. Scales as shown.)

Fig. 3.2. Elaborate finger-rings became more frequent in the late sixth and seventh centuries, though they were never common, there being few in base metals. This gold one from north London, near Euston Square, is probably seventh-century and may have belonged to someone wealthy with an interest in the re-emerging port or the newly founded St Paul's Church. The gold *solidus* was struck in Constantinople for the Emperor Theodosius II (408–50), but it is very worn so must have been quite old when set into a ring by a goldsmith skilled in making very fine beaded and twisted wires. It may have been made in Frisia or Francia, where work of that quality was done, but could have been made in Kent, or by a peripatetic craftsman like the Tattershall Thorpe smith. (Photograph reproduced by courtesy of the Ashmolean Museum, Oxford. Actual size.)

Another grave at Harford Farm had two coins of about the same date as that in the Boss Hall grave; others were found in the Southampton cemetery, in a grave which had a range of objects including a gold pendant that had probably come from Frisia (Col. pl. C.3). They provide welcome evidence that the custom of depositing grave goods continued sporadically at least to the end of the seventh century. Not all the brooches were being worn on costume when buried; even more than before, things were placed in purses or pouches, or in wooden boxes. The Harford Farm, Boss Hall, and London brooches were all found beside the women's necks, all with silver-wire rings, and the first two with toilet sets; presumably all were in small containers of some sort.[14] These collections seem different from the medleys of objects such as crystal balls and silver spoons occasionally buried dangling on festoons from the waist, and from the purse collections of odd scrap items, or of very odd items.[15] In pouches or boxes brooches would not have been visible—and so would not have been open displays of wealth at funerals. In these cases it may have been deemed more important to dispose of things particularly associated with the dead person than to emphasize their social pre-eminence publicly.

Although there is no great precision in the dating, it appears that supplies of E-ware pottery and of glass from south-west France petered out during the eighth century. Trade to sustain the British and Welsh hillforts may have depended on sea-crossings that were no longer worth risking if merchants could find greater security and a more guaranteed supply of slaves and other things for exchange at the English *wic* and other sites. A few coastal places may have been landing-sites for goods, or even beach-markets, such as Dunbar and Aberlady, Lothian, in the east of what was by then becoming Scotland,

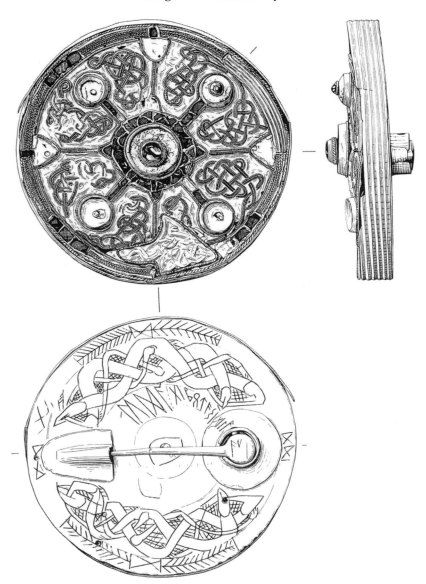

Fig. 3.3. The composite disc-brooch from Harford Farm, Caistor St Edmund, Norfolk. The front shows that it had been repaired, and the back, as well as having a rough-out of a Style II animal, has a runic inscription revealing that the secondary work was done by someone named Luda (or Tudda). He had enough gold, perhaps supplied by his patron, to make a patch, which he roughened to make it look more like the original work, and he put a beaded wire round it that is an approximate match. He seems to have funked replacing the missing herringbone wire, however, nor did he have garnets with which to replace those that had dropped out. (Drawing by Steven Ashley reproduced from Penn 2000, 109, by permission of Norfolk Museums and Archaeology Service. Actual size.)

but the finds made at them do not testify to overseas trade. Very few eighth-century coins have been found north of Hadrian's Wall, and only one in Pictland north of the Firth of Forth.[16]

Pictland was not unprosperous, however, in the eighth century; even though some resources may have been diverted from the most elaborate personal display to the support of monasteries and other churches, and to the creation of elaborate stone sculptures,[17] the remarkable hoard discovered on St Ninian's Island in 1958 shows something of the metalwork that was available (Fig. 3.4).[18] There is every likelihood that most if not all of the objects that it contained had been made in Pictland; its twelve silver-gilt penannular brooches, for instance, came from moulds similar to some found at Birsay, and two are like the Dunadd motif-piece (Fig. 2.5). Admiration for this display of wealth is tempered by analyses that have shown that most of the brooches were made from low-silver alloys, despite the gilding.[19] The other silver includes two chapes, one with 'Resad' inscribed on it, which is generally reckoned to be so unlike anything in any well-known language that it must be Pictish, probably its owner's name[20]—though an alternative is that the 'name' is actually two Latin words.[21]

The adoption of penannular brooches by the Picts is an example of their willingness to accept new ideas, in that case from Ireland and Dàl Riata. Influence from further away can also be seen. The St Ninian's hoard contained eight bowls, seven of which have animal and interlace ornament punch-dotted into them, an unusual technique, though the shapes are comparable to southern, Anglo-Saxon work, where speckling on animal bodies may be the origin of the dotting. The two scabbard-chapes and a sword pommel show southern influence even more strongly in the formers' finely modelled animal heads and the latter's speckled, long-limbed creatures and swirling interlace.[22] A hanging-bowl is the last in the series known, smaller than most and with three external ribs unlike any of the others. As with those, so here its intended use is

---

Fig. 3.4. The St Ninian's Isle Pictish eighth-century hoard, found in 1958, contains eight silver bowls (one not shown), including the hanging-bowl which has three suspension loops gripped by silver-gilt animals peering over its rim. Most of the other bowls have patterns created by punched dots. A loose mount with Celtic spirals from the centre of a bowl is also shown. The function of the three conical objects is unknown, but slots on their backs suggest that they fitted on straps, and as the hoard contains a sword-pommel and two beast-headed chapes, they may have been intended for a sword-belt or baldric, although ecclesiastical use has also been suggested. The twelve penannular brooches have a variety of terminals, some with glass settings, including two which have wide flat plates (cf. Fig. 2.5), and one, second from top, has snarling beasts' heads. A more benign creature is holding the bowl to the stem of the spoon; the claw-ended object next to it harks back to Roman implements and might have been used for opening shellfish, or as a toothpick—though again, a liturgical role has been proposed. Next to them is a porpoise's jawbone, included in the hoard for no very obvious reason. (Photograph reproduced by courtesy of the Trustees of the National Museums of Scotland, Edinburgh.)

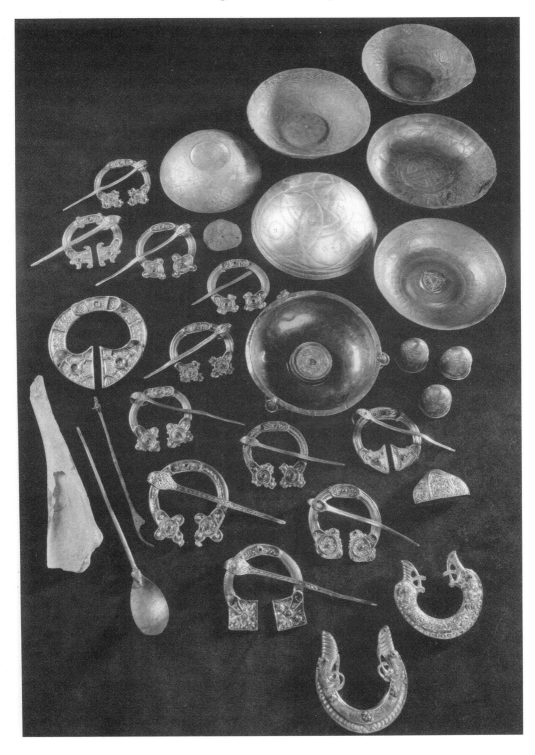

uncertain and it could have been either religious or secular, as could a spoon and a pronged instrument like those with which the Romans had eaten shellfish, but for which Eucharistic use has also been argued. There are three cones which might have come from a *flabellum* used in church services.[23] A porpoise's jaw in a box made of larchwood—not a native timber—is unexplained.

Other hoards with Pictish silver have been found in the far north; little is known of one of them, but surviving pieces from another, at Rogart, Sutherlandshire, include two large silver penannular brooches with interlace decoration, one also with cast heads in relief that look as though they are drinking from the cross patterns on the terminals, and may refer to baptism and eternal life through Christ. There was also a strap-end of Anglo-Saxon type in the hoard. Two penannular brooches from near Dunkeld, Perthshire, one of which has relief heads similar to those at Rogart, might also be from a hoard, but one from Aldclune in the same county was found in a hillfort excavation.[24]

The St Ninian's hoard was hidden under a stone in a church, probably chosen as much for the extra security offered by its stone walls as for its spiritual protection, since one likely reason for its deposition is viking raids, first recorded in Britain in the 780s, which caused levels of destruction and disruption that outraged chroniclers and continue to preoccupy historians and archaeologists. It might have been a viking raider who took south a Pictish brooch, part of which was found in Canterbury, or it might be a record of coastal trading; the same is true of two brooch terminals found in York.[25] The vikings' effect is partly to be seen in the booty that they took home, a little of which ended up in their graves. These pieces show that England and Ireland suffered, but none have been identified as Pictish—probably not because there were none, but because of the difficulty of attributing treasures specifically to a kingdom that is best known for its stone sculptures. At the same time, things such as a set of gilt copper-alloy mounts, probably from an object in a church treasury, that have decoration similar to some in the Book of Kells, and are therefore dated to the later eighth or ninth century, need not be Pictish just because they were found at Crieff in Perthshire; they could have been Irish, brought by a marauding viking, but they could show the influence of Dàl Riata on the Pictish church.[26]

Although the Hunterston brooch and the St Ninian's hoard show considerable Anglo-Saxon influence, they do not show Anglo-Saxon cultural domination of northern Britain. In the west the Britons were much less able to retain their distinctiveness. Partly this was because of direct conquest: Dorset, Somerset, and east Devon fell under the political control of the kings of Wessex during the second half of the seventh century, and the peoples of the Severn valley came to be dominated by the Mercians, just as the Northumbrians had pushed up to the Firth of Forth, though only to be pushed back again.[27] The Cannington cemetery in Somerset continued in use into the eighth century, and adoption of new customs can be seen in it, rather than just the acquisition of a few Anglo-Saxon objects as previously; the placing of small bags containing assortments of objects by the necks of two children must be linked to such purse-collections in the east, though several of the objects in the bags are not specifically Anglo-Saxon. Knives were deliberately put into twenty-two of the late graves in the Cannington sequence, another custom that must have derived from seventh-century English practice. Against this cultural onslaught, a penannular brooch of late seventh- or eighth-century type seems like token resistance, particularly since it was with one of the children.[28]

Somerset has a number of other finds that probably came from the Anglo-Saxon world in the seventh century, such as glass jars at Banwell and Chew Stoke.[29] Glass vessels could have come by exchange, but Cannington is not the only Somerset cemetery to suggest that deeper change was occurring: Camerton, in the north of the shire, had graves with prestigious-looking objects in it, including bracteates, pendants, and an inlaid glass stud.[30] So far as can be told, all the western hillforts went out of use.

West Dorset also has cemeteries with Anglo-Saxon material, suggesting a new elite practice, if not a new elite altogether. On Maiden Castle a male buried with a long *seax* could be another example of an Anglo-Saxon king's reeve, here brought in to control newly won territory.[31] There is nothing comparable in east Devon, but there is nothing 'British' either. These areas were not necessarily being swamped by English migrants, nor was Anglo-Saxon culture necessarily forced upon them, but their new rulers may have imposed heavier burdens on those whom they regarded as conquered people. King Ine's laws differentiated against the Welsh, who had lower *wergild* compensation values; consequently, Britons may have had good reason to adopt new modes, including the language, of their rulers, so that they would be better able to merge with the Anglo-Saxons and avoid discrimination.[32]

In west Devon and Cornwall the British kingdom of Dumnonia survived, and for a little longer preserved some of its cultural distinctiveness, not only in monuments such as sculptures, but, in Cornwall, in lesser things such as grass-marked pottery and stone mortars.[33] Unfortunately, however, lack of surviving evidence limits the extent to which it can be seen whether Anglo-Saxon influence was accepted but reshaped, as in north Britain, or was rejected completely, since there is a dearth of objects that can be positively attributed to the later seventh and eighth centuries. No coins or other artefacts such as E-ware pottery that had attested trade at Bigbury Bay and Bantham in south Devon show that it continued; the supply of E-ware seems to have dried up everywhere.[34]

Similar difficulties from lack of evidence beset study of the British kingdoms in Wales; pressurized by the Mercians, with whom they may have been forced sometimes into making alliances that pitted them against the Northumbrians,[35] and without the ability to exploit such mineral resources as existed, the kings' material wealth may have been exclusively in agricultural products, and the disappearance of French merchants gave them no means to dispose of those outside their kingdoms, except through England. Consequently, there may have been feasting, and gift-giving of native cows and horses, but not of imported gold and silver. As everywhere else in the eighth century, resources were also needed for churches, and stone sculptures show that some culture was maintained. A few establishments may have been large in numbers, but none has produced evidence that they were rich in church treasures.[36]

Secular sites in Wales are no different;[37] at the highest social level, it is uncertain when Dinas Powys was abandoned, but even if it continued into the eighth century there are no rich finds from it, and the Anglo-Saxon objects there are all likely to be earlier.[38] One piece of glass at Longbury Bank could have been landed there in the eighth century, but that is the lone possibility;[39] the only glass at Hen Gastell, probably an aristocratic fort and one of the few Welsh sites with good evidence for use in the eighth and ninth centuries, was beads of a type that suggests that they may have been brought there from Ireland, like a piece of amber.[40] There is little sign of much trade with Ireland, though another site still occupied, Caerwent, had copper-alloy pins of Irish type, as well as others suggesting Anglo-Saxon influence.[41] Such influence was slight, however, even in south-east Wales; there is no record of any eighth-century coins being found anywhere west of the Severn.[42] So limited is the evidence of Welsh artefact production that the frame of an annular brooch with expanded terminals somewhat like those made from the Dunadd moulds, found at Llys Awel on the north coast, is interpreted as very likely to be Irish, looted by vikings.[43]

That several recently excavated cemeteries—Southampton, Harford Farm, Boss Hall, and Canterbury[44]—all had graves in which were coins datable to c.700 might seem another example of coincidence. Unlike the scabbard-studs, however, they are not quite the first known English examples, and in any case improved recovery techniques may be a factor, for the coins are not gold but silver, and less easily seen in the ground. Even less likely to have been noticed except by skilled excavators is a pierced copper-alloy imitation coin of about the same date in a grave at Lechlade.[45] Its piercing shows that it was an ornament; a few silver coins with added loops must have been converted for similar use, despite having a much lower intrinsic value than the earlier gold thrymsas, but as familiarity with the coins increased, so their use as ornament seems to have died away.[46]

The replacement of gold thrymsas by silver coins late in the seventh century seems in one way to have been a smooth transition, the size of the flans staying the same and sometimes similar designs being used. Two Kent coins illustrate the progression: one is called 'pale gold' because of the amount of silver alloyed with the gold in it, while the other is silver with almost no gold, but both are copies of the same design, a late fourth-century coin with two emperors' heads, showing respect for the imperial past rather than merely imitating Merovingian practice (Fig. 3.5).[47] Neither has an inscription to give absolute dates, however, and the process of moving from gold to silver probably happened at slightly different dates in different kingdoms, with the change generally complete by no later than 700.

The transition was more than a change of metal. If silver had been intended merely as a substitute for gold, the new coins would have had to be some ten times heavier if they were to have the same value.[48] The weights were practically unchanged, however, so the intention seems to have been to facilitate lower-level transactions. Merchants could have used them to make small toll payments and buy goods of considerably less value per unit than a gold coin would have bought. Increasing use of coins is shown by their widening distribution: pale gold coins are quite rare and mainly found in Kent, around London, and in Suffolk;[49] silver coins issued up to about 710 are found also in Norfolk and the south-east Midlands, with a few further afield in Yorkshire and round the south coast;[50] thereafter they are found as far west as Dorset, Somerset, and up to the River Severn, and in the north up to Hadrian's Wall and at Whithorn.[51]

A change in the nature of trade is also implied by the numbers of coins found in particular places. They seem to have been quite freely used in the *wic* sites (Fig. 3.5).[52] Other places where they have been found in quantity include Whitby, where recent excavations have shown that the abbey had a coastal trading-place attached to it; churches had need not only of imported goods such as wine for the Mass, silk for vestments, and metal for altar plate, but also of regular supplies of food and other commodities which could be obtained both by consuming the produce of their own estates and by trading some of that produce for coin with which to purchase other requirements. Secular estate-owners could also turn surpluses into a more negotiable medium, and kings could convert the tribute due to them in kind into cash rents, giving them greater flexibility. Quantities of coins found at newly identified sites such as South Newbald, near the River Humber, where 126 eighth- and ninth-century coins have been recorded, suggest substantial amounts changing hands even at places with no institutions to support, at least on the eastern side of the country.[53]

Although now usually referred to as sceattas, the early silver coins were probably called pennies, since that word begins to appear in contemporary documents. Most of King Ine's late seventh-century laws still talked of shillings, but pennies were used to value an ox horn (ten pence) or a cow's (two pence).[54] The sceattas must have been awkward to handle and easy to lose, which may help to account for their relatively frequent discovery. Large numbers would have been needed for higher-value transactions, and a few travellers must have had quite large quantities with them; one hoard at Aston Rowant, Oxfordshire, had at least 175 in it.[55] Nevertheless, this was not a particularly large sum; eighth- and ninth-century charters show that land was increasingly being

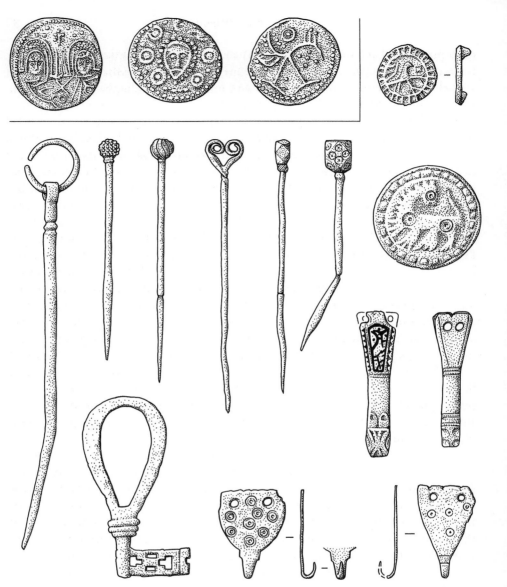

Fig. 3.5. A late seventh-/ninth-century miscellany. Top left: 'Two Emperors' gold thrymsa, a design also used on silver sceattas; right: obverse and reverse of a silver sceat or penny of Series H Type 49, probably minted in *Hamwic*, Saxon Southampton (cf. distribution map, Fig. 3.6). Centre: a selection of pins from *Hamwic*—though most could have come from almost anywhere in Britain. On the left is an Irish type of ringed pin, in the centre a spiral-headed pin, both of which are very similar to examples in Caerwent, for instance. Most have a swelling or hipped shaft, which is thought to have made them less likely to slip through textile weaves. All are copper-alloy, except the second left, which is silver. Top right: lead alloy brooch with a crude bird in relief, from Upavon, Wiltshire. Right centre: copper-alloy brooch with a back-turned animal, from Icklingham, Suffolk. Lower right: two copper-alloy strap-ends from Winchester, Hampshire. The one on the left has a 'Trewhiddle-style' animal on its plate, and a terminal that seen from above can be recognized as a three-dimensional animal head; the strap-end on the right has vestiges of such a head. Bottom right: copper-alloy hooked tags from *Hamwic* and Winchester. Bottom centre: copper-alloy key from *Hamwic*. (Drawings by Nick Griffiths from the collections of the British, Southampton City, Wiltshire Heritage, Ashmolean and City of Winchester Museums. All actual size except the coins which are 2:1.)

exchanged, and payments are sometimes referrred to as being made in *mancuses*, a unit of account equivalent to thirty pennies. The Aston Rowant hoard would have amounted to less than six *mancuses*, not enough to buy a decent estate. Some charters refer to payments in rings, of twenty-three, thirty, seventy-five, and even a hundred *mancuses*.[56] Although there are decorated finger-rings from the mid Anglo-Saxon period (e.g. Fig. 3.2), there are almost no plain rings, whole or in segments, likely to have had value only as bullion units;[57] nevertheless, they are sometimes mentioned in terms that must mean that they existed physically, because their transfer was linked with other objects, such as vessels, or the gospel-book that King Offa gave to one of his churches together with two gold *armillae*.[58]

Doubts over the extent to which the gold coins had been controlled in detail by kings continue to apply to many of the sceattas. A few of the latter have inscriptions, such as some issued by King Aldfrith of Northumbria (685–705),[59] but the wide range of designs could indicate unregulated production. On the other hand, both weights and metal alloys have a consistency that argues for control, though with enough variation to suggest that the sceattas were accepted at face value, not weighed before being accepted;[60] if that had been happening, many more balance-sets would be found.[61] Although early designs had recognizable Roman models, they reverted to imitating continental coins which had already diverged far from Roman prototypes; increasingly, images were adopted from other works of art, more akin to Germanic styles, such as a combination of a fantastic bird on one side and a gaunt moustachioed head on the other (Fig. 3.5).[62]

Sceattas continued to be placed occasionally in graves, probably until about 730, not only in cemeteries with seventh-century or earlier origins, but also at what are probably new sites with churches, like Repton, Derbyshire, where one corpse had a coin in its hand[63]—placed there by a mourner, unless it had been gripped convulsively at the moment of death. They sometimes turn up in churchyards, as at Wharram Percy, Yorkshire, where it is just possible that they derive from graves disturbed by later burials, but are more likely to be casual losses by people taking their offerings to the church, or using its yard as a meeting-place.[64]

Although objects were very occasionally deposited in graves after the early eighth century,[65] the near-absence of costume jewellery suggests that most people were being buried in shrouds. One consequence is that things found in excavations are mostly those that were least worth keeping or looking after, such as broken pottery, bone combs beyond repair, or iron nails and copper-alloy pins too trivial to be worth picking up if dropped (Fig. 3.5). The only gold object that had been found in the whole of the *wic* at Southampton was a single ninth-century coin, until 1999, when a rubbish-pit on the stadium site yielded a skein of thin strip, twisted for use in embroidery, and even that quite probably derived from a grave disturbed by pit-digging during the eighth and ninth centuries. Gold thread has been found in some seventh-century graves, notably in Kent, in positions that show that rich women were wearing sleeve-ends and headdresses with embroidered bands, and reference to the latter as *vittae*, apparently worn by both men and women in some religious houses, drew condemnation from St Aldhelm; fragments have recently been excavated at Barking Abbey, Essex, one of the principal mid-Saxon nunneries.[66]

Some gold was available to *Hamwic*'s metalworkers, as it was used for gilding, but apart from coins the only solid silver items discarded were a few pins and a couple of strap-ends (Fig. 3.5). The problem becomes the opposite of the earlier period, in which objects in graves may be grander than what was in everyday use; now the losses may be of the most everyday things, although more valuable brooches and the like could still have been owned. A few probably were; but earlier occupation sites like West Stow and Mucking are a corrective to the view that nothing of any consequence gets accidentally mislaid. The *wic* sites may indeed have been places in which most personal jewellery was of little value.[67]

A different picture is given by the large numbers of broken glass fragments, mostly from funnel-shaped beakers and palm cups, variously coloured and often with white trails. Analyses of their composition suggest that those in *Hamwic* were nearly all coming from the same source. Surprisingly, that source does not seem also to have been supplying Quentovic, the trading-place in north France with which *Hamwic* was likely to have been in close contact.[68] Possible manufacturing centres are the Rhine–Meuse region,[69] Kent, Glastonbury Abbey,[70] and south-west France,[71] but nothing yet explains why there should be different compositions at different sites, so that glass in *Hamwic* is similar to that in Ipswich but not to glass in London.

Glass residues fused to crucibles are sometimes excavated,[72] but this does not mean that hollow vessels were being blown at the sites where they are found, only that solid beads were being rolled, or inlays cut. The most intense colouring is in the thickest part of a vessel, its base, so fragments from it are the most sought after for recycling. The Tattershall Thorpe smith was carrying a broken beaker base, deep blue from the use of cobalt, a rare mineral. There was no trace of any of the rest of the vessel, so probably only that one part was worth keeping for reuse.[73]

The glass vessels landed at *Hamwic*, *Lundenwic*, and elsewhere might either have been for use by their residents or by the merchants who brought them, or were intended for trading on to royal, church, and aristocratic sites, so that what is found at the ports is mostly what was damaged in transit. The last seems most likely, but too little is found at inland sites to be sure, in the same way that it cannot be certain that such things were acquired by kings as part of their pre-emption rights to goods landed at the *wics*.[74] Although the glass is quite durable, its tendency to break into tiny pieces militates against its recovery, and a lot has probably gone unrecognized because it is difficult to distinguish very small fragments of the Anglo-Saxon period from Roman.

The concept of a social elite bolstering its position by offering wine or mead in suitable drinking vessels is expressed in *Beowulf*, especially when the hero is offered a cup by his hostess in a gesture clearly redolent of a tradition of honourable hospitality.[75] Unbroken vessels may disappear from the archaeological record because they ceased to be buried, but the poem suggests that they still had a social function, and the ban on the use of glass for communion chalices in the eighth century may partly be because of its secular feasting connotations. A similar ban was imposed on horns, in that case explicitly because they were bloody, from the slaughter of the animal.[76] There is no doubt that horns continued in use, though the seventh-century law that a stranger was to shout or blow one when off the beaten track is a reminder that drinking was not their only use.[77]

The problem raised by the glass over the extent to which the trading-places were passing goods on to an elite is part of the wider question of their interrelationships with their hinterlands. The distribution of imported pottery is another. Although unglazed and therefore only different shades of brown, grey, and black, wheel-throwing and burnishing meant that in some respects such pottery was distinctively different from the much commoner indigenous wares. At the *wics* and other, smaller landing-places such as *Sandtun*, near Hythe in Kent, pottery from the Rhine and Meuse valleys and from northern France has been found in varying proportions.[78] Some then travelled inland, and because it is more durable than glass, and cannot be recycled, it may be a better barometer of trade and exchange. The uplands site in the Yorkshire Wolds, Wharram Percy, had about ten black, north French sherds, for instance, despite its distance from the sea and its isolated position. It also had a sherd of Tating ware, very distinctive because of the tinfoil pressed into it.[79] That seems sufficiently distinctive to have been worth trading or giving as a present, but the more ordinary imports may not have had such appeal.

Another type of import that can be quite readily identified is basalt lava, brought from the Rhineland outcrops in the Eifel region, near Mayen, and used for quernstones. It may have been preferred to British stones because most limestones and sandstones are too soft to produce good grinding surfaces, and most gritstones and granites are too hard to be worked easily, though they were certainly used. Basalt lava is softer, and retains a grainy surface during use.[80] It has been found at many inland sites now, so is unlikely to have been particularly prestigious, as used to be thought on the assumption that it was referred to as 'black stones' in a letter written by the Emperor Charlemagne to King Offa of Mercia in 796. In fact the letter speaks of 'lengths' of stone, an inappropriate term to use of round querns, and more probably means columns, perhaps of imperial purple porphyry, for use in a prestigious building. In exchange, Charlemagne wanted Offa to make sure that the *saga*, cloaks or lengths of cloth, coming to his people from England, were of the same size as they used to be. That could refer to a regularly traded commodity, but the context suggests that Charlemagne was concerned about high-quality woollens wanted for his court, and that the royal discourse was about gift exchange.[81]

One commodity that was not an import from overseas, but was traded widely, was Ipswich ware pottery. Produced on the fringes of the *wic*, it was made on a wheel—not thrown, but by turning—and fired in permanent kilns, not in bonfires as were most handmade wares. It is found mostly in East Anglia, but some has come from Kent, Lincolnshire, and up the rivers that flow into the Wash, as well as small amounts from even further away at Wharram Percy, Southampton, London, and the upper Thames valley (Fig. 3.6). Although now thought not to have begun production until *c*.700, some of this pottery has stamped decoration like that on cremation urns, which has

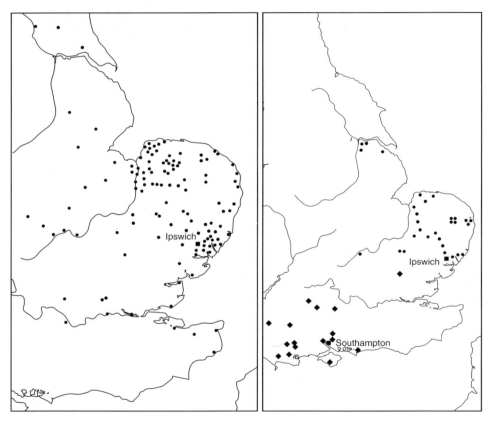

Fig. 3.6. Distribution map of Ipswich-ware pottery (with some omissions for clarity) and of two sceatta coin types, Series H, Type 49, probably minted in *Hamwic* (cf. Fig. 3.5), and Series R, Types 7–11, some at least probably minted in Ipswich. (Drawn from data in Newman, J. 1999, Metcalf 1994, and the Fitzwilliam Museum, Cambridge, Early Medieval Coin Corpus.)

Fig. 3.7. Eighth-century Ipswich-ware pottery sherd with face-masks below the rim. Although they have been compared to the heads on the earlier Sutton Hoo whetstone, the head on the *Hamwic* sceat is more closely contemporary with the sherd (Fig. 3.5). (Photograph reproduced by courtesy of Ipswich Museum. Actual size.)

led to the proposal that it was at least initiated by people who recalled earlier ways of doing things (Fig. 3.7).[82] Any association of that sort might have made the pottery unacceptable in Essex, which has nothing like the quantity in Suffolk, although Ipswich is close to the boundary between the two. Because Essex was a different kingdom, however, the explanation may be that toll restraints, or active discouragement of exchange for political reasons, acted as a barrier to normal market conditions. Within Suffolk itself the distribution is uneven, which suggests that a market system had yet to be established;[83] maintenance of contacts between families may still have been as important in the circulation of goods. Production of the pottery seems to have ceased in the middle of the ninth century. Why it had no imitators in England, either at the other *wic* sites or elsewhere, is far from clear; the earlier hones and Charnwood Forest ware show that networks either already existed or could be quickly established for distribution, and the lava and the coins show that Ipswich was not uniquely well placed.

The argument that a frontier restricted but did not altogether prevent Ipswich ware's passage into Essex gets some support from the distributions of certain types of sceat, which could reflect embargoes on the use of a rival king's coins (Fig. 3.6). There are distinctive types that look likely to have been minted in York and Ipswich, which are nearly confined to Northumbria and East Anglia respectively.[84] Most of those with a bird on one side and a moustachioed head on the other have been found in Southampton, and most of the rest in Wessex,[85] but too rarely to prove that they were totally unacceptable in Mercia. Most sceattas cannot be associated with particular kingdoms in this way, however, and very few have inscriptions to make an explicit link between a coin and a kingdom for those who could read letters but would not necessarily understand the meaning of the images, if indeed they were intended to be meaningful.[86]

Some other types of object, not necessarily important-looking ones, may also have been associated with a particular kingdom. An undistinguished copper-alloy disc-brooch cast in relief with an animal looking back over its shoulder is a type mostly found in East Anglia, though discoveries in York, Winchester, Oxfordshire, and elsewhere have also been made, so their frequency in Norfolk and Suffolk might be as much a factor of the large number of finds in those counties generally as a factor of any specifically regional sense of identity (Fig. 3.5).[87] The case for regional production in East Anglia of strap-ends with silver-wire inlay is a good one on the basis of their distribution,[88] but it is a variation within a very standardized range. A northern preference for larger strap-ends is shown by the discovery of a mould for producing them found in Carlisle, and by a group of four at Lilla Howe, Yorkshire, and a single one in York—where, however, there are several of the more usual slightly smaller ones.[89] Arguments that a particular type of brooch can be linked to a particular kingdom can easily fail because of the coincidence of a new discovery; a lead-alloy brooch with a bird design was once attributed to *Hamwic* on the basis of two examples found there (Fig. 3.5), only for a bone mould for casting similar ones to turn up a year later in London.[90]

Most of the mid-Anglo-Saxon metalwork shows no sign of regional variation; overall similarity is well shown by spiral-headed pins (Fig. 3.5); although few in number, they have been found from Southampton to Caerwent to Carlisle,[91] occasionally in graves, where they could have been used as shroud pins. The vast majority of pins are equally ubiquitous, but are not in graves—with the consequence that there is no idea of quite how they were worn or used. Nevertheless, the broad picture is that everyday material culture was standardized throughout England, with minor geographical differences in some instances, as it had been at aristocratic level at least in the seventh century, despite political divisions. The quantities of base-metal objects now being found suggest large-scale production and probably specialist workers, some beginning to concentrate at the *wics* and at churches, as well as at royal and aristocratic centres such as Ramsbury, Wiltshire. Technology was also more widely applied, even if it was not actually new; the range excavated in the *wic* at York is instructive: the non-ferrous plating of iron objects; the making of iron knife-blades by piling, that is, mixing ores of different qualities to get a homogeneous structure; the use of tin-lead alloys; and perhaps enamelling.[92]

Just as lava for quernstones can no longer be seen as especially prestigious because it is now known to have been widely available, so also Ipswich ware is not usually thought of as something special and sought-after, but as merely an alternative to locally produced pottery, perhaps slightly preferable to organic-tempered and shell-filled wares if its greater refinement was noticed. That it has been reported from various ecclesiastical sites is just a reflection of the greater attention that they had received from excavators until recently. Bede's Jarrow, its twin foundation Monkwearmouth, Hild's Whitby, and Augustine's Canterbury were obvious targets for archaeologists; Yeavering had its known royal connection; Southampton and the other *wics* are recorded as trading-places. The work at rural Wharram Percy is different, partly because the settlement is not mentioned in any document until the end of the eleventh century, and partly because its excavation began as long ago as 1950 to investigate late medieval earthworks; the Anglo-Saxon discoveries there were a bonus.

Wharram raises the considerable problem of attributing a particular status or set of functions to a site; it was on a royal estate in the late eleventh century, but that ownership may have no bearing on conditions 300 years earlier.[93] Nevertheless, if a king owned the estate, he might have stayed there occasionally, bringing with him an entourage that carried with it what the royal court needed, including the Tating ware, the coins, and even the lava querns and the Ipswich ware found there. That would help to explain why a part of the site was given over to blacksmithing, producing not only the tools and equipment needed for farming and working the estate, but also sword fittings, things that only an aristocrat would have expected to use.[94] Other objects excavated that seem more than might be expected if the place amounted to no more than an isolated couple of farmsteads include two imported Frisian bow-brooches,[95] glass beads—but only a single fragment of vessel glass—and an imported sceat.[96] An elite presence is also indicated by copper-alloy working, in the form of crucibles and notably moulds for casting interlace patterns, things otherwise found at sites like Hartlepool assumed to be ecclesiastical, in that case because Hild is recorded as its abbess.[97] At Wharram no church is known from documentary evidence, but part of an eighth-century carved cross-head with Whitby parallels[98] must demonstrate that an important person was commemorated there. Either craftspeople and imports arrived because clients like that lived at Wharram, or visited it from time to time; or the amount of trade and contact enjoyed by ordinary farming folk has been underestimated, in which case Wharram's richer items need not imply a richer social stratum.

Another Yorkshire Wolds site, Cottam, is a contrast to Wharram in that it was identified first from metal-detectorists' discoveries of coins, pins, and strap-ends in quantities comparable to those from *Hamwic*. The number of features was shown to be nothing like comparable, however, when the site was excavated in the 1990s.[99] Its mid-Anglo-Saxon ownership is unknown, but as it seems not to have the evidence of an elite presence, such as stone sculptures or sword fittings, it may have differed from Wharram Percy. Nor did it have any Ipswich ware, yet thirty eighth- and ninth-century coins must show that it had involvement with trading networks, and some of the strap-ends were of the type identified as probably coming from East Anglia, and, as they involve silver-wire inlay, were not valueless items.[100] A little further south, South Newbald indicates that goods were being landed in the Humber estuary, so not all were going up the river to the *wic* at York for redistribution.[101]

On the opposite side of the Humber, Flixborough is another site that has been excavated as well as metal-detected. It has produced coins, pins, and strap-ends, but also evidence of a wide range of craftworking. Unlike Cottam, it had a small cemetery for at least part of its period of use, and a building that could have been a small chapel. A lead plaque inscribed with a cross followed by some names, at least one of which is female, may be listing members of a community, or benefactors of one, for whom prayers were sought (Fig. 3.8).[102] That community might not have been at Flixborough, however, and other indications of literacy there, such as styli, and a silver ring with the first half of the alphabet on it (Fig. 3.9), might be a consequence of secular use of

Fig. 3.8. X-ray photograph of the lead plaque excavated at Flixborough, Lincolnshire. The list of names inscribed into it starts with *Alduini*, a man's name, but the first in the third line is a woman's, *Edelgyd*. The style of the letters is closest to that used in the handwriting in late eighth- and early ninth-century charters. (Photograph reproduced by courtesy of Humber Field Archaeology and of English Heritage. Actual size.)

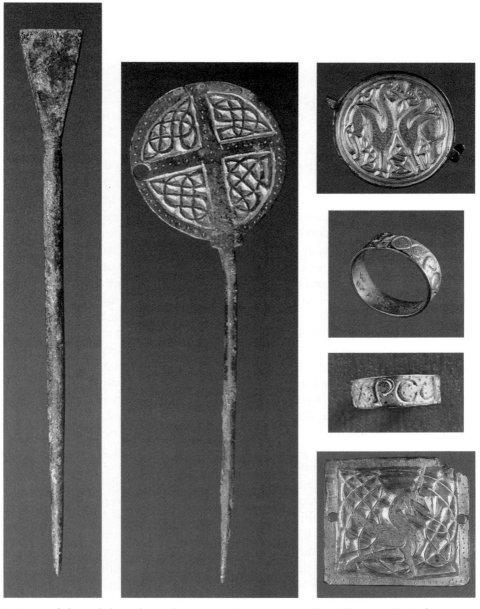

Fig. 3.9. Some of the eighth-/early ninth-century objects excavated at Flixborough. Left: a copper-alloy stylus, further evidence of literacy at the site, as the pointed end would have been used for writing on wax tablets or to make lines on parchment, the wide end for erasing. Next to it is a gilt copper-alloy disc-headed pin, with interlace knots between the arms of a cross. Top right: silver-gilt brooch with two confronting animals, their bodies speckled, and their tongues forming a knot and then seeming to pass through their heads to interlace with lappets and entwine their way around the animals' bodies. Centre right: two views of a silver-gilt ring incised with alphabet letters; the lower picture shows an 'a', formed in the same way as the first letter on the lead plaque (Fig. 3.8); next to it, visible on the upper photograph, is a 'b', upside-down in relation to the 'a' and the following 'c'. The ring was made by bending a flat strip of metal and securing the ends with two rivets, a fitting that strongly suggests that it was not a finger-ring, though its actual use is unknown. Bottom right: a gilt copper-alloy plaque, with a single winged creature in the same 'Mercian' style as the animals on the brooch. (Photographs reproduced by courtesy of Humber Field Archaeology and of English Heritage. All actual size.)

documents; the range of objects perhaps indicates that the burials were those of the owning family, as may be suggested for Wharram Percy, and not those of a major but unrecorded church establishment.[103]

Other sites that have produced evidence of metalwork in quantities that were unanticipated only twenty-five years ago include several in East Anglia,[104] while various others are suspected though not proven.[105] One where excavation has taken place, Barham, Suffolk, produced layers of dark earth suggesting occupation, but no evidence of structures, so could have operated primarily as a fair, a neutral place not too close to any one settlement. By contrast, some sites of the same period have produced features, but very little in the way of artefacts; Tamworth, Staffordshire, the site of a royal watermill, is one example of a high-status place where more might have been expected. Whether mid-Anglo-Saxon Northampton was primarily a royal centre, or a church occasionally visited by kings, is not clear from the written sources, from the excavated features, or from the artefacts—three eighth-/ninth-century coins, a strap-end, a stylus, and a triangular piece of rock crystal which seems likely to have had a metal setting and to have been a pendant, perhaps for personal use, perhaps to suspend from an altar or reliquary. Much more surprising is that the bishopric centre at North Elmham, Norfolk, had very little metalwork in the backfills of its ditches and wells, despite being in East Anglia; there were only two coins, but at least a small piece of silver strip with an impressed plant-scroll looks as if it may have been snapped off a casket or a book appropriate to its context. In Buckinghamshire, a site at Pennylands with enclosures and buildings not unlike Cottam's had some lava, some Ipswich ware and other pottery, a bone comb, and a lot of textile-working equipment—but no coins, and only a single pin, although there were wells and pits in which rubbish and losses could have accumulated. These places were not simply too far inland to participate in trade and exchange; all except Tamworth were well within the coin-using area, and Pennylands is not far from the River Thames, where a number of pits at Lot's Hole near Eton have recently produced enough pottery to suggest that it was a landing-place for goods, perhaps operating much like a fair.[106] One difficulty is that fewer sunken-featured buildings were used in the mid-Anglo-Saxon period, so the rubbish deposits that so informatively filled them disappear from the archaeological record.

All these new sites, the *wics*, the coins, and the plethora of metalwork indicate solid prosperity in eighth-century England, despite the decline in the availability of gold. How far the distributions reflect different regional wealth levels in the eighth century is not yet clear: sceatta finds may show where coins were used, but non-monetary systems must have continued for most purposes in most areas. East Anglia, Lincolnshire, and south Yorkshire seem to have the most sites prolific in discarded objects and coins; Kent, however, has a fair number of coins but many fewer objects, as the recently excavated seashore site at *Sandtun* indicates.[107] Even excavations in Canterbury have not produced many eighth-century coins or objects, and the most interesting, a metalworker's die, is not in precious metal.[108] Yet Canterbury was almost certainly responsible for many of England's very fine manuscripts of the period, which involved considerable investment. The best-quality animal skins and great care in their tanning were needed for the parchment, long hours had to be spent in the scriptorium by the scribes, who had to be fed as well as supplied with inks and colours for the pictures, including, for the most exceptional, purple dyes from the *murex*, a shellfish, to stain a whole page with the imperial colour for the Majesty of Christ, with gold leaf laid over it. The same dye was used for textiles, drawing disdain from St Aldhelm.[109]

The number of prolific sites in East Anglia helps to explain why Mercia was anxious to expand eastwards in the eighth century, having taken over Lindsey (north Lincolnshire) in the seventh. The Mercian kings' increasing dominance is not reflected by subsequent finds in their west Midlands heartland, but the wealth already implied by the string of rich seventh-century burial sites for the Thames valley—Taplow, Cuddesdon, Asthall—is reflected by new church foundations[110] and by secular finds—though not so much by secular sites; Lot's Hole looks meagre alongside Barham or Coddenham. To the south, Wessex is not strongly represented either. There are several late seventh-century rich burials—Swallowcliffe and Roundway Down in Wiltshire,[111] the Brooks in Winchester,[112] the football stadium in Southampton—but if the *Hamwic* range is representative, the kingdom's rather modest eighth-century political and ecclesiastical achievements were matched by the quality of its disposable resources, although Ramsbury and some other sites show intensification of output.[113]

The rich burials effectively ceased at the end of the seventh century. Scarcity of gold might have been a factor in this, silver being less able to make a great impression, but probably far more significant was the completion of the process of acceptance of Christianity and Christian burial practice, with commemoration and status display by crosses, as at Wharram Percy, and by benefaction, with the lead plaque at Flixborough perhaps an example of an aide-memoire of names to be remembered in prayers.

One site which has stronger claims than Flixborough to have been an important church, despite not being named in any surviving document, is Brandon, Suffolk, where many of the finds are no different from those at Cottam and elsewhere, but where excavations have shown that there were at least two cemeteries and probably a church building.[114] As at Flixborough, there were signs of literacy at the site, such as the first sixteen letters of the 'futhorc', the runic alphabet, inscribed on the back of a silver disc-headed pin.[115] Part of a pair of tweezers at Brandon had the name 'Aldred' on it in runes, presumably for its owner or maker; whoever had cut them was familiar also with Latin letters, as he had added serifs to the runes.[116] A small gold plaque on which is shown in black niello outline a haloed figure with an eagle's head, holding a pen and identified as St John by a Latin inscription, must have been part of a set showing the four evangelists, perhaps from the arm of a cross. On formal Christian texts, Latin was used. For informal messages and secular objects, runes were appropriate, as on the Brandon pin and tweezers, and on the Harford Farm brooch. The dichotomy was not absolute, however, a few runic letters being added to the Latin alphabet. But even the scratching of someone's name in runes on a brooch put that person into the ambit of the venerated Word.[117]

The front of the disc on the head of the Brandon pin was gilded, and incised with a symmetrical pattern of two birds, their legs and tails interlaced, pecking at a plant; the reference is to the Tree of Life, and to the trees of the Lord offering shelter.[118] Designs like these were coming into western Europe embroidered on Near Eastern textiles, and although the interlace was retained from seventh-century traditions, animals and birds were more lifelike and less sinuous than those in Style II (e.g. Fig. 3.9). The pin's owner may have understood its message without necessarily being a priest, just as the owner of another gilt-silver disc-headed pin from the site must have known the significance of the round-headed cross on it.[119] In the spaces between the cross arms are various contorted creatures, including a humanoid, which have no obvious message unless as very generalized warnings of evil demons. The same is true of the many other eighth- and ninth-century pinheads with patterns of various kinds, many of which are like miniature versions of stone sculptures. The humanoid is interesting because it is still unusual for a whole figure to be shown, unless it is one of the evangelists or other saints; Brandon has another example, a naked male on a strap-end,[120] but it is as though the taboo that restricted earlier representations of bodies rather than just masks from appearing on Anglo-Saxon metalwork was still felt—perhaps reinforced by Christianity's view of humans as different from and superior to the beasts of the field.

One of the difficulties of the eighth century is that the known hoards, like that at Aston Rowant, contain only coins;[121] without any grave-good sequences, dating of metalwork is heavily dependent on comparisons with manuscript illuminations, which are themselves not beyond dispute as to origin or date, or with stone sculptures, which have the merit of not being likely to be moved far from their original context, but which also have to be dated mainly by style. The anthropomorphic figure and the letters on the Brandon gold plaque, for instance, are very like evangelist portraits in the Book of Cerne, usually taken to be an early ninth-century gospel-book written and decorated in Mercia.[122] Book decoration was not only internal: covers were likely to be set with gems and glass studs, such as the dark green domed glass oval inlaid with yellow, found at York Minster,[123] or a cameo and a rectangular dark blue glass mount inlaid with gold from Whitby Abbey.[124] Establishments like those needed

Fig. 3.10. The front panel of the late seventh- or eighth-century Franks Casket shows the importance of storytelling, Christianity, and material objects. On the left is Weland the Smith, killing and abusing royal children to revenge himself on the king who had injured him, a form of anti-gift. On the right the three Magi are bringing their good gifts to Jesus. Weland had special powers to make wonderful things for a king, but the Magi put their skills to better use by recognizing the King of Heaven. The runic inscription round the two scenes describes the fate of the whale which provided the raw material for the casket. (Photograph reproduced by courtesy of the British Museum, London. Slightly less than half size.)

their own craft workshops, and some who worked in them were permanent members of the community, for whom a peripatetic existence was not an option.[125]

One smith who was peripatetic until hamstrung to prevent him from escaping was the legendary Weland, whose story is carved on one of the whalebone panels that make up the late seventh- or eighth-century Franks Casket (Fig. 3.10).[126] He is shown with an anvil, hammers, and tongs like those carried by the Tattershall Thorpe smith, in the act of making a cup out of his captor's son's head,[127] so that he could offer a drugged potion to the boy's unsuspecting sister. This story is typical of its time in illustrating both revenge and how people can unwittingly bring their own fate upon themselves, since the children were unknowingly taking part in events that would bring them tragedy, just like the whale which, by casting itself up on the shore, had provided the material for the box from which the Casket was made. The downfall of 'the king of terror' was recorded in an inscription written in runes around the front panel. Other texts on the Casket explain some of the scenes. They are not scriptural, so Latin was only used once, when Jerusalem, the Holy City, is mentioned.

Other themes that can be recognized from the scenes on the Casket include an archer defending an enclosure, which may be a reference to protection of the box's contents, perhaps holy relics, which would provide one reason to think that it was from a church treasury, despite the inclusion of stories from the non-Christian world like that about Weland. Next to the Weland scene is one showing the Three Magi bearing gold, incense, and myrrh to Mary and Jesus, the message probably being that Weland misused his skills by making gifts for his enemies that would bring them evil, whereas the Wise Men's offerings symbolize the good things that God bestows on humankind through His son. This was using the familiar concept of gift-giving to create a contrast between the Old and New Worlds, comprehensible in the secular as well as the church environment. Some of the Casket's deeper meanings, however, such as its possible Eucharist references, would not have been picked up by those without education and familiarity with the Church liturgy; a Beowulf would have understood the significance of the Magis' gold, but would not have known Pope Gregory's reflections on incense and myrrh.[128]

Although the Franks Casket has many similarities to pictures ranging from stone carvings in Gotland to mosaics in Ravenna, no single direct source has been identified, and some details may have been devised by its designer; smith's tools, for instance, are shown on Roman pots and grave-slabs, but not in surviving manuscripts or on ivory carvings or textiles, even though those were portable things either known in or likely to have been brought to England. Consequently the clothes worn by Weland and some other figures, the weapons being used, and the earth barrows in one complex scene are likely to be closer to what was part of Anglo-Saxon experience than anything shown in manuscript illuminations. On the other hand, the prominent round brooches fastening the Magis' cloaks are more probably copied from some Mediterranean import, such as an ivory plaque, as they are almost absent from the archaeological record of the eighth century, and are found almost entirely in women's graves in the seventh.[129]

A few other church items survive, and show the importance of having things that caught the light and the eye in dark buildings, concentrating attention upon the altars and the message of the Cross. Some of the material was not actually precious; the largest surviving item is the Rupertus Cross, probably Anglo-Saxon workmanship although now in Germany. At first glance it might seem to be solid gold studded with precious gems, but it is actually wood with gilded copper-alloy sheets nailed to it, and set with glass studs much like those from York and Whitby.[130] Other examples are a reliquary from Winchester and the earlier one now in Mortain, and an ornate gilt copper-alloy chalice cast for Duke Tassilo of Bavaria between 777 and 788.[131] Combined with coloured window glass, such things created a jewelled effect for church interiors, awe-inspiring for the visitor, and difficult to emulate in the secular context of the feast-hall. Consequently there was no particular reason why secular items should follow the same trends, though some of the same ideas can certainly be recognized, and an object like the Ormside bowl, a gilt-silver vessel with glass settings and an embossed cross on its base,[132] could have been used in either context, since it is not specifically liturgical. Chalices may also have crossed the boundary; one is shown in the barrow scene on the Franks Casket, while one in gilt copper-alloy from Hexham Abbey seems from its find-spot to have been for communion use.[133]

Both the Ormside bowl and the Rupertus Cross have embossed decoration of birds and animals in plants, like the Brandon disc-headed pin. Here, however, the plants include bunches of fruit off which the creatures are feeding, an allusion to the vinescroll and Christ's words in St John's Gospel, 'I am the true vine . . .'.[134] Very fine gold granulation on a sword-pommel from the River Thames at Windsor, Berkshire (Fig. 3.11),[135] may be another allusion to

Fig. 3.11. Late eighth-/early ninth-century copper-alloy and silver sword-pommel with a gold panel in the centre, from the River Thames at Windsor. In the panel, a snake's head can be seen on each side, both having eyes made of grains of gold; each long wire body loops and interlaces before being devoured by its opposite number. Finer twisted filigree wires go over and under the bodies, sometimes sprouting clusters of gold granules. The outer border of the panel is a vertical strip of gold soldered to the back-plate, with its top cut to make it look like a beaded wire, a technique referred to as 'serrated band'. The panel is flanged, and slides into grooves in the silver dome which fits over the copper-alloy core of the pommel, which may originally have had silver plates over its ends like those on the Abingdon sword (Fig. 4.2). (Photograph reproduced by courtesy of the Ashmolean Museum, Oxford. Twice actual size.)

grapes, with snakes that have not grasped the message that they can feed off the fruit and are devouring each other, just as Mankind will destroy itself if it does not heed the Word of God. The composition perhaps therefore alludes to the evil that threatens God's creation, which it is the Christian warrior's duty to defend. It is also a sword's job to provide corpses for carrion-eaters to feed on, and animal heads on some pommels may refer to that image, which occurs in poetry (cf. Fig. 4.2). The snakelike creatures may be corpse-devouring *wyrms*, given a Christian interpretation because the body was an analogue for the soul devoured by sin, especially by Gluttony.[136] Transition from whatever meanings Style II had originally had is further shown by two pairs of interlaced snakes on either side of the door into the church at Monkwearmouth, which may be warnings of the evils of the world being left behind by those who enter—but as they are carved to form a T-cross, they may also allude to the beasts that recognize Christ, and thus become symbolic of the promise of eternal life.[137] Again, the difference may be in different layers of meaning.

The Windsor pommel is usually dated to the late eighth or early ninth century, on the basis of its similarity to manuscript decoration.[138] A similar pommel, but in iron with silver inlay, has recently come from lower down the Thames at Chiswick.[139] Also from the Thames, at Westminster, is a mount with a fearsome beast's head terminal comparable to those on the Pictish chapes; it has a runic inscription, unfortunately incomprehensible, but adding to its aura.[140] Several other high-quality objects, including the now-lost hanging-bowl and a set of three linked disc-headed pins from the River Witham in Lincolnshire, are from streams and rivers. This may not be coincidence; despite their value, some objects may have been disposed of because of their association with owners who presumably had no further use for them; bad luck in battle would not be passed on if a weapon that had failed in its duty were disposed of. This would not have been 'sacrifice' in propitiation of anti-Christian gods, but was perhaps nevertheless a residue of older ideas about personal property taking on something of that person's character. The number of objects inscribed with owners' or donors' names seems very high; they may just be casual losses, but could be deliberate discards, not necessarily always in water. Gold finger-rings, such as one inscribed 'Aedred owns me, Eanred engraved me', are the most frequent, but there are also knives, such as one inlaid in silver with 'S[i]gebereht owns me, Biorhtelm made me'.[141]

Many of the finest eighth- and early ninth-century objects have been found in areas controlled by Mercia, and may well be a direct reflection of that kingdom's supremacy.[142] The Windsor and Chiswick pommels are not the only elaborate sword trappings to survive from the eighth and ninth centuries. Another, from Fetter Lane, between the City and *Lundenwic*, has gilt-silver plates over the handgrip and the pommel, with a whorl of snakes and other animal ornament that puts it into the same general date range.[143] A pommel discovered recently at Beckley, Oxfordshire, in gilt silver has an openwork frieze of animal heads unlike anything seen before.[144] Clearly swords continued to be very prestigious, their ownership still symbolic of self-protection and the right to defend oneself against insult.[145] The old custom of tying a bead or fixing a ring to the pommel probably ceased, however, perhaps because such amulets were frowned upon.[146] More surprisingly, belts seem to have lost their status. None of the large, elaborately decorated buckles such as were found at Sutton Hoo and Taplow is attributed to the eighth century, and there are not many of any sort. Those in York's Fishergate area and *Hamwic* suggest use on much narrower straps.[147]

One item of warriors' equipment to maintain its status implications was the metal helmet, to judge from one found in a well at Coppergate, York, apparently hidden just below the water level rather than thrown in to dispose of it. It had been partially dismantled after long use, and may have been concealed while awaiting repair in the ninth century, having been made in the eighth. Animal patterns comparable to those on the St Ninian's chapes and other objects occur on its nasal, over the eyebrows, and at the end of the crest (Fig. 3.12). Inscriptions in brass strips forming a cross over the top of the helmet invite prayers for Oshere, assumed to be its first owner. Some of the letters are back to front, others upside down, so presumably the text was composed and written out by a cleric, and imperfectly copied by an illiterate craftsman, though well enough for Oshere not to know any better.[148]

In Old English poetry a warrior's helmet invariably had a boar image; his 'boar-helm' was the first thing that a hero reached for when rudely awakened.[149] Three-dimensional boars stand on the crests of two of the English seventh-century helmets,[150] the animal's fierce courage and boldness in protecting its territory being qualities that a warrior most needed. Fertility associations probably account for occurrences of its tusks in some earlier female graves. Some of its associations may have been too close to pagan deities for it to be incorporated within Christian iconography, which would account for its absence from the Coppergate helmet and from other metalwork.[151] The stag was similarly viewed askance,[152] and made no appearance after Sutton Hoo until rehabilitated by the popularity of Bestiaries after the tenth century.[153]

That helmets had high status is evident from the few survivals, but whether they were yet symbols of kingship, as has been asserted of Sutton Hoo's, is more doubtful. When coronation rituals begin to appear, the Latin word for 'crown' was translated as Old English *beag*, 'ring', which could be a reference to a circlet or diadem.[154] On coins, royal images continued to show variations of the classical diadem and wreath ties, and the mounted figure on a broken cross-shaft discovered at Repton in 1979 seems to be wearing a band like a diadem, rather than a helmet, and the pose has been likened to that of classical emperors trampling barbarians (Fig. 3.13). The sculpture's context, a church known to have been used in the eighth century as a royal mausoleum,

Fig. 3.12. Reconstructed side view of the helmet found in a pit at Coppergate, York. Made of iron sheets riveted together, it also had an iron ring-mail neckguard—each ring laboriously riveted—and copper-alloy fittings including inscriptions and snarling beasts' heads. The part of the text shown here ends with the name OSHER, the letters back to front. (Drawing by Helen Humphreys reproduced from Tweddle 1992a by permission of the York Archaeological Trust. About half actual size.)

Fig. 3.13. One side of the cross-shaft fragment excavated at Repton, Derbyshire, showing a moustachioed mounted figure wearing a diadem, a kiltlike skirt, and what may be ring-mail body armour or a jerkin padded with leather scales. In his missing right hand he was wielding a long sword, part of the blade of which survives above his head; there is a small shield in his left hand. His control of the horse would have been limited if the reins really were draped across his elbow, but the details of the bridle-bit are also strange and suggest a sculptor who did not fully understand them. The *seax* the rider has at his waist is clearly shown as a single-edged weapon by the angle on the underside, so it was being worn with the blade upwards. The weapons seem Germanic, the pose imperial. (Drawing by Judith Dobie reproduced with the authors' permission from Biddle and Kjølbye-Biddle 1985. One-sixth actual size.)

sanctions the claim that it is the earliest representation of an individual English king—not a likeness, but an icon with appropriate attributes.[155] His horse, the decorated shield that he is brandishing in one hand, the sword in his other, and the long, single-edged seax at his waist like those at *Hamwic* and Ipswich all suggest authority. He seems to be wearing armour on his upper body, either iron ring-mail like the coat at Sutton Hoo,[156] or leather scales, a short skirt or kilt, and his legs appear to be cross-gartered. He also has exuberant moustaches, recorded again in the eleventh century as an aristocratic military custom.[157]

If the Repton sculpture is indeed of a king, it is indicative of their increasing authority and position at the top of an administrative hierarchy, emphasized by changes made to the coinage in the second half of the eighth century. An obscure East Anglian king named Beonna seems to have taken a lead in the late 750s by imitating the new continental practice of striking on broader, thinner flanges than was used for sceattas. One of his moneyers is soon afterwards found striking coins for King Offa of Mercia, and Beonna's name disappears from history. His gesture of defiance by producing coins without the approval of his overlord may well have been one reason why he was ousted, probably with extreme prejudice.[158]

The new pennies almost invariably had both a king's and a moneyer's names on them, and they can therefore usually be linked to particular kingdoms, if not yet always to particular mints, with more assurance than can most of the sceattas. There can be little doubt that from now on kings controlled the coinage, presumably making a profit by charging the moneyers a fee for their licences, and occasionally granting the right to churchmen as a benefaction. King Offa even gave his wife the right to a licence, so that there are a few coins with Queen Cynethryth's name on them.[159] They were struck for her by Eoba, who also produced coins for the archbishop, presumably at Canterbury. Offa was probably both underlining his control of Kent, and building up his attempt to establish a third archbishopric, at Lichfield, by making a gesture against one of the existing archdioceses.

In general, there are fewer of the new, larger silver pennies than of the old sceattas, which could indicate economic decline, or merely that people were learning to take better care of their coins, for their distribution is no less widespread.[160] Finds become even scarcer after about 830, however,[161] and after that southern English pennies became seriously debased; King Offa achieved 95 per cent silver in his new issues, and 92 per cent was standard thereafter until about 840, when a movement began that took the silver content down to little more than 60 per cent.[162]

A few special-issue gold coins were also produced, mostly in the ninth century as imitations of *solidi* struck on the continent by the emperor Louis the Pious. The most extraordinary is late eighth-century, having King Offa's name on the obverse, and on the reverse a blundered Arabic inscription miscopying a dinar, a coin probably minted in Spain. Presumably Offa was impressed by one that he saw and by the distance it had travelled, so ordered some like it for himself; the only example known was found in Rome, probably sent there as part of the annual Peter's Pence offering—although the pope would not have been pleased by the inscription, had he known about it.[163] The coin may have been meant as a *mancus*, as it weighs about the same as three silver pennies, but the later *solidi* imitations are too heavy for that, and may have been weights.[164] Gold coins from the continent are also occasionally found, some presumably traded, others quite probably residues of viking loot.[165]

Northumbria only partly adopted the new coinage. From the 790s kings' and moneyers' names both appeared regularly, but the size of the coin flans was not changed. Although production continued despite viking raids, it may have been intermittent. Most problematical is the change that took place during the early ninth century, because unlike that of any of the other kingdoms, Northumbrian coinage became so debased that it descended into a base-metal series, usually called 'stycas'.[166] Those are found in large number, so they were in frequent use despite their low value, and as they were made of brass from newly smelted ores, not just from scrap metal, considerable care went into them. They are increasingly being found outside Northumbria; even if that is because no one elsewhere would accept them and they were not looked after, they still show considerable commerce between kingdoms[167]—it seems unlikely that viking raiders would have moved them round in the same way as they might have carried gold.

Gold remained a word that resonated for raiders and poets. *Beowulf* implies that gift-giving and feasting were still understood as social mechanisms,[168] even if kings could not lavish gold on their followers to quite the extent that they seem to have been able to do in the first part of the seventh century. Weapons were doubtless still welcome presents, and had the advantage of making their recipients more effective in their lord's service.[169] Charters, however, show that estates and the control of their produce became the means of power as the smaller tribal or political units had their independence reduced or removed.[170] A king needed regular supplies and services to maintain a position beyond that of warband leader. Whatever 'folk-land' had once meant,[171] by the mid Anglo-Saxon period any concept of tribal ownership was an anachronism; unless it was part of a family's inheritance, land was the king's to grant to followers or to churches, but once granted to the latter it was held by them in perpetuity, and unsurprisingly the laity sought similar privileges. Coins, *wics*, and the newly identified prolific sites show one of the mechanisms that made all these changes possible.

4

Alfred *et al.*

From the Mid-Ninth Century to the Mid-Tenth

A distinguishing feature of the ninth century is the amount of precious metal that has survived from it. Some of this comes from hoards, for in contrast to the eighth century there are several with both coins and objects, as well as some only with coins and some only with objects. The latest coin in a hoard provides no more than the earliest possible date at which it could have been deposited, but at least that is a fixed point in one direction, and its owner was unlikely to keep a store of coins for long without occasionally taking some out or putting others in. Objects in hoards, of course, may always include some treasured heirlooms, as may furnished graves, but at least perceived similarity to works in other media is not their only dating criterion.

A few objects can be dated because they have an identifiable name on them. A gold and niello ring inscribed *Ethelwulf R[e]x* at the bottom of the bezel associates it with King Aethelwulf, ruler of Wessex from 839 to 858 (Fig. 4.1, right). The ring was not necessarily made for him to wear himself, but for him to give to a follower as a permanent reminder of the service owed to its donor, though a Beowulf seeking a 'generous ring-giver' might not have thought its inscription sufficient compensation for its modest weight. Alternatively, it could have acted like a seal, to accompany a royal messenger and validate that his news or instructions came from the king; or have been used as a guarantee of a land donation and a physical reminder of the event at which the grant had been made.[1] That might have been the reason why the name of Queen Aethelswith was added to the back of another gold ring, thus associating it with Aethelwulf's daughter, who was queen of Mercia from 853 to 874 (Fig. 4.1, left).[2] The inscription may have been an afterthought, needed when the ring was used for an unanticipated purpose. A third explanation is that both rings were baptismal; above Aethelwulf's name are two birds at the Fountain of Life, and the bezel of Aethelswith's ring has the Lamb of St John the Baptist.[3]

With diameters of 28 mm and 26 mm, these royal rings are too big to have been worn on most fingers, unless over a glove as was done later in the Middle Ages. They may have been meant to wear on the thumb, but there are no illus-

Fig. 4.1. Two royal gold rings, both with black niello filling the backgrounds to the designs (cf. Col. pls. D and E). On the left, the bezel of the ring from Aberford, Yorkshire, has the *Agnus Dei*, the Lamb of God, identified by the letters 'A' and 'D', and by the halo, which has the bars of the cross through it, an attribute specific to Christ. The name inside the hoop is Aethelswith—the crossed 'D's here are standard Old English signifiers of the 'th' sound—with REG for the Latin *Regina*, the last two letters looking like an afterthought. The larger ring, from Laverstock, Wiltshire, has the name of her father Ethelwulf, with his title '*Rex*' abbreviated. (Photograph reproduced by courtesy of the British Museum, London. Drawings from Jessop 1950. Actual sizes.)

trations that suggest such a practice. One in the minster churchyard at Exeter seems to have been deliberately placed in a grave, but by the person's right arm, not on a finger. Although it was not with coins, it can probably also be dated to the ninth century.[4]

As well as the two royal rings, there are several others on which are the names of their owners or makers, but most are not those of people who can be positively identified in other sources. One from Bossington, Hampshire, has a Latin text, and seems to have some baptismal meaning. About as many uninscribed rings attributable to the ninth century by their decoration are known. Gold was also used on other objects, such as a sword from Abingdon, Oxfordshire, which had a gold plate set into its silver pommel, rather like the one on the Windsor pommel (Fig. 3.11). Somewhat similar gold panels are fitted into two silver strap-ends found at Ipsden, Oxfordshire; both have a central filigree-wire plant stem, with sprouting leaves and tendrils. Although the panels are slightly different, the strap-ends must have been used as a pair, though despite what now amount to hundreds of finds of strap-ends in silver and copper-alloy, what uses they had remains uncertain.[5]

The recipients of the royal rings may have been expected to appreciate the symbolism not only of the gift-giving act but of the royal mystique enhanced by the inscriptions.[6] The craftsman who made Aethelwulf's was not literate enough to know which way up a 'T' is meant to go, so it was presumably not his choice to use an abbreviation of the Latin *Rex* rather than the vernacular for the king's title. Whoever set out the inscription for the craftsman to copy deliberately chose the greater formality. So too did whoever ordered *Reg[i]na* to be put with Aethelswith's name. The Christian devices on their bezels need not mean that the two rings were intended for ecclesiastics; the Abingdon sword's upper guard has the four symbols of the evangelists on it, as though to show that its owner saw himself as a soldier of the Church in the fight against the pagan vikings (Fig. 4.2). Some of its other imagery, however, seems more expressive of the exultation of a warrior at his anticipated success in battle; the creatures modelled on the ends of the pommel may represent the scavengers that will feed off the weapon's victims—'the dusky-coated one, the black raven with its horned beak, to share the corpses, and the dun-coated, white-tailed eagle, the greedy war-hawk, to enjoy the carrion, and that grey beast, the wolf of the forest'.[7]

More complex ideas are expressed on the Fuller brooch, a large silver disc on which a half-length figure with staring eyes that is generally taken to represent Sight is surrounded by four full-length figures in various active poses, which represent the other four Senses (Fig. 4.3). Other elements may represent

Fig. 4.2. The Abingdon sword. Part of a gold panel that would have fitted into the centre of the pommel was found with it, but is now missing. The two enlarged photographs are panels on the other side of the sword, equivalent to the positions of panels 10 and 12; they can be taken as Man, symbol of the evangelist Matthew, and Eagle, St John's symbol. It may need the eye of faith to see a Bull in panel 12, though the head on the pommel immediately above looks slightly more bovine. That the snake in Panel 10 is actually St Mark's Lion has to be taken on trust. The way that its neck penetrates its own body is a trick used in the period (cf. the Flixborough brooch, Fig. 3.9). The other panels on the upper guard have foliage of various kinds, panel 13 being an example of the acanthus leaf, which was often used, derived from classical and Carolingian art; panel 9 looks as though the artist could not work out how to complete it. On the lower guard, the creatures in panels 24 and 26 do not seem to have explicit symbolic meaning, though beautifully crafted; the self-destroying two-headed winged fantasy in panel 24 is certainly enough to scare anyone taking it to represent the terrors of Hell. On the top of the pommel are the remains of a creature's head, with an upstanding ear, a round eye, and a nose. (Drawing by Pat Clarke reproduced from Hinton 1974; drawing and photographs reproduced by courtesy of the Ashmolean Museum, Oxford. Drawing actual size.)

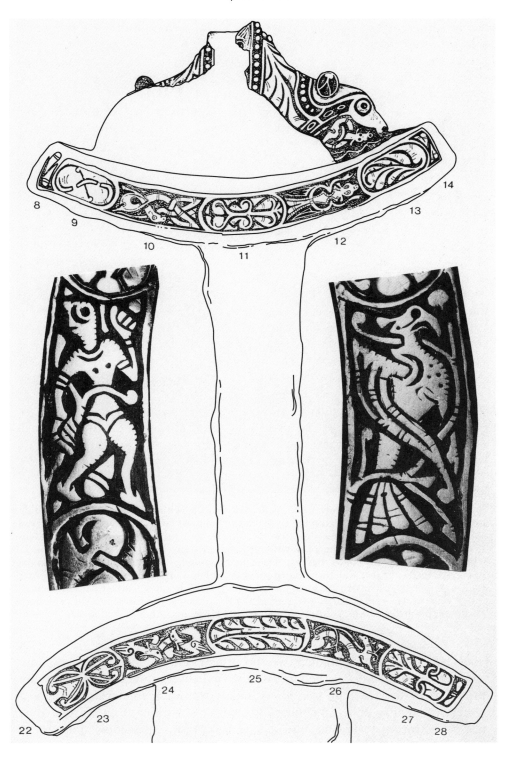

Fig. 4.3. The Fuller brooch. Silver and niello disc-brooch, with Sight in the centre holding flowering branches, perhaps signifying Christ as the Fount of Life. The frame with its curved sides forms a round-armed cross (cf. Col. pl. D). The four full-length figures can be identified as Smell, top right, sniffing a leaf with his hands held carefully behind his back; Touch, lower right, rubbing his hands together; Hearing, cupping his ear and running towards the sound that he has heard; and Taste, unsubtly with his hand in his mouth. The outer border has four segments, each with a human bust, an animal, a bird, and abstract patterns which, if they are flowers, would constitute the fourth of the principal life-forms of God's creation. (Photograph reproduced by courtesy of the British Museum, London. Actual size.)

God's creation.[8] Sight is holding two sprouting plants ending in leaves that are very similar to the tails of the birds on the Aethelwulf ring, which in turn are like those of the eagle on the Abingdon sword. Such similarities suggest a maker or makers with royal connections, perhaps working for a Wessex court able to patronize craftsmen enriched by successful expansionist policies. A

Fig. 4.4. Silver strap-end from Cranborne, Dorset. The man in the panel seems to be struggling with a plant that threatens to engulf him, and is wielding a *seax* above his head as though to cut himself free, like a Christian soul cutting itself free of the bonds of Hell. The shoot under his nose, however, can be read as a bunch of grapes, which he is about to harvest, a reference to the much-favoured vinescroll image based on Christ's words 'I am the true vine', a passage that goes on to describe the husbandman's pruning of the branches (a stone cross-shaft at Codford, Wiltshire, has a similar theme, the figure having a knife slung round his neck). It can be compared to the Man on the Abingdon sword (Fig. 4.2). The strap-end has two rivet-holes at the top to hold it to a ribbon or to a thin strap, and an animal-head terminal seen from above—compare the ears to those on the pommel of the Abingdon sword (Fig. 4.2). (Drawing by Nick Griffiths. Actual size.)

newly discovered strap-end from Cranborne, Dorset, adds to the Wessex corpus (Fig. 4.4).[9]

The style of metalworking on all these objects, using niello as background to a wide range of contorted animals, birds, plants, leaves, knots, and occasional humans, takes its name from a hoard of coins and objects found at Trewhiddle in Cornwall in 1874, deposited in or very soon after 868.[10] The origins of the style lie earlier than that, and provide another example of metalwork's close connections with illustrated manuscripts, in this case mainly early ninth-century work (Col. pls. D and E).[11] In books the art form was not pursued, since, whether from poverty, viking disruption, or clerical indolence, none with full-page illustrations is known to have been produced in England for a hundred years after the Book of Cerne. The pristine condition of many of the objects in the Trewhiddle hoard, however, shows that the style was maintained by metalworkers well after the middle of the ninth century. Another hoard, deposited at Beeston Tor, Staffordshire, *c.*874, included two brooches, both ornamented in the Trewhiddle style.[12]

Made of thin silver sheet but with a diameter of 114 mm, the Fuller brooch is somewhat impractical for costume use, and indeed at some time it was remodelled for use as a pendant.[13] There are other brooches of the same period that are almost as large, but more substantial. The Strickland brooch is of thicker silver, but with gold inlays and ornament of animals and beasts' heads cut so deeply into the metal that in places it has gone right through, making some of it openwork. Although it has the same round-armed cross format as the Fuller brooch, it seems to lack a complex iconographic meaning, despite the skilful symmetry of its design.[14] A hoard of six brooches, unfortunately without coins, was found in a churchyard at Pentney, Norfolk (Col. pls. D and E). Five are silver and have similarities to those in the ninth-century coin-dated hoards, but the sixth is differently made and looks earlier in date, and is indeed quite worn.[15] It is also by some way the smallest, and seems to confirm that it is not mere accident of survival that accounts for the difference in the quantities of precious-metal objects attributed to the eighth and ninth centuries; after the composite disc-brooches of the seventh century had passed beyond repair, there really were no large brooches again for a hundred years. It is difficult not to see in this a return to more ostentatious costume display in the ninth century.

Despite strictures by Alcuin, who blamed it for the viking raids,[16] ostentation is also shown in such things as swords with Trewhiddle-style fittings, of which that from Abingdon is the most sophisticated. As well as the numerous silver strap-ends, there are also silver hooked tags; both categories are commoner in copper alloy and are not confined to the ninth century (Fig. 3.5), but the precious-metal ones nearly all have versions of the Trewhiddle style.[17] Six strap-ends with particularly imaginative designs were found recently at Upper Poppleton, North Yorkshire.[18] This ever-increasing number of finds is in contrast to the coins, which seem to decline in quantity, both in excavations and as isolated single finds.[19] Furthermore, the amount of silver in them up to the 870s decreased, as though it was more difficult to obtain.[20] Whatever the problems for the currency, however, the objects show that there was a great deal of precious metal in England, which must have been a target for the vikings; concomitantly, the crises that they brought may have caused people to revert to investment in personal display, a means of boasting of success and of boosting self-confidence. Much of the silver came from churches, mostly 'liberated' by vikings, but some by the English themselves.[21] Although the vikings were raiders, they also brought silver into the places that they were attacking, and some of this portable loot from other countries did not get taken away again.[22] Declining silver ratios in the coinage may have been a means for kings to increase their own stocks of the metal, or because of difficulties in maintaining governmental structures in times of crisis, and a consequent need to reward secular followers with treasure to retain their service and loyalty.[23]

The Pentney brooches raise a number of questions. Two are effectively pairs, which could mean that they were designed to be worn on each shoulder—unless members of the same family wore matching jewellery. All the representations, however, from the Franks Casket onwards, show them worn singly by men on their outer cloaks in classical style, in some cases with a neat loop of drapery behind them.[24] An alternative is that the hoard was a metalworker's, and that most of the brooches had been made to display to potential customers.[25] For the smith to invest so much in time and materials by making brooches speculatively would imply considerable confidence in the availability of a market, but there is the possibility that at least one of the other hoards, found at Sevington, Wiltshire, was also an Anglo-Saxon metalworker's, since there are unfinished strap-ends in it.[26] There may have been another at

Talnotrie in the part of south Scotland that was perhaps still under Northumbrian control when the hoard was deposited in the 870s, but as well as Trewhiddle metalwork it contained fragments of coins and a weight of types suggestive of viking ownership.[27] Peripatetic smiths were perhaps temporarily halting the trend to permanent workshops at monasteries and *wics*.

Because of the overall decline in coin numbers, the level of activity at the *wics* is difficult to measure, but at least from the middle of the ninth century seems to have been falling off. In Ipswich production of the distinctive wheel-made pottery seems to have died out around then, with the implication that the demise of its distribution network reflects internal trade decline as a whole.[28] Metalwork at Saxon Southampton does not include anything necessarily made later than that, though a little pottery and glass is consistent with the tailing-off of coin finds through the second half of the ninth century. A broadly similar picture has emerged from York's Fishergate and at Beverley in the same county, a major church site where excavations have suggested almost total abandonment, a decline marked by a hoard of stycas hidden in the 850s.[29] Excavation within *Lundenwic* has revealed that a new fortification was constructed, either against viking raids or itself a viking encampment;[30] here too was a hoard of 850s stycas, which in this case could have been brought by one of the last Northumbrian merchants to visit the *wic*, or have been viking loot, though the metal value of the coins was so slight that it is difficult to see why anyone bothered to bury them.[31]

Presumably because of their low value, stycas are common enough on Northumbrian sites to provide a more reliable barometer of usage than silver pennies do for the south. Even the very isolated Ribblehead site at Gauber had four of them. There were small iron objects there which might have been made on the site, though if so either smelted ore or scrap items had to be taken to it, and a rotary quern is further evidence that even a farmstead near the highest point of the Pennines was part of a wider economic system.[32] The decline of the stycas may have been quite abrupt; although the numbers are small, Wessex pennies of the 850s and 860s have been found at Cottam, York's Fishergate, and Green Shiel on Lindisfarne, suggesting that Northumbria could no longer exclude coins from other kingdoms.[33]

By the 870s Wessex and Mercia were operating very similar coinages,[34] so it is not surprising that the Trewhiddle hoard should have had roughly two-thirds of its coins from the latter, with only one-third from the former. There were also a couple of continental interlopers.[35] Also an interloper was a copper-alloy 'Celtic' penannular brooch,[36] but all the surviving decorated silver objects are likely to be Anglo-Saxon.[37] Some of them are unique; a length of knitted silver wire chain, one end tied round a glass bead and the other ending in four knotted strands, may be a scourge. Perhaps but not necessarily also ecclesiastical is a chalice, so the whole hoard, which included silver mounts, strap-ends, two rings, a pin, and a small ingot of gold, could have come from a church but have included some things that were privately owned, much like the St Ninian's hoard.[38] The predominance of Trewhiddle decoration, and of the Anglo-Saxon coins, shows that Cornwall became integrated with the English world after its conquest and loss of autonomy early in the ninth century, though the penannular brooch could be taken to mean that integration was not complete.[39]

Some of the ninth-century hoards found in England are likely to have been hidden to conceal them from viking raiders, dramatically shown on a Lindisfarne grave-marker brandishing their weapons aloft.[40] The Beeston Tor hoard, with its latest coin pre-dating 875, was buried very near to Repton, where a viking army spent the winter in 873–4, a date consistent with five coins of c.873–6 in the grave of a man who also had a gold ring, and of others in a mound a short distance away.[41] Few other discoveries can be tied to such well-recorded episodes; the latest known coin at Trewhiddle was minted c.868 and therefore, unless nothing was added to it for the ensuing six years, the hoard was not hidden from the army that spent the winter at Exeter in 876–7.[42]

Of the decorated metalwork at Trewhiddle, everything apart from the penannular brooch can be described as 'Anglo-Saxon', as is true also at Beeston Tor and Sevington. Rather different is the hoard from Croydon, Surrey, certainly deposited after 871 and probably in 872–3;[43] it contained some 250 coins, which had come not only from different parts of England but also from Francia and the Near East. Such a wide mixture is unlikely to have been carried by an English merchant, but could be expected of a viking who had been raiding far and wide, taking plunder or subsidies from wherever there were pickings to be had. The Croydon hoard also contained bits of stamped rings and rods, usually called hack-silver, variations of which are found throughout the parts of the world that the vikings visited themselves upon. By contrast, a hoard from Gravesend, Kent, of much the same date has English and continental coins, but no 'kufic' ones from the Near East or hack-silver, and is therefore as likely to be a merchant's as a viking's; it included a small pendant cross cut from a thick sheet of silver, set with a marbled glass stud in the middle, which might have been a bit of personal property, not something looted from a church.[44]

In 871–2 a 'great army' took control of London and an 'immense tribute' was levied to pay them off.[45] Their demand was probably not for a random amount, but a carefully weighed sum such as the '4,000 pounds according to their scales' paid to a viking army raiding in the Seine valley.[46] It is likely that tributes were divided up amongst the members of the armies, and that the Croydon hoard contains the share-out which one of the London victors added to what he was already carrying. Although status for raiders like him appears to have been won by quantity rather than quality, some ingots and hack-silver seem not to be of random weights, but to be multiples or subdivisions of units in known systems.⁴⁷ One of two lead weights recently found near Wareham, Dorset, weighs about 100 g, closely equivalent to four times an *eyrir*, or ounce, of 26.6 g; the other is incomplete but was possibly for 3 ounces.⁴⁸ The whole one was capped with a Mercian coin held in place by a silver rivet as though to authenticate it. In areas where coins did not circulate as currency, weights were usually capped with decorative Celtic mounts, perhaps to make them identifiable to their owners, but since most of the mounts were pillaged from churches, just possibly to verify the units by their sanctity.⁴⁹ An undecorated gold ring in the Beeston Tor hoard may have been some sort of bullion unit, as it is larger than King Aethelwulf's and, being lozenge-shaped in section, not suitable for a finger.⁵⁰ There is also the small gold ingot at Trewhiddle, so bullion had its uses for the English as well as the vikings.

As well as hoards, a few burials in England may provide evidence of vikings because Scandinavian-style objects were found with them,⁵¹ although Anglo-Saxon, British, Irish, or Carolingian renegades who saw a chance to better themselves by joining the enemy, or who in a time of crisis accepted viking culture because it was proving more successful than their own, might also have been buried in a viking mode.⁵² The gold ring at Repton, for instance, is not in the Trewhiddle style, but is a flat, tapering sheet, punched and with overlapping ends, a type unlike anything in the Anglo-Saxon world at the time. Outside Reading, Berkshire, a man was buried with a horse and a sword with worn guards, distinctive both for being a solid copper-alloy casting and for its decoration of a chain of little animals, in the Scandinavian late eighth-/ninth-century style called 'Gripping Beast'. Despite the sword's age, the burial could be that of a leader who died while the vikings were camped at Reading in 870–1, a time when one of them probably deposited a small coin hoard inside their enclosure.⁵³

There are also a few instances of Scandinavian objects normally associated with women, as at Santon Downham, Norfolk, where two very distinctive oval brooches were found in 1867 (Fig. 4.5).⁵⁴ The obvious conclusion that the viking armies had Scandinavian women with them might not be correct; a warrior might have bedecked a woman, whether a slave or a pawn in a treaty, whether English or continental, with ornaments symbolic of his origins and success. In some cases brooches may have been burial offerings, as in the case of an assemblage at Claughton Hall, Lancashire, where a pair of oval brooches was found with a sword and other weapons, but also a hammer-head, a prehistoric stone axe-hammer, a silver pendant, and at least two beads. Nevertheless, it seems unlikely that many Scandinavian warriors would have travelled round with such female gear to bestow on an uncomprehending native, so it is more likely that at least a few Scandinavian women were with them.⁵⁵

Burials like that at Repton where the grave with the coins and ring was alongside the wall of the existing church need not mean that its presumably

Fig. 4.5. Two ninth-century oval brooches found at Santon Downham, Norfolk. They are complex castings of part-openwork copper-alloy, gilded, and embellished with silver wire. They are associated with high-status Scandinavian women. (Photograph reproduced by courtesy of the British Museum, London. About two-thirds actual size.)

viking occupant had embraced Christianity, but that the place was acknowledged to be a sacred site, an interpretation strengthened by the discovery in another man's grave there of a silver Thor's hammer pendant, presumably a symbol of the northern god, with a sword and other items.[56] In some cases where viking burials have been found in churchyards, the site might not have been a burial ground when the pagan was interred, but his descendants may subsequently have 'Christianized' him by building a church. The Ormside bowl, probably eighth-century Mercian work but dug up in a churchyard in Westmorland, may have been a piece of loot buried in the grave of such a 'founder', but when such things are not found with a body in a grave, there is always the possibility that they were concealed with the idea of returning for them.[57] Similarly, a group of two pairs of silver strap-ends and two gold discs may have been buried at a prehistoric barrow on a moor at Lilla Howe, North Yorkshire, because it would be easy to relocate them, rather than because they were with a burial.[58] Those could have been hidden either by or from vikings, just as swords like those at Fiskerton, Lincolnshire, and West Gilling, North Yorkshire, may have belonged first to Englishmen and then to their killers.[59] The first was found in a river, and like many others could have been a ritual deposit, but the latter was from the bank of a small stream, so was perhaps just a casual loss, if it was not from an otherwise unrecorded viking burial.[60]

Shifts of fortunes were political as well as personal. After the 870s there are no hoards in southern or Midland England for a while, but several in the north. The largest was found beside the River Ribble at Cuerdale, near Preston, Lancashire; unfortunately it was not all kept together, but there were probably over 7,000 coins and about 1,100 bits of bullion in it.[61] The coins are a mixture from the Anglo-Saxon kingdoms, from the Norse kingdom based in York, from the continent, and from the Near East; they suggest deposition *c.*905.[62] It may have been the treasure-chest—fairly literally, for it was in a lead container when found—of a particularly successful viking, or it may have been amassed to pay for an expedition against Dublin.[63] The bullion pieces have a geographical range almost as wide as that of the coins; a few are still recognizable as Anglo-Saxon, Irish, Pictish, and Carolingian objects not yet melted down, but most are ingots, many of the larger with a relief cross on the top, and rings, again of various kinds, some stamped like those at Croydon, others spiral and recognizable as Baltic types, as are some of the brooches.[64] There is also a wide range in the alloys used in the ingots, which generally have lower traces of gold than would be expected if they contained many melted-down Anglo-Saxon coins. That might suggest that they were predominantly made from Arabian kufic coins, yet this is denied by their very low levels of bismuth.[65]

Other hoards of the first half of the tenth century show a similar interest in silver, though they are on a smaller scale. Thus at Goldsbrough, Yorkshire, hack-silver and brooches were deposited *c.*920 with coins that included none from the York mint despite its proximity, suggesting someone newly arrived from Dublin with King Sihtric. Subsequently hoards may have been buried in response to the threat of English conquest of the north, Norse leaders deciding that it was prudent to conceal some of their wealth, as in the unfortunately lost Bossall/Flaxton hoard. Others could be part of the same response, but are not datable by coins.[66]

The whole emphasis in the hoards seems to be upon silver for use within a 'bullion economy', as a commodity to be used to make payments and give as rewards. The rings are sometimes called 'ring-money', but that does not mean that they were direct alternatives for officially issued coins which had authenticating images, and precise weights and alloy mixtures; the rings do not have the first, and vary widely in the second and third.[67] One measure of the extent to which an individual piece of bullion had been used in exchanges is the number of nicks or peck-marks on it, for a recipient needed to be sure that it was solid silver throughout, not merely base metal with plating; another is the size of the pieces, because if cut up into small fragments they are likely to have been used in small-scale exchanges. On those criteria, much of the Cuerdale hoard had been through several hands.[68]

The bullion-rings are also called finger-, arm-, or neck-rings because they are generally approximately in one of those three sizes, though how many were ever actually worn is another matter. Repton is one of the very few examples of any sort from a grave, and there are only two in the whole of Britain found *in situ* on skeletons.[69] By contrast, the grave-finds and possible grave-finds are weapons, horse-gear and riding equipment, or oval brooches and beads. The brooches must have been highly regarded, for they are found widely throughout the viking world, and involved intricate and skilled casting,[70] yet have not been found in hoards in Britain despite being easily portable in chests (which could be used to explain away the absence of swords, for instance). Vice versa, bullion silver is not found piled up in British graves, so it was not appropriate to take it permanently out of circulation, even though amassing it seems to have been so important to the vikings. Consequently some of the silver brooches in the hoards may not have been chosen with an eye to their costume use. Although the large Irish bossed penannular brooch in the Orton Scar, Cumbria, hoard had had its original pin replaced with one of Scandinavian type (Fig. 4.6),[71] which would hardly have been done by someone who did not intend to wear it, the final owner may only have cared about it as bullion, since no brooch of this type has been found in a grave. Similarly, brooches in the Goldsbrough hoard are of Irish types,[72] so again were probably carried for their silver, not for their ornamental use. These things do not seem to have been copied even in northern England.

One effect of the vikings was to check, though not entirely to halt, the advance of Anglo-Saxon culture in Wales. The artefacts present questions similar to those raised elsewhere in Britain. At Caerwent, for instance, an axe and a spear in a grave could have accompanied a viking who sought either integration or an expression of domination by being buried in the native cemetery, or the burial could be that of a native who had observed viking customs.[73] The Caerwent cemetery also had a knobbed pin of distinctive Hiberno-Norse type, perhaps brought by a viking, or the result of continuing contacts between Welsh and Irish.[74]

When an isolated Anglo-Saxon object is found in Wales, such as a gold and niello Trewhiddle-style ring inscribed with the Old English name Alhstan found in Denbighshire,[75] it could have come as a result of continuing interaction like that which took Bishop Asser from St David's to King Alfred's court in Wessex.[76] Equally, it could have been booty brought by a viking, just as a gilt mount might have reached Monmouthshire from Mercia directly in the eighth century, or indirectly through a raider in the ninth.[77] In the same way, a silver penannular brooch with gold filigree in its terminals found at Newton Moor, Glamorgan, has nearly all its parallels in Ireland; it was quite worn, so probably entered the ground in the ninth century even though it could have been made in the eighth. A second, base-metal penannular was found nearby, and

Fig. 4.6. What might politely be termed viking flexibility is shown by this bossed penannular silver brooch, found with a large silver ring hidden in rocks at Orton Scar, Westmorland, in 1847. The frame is almost certainly ninth-century Irish work, the flat terminals developed from such forms as the Hunterston and other brooches (Figs. 2.5 and 2.6). The bosses on the terminals obscure writhing interlaced creatures set against a hatched background. Two open-jawed animal heads at the ends of the hoop seem to be swallowing the terminals (cf. Fig. 3.4). The pin, however, is a replacement, the stamping on its swivel being typical viking work, much used on hack-silver. It swells out between the terminals to make it less likely to slip out of the material it pierced when worn. (Photograph reproduced by courtesy of the Society of Antiquaries of London. Half actual size.)

this too has Irish parallels, although some of its details could indicate manufacture in Wales.[78] A lead weight may have belonged to a viking raider, as it has an Irish-derived copper-alloy mount.[79]

A site excavated in the 1990s on Anglesey at Llanbedrgoch has produced one or two Anglo-Saxon coins, but a larger number are Carolingian of the first half of the ninth century, including a small hoard deposited c.850.[80] This may indicate that even if the place was under the control of Welsh kings, its contacts were not so much with England as with Ireland and the vikings—direct trade between the Isle of Anglesey and the continent seems unlikely,[81] and the evidence of lead weights, enamelling, and hack-silver seems different from

Fig. 4.7. Five early tenth-century silver rings from Red Wharf Bay, Anglesey. Four have various stamps punched into them and the fifth is rather roughly grooved. None has a terminal of any sort. Although they are all of a size to fit on an arm, the quality of the workmanship implies that they were valued primarily as bullion, even if they were sometimes worn to show off a successful raider's booty. (Photograph reproduced by courtesy of the National Museums and Art Galleries of Wales, Cardiff. Diameter of largest, 73 mm.)

what is found at Meols on the Wirrall peninsula, even though the areas are easy to get between by sea. Something special about Llanbedrgoch is hinted at by a most unusual whetstone with a copper-alloy mount to turn it into a pendant.[82] Five punch-stamped silver rings also found in Anglesey, at Red Wharf Bay (Fig. 4.7), confirm viking involvement in north Wales in the late ninth and early tenth centuries. Two have quite a high gold content, unlike almost all others in the British Isles, and the remaining three have varying alloys, indicating that they were made from different combinations of a wide range of coins and objects.[83] Nevertheless, they show that north Wales was part of the bullion economy of the Dublin–Isle of Man–York axis, as does a hoard deposited at Bangor probably soon after c.925 that had Anglo-Saxon, viking York, and Near Eastern coins, with a similar polyglot mixture of hacksilver.[84]

Further south, a crannog at Llangors, Breconshire, is dated by the dendrochronology of its waterlogged timbers to the late ninth and early tenth centuries.[85] Waterlogging also allowed the survival of a substantial part of a fine linen garment, delicately embroidered in silk and with designs of lions, birds, and vinescroll like those on Byzantine and Near Eastern textiles, though the stitching details show that the work could have been done in Britain.[86] If it was, the garment might have been an English gift, as was a silk robe given to Bishop Asser by King Alfred.[87] Like Llanbedrgoch, Llangors yielded metal-working evidence, but in most ways its assemblage is slightly different, as befits a site recorded as being in royal ownership. It includes an enamelled hinge from a shrine, probably Irish but in this case perhaps something taken there for safe-keeping from a neighbouring church rather than as viking loot.[88] Pins are comparable to Anglo-Saxon ones, but there is also an Irish-style brooch. Some things may have been made on the site, or at least in Wales, not imported, since the metalworking evidence here and at Llanbedrgoch shows that skills did not vanish when the hillforts were abandoned.

There are no settlements apart from Llanbedrgoch to show how culture continued to develop in Wales, for Llangors was overwhelmed by an English army in 914. Llanbedrgoch was still lived in for a while, but probably by vikings, not native Welsh. Although beads and ringed pins there could have been made in Dublin and arrived as traded goods, a fragment of an oval brooch suggests something more, since it seems so specifically associated with Scandinavian women.[89] Elsewhere, Welsh kings who survived viking onslaughts reacted to them by becoming more like their English contemporaries in their taxation and service demands.[90] South Welsh charters hint at the use of silver in weight units, but cattle seem to have been a more significant medium of exchange.[91] Hywel Dda in the mid-tenth century had a coin minted for him in Chester, but the initiative was not maintained,[92] and so few English coins entered Wales that it cannot have been drawn into the Anglo-Saxon network until after the middle of the tenth century.[93]

The St Ninian's hoard showed that Anglo-Saxon influence was having its effect as far north as the Shetlands by the end of the eighth century. As in Wales, viking loot rather than trade or gift might explain occasional ninth-century finds, such as a circular silver mount with Trewhiddle ornament found at Burghead, Morayshire, fitted with suspension loops that make it more likely to have come from a blast-horn than from a drinking-horn.[94] The Talnotrie hoard contains Trewhiddle-style silver, but the weight and the kufic coin fragments point more to a viking than to a Northumbrian owner.[95]

Certainly viking are the oval brooches found mostly in pairs in female graves in the Western and Northern Isles, testimony to the sea-routes of the Norse between Ireland, the Isle of Man, and their homelands.[96] Also different from Pictish styles are long combs and ringed pins,[97] and one grave had a Thor's hammer.[98] When there are other items, they are often tools for textile production, occasionally including large, flat, whalebone plaques, interpreted as for use with heated bun-shaped glass or stone smoothers known as slickstones, thought to have been for pressing linen. They are well known in

Norway, but a particularly impressive one carved with animal heads, their lips snarling to reveal teeth and fangs, was excavated recently in a boat-grave at Scar, Sanday; its quality may link it to the goddess Freyja, because flax for the best clothes had to be sewn on Fridays.[99] Most plaques date from the mid-eighth century to the early ninth, and a really fine one might have passed down two or three generations. At Scar the woman was elderly, and also had a gilt copper-alloy equal-armed brooch, intricately cast with 'Gripping Beast' ornament, comparable to that on the Reading sword. These artefacts suggest an earlier date than did radiocarbon analyses, and may have been quite old when buried between about 875 and 950; the tenth century would be very late for them, but perhaps not inappropriately so for an elderly lady who may have regaled her family with memories of how things used to be done. Some of that family may have been buried with her, as a man in his thirties and a child were also in the grave.[100]

So many of these special graves are quite unlike anything from Ireland or Scotland of the eighth or early ninth centuries that they are probably those of women of Norse origin rather than those of indigenous 'peace-weavers', let alone slaves.[101] Furthermore, the burial of men and women together, particularly that of the elderly lady at Scar, suggests equality, not male domination.[102] The textile equipment, and occasionally other tools, particularly sickles,[103] should not necessarily be taken to mean that the higher-status women had to do manual work themselves, for the things may symbolize their supervision of others; agricultural items, for both genders, could signal land-ownership. The assemblages in these graves do not mean wholesale replacement of Pictish natives, however, as indigenous objects continued to be used at settlement sites.[104]

Some of the male graves in the north are also highly distinctive, with an emphasis on weapons, particularly swords, and horses. Some of the swords had originated in Norway, like one found on Eigg with silver and copper-alloy fittings.[105] Social rank may be directly reflected by the types and quantities of artefacts in the graves. The man in the boat-burial at Scar had a sword, arrows, and a set of bone and antler gaming-pieces, presumably indicative of his aristocratic leisure time, as in earlier Anglo-Saxon graves. He had a set of lead weights also.[106] Like many of the women, men sometimes had sickles, and occasionally other equipment such as carpenters' adzes and the smiths' tongs and hammers at Ballinaby, Islay; this was not the grave of a mere artisan, for he had a sword and a shield (Fig. 4.8). Alongside this well-equipped male was a woman with a pair of oval brooches, a silver ball-headed pin, and a chain made of several strands of silver wire knitted together and knotted at the ends, reminiscent of the putative scourge at Trewhiddle. She also had a ladle that had probably come from an Irish church.[107]

Other Irish loot in these northern graves includes shrine-fittings converted into brooches, and mounts fitted to lead weights, a set with its balance in a

Fig. 4.8. A man's grave at Ballinaby, Islay, included a sword and shield, the latter represented by the central boss seen here from the back with the long copper-alloy grip ending in round terminals. The curved iron object is part of the handle of a cauldron, perhaps symbolic of feasting like the vessels at Sutton Hoo. High-status consumption is also shown by the copper-alloy terminal of a drinking-horn, to the left of the sword's lower guard. The two axeheads were not from weapons, but from woodworkers' tools, like the adze-head below the one on the right. Other tools include a blacksmith's tongs, a hammer-head, and a hone for sharpening blades. The man was buried with a woman, who had silver items as well as tools, in her case for textile production. (Photograph by courtesy of the Trustees of the National Museums of Scotland, Edinburgh.)

boat-grave at Kiloran Bay, Colonsay, one of the Inner Hebridean islands, being especially impressive.[108] Three Anglo-Saxon mid-ninth-century stycas found nearby may have been part of the same set; one at least had been pierced, possibly for suspension, possibly to reduce its weight to a specific amount.[109] This man had a horse, a sword, an axe, and a shield as well as a boat, so was no mere tramping pedlar.

Probably the most striking of the Irish objects in the Norse graves is the silver brooch set with gold filigree panels, amber, and red glass, found on Orkney at Westness, Rousay, in the burial of a rich woman whose other costume fittings included oval brooches and a necklace in the usual Norse style, but also two Anglo-Saxon strap-ends, so her cultural signals were fairly mixed (Fig. 4.9).[110] The brooch was made in the eighth century, and is more or less

Fig. 4.9. A woman's grave at Westness, Rousay, included an Irish brooch, presumably looted, and a hundred years or so old, but still appreciated, like the Hunterston brooch (Fig. 2.6). The oval brooches, the bone comb, and the amber and glass beads on her necklace may have been obtained peacefully, but the two Anglo-Saxon silver strap-ends next to the last may have derived from a raid southwards. Her equivalent to a man's sword was a weaving batten (cf. Fig. 2.17), and other textile equipment included the very corroded heckle comb for use with flax—the sickle on the right may have symbolized the plants' harvesting, with the shears below it to represent the final trimming of the linen. (Photograph by courtesy of the Trustees of the National Museums of Scotland, Edinburgh.)

a contemporary of the Hunterston brooch (Fig. 2.6). That was found close enough to the sea, in Ayrshire,[111] for it to be considered as something deliberately hidden, like the ninth- to eleventh-century hoards on the coastal fringes of the western Highlands and Islands.[112] The physical expression of conquest that the use and reuse of loot implies is in one way made explicit on the Hunterston brooch, to which an inscription in tenth-century Norse runes was added, 'Melbrigda owns [this] brooch', and another name that is not fully legible but may also have been an ownership statement. There is an ambivalence in the message, however, for although the alphabet is Norse, Melbrigda is a Celtic name.

As well as Irish-made objects in the graves along the northern seaways, there begin to appear various silver rings and ingots that are likely to have originated amongst the Scandinavians in Ireland; the former include plain, thick, penannular shapes, as well as stamped forms comparable to those in hoards in northern England. There are many isolated finds, and also some impressively large hoards, mostly of silver but with some gold as well. They can only be dated if they include coins; some may pre-date one from Storr Rock on Skye, which had over 100 Anglo-Saxon and kufic coins, and must have been deposited after *c*.935, but the evidence is patchy.[113] Metallurgical analyses do not invariably show trace elements of the bismuth typically found in Arabian silver, but instead indicate a wide mixture of Anglo-Saxon and continental coins, as well as kufic, mixed with various looted and traded brooches and church treasures in most of the material.[114]

There is also a question about the extent to which the Scottish material had been used in exchanges; some has been less pecked and nicked than is usual if such silver had been used quite frequently, and Storr is one of the few hoards to contain small pieces of hack-silver, needed for use in smaller transactions; furthermore, those few include the only ones with coins that pre-date the 970s.[115] Nor can the ingots be shown to be weight-related.[116] The hoards place the sea-routes between Ireland and Scandinavia into the society of the northern world, but participation in the bullion economy of northern England, Dublin, and Man is harder to show, and may have declined rather than developed during the course of the tenth century.[117]

When decorated at all, this metalwork usually has only punched stamps, though some of the rings are carefully twisted, with two or more strands. Why were so many hoards deposited and not recovered? They may show turbulent times, but without reliable chronicles, particular events cannot be associated with them. Some could perhaps have been votive offerings, as some single finds may have been, but rings and ingots are almost completely absent from the well-furnished Norse graves.[118] One fragment, from Crossmichael, Kirkcudbrightshire, is from too far south to be part of the hoard pattern, and otherwise there is only a plain ring from Unst, Shetland, which is also the only one north of York reported as found on a skeleton, on the wrist.[119] As though to confirm that the hoarded silver was not thought appropriate for burial in graves is the necklet worn by the rich woman at Broch of Gurness, which was of iron.[120] If people went to their graves wearing what they had worn in life, the rings were not parts of their costume. Nor did a chieftain get buried with the spoil that his success had allowed him to accumulate.

As well as graves and hoards, there are Norse settlements such as Jarlshof in Shetland from which artefacts have been recovered. An everyday range of pins, including a few ringed ones similar to Irish examples,[121] and a few other objects are metal, but bone and stone played an important part in the equipment of the people of the northern isles. Their Scandinavian affiliations are shown most strongly by their preference for cooking vessels made of steatite, or soapstone, rather than of pottery. Steatite was quarried in Norway, and probably in Sweden, and was exported to Denmark, so it was not a taste limited to a particular viking group. The stone can also be quarried in the Shetland islands and north Scotland, and unfortunately what was taken west and south from there cannot yet be distinguished from what was shipped across the North Sea.[122] Amber, however, from the Baltic hardly occurs.[123]

Away from the Norse areas, there is considerably less information about Scotland and its artefacts. At Whithorn the range of finds changes noticeably after the middle of the ninth century, a period of retrenchment after a fire. Many of the objects show contact with Ireland and are likely to have come from Dublin, such as ringed pins and a piece of steatite;[124] perhaps more surprising is that coarse pottery known as Souterrain ware seems to have been made at or near Whithorn, which seems to imply people from Ireland moving into south-west Scotland who were used to cooking in it.[125] The apparently complete absence of anything identifiable as English, including coins, is marked. The same is true of Iona, where Souterrain ware has also been found. Away from the south-west evidence is sparse.[126] This should probably not be taken to mean a time of quiet prosperity; the area was seeing the transition from Pictish to Scottish sovereignty and culture, as well as viking raids. As the latter did not lead to a transfer of power, as they did both further north in the islands and on the coastal fringes of the highlands, and in Northumbria to the south, no distinctive graves and no hoards of silver suggest people with much wealth to display or the wish to create new identities for themselves as members of a new elite.

Whatever the uses of the various rings in their hoards, the vikings had one ring that they valued differently. In 876 they swore an oath to King Alfred on 'the holy ring', something that made the occasion especially symbolic as they had never done so before.[127] Probably it had Odin associations, like the 'Raven' banner captured in the following year.[128] If the Christians could use their religious symbols to bolster warrior morale, as the Abingdon sword implies, so too could the vikings.

When the *Anglo-Saxon Chronicle* says that 'peace was made with the army', it usually leaves unstated that Danegeld was paid; the 'immense tribute' levied to pay off the Danes who had taken London is only revealed in a charter.[129] Some of this tax was probably not passed on to them, but was retained by the king, and may explain how he was able to increase the silver content of his coinage before rather than after his great success against Guthrum in 878.[130] Alfred was well aware of the need for kings to have worldly goods, finding justification for his acquisitions in one of the books that he studied.[131] The gifts with which he 'greatly honoured' Guthrum may not have been merely honorific, but a substantial Danegeld to enable the latter to set himself up in East Anglia, his acceptance of baptism being a signal that he accepted some sort of dependence upon Alfred, a practice with continental precedent. Although conversion was not involved, Alfred seems to have used gifts to cement an overlordship arrangement with Welsh princes as well, though the nature of the gifts is not divulged.[132]

Gifts other than money and bullion were certainly made by Alfred. Bishop Asser records how he received 'an extremely valuable silk robe' and incense from the king, as well as estates (cf. Col. pls. F.1 and F.2),[133] and although Bishop Wulfsige was not specific when he called Alfred his 'ring-giver' and 'the greatest treasure-giver of all kings', he was probably not thinking only of the book which the king had just sent him.[134] In a letter to all his bishops, Alfred said that he would send to each an *aestel* with his translation of Gregory the Great's *Cura Pastoralis*, although unfortunately he omitted to tell posterity what this actually was, apart from being worth 50 *mancuses*.[135] A later scribe called it an indicator, so perhaps it was an aid to reading or copying a book. The gold, enamel, and rock-crystal object known as the Alfred Jewel might be one of them; it has a beast's head terminal holding a short, narrow nozzle pierced by a rivet, which could have held an ivory or wooden rod to be used to point at a word or line in a text (Fig. 4.10).[136]

The Alfred Jewel gets its name from the Old English inscription in openwork gold letters round its side, *Aelfred mec heht gewyrcan*, 'Alfred ordered me to be made', a phrase similar to the one in Wulfsige's poem praising the king, 'Bishop Wulfsige commanded me to be written . . .'[137] This format was not only used by King Alfred and his circle, however,[138] and there were many personified objects, such as the knife from Sittingbourne with 'Sigebereht owns me' on one side and 'Biorhtelm made me' in conspicuously larger letters on the other.[139] The king was not the only man with the name Alfred; another was the ealdorman of Surrey in the 870s, who with his wife ransomed the *Codex Aureus*, a gold-ornamented gospel-book, from a party of vikings—a benefaction commemorated by an inscription added to the book at Canterbury, and one that shows not only that negotiations could take place over such treasures, but the high regard in which they were held even among the laity.[140] If someone of the ealdorman's standing had commissioned the Alfred Jewel, the absence of the royal title from its inscription would be explained.[141]

The text of the Jewel's inscription, however, has Mercian grammatical elements, and there were Mercians at Alfred's court, just as there were craftsmen in 'almost countless quantity from many races', who were 'skilled in every earthly craft',[142] as would be expected of a king building on the work of his predecessors.[143] Its goldwork is technically good, though not outstanding. The enamel, on the other hand, is the first known use in England of the technique of fusing the colours into cells, not setting pieces of glass in as inlays, like garnets, and was almost certainly done by someone trained in Italy. If the figure represented in the enamel is Wisdom, it is personifying one of Alfred's favourite topics, and the two flowering plants that it holds would link it to the figure of Sight on the Fuller brooch.[144]

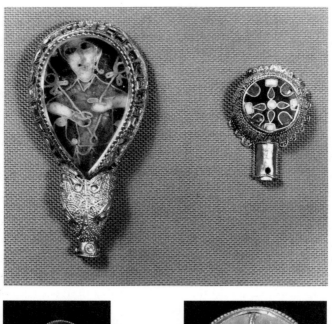

Fig. 4.10. The four *aestels*, all viewed from above to show how each has a short open nozzle pierced for a rivet-hole, the rivet remaining in two. Above left: the first found, in 1693, at North Petherton, Somerset, and known as the Alfred Jewel because of the inscription, not visible in this photograph, which shows the cloisonné enamel figure partly obscured by the sloping edges of the large rock crystal that covers it. The nozzle is held by a beast's head, unlike any of the others. Top right: the Minster Lovell, Oxfordshire, jewel, found in 1860, also has cloisonné enamel, making cross patterns; because it does not have a crystal, the gold cells forming the cloisons are more clearly shown. The gold filigree and granulation on the sides and on the engrailed edge can be seen; the goldwork is similar but not identical to that on the Alfred. Bottom left: the Bowleaze Cove jewel was found near Weymouth, Dorset, in 1990. It is a little smaller and a lot simpler than the Minster Lovell, but has the same sloping sides. Granulation clusters and a blue glass stud take the place of enamel. Bottom right: the Warminster, Wiltshire, jewel was found in 1997. It has a blue glass stud at the centre like the Bowleaze Cove jewel, and a crystal; although a milky bead, not flat, clear, and polished like the Alfred Jewel's, it is like it to the extent that it was not new when fitted into its frame. Because it is a bead, it has curved, not sloping sides, and does not have a flat back like the other three, one consequence being that its nozzle is round, not flat-backed, and being in the middle of the side would not have rested comfortably on a flat surface such as the page of a manuscript. (Photographs by courtesy of the Ashmolean Museum, Oxford, of the British Museum, London, and of the Salisbury and South Wiltshire Museum. Actual sizes.)

Also entirely appropriate for an object made for the king is the rock crystal. This was a reused Roman panel, something of extreme rarity which exemplifies the value attached to such *spolia*.[145] That its best parallels today are in the Vatican collections may be coincidence, but the pope exchanged gifts with Alfred, who was especially interested in Pope Gregory.[146] Respect for Rome is also shown in the way that Alfred copied imperial coin designs, one of his earliest following particularly closely a 'two emperors' fourth-century *solidus*; that image had been used before, but later he adapted Roman designs not previously known in England, such as a monogram composing London's name.[147] Who but King Alfred would have ordered craftsmen to mount a precious crystal in a way that reflected so many of his interests? Is it just coincidence that the Jewel was found in south Somerset, only a few miles from Athelney, where the king established a monastery?

Three other objects have short gold nozzles pierced by rivets, and though all are smaller than the Alfred Jewel and do not have beast-head terminals, two were found in Wessex, and the third, from just over the border at Minster Lovell in Oxfordshire,[148] has cloisonné enamel, and its filigree goldwork could well have been done in the same workshop (Fig. 4.10). A third, from near Weymouth, Dorset,[149] is very similar in size and shape, but has a blue glass stud at its centre, not enamel, and lacks filigree (Fig. 4.10). The fourth, from near Warminster, Wiltshire, is rather different, for its nozzle is held to a large crystal bead by gold straps, though it also has a blue stud in the centre (Fig. 4.10). The crystal is not clear and polished like the Alfred Jewel's, but is very milky. It is also a reused item, but this time more likely an English heirloom, from a necklace or a sword.[150] None is anywhere near the weight implied by the 50 *mancus* value of the *aestels* referred to in the king's letter to his bishops, but pre-sumably the bullion content mattered less with such gifts than their opulence and meanings. Nevertheless, it is increasingly difficult to explain why these things have no equivalents in surviving church treasuries on the continent, if they were so profligately lost by bishops in England, and that some at least were secular property has to be countenanced simply because of their numbers.

When Alfred said in his will that he was bequeathing a sword worth 100 *mancuses* to his son-in-law, the weapon was clearly something special, but surely not vastly more ornamented than the Windsor pommel or the Abingdon sword. On the continent bequests of swords were becoming a way of passing on symbols of family superiority,[151] and something like that might have been in Alfred's mind. At the Carolingian court investing an heir with arms had replaced hair-cutting or the first shave as a way of marking a prince's coming of age, and Alfred may have performed some such ceremony for his grandson.[152] When he wrote of the three orders of society, the 'fighting men' that he was thinking of presumably formed an elite group as on the continent, not merely those who had to perform army-service.[153]

Continental records speak also of belts, which were becoming a mark of nobility. For the English, the early seventh-century gold buckles like those at Sutton Hoo, Taplow, and Alton seem to have implied belts symbolizing authority, but eighth- and ninth-century buckles are small and few.[154] But even if no sword-belt is known, amongst the textiles in St Cuthbert's coffin is one elaborately embroidered band, usually called a girdle, recently identified as being as likely to be an item of secular as of ecclesiastical dress, worn with cloaks by kings and queens as well as priests, and treasured enough to merit presentation to the saint's shrine.[155] A complicated law-case began in Alfred's reign with a theft; this may have been more of an insult than a financial injury, but the item stolen was a belt, so if belts were already reacquiring some kind of symbolic status, it would help to explain why the theft of this one caused so much fuss.[156]

New concepts of the symbolism of artefacts include tenth-century developments in the use of regalia in royal inauguration ceremonies. Edward the Elder (899–924) may have been the first English king to be crowned, rather than anointed,[157] but if so he was too traditional to have himself represented wearing a crown and carrying a sceptre on his coinage. His son Athelstan (924–39) made a significant change by being shown wearing a crown, a band with upright spikes ending in knops; he did not dispense with tradition altogether, however, as the crown had diadem ties at its back.[158]

Coin designs were important also in the areas not controlled by the Wessex kings. Some viking rulers involved themselves in, or at least permitted, the minting of coins in the areas that they controlled. Some of their designs in the late ninth century were very similar to Alfred's and used his name; Guthrum put his baptismal name, Athelstan, on some of his issues, hardly a declaration of independence, and his successors reverted to copying, as with an imitative coin of Edward set into a brooch, found in Rome. Others allowed production of a design with a cross and the name Edmund that seems to commemorate the last English king of East Anglia, even though vikings had killed him—or rather, as legends developed, martyred him. In York some early tenth-century designs have a cross and St Peter's name, which suggests that the archbishops had come to an accommodation with their new rulers that allowed them to continue their minting rights. All these late ninth- and early tenth-century coins imply viking rulers almost ingratiating themselves with their Christian subjects. Briefly in the 920s there were issues that asserted Norse kings' authority; a sword could be read as a conquest symbol, or as St Peter's, but may represent a viking cult-object, 'the sword of Carlus', and a Thor's hammer on the other side was unequivocally pagan.[159] These deviations disappeared when Athelstan took control of York.

The Wessex kings' conquest of the north was underlined by the visits of King Athelstan and of King Edmund (939–46) to the principal shrine of northern England, St Cuthbert's, with appropriate gifts. King Edmund donated two

'Greek robes' and two gold arm-rings. The embroidered girdle, and perhaps other surviving silks, may have arrived at this time. King Athelstan probably presented the priest's vestments embroidered in silk and gold thread that had certainly been produced in southern England, as they have inscriptions that include *Pio Episcopo Frithestano*, 'for the worthy Bishop Frithestan', and *Aelfflaed fieri precepit*, 'Aelfflaed ordered [these/me] to be made' (Col. pls. F.1 and F.2). Frithestan was bishop of Winchester from 909 to 931, and Aelfflaed is probably Edward the Elder's second queen, who died in 916, though the name was a common one amongst the nobility.[160] If the queen really did give the vestments, they would show continued royal munificence to the Church, otherwise only recorded of Alfred's son in his building of the New Minster at Winchester.[161]

Doubts over whether Frithestan's vestments were actually embroidered in Winchester itself follow from reattribution of a number of early tenth-century manuscripts formerly taken as products of its churches. The use of Carolingian-inspired acanthus-leaf ornament may not have developed at Winchester, therefore, despite having acquired the name 'Winchester style'. Nevertheless, some significant changes in metalwork probably did originate there. The finest of a number of large, tongue-shaped, cast openwork strap-ends was excavated in a mid tenth-century grave at the cathedral cemetery; it has pairs of birds and animals on either side of a plant stem, presumably a Tree of Life, very similar to the borders of the contemporary manuscript showing the crowned king (Fig. 4.11).[162]

By the end of the ninth century Winchester was emerging as a town, as well as a church centre. One of the openwork strap-ends came from the Brooks area, for instance, where an urban sequence from the late ninth century onwards was excavated.[163] Mundane pottery, locally made and sometimes tempered with shell, begins to be found, not only at Winchester but at some of the other places starting to become urban in the south. In London activity moved back inside the Roman city walls, mainly at first close to the river south of St Paul's, and to a lesser extent at Southwark on the opposite side of the Thames. Expansion seems to have been less rapid than in towns further north boosted by viking presence and commerce, however. In some of those places pottery production using the wheel began; at Stamford, Lincolnshire, one of the major centres, it included some with red-painted decoration, and then with glaze. These innovations were not brought by Danes, who did not have the technology, but they probably came with contacts created by them, from the Rhineland and the Low Countries.[164]

The most prolific source of data on late ninth-/early tenth-century towns is York, where the Fishergate area was replaced for trade and craft activity by sites closer to the minster, though not confined within the old Roman circuit. Excavations in Coppergate have shown that in the second half of the ninth century there was a glass-working hearth, not making the raw material but

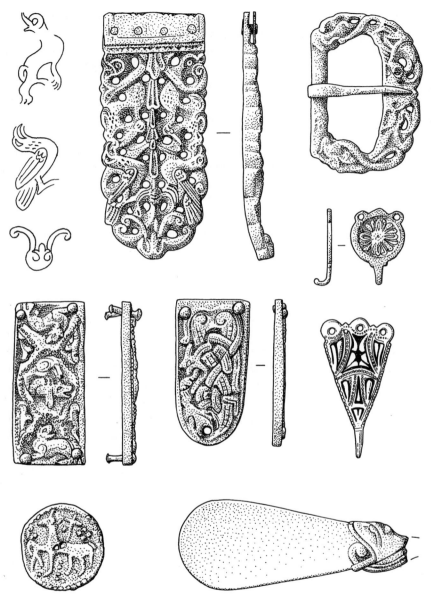

Fig. 4.11. A selection of objects showing the high quality of work available in late ninth-, tenth-, and eleventh-century Winchester, Hampshire. Top left, cast copper-alloy strap-end from a mid-tenth-century grave at the Old Minster; on each side of a plant-stem sprouting from an animal mask are a bird and a four-legged creature (the details are clarified alongside). Top right: a cast copper-alloy buckle with a similar inhabited plant forming its frame; it appears to be unfinished, but had been fitted with a silver pin, so must have had use. From a New Minster grave, early to mid-eleventh century. Centre right: two hooked tags, the upper cast copper-alloy with a symmetrical pattern derived from acanthus leaves, the lower one of a silver pair, also with leaves, but picked out in niello; both from the Old Minster, the latter in a grave attributed to the ninth century, which is consistent with the

melting down Roman and other glass, though there was no evidence about its products.[165] Some time after the hearth went out of use the site was subdivided into long, narrow tenements; the distribution of debris inside each of those suggests that particular crafts can be linked to particular properties, so there was already specialization. Usage changed regularly, however, so that there was no permanent zoning for individual activities, though those like tanning that demanded a flow of water would have concentrated closer to the rivers than the Coppergate street frontage, where bone and antler waste from comb-making suggests that customers could deal directly with the craftspeople in their workshops.[166] Gold, silver, copper alloys, iron, and lead were all being processed; gold occurs on crucibles and on sherds used to part it from silver; its refinement was tested in shallow 'cupel' dishes. Haematite was found in some quantity, used to give things a final polish. Hearths and bellows fittings, mould fragments, ingots, bars, and the like indicate a busy, noisy, and unhealthy environment.[167]

Metalworking included coin production. When two iron dies, and lead sheets struck with other dies, were found, it was assumed that the York coins had been minted at Coppergate, the lead either being 'trial-pieces', used while a die was being cut to check how it was progressing, or as a record for future comparison.[168] One of the dies had been deliberately defaced to make it useless, however, and the other needed repair, so both could have been lost while awaiting recycling.[169] A possible alternative use of the lead pieces was as a record of official transactions, such as a customs payment;[170] presumably they would have become redundant as the likelihood of a dispute faded, so may also have been intended for recycling. The moneyers were handling large amounts of precious metal, so were probably wealthy enough to live somewhere that was both more secure and more salubrious than Coppergate.

The designs on the York-minted coins changed frequently, unlike the moneyers responsible for them. The Scandinavian kings who controlled York from

---

(continued)
Trewhiddle style of its decoration. Centre left: a silver-gilt belt- or strap-mount cast with contorted animals, and a silver-gilt strap-end with a contorted interlace Jellinge-style creature, its head centre left; both are from the Old Minster's final phase, and were probably worn together although the Jellinge style of the strap-end is a bit earlier, and the object shows more signs of use; both have Scandinavian rather than Anglo-Saxon parallels, and could have belonged to one of King Cnut's followers in the first half of the eleventh century. Bottom left: an embossed disc of thin copper alloy, probably from a brooch. The design is an *Agnus Dei* (cf. Fig. 4.1), with a cross behind it, a design used on some of King Aethelred's coins of *c.*1009. Bottom right: ivory spoon, broken off at the junction of the bowl and the stem, where a finely carved beast's head with scrolling tongue can be dated to the late tenth or early eleventh century, and like the strap fittings came from the soils that filled the emptied trenches when the Old Minster was removed in 1093–4. (Drawings by Nick Griffiths from the collections of the City of Winchester Museum. Actual sizes.)

the 870s did not have their own die-makers, and would have had to rely either on indigenes or on immigrants from Francia. Licences could have been awarded to some of the fighting men who came with the kings, and who therefore took part of the profit, though not themselves being part of the production process; at any rate, one monopolist whose name is on some of the York coins in the 930s was Ragnald, who sounds Scandinavian—though he had no problem in transferring his allegiance to serve King Athelstan. Some vikings are presumably represented in a small group of burials that is unlike anything native; it included a man with a penny issued between 905 and 915, who was also furnished with a knife, whetstone, and buckle-plate. Another skeleton had a silver ring, with a smaller ring attached to it, round its upper left arm—unequivocally an arm-ring; part of another ring was found nearby. Despite these customs, the graves were found in a churchyard. If the church and its cemetery already existed, the vikings in it had chosen some degree of assimilation, even if it was only to acknowledge the sacredness of the site, as earlier at Repton.[171]

Burials of men likely to have been York's viking leaders have not been identified, however, and women of equivalent social standing are even less visible in the archaeological record—there are no oval brooches or whalebone smoothing-boards in York. A few exotic items have origins not always as obviously pagan and viking as a first glance might suggest. A curious lead figurine might be a god of some sort, but may be a much later pilgrim's badge, despite its tenth-/eleventh-century context.[172] A gold ring with a human head between animals, found at Fishergate long before the archaeological excavations took place there, was once thought to be of the viking period, but is now usually ascribed to the early ninth century on manuscript parallels.[173] There are no Thor's hammers, but a coiled snake pendant made from jet has some Scandinavian parallels,[174] and a miniature lead axehead may be a viking pendant amulet.[175] A scabbard-chape for a sword is of a type generally found in Scandinavian graves, and may be something that came to York on a viking's weapon (Fig. 4.12).[176] An upper social stratum of conquering immigrants is generally difficult to detect in this evidence, and the way that grave-markers were used is instructive. Various sculpted stones have been found in York, and like the small group of graves with artefacts, some suggest that churchyards were already being used; furthermore, the stones—which must have been expensive, and therefore exclusive to the better-off—do not express anything distinctively Norse or Danish, but developed a mode of their own.[177]

At a domestic level, it might be expected that Scandinavians would have cooked their food in soapstone vessels such as they would have used at home; all the fragments from Coppergate, however, came from post-930s contexts, not those associated with a 'first generation' of immigrants, and the numbers of pieces are too small to suggest widespread use.[178] A sock from Coppergate was made of looped woollens, a Scandinavian technique rather like knitting

Fig. 4.12. Four York objects with viking elements. The first was found in Coppergate in the early twentieth century, the third and fourth were found there in the late twentieth-century excavations; the other strap-end came from St Mary Bishophill Senior. Left: a sword-scabbard chape in cast copper alloy, with two openwork Jellinge-style animals; the back foot of one is centre right, and its body curls round to end in the relief head at the top; the other's tail is at the bottom, and snakes in and out, apparently ending with a head and eye at top right. Centre left: copper-alloy strap-end with a knot pattern incorporating a circle at the top, a Borre-style identifier. At the bottom, however, the two dots are probably vestigial eyes, remnants of the beasts' heads that had been a feature of English strap-ends since long before the late ninth century (cf. Fig. 4.4). Centre right: the animal-head terminal on this lead-alloy strap-end is more obvious, but it too has a form of Borre-style ring-chain. Right: a copper-alloy strap-end, with a more three-dimensional animal head and a ring-knot which is as close to Anglo-Saxon interlace as to Borre-style knots. (Drawing of chape reproduced from *Proceedings of the Society of Antiquaries*, 23 (1907); of left centre strap-end from Wilson (1965a) by courtesy of Eva Wilson; right strap-ends from Mainman and Rogers 2000 by courtesy of the York Archaeological Trust. Actual sizes)

but using a single needle;[179] so far, however, no other finds suggest that this method of production was taken up in England, textiles otherwise showing no changes from previous practice. Assuming that cloth- and linen-making were predominantly female activities, this would imply a large majority of Anglo-Saxon women.[180] Another raw material reflecting the homelands of the vikings is Baltic amber, much used for beads, and imported for working in York, as waste has been found.[181] Although it had been used by the Anglo-Saxons,[182] its quantity in York suggests a new level of demand—but not one specifically viking, as there is almost none in the Norse graves in the Scottish islands.[183] Some of it was cut into long rectangles and perforated for use as pendants, very different from almost anything Anglo-Saxon. If these were amulets, so too probably were some of the hones worn as pendants, such as the schist example from the early tenth-century male grave. Schist and phyllite for hones were other imported raw materials, from Norway.[184] Jet, although native to Yorkshire, was also worked in much greater amounts than previously.[185] Some types of glass bead are unlike any earlier English examples, in particular two with gold foil over them, similar to some found in Scandinavia.[186] Costume items like these may have originated in the tastes of a few incomers, but have been rapidly adopted by a much larger number of indigenous townspeople with no wish or need for their own distinct identity; medieval towns always depended on large numbers of local immigrants for their populations, and in York's case there would have been few people left in Fishergate to tranfer into the new area. Most natives would therefore have been uprooting themselves almost as much as overseas immigrants. Since the latter certainly included the ruling elite, integration may have been politic ingratiation.

Other ornaments, such as ringed pins, probably derive from the Dublin Norse links,[187] and like the steatite vessels were perhaps occasional trade goods, not specifically demanded by Scandinavians but a consequence of the wide contacts and long-distance networks that the vikings were establishing even while they were raiding.[188] Two pieces of silk with such similar weaves that they probably came from the same bale have been found at York and Lincoln; a merchant had gone from one to the other, selling lengths of material that had originated in the east Mediterranean or beyond for making up into headdresses and other small items.[189] A cowrie shell had come from the Red Sea,[190] direct evidence of contact with the Arab world, as is a forged Samarkand *dirham* which someone had tested by nicking.[191]

Among the influences coming into Anglo-Scandinavian York were Carolingian and southern English. An openwork copper-alloy strap-end with acanthus-leaf ornament would not be out of place among the Winchester examples, for instance,[192] and another with relief ornament may well be a Carolingian import.[193] The Trewhiddle style seems to have remained current in York; a bone strap-end has it, but in the new, wider, tongue-shaped size used in the cast copper-alloy Winchester series, and a piece of bone had Trewhiddle animals cut into it, a craftsman's die or motif-piece. Both were from Coppergate, a site at which damp conditions preserved some organic items, including a wooden saddle bow with Trewhiddle panels of ornament containing triquetra knots.[194] Practice of that Anglo-Saxon style may therefore have overlapped in time with two others given Scandinavian names, the Jellinge and the Borre; the former was used on the York chape (Fig. 4.12), on another Coppergate bone motif-piece, on stone sculptures,[195] and on some small metal items;[196] the latter on such things as strap-ends (Fig. 4.12), two of which are so similar that they may well have come from the same mould, and two open-work cast lead badges, very like one found at Beverley.[197] Even further afield, but at least with a York connection, is another lead object, a disc-brooch found near Bury St Edmunds, Suffolk, cast with an imitation of one of Ragnald's coins, of c.919–21.[198]

York was probably the largest centre to attract a new urban population, and is therefore the most likely to be where a Scandinavian element could be most clearly recognized in the surviving material culture. Integration rapidly created a recognizably Anglo-Scandinavian idiom, however. The same can be said of Lincoln and other towns in the territory that is usually called the Danelaw.[199] A gold ingot from Norwich is one of the best bits of evidence for viking involvement there, rather than any costume items or manufacturing styles; at Torksey, Lincolnshire, ingots and Arabic *dirhams* have also been reported, but the evidence from what was clearly an important port on the River Trent is much less valuable than it would be from properly conducted excavations.[200] Chester is, after York, potentially the most directly relevant to the problem of identifying a significant Scandinavian element, because of its close links with Dublin, its trade stimulated by the Church and by its easy connections to Wales, Peak District lead, and Cheshire Plains hides and cattle. The nature of the artefacts is not very different from the York assemblage; ringed pins, an ingot mould, and a Jellinge-style brooch show the Irish–Scandinavian link, but there are also a silver brooch that is probably English work of the second half of the ninth century, and a slightly later, well-cut bone strap-end with Winchester-style ornament.[201]

All this information shows that the new towns may have had very mixed populations, with relatively few Scandinavian settlers. Were the conquering armies likely to have turned themselves into townspeople, adopting a lifestyle with which nearly all would have been unfamiliar except from their destruction of it? The *Anglo-Saxon Chronicle* says that 'they proceeded to plough and to support themselves', with no mention of their towns and army centres. The same question about the numbers involved applies to the countryside; the *Chronicle* need not mean that they worked the land themselves, but that they became a landowning elite.[202] Were there large numbers of Danes, and did they invite their families to join them? Until recently it was possible to point to the very few artefacts recorded from the Danelaw countryside, and to argue that the Scandinavian settlement must have been only of some new landowners. It is still true that Thor's hammers, seemingly the most overtly pagan and Scandinavian of symbols, are few, though those datable do seem to be 'first-generation' objects.[203] If women joined the new settlers, they were mostly below the social level that could expect to wear oval brooches.[204] Much more controversial now is whether the large number of 'Anglo-Scandinavian' objects found principally by metal-detectorists, especially in Lincolnshire and East Anglia, betoken a large immigrant element. The more parallels that are found between these items and objects found in Scandinavia, the more likely it might seem that many people came across the North Sea; but it has to be demonstrated that the objects were not being made in the Danelaw towns and are not simply evidence of a growing population going into them and buying trinkets like those worn by the townspeople.[205]

Instructive in this debate are the results of controlled excavations at rural sites in Yorkshire, which do not suggest a culture different from that of York. Cottam is a particularly useful example, because occupation of one area there seems to have ended around the middle of the ninth century, and a new zone was used in the later ninth and tenth centuries. Consequently the different objects recovered will be indicative of any cultural changes that the transition to the Anglo-Scandinavian period entailed. All the coins were found in the earlier zone, as were the strap-ends with silver-wire inlay of East Anglian type. Other types of strap-end were in both areas, but a characteristically late ninth-/tenth-century Jellinge-style brooch and a slightly later Borre-style buckle were all in the second, as were Norwegian hones and a small bell. All these could have come from York, not directly from Scandinavia, as could pottery and a pewter brooch.[206] At another Yorkshire Wolds site, however, Wharram Percy, two Borre-style strap fittings are considered Scandinavian rather than things likely to have been made in York, but they are quite fine objects, and suggest an owner of high status rather than things representative of the majority of the population. A sword-hilt, not closely datable but ninth- or tenth-century, is further evidence of high-status people at Wharram.[207] Unfortunately, other towns in the Danelaw do not have the same hinterland excavation evidence as York, without which the pattern provided by detectorist finds is incomplete. A culture change certainly took place; whether it was accompanied by a wholesale population change is another matter.

5

An Epoch of New Dynasties
From the Later Tenth Century to the End of the Eleventh

The Wessex kings' conquest of the whole of England during the first half of the tenth century created conditions that led to a nation-state being recognizable by the end of the eleventh. In Scotland this was a much longer process, and Wales remained fragmented. The differences between them are mirrored by coinage; increasingly regulated and systematic in England, but not even produced in Scotland or Wales. The nation-state remained focused upon kings, however, elevating their status but exposing society to the haphazard behaviour and ambitions of an individual. They might still be seen as leading their 'people', English, Norman or whomsoever, but in reality they depended upon the support of a military elite and legitimization by the Church, rather than upon an efficient bureaucracy, let alone upon popular acceptance.[1]

Physical expression of royal supremacy was provided by increasingly elaborate inauguration rituals, and by crown-wearing ceremonies held on major feast-days at Gloucester, Winchester, and elsewhere, when the king represented his elevation by displaying himself with his emblems of power.[2] A crown had been used as an image on coins by King Athelstan in the 930s,[3] though his immediate successors stuck mainly to the traditional diadem. Ethelred (978–1016) added a staff, symbolizing a king's pastoral duties to his people, and was occasionally shown wearing a round cap, usually taken to represent a helmet based on Roman coin images rather than on contemporary armour. The 'hand of Providence' on the reverse of some of his coins implied God's blessing on an anointed king (cf. Col. pl. F.2). Cnut (1016–35) began his reign with a coin showing him crowned, as though to emphasize that his usurpation of power was legitimized by God through his coronation; the crown was a new type, an open circle surmounted by gold lilies.[4] He followed it with a coin that has him wearing a tall, pointed helmet, this time a form that was in contemporary use.[5] The lily-circlet crown had already been shown in a manuscript picture being worn by King Edgar in c.966, and a domed version was drawn being brought down from Heaven to crown Cnut in a painting that commemorates his donation of a gold cross to the New Minster at

Winchester. In that picture Cnut is shown also grasping a trilobe-pommelled sword, to show where his earthly power came from, as well as his munificence towards the Church.[6]

Apart from a change to a sceptre with identifiable fleurons, the next major development in coin representations was not until the reign of Edward the Confessor (1042–66), who after c.1053 was shown bearded, a touch of realism that emphasized his age and venerability (Fig. 5.13). Soon afterwards a coin portrayed the king crowned and enthroned, holding the orb and staff; this was ultimately a design inspired by the Byzantine Empire, more directly by images of the German emperors, and was chosen to stress Edward's and England's independence of them.[7] An imperial pose was not used on coins again, though a front-facing bust was an occasional variant. Edward's successors, Harold (1066) and William I (1066–87), did not follow these changes in the 1060s; because neither had a secure claim to the throne, both needed to establish the legitimacy of their rule, for which traditional designs served best. Only when William felt more confident in the 1070s did a new type appear, with the king front-facing and wearing a crown (Fig. 5.13). He added a sword to this image, presumably by now feeling safe in a secured conquest, before reverting to the traditional staff.[8]

Some of these representations may have been the work of overseas craftsmen, such as Theodoric, a German known to have been in Edward the Confessor's service.[9] One of them was probably responsible for the creation of Edward's great seal, the first English one known and an instrument of state development, which was closely modelled on those of the Ottonians and, like the 1050s coin, showed the king enthroned with orb and staff.[10] A craftsman with a very different background, named Spearhafoc, 'sparrow-hawk', was apparently an English monk trained as a goldsmith, who became bishop of London. When commissioned to make Edward a new crown, he was entrusted with gold and jewels for it, with which he promptly absconded. William I had a crown made by a Byzantine smith which included twelve gemstones, a reference to Aaron's breastplate as well as evidence of renewed interest in gems and their significance.[11] The 1070s coins give an indication of how this crown looked, including ornaments dangling on each side, amongst which were probably little bells.[12] The smith who made it may also have made William's great seal, on one side of which the king had himself displayed on the throne with the symbols of power, and on the other as a mounted warrior with raised sword.[13]

These regal images became well enough understood to be used in the Bayeux Tapestry, which opens with a scene of the elderly, bearded Edward on his throne, as though at a crown-wearing, holding in one hand a sceptre, the symbol of a king's power to command, rather than a staff. He is not shown holding the orb, as he needed his other hand to give instructions to Harold, who later accepted the offer of the throne, thus bringing his destruction upon himself like someone in a traditional Old English story. The turning-point is the moment when Harold was given the crown; he is next shown enthroned, crowned, and carrying the orb and staff, while one of the nobility offers him the sword of state. Clearly these symbols had deep significance by the 1060s.[14]

Most of the male figures in the Bayeux Tapestry are shown wearing cloaks, attached on one shoulder by what look like large disc-brooches. A number of the key figures, including the continentals like Count Guy and Duke William, as well as Edward and Harold when in their finery, are wearing square clasps that hold their cloaks centrally below the throat. No fitting like that has survived,[15] and, although there are several large tenth- and eleventh-century disc-brooches, none seems grand enough for kings and earls. Only the King's School, Canterbury, brooch contains a significant amount of gold, flanged panels with filigree scrolls held in place between two convex silver sheets secured by rivets, a method not known on other brooches. Its use of niello on silver continued a long tradition of panelled decoration, but the contorted animals in some of the frames show Jellinge influence that perhaps favours a date in the early part of the tenth century.[16]

Another large disc-brooch, probably but not certainly from Canterbury, has a disc at its centre that looks at first like a coin because of the diademed bust on it, but has the inscription *Wudeman fecit*, 'Wudeman made [this/me]', not a king's name and title (Fig. 5.1). Nevertheless, it is in other ways similar to coins of King Edgar (959–75), so it was probably made in his reign. The reverse has an inscription round a small cross in the centre, *Nomine Domini*, 'In the name of the Lord'.[17] Rather like it but smaller is a cast silver brooch with an imitation of a Valentinian III *solidus*, thought to be from York; it too has strips on the back, though structurally they are much less necessary.[18] These seem to be the last of the precious-metal brooches with coins or simulations of coins at the centres.[19] Wudeman's, however, was the first to invoke the holy name as though to make it a talisman to ward off evil.[20]

The last of the big disc-brooches to have been found in a dated context has an owner's name added to the back in a long inscription that proclaimed the ownership of Eadwynn, a female name, and invoked the Lord's curse upon anyone who stole it from her. It was found at Sutton, Cambridgeshire, with a hoard of coins of William I, deposited c.1070; although the script allows it to have been as much as a hundred years old when hidden, the Ringerike- and Urnes-style animal ornament on the front puts it into the eleventh century. Not only is it interesting for the attitude to her possessions shown by Eadwynn—and the acknowledgement that theft was a strong possibility—but it also continues the tradition of personifying objects—'Eadwynn owns me'.[21]

The Sutton brooch cannot have had much value; its weight in silver is slight, while the design on the front is too poorly executed to have done much to

Fig. 5.1. Silver brooch of *c*.960–75, probably found in Canterbury, made by soldering beaded wires around a central coinlike disc with the inscription *Wudeman fecit*, 'Wudeman made [this/me]', on the obverse and *Nomine Domini*, 'In the name of the Lord', on the reverse; the effect of the latter and the small cross with it seems diminished by the reinforcing strips that partly obscure them. Presumably it mattered more to the owner to know that the protective text was there than to have it clearly visible (cf. Fig. 2.12). Wudeman may have been the maker either in the literal sense of being the smith or metaphorically as the patron who commissioned it. (Photograph, and drawing by Pat Clarke, reproduced by courtesy of the Ashmolean Museum, Oxford. Actual size.)

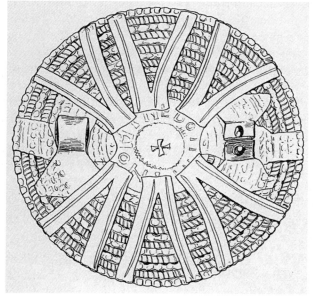

enhance it, and is too simple to suggest significant hidden meanings. Even so it was worth hoarding, as was another disc-brooch, from Barsham, Suffolk, which was found with coins of *c*.1002–3, and weighed approximately the same as thirty-seven standard pennies, a little more than a single *mancus*. As there was a hammer in this hoard, and its panels are marked out but unfilled, that brooch could be taken as a jeweller's unfinished stock item but for the damage and modifications already made to it before burial.[22]

That Eadwynn felt so strongly about the possible loss of her brooch may emphasize how unprotected some women felt.[23] Many whose marriages ended had enough control over their own destinies to be able to own property, and their few surviving wills provide some of the most graphic information about attitudes to possessions.[24] Best-known is that of Wynflaed, who died around the middle of the tenth century. As well as estates and money, she made bequests of things such as offering-cloths, probably from her altar; but the first thing that she listed in her bequests to her daughter was her *agrafen beah and hyre mentelpreon*, her 'engraved ring and her cloak-fastener',[25] as though they were personal to her and in that way more precious than the estates (let alone the men who worked on them) that followed. Later in the will comes a bequest of an *ealdan gewiredon preon is an vi mancussum*, 'an old wired fastener worth six *mancuses*'; *gewiredon* could mean filigree, like that set into the King's School, Canterbury, disc-brooch, or concentric wires, like Wudeman's. 'Old' could be dismissive of the object's age, but Wynflaed was very precise about its value—theoretically five times that of the Barsham brooch, so not inconsiderable. The bequest was to a granddaughter, so perhaps it was considered an important heirloom, around which family memories were constructed.[26]

Wynflaed's will has several references to cups, probably an indication that she and her family were part of hall society and could offer appropriate entertainment to guests. Her granddaughter was to receive two *treowan gesplottude cuppan*, 'two wooden cups ornamented with dots', her grandson a *goldfagan treowena cuppan*, which suggests gold bindings. Alternatively, he could have sixteen gold *mancuses* in lieu of the cup, as 'that amount has been attached to it'.[27] Another bequest was of *twegen wesendhornas*, 'two wild-ox horns', presumably set with decorative mounts as those at Taplow and Sutton Hoo had been, and as are shown on horns in the Bayeux Tapestry and other eleventh-century illustrations. Their value is unstated, but the same recipient was to get a horse and a red tent, which must give some indication of their relative worth.[28] Drinking-horns are bequeathed in other wills; King Ethelred's son, the aetheling Aethelstan, had bought his from the Old Minster at Winchester, suggesting that the craftsmen in monasteries made things for the secular world as well as church treasures.[29]

The men and women who owned property and drew up wills were coming to need the same means of making permanent records as the clergy. Not only were they increasingly recording their transactions in written charters, they

Fig. 5.2. An ivory seal-matrix from Wallingford, Oxfordshire, late tenth or first half of the eleventh century. The obverse, left, has a Latin inscription (with the letters cut 'retrograde' but here shown reversed so that the text can be read) *Sigillum Godwini Ministri*, with a runic letter used for the *w*, 'the seal of Godwin the thegn'; the cloaked figure in the centre carrying a sword is broadly comparable to coin designs. On the handle is a scene showing God the Father and God the Son making a footstool out of a downtrodden enemy, illustrating Psalm 109. The reverse has a longer inscription (not reversed), 'The seal of Godgytha a nun (*monache*) given to God'. It shows women's needs to be involved in business, for instance when widowed. (Photographs reproduced by courtesy of the British Museum, London. Actual sizes.)

were likely to use seals to verify them, though a knife might be sent instead, and symbolic actions like placing an object as a memento on an altar were still seen as creating a tangible and therefore permanent record.[30] An ivory seal-die found in Wallingford, Oxfordshire (Fig. 5.2), is inscribed *Sigillum Godwini ministri*, and must have been cut for someone in a high social position; *minister* translates as 'thegn', and Godwin was probably a man close to the centre of the king's business, or that of one of the great earls.[31] The die's handle was intricately carved to illustrate a text from one of the psalms, and can also read as a judgement scene, appropriate for the seal of someone likely to have had a role in the shire and hundred courts. The biblical scene and the well-cut Latin inscription could well place the production of this object within a church context, something Godwin commissioned in much the same way as the aetheling bought his drinking-horn from the Old Minster. On the back is another die, for Godgythe, 'a nun given to God', possibly Godwin's widow needing a seal to conduct her business after his death.[32] Two other seal-dies for secular owners are known; all three have busts in the centre which are based on coin designs, presumably contemporary ones, and therefore all of c.980 to c.1050.[33]

Another woman whose will survives drew hers up slightly later than Wynflaed, probably between 966 and 975.[34] She also had cups to bestow, but did not describe them or state their value. She was more precise about various *baegas*, 'rings', presumably because they were part of the *heriot* that she had to pay for permission to make the will, since the rings went to the king, the queen, and the king's eldest son. Two were worth 120 *mancuses* each and two 30 each; a *swyrdbeage*, 'neck-ring', was also worth 120.[35] Similar bequests of valuable rings continued to be made until the end of the tenth century.[36]

A few rings made of twisted gold wires and rods are heavy enough to be survivals of the kind of ring to which the bequests may have been referring. None weighs enough to be worth 120 *mancuses*, but the largest known, from Wendover, Buckinghamshire, could be a 40 *mancus* ring, one from Brightlingsea, Essex, a 15 *mancus*.[37] High-value rings had apparently been used for payments in eighth-century charters, and the wide variety coveted by the vikings, as the ninth- and tenth-century hoards demonstrate, may have revived their use generally. There are also silver rings, and smaller gold ones. Examples turn up occasionally in archaeological contexts, such as an eleventh-century silver one made by plaiting together six different wires and fusing the ends, excavated in Winchester.[38] They have no decoration beyond the twisting of the often tapering wires; their ends are simply knotted or fused together, or they may be penannular, like a six-strand gold ring found in Oxford (Fig. 5.3).[39] Presumably such rings were worn on ears, fingers, and arms despite being so plain; they would not otherwise have been made in base metal as well as in gold and silver.[40]

English warriors were remembered as having been arrayed in arm-rings in 1039 and 1066, and the *Battle of Maldon* poem has several allusions to them.[41] There are no survivals of inscribed personal finger-rings like that of ninth-century King Aethelwulf, however, and none with decorated bezels like those with Trewhiddle ornament.[42] Wynflaed expressly gave the *goldfagan* cup to

Fig. 5.3. Penannular six-strand gold ring, tenth-/eleventh-century, from Oxford. The ends of the strands are fused together; others of this general type are complete circles, or have their ends twisted together. (Photograph reproduced by courtesy of the British Museum, London. Actual size.)

her grandson so that he could 'enlarge his *beah* with the gold', as though a ring could be melted down and have its weight increased because its principal value was as a bullion store, albeit one that might be publicly displayed; this could have been done quite easily to rod or wire rings that did not have bezels, or filigree soldered to their hoops.[43] Their lure seems to be borne out by a painting in an eleventh-century manuscript that shows three twisted gold rings among the things with which the Devil tried to tempt Christ.[44]

The Devil's other temptations were also frequent bequests in wills: a drinking-horn with what are clearly metal mounts, a chalice-like cup, a bowl, a shield, and a sword in its scabbard, on which a curious oval has two tapes with wedge-shaped ends hanging from it, presumably 'peace-bands'.[45] Other illustrations show that swords remained the aristocrat's weapon of choice, and there are many survivals despite the absence of grave-goods, the quantity dredged from rivers suggesting some sort of continuing ritual practice. Consequently enough are known for it to be fairly clear that, despite contemporary descriptions, they were not actually 'gold-ornamented' in the way that the earlier Windsor, Seine, and Abingdon pommels had had inset gold panels; nor did they have elaborate silver plates over their grips, like the Fetter Lane handle. The most elaborate known has silver wires wound round the grip, as well as between the lobes of the pommel.[46] Some pommels and guards had plain silver plates, others silver wire, but most of those that had any decoration at all had copper alloys or tin of various colours making patterns in the iron surfaces. A few had cast copper-alloy guards, and there is a whalebone pommel from York.[47] A copper-alloy mount from Lincoln could be a scabbard-mount (Fig. 5.4).[48]

Despite what survives, a few bequests of swords suggest that they had fittings with more than base-metal value. Aelfgar had already given 'the sword that King Edmund gave me' as part of his *heriot* when he drew up his will in c.950, and was anxious for the king to recall that it 'was worth 120 *mancuses* of gold and had four pounds of silver on the sheath';[49] that scabbard might have had silver plates, an intricate chape at its end, or perhaps an oval ring attached to it like the one that seems to be shown on offer by the Devil. It was valued partly for its association, as was one which King Ethelred's son

Fig. 5.4. Cast, gilt copper-alloy mount from Lincoln which might have come from the mouth of a scabbard, though there are no decisive parallels. Its openwork decoration is in the eleventh-century Urnes style—the head of a snake-like creature can be seen dangling from the centre, its body coiling round that of one of four other creatures, difficult to make out because the object is curved; another head can be seen projecting upwards on the right. (Photograph reproduced by courtesy of Lincolnshire County Council, City and County Museum. Actual size.)

Aethelstan promised to his brother in c.1014, which he believed to have belonged to King Offa. A weapon like that may have carried family memories, like the women's brooches. The king's son had a number of other swords to hand out, including two with silver hilts, but not with gold ones. One had been made by Wulfric, presumably a well-known smith. Makers could become famous; the names Ulfberht and Ingelrii were hammered into some blades, because they had acquired reputations like Weland's. The inscriptions were often pattern-welded, though the blades themselves were increasingly likely to be plain steel.[50] One of Aethelstan's had the mark of a hand on it, probably another form of maker's identifier. Aethelstan also had a sword-polisher, Aelfnoth, in his household retinue, presumably to keep its weapons in good condition.

Sword-guards and -pommels could be fitted to older blades, so the Eofric or Eofrid who added his name to a sword-pommel found in Exeter may not have been the maker of the killing part.[51] The horn handle grip which unusually survives on a sword from another defended Anglo-Saxon burh, Wareham, has an ownership inscription, unfortunately flaked off halfway through the name, leaving *Aethil . . . mec ah*, but the element that survives means 'high-born' and was used for important people like King Ethelred and his son, Aethelstan.[52] Despite that, the decoration on its guards consists of geometric shapes, well enough executed but not using much, if any, precious metal.[53]

High-value rings were not used only in England. Hoards continued to be deposited on the Scottish islands and coasts, mostly of silver, but some with gold. The largest was found at Skaill, Sandwick, in the Orkneys, weighing over 8 kg in total, all of it silver (Fig. 5.5).[54] It included a few Arabic *dirhams* and two English pennies, which suggest burial in the twenty years after c.950. Its contents are more varied than those of any other hoard; particularly distinctive are seven complete thistle-brooches, together with pins and fragments of others. Several had been decorated with incised interlace knots and animals in the Mammen style: the Skaill hoard is important evidence for that style's introduction and its probable evolution in Ireland.[55] It also appears on the flattened terminals of a penannular ring-brooch in the hoard, but apparently not on any of the large number of twisted rod and wire rings, although several of them have punchmarks, like those in earlier hoards. Most of the rings are neck-sized but, unlike most of the rings found in England, have hooked terminals, suggesting that they were put on and taken off.[56] The Mammen ornament was not used on them, so presumably either it was considered inappropriate for neck-rings, or their makers simply did not know the style because they were working independently of outside influence. There is one ring which is a complete circle, its terminals being replaced by two very unusual animal heads, joined together. Otherwise the hoard contains a ringed pin, various fragments

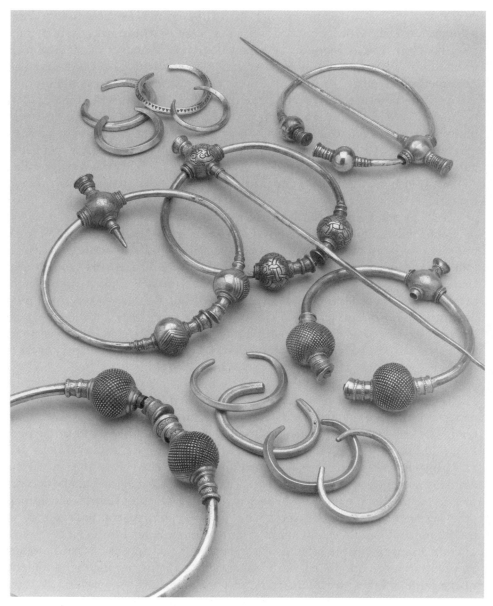

Fig. 5.5. Part of the Skaill, Sandwick, hoard, deposited soon after the middle of the tenth century. Shown here are examples of the penannular 'ring-money', some of it stamped but mostly plain, and of the large penannular brooches with very long pins. Most have ball-shaped terminals, 'brambled' as though to look like thistles, but one in the centre has incised interlace of Mammen-style ornament. (Photograph reproduced by courtesy of the Trustees of the National Museums of Scotland, Edinburgh.)

and ingots of different sizes, a length of trichinopoly chain, and twenty-eight stamped and plain penannular silver rods, of the sort usually called ring-money. Why this should be the only hoard to include such a range of objects is like the wider question, why were so many hoards deposited and not recovered generally?

Ring-money, in the Skaill and other, later hoards, seems too simple and poorly finished to have been worn as jewellery. The extent to which it was used for exchange or payment of tribute rather than merely as a slightly curious way of storing bullion is a moot point. Although the pieces are much the same size, they weigh varying amounts and do not seem to conform to a weight-unit system, either of their own or one compatible with ring-money in Ireland.[57] Most are pecked and nicked less than would be expected if used regularly, as they would have had to be checked for purity. Furthermore, few of the hoards have the smaller pieces of hack-silver needed for small-scale transactions—and of those few, it is the earlier, such as that from Storr Rock, that contain the smallest pieces, just as they also have the most coins.[58] The later tenth- and eleventh-century Scottish seaway hoards seem to be evidence that the islands were less rather than more drawn into north-western European trade and culture. Skaill is the only one to contain thistle-brooches or similar ornament;[59] English coins began to reach the Scottish margins a little more at the end of the tenth century, but not in enough quantity to suggest regular contact, let alone participation in the raids that took huge numbers into Scandinavia.[60]

On the mainland of Scotland the coin record is meagre for the tenth and eleventh centuries, suggesting little opportunity to acquire goods and commodities.[61] Such hoards as have been found are mostly inadequately recorded, some with vague mentions of bracelets or ring-money. Iona Abbey has a hoard of more than 360 coins, nearly all from England, probably concealed at the time of a raid in 986. Also in it were an ingot, a small gold rod, and the bezel of a silver finger-ring with gold filigree and a green glass centre, which may have been quite old when hidden.[62] In the Whithorn excavation, the second half of the tenth and the eleventh centuries produced only two English pennies and one Irish, all clipped, like many in the Iona hoard, which probably means that they were treated as bullion, not at face value;[63] there was also a piece of ring-money.[64] Generally, the material record from the site continues to show more contact with Ireland than with England; a few things, such as a board for playing *tafl*, would not have been out of place in York. But they would not have been out of place in Dublin, either, and such objects as a ball-headed pin, stirrup-shaped ring-pins, stick-pins, and combs all suggest that Hiberno-Norse influence continued to remain much stronger than English, while place-names and the like suggest a reassertion of native Gaelic culture.[65] Small hoards of English coins at Jedburgh, Roxburghshire, and at Lindores, Fife, are evidence of contact, perhaps less than peaceful, in Cnut's reign.[66] In this limited amount of information from Scotland generally, it is difficult to see much sign of economic or social change, despite the political changes that are recorded.[67]

For Wales the picture is rather different. There is hack-silver in a Bangor hoard deposited with coins of *c*.970,[68] but thereafter the hoards in the north-west contain only coins, usually English and mostly minted in Chester.[69] The Welsh were in the unfortunate position of being liable to attack both by viking Norse and Anglo-Saxons, and having to pay tribute to both.[70] With silver being drawn out of Wales, the paucity of single coin finds is understandable; there are only two datable to the second half of the tenth century, and one of those was almost certainly deliberately placed in the mouth of an adult male burial on Bardsey Island, which does not suggest everyday familiarity.[71] A Borre-style buckle from Llanbedrgoch and a Jellinge-style bone motif-piece from Rhuddlan, Clwyd, could result from ongoing Hiberno-Norse links, and two cast copper-alloy lobed sword pommels cannot be attributed to one area rather than another.[72] Apart perhaps from a locally made deviation from the Ringerike style, used on an object from Llanelen, Gower,[73] there is little to suggest anything specifically Welsh in the material culture of the tenth and eleventh centuries, despite contemporary beliefs in Welsh unity, tradition, and identity.[74]

The British in the south-west, Cornwall, were already following a different path from those in Wales, as their political autonomy had disappeared in the ninth century. Relative isolation always meant that the peninsula was likely to have distinctive elements in its culture, and despite its tin and other metals there is not much direct sign of economic involvement with the rest of England; the growth of Exeter may show wealth being drawn out of it, but there is little evidence.[75] After the Trewhiddle hoard of *c*.868 no coins are reported from the shire for over a century; a penny of *c*.991–7 excavated on the north coast at Mawgan Porth, minted close by at Lydford, was the first to be found—significantly, there were no mints in Cornwall itself.[76] The site at Mawgan Porth was remarkable for the survival of stone buildings, farms grouped round small courtyards unlike anything else excavated, and for the near-absence of metal; iron would not have survived well in the sandy conditions, but copper alloy was also almost totally lacking. It was largely a 'stone and bone' economy, except for pottery. This consisted mainly of the very distinctive 'bar-lug' pots, the sides of which were drawn up and pierced so that they could be suspended over a hearth; they are unknown outside Cornwall and the Isles of Scilly. Before the site was abandoned in the eleventh century, sherds of sandy ware similar to contemporary pottery produced elsewhere in England were just beginning to appear.[77] Cornish 'grass-marked' pottery, such as some of the bar-lug vessels were made of, petered out during the eleventh century, perhaps running on into the twelfth, like the bar-lugs themselves.[78]

One contrast between tenth- and eleventh-century Scotland and Wales seems to be that the former has yet to produce examples of horse-riding equipment. From the latter, however, there are spurs and at least one pair of stirrups, as well as the Llanelen object, which may be a bridle fitting.[79] This evidence of changes in riding equipment is fairly widespread in England.

The reintroduction of spurs after the Roman period has been attributed to the early Anglo-Saxon period on the basis of one or two iron objects from fifth-/sixth-century graves, but these are spurlike rather than definite examples.[80] The well-equipped young man with the horse in Mound 17 at Sutton Hoo did not have any.[81] By the ninth century on the continent, however, a Carolingian count's equipment included spurs,[82] and the silver strap-ends and slides in the Trewhiddle hoard could have been a set of spur fittings.[83] A cast copper-alloy object from Pakenham, Suffolk, has short, curved arms ending in open-jawed animal heads with blue glass eyes, each having a single rivet through it (Fig. 5.6). The heads resemble those on some of the common ninth-century strap-ends. In the centre is another well-executed animal head holding a short, pointed rod—but flat-backed, not round like a normal spur-goad.[84] Rather different is an object from the Thames at Kingston, also in copper alloy but with much longer arms ending in slotted terminals. Buckle-frames swivel

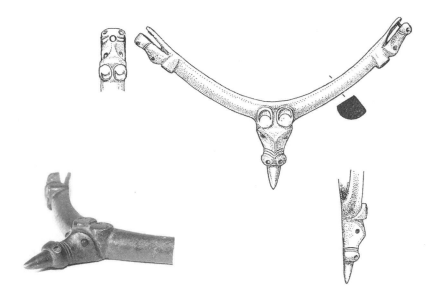

Fig. 5.6. Cast copper-alloy object from Pakenham, Suffolk; its neatly modelled animal heads with blue glass eyes suggest a date in the ninth or tenth century—cf. the head on the Alfred Jewel (Fig. 4.10) or the ears on the Abingdon sword (Fig. 4.2)—but the shortness of its arms, and other details, make its identification as a spur uncertain. (Photograph, and drawings by Pat Clarke, reproduced by courtesy of the Ashmolean Museum, Oxford. Actual size.)

on the terminals, and it makes a much more convincing spur.[85] The first in a proper archaeological context is a single iron spur in the 'viking' grave at Middle Harling.[86] Others, complete and broken, have been found, but are attributed to the eleventh century.[87] The earliest pairs of spurs in England are iron ones in viking graves in Cumbria that were also furnished with weapons and other objects, including horses' bridle-bits.[88] This does not make them a late ninth- or early tenth-century Scandinavian introduction, but they are to be associated with the raids and the use of horses both by attackers and defenders who observed spurs being used on the continent.[89] Iron is a much better metal for spurs than copper alloy, particularly if given a coating of tin to inhibit rust and to flash in the sun. Iron spurs with straight arms and short, sharp goads became the norm until the thirteenth century (but cf. Fig. 6.2).[90]

Iron was also standard for metal stirrups, which are quicker to get the feet out of than looped straps. As they have not been found in the earliest viking graves, they may be later introductions than spurs, although they too had been used by the Carolingians.[91] Two found just outside Oxford with a spur and other items are not quite identical, but were probably worn as a pair (Fig. 5.7).[92] They have long arms, a rectangular strap-loop at the tops, and expanded side-plates at the ends of the arms, a form that is sufficiently common for manufacture in England to be fairly certain, even if similar ones were also being made overseas. They were ornamented with plant and scroll patterns made by beating brass or other copper alloys into the iron. No stirrups have definitely come from graves in England, but the number dredged from rivers suggests that, as with swords, some unrecorded deposition ritual may have been practised.

Until ten years ago it seemed that there was little more to be learnt about stirrups. Then it was realized that the leather straps that passed through the rectangular slots at the tops had been riveted into place using flanged cast copper-alloy mounts, objects previously identified as book or shrine fittings.[93] This in turn led to the collation of reports of very large numbers of them, of different types, such as a triangular form often cast with a lion-like creature on the front, or a rectangular open-cast form with animal heads (Fig. 5.8).[94] Others have animals clambering up the sides, or human faces or plants, and there is even a small group of naked human figures. Some have small areas inlaid with silver wire, the only use of precious metal on any of the mounts despite their elaborate casting.[95] They were things that were easily lost, and which had to be robust, but it is symptomatic of changing ways of expressing status that they were not even gilded.

As well as the tall stirrups with side-plates like the two from Oxford, there was a more triangular form on which the side arms often ended in cast animal heads (Fig. 5.8). Again, one or two have niello and silver-wire inlay.[96] Heads of similar shapes also appear on many of the flanged mounts, on bridle fittings such as cheek-pieces,[97] and on buckles, but apparently not in the same

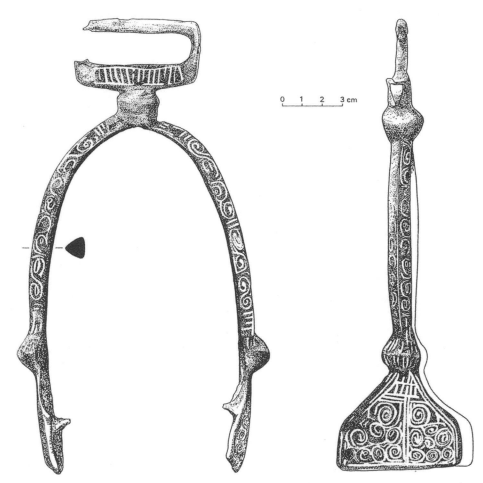

Fig. 5.7. Eleventh-century iron stirrups with copper-alloy scroll decoration, as was also used on contemporary swords. (Drawing by Pat Clarke reproduced by courtesy of the Ashmolean Museum, Oxford. Scale as shown.)

numbers. Small buckles are needed for spur-straps, so it may be that fewer have been found because not many people wore spurs, although many used stirrups. In Aelfric's *Colloquy*, a school-book written *c*.1000 as a series of dialogues in Latin and Old English between different craftsmen and traders, the leatherworker listed spur fittings among his products, so they were reasonably familiar, but the book was only aimed at the small educated minority. As spurs are so clearly shown being used by the mounted Norman knights in the Bayeux Tapestry to urge on their specially bred horses, the archaeological record may be confirming that the English did not rely on mounted warriors, with the

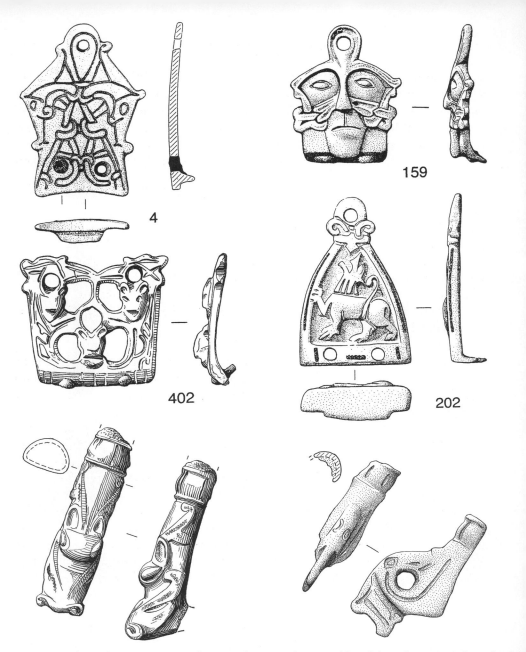

Fig. 5.8. Various eleventh-century stirrup fittings. The upper four would each have been riveted to a leather strap that passed through the loop at the top of a stirrup; no. 4, from Hastings, Sussex, has two Urnes animals, heads to left and right, their bodies knotted together; no. 159, from Deal, Kent, has a human mask with leaves on either side of its nose making it look rather like one of the Green Men popular later in the Middle Ages, but with those the leaves come out of the nostrils, mouth, or ears. Traces of niello and silver-wire inlay survive around the rivet-hole at the top; no. 202, from Cliffe, Kent, has a roaring lion, which was used on many of these mounts. Like no. 159, it has silver inlay in the borders; no. 402 from Legsby, Lincolnshire, has three animal heads in relief, and two surviving iron rivets.

Below are two examples of copper-alloy terminals from the ends of stirrup arms. On the left is a well modelled Urnes-style animal head from Binbrooke, Lincolnshire. Like some of the mounts, it has niello and silver-wire inlay refinements. On the right is a more vestigial head from Donnington, Lincolnshire. In this case, the head is looking back up the arm of the stirrup. (Drawings by David Williams reproduced with his permission; mounts from Williams 1997a, terminals from original drawings which he kindly supplied. Actual sizes.)

social consequence that there was less separation of a highly trained and expensively equipped military aristocracy from a much wider group of horse-owners who had, for instance, to perform 'riding services' for their lords.[98]

The Ringerike and Urnes styles seen on many of these fittings also appear in manuscript illustrations, though perhaps as the choice of one or two particular artists rather than as part of a standard repertoire. The styles takes their names from sites in Scandinavia, but their similarity to the Winchester style do not preclude an origin in the south of England in the late tenth century, just as the earlier Mammen style may have evolved in Ireland, despite its name.[99] But even if the styles really were originally Scandinavian, their rapid adoption in a range of different media throughout England would not be evidence of a large Scandinavian immigration after Cnut's conquest. There are many fewer brooches than there are earlier in the Jellinge and Borre styles.[100] That more stirrup fittings have been found in the southern 'Danelaw' may only be because more people lived there than in other parts of England, as Domesday Book shows.[101]

The *wic*-using trading and production system of the eighth century had been disrupted in the ninth, but the urban network that re-emerged in the late ninth and the tenth centuries proved permanent. Markets and fairs were increasingly used, probably stimulated by the widespread need to acquire coins to pay rents and taxes, and population increase not only created a means of peopling the towns but also expanded the scale of demand.[102] Many types of artefact were increasingly likely to be perceived as items to be bought at agreed prices rather than acquired by gift or reciprocal exchange, a process that was a major factor in changing social relations generally.[103]

Attribution of small items of no great value to production at particular centres can be difficult; the stirrup fittings, for instance, have been recovered in numbers that imply large-scale production, but no moulds for making them have been found. The wide distribution of the mounts with a rampant lion (Fig. 5.8) suggests that the design was generally acceptable, with no exclusion caused either deliberately or by restricted marketing; the similarly wide distribution of contemporary pennies, on which mints are invariably named after *c*.973, suggests the same.[104] Even the nine examples of the type of mount with a human figure, naked, bound, and apparently attacked by monsters, have come from six different counties, from Lincolnshire to Hampshire.[105] Recognitions of circulation areas can still be made, however. One subtype of the lion is found mostly in southern England, suggesting distribution around a region, with a few being taken further, while another subtype is mostly in Norfolk, but again with a few outliers;[106] the first has no obvious centre to its distribution, the second concentrates around Norwich. The first might have been made by travelling smiths, or carried around by pedlars; the second is much more likely to have been made and sold in a workshop in the emerging town.

Coins again provide a useful comparison, as those found in rural sites are a little more likely to have come from the nearest mint than those in towns or in hoards.[107]

The only metalworking craft that had to be practised in specific places was the production of iron coin-dies, to prevent forgery. The dies were either then sent to the mints, or the moneyers had to travel to collect them. Dies were also sent from England for use in mints in Dublin and Scandinavia, a tribute to their high quality.[108] Minting itself was sometimes permitted at places too small to be considered towns, and a few moneyers seem not to have stayed at one mint, instead travelling from one to another with their dies. Most coins, however, were produced at the few large mints, London, York, Winchester, and so on, and a similar pattern of production might be expected of other metalworking—that it was mostly but not exclusively practised in the larger towns.[109]

Die-cutters may also have been responsible for the lead weights that are occasionally found, which are not—like the earlier viking raiders' weights—set with coins or ornaments, but have been stamped with official coin dies. They may have been for use at the mints, since they may be equated to *mancus* or to shilling multiples,[110] but the tolerance is so wide that this cannot be certain, and there were variations within the issues of the coins themselves, with slightly different standards applied in different shires. Nevertheless, the weights are part and parcel of the increasing use of precision in everyday dealings. Unofficial everyday weights also continued to be used; in York some were of iron with shiny copper-alloy casings, including two from what was probably a set stamped with patterns that may have been personal identifiers. Some of these weights conform to Scandinavian mark and øre systems, probably introduced by Cnut. Some of his followers demanded payment in silver, which had to be carefully weighed; they were not prepared to take coins at their face value.[111]

The number of halfpennies and even farthings shows that coins were increasingly likely to be used in everyday transactions, though what small objects were valued at is not recorded. The stirrup-mounts, for instance, are sufficiently common to be regarded as commodities produced in some volume, and easily replaced if lost, not items made for a specific patron, like an inscribed brooch or ring. The same is true of other base-metal products, such as brooches in York which include a large one cast in lead alloy but plated with silver.[112] A mass of castings for pewter brooches, rings, and beads was found in 1838 with coins of *c*.1000 in London's Cheapside, clearly from a maker's workshop (Fig. 5.9).[113] Antler moulds for casting tin-alloy brooches have been found in two towns, Southampton and Ipswich, but brooches likely to have come from such moulds are widespread, from York to Milton Keynes, Thetford, Taunton, and Steyning.[114] Pewter was also used in at least one instance for a direct copy of a silver coin of *c*.1029–36, found in London.[115]

An Epoch of New Dynasties

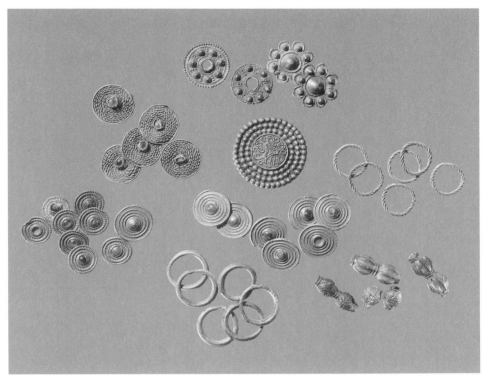

Fig. 5.9. Hoard of lead-alloy rings, brooches and beads, part of a large number found in Cheapside, London, in 1838, some unfinished and clearly a maker's stock-in-trade. Some of the brooches have coloured glass studs in their centres. Low-value trinkets like these have been found in many of the emerging towns of the late Saxon period. In London, Cheapside was to have a long history as the metalworkers' street. (Photograph reproduced by courtesy of the Museum of London. About two-thirds actual sizes.)

As well as being made in base metals, brooches were contrived by putting pin fittings on a coin or coins, something occasionally done before the eleventh century,[116] but seemingly particularly favoured in Edward the Confessor's and William I's reigns. These coin-brooches are mostly found in the south of England. They are gilded and worn so as to display the cross on the reverse, not the king on the front, so they were not statements of loyalty to the changing dynasties but conventional displays of piety, or talismans.[117]

Another range of small brooches, not so readily datable but apparently made in the later tenth and eleventh centuries, have gilt copper-alloy frames holding cloisonné enamel of various colours, often also with tiny beads of glass in surrounding lobes. Some of the enamels are floral patterns, but others are crosses, some have heads reminiscent of earlier coins, and a few have pointed ovals. The floral patterns are mostly in cruciform designs, and the ovals can be interpreted as eyes, possibly to ward off evil, so the whole series may also be talismanic in one way or another.[118] They are less confined to the south of England than the penny-brooches appear to be, but there is no way of knowing who was wearing either type. Bright colours certainly appealed in the north as well, however, and glass answered the demand in a different way in York, with a range of polychrome beads and some covered in gold foil.[119]

Some things were probably still home-produced; anyone with a knife could have made one of the commonplace bone pin-beaters needed for weaving on upright looms.[120] Combs, on the other hand, required a small saw to cut the teeth, rivets to hold the pieces together, and therefore some experience as well as equipment. Partly because little waste from the comb-makers' activities has been found, it has been argued that the comb-makers' scale of output was insufficient for year-round employment. They therefore had two possibilities: to have another occupation as well, or to be itinerant. They may have gone from market to market and to fairs, answering demand as they met it. Collecting shed antlers on their travels may have been better for them than having to rely on other people bringing supplies to a permanent centre. Theirs was an old craft, and may have gone on in traditional ways for longer than some others. Nevertheless, their transactions could have been facilitated by coins.[121]

Pottery was another commodity that probably reached down to the bottom of the economic hierarchy. It demonstrates that the emergence of a broad-based market, and of towns like Norwich to provide permanent centres, does not mean that there is a single path of development for a craft to follow. In many of the towns north of the Thames kilns have been excavated showing volume production, but also a variety of manufacturing techniques and finishing processes. At Stamford, for instance, the red-painted pottery being made in the late ninth century was not copied elsewhere and was not maintained. The particular qualities of Stamford-area clays were especially suitable for crucibles, and for production of wheel-thrown white pitchers and other vessels notable for the application to them of lead glazes giving a glossy finish (Fig. 5.10). They are regularly found at tenth- and eleventh-century sites up to 100 miles from Stamford, occasionally getting further. They were constrained neither by old political barriers nor by cultural preference, only ultimately by transport limitations.[122] The Stamford-ware glazed pitchers are the only pots that seem likely to have been regarded as anything special; one from Oxford was only broken in the thirteenth century, which suggests that it had been carefully looked after.[123] Pottery produced in other midlands and northern towns was not so distinctive, and was unglazed. Large quantities were made, particularly in Lincoln, Thetford, and Norwich, but also in towns further west such as Northampton, Stafford, and Gloucester, from which generally it did not travel nearly so far.

Southern England is different, for most of the pottery kilns found have been in the countryside, possibly because older practices and distribution systems

Fig. 5.10. Eleventh-century spouted pitcher with small side-handle, made in Stamford but found in Oxford. It is wheel-made and lead-glazed. (Photograph reproduced by courtesy of the British Museum. Actual height 170 mm.)

had been less disrupted in the ninth century. As the eleventh century progressed, however, urban potters were liable to be pushed out to the edges of towns, probably by a combination of fire risk, smell, water pollution, high central rents, and transport costs of fuel and clay. Even well-established industries came to face rural competition, as Thetford and Norwich did from Grimston, Langhale, and other country places. Nor was the superior technology of wheels, lead glazing, and updraught kilns generally adopted; proximity to a market was presumably not enough to compensate for investment of time, rent, and materials.[124] A few continental vessels widened the range available in ports, but quantities varied.[125]

For many purposes wood, leather, and horn were rivals to clay for making pots but, being organic, do not usually survive. Well-preserved wooden cups and bowls at York show what was available, turned by makers who were probably already specialists and working within the town, the large number of cores demonstrating the veracity of the name *koppari* or cup-makers' street, for Coppergate. Most of the cups had a fairly small capacity, presumably for use with a strong drink, and were made from yew and other carefully chosen woods; they were sometimes painted, but perhaps surprisingly were very rarely fitted with metal mounts.[126] Glass can be assumed to have been a lot more expensive, but in any case potash was coming to be used for vessels, which is less durable than soda-lime mixtures, and means that there is even less evidence in the archaeological record than earlier. At the same time, however, there was greater diversity, as glass with a higher lead content was also being made, and from the middle of the tenth century was being used in London, York, Winchester, Gloucester, and elsewhere, mostly for the manufacture of rings.[127] For that purpose, therefore, glass provided an alternative to amber, jet and shale,[128] metal, or bone, just as bone and antler could be used as alternatives to metal for small items such as strap-ends and buckle frames. Some of these were skilfully made, and probably go beyond what anyone with a sharp knife could produce. This is even more true of bone spoons, some of which have Winchester-style patterns cut into the bowls; one has a fine beast's head with scrolling tongue between the stem and the bowl, which is very like designs in manuscripts of *c*.1000 (Fig. 4.11).[129] In such small ways was the range of consumers' choice increasingly extended.

Choice in everyday items can be seen in various other products, notably textiles. The preference for the brightness of Stamford ware over the dull pottery of Thetford and other centres has a counterpart in the colourfulness of dyed cloth, linen, and even silk. Londoners in particular had a wide choice, but so too did the townspeople in York. The number of different weaves giving different surface finishes to woollen cloths grew as the horizontal loom was adopted during the eleventh century. Surviving fragments imply that these fabrics were not confined to the very rich.[130] Glass 'calenders' or slick-stones used for ironing linen could indicate that pleated dresses were already being worn.[131] Silk came from Italy or the Near East; urban finds show that it was not confined to ecclesiastical vestments, and contemporary descriptions show that King Edward was not alone in sumptuous dressing.[132]

In footwear, too, there was an element of choice; there was no alternative to leather, but the range of ankle-boots and shoes, some of which were given toggle fastenings, embroidered strips, or pointed toes, shows that fashion already counted for much; pointed toes are prominent in late eleventh-century London asssemblages, precisely when they are recorded as a source of scandal at the royal court, so the courtiers' folly was not disavowed by the citizenry (Fig. 5.11). Londoners seem to have been more susceptible than the citizens of York or Winchester.[133] Another leatherworking craft was scabbard-making; the most highly decorated survivals are for knives rather than swords (Fig. 5.12). The best had raised patterns, very like those seen in manuscripts, and showing

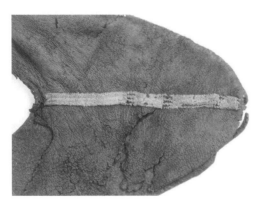

Fig. 5.11. Late eleventh-/early twelfth-century Londoners' footwear.
Above: everyday leather ankle-boots, with leather drawstrings. The stubby toes show that even these make some concession to the whims of fashion, and the one on the right has a side opening in the quarter for a decorative thong of two plaited leather strips. The boot on the left was probably a child's.
Below: an almost pointed toe on this leather shoe upper suggests something even more stylish, as the embroidered three-coloured silk strip emphasizes. (Photographs by Jon Bailey reproduced by courtesy of the Museum of London Archaeology Service. About half actual sizes.)

that in this dress item also people kept up with fashion, again apparently with Londoners to the fore, though the most elaborate example is in the treasury at Aachen.[134] Seaxes and knives continued to have inlaid wire decoration,[135] though the acanthus leaves that Biorhtelm had used to embellish Sigebereht's knife were never seen again.

How far people in the countryside shared in the range of urban choice is not clear. Flixborough, for instance, had tenth-century levels with large quantities of buildings and bones, but much less metalwork than before. There are a few lead weights and a small silver ingot, but no coins from c.880 until the

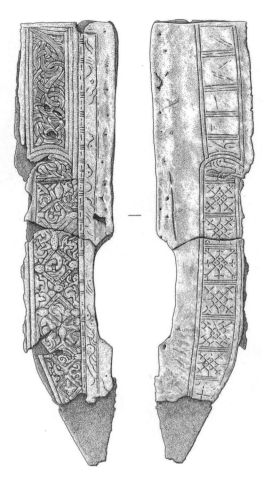

Fig. 5.12. Embossed leather tenth-/eleventh-century knife-scabbard from London. The decoration on one side has a panel of interlace at the top, the rest being lozenges with bosses at the corners, containing leaf patterns and what may be animals (cf. Fig. 4.11). (Drawing by Nick Griffiths from the collections of the Museum of London. One-third actual size.)

late 970s. Either much less metalwork was being used, or it was being looked after and recycled.[136] Wharram Percy also seems to have had much less metalwork in the tenth and eleventh centuries—a contrast that makes the limited evidence from Mawgan Porth look as likely to reflect a general trend as to result from the place's isolation. A smaller rural site in Hampshire at Swaythling, between Winchester and Southampton, was less isolated, which is probably reflected in the slightly larger number of finds and the range of pottery there; it had copper-alloy tweezers, a buckle and a key, an iron knife, and a bone weaving tool not very well decorated with a version of the Ringerike style.[137] In Norfolk, Middle Harling has about a coin per major reign in the second half of the tenth and in the eleventh centuries, but only an open-work strap-end seems a personal ornament certainly attributable to the same period.[138] Minor rural sites of the period have not been much excavated, however, so an overall perspective is difficult to achieve.[139]

One of the estates that Wynflaed bequeathed in her will was *Faccancu* . . . , Faccombe in Hampshire,[140] where major excavations on a site next to the church revealed the development of a high-status residence. The discovery of a number of well-made objects might have been anticipated at such a place, but not necessarily evidence that some were being made there. Hearths and crucibles were found, however. Cast copper-alloy objects included a strap-end, and part of a key with openwork Winchester-style ornament, probably of the late ninth or first half of the tenth century, suggestive of the range of small fittings that someone like Wynflaed needed; another loss was a gold ring of twisted wire with knotted ends.[141] A smith was certainly working at Faccombe, probably as an occasional visitor, either as a member of its owner's travelling household or as a freeman seeking out a patron.[142] Another late ninth-/tenth-century residential complex, this time owned by the king, that had evidence of metalworking, including gold, was Cheddar, Somerset.[143] The smith called Wulfric, who had made a gold belt and a ring as well as sword parts bequeathed by Ethelred's son Aethelstan, may have been active at places like that, not necessarily as a permanent part of the aetheling's household, as the sword-polisher Aelfnoth seems to have been.[144]

Metalworkers' skills were also in high demand by the Church; a few survivals show the standard of what could be produced, such as the silver mounts on a portable altar that are incised with the Crucifixion, figures and symbols similar enough to drawings in manuscripts to have led to the suggestion that the same people were responsible for work in both media. The panels surround a slab of purple porphyry.[145] Some of the craftsmen reached high office, for better or—as in Bishop Spearhafoc's case—worse.[146] Gifts like Cnut's of a gold cross to the New Minster at Winchester[147] may have been expected of the laity generally—the stone sculptures could be other examples, highly visible if painted, gilded, and set with metal mounts, and not all in the greatest churches, showing the wide spread of patronage. Such expenditure may have taken significant wealth out of secular circulation. Aethelstan's will shows that dealings could be commercial, if his purchase of a drinking-horn from the Old Minster was typical; sometimes churches realized their assets to meet expenditure.[148]

Partly because of connections like Aethelstan's, it is not always possible to assign an object to the Church rather than to the secular world; an exquisite gold portable sundial found in the precinct of Canterbury Cathedral has Latin inscriptions as well as its computation system to show its origins in a centre of learning, and its context suggests that it stayed in one.[149] Unrecorded gifts may have been made by churches to secure the favour and protection of a secular patron. An example could be a cast copper-alloy pendant reliquary from Sandford, Oxfordshire, since its size implies personal use and it was not found at a church site.[150] On the other hand, a gold cloisonné enamel mount from St Augustine's Abbey, Canterbury, probably is from a church treasure such as a shrine or a reliquary casket, as is an enamel disc from Oxford. A cabochon crystal from Castle Acre, Norfolk, however, and fragments of crystal from both Lewes, Sussex, and Rhuddlan are less certainly ascribed to such a function, as they could demonstrate new secular interest in gems and their properties generally. The Rhuddlan crystal is particularly interesting because it was found with the remains of a leather bag and two coins of 1092–5 in a grave.[151]

The development of towns and their markets, and of fairs, during the tenth and eleventh centuries began to create an alternative system through which the aristocracy could acquire their needs. By the middle of the eleventh century they did not have to have smiths in their retinues or visiting their residences, as they could get their swords and shields in at least some larger towns, as well as gold cups and drinking-horns. Winchester already had a 'street of the shield-makers' by 996, and goldsmiths had houses in the town. By *c*.1057 a man named Spileman was working there as a swordmaker, if *brandwirchte* is correctly translated.[152] In York, iron pommels, guards, and bits of blades could be evidence of the same craft, with the whalebone pommel as an alternative material for the top of the handle.[153] London was regarded as a weapon-store by the early eleventh century, which implies manufacturing there. In 1016 there were reputed to be 24,000 chain-mail byrnies within the city. The weaponry may have become cheaper as a consequence, but the cost of a horse and its maintenance far outweighed any savings for anyone who expected to have to fight mounted.[154]

Apart from the penny-brooches, there are practically no small dress items made of precious metal after the end of the tenth century, by which time even the little hooked tags seem only to have been made in copper alloy.[155] Some objects have yet to be found in contexts that allow them to be properly dated, but a fairly common type of silver-gilt pin with a globular head and delicate filigree seems not to occur in the new towns and may have stopped being made by the middle of the tenth century.[156] Nor are there more than a couple of new precious-metal finds attributable to the eleventh century recorded by detectorists, except the penny-brooches.[157] Two of the last really fine items known are silver-gilt cast belt fittings found in the cemetery at the Old Minster in Winchester, one a Jellinge-style strap-end probably worn with the other, a rectangular mount on which neat little animals seem later in date (Fig. 4.11); they could have come from a sword-belt worn by one of the Anglo-Scandinavians who served King Cnut in the early eleventh century, but they could equally have been the sorts of thing that Wulfric put on Aethelstan's gold belt.[158]

The Scandinavian followers of Cnut, and before him his father, Swein, were certainly interested in gold and silver, like those who demanded payment in weighed metal, not coin. All the more extraordinary, therefore, is it that while there are plenty of hoards in Scandinavia which show that very high numbers of silver coins left England, very few contain anything else identifiable as

English. Within England, only the silver disc-brooch at Barsham and a silver bowl, neck-ring, and pendants at Halton Moor, Lancashire,[159] are recorded in hoards of the 980s to 1020s. This is very different from the later ninth and early tenth centuries, with their rings, ingots, and hack-silver. The last hoard of that type is one found in Chester, dated to *c*.965, which had about forty silver rods, ingots, and ring-pieces.[160] Silver seems to have been plentiful in Europe after the discovery of fresh sources in the Harz Mountains in the 960s, and a reason for the renewed viking raids was to acquire it, since Near Eastern supplies had diminished. Why was it not flaunted in England by those who prospered from Swein's and Cnut's successes? Although the two silver-gilt belt fittings in Winchester could hint at a funeral that the bishop would not have enjoyed taking, burials like the earlier raider's at Reading and elsewhere have not been found.[161] The new generation, many if not most already Christian,[162] took up the tradition of munificence to churches, like their king, and emphasized their status by their estates and residences, assimilating with what they found in their new country rather than harking back to what they had known in their old ones.[163] Even if they married English women, however, they could not pretend to long-term family memories or claim to have inherited heirlooms; the resonance of antiquity gave them no status.[164]

That there was a trend away from using precious-metal jewellery with costume continues to be borne out by the coin hoards, which are quite prolific throughout the eleventh century, especially in the troubled times around 1066. A few then contain objects other than coins, such as that from Soberton, Hampshire, which had in it two small plaited gold-wire finger-rings.[165] The Sutton brooch is said to have had rings with it, now lost; other losses are a disc-brooch said to have been with the Oving, Sussex, hoard, and a gold filigree brooch recorded as set with pearls and a sapphire, from near St Mary Hill Church, London (Fig. 5.13).[166] Unless the gold disc found in 2001 at Holberrow Green, Worcestershire, is from a brooch (Col. pl. F.3),[167] the only other known is also from London, finely made from filigree with an enamelled figure in the centre and small pearls round the outside. As it was found close to the Thames at Dowgate, it may well be an import mislaid at the dockside.[168] It shows a much higher level of craftsmanship than the Sutton brooch, but unfortunately it was not found with any coins. There are some very well-cast three-dimensional objects, such as the mount excavated in Lincoln (Fig. 5.4), some of which have gilt finishes like a brooch from Pitney, Somerset,[169] but they have no solid gold or silver equivalents.

Another change is that, apart from sword-blade makers, and moneyers for whom it was a condition of their licence, metalsmiths ceased to put their names on their products, as though objects were no longer special enough to be distinguished as the work of an individual. If Wudeman was the maker and not the commissioner of the rather undistinguished brooch that bears his name (Fig. 5.1), he is the last Anglo-Saxon known to have put his name on a piece

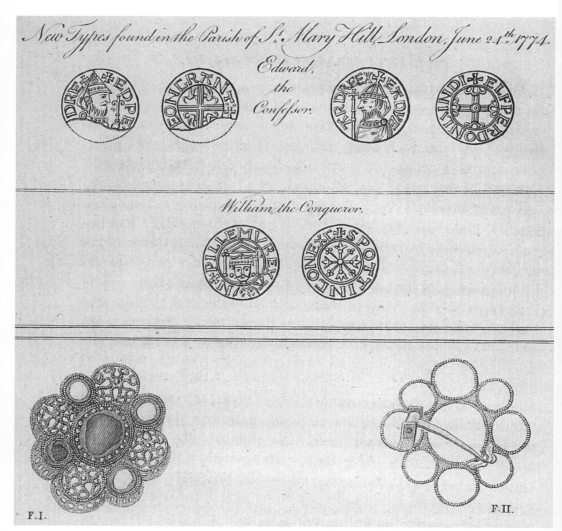

Fig. 5.13. Late eighteenth-century engraving of some of the St Mary Hill, London, hoard found in 1774. Between 300 and 400 coins were found, but only about fifty have survived. The two at the top are Edward the Confessor types of the 1050s: on the left, he is wearing a pointed helmet and holding a fleur-de-lys headed sceptre, the reverse having 'eagles' between the arms of a cross—the letters GRANT above are the name of the mint, Cambridge, then called *Grantebrycge*; on the right, the king's helmet now has a cross on it, as though progressing towards a crown, and the sceptre is much longer. The moneyer is Elfwerd—the third letter should be a runic *wyrm* rune, not a Latin P—of (ON) London (LUNDI). Below is William the Conqueror in 1071–4 wearing a 'canopy' crown of ultimately Byzantine style; the moneyer was Swottinc (not Spottinc) of Exeter (EXC—'c' for *ceastre*). The engraver of the plate may have been wrong to give William a moustache. At the bottom is the only record of the gold filigree brooch found with the hoard; the patterns in the larger panels were probably more cruciform than they appear. (Reproduced from *Archaeologia*, 4 (1786), opp. p. 357.)

of personal jewellery. Owners' names also disappear, one of the last being on the Wareham sword.[170] This is not only true of metal; a few knife scabbards have their makers' names, intriguingly, all the latest examples being overseas at Aachen, Dublin, and Trondheim.[171] At the same time, very few objects were still personified,[172] as though they were becoming too commonplace for individual identification.

Because these changes were in train before the Norman Conquest, they cannot be ascribed solely to William's heavy taxation. Clearly there were landowners as well as townspeople with money to spend before 1066; the number of stone grave-markers in a rural churchyard like that at Raunds, Northamptonshire, is an indication of that, and of their wish to be remembered.[173] Their heirs were downgraded by land reallocation after the Conquest, and urban records of 'waste' tenements, from which rents could not be obtained, and of fleeing burgesses show that spending power would have declined. The many 1060s hoards, including several from London, are a record of pre-Conquest wealth. Some have large numbers of coins; in towns it might be argued that they belonged to merchants who were rich in money but not in the gold and silver ornaments, vessels, drinking-horns, and other items recorded in the aristocratic wills—but such things are not found in the country hoards either.[174] The contrast to the contents of the ninth-century hoards is very marked. Only the Dowgate Hill brooch seems good enough to be the sort of thing that the Bayeux Tapestry and coins (Fig. 5.13) show being worn by kings and their courtiers; the wills and the Sutton brooch all point to women, not men, being brooch-owners, however, so representations may not be reliable in this detail.

The Bayeux Tapestry may have been more concerned to present iconic images of kings than the precise details of contemporary costume fittings, but it was certainly keen to emphasize the importance of people's appearance in other ways. The contrast between the haircuts of the Normans and the English is consistently shown. The long moustaches favoured by Harold and many of the English with him are not so invariable, but are confirmed by occasional descriptions, like that of a bishop who died in battle in 1056, who still 'wore his moustaches during his priesthood'.[175] Facial hair was an identifier, to the extent that in 1086 the English were ordered to shave so that, in the event of a Danish invasion, they could not be told apart from the Normans.[176] Such accounts can be exaggerations, however,[177] and differences do not seem apparent in other ways. Nor are the colonies of French and Flemish settlers in Norwich and other towns distinguishable in material remains, such as different brooches, pottery, or foodstuffs. A different identifier, perhaps associated with particular families but not distinguishing English from Scandinavian or Norman, was the display of dragons and other mythical beasts, or elaborate geometrical patterns, on shields, pennants, and ships' figureheads, described as being of solid gold but presumably painted or gilded. Sails were brightly coloured too. These were displays to embolden those who fought with them and to overawe the enemy.[178]

Costume display was also important, but was not so personal as an object that could be associated with an individual. That no wills mention brooches or the like after the early eleventh century could be because, by chance, the only extant later wills are not those of greater lords, but the three seal-dies to have survived that belonged to people near the top of the social hierarchy show that the paucity of appropriate jewellery cannot be explained away so readily. Also surviving are the Wareham and other swords, and these show the same trend away from rich ornamentation. A few have lively animals on their guards, but they are fairly stereotyped and meaningless; they do not seem like the swirling individuals on the Fetter Lane pommel or the carefully crafted evangelist symbols on the Abingdon sword. Gold finger-rings with personal names and Trewhiddle-style decoration are relatively frequent ninth-century finds, but only the plain twisted rings succeed them.[179] A man might go into battle with weapons which his lord had given him at a commendation ceremony, but they were for use rather than display of personal loyalty, and were not individualized by either inscription or unique ornament.

Treasure did not become less important for political manipulation, but its value was as coin and bullion.[180] The Dowgate Hill brooch and the few other pieces may show that the tradition of wearing valuable ornaments did not completely cease in the eleventh century, but such display was not necessary unless symbolic of royal power, as crown, orb, or staff. Gifts were still important, not only to churches; but while Edward the Confessor gave rich presents to his fellow kings and princes, he is not recorded as handing down gifts to his own people. Did anyone think of him as their 'ring-giver'? He was a recipient, but of fully equipped ships.[181] By the middle of the eleventh century status came from land and the exercise of power that went with it, and a display of elaborate jewellery was no longer the means of expressing competition or showing personal prowess and the ability to dispense patronage. The Germanic world of gift-giving, tribute-taking, and shifting personal relationships had ceded to one in which values could be measured and paid in coin, services commuted, and subjects taxed, with social position even more likely to be dependent on birth than on attainment.[182]

6

Feudal Modes

The Twelfth Century and the First Half of the Thirteenth

The trend away from ornamented brooches, rings, and swords that demonstrates changing social pressures and expression during the eleventh century was maintained in the first half of the twelfth. The Anglo-Norman aristocracy had considerable wealth for its castles and churches, but the spending power of the Anglo-Saxon majority was very much diminished by the impositions that followed the Conquest. Social relations among the former were based primarily on land, and although sentiments of personal loyalty were defined by oaths of fealty, there is no record of gift-giving from lord to retainer other than the increasingly formalized bestowal of arms. Towns were growing both in size and number, but only a few merchants were really rich, and the peasantry in the countryside was increasing in number but had decreasing opportunity for individual advancement.[1]

Excavations at castles and other baronial residences generally yield the evidence of martial appearance and activity that would be expected, like spurs, and slightly more evidence of wealth, with coins a little more profligately lost, than at other sites. There are also luxuries like gilt strips, from caskets of bone or wood, and evidence of leisure activities, such as gaming-pieces; chess was being introduced into western Europe, and appealed to the aristocracy because it was a complicated pastime that only the educated would have time to learn and indulge in. Furthermore, it could be played by both sexes, though ladies were expected to show their inferior skill and intelligence by losing to the men; it echoed feudal society and its courts; and it could be played for stakes. An occasional urban chess-piece find, not always well dated, shows that a few burgesses might seek to emulate the aristocracy. Other predominantly castle finds include small bone and copper-alloy pins with decorated heads that have been interpreted as hairpins, as at Castle Acre, attesting a female presence, but other personal ornaments are infrequent.[2]

Some pictures in manuscripts suggest that in the early twelfth century the highest ranks of the aristocracy were wearing brooches. These were probably conventional representations, however, as there are no valuable brooches or finger-rings in the archaeological record, as there had been earlier. The implication is that the Norman barons were secure enough in their estates to feel no need to wear things designed to emphasize their status and to impress those below them, nor to have easily portable wealth.[3] Facial appearance was still important, however, so that when Henry I (1100–35) and his barons cut off their long hair it was an overt rejection of decadence.[4] Manuscript illustrations of kings show them wearing costumes in resplendent reds, blues, and greens, elaborately embroidered and often apparently with coloured stones sewn on them.[5] They glowed like the stained-glass windows that were beginning to appear in churches.[6]

The Norman knights can be considered part of the aristocracy, though they often had interests different from the barons', as well as different spending powers. It is telling that when Henry I had a nightmare, one group whom he saw petitioning him against his taxation were the knights, whose ability to sustain themselves, their arms, their horses, and their grooms, let alone their families, was precarious (Fig. 6.1). Their initiation ceremonies helped to set them apart, and became more elaborate and therefore more expensive. Gilt spurs are first recorded as being part of their investiture in 1128, and became a symbol of rank for them, though one that was a little too accessible, as wealthy merchants might also sport them (Fig. 6.2).[7]

The aristocracy and their immediate families were buying commodities such as silk, glass, wine, and spices, either at the great fairs or from merchants based in London and a few other cities.[8] Their patronage did not benefit urban craftsmen and artisans, for whom the volume market shrank very markedly after the Conquest and remained depressed well into the twelfth century even in the largest towns, as the excavation record of metal and bone objects shows. Only a single disc-brooch seems to be known, a copper-alloy imitation of a coin of Henry I, found in London, where otherwise the metalwork amounts to little more than a few buckles, and none of those even has a decorated plate.[9] Much the same can be said of York or Exeter. In some cases in such towns, objects attributed to the tenth or eleventh centuries are found in twelfth-century and later contexts, so that it might be argued that they are not residual, but misdated. If that were the case, however, they would be found in the new towns like Lynn, Norfolk.[10]

The only exceptions are a few fairly simple buckle-frames cast with animal heads to hold the pin-bars, which have been found in Winchester and Norwich, for example. They are not usually closely datable, but may have been current by the beginning of the twelfth century.[11] Also from Winchester is a clasp that might be from a belt and have been a personal ornament, or might be from a bookbinding strap and therefore have been for ecclesiastical use (Fig. 6.3); it is certainly comparable in quality to such church treasures as the magnificently complex Gloucester Abbey candlestick.[12] There are various Romanesque

Fig. 6.1. Illustration from a manuscript of c.1130–40 showing two scenes from Henry I's nightmare about protest against his taxation demands. In the lower register armed knights are threatening him; in the upper, peasants are more humbly presenting a petition. While the pictures are not realistic—kings did not sleep in their crowns—they present images that are no less interesting for being stereotypes. The wide-brimmed straw hat worn by the peasants' leader betokens a countryman as surely as does his sunburnt face and scythe—its two side-grips being features derived from knowledge or observation, like the metal 'shoe' on his companion's spade. The broad foreheads of the other two peasants suggest boorishness; the cloak of the man in the centre appears to be held by a small disc-brooch, more typical of the eleventh than of the twelfth century. (Photograph reproduced under licence from the Bridgeman Art Library by courtesy of Corpus Christi College, Oxford. Actual size.)

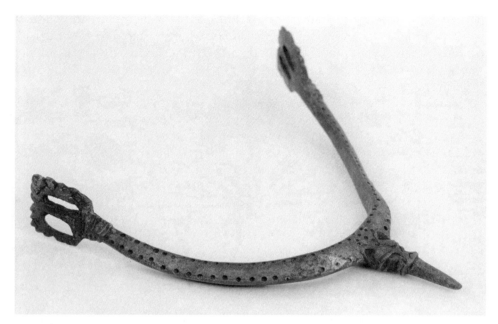

Fig. 6.2. A gilt copper-alloy twelfth-century prick-spur from Perth, with a finely modelled animal head holding the goad (the difference between a Romanesque head and an Anglo-Saxon one, e.g. Fig. 5.6, can be very minor, but slightly more realistic features such as ears and more rounded features provide pointers). It is recorded that a Fleming, Baldwin the lorimer (usually meaning spur-maker or more generally maker of metal harness-fittings), who worked for King David I, had a property in Perth. (Photograph reproduced by courtesy of Perth Museum & Art Gallery, Perth & Kinross Council, Scotland. Slightly reduced.)

cast copper-alloy pieces, including crouched dragons holding styli. Other dragons were parts of pins and needles, and these could have been for secular use.[13]

Very limited post-Conquest secular spending can also be argued from pottery. London continued to be a market supplied by different producers, most of them fairly local and making unglazed vessels for cooking or storing foods and liquids. Glazed wares still arrived from Stamford, but they were changing, from high-quality, evenly coated spouted pitchers to sparsely glazed jugs that were presumably cheaper because they used less lead. One Stamford potter nevertheless had the initiative to make vessels with moulded birds decorating the outsides, which were shipped round to London. Other large towns experienced the same market limitations: in Lincoln sparsely glazed jugs and pitchers were also used, to the general detriment of Stamford ware. York too saw a change, to splash-glazed and gritty wares, perhaps made by a larger number of potters than in the eleventh century, but working individually rather than in workshops, a change that suggests a market for cheaper but less accomplished vessels. In East Anglia, too, production of superior urban products petered out in the twelfth century. Thetford's potters suffered from the town's overall decline, but although hanging-lamps and ring-vases show some attempt to diversify, the dearth of jugs seems to indicate no ambition to meet competition from rural kilns like Grimston.[14]

One factor in the pottery market that can never be measured is the extent of competition from other materials, especially wood, with leather a possible alternative for costrels or jugs.[15] Organic deposits in Winchester led to survival of a selection of turned cups and bowls from late Saxon deposits, but lack of suitable twelfth-century preservation conditions precludes comparisons of quantities either there or in other towns, such as London and York. Competition could be reflected in a decrease in the number of pottery bowls and dishes found, for instance in Lincoln; as they are not usually covered in a layer of soot on the outside, bowls were probably used for drinking, or serving at meals, not for cooking, so wood was a viable alternative to clay. The proportional increase in jugs and pitchers is partly at least a factor of decline in some other ceramic products rather than a sign that the partially glazed vessels were being bought in greater quantities.[16]

If there had been enough demand in the early twelfth century, glazed pottery could have come from sources other than Stamford, principally from Andenne in modern Belgium. The quantity of pottery from France and the Rhineland in London may be just enough to suggest that some was brought in to sell in the market-place, and was not all merely dropped overboard by careless sailors. Even in ports like London or Southampton, however, the quantity of imported pottery is never more than 10 per cent, less than it had been in the eleventh century, and the unglazed imports are often sooted, so they were used for cooking, not reserved for serving and drinking from at meals.[17] Despite the increase in political traffic with Normandy that the Conquest produced, there was no immediate increase in the quantity of pottery imported from northern France rather than from the Low Countries. In the same way, Exeter is said to have had close ties with Brittany, but there is no sign of this contact in the imports of pottery.[18] Away from the ports, even in the relatively densely populated and wealthy East Anglia, imports were minimal.[19]

One possible exception is a curious small pot with a long, curved handle in a 'blue-grey' fabric thought to have been made in the Rhineland that is found sufficiently often in London and elsewhere to suggest that it was quite a well-known type; these ladles, if that is what they were, do not seem special enough to have been regarded as things that it was not appropriate to copy, yet none in clay are known.[20] There are one or two wooden ladles, however, and it may have been those that dissuaded the English potters from competing.

Further west, tripod pitchers rather than jugs were being made (Fig. 6.4). They are handmade, not wheel-thrown, and look lumpy because of their size, but their appearance is enhanced by sparse glaze and often by applied strips

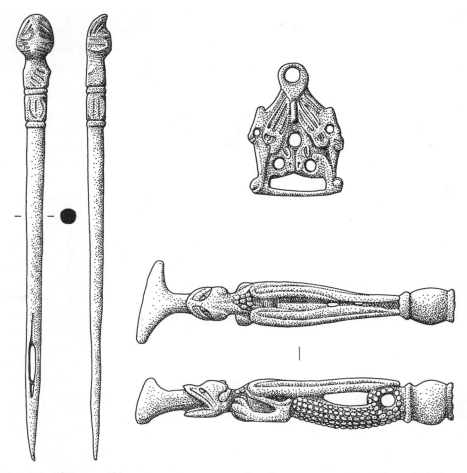

Fig. 6.3. Three twelfth-century cast copper-alloy Romanesque objects from Winchester, Hampshire. Top right: a hasp with two symmetrical birds, a loop for a strap at one end, and attachment-holes for rivets. Left: a long needle with animal-head terminal; the eye in the shaft indicates its function. Lower right: a broken-shafted stylus (cf. Fig. 3.9) with the eraser held in the mouth of a winged, scaly-bodied dragon curling its tail. (Drawn by Nick Griffiths from the collections of the Winchester City Museums. Actual sizes.)

of clay; many also have stout handles with an eye-catching coil of clay looking like a rope down the middle. Their three stubby feet imply that they were expected to stand on flat surfaces; because it was becoming acknowledged that to eat off the lap was a mark of peasantry, the tripod jugs may be showing a widespread change to the social aspiration of eating at a table.[21] Some of the

Fig. 6.4. Twelfth-century pottery tripod pitcher from Loughor Castle, West Glamorgan. Vessels of this type were favoured in the west rather than the east, and one possibility is that they were used for cider as much as for ale. This one was probably made in Gloucestershire or north-west Wiltshire, and has a thin lead glaze and wavy lines incised into it by a comblike tool. Not only is it very worn, but a hole in the side had been plugged with lead—someone may have deliberately cut the hole so that a bung could be inserted. Certainly it would have been very heavy when full and thus awkward to empty; wear patterns suggest that it was tipped forward on two of its feet when emptied from the top. (Photograph reproduced by courtesy of the National Museums and Galleries of Wales, Cardiff. Actual height 175 mm.)

western towns, like Worcester, received less of their pottery from far afield after the middle of the eleventh century, with cooking vessels made in the same places as the tripod pitchers cutting out the trade of anyone specializing in better-quality jugs.[22] The potters in these areas were often forest workers, but if their kilns were close enough to a large town they could dominate its market. Potters recorded in Domesday Book on the manor of Bladon, who probably operated first in the forest of Wychwood and then in that of Woodstock, sold their lumpy and coarse cooking vessels in Oxford to the exclusion of most competitors until the middle of the twelfth century.[23]

The higher spending power of members of the aristocracy is not usually going to show in their use of pottery, as excavated at their castles, because most of it would have been kitchenware and did not reflect an owner's status. The jugs found at Goltho, Lincolnshire, with coins of King Stephen (1135–54) were nearly all splash-glazed, coming either from Nottingham or Lincoln, but a broken ewer from the east Mediterranean may be the remains either of a curiosity brought back by a crusader or of an exotic bought at a fair from one of the Italian merchants who were beginning to trade in England.[24] The aristocracy formed only a tiny percentage of the overall population, however, whatever its spending power. Clerics, who formed another group in Henry I's nightmare, were slightly more in number, and the Church overall had enormous resources, but also enormous costs in building and maintaining its institutions, which necessitated some involvement in the market, stimulating trade and adding to urban activity.

Townspeople made up somewhere between 7 and 10 per cent of the total population in England, leaving the peasantry in an overwhelming majority; no wonder a group of rustics formed the third element in Henry I's nightmare (Fig. 6.1), the only time that any concern about the reaction of such people to their Norman lords was expressed; and even then the moral was that they should be kept at a distance, not that they should be listened to. One of them is shown wearing a cloak which seems to be held by a circular brooch or clasp, as is the king, though in other respects a very obvious distinction was made between the costume of the peasants and the other groups, to express their differences.[25] The actuality was that a peasant was even less likely than a townsperson to have a brooch. Few rural sites have clear evidence of specifically late eleventh- and early twelfth-century material; one recently excavated at Westbury, Buckinghamshire, is a valuable example, as the archaeologists used metal-detectors and located very small things, like an Edward the Confessor cut farthing and a Henry I cut halfpenny, that might have been found more often if the same technology had been used at other such sites. Nevertheless, a buckle was the only other metal object identifiable as 'Saxo-Norman' at Westbury, nor was there much pottery.[26] At such places paucity of finds may get attributed to low density of occupation, but in fact it may indicate the inhabitants' lack of buying power. A village like Westbury is particularly useful for this sort of analysis, as it does not seem to have had a manor-house nearby, from which 'elite' material might have been spread as rubbish or even as curios into the peasants' crofts.

The royal taxation about which the knights, churchmen, and peasants were protesting in Henry I's dream was one reason why economic depression restricted any surplus expenditure by those with incomes less than that of the barony. Another problem may have been a run of poor harvests and high disease rates, though chroniclers were prone to exaggerate such things.[27] Shortage of silver, already a factor in the Conqueror's time, would have been another. Despite that, the coinage was maintained at a reasonable level, and some of Henry I's coins seem to express the same wish to portray an image of kingship as his predecessors had shown. That the symbolic meaning of coinage as an instrument of power was understood was graphically demonstrated in Stephen's reign, as the breakdown in law and order led to some of the barons making their challenge to royal authority overt by issuing coins, albeit not very good ones.[28]

As would be expected, there is an increase in the number of known coin hoards from the mid twelfth-century civil war years, but there are several from Henry I's reign as well. Although some contained quite large numbers of coins, none has any gold or silver object, even a ring or brooch like the occasional ones in some of the Conquest-period hoards.[29] A few households may have kept a few old jewellery pieces, but if they had been in any numbers their owners would have hidden them with their money when they anticipated the need. The hoards seem to support the other evidence that in the century after the Norman Conquest most people could not acquire valuable objects, and that the few who could have afforded them were unconcerned about expressing social status through that form of display; for them, personal relations were defined by land, vassalage, and the extent of their 'honours'.[30]

Such distinctiveness as the material culture of modern Scotland displayed in the eleventh century largely disappeared during the twelfth. The use of ring-money and ingots in a northern bullion economy may have continued for a while, but the only coin-dated hoard is from the island of Bute at the mouth of the Clyde, well to the south of the other ring-money hoards and not necessarily part of the same economic system, although it contained a silver ingot and a plain penannular ring as well as mid-twelfth-century coins and some other things.[31]

The effect of English practice on notions of Scottish kingship were already apparent in the 1090s when Duncan II (1093–4) began to use seals, but more systematic efforts to create a nation-state were made by David I (1124–53). He brought in knights, founded towns, and established churches belonging to the new European orders. In 1136 he was able to take advantage of King Stephen of England's weakness and annexed swathes of northern England, including silver mines in Cumbria which allowed him to further his ambitions to be a European king by issuing his own coins. As images of kingship they are not very inspiring, but it was more important that they should look sufficiently like English pennies to be acceptable as currency. Partly because Cumbria had to be ceded back to England, Scottish coins were issued only fitfully after David's death until the 1170s, after which silver became more readily available in Europe generally.[32]

The burgesses in the new Scottish towns had consumption patterns very similar to those of their counterparts in England. In St Andrews, for instance, which had a large Fleming contingent involved in its commissioning and laying out in the mid-twelfth century, some Stamford-ware pottery of the kind known as Developed, some London pottery, some from north-east England, and some from the Low Countries was available, though increasingly the bulk of what was used was locally made. Towards the end of the twelfth century, or in the thirteenth, clay copies of metal aquamaniles, for washing the hands, were being used in St Andrews (cf. Fig. 6.9); similar vessels have been found at Scottish castles, so urban finds might show polite baronial behaviour being taken up by townsfolk, unless they were using them merely as pouring-jugs at table, despite being rather impractical for that function.[33]

Inland of St Andrews, Perth was already important as a royal centre when a town was grafted on to it. Telling evidence of its administrative role and of a citizen's need to conduct business formally is the matrix of a seal cut in c.1200 for William de Brun, perhaps significantly a citizen with a French-sounding name (Fig. 6.5). Some other finds, such as the well-made spur (Fig. 6.2), may reflect the town's aristocratic connections, as do some of its textile remains, which include tablet-woven braids with silver threads. A few things do not seem English in character, such as a pin with a semicircular head attributed to the thirteenth century and other pins with long shafts and grooving below the heads, but copper-alloy ring-brooches and moulds for making them are exactly like those found in England (Fig. 6.6), and the coins are a mixture of Scottish and English.[34] The pottery is similar in range to that from St

Fig. 6.5. The copper-alloy seal-matrix of William de Brun, excavated in Perth. The inscription starts at the top with the star, followed by 'S' for *sigillum* (cut with the letters retrograde, but the photograph here reversed so that the text can be read). The star device in the centre was commonly used and probably had no especial family or other significance for William. (Photograph reproduced by courtesy of Perth Museum & Art Gallery, Perth & Kinross Council, Scotland. Actual size.)

Fig. 6.6. Stone mould from Perth for casting the frames and pins of ring-brooches and other small rings. It was used with a 'partner'; one of the lead plugs that ensured a tight fit by matching a hole in the other half can be seen at the bottom. Broken off at the top is the in-gate into which liquid metal was poured to flow down the runners—when the metal had cooled and solidified the stones were separated, the rings and pins removed and filed smooth, and the surplus metal in the runners could be put back into the melting-pot for reuse. (Photograph reproduced by courtesy of Perth Museum & Art Gallery, Perth & Kinross Council, Scotland. Actual size.)

Andrews, as indeed it is even further north at Aberdeen, where Scarborough ware made up as much as 16 per cent of the overall total, including late twelfth- and thirteenth-century jugs moulded with figures of knights. Scottish local wares predominated, however, including some very locally made at Rattray, Aberdeenshire, but all in forms no different from those produced in England. Good organic preservation means that a range of textiles can be recognized, including silk.[35]

Only north of Aberdeen, in Caithness and on the islands, was locally made pottery distinctively different, mostly handmade, grass-marked, and coarse, though even Kirkwall was receiving southern wares in the thirteenth century.[36] The outer isles were not incorporated within Scotland until 1268, so traditional Norse links were maintained for longer. The remarkable walrus-ivory chess-piece sets found on Lewis were presumably goods in transit, however, not an indication that a feudalized local elite appreciated the game's social implications.[37]

One of King David's early coins was excavated at Whithorn, where other finds also show the site drawn away from the Hiberno-Norse sphere after its refoundation as a cathedral; metalworking was practised there, a draw-plate with residues of silver wire in its holes being the first definite evidence of that particular tool in Britain.[38] There is nothing from it as fine as the liturgical comb made of walrus ivory found at Jedburgh Abbey, one side of which has a knight fighting a dragon, the other a griffin attacking some other creature. This is a Romanesque piece of outstanding quality, comparable to any of the best twelfth-century work.[39] Another example is a cast copper-alloy swivelling strap-distributor with silver inlay, found at Rattray Castle, not in the borough (Fig. 6.7).[40]

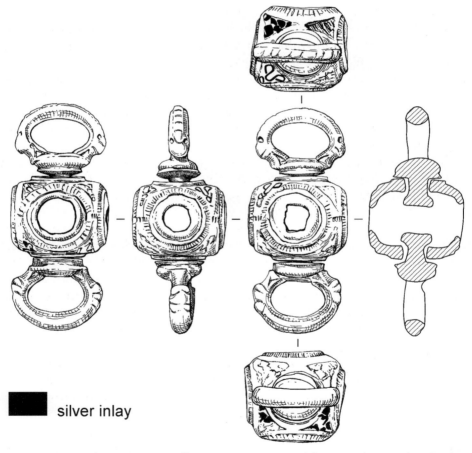

Fig. 6.7. A complex cast copper-alloy Romanesque swivel from Rattray Castle, Aberdeenshire. It is thought to have been used with a hound's leash. The loops at the top and bottom have animal-head terminals like those that appear on a few contemporary buckle-frames. (Drawing by Jan Dunbar reproduced by courtesy of Aberdeen City Council. Actual size.)

As well as mid-twelfth-century coins, the silver ingot, and the plain gold penannular ring, the Bute island hoard contained a plaited gold ring and three thin gold strips embossed with geometric ornament and six-armed crosses. One is about 430 mm long, but only 5 mm wide. The second is a little shorter, the third broken. All have a single perforation at the ends. The only objects like them also came from western Scotland, and are also from a hoard, this time found within the precinct of the nunnery church on Iona; one is a fragment decorated rather like one of the Bute strips, the other is complete though broken in two, and is embossed with a scroll pattern, but has the same single perforations at the ends (Fig. 6.8). They were found scrumpled up within a four-plait gold ring, with a length of gold wire and four silver spoons with Romanesque animal heads and other ornament, but unfortunately no coins. The gold strips and the silver spoons put this part of Scotland firmly into Romanesque Europe, despite the continued use of old-fashioned rings and ingots. The function of the strips is another matter; the holes at the ends could have been for threads rather than nails, and the gold is thin enough to be flexible, so they may have been tied round something. One possibility is that they are hairbands. Certainly, if they had been attached to something like a shrine they would have had more nail-holes, and even if they had been stiffeners for a veil they would have needed more attachment-points. On the other hand, if they were hair ornaments they would make that part of Scotland the leader of European fashion.[41]

Thirteenth-century Scottish coin-hoards are complimentary to the urban excavations in showing the penetration of European modes in the twelfth and thirteenth centuries. In one, found at Tom a'Bhuraich, Aberdeenshire, loosely dated to between 1210 and 1250, were included two rings, not twisted rods of the traditional type, but in the 'stirrup' shape by then familiar elsewhere in Europe (cf. Col. pl. F.5); both are said to have held blue sapphires in their settings.[42]

Whereas in Scotland internal changes moved towards a formally unified state, in Wales in the twelfth and thirteenth centuries the struggle was to avoid having one imposed from outside. Although Gruffydd ap Llywelyn (1039–63) had almost achieved unification, there was little subsequent prospect of a kingdom ruled by a Welshman that would encompass the whole area from Glamorgan to Gwynned. In the 1060s and later, however, Norman expansionism led to alien control of most of the south, and fleetingly of a northern coastal strip west of Rhuddlan.[43]

The Welsh princes were as likely to resist assimilation by stealth as by direct conquest, slowing changes in material culture. Welsh law-books were written with a view to resisting Anglo-Norman pressure and retaining Welsh tradition. Their ponderous and artificial statements about the products and privileges of the kings' smiths are more interesting for their language than for any sense

Fig. 6.8. Two objects from a twelfth-century hoard found on Iona.
Above: a gold strip embossed with a running scroll pattern. The holes at each end seem to have been its only method of attachment. (Photograph reproduced by courtesy of the Trustees of the National Museums of Scotland, Edinburgh. Reduced from actual length of 352 mm.)
Below: one of the four partly gilt silver spoons. A Romanesque animal head holds the bowl to the shaft, on which a rectangular plate has niello background to leaf patterns. The stem ends in a knop, unlike e.g. the earlier St Ninian's spoon, though the hooked object there has one (Fig. 3.4). (Photograph reproduced by courtesy of the Trustees of the National Museums of Scotland, Edinburgh. Actual size.)

that they dealt with reality. When they speak of costume, however, they show that it played an important role in princely society, denoting rank and providing a means of gift-giving, usually from superior to inferior, but occasionally to secure an alliance between equals. What the clothes were actually like is not revealed, nor what was meant by a gold ring.[44] Although Giraldus Cambrensis wrote slightingly about the absence of tables from Welsh princes' halls, an aquamanile from Nant Col, Gwynned, suggests a very different level of social behaviour, if it arrived soon after it was made in the thirteenth century (Fig. 6.9).[45]

Like Aethelberht's Kentish laws of *c.*600, the Welsh laws state values in terms of a currency which the Welsh were not producing, nor often handling. There are twelfth-century hoards and single finds in the Anglo-Norman areas, but very few of the latter are known in the Welsh areas, and the earliest hoard is one buried outside Wrexham, Clwyd, around 1245. It contained only pennies and halfpennies, showing a change from earlier periods when ingots or ring-money would have been included; although such things might still have been circulating as a form of currency in the twelfth century, they were presumably not doing so in the thirteenth.[46] Silver extraction is possible in north Wales, but it is the English King Richard I (1189–99) who is recorded as opening a mine at Carreghofa at the end of the twelfth century, which probably reduced even further the opportunities for a Welsh prince to build up a treasure hoard.[47] They knew coins as images rather than as currency, and cattle were more important to them than silver, the animals being literally synonymous with wealth.[48] Most princes have left no records of themselves except of their constant warfare, though some were issuing charters and using seals by the thirteenth century,[49] presumably indicating that they were now operating like their Anglo-Norman counterparts; kinship, however, remained the most powerful bond for the free Welsh.

It is only to be expected that the Anglo-Norman town and castle foundations would reflect the culture of their owners and burgesses, a process probably intensified after the 1169 invasion of Ireland opened up trade with Dublin.[50] As in Scotland, so in Wales potters making copies of English vessels soon followed the first settlers (Fig. 6.4). In south Wales the Severn drew some pottery from and through Bristol and Gloucester; Newport, Dyfed, is probably fairly typical despite being so far west, as a small assemblage there included vessels from Ham Green, a kiln-site just outside Bristol, from north Wiltshire, and from France, but with the great majority being locally made.[51] In central Wales excavations in New Radnor, Powys, have shown that there too most of the pottery was locally made, but with some variety provided by Herefordshire and, even that far inland, France.[52] If late twelfth- and thirteenth-century pot-making did take place outside the defences of these places, interaction with the hinterlands must have been happening, albeit on a limited scale.

Fig. 6.9. A large hoard of scrap metal found at Nant Col, Gwynned, included this copper-alloy aquamanile, probably made in Germany in the thirteenth century. It was a hand-washing vessel (*aqua* = water, *manus* = hand), this one in the form of a stag, its antlers broken off, with a hound leaping on its neck and forming the handle. It was found with other metalwork, some much later in date, and was probably part of a collection being gathered for recycling, but where it had come from is unknown. (Photograph reproduced by courtesy of the National Museums and Galleries of Wales, Cardiff. Actual height 260 mm.)

The Welsh peasantry, formally but not actually excluded from the new towns,[53] seem to have been slow to take up pot usage, which may be a mirror of their attitude generally to changes in their culture and custom. The only excavation of a Welsh rural site, at Cefn Graenog, Gwynned, between

Snowdonia and the Lleyn peninsula, revealed reasonably substantial farmstead buildings, but very few artefacts—a handful of straw-impressed coarse pottery sherds fired to a low temperature, some lead scraps, and some iron tools and other equipment.[54]

The two rings in the Tom a'Bhuraich hoard said to have held blue sapphires are symptomatic of a new European interest in gems. Bede had written about the twelve stones of Aaron's breastplate symbolized by Jerusalem's twelve gates, but those ideas derived from Jewish lore were now augmented by new awareness in western Europe of Greek and Egyptian tradition. Particularly influential was a Latin poem composed by Marbode, bishop of Rennes, who died in 1101; it was copied frequently in England and Normandy during the following century. The number of stones described increased to sixty, including some which would now be differently classified, such as coral. Most gems were thought of as marvels because they came from the far ends of the earth, such as emeralds from India and sapphires from Ceylon, or because they were natural but wonderful phenomena, such as toadstones, said to grow inside the toad's head and to be efficacious against poison, since the toad was believed to be venomous; surviving examples are now recognized as fossils.[55]

In the lapidaries, as the texts on the stones are called, the simple expedient of converting references to pagan gods, *dei*, into the singular *Deus* with a capital letter turned the stones into the creation of the Christian God. He had imbued them with various properties that made them active agents in human affairs. Sapphires, therefore, were particularly appropriate for the religious, because they helped to concentrate the mind upon thoughts of the heavenly kingdom, for blue is the colour of the sky; they also aided concentration, because the stones were taken to be cold, and so would cool ardour for human love; and they could ward off the sin of Envy; but their wider appeal included their ability to guard against various kinds of sickness, and even to help someone to escape from prison.[56] Because of the particular relevance to churchmen of sapphires, several gold rings set with them have been found in bishops' graves, though unfortunately the ascriptions of most of the rings to specific individuals may be wishful thinking.[57] A buried ring was probably not its owner's best; his consecration ring was supposed to be sent to the king after a bishop's death.

Most of the stones that percolated through to England were small, so stirrup-shaped settings were particularly suitable for holding them, as it was scarcely necessary to widen the hoop of a ring merely to bulk it up to give the stone more prominence (Col. pl. F.5). Some of the bishops' rings were of this type, so it was probably current by the second half of the twelfth century.[58] Larger stones either needed a separate collet, usually rectangular or square, soldered to the hoop (Col. pl. F.4), or they could be gripped in a claw setting (Col. pl. F.6). By the beginning of the thirteenth century a few rings had smaller stones set round a large one. Gems might be shaped and polished, but intricate cutting into facets was a later development. Some bezels were open-backed so that the stone touched the wearer's finger, as its property was enhanced by direct contact.[59] Ideas about the correct fingers on which to wear rings were developing, but were not consistently applied.[60]

Classical gemstones continued to be used to ornament shrines and other church fittings; Bishop Henry de Blois wanted to acquire Waltham Abbey's 'great carbuncle', not to wear it, but to enhance his prestige by presenting it to Winchester Cathedral.[61] Also highly valued were classical cameos, such as one owned by St Alban's Abbey, probably a three-colour sardonyx, its upper layers cut back to leave figures in relief against a contrasting background. A mid-thirteenth-century drawing shows its design to have been a Roman emperor supporting a small female figure symbolizing Rome. Somehow it had acquired the reputation of being an aid to women in childbirth, perhaps because 'Rome' was misinterpreted as a baby.[62] More common are engraved classical gems, not least because they could be used as seals by setting them into metal frames into which inscriptions were cut. Conventionally, these would be their owners' names, but came increasingly to be allusive messages in Latin or French. The earliest identifiable is a gold finger-ring holding a gem engraved with the god Mercury, with an inscription ascribing it to King Richard I (1189–99), which is also the first surviving piece of jewellery that can be linked to royalty since the ninth century.[63]

Six silver finger-rings were found in a hoard at Lark Hill, Worcester, with coins of the mid-1170s, the first hoard in England for a hundred years to have anything but coins in it (Fig. 6.10). One ring held an amethyst, one a crystal, and one a yellow glass or paste. With a foil set behind it crystal takes on a colour, though it was valued in its own right, not least for its ability to revive the properties of other stones when exhausted by their owners' wickedness.[64] Another ring was either an old one retained for its metal value, or one that represents an undercurrent of older fashions, as it is made of two tapering twisted rods, soldered together at the ends in the way that viking-period rings had been. More surprising are the other two rings, since they show that people were already wearing new modes. One is symbolic, showing two clasped hands in token of good faith, possibly a marriage-ring and a symbol of troth plighted, originally a Roman design and known as a *fede* ring. The other has niello-inlaid Maltese and saltire crosses.[65] Finger-rings begin to appear in other contexts at this time, but they are still very infrequent; a silver one from a twelfth-century Norwich context is so small that it has been identified as a child's.[66]

The seventh piece of jewellery in the Lark Hill hoard was a small ring-brooch made of two twisted wires like earlier finger-rings, but with a slot for the pin. It is the earliest dated example of a type that begins to appear on sculptures in the second half of the twelfth century, first shown worn on women's costume

Fig. 6.10. The six silver finger-rings from Lark Hill, Worcester, found with mid-1170s coins. The ring in the centre at the back was probably at least a hundred years old when buried (cf. Fig. 5.3), but the others are likely to be twelfth-century, the *fede* ring with two clasped hands, top right, being the earliest example known in Britain. The niello-inlaid panels of the ring at top left have some likeness to the Iona spoon (Fig. 6.8). The front three rings have square bezels holding, from the left, an amethyst, a crystal which glints because a foil had been placed behind it, and a yellow paste. (Photograph reproduced by courtesy of the British Museum, London. Actual sizes.)

at the throat.[67] Versions of its use of wires have been excavated in York and London in twelfth- and thirteenth-century contexts (Fig. 6.11).[68] Ring-brooches could also be created by Romanesque-style creatures, head-to-head and tail-to-tail, their curved bodies making the frame. One in cast copper alloy at Norwich is similar to one of two in silver found together at Benington, Hertfordshire.[69]

The most frequent type of ring-brooch is a flat band, popular because it could incorporate gemstones or inscriptions (e.g. Fig. 6.12). Some early ones also had filigree wire, like a gold example excavated in Waterford, Eire, which is set with four green and blue glass studs, presumably to be taken for emeralds and sapphires. It may be a hundred years or so earlier than its mid- to late thirteenth-century context.[70] Another in a context considerably later than its probable date of manufacture is in silver-gilt, with filigree but with silver pellets in lieu of stones. It was found within a late thirteenth-century pottery-kiln at Laverstock, Wiltshire, an extraordinarily unlikely place for such a loss, even though it is not far from a royal palace at Clarendon.[71]

The ring-brooch was not confined to the most wealthy and was not only worn by women; a thirteenth-century woodcarver is shown wearing one at the throat on a misericord in Wellingborough, Northamptonshire, and as a type it was already well enough known by the end of the twelfth century to to be copied in clay on the front of a sparsely glazed jug in York.[72] One reason for its popularity was that those who were abreast of twelfth-century intellectual development would know that its circular shape fitted the geometrical theory of beauty, undisrupted by angles, as well as being 'unbroken' as a testimony of faith, like a crown or a finger-ring.[73] Ring-brooches could therefore be unspoken testaments of undying love, sentiments enforced by appropriate inscriptions. The use of the French language and Lombard lettering for these texts made them unreadable even by those few people who had a smattering of English or Latin, so they were a means of restricting understanding to an even smaller group.[74] At one level such inscriptions were expressions of courtly love and devotion, from an admirer to someone who was flattered by the assumption that they would understand it. The sentiment was a secret between them, no one else knowing who the brooch had come from, and it might even be worn out of sight to keep the secret still more private. At another level they could be an expression of male concern over female purity and chastity. A ring-brooch that fastened a woman's robe below her neck prevented her bosom from being seen, so that her modesty was preserved for her husband's gaze; *Jeo sui fermail pur garder sein | ke nus villein n'I mette mein*, 'I am the brooch to guard the breast, that no knave may put his hand on it', on a gold thirteenth-century brooch from Writtle, Essex, is perhaps the most direct expression of such male possessiveness.[75]

Another way of using the brooches to express devotion was to add two projecting hands, a device perhaps adopted from the clasped hands of the *fede* rings. Clasped hands could also be taken as being lifted in prayer. They often held a stone, as though offering it to the object of devotion (Fig. 6.11). Many ring-brooches have religious formulae, such as Ihs Nazarenus, often abbreviated to IHS or IHC, an invocation using Jesus's name as protection against sudden death that was current by the end of the twelfth century. Justified by

Fig. 6.11. Gold ring-brooch excavated at the Bedern, York, made by coiling twisted wires round a central core, a technique clearly seen where a gap for the pin was made by fusing the ends of the wires together. The silver ring-brooch in the Lark Hill hoard was probably quite similar to this except for the pin attachment method. (Photograph reproduced by courtesy of the York Archaeological Trust. Actual size.)

Fig. 6.12. Gold ring-brooch, thirteenth-/fourteenth-century, with a ruby in the collet, two Gothic leaf appliqués, and two hands clasping an opal. The text engraved in the frame is the Angelic Salutation 'AVE MARIA G[RATIA PLENA]'. (Photograph reproduced by courtesy of the British Museum, London. Twice actual size.)

Apocyphal texts though not by the Bible are the names of the Three Kings, efficacious against the falling sickness, probably epilepsy. Very frequent is AGLA, Latin-letter equivalents for the first letters of the Hebrew 'Thou art mighty for ever, O Lord', as protection against sickness or sudden death. Such Hebrew or pseudo-Hebrew inscriptions, taken from Gnostic lore, were permissible despite being Jewish, because the earliest 'sacred' language had been Hebrew and had been used with Latin and Greek on Christ's cross.[76] Other 'charm' words had no actual meaning, the very fact that they appeared to be words giving them authority. Jewellery could be used to express conventional piety, and it was partly for that reason that many items were bequeathed to a church, to hang on an altar or shrine. Brooches were less useful as settings for protective stones than rings, however, because they were not worn next to the skin unless dangled secretly under a robe.

Lapidaries are not the only written sources to show the increasing interest in jewellery. A technical treatise attributed to a monk, Theophilus, was written in Germany in the early twelfth century.[77] Later in the century an Englishman, Alexander Neckham, wrote about Paris goldsmiths and their craft.[78] Neckham shows great concern about display and costume, condemning court fops. He is also one of the first writers to show awareness of property more generally, supplying a list of what a well-supplied household should contain—pots and a mortar in the kitchen, dishes and candlesticks in the pantry, spoons, cups, and basins in the cellar.[79]

Information on jewellery also begins to come from royal expenditure records after the middle of the twelfth century. In 1158–9 Henry II (1156–89) bought a *zona*, presumably a belt, which at £16. 6s. 8d. was considerably more than just a leather strap, though how it was embellished is not described. Much was spent on gold for special occasions, such as £8. 6s. 0d. paid in 1161–2 to

William Cade, then London's greatest capitalist, for the king's daughter's crown and other unspecified regalia. Mostly the purchases were made in bulk, so exactly what an individual piece was worth, or what it looked like, is not stated, and the totals often include cloth, furs, and sables as well as rings, stones, and gold, on which £108. 13s. 8d. was spent in 1186–7. These sums are difficult to see in proportion to the king's annual income, but some idea of what they mean can be gained from comparison with expenditure on building and repairing castles, which in Henry II's reign averaged about £650 a year.[80] Gold rings were also received as part payments for sheriffs' and other accounts.[81] Whether any of Henry II's acquisitions were passed on as gifts is not recorded; it is known that he was himself a recipient, getting a gold ring with an emerald from the pope in 1159.[82] This was a gift between social equals, not implying any superiority in the donor.

One gold object that might have been a gift is a brooch found at Folkingham Castle, Lincolnshire, that can be dated to between 1156 and 1185 (Fig. 6.13); precision is possible from a combination of reasons: the brooch is a miniature kite-shaped shield imitating a design that passed out of use towards the end of the twelfth century; on it is a heraldic lion, an emblem used by a family of whose members one married a Folkingham heiress who died in 1185; and because its small size and delicacy suggests that it may have been intended for wear by a woman, it may have been a present to her from her husband.[83] Despite the appeal of the shield as a shape, and the popularity of heraldic designs which would seem likely to have made such brooches popular as tokens of support in the tournaments and 'hastiludes' that were such important opportunities for display, other examples are very few. Presumably ring-brooches fitted the ethos of 'courtly love' better, precisely because their

Fig. 6.13. The Folkingham brooch. Gold, engraved with a rampant lion, third quarter of the twelfth century. An early example of heraldry, its delicacy could mean that it was worn by a lady of the Folkingham family, at whose castle in Lincolnshire it was found. (British Museum photograph, reproduced by courtesy of the owner, Lady Thomas. Actual size.)

expressions of devotion could not be attributed to a specific person, breaching the code of honour that required secrecy.[84]

The lion on the Folkingham brooch was not a badge confined to a particular family, and its use on the brooch shows a transitional phase between such things as the dragons on shields and pennants that might generally represent a concept like the kingdom of Wessex, and the specific identification of an individual by a combination of devices and of colours. The knights in Henry I's nightmare have painted chevrons on their shields, a simple motif that could become specific to a family by use of different colours (Fig. 6.1).[85] Heraldry was taken up for ornamental horse-harness pendants (Fig. 6.17), which were beginning to appear in the twelfth century; an early example has two Romanesque rampant lions in relief, found at Old Sarum, Wiltshire, appropriately from within the castle there. Later ones were enamelled, and some can be linked to particular families if not to individuals, though the more complex designs were too difficult to achieve cheaply, and the simpler arms were probably carried indiscriminately.[86]

Allied to the development of heraldry was increased use of personal seals, from the occasional late Saxon examples, through one found in York cut for Snorri the tax-gatherer, showing him with an appropriately large purse, to those that used coats of arms as identifiers. Others used animals as devices, some probably a play on personal names, some, like a squirrel with the text 'I crack nuts', probably sexual allusions. They came to be used far down the social ladder, even thirteenth-century peasants as well as urban citizens having them. This participation in legal affairs is an indication of the way that traditional customs and modes of doing things were no longer sufficient; now, a visible, physical reminder of an agreement was needed to reassure those who could not read the text of the document.[87]

A coat of arms identified an individual, but the right to its possession identified that individual as a member of a particular social group, the barony and the knights. From the late twelfth century badges were also being worn to identify other groups: crusaders, for instance, took to wearing a red cross made of linen, cloth, or parchment sewn on their clothing. A natural progression was for pilgrims, as spiritual crusaders, to adopt a similar practice (Fig. 6.14). Small pottery containers known as *ampullae* had always been brought back from holy places filled with oil or water blessed at the shrine, and might sometimes have been worn suspended round the neck. Some of the tin and pewter ampullae that appeared in the twelfth century were worn in this way, or were sewn on a hood or cloak to show which shrines a pilgrim had visited. Those who went to Compostela in Spain were expected to return with a scallop-shell, St James's device; during the twelfth century lead-alloy imitations started to become acceptable as substitutes for real shells. Other churches followed suit, authorizing pewter badges imbued with the healing qualities attributed to their saint's shrine by being pressed against it. In England the new cult of Thomas

Becket meant that Canterbury already by the end of the twelfth century had mould-makers whose output was sold to visitors. During the thirteenth, both shrines and badges proliferated.[88]

As people became more used to seeing pilgrim badges, so they were more likely to take to wearing badges that identified themselves with a group, such as a guild. Among the earliest were royal emblems, such as the broom-cod, the plant's French name, *plante à genet*, being a wordplay on the dynasty's Plantagenet name. Familiarity eventually bred contempt, so that some badges were worn to mock others' pretensions, with erotic and obscene images— though someone would have had to look closely to recognize such 'subversions'. Londoners are still known as cockneys because of the derisive badge of a cock laying an egg, implying townspeople's ignorance of the natural world.[89] What anything like this cost to buy seems not to be recorded, but it was presumably trivial. One group of cheap objects that may be lead-alloy badges are usually called 'spangles'. They are small thin discs with designs like those on contemporary tokens, but are only one-sided and each has an extension with two attachment holes, either so that they could be sewn on to something or so they could have a cord passed through them (Fig. 6.15). They came into use in the late twelfth century in London, and have been found in various towns, including Perth, so they are very widespread, but their apparent absence from inland towns like Winchester which have large twelfth- and thirteenth-century assemblages makes their costume use questionable. They could perhaps have been used on tags to attach to bales of cloth or sacks of wool to show ownership, or that a toll or customs payment had been made.[90]

Fig. 6.14. Pilgrims' badges became increasingly common in the thirteenth century. Some were ampullae, like that shown top left, for containing holy oil or water. The scallop-shell was associated with the shrine of St James at Compostela, but became a token of pilgrimage generally. The crowned W on this example shows that it probably came from Walsingham, where Mary, the Queen of Heaven, had a much-visited shrine. Even more popular in England was Canterbury Cathedral's Archbishop Thomas Becket, usually symbolized as his mitred head, but also often shown at the moment of his murder, or sometimes, as here top right, in the ship that brought him back to England; in the forecastle is a knight acting as lookout. The rear deck with its stern rudder, and the lines of the planks, show that the vessel is a cog, the workaday haulier of the high Middle Ages. Another Canterbury emblem was a bell, bottom left; whereas badges were usually made of a pewter alloy with a high lead content, the bells were predominantly tin so that they could be rung, adding to the cacophony at shrines that was often remarked upon. Bottom right is a crucifixion from Bromholm, Norfolk, where a miracle-working relic of the True Cross was kept. In the centre is an abbess, probably St Etheldreda of Ely, where a fair held on 'St Audreys' Day' has given us the word 'tawdry' because of the dubious quality of some of the goods sold there. (Drawings by Nick Griffiths from the collections of the Museum of London and of the Salisbury and South Wiltshire Museum. Actual sizes.)

Fig. 6.15. Late twelfth-/thirteenth-century pewter spangle from Perth, with a crude relief creature and two attachment holes at the top. Despite its fishlike head, the creature is probably a dragon, with two legs ending in claws and a tail borrowed from a rampant lion. (Photograph reproduced by courtesy of the Perth Museum & Art Gallery, Perth & Kinross Council, Scotland. Twice actual size.)

Badges could be forced upon groups outside the social norm, to identify those liminals with whom Christians should have few if any dealings: lepers, whose sickness was a mark of sin; prostitutes, who tempted men to sin; and Jews, who had been blind to Jesus and God's promised salvation. Conditions for the last of those groups were made increasingly difficult throughout the thirteenth century, and from 1218 they were forced to sew a double rectangle, symbolic of Moses's tablets of stone, on their outdoor costume. Caricature drawings show Jews wearing these badges, though none survives because they were made of textile or parchment. The Jews had only been in England since the Conquest, and retained cultural practices in the twelfth century that would have helped to make people more aware of group identity generally; in particular, they wore a pointed hat, the *pileum cornutum*, a self-chosen identity marker that had been worn with pride in the twelfth century when there was little reason to fear discrimination. The *tabula* badge was material culture used against them.[91]

Some of the Jews were extremely rich, as were merchants like William Cade. The country was prosperous in the second half of the twelfth century, largely avoiding internal wars and overseas adventures until Richard I went on crusade; his ransom for £100,000 was a serious drain, but was paid—in silver pennies. The logistics of getting more than 2 million coins to London was a major transport feat. That so many were actually available, or could hastily be minted, is an indication of the amount of silver that was again coming into the country, after the discovery of new European mines in the 1160s. As this could be exported to the Arab world as well as supply Europe, a return flow of gold from the Near East and the south Mediterranean made the materials for making jewellery more available.[92] The Lark Hill hoard shows one of the direct consequences.

The Lark Hill hoard is still the only one known that was deposited in the twelfth century and had jewellery in it, though it has now been joined by a few which from their coins date to the early thirteenth: at Fillongley,

Warwickshire, a silver finger-ring and two silver brooches, including a ring-brooch; at Brackley, Northamptonshire, a silver finger-ring with two rudimentary animal heads holding a rectangular bezel with a crystal; and near Stratford-upon-Avon, Warwickshire, a stirrup-shaped gold ring holding a sapphire and a silver seal holding a Roman intaglio gem. The last has an inscription cut into the setting which identifies it as 'Christ, Head of All', although the figure on the gem is actually Apollo. It was inappropriate for a gem like that not to be in a gold setting, though as it was found with over a thousand coins as well as the ring, its owner was no pauper—but had perhaps become too deeply involved in the baronial problems of King John (1199–1216) and their aftermath.[93]

From the beginning of the thirteenth century come the first reports of cases heard by the king's justices in the royal lawcourts. Stolen property is often itemized, and although some values may have been exaggerated in the hope of restitution, they cannot have been totally incredible or they would have discredited the claim. They show people owning quite costly articles: Elias Marshall asserted in 1200 that he had been robbed of a gold ring worth 5s. But most things were given much lower values: in an affray at Newcastle, while one man lost a gold ring worth 2s., another lost one worth only 6d. (cf. Col. pls. F.4–6).[94] Thefts on the way to and from market were quite common, one loss being £10 in coin, five rings worth 1s. 6d., and a belt worth 1s. Richard de Lancell had the rings taken off his fingers, and his wife's clothes and their silver spoons stolen, as well as other rings and clasps. Someone who laid a claim for a lost clasp worth 2s. may have lost a lot more by drawing attention to himself, as in a subsequent case the abbot of Waltham declared the man to be one of the abbey's runaway villeins—which would have meant that the abbey could confiscate his property for disobedience and failure to do the service he owed it. That such a person could own a valuable object was obviously not beyond the court's belief, any more than that another had been fool enough to go out working in the fields while having a gold cross and three gold rings on him. General belief in the efficacy of stones is shown by a boy who wore a gold ring round his neck because he had bad eyes, and by a woman who had been loaned sapphires to cure her sickness.[95]

Because there are no comparable records for the twelfth century, the court proceedings of the early thirteenth cannot show whether jewellery was more commonly carried and worn than it had been previously, but the Lark Hill hoard suggests that it was already becoming more widely available by the 1170s. In Southampton a gold finger-ring faceted to catch the light and set with three oval garnets came from a late twelfth-century rubbish-pit, where it is likely to have been lost by a merchant, and either an import that he intended to trade or an object that he wore himself (Fig. 6.16). Another gold ring, set with a single garnet, was lost at Llantrithyd, Glamorgan, presumably some time before the early thirteenth-century abandonment of the castle in which it

Fig. 6.16. Left: gold finger-ring from a late twelfth-century rubbish-pit excavated in Southampton, Hampshire, one of the earliest to be found in a secular context that is set with stones, three polished cabochon garnets in this case. The hoop was cut so that the facets created would catch the light. (Photograph reproduced by courtesy of Southampton City Museums. Actual size.)
Right: gold finger-ring with a hoop cut into ridges with a file, holding a slightly damaged oval garnet in a cabochon bezel. It was excavated in the Norman ringwork castle at Llantrithyd, South Glamorgan, a site abandoned early in the thirteenth century. (Photograph reproduced by courtesy of the National Museums and Galleries of Wales, Cardiff. Actual size.)

was found (Fig. 6.16).[96] There are never very many such things from excavations, partly because in elite buildings paved or wooden floors made recovery of lost objects easy, and metalled roads and yard surfaces in towns made the sharp-eyed more likely to see and pick up anything dropped by a passer-by. In all the great assemblage of twelfth- to fifteenth-century objects now published from London, there are only five gold finger-rings and two silver ring-brooches; Winchester had three gold rings and one partially silver ring-brooch; York two gold rings (Fig. 7.1), one gold brooch, and two of silver. Someone in Canterbury mislaid a simple gold ring set with a sapphire, which turned up in a quarry-pit in a backland area. Someone in Carlisle suffered a similar loss. Rings are also being increasingly found in the countryside by metal-detectorists (Col. pls. F.4–6).[97]

The tally of precious-metal objects excavated may be low, but people were much more profligate with their base-metal things. Against London's five gold rings can be set seventeen in lead alloys and fifteen in copper alloys; against its silver annular brooch, fifteen and twenty. Londoners made more use of pewter for everyday things than townspeople elsewhere; in Winchester nine rings were in copper alloy but only three in lead, and twenty annular brooches were copper-alloy, only three pewter; in York there was one lead-alloy ring and six in copper alloy, four lead-alloy annular brooches, and five in copper alloy. This difference may only reflect the London merchants' dominance of the tin trade, at least after the late thirteenth century, and the production in the city of pewter vessels, rather than any significant difference in taste. The rings and brooches can be found throughout Britain, just as stone moulds are found from Exeter to Perth (Fig. 6.6). Even rural sites produce them.[98]

As well as rings and brooches, many other small decorative dress items began to reappear. A few buckle-plates cast with figures in relief are dated to the later twelfth century by their style. If those designs were to have any meaning for their wearers, they either had to have some familiarity with Christian iconography, or to be able to recognize the way that a seated king was an image derived from the royal great seal.[99] This suggests that they had a restricted market, unlike some thirteenth-century thin sheet-metal buckle-plates with embossed decoration, which were cheaper to make and are more numerous. One favourite pattern was a striding lion, looking back over its shoulder or facing the spectator, another a hunting dog, both presumably taken from heraldry but not showing any particular family allegiance. Such things cannot be attributed either to a particular craftsman or to a particular production centre; there is a die from London, but another is said to have come from rural Horndon-on-the-Hill, Essex.[100] These buckle-plates seem to be following elite fashions in cheaper forms. In the same way, many base-metal finger-rings and annular brooches had glass studs or pastes set in them in imitation of proper gems, just as many were gilded to make them look at first glance like gold. AGLA and other inscriptions appear on base-metal objects as well as on gold and silver, though the letters are even more prone to misrendering.

As with badges, so with other base-metal objects there are no records of what was paid for them, but if a gold cross could be valued at only 6*d.*, it cannot have been much. Nevertheless, despite generally low incomes, a market existed; little direct information survives, but in Lincolnshire in 1225 there were a few peasants with a few pennies in their purses as well as some animals in their fields.[101] This is borne out by increasing finds of coins; at Westbury the two pre-1150 fractions are joined by five halfpennies and farthings for the subsequent thirty years.[102] Absolute quantities cannot be reckoned, but in Winchester the total number of non-ceramic finds rose from about 500 in the twelfth century to 800 in the thirteenth; on its domestic sites, however, the rise was much more dramatic, from about 200 to 600.[103] A facet of market development was probably the change in urban specialization for some crafts, especially those organized into guilds; instead of being a worker in a particular material, a master or artisan became a maker of a particular product, whatever it was made of.[104] Familiarity could, however, breed contempt; even though the moneyers continued to be named on the English coins, the designs were allowed to degenerate in the second half of the twelfth century, too widely used at all social levels to be noticed any longer as significant images of kingship.

The same wish for a little colour and display is shown by pottery. The sparsely glazed wares of the earlier twelfth century were generally replaced by jugs with a spread of glaze around most of the body, clays of different colours were used to produce different finishes, and applied decoration became more common. A few, particularly in London where French pottery from Rouen was both used and imitated, were positively gaudy. Again, what had to be paid for such jugs individually in the market-place is not known, but a few royal expenditure records give some idea; in 1270 it cost 25s. for 1,000 pitchers to be delivered to Winchester Castle from the potteries at Laverstock, a figure that included the twenty-mile carting cost, probably at least 25 per cent of the total. Presumably those vessels did not reach the king's high table, where metal would have been expected, but they may have been satisfactory for the lower end of the hall. Wine deposits are said to have been identified in one or two pottery jugs, so perhaps a few were used by servants pouring deferentially on bended knee in front of their lords. As well as glazed jugs there are a few pottery aquamaniles like those in Scotland, copying metal vessels (Fig. 6.9), but with the same uncertainty over whether they were used in the same way for washing the hands, a gesture towards polite behaviour in town houses as well as castles.[105]

Many pottery aquamaniles were made in Scarborough, which suggests that the place had become known for that particular product, just as other towns are recorded as having a name for other things. Scarborough competed more directly with rival kilns in making jugs decorated with face-masks or parades of knights. A few very elaborate jugs are known (Col. pl. G). Dancing figures and hunting scenes also appeared. Lettering is occasionally used on a few thirteenth-century jugs, one in Coventry being possessively inscribed MEAMQOD, an abbreviation for a Latin tag, 'What's mine is mine'. More surprisingly, someone had scratched something like 'Adam and Eve' on a large Norwich cooking-pot. Labour was cheap, so the time spent making more elaborate vessels was not a major factor, but lead for the glaze had to be bought somehow, and rent had to be paid, even out in the country; ten kilns in Bernwood Forest were charged 3d. each in 1255, and most manors would levy a payment for clay-digging. Then a market stall had to be rented, for perhaps as little as 4d., but still a cost that had to be passed on to the consumer.[106]

King John is the first English king known to have had a personal interest in gemstones and their properties; he received several from the pope in 1205, with a letter explaining their significance. Like some of his subjects, he is recorded as wearing stones round his neck, and he believed that he had been saved from eating a poisoned dish of pears because he had noticed one of his stones sweating to warn him.[107] Gold clasps, rings, and gilt belts were frequently bought for him, and by the later part of his reign were major items of expenditure; in 1211, £40 was paid for a 'balas ruby', another ruby, and an emerald, all in gold settings—it is not recorded whether those were to wear or to set into plate, of which the king was also very fond. In the same year, two gold clasps cost £13; three gold rings set with sapphires that cost £2. 15s. 0d. were sent as gifts to the king of Norway, his brother, and an archbishop; various repair bills were met; and two merchants were paid £226. 13s. 4d. for precious stones and rings.[108]

Gifts received from a pope or made to an archbishop or a fellow king were between social equals. Other gifts could emphasize the donor's social superiority; John is the first king known to have made regular distributions—of robes—to his household; his generosity was important symbolically, though the main reason for serving a king was to acquire grants of land and profitable rights such as wardship of heirs. John used material things in other symbolic ways, trying to boost his position by associating himself with the Arthurian legends and claiming to own Tristram's sword.[109] Wardship could work against the Crown, since John's successor Henry III (1216–72) was a minor and the royal stock of rings and stones was dispersed, used by his guardians in lieu of cash payments, as well as for gifts that included a ring with a 'large and good' ruby to the pope. Another was a 'gimmel' ring, with two stones.[110]

Henry III developed his father's love of jewels, and received various valuable ones from his subjects, sometimes as forfeits for their disloyalty, sometimes as gifts that were in effect bribes, and used his own as pledges for loans, as he did with his plate and crowns. When he could, and even when he could not, he bought lavishly, for himself, for his family, for envoys, and for churches, especially his favoured shrine of St Edward at Westminster, where it was later to become a custom for the coins distributed by the king on Good Friday to be turned into 'cramp rings', which he blessed, emphasizing his association with the Confessor, whose charity had notably included the gift of a ring to a beggar.[111] In 1241 Henry paid £99 to a Paris merchant for stones, including a 'gimmel' ring set with a ruby and two emeralds valued at £5, given to the count of Gysnes. Sometimes the sheer quantities that were bought leave more impression than the values—fifty-six gold brooches, but only worth £12. 12s. 0d., ten 'staves' holding 208 rings with rubies, and others holding emeralds, sapphires, topazes, and 'various stones'. His expenditure records do not seem to state it, but presumably these were for distribution to Henry's household members, as many were bought for feast-days, such as the £160 spent for Christmas 1247. Direct evidence comes from Matthew Paris, writing in 1251, who recorded what would seem to be an unfair complaint against the king that he was mean with such largesse.[112]

Kings were not the only heads of households who distributed robes. William Marshall, one of the great barons of the early thirteenth century, was one who gave them out to his knights, and in the 1240s Bishop Robert Grosseteste was recommending to a countess that she should supply liveries: he did not mean uniforms by this, but cloth of different colour and quality according to the status of the members of her household. So far as is known, only materials or clothing were handed out in these circumstances, not yet badges, though royal messengers had an 'R' embroidered on their collars, and horse-harness pendants were frequently armorial (Fig. 6.17). To wear a livery was not a mark of servility, but rather of someone who knew how to behave appropriately, with due courtesy and reverence to their lord—in fact, to be a *gentis homme*.[113]

The almost complete absence of jewellery from most of Britain at the beginning of the twelfth century had changed by the middle of the thirteenth to the point where it can be recognized as worn at all economic levels, except perhaps the very poorest.[114] Reasons for this change are partly due to supply—more silver in western Europe, more of it to exchange for gold and gems with the Muslim world. Demand is more difficult to understand. Writers like Marbode could stimulate interest, but a kernel of the wish to know had already to exist. Court poetry might help to create concepts of chivalry, but could only do so if elements of the court were prepared to listen. Even if the king, barons, prelates, and knights introduced new modes amongst themselves, the adoption of similar ideas at lower social levels would have been impossible had there been no interaction. Since the aristocracy's spoken language, French, was not understood by the majority of the population, why should the unspoken 'language' of behaviour patterns and semiotics have been different?

One part of the answer is that the lore of gemstones encouraged beliefs about magic; if wearing a gem could protect against sudden death (Col. pls. F.4–6), or a mystical incantation like the names of the Three Magi on a brooch could ward off the falling sickness, the owner had acquired a powerful supernatural defender. Furthermore, it was one that was a constant presence, and did not need a priest's intervention. A reason for the Church's promotion in the thirteenth century of the Eucharist as the supreme element was that it restored the centrality of the priest as intercessor between man and God, at the Mass. Another example is clerical blessing of the marriage-ring, making family alliances more than secular contracts. A similar motive underlay new insistence upon preaching in the vernacular, so that the only doctrines that people would hear expounded were their priest's. Some of those might be strange and eccentric if the priest had not had enough education, or had been too long in an isolated living, but in principle at least the teaching that was heard in Penzance

Fig. 6.17. Copper-alloy pendants made to dangle from horse harness became increasingly common from the second half of the twelfth century. Some are simply decorative, like the acanthus pattern at the top left, from Darenth, Kent, and the lion mask, middle centre, from Northampton. Many are heraldic, and the arms can often be identified, though when without enamel colouring may be unattributable: top centre, from Salisbury, the Trubleville family; top right, from Old Sarum, Wiltshire, the Mauduit family. Others express different affiliations: left centre, from Horning St Benet, Norfolk, the See of Norwich; bottom right, from Bury St Edmund's, the arms of the abbey there. Some seem devotional: right centre, from Winterbourne Dauntsey, Wiltshire, may be intended as the Crown of Thorns around the Cross; the more obvious Cross with its suspension loop still attached is from Swan Lane, London; more uncertain is bottom left, from Essex, which may be a pilgrim's scallop-shell badge. (Selected and drawn by Nick Griffiths from private collections and those of the Museum of London, the Salisbury and South Wiltshire Museum, Northampton Museum, and Bury St Edmund's Museum. All actual size.)

was the same as was heard in Perth, whatever language or dialect it came in. Sermons were therefore a means to control the spread of unorthodox ideas and practices, such as any tendency to worship rather than to revere gemstones. To some extent the success of this control over any idolatrous deviation is shown by the way that popular modes of behaviour followed the aristocratic, rather than creating a distinct mode through which to express differences, with churchmen as ready as the laity to believe in the efficacy of stones and other prophylactics.[115]

Another change was in attitudes to property and possessions generally, and in the way that they were valued. Royal taxation demands did more than give Henry I nightmares about his subjects' reactions to them; 'geld' on land was not yielding enough, and as early as 1166 a levy based on people's income and movable property was introduced. The exclusion of precious stones and clothes from the valuations of these levies shows that already these were considered differently, either as too personal or too special to tax, or as too mystical in the case of the stones. Another such levy was imposed in 1185, and then in 1188 came the much heavier demand to support a crusade. By then a knight's horses and arms were exempted, since the royal need was for their service to be effective. King John used the new tax twice, and it was renewed under his successor. After 1225 the levies became routine, though the proportions varied from a fifteenth part of the total of someone's taxable property to a fortieth, and later to a tenth and even a sixth.

A consequence of the new tax was that everyone had to be individually assessed. Only a few fragments of the early records that were made of people's property have survived, but in theory the procedure involved each householder taking an oath in front of the justices to declare what they owned. As honesty was unlikely to be absolute, assessors were appointed to work out what possessions each person had and thus what they owed. The list of exemptions grew, and the exclusion of what a family had in store for its own consumption means that the lists do not say what anyone actually owned, only what could be considered part of their surplus. Nevertheless, a new source of data on people's property was being created. Furthermore, everybody became inured to having their possessions regularly assessed by their neighbours. What a man or woman owed became a way of placing him or her in their local society. To be taxed was unpleasant, and under-representation was rife; but not to be taxed at all would have carried the stigma of poverty, and probably exclusion from those small signs of status such as being a village juror that gave a person a sense of substance.[116]

The new taxation also emphasized the household, rather than the land that someone owned or worked. This may not at first have had much effect on people's thinking, but was certainly one factor in the growth of the household's importance as an institution and social unit. At the aristocratic level this can be seen more clearly, partly because of such writers as Neckham and

Grosseteste. The barons who issued liveries were already creating a visible sign of their 'affinities' or relations of power, with the potential to challenge and subvert the new authority of the royal courts of justice.[117]

What a man or woman owned and wore therefore mattered, and was something to be observed and scrutinized. People's roles could be identified, so awareness of appearance was heightened. In parallel went greater awareness of the body generally, with John of Salisbury using it as a metaphor of society, at the bottom being the workers as the feet who supported the rest, but who also therefore were literally the lowest, closest to the ground, and most in contact with its polluting dirt and the animals who lived on it.[118] Costume and display became, in such thinking, a means for the better-off to dissociate themselves from the poor, who were in both senses the base.

7

Material Culture and Social Display[1]
From the Mid-Thirteenth Century to the Beginning of the Fifteenth

The trend towards increasing secular interest in jewellery was probably maintained throughout the thirteenth century, though precise dating of individual pieces remains difficult. With only small amounts of gold to be found in the south of France and Hungary, western Europeans continued to depend upon both gold and gems coming by overland routes from or through the Arab world, with Italian merchants acting as intermediaries. In 1257 Henry III was able to attempt to imitate continental kings by issuing gold coins, not to facilitate trade but to attract gold into the mint to back up his loans and pledges, and to use as alms. The care that went into the coins' design shows that they were thought of as having prestige value, and the decision to represent the king carrying the orb and sceptre was most probably made in homage to one of the issues of his revered predecessor Edward the Confessor; the royal seal was also changed, to a design that adapted Edward's image of an enthroned king ruling as a judge like Solomon rather than as a military leader with a sword. Henry's gold coins were only produced in small numbers and for a very short time, but they show that the importance of the symbolism of a currency was still understood, though no more effort was made with the designs of everyday silver coins than in previous reigns.[2]

The amount of coinage in circulation is shown both by single finds and hoards, not only in England but in Wales and Scotland as well. Excavation of the church at Capel Maelog, Powys, produced coins of Henry III, Edward I (1272–1307), and Richard II (1377–99), suggesting that the use of English money had spread into Welsh culture. The Welsh kings did not mint their own coins, however, unlike the kings of Scotland, whose coins were allowed to circulate in England just as English ones did north of the border. Presumably exclusion of a rival's image was no longer a matter of pride.

No hoard in Britain hidden during the middle part of the thirteenth century has objects in it to help to establish a chronology for jewellery. One from

Coventry, deposited in c.1298, included two silver ring-brooches, both with quite wide diameters but very narrow, rod-like frames, one of which had intermittent stamps and niello inlay, the other being divided into alternately plain and cabled segments (Fig. 7.1). Stamps and niello were also used on a gold brooch from Perth and a ring from York (Fig. 7.1), the latter from a mid-thirteenth-century context; the technique may have been used for only fifty or so years, but the three examples are so widely separated that a single workshop is unlikely to have been responsible. A coin-dated hoard probably of the 1330s from Dumfries included a whole rod-framed brooch and segments of two others, so they were quite common, probably because they did not contain much metal and did not take long to make. Coventry was a manufacturing centre, where moulds for casting various different kinds of ring-brooch in both silver and copper alloy have been found. A remarkable stack of the rod-like type in copper alloy was found recently in a small pit in Hambleden,

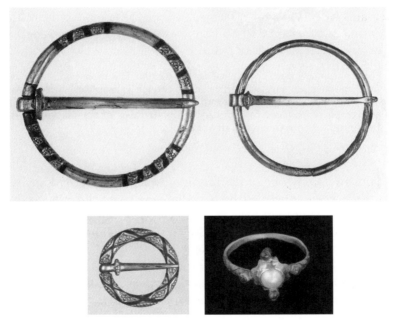

Fig. 7.1. Top: two silver ring-brooches from Coventry found with coins of c.1298. The larger one has niello-inlaid grooves and ring stamps on the frame. (Photograph reproduced by courtesy of the British Museum, London. Actual size.)
Lower left: gold ring-brooch from Perth, using a very similar technique. (Photograph reproduced by courtesy of the Perth Museum & Art Gallery, Perth & Kinross Council, Scotland. Actual size.)
Lower right: gold finger-ring from Coppergate, York, also with niello and ring-stamps. The central setting holds a large pearl, particularly well preserved, surrounded by four small garnets. (Photograph reproduced by courtesy of the York Archaeological Trust. Actual size.)

Fig. 7.2. The Canonbie hoard, coin-dated to the 1290s. The three rodlike brooch-frames have various appliqués, cf. Fig. 6.12. The other brooch is inscribed 'IHESUS NAZARENUS REX'. One of the two gold rings is an example of a stone held in a claw setting. The beads are jet. (Photograph reproduced by courtesy of the Trustees of the National Museums of Scotland, Edinburgh. Approximately half actual size.)

Buckinghamshire. Only one of the fifty-nine seems to have had any wear, and they may have been concealed by a pedlar—as some did not yet have pins fitted, their owner may have been their maker, who waited until he had a customer before he completed them. If he was travelling with his moulds, however, he did not hide those at the same time.[3]

Another Scottish hoard, deposited at Canonbie, Dumfriesshire, at the beginning of the 1290s, had one complete rod-like silver ring-brooch to which were applied knops and rosettes, and segments of two others (Fig. 7.2). A hoard at Langhope, Roxburghshire, with coins that show that it was hidden at least thirty years later than the Canonbie hoard, also contained rod-like ring-brooches and segments with applied decoration, so that for a time it was thought that that type was specifically Scottish, a view reinforced when one was excavated in Perth. Excavation of one in Hereford in the 1970s, however, showed that ring-brooches with applied decoration were not confined to Scotland, and subsequently one has been reported from Boxley, Kent. As with the Coventry type, so too there were base-metal copies, like ones found in

Fig. 7.3. Small silver-gilt quatrefoil-framed brooch, with feline head appliqués, from Rattray Castle, Aberdeenshire. A parallel for this brooch has not been found, and like the Perth brooch (Fig. 7.1) and mirror (Fig. 7.5) shows that rich people in thirteenth- and fourteenth-century Scotland could obtain high-quality objects in the mainstream of European culture. (Photograph reproduced by courtesy of Aberdeen City Council. Twice actual size.)

Hereford, Norwich, and Leicester, in Aberdeen, and in Rattray, the Aberdeenshire burgh; excavation at the castle there produced a silver-gilt brooch with a quatrefoil rather than a circular frame, little feline heads in relief disguising the joins (Fig. 7.3).[4] Material culture was no longer restricted in any way by political frontiers, only by wealth and affordability, though the hoards hidden in southern Scotland and northern England reflect the frontier problems brought on by the campaigns initiated at the end of the thirteenth century by Edward I.

Also in the Canonbie hoard were fifteen jet beads, all oval except for two that are slightly larger and faceted. They are almost certainly the earliest identifiable British examples of 'paternoster' (or rosary) beads, which were usually strung in three sets of fifty, with a larger bead, the 'gaud', every tenth; the three sets stood for the psalms, and each bead was to be counted off by the pious as they repeated the *Pater Noster* and *Ave Maria* prayers. The sombre black of jet might have made it seem particularly suitable for devotional purposes, but the lapidary texts stressed its bright shine as much as its colour, and it was only one of many materials used for the beads. A London jeweller in 1381 stocked them in amber, coral, glass, jet, bone, wood, and precious metal, and beads of all those materials except the last two, but also in crystal, tin, and pearl, have been excavated in the city. As the fourteenth century was a time when necklaces were not much worn, all these beads would have been rosaries. Amber and bone beads were certainly being made in London, and two unfinished beads in York suggest that jet was worked there in the thirteenth and fourteenth centuries, though only on a small scale, despite its proximity to the source at Whitby. Whitby jet cannot easily be distinguished from other similar geological strata such as lignite, or from Spanish jet, which is found near Compostela and was used in quantity at that shrine, not only for making beads but for scallop-shell badges and probably small crucifix pendants like one found in Winchester.[5]

Compostela was a hard journey, taking over four days in a boat from Plymouth, or fifty by the overland route through Calais, so scallop-shell badges were hard-won. A 'palmer' could be hired to undertake the journey on someone else's behalf, however. Canterbury and Walsingham were the main shrines in England, and the number of ampullae and badges from them shows their popularity (Fig. 6.14), but smaller local cults also developed, some with more dubious sanctity and with messages less obviously likely to be promoted formally. At North Marston, Buckinghamshire, was a shrine to John Schorn, an exorcist who had conjured the devil into a boot (Fig. 7.4); a stone mould for making the cult's badges was found in a nearby village. At least Schorn had been a priest; Thomas of Lancaster, executed by Edward II (1307–27) in

Fig. 7.4. Pilgrims were not the only ones to wear badges in the fourteenth and fifteenth centuries. Some people wore insignia of great households, like the ostrich plumes, top left, of the Prince of Wales, introduced by the 'Black Prince' and usually with his Flemish motto ICH DIEN, 'I serve', but here with his name 'Edward'. Another that may be a livery badge is the padlock, bottom right, associated with the Lovel family, a variant of the commoner 'fetirlock' which might be amatory as well as being a Yorkist device. To its left is a badge from the surprisingly popular cult that developed in the fourteenth century from the feat of John Schorn, vicar of North Marston, Buckinghamshire; he is shown in his pulpit, with the Devil whispering temptations in his ear prior to being 'conjured' by Schorn into a boot, shown on the left. The other two badges seem to be secular: the female figure is holding an overflowing jug and a garland of flowers, the latter the insignia of Mayday milkmaids, perhaps in reference to the flower-sprinkled meadows on which cows grazed. The other is a currycomb, with 'Favel' on it; Favel was a horse associated with deceit, so to groom it was to be a false flatterer. That badge was probably worn ironically, not necessarily on a hat or hood, as by this time badges were being sewn to clothing and belts as well. (Drawn by Nick Griffiths from the collections of the Museum of London and of the Salisbury and South Wiltshire Museum. Actual sizes.)

1322, was not someone to put on a par with the martyrs, but his cult was promoted for political reasons by Edward III (1327–77). Shrines like these suggest a level of popular culture uninformed by educated Church teaching, but the latter also shows a surprising lack of resistance to royal doctrine.[6]

Also an undoctrinal practice, or at least not known to have been formally acknowledged by the Church, is the use made of tokens as a physical metaphor for the pilgrim's spiritual journey. A coin would be bent when the vow to undertake a pilgrimage was made, as an 'earnest of intent' to be given to the shrine as a sign of the completion of the task. Bent pewter tokens found in some number in London could represent a superstition in that city to wish for good luck before any sort of journey, an unrecorded derivation from the pilgrims' 'earnests'. The badge or ampulla brought back from a shrine had magical properties because of its association with the saint revered at it, and could be used for healing, as could a bent coin in emergency. Badges might be buried to deter weeds after ploughing, or be fixed to stockyard gates to protect cattle. Some, being of an appropriate alloy, were melted down and incorporated into new church bells that rang officially to mark the hours and summon people to church, informally to frighten away demons. Occasionally badges are found in graves, and many are found in streams and rivers, perhaps deliberately thrown in just as weapons had once been.[7]

Small mirrors could be bought at some particularly popular churches where the crowds of pilgrims prevented everyone from touching the shrine itself; the mirror was held up to catch the sacred feature's reflection, so that its 'radiated grace' passed into and sanctified the physical object, which could then be shone on a piece of bread to turn it into a cure, a simile for the Eucharist. Small circular copper-alloy and pewter boxes with a piece of glass inside may have been produced for this purpose, but the large number now recognized, and the record of bulk imports, could imply use as forerunners of modern vanity mirrors. Larger ones were certainly used in that way, and are shown in manuscripts like the early fourteenth-century Luttrell Psalter, and the finely carved ivory backs of some survive. A rare variation had an openwork disc fixed to the back of the glass, like one found in Perth (Fig. 7.5). A mirror could both flatter and deceive; towards the end of the fourteenth century the poet William Langland had Piers Plowman looking into Fortune's mirror and seeing Lust and her delights, but being warned off by Old Age. Geoffrey Chaucer's almost contemporary *Canterbury Tales* include one in which a mirror could show who was false and who was true—but the story was told by the Squire, who was himself a vain character and not to be trusted. A broken mirror stood for shattered illusions—but a mirror could also be an aid to self-contemplation by providing a window into the soul, though that search might too easily prove to be a devil's snare leading to self-delusion. More obvious moral problems were that mirrors encouraged Pride, and because people—especially women, in medieval thinking—wanted to look

Fig. 7.5. Openwork pewter 'valve' from a mirror-case, found in Perth. It would have been glued to the foil on the back of the mirror's glass, and hinged to another valve that acted as the lid. The scene is from the Arthurian romance story of Tristram and Iseult, identified by labels in the horizontal bands, though the names are misrendered by a craftworker who did not know that an upside-down 'M' looks like a 'W'. On the right, the mounted knight in early to mid-thirteenth-century armour is Tristram, a name sufficiently similar to the much older Pictish Drystan to suggest that the legend had particular connotations in medieval Scotland, where it was adopted by various aristocratic families. Nevertheless, the mirror may have been owned by a prosperous Perth citizen rather than by a visiting lord or lady. (Photograph reproduced by courtesy of Perth Museum & Art Gallery, Perth & Kinross Council, Scotland. Actual size.)

their best, they would not spoil their looks by working, thus succumbing to Sloth.[8]

Jewellery itself could be an illusion, if it was not what it seemed on the surface. Gilt copper-alloy can be mistaken for gold, and tin for silver. Goldsmiths' regulations of the fourteenth century complained of counterfeits being sold to mercers, and some glass pastes and beads were probably passed off as gems by smooth-talking pedlars. The medieval sense of what was proper did not merely proscribe cheating, but made it inappropriate and thus illegal to put a noble gemstone into an ignoble setting of base metal. Regulations seem generally to have been obeyed, as no gold brooch has yet been found in Britain that contains a false gem. The same cannot quite be said of rings, Winchester for instance having a gold one identified as set with blue glass rather than sapphire. The difference between red glass and garnet is especially difficult to tell, but so far no significant examples of malpractice have been found, probably because good ruby-coloured glass was rarer than garnet, so that the placing of a tiny chip of the latter in a copper-alloy ring in Lynn was only a very technical infringement. An unfinished copper-alloy ring-brooch with at least one emerald was found in London, however. There were various ways in which gold leaf or some other foil could be put behind a stone or glass to enhance it (Fig. 6.10), or a lead lining added to give extra weight. These techniques were only supposed to be used to make 'doublettas' for the royal family, sewn on their robes to look at a distance as though they were encrusted with gems when they appeared in front of their subjects—both in life and when being carried to their funerals. Doubtless cheating was practised despite prohibitions, though examples have not been found. Copper-alloy can be given various

A.1. Segment of silver-gilt quoit-brooch from Sarre, Kent; probably early to mid-fifth century. The two outer rings have panels of crouching animals looking back over their shoulders, in 'late classical' style. The two little birds riveted to it would not have stayed in place for long if the brooch had much use—other examples have empty rivet-holes showing their loss. (Photograph reproduced by courtesy of the British Museum, London. Actual size.)

A.2. Gilt copper-alloy equal-arm brooch from Collingbourne Ducis, Wiltshire, probably made between the mid-fifth and early sixth century. Although the gilding is in good condition, the broken terminal shows that the brooch was not new when buried, and there is a repair to it on the back. See Fig. 1.7 for the ornament. (Photograph reproduced by courtesy of the Wiltshire Heritage Museum, Devizes. Actual size.)

B.1

B.2

B.3

B.4

B.5

B.1 and B.2. Two gold and garnet composite disc-brooches from Kent; both also have a few coloured glass inlays. B.1: the Sarre (Amherst) brooch shows how gold foils were placed in the gold cells to make the flat red garnets reflect the light better. Its gold panels have filigree scrolls. B.2: the Monkton brooch has two imported shells as white bosses, and its filigree wires create Style II snake-like creatures. The difference in the gold alloys of the two brooches suggests a time difference, the much whiter gold of the Monkton brooch containing more silver, and probably dating to the middle of the seventh century rather than to the end of the sixth or first third of the seventh. (Both photographs reproduced by courtesy of the Ashmolean Museum, Oxford. Actual sizes.)

B.3 and B.4. Two further examples of high-quality goldwork of the first half of the seventh century. B.3 is a sword pommel said to be from Aldbrough, East Yorkshire. It has a filigree gold pattern on the side shown, and cells for garnets on the other. B.4 is a pyramid stud found near Bury St Edmunds, Suffolk, probably one of a pair that would have fitted onto straps attached to a sword scabbard. Its filigree animal is more tightly coiled than those on the Monkton brooch. (Photographs reproduced by courtesy of the Portable Antiquities Scheme and the British Museum. Actual sizes.)

B.5. Gold finger-ring from near Norwich. Its bezel pivots, and is engraved so that both front and back could be used as a seal matrix. Nothing like it had been found before 1998 in England, and it was probably made in Francia. The inscription is *Baldehildis*; an Anglo-Saxon named Bathilda married the Frankish King Clovis II in about 648, but the name is not quite hers, and the purity of the gold, 98%, could suggest an earlier date. The two apparently naked figures may be a married couple, as such devices are known on the continent. (Photographs reproduced by courtesy of the Portable Antiquities Scheme and British Museum; now in the collections of the Norfolk Museums and Archaeology Service. Twice actual size.)

C.1

C.2

C.3

C.1. Some of the many and various things found in an isolated grave at Tattershall Thorpe, Lincolnshire, probably the property of a smith who was buried in the second half of the seventh century (see also Figs. 2.18–20). Prominent are a pair of snips for cutting sheet metal, its handles curved to give a more comfortable grip, and a file with parts of its wooden handle surviving. The copper-alloy disc is a scabbard-mount with Style II ornament. There are also several lengths of copper-alloy sheet, perhaps wrested from a vessel, and various other bits of scrap for recycling. Underlying the rest of the group is a flat lead plate, perhaps used as a cushion by the smith when using a punch. (Photograph reproduced by courtesy of Lincolnshire County Council, City and County Museum.)

C.2 and C.3. Two gold pendants from women's graves excavated at the new football stadium in Southampton (cf. Fig. 3.1). C.2: the rather rough cutting and chipping of the garnets on the disc-pendant suggest the same sort of date as those in the Monkton brooch, which are a contrast to the much finer workmanship shown in the Sarre brooch (Col. pls. B.1 and B.2). The outer border has four Style II filigree snakes, their heads identifiable from the raising of an outer wire to look like an eye-brow. C.3: the smaller pendant has a parallel at a royal site in the Netherlands, so it may well be a Frisian import made around 600 to judge partly from the purity of its gold. The larger pendant is as likely to have been made by an itinerant smith like the one buried at Tattershall Thorpe as by someone working in a permanent centre. (Photographs reproduced by courtesy of Wessex Archaeology. Actual sizes.)

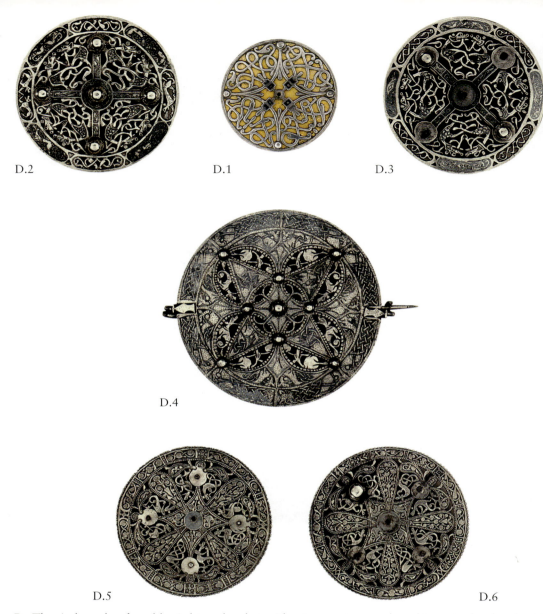

D.2 D.1 D.3

D.4

D.5 D.6

D. The six brooches found buried together, but without any coins or other objects, in the churchyard at Pentney, Norfolk, where they had presumably been hidden for safekeeping. The one at the top (D.1) is unlike the others, not only in size but in its design, a round-armed cross with symmetrical plants; it is also differently made, the cross and plants being openwork, riveted to a gilt copper-alloy background. The other brooches are all solid silver, though all have bosses, some covering rivets holding pin attachments, some merely decorative. The next two (D.2–3) have paired animals in the segments of a square-armed cross. The other three all have round-armed crosses, but which take more time to see. Their patterns are formed partly in openwork, partly in black niello. They have small bosses riveted onto them. The group seems to make up two pairs and two singles, which is curious since it was not realized before their discovery in 1977 that pairs of brooches were likely at this time—almost certainly the ninth century, as the ornament on most of them is the Trewhiddle style that occurs on brooches and other objects in hoards coin-dated to the 850s and 870s, most probably concealed to hide them from viking raiders. The small brooch looks earlier than the others, however, and the paired animals in D.2–3 also look as though they owe a lot to eighth-century, mainly Mercian, work (cf. Fig. 3.9). (Photographs reproduced by courtesy of the British Museum, London. All half actual sizes.)

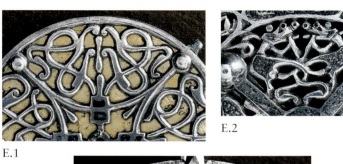

E.1   E.2

E.3

E.4

E. Segments of the Pentney brooches, to show the workmanship and design elements more clearly. E.1 is from the probably eighth-century brooch (D.1), and shows it as having elegant symmetrical double-branching plants, ending in leaves with volutes at the ends—perhaps meant to be seen as Trees of Life. E.2, from one (D.2) of the pair that may be next in a time-sequence, shows back-to-back paired and interlaced creatures with prominent eyes and nostrils, details shown up by the niello background. Niello is more obvious in the largest brooch (D.4), E.3, which is also the closest to the Trewhiddle style, with its less robust creatures; the speckling all over the bodies of those in the flat panels is typical, as is the way that some dissolve into interlace strands, and the beaded borders. The subtlety of the layout, with intersecting circles and triangles shows well, as it does on the final example, E.4 (D.6), which also has openwork creatures ending in interlace, a flowering plant in the kite-shaped panel, and a range of plant patterns in the outer border (cf. Figs. 4.1–4). (Photographs reproduced by courtesy of the British Museum, London. All actual sizes.)

F.1

F.2

F.3

F.4   F.5   F.6

F.1 and F.2. Two panels from the best surviving example of Anglo-Saxon use of coloured silk and gold-thread embroidery, for ecclesiastical vestments called a stole and a maniple. The gold is 1/7000 inch thick and 1/150 inch wide, spirally twisted round a silk thread. F.1 shows St John the Baptist, holding a palm for martyrdom and a book for God's word (strictly, he was not entitled to either; he did not die for the Faith, and he did not write one of the gospels). He is identified by his name in Latin capitals, *Iohannes B*, with a bar over the B to show the contraction. The panel in F.2 shows the *Dextera Dei*, the Right Hand of God, descending from the clouds to bless Christ at the Crucifixion, and thus to redeem Mankind. This was a favoured motif used also on sculptures and on secular things such as coins to show God's blessing of the kings who issued them. Another inscription, not shown, says 'For the holy Bishop Frithestan', who was bishop of Winchester from 909 to 931, and his stole and maniple may subsequently have been taken to the shrine of St Cuthbert, then at Chester-le-Street, by one of the kings of Wessex who wanted to show his patronage of the northern saint. A fourth inscription records that the work was done to the order of Aelfflaed, a lady who may have been a wife of King Edward the Elder and who died in 916, so the stole and maniple probably had a royal connection, like the silk cloak given by King Alfred to Bishop Asser. (Photographs reproduced by courtesy of the Dean and Chapter of Durham Cathedral. Actual sizes.)

F.3. Few ornamented brooches are known from the eleventh century, and if this gold disc found at Holberrow Green, Worcestershire, was from one, it must have been soldered to a back-plate that is now missing, as there are no signs of attachments for a pin (cf. Fig. 5.13). The filigree scrolls set round grey glass studs are not exclusive to either the secular or ecclesiastical worlds, and it may have come from a shrine or some other church object. Its centre presumably held a gemstone, a larger version of the one in the ring next to it, F.4. (Photograph reproduced by courtesy of the Portable Antiquities Schemes and British Museum. Actual size.)

F.4–6. Gold finger-rings with small gemstones in their bezels spread from the ecclesiastical world into the secular, and these examples, all recent finds reported by metal-detector users to the Portable Antiquities Scheme, are typical of the relatively low-value jewellery that became increasingly common after the middle of the twelfth century. F.4, from South Kyme, Lincolnshire, has a rectangular garnet set in a collet; F.5 from West Lindsey, Lincolnshire, has a sapphire in a stirrup-shaped ring. F.6 is from Shrewsbury and has a ruby in a claw setting. (Photographs reproduced by courtesy of the Portable Antiquities Scheme and British Museum; the first two are now in the collections of Lincolnshire County Council, City and County Museum. All actual sizes.)

G. Polychrome jug from Exeter, late thirteenth or early fourteenth century, made in the Saintonge in south-west France, and imported with wine from the English kings' lands in Gascony. The top, decorated with heraldic shields as though with pendants at their tops (cf. Fig. 6.17), acts as a basin, and liquid entered the container at the bottom through the handle, which is a hollow tube. The head at the end of the long spout is probably meant to be a donkey, from the long ears (the stripes may make it look like a giraffe, but the creature was not yet known in northern Europe, unlike lions, leopards, and a few other unfortunate beasts). Musicians serenade a woman leaning out of the tower, inside which are two figures revealed to be bishops by mitres and crooks, though by nothing else. The jug may be an anti-episcopal satire that would have been appreciated by Exeter's richer merchants. (Photograph reproduced by courtesy of Exeter City Museums. Height 460 mm.)

H.1

H.2

H.3

H.4

H.5

H.6

H.7

H.1–3. Three gold posy-rings, probably all fifteenth-century. No. 1 is from Kirk Deighton, North Yorkshire, and retains much of its original white enamel in the engraved flowers and inscription *nul ce bien*, 'none so good'. No. 2, from Alkmonkton, Derbyshire, is engraved with sprays of flowers and a black-letter inscription, not visible. No. 3 is from North Warnborough, Hampshire, and has engraved flowers and the text *fortune le voelt*, 'fortune wishes it'. (Photographs reproduced by courtesy of the Portable Antiquities Scheme and British Museum. Actual sizes.)

H.4–5. Two gold iconographic rings, also probably fifteenth century. No. 1, from Carisbrooke, Isle of Wight, shows St Christopher wading across a river with his staff in one hand and the Christchild (obscured by wear) on his back. No. 2, from Scotton, Lincolnshire, has St Katherine with her wheel on the right and St John the Baptist with the Lamb of God on his shoulder. (Photographs reproduced by courtesy of the Portable Antiquities Scheme and British Museum. Actual sizes.)

H.6. A gold seal-ring recently found at Raglan, Monmouthshire. It has a lion passant flanked by letters, 'W' and 'A', and '*to yow feythfoull*' in retrograde black letter—an early example of a text in English. The weight and quality of the workmanship put this ring in a much higher league than the ones above. (Photograph reproduced by courtesy of the Portable Antiquities Scheme and National Museums and Galleries of Wales. Actual size.)

H.7. Silver-gilt badge found at Chiddingly, East Sussex, probably worn by a supporter of King Richard III (1483–5), the last of the Yorkist kings. Richard is known to have issued several thousand of his boar badges to adherents. (Photograph reproduced by courtesy of the Portable Antiquities Scheme and British Museum. Actual size.)

finishes as well as gilding to colour metal objects or to make them black, but again no intention to deceive can be proved.[9]

The later twelfth-century vogue for finger-rings was maintained throughout the thirteenth and fourteenth centuries. Engraved inscriptions began to appear on some of them, although the only well-dated example was in a lost hoard from Tutbury, Staffordshire, deposited in the 1320s, that contained a single gold ring with a scroll pattern, and a Latin text inside the hoop, *Spreta vivunt*. Rings with personal seals on the bezels were another new development. Some which look like seals at first glance had single letters that are not cut retrograde, so were a device to be read, not to be used as a seal.[10]

By the time that Langland and Chaucer were writing, English vernacular poetry had become well established and was another means of spreading lore about gemstones. Love poems extolled a woman's white skin, against which 'coral of godnesse', 'rubye of rightfulnesse', and 'crystal of cleannesse' could presumably shine. Mostly it was costume that drew writers' attention, for admiration or censure, but in one passage Piers Plowman observed Lucre prettily adorned with gold-wire rings, rubies, diamonds, sapphires, amethysts, and beryls. This was taken from the Book of Revelation's description of the Whore of Babylon, however, so does not mean that Piers often saw such women in the street. Nevertheless, everyday awareness of the symbolism that objects could have was such that a fraudulent pilgrim could be put in the pillory with a whetstone tied round his neck, with the implication that the allusion to his sharp, lying tongue would be understood. The practice of *deodand*, whereby the value of an object that had caused a fatal injury was forfeited to the king as compensation for the damage it had done to him by depriving him of a subject, is another indication that something physical could stand as a metaphor for an action.[11]

The assessments made of people's movable property for the Lay Subsidy taxes continue to be a useful, though sporadic, source for what might have been seen in the streets, or at least in houses, until individual inspections ceased in 1334. Exemptions increased, however: the threshold for non-payment rose, and rural dwellers did not have their 'treasure, riding-horses, bedding, clothes, vessels, tools . . .' taken into account, unlike townspeople, and from 1290 even they had a personal allowance for man and wife of their bed, and for each a silver cup and a ring, a gold or silver clasp, and a silk girdle, provided that they wore these things daily, which suggests a concession to the better-off. Even when both urban and country records survive, as they happen to do for Bedfordshire in 1297, the exemptions mean that what the peasants and townspeople owned cannot be compared directly; brass, lead, and wooden vessels worth a shilling or two were quite common in towns, but only in 1301 is a rural Bedfordshire vill recorded as having a few peasants with copper pots. At the top of the social ladder, knights and gentry did not have to pay tax on any of their jewellery, plate, and clothing, or on their armour and horses; they were expected to be able to maintain their position, and had other payments to make as well. When Sir Geoffrey Luttrell commissioned his psalter between 1320 and 1340, he could have himself shown with a display of plate and spoons on his table without fear of having to pay tax for the privilege.[12]

The richest individuals for whom late thirteenth-century assessments survive lived in the port of Lynn, Norfolk, but no distinction was made between what was merchants' stock intended for sale and the jewellery, plate, and other items to be seen by visitors to people's houses. Many had jewels, to the value of just over £7 in one case, but the only piece individually valued is a silver clasp at 7s. 6d. Silver spoons had an average value of less than 1s., and although they seem to have been carefully counted, no one had more than twenty-five. Brass and lead vessels were relatively frequent, wooden mazers rather less so, and only a few people had silver plate, valued from 18s. for two pieces to £17. 10s. 4d. for seventeen. The latter belonged to an innkeeper, as did the next largest quantity recorded; these men were the second and tenth richest men in Lynn according to the assessment, but they were probably being penalized for having their goods on public display and for not being part of the merchant clique. Such factions are even more visible in Shrewsbury, for which more than one assessment survives, allowing it to be seen that gross underestimates were rife, especially for the better-off. Shrewsbury lacked Lynn's very rich group of citizens, but a few owned plate and jewels. Variation of recording between towns means that in Colchester such things were individually recorded, to the level of gold rings ranging in value from 8d. to 1s. and silver clasps from less than 3d. to 3s.—nominally.[13]

Inquisitions, usually drawn up when someone died, show the same concentration upon silver plate and spoons. One or two early examples are from Lynn, but unfortunately not those of people whose assessments survive, so the two cannot be compared. Only the relatively wealthy had enough goods to be worth recording, such as Dame Christina of Stikelayne, who lived in Bridport, Dorset, in 1268 and owned three gold buckles as well as several silver spoons, a silver cup, gold cups, and brass pots, not individually itemized; more informative is the inventory of John de Digby of Derby, who in 1323 had plate and spoons valued at £3. 16s. 0d., jewels at 13s., and a silk girdle and a tunic at 8s. and 5s. respectively. Even a bishop of London who died in 1303 did not have much individually valuable jewellery—three gold clasps worth 18s. in total, and gold rings worth 1s., 2s., and 7s. 6d.; even a ring set with diamonds was only valued at 26s. 8d. He had a penchant for beryls, the stone which St John placed highest in the firmament, but which had practical properties such as being good for the liver and sore eyes; less relevant to a bishop was that it stopped a man from becoming angry with his wife. The bishop believed in the efficacy of serpents' tongues, and owned several; actually fossilized shark's teeth, they were an antidote to poison—if the snake could survive its own venom, then its tongue must make it invulnerable. More appropriate was his pontifical ring, worth £1, which was to go to the king, his paternosters valued at 3s., and a small jet cross. In sum, his jewels, clothes, and plate were worth £1,242. 0s. 6d.[14]

A few silver spoons survive that show what was meant by the items in the valuations (cf. Fig. 6.8); an acorn at the end of the stem enhanced one from Coventry, not found with the two brooches, though probably of much the same date. The earliest piece of silver plate with a punch-mark to vouch for its quality happens to come from a context in Shrewsbury deposited at much the same time as some of the city's surviving Lay Subsidy records were written; as it came from the site of the abbey, it need not have been owned by one of the townspeople, but it shows the sort of thing that they were being assessed for. It has been identified as a 'saucer', to which references first occur in the early fourteenth century. Contemporary with it are the earliest pieces of pewter plate, of much the same shape and size, which show that trends in precious metal were closely followed by those working in cheaper materials. That need not mean that it was getting into poorer households. Of the earliest examples known, a saucer from Southampton is from the property of one of the richest merchants (Fig. 7.6), and the other pieces are from Exeter, a castle, and an abbey.[15]

Fig. 7.6. An early example of pewter, a saucer of c.1300, excavated from a rubbish-pit in Southampton, Hampshire. The letter 'P' on the left is probably the maker's mark, rather than the owner's. Pewter is a soft metal and cut-marks made by knives can be seen scored into the surface. (Photograph reproduced by courtesy of Southampton City Museums. Slightly smaller than actual size.)

The distribution of early pewter vessels seems comparable to that of a very distinctive pottery from the south-west of France, Saintonge polychrome, which is also of the later thirteenth and early fourteenth centuries (Col. pl. G); with very few exceptions, it has been found in ports like Southampton or at castles and moated manors. It was coming from the area which was by then England's main wine supplier, and that association probably made it acceptable to those who could afford the most expensive drink; it must have seemed inappropriate for ale or cider, therefore, and so was inaccessible to the less wealthy, not merely for cost reasons. Much of the polychrome pottery destined for England was decorated with shields and vaguely heraldic birds, to appeal to the interests of those eligible to bear arms. Almost the only English pottery to imitate those designs was made at Laverstock—which is also one of the only kiln-sites known to have been supplying the royal court. Potters in the second half of the thirteenth century continued to produce some highly decorated jugs, with applied decoration. Some of this shows familiarity with personal seals, others show bearded men, but whole figures are usually dancers or from religious scenes. A few are mildly scatological, but there is nothing to suggest that, despite their low status and the cheapness of their raw materials, the potters expressed subversive popular ideas; even face-jugs with noses that dripped when the jugs were poured do not seem to be parodies of anyone in particular.[16]

One exception could be the elaborate jug from Exeter which imitates a tower, inside which can be seen the figures of two bishops with mitres and croziers (Col. pl. G). Women are leaning out of the windows, watching musicians below. It may be a wholesome carnival scene, but it may be an attack on episcopal morals. This jug would almost certainly have been imported by a rich merchant, however, so the representation need not have been part of any popular anticlericalism, but have expressed the specific resentment of would-be oligarchs in a few towns like Exeter where civic freedom conflicted with church administration.[17]

A polychrome jug might have been acceptable for containing wine, but in most households it would have been drunk from gold and silver cups, which feature in royal and baronial records, and are shown in illustrations. Silver cups may have been used also for lower-status ale, as they feature in so many inventories, as in Lynn, and they could be found even in taverns, Robert Dicoun being hanged for stealing one from a London inn. Such crime records continue to show the same sort of occasional ownership of items of small but worthwhile value, cups and spoons still being the most frequent.[18]

What seems to be unmentioned in all these sources is vessel glass for table use; there are not many survivals, but some extremely fine enamelled beakers of the early fourteenth century were excavated in the London goldsmiths' quarter, where they may have been in a shop waiting to be fitted with precious-metal mounts. Those beakers were probably Italian imports; others came from the Islamic world. Being soda glass, they survive much better than the potash, or forest, glass made in northern Europe, so it is impossible to be sure that more glass was not being used than seems likely either from finds or from written records. Some potash glass was very high-quality, like a fourteenth-century goblet with a long, delicate stem and flanged bowl excavated at Ludgershall Castle, Wiltshire; a fragment of a cobalt blue forest-glass jug was also excavated there, which is like one found at a moated manor site at Penhallam in Cornwall. At the other end of Britain, a fragment of a stemmed goblet was excavated at Rattray Castle. Some lead glass was also being made, probably in Germany, used for goblets and beakers such as those found at the castles at Old Sarum and Knaresborough, Yorkshire. The sites where high-quality glass has been found are very similar to those that produce polychrome pottery, and the same association with wine would have meant that there was no wish for glass at a lower social level, even if the native forest glass made less elaborate vessels more affordable.[19]

That enamelled beakers and polychrome pottery should seem closely linked to wine-importing merchants is one indication of the way that social groups could use material culture as a means of making themselves distinctive. The right to carry certain types of weapon was a long-standing example of this practice, reformalized in a 1285 statute on a sliding scale according to what men had in lands and chattels—anyone with more than £2 worth should have a sword, a bow, arrows, and a knife; anyone with land worth £15 or over was to have a horse and armour, in other words, to be a knight. To qualify for that status, anyone who did not have land had to have goods worth 40 marks (£26. 13s. 4d.), almost twice as much as was required for the landed, who were considered likely to have the training to use the equipment. Judging from inventories and Lay Subsidy assessments, in most years very few townsmen would have had 40 marks in goods, so although many had much more than that tied up in urban property, they were excluded from potential knighthood.[20]

From the government's point of view, the need was to ensure that men could fight for it, and throughout the Middle Ages there were intermittent expressions of concern that people should not reduce their ability to serve by unnecessary expenditure; in 1188 English law had already tried to proscribe certain dyes and furs, so as not to squander money better spent on a crusade. Similar wording was used in the fourteenth century to justify legislation that sought to codify what was appropriate to different ranks, because if people spent too much money on food or dress they would not be able to 'help their liege in battle', as the 1337 Act expressed it. The 1363 Act was more explicit in its social statement, fulminating against 'outrageous and excessive apparel of divers people against their estate and degree, to the great destruction and impoverishment of the land'. In other words, the problem was not so much the need to serve the king as to avoid the threat to the social order implied if people wore furs, clothes, and jewellery inappropriate to their rank and 'everyone tried to imitate the other'. Equally, it put an unspoken obligation upon lords to dress up to their status, so that they had to spend money to distinguish themselves. There remained, however, concern that the kingdom should not be 'impoverished' by exports of gold, silver, jewels, arms, and grain needed for its own wealth and security.[21]

This sumptuary legislation was explicitly hierarchical: 'people of handicraft, and yeomen' should have 'no stone, nor cloth of silk nor of silver, nor girdle, knife, button, ring, garter, nor ouche [brooch], ribbon, chain, nor any other such other things of gold or of silver'. Clauses like those would not have been enacted if no ordinary townsfolk and country people had been observed flaunting themselves. Even if they were excluded from taking part in the pageants and processions that were the main public opportunities for the oligarchies to show themselves in their hierarchical position wearing their best costume, the poorer sort were on view too, albeit as spectators. It was then, or in church if they attended, that everyone could be seen for what they were; to appear in public inappropriately arrayed could be interpreted as a deliberate challenge to the established order which the processions sought to demonstrate, but the motive was usually social aspiration. Indeed, the intention of the laws was not to prevent individuals from bettering themselves; as far as is known there were no prosecutions, and the 1363 Act was repealed, though its sentiments remained. Chaucer, for instance, noted the silver-decorated knives, girdles, and purses carried by the five burgesses on their pilgrimage to Canterbury, which they used as one way of showing their sense of self-worth and their pretensions to be aldermen. They were not wishing to undermine those above them, but to demonstrate that they had the wherewithal to maintain that social estate, as much for the benefit of their guild brothers to observe as for those outside it.[22]

In the Prologue to the *Canterbury Tales* Chaucer gave the most explicit view of the link between costume and social place: 'What their condition was . . . according to profession and degree, and what apparel they were riding in.' This was the same thinking as lay behind the sumptuary legislation. Ranking also formalized taxation when poll taxes replaced the Lay Subsidies in 1377; a graded scale was set out in 1379, headed by dukes and passing through esquires, lawyers, mayors, merchants, farmers, artisans, and innkeepers. Apart from the magnates, all these and more were in Chaucer's company, a microcosm of a nation to be measured by the extent that their appearance matched their social rank and conduct.[23] The fourteenth-century statutes articulated contemporary opinion that people could be recognized by the value of what they wore as much as by the land that they owned or the houses that they lived in. Like getting a licence to crenellate a house or for a private chapel, having silver plate on a table, or fencing off land for a deer-park, jewellery and clothing were a means of using physical appearance to define status. Such definition was needed in a state in which oaths of fealty, honours, and vassalage were ceding to the exercise of control through legal precision rather than through feudal relationships.[24]

The silver and base-metal ring-brooches with applied knops like those in the 1290s Canonbie hoard may have been a response to more elaborate ones in gold, such as a brooch with three cameos alternating with rubies found at Oxwich Castle, West Glamorgan (Fig. 7.7). The cameos were not reset antiques, as the heads on them are wearing coifs in thirteenth-century style, and are probably an indication that the art of gem-cutting had been relearnt in Italy and passed on to Paris, and perhaps to London. They are the only such cameos yet known in Britain, but they mark the beginning of more elaborate cutting and shaping of gems generally, soon followed by new colouring methods achieved by new enamelling techniques. Such finery might be expected to have been well beyond the purchasing power of any but the richest, except that the owner of Oxwich Castle was not one of the country's leading magnates.[25]

Cameos would have been almost impossible to reproduce in a cheap material such as glass. Similarly, elaborate gold fruit-pods on a brooch from Manchester would have been very difficult to emulate in a less malleable metal (Fig. 7.7). Its stones are set in high collets, which seem to have gone out of

 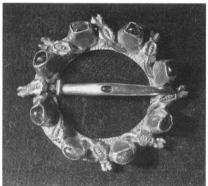

Fig. 7.7. Two late thirteenth-/early fourteenth-century gold ring-brooches.
Left: from Oxwich Castle, Glamorgan, set with three rubies (one missing) and three cameos, the pin missing. The frame was made in separate segments, soldered together, and the cameos are so tightly fitted into their frames that they had probably been taken from some other object and been reset. King Edward III owned a brooch with four emeralds and four cameos which could have looked like this. (Photograph reproduced by courtesy of the National Museums and Galleries of Wales, Cardiff. Actual size.)
Right: from Manchester, set with alternate garnets and sapphires (two missing) in high collets, with pea-like gold fruit-pods in between that could be the Plantagenets' broom-cod emblem, the *plante à genet*, but which at this time was also and perhaps only used by the French monarchy. (Photograph reproduced by courtesy of the Manchester City Art Gallery. Actual size.)

fashion in the early fourteenth century; otherwise it would be very difficult to attribute the Manchester brooch to the same period as that from Oxwich.[26] Most others, unless they have inscriptions with letters in forms that can be matched with seals or other things of known date, can only be given fairly broad date ranges.

The fruit-pods on the Manchester brooch might be representations of the broom, possibly the royal Plantagenet family's emblem, but also used by the kings of France. Such devices were becoming more commonly worn. Particularly well known was the use of the swan, derived from various legends including that of a knight whose boat had been pulled by one when he had come to the rescue of a duchess in distress. The Swan Knight was supposed to have been the ancestor of one of the early crusaders, so the swan was used in various countries as a badge by people who sought an association with Christian militarism. Edward I created some 300 'Swan knights' when he dubbed his son in 1306 at the Feast of the Swans, the sort of occasion that led to the bird being linked with Gluttony. It had other associations; the Middle Ages expressed abstract ideas by physical representation, so that Lust, Pride, and other vices appeared in human guise, paired with the less interesting virtues. For instance, Tranquillity figured on the wall of Henry III's Painted Chamber at Clarendon Palace wearing a swan badge, so in other contexts the serene swan could represent a virtue. There was also a story about a swan that attached itself to St Hugh of Lincoln, with the consequence that some surviving pewter badges of swans may be pilgrims', not things issued to retainers.[27]

The swan became the family emblem in England of the Bohun family, and subsequently of the Lancastrian earl of Derby, who became Henry IV by deposing Richard II in 1399. An enamelled white swan brooch, with a crown around its neck and a short chain, found at Dunstable, Bedfordshire, is probably to be associated with the Lancastrian faction, therefore, perhaps lost during a royal visit (Fig. 7.8). It illustrates the importance attached to the symbolism of an emblem worn to show allegiance, as well as the expense in the best of such work, for the technique of enamelling to achieve the swan's feathers puts it in the forefront of western workmanship, most probably Parisian of c.1400. The profit that goldsmiths from the French capital could make in England was considerable: in 1397 two of them paid customs and dues for permission to sell jewels with pearls and marguerites to the value of 1,000 marks.[28]

The Dunstable swan shows the developing political problems of the fourteenth century. One view is that a turning-point came in 1265 if Simon de Montfort had his throat slit after losing the Battle of Evesham. Conventions of behaviour were thus overturned, because rebels could now expect a punishment worse than forfeiture of lands or banishment. The only way to avoid retribution by murder or judicial execution, like that of Thomas of Lancaster in 1322, was to remove the king permanently from the scene, as were two English kings in the fourteenth century, the first since perhaps William II in

Fig. 7.8. The Dunstable swan: late fourteenth-/early fifteenth-century. Gold, with its feathers created by white enamel, its eye by black enamel. It was worn as a brooch: the end of its pin can be seen projecting below the tail. The coronet round its neck helps to identify it as a Lancastrian emblem; the gold chain was partly for security, in case the pin came loose, but could also have allowed it to be worn dangling from a necklace. It may have been lost at a tournament, as Dunstable was a centre for such occasions at least until the early fourteenth century, or during a royal visit, of which several are recorded in the fifteenth, but its findspot, a friary, may mean that it had been entrusted to the treasury there for safekeeping and it was overlooked when the house was dissolved in 1539. (Photograph reproduced by courtesy of the British Museum, London. Actual size.)

1100.[29] With failure having such awful consequences, it was more and more important to have protection: a magnate derived it from his supporters, lesser lords from a magnate. This volatility needed new expressions, not least the wearing of a badge to show affiliation: a threat to rivals and a comfort to friends.

The tradition of expenditure on plate, furs, and jewellery for royal display was maintained by all Henry III's successors. In 1281 the £112 which Edward I paid to Italians included what are described as square-cut rubies, an early reference to that technique; in one year he spent £631. 2s. 4d. on jewels. Like his bishop of London, he was a believer in the efficacy of stones, having a 'serpent's tongue' as an antidote to poison. His wife, Eleanor of Castile, spent money with merchants from Palestine as well as Paris and London. She died in 1290 owning jewels, carpets, and hangings that sold for over £600, probably having set new tableware standards with her jade-handled and enamelled knives. Any restraint that she may have exercised over Edward's behaviour was lost, and his temper is suggested by the incident when he threw his daughter's coronet into the fire in 1297, regardless of its value.[30]

Edward II was a reckless spender, as was his favourite Piers Gaveston.[31] His wife, Queen Isabella, had a gold brooch (*firmaculum*) with rubies and emeralds valued at £20, and two others at £10 were made available to her from the king's store; on one of her robes she had fifty gold knots, bought for 15s. Knots implied everlasting devotion, and passed into the secular world from Franciscan friars, who wore three on their girdles, for poverty, chastity, and obedience, qualities that Queen Isabella conspicuously lacked. She ensured that her household reflected her importance, disbursing robes to her ladies, knights, clerks, and servants both in summer and winter; grooms merely received money for shoes.[32]

Edward III behaved like his predecessors, buying jewels and using them as pledges; in 1348 jewels worth nearly £200 were stolen from the Tower of London, and the king subsequently issued a pardon to the man who killed the thief. It would have been very serious if doubts about the Tower's security had made merchants reluctant to accept the king's pledges; in 1326 the Bardi of Florence had lent £4,000 against the king's jewels there, and there were many other occasions when lesser sums were involved.[33] The royal image was again presented on gold coins, partly because it was felt right to match what the French were doing. The first, struck in 1344, echoed Henry III's earlier attempt, showing the enthroned king with the emblems of state. Later issues used heraldry to emphasize the king's claims to the French throne, and a ship to proclaim his superiority at sea. Also in line with kings on the continent, Edward established the chivalric Order of the Garter, an Arthurian conceit of a closed companionship. Its origin is obscure, but the garter could be replicated as a badge, so was not just a leg ornament, though the concept of binding with a round band for unity was a particularly apt metaphor for the special band of knights. Edward III's sense of a created elite was expressed also in his free use of titles, bestowed at elaborate ceremonies at which physical insignia expressed the new rank. The phrase 'He who gives, dominates' applied to Edward, though as his grandson was to find, giving alone could not guarantee that domination in the long term.[34]

Edward was a big spender, paying £20 for a single ring with a ruby in 1350, but his sons could match him. The Black Prince spent as much in a single year on jewellery as he did in building Kennington Palace over four. He was clearly using some of his purchases to bind men to him, his New Year's Day gifts in 1351 including brooches for a number of knights, such as Sir Richard de Bere, whose 'ouch of gold' was for some reason described carefully as 'without pearls', with 'a rose in the middle and a crown above it, set with a beast and two birds'. The rose was already a favoured device, but eagles and a lion on a staff are also mentioned; both were creatures with imperial and royal associations. 'Three rings with the prince's motto' sound like obvious things to hand round, but in fact he kept two for himself. Pearls might be large ones for setting in jewellery, or smaller seed-pearls for sewing on costume, such as hoods. In 1353 gold, silver-gilt, and silver buttons occur, an innovation that went together with more tightly fitting and tailored clothes. In 1362 he spent £200 on them. Three years before that, a helm set with 'many great pearls and a leopard' cost £70, and the prince spent £5 on a long ostrich feather, a conceit which served as a helmet plume, presumably so that he would make a bigger show at tournaments, and which became his badge (Fig. 7.4). In the same year he paid £28 for a single gold ring with a diamond and two rubies, and acquired brooches that cost £35 or even more, which are described as enamelled, the first mention of the application of colouring in the prince's records. By 1361 he owed £1,906. 15s. 8d. to an Italian of Pistoia.[35]

It is not possible to be sure, but Edward's sons seem to have been using lavish display as a means of competing with each other. In part-payment of his debts, Edward's second son, John of Gaunt, 'released' jewellery to the value of £1,671. 13s. 4d. in 1379. His dealings with Herman of London show old items being melted down for reuse, a gold brooch with a 'lece' (?fleur-de-lys) being made out of an old 'fermail', a brooch or buckle. Unless something either mystical, like an antique gem, or associated rightly or wrongly with an ancestor or an ancient hero, old things had no value in the medieval world, but were better replaced by something new. Herman was paid 20s. 8d. for the gold from which to make a ring-brooch, 'in the guise of two clasped hands with a diamond and a ruby' and a 'certain reson' (presumably a motto or other text) on the 'roule' (hoop), and £1 for making it, whereas he had £3. 3s. 4d. for a gold ring set with a ruby, a present to the duke's daughter on her wedding-day. Herman's other work included a gold belt with links in the shape of the letter 'J', for which he was paid £28. 4s. 10d. Gaunt is associated with another letter, S, which was used as a series of links to form a collar, by the end of the fourteenth century a familiar livery. Other collars might have badges dangling from them, or forming centrepieces. Minor items were given away, including a pair of paternosters to the duke's confessor. Clearly it was very important for the duke, who was a king but not in his own country, that he and his family should impress anyone who saw them wearing their gold and gems on their sumptuous robes, with their plate on the table before them and on the open shelves in the buffet behind, all glinting in the firelight and set off by expensive hangings, especially tapestries, in a great hall such as the one at Kenilworth which he built for this kind of occasion and display. The more that normal dining became 'withdrawn', with access to a lord and his family at meals made a special privilege, so it became more important to make the most of the formal occasions when a household and its guests dined together.[36]

Edward III's youngest surviving son, Thomas, was one of the nobility who paid with his life for crossing the king; he was smothered at his nephew's orders in 1397. Although he had no family connection to it, he used the swan as his badge; it is recorded as being on the tapestries hanging in his castle at Pleshey. The inventory of what he had there shows the opulence that a royal magnate could command; carpets, silk bed hangings, embroideries with badges, coats of arms, scenes from popular romances and religious images, silver vases, maces for his sergeants, books, a chessboard, mirrors, gowns trimmed with fur, caps, arms and armour including Bordeaux steel, and in his chapel plate, tablets, books, and vestments.[37]

Richard II (1377–99) was himself murdered only two years after Thomas; his over-reliance on an exclusive clique and his fondness for secretive affiliations for which he issued badges were among the criticisms made of him. Gifts for his young queen to distribute at Christmas 1397 cost £116. 6s. 8d., and included tablets, studs, and rings, all set with gems. Such donations could not guarantee his safety, however, not least because they excluded from power and favour those who were not recipients; but also because gifts, except of land, were no more a means of creating permanent obligations than they had once been to Saxon kings. They set up expectations: Piers Plowman noted how people came to expect New Year gratuities, in effect bribes, and how Lucre supplied them. Gift-giving was not only from kings to subjects, but could work in reverse; the London citizens who gave the king and queen jewels shaped as a dromedary and a bird, presumably enamelled like the Dunstable swan, were seeking short-term favours, whereas the courtiers who felt obliged to lavish jewels on Richard's child-bride in 1396 were probably looking to the longer term. Formal gift-giving was by social superiors to inferiors, though the latter might offer a token present in exchange, its lower value acknowledging their inferiority. This stress on hierarchy was particularly clear in households, with careful grading of what was handed out, to reflect the level of service expected of the recipients. Christmas and New Year had become established as the time for these distributions, as they were for gift-giving between social equals: 'Christmas was celebrated anew . . . nobles came forward to offer good-luck tokens, called aloud "New Year gifts".'[38]

Richard II was another king with a close personal interest in his jewellery and plate, if his 'secret' visit to inspect them is anything to go by. He appears in the first surviving portrait painting of an English king intended for public view, at Westminster Abbey, in the full robes of state. A different, more private self-image, wearing insignia of various sorts, is shown on the Wilton Diptych (Fig. 7.9).[39] If the Dunstable swan can be taken as a surviving example of such

Fig. 7.9. Part of the Wilton Diptych. In one of the earliest lifelike images in Britain, Richard II is shown kneeling in prayer, sumptuously robed and crowned, supported by John the Baptist with the Lamb of God, an ermine-clad Edward the Confessor with his ring, and King Edmund of East Anglia, with the Danish arrow that had martyred him in the ninth century, wearing a very fine oval brooch set with large pearls. Richard is wearing a chained hart badge as a pendant from a gold collar of broom-cods, the former his own badge, the latter perhaps a gift from the king of France. (Photograph reproduced by courtesy of the Trustees of the National Gallery, London. Approximately actual size.)

people's jewellery, the splendour of their plate can be seen in the 'King John' cup at King's Lynn, though its fourteenth-century ownership is debatable; it includes outstanding translucent enamelwork, a new fourteenth-century technique.[40] More certainly attributable is the crown which Henry IV (1399–1413) gave his daughter; it was one that he had acquired with the crown jewels, and was so recently made as to be still appropriately modish, though the best reason for thinking it English craftsmanship is that eight of its stones were noted as counterfeit.[41] Henry's rival Henry Percy had fewer precious things in his London house, but they included signs of the dining etiquette known to Eleanor of Castile, with four knives with amber hafts and a fork for eating green-ginger.[42]

Information about the expenditure of the aristocracy comes from a few surviving household accounts, though those for the later thirteenth and fourteenth centuries record the costs of food, plate, clothes, and travel rather than jewellery.[43] Nevertheless, Bogo de Clare, member of a magnate family, spent 55 per cent of his £375 London outgoings in 1285–6 on clothes and furs, 12 per cent on silver and plate.[44] This was not his total household expenses, however, merely what his agents took to his London house, and it is not usually possible to establish what proportions of income and expenditure went on such things, though scattered references show that jewellery featured amongst New Year's Day gifts. The earl of Arundel who was executed in 1326 was found to have £524 and £52 worth of jewels in Sussex, yet fifty years later his successor had £30,000 worth of gold and silver in his tower at Arundel. This sort of increase cannot be taken as an absolute indicator of increased expenditure and holdings, but is certainly indicative.[45] Thus the earl of Kent owned five gold rings set with precious stones worth 100 marks in 1399. No wonder that Piers Plowman compared the rich to peacocks, weighed down by their finery but praised and flattered for their plumage, which is superficial.[46]

The wearing of all this jewellery was governed by convention, though the niceties cannot always be discerned from the records. Rings, brooches, pendants, and even circlets on the head might be worn by either sex, and by children, though hair-ornament was mostly for women. Otherwise, gender differentiation was slight; the lapidaries associated certain stones with sexual appetite or its outcome, such as childbirth, but did not gender any stone in the sense of giving it properties that made it totally inapposite either for men or for women. Sumptuary laws could be a male-enacted means of controlling women's dress and expenditure, but do not seem to have been used in this way in England. Piers Plowman inveighing against Lucre shows one view about women wearing too much jewellery, but it was an extreme one.[47]

The inscription on the Writtle brooch is the only one which makes explicit the intention that it was to be worn by a woman, and the supposed association of the Ave Maria prayer with religious women might possibly mean that that text was more likely to appear on women's brooches (Fig. 6.12). Chaucer's Prioress had a brooch shaped as a letter 'A' dangling from her rosary, but that was the first letter of a different text, spelled out below it, *Amor vincit omnia*, 'Love conquers all'; this slogan could have many meanings, from the amatory to the implied threat that love and friendship, in other words a lord's power, would settle any dispute. What it meant to the nun and to those who saw it may therefore have been different things. A brooch from Cliffe Hill, Sussex, that includes the *Amor* text certainly had mixed meanings, as the inscription begins with an incomprehensible *Rei*, and ends in the French *Pensez de mei*, 'Think of me', with two other words, *Avuz meiot*, that defy explanation. Sandwiched in between is some Latin, *Johannes me fecit*, the only use of that formula since the Saxon period, though one which leaves the same doubt as to whether 'John' was the maker or the patron who caused the brooch to be made.[48]

Older women, like the Prioress, were expected to be restrained in what they wore, and unmarried girls were not supposed to disturb their maidenly modesty by wearing anything that would attract improper attention. Men might wear their jewellery only on feast-days. At any rate, this was behaviour expected on the continent, and as the courts were as much French as English or Scottish, was probably expected in Britain as well. Nevertheless, practices may have varied; the aristocracy generally used different types of hall for their feasting and entertaining, depending on which country they were in, and may therefore also have varied their concepts of proper convention. At the level of the knight, the painting of Sir Geoffrey Luttrell shows him at a meal with his family when the only visitors were two friars, and jewellery seems to have been limited to pearls in the hairnets of the ladies.[49]

Male costume could be very gaudy in the fourteenth century, with robes of more than one colour, so that Chaucer's Man of Law was content to be seen looking like a walking chequer-board. It also provided flatter surfaces on which appliqués and bells could be sewn (Fig. 8.9). Chaucer's burgesses' 'full fresh and new geer' was 'apiked', which suggests coloured costume perhaps adorned with metal fittings like the base-metal mounts and bells found in some number in London. Hats tended to be preferred to hoods, and gave another surface for the display of jewels. In many respects these trends made men much showier than women, and more fitted for public display; this can be seen as males seeking to keep women in their 'private' domain, but at the same time being expected to provide them with finery that often led, as in Chaucer's tales, to inconstancy and deceit. The young wife in the Miller's Tale was bedecked with a silk girdle, a tailored dress with ribbons, a leather purse with silk and pearls, and '. . . her collaret revealed | A brooch as big as boss upon a shield'. Who can blame the clerk Absolon for exchanging his mother's ring for a kiss? But the poignancy is that the ring was a symbol of eternal love, and this one was 'engraved' either with a reminder of constancy or with a religious text intended to inspire thoughts far removed from Absolon's.[50]

To some extent jewellery was responding to changes in costume design. New dress fashions at the aristocratic level created a need for new types of fastening, in particular as clothes became tighter-fitting and more tailored to the body. This was wasteful of cloth, as was greater use of 'dagging', cutting hems into semicircles or triangles, because of all the offcuts that resulted—and thus was perversely encouraged by the fulminations of moralists against it. To achieve a close fit, the dress could not merely be slipped over the shoulders but had to be fastened. One way to achieve this was by laces, which might be fitted with metal ends to prevent fraying; several in London still have silk residues trapped inside them. A few are thirteenth-century, but most coincide with the first, fourteenth-century, documentary records of their being purchased and owned. The alternative was to use buttons, either of metal or of fabric, which had less scope for causing scandal by exposing flesh. They are first mentioned in the 1330s, though the term may not by then have acquired its later meaning, so that some thirteenth-century small cast double-convex discs in London, York, and Winchester might have been sewn on to be ornamental rather than functional (Fig. 8.9).[51]

Buttons and lace-ends have been found in London in greater numbers than in other towns, which is partly a reflection of its larger population, but mainly of the circumstances of excavation opportunities. Norwich, for instance, often the second city in size, has yielded neither buttons nor lace-ends earlier than the late fifteenth century, and only a dozen or so belt-mounts, while York has produced lace-ends and buttons as early as those in London, as well as various mounts and base-metal bars for stiffening belts of types which are also known in silver. Bars, buckles, and chapes were bought from their makers by the girdlers who cut the leather or sewed the textiles from which the belts were made, and who were among the most prosperous artisans in fourteenth-century York, as they controlled the final selling-price of the finished product. They usually sold small metal fittings as well (Fig. 8.9). By the end of the fourteenth century, wills and inventories were being drawn up even for better-off artisans; clothes, beds, and coverings are most frequently mentioned, but in York a good many owned at least a silver spoon, pewter was becoming widespread, and a seamstress had two gold brooches as well as six silver spoons to bequeath in 1398. Goldsmiths were, of course, always likely to be among the wealthiest citizens; one in Carlisle in 1379 left half of his tools and equipment to his son—he was lucky to have had one to inherit his trade—and made a special mention of a silver baslard, a kind of knife that Chaucer's burgesses would have been proud to own.[52]

Londoners may have been more sensitive to fashion changes than most other townspeople. The king and aristocracy were more often to be seen in the city's streets than anywhere else, and everyone could look into the shops in Cheapside that served them. Many magnates owned London houses; in the thirteenth century they were 'wardrobes' from which trade was conducted, but as institutions like lawcourts and parliament increasingly turned London into a true capital, so the magnates themselves were more likely to stay either in the city or in its suburbs. To some extent Perth served the same function in Scotland, with Scone as the equivalent to Westminster. A finely carved fourteenth-century ivory knife-handle probably indicates the taste of a wealthy merchant, though in Perth a magnate owner is also possible (Fig. 7.10). In these two towns there was an aristocratic market to supply that scarcely existed elsewhere, and many of the buttons, laces, and other objects from London rubbish-dumps may have come from or been intended for the great households: so too may many of the silks, linens, and 'dagged' costume fragments from organic layers, leather shoes with openwork cutouts or long, moss-stuffed, pointed toes, and decorated leather scabbards (Fig. 8.9).[53]

The Perth knife-handle is like several bone ones carved with human figures of various sorts that could be examples of the spreading use of table cutlery, following Eleanor of Castile's example. Knives and daggers were, however, also worn very prominently as costume fittings because men's tight-fitting tunics were shown off by low-slung belts. The upsurge in decorated leather knife-sheaths, some painted as well as embossed, may have begun before this fashion developed, but have been promoted by it; London has produced a particularly large collection. Chaucer's five burgesses evidently made a great display of theirs.[54] Purses also became even more prominent.

Although many of the London finds of mass-produced base-metal belt-mounts and suchlike can be described as 'shoddy', they may nevertheless have been made for household servants and retainers who would not have cared much about the quality of things that would soon be thrown away. People were prepared to sport things that were almost literally valueless, such as the late thirteenth-century copper-alloy jetton turned into a brooch, discarded in Norwich. Such things existed below the level of quality control that was being exercised on many commodities, which is shown by the makers' marks on the silver and pewter saucers, and increasingly on other things such as knives. This was not only a guarantee for the customers, but preserved the good name of the London manufacturers—and their oligarchical control. Making things in public view was supposed to be another way of guaranteeing quality, and helps to account for the concentration of crafts in and around Cheapside. Amongst the uncontrolled manufactured products, lead-alloy toys can be recognized, and children can begin to be seen as having a group identity of their own.[55]

Just as urban finds may indicate production for great households as well as for bourgeois and artisan, so rural finds cannot usually be attributed to particular owners and therefore to the different strata within the peasantry; even the rubbish from the house of someone like Chaucer's Franklin might get mixed up with that of the villagers. Sites like Wharram Percy do not produce

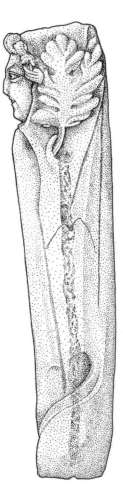 

Fig. 7.10. Front and side views of a finely carved fourteenth-century ivory knife-handle from Perth, probably an example of increasing use of high-quality table cutlery. The grinning male head emerging from leaves may allude to Mayday festivities. (Drawings by Dave Munro reproduced from Hall 2000*b* by permission of Perth Museum & Art Gallery, Perth & Kinross Council, Scotland. Actual size.)

very large quantities of finds, but the range of iron fittings, a copper-alloy vessel rim, and glass beads are typical enough. Another find was a scallop-shell pendant, probably a harness fitting rather than a pilgrim's badge brought back from Compostela, but even people from a fairly isolated village might make a pilgrimage, or be conscripted for service in France, which would take them into a wider culture than merely their local market-town. Metal-detecting of the excavated soils at Westbury again led to the collection of a larger assemblage than usual, including a mirror-case, a ring-brooch, a *fede* finger-ring, pilgrims' badges and ampullae, a seal matrix . . . in fact, anything that might be found in a town, and nothing that would not be. The better-off peasants could do quite well for themselves, one at Gomeldon, Wiltshire, managing to acquire a gold coin, and even some in the troubled Borders had a few silver pennies to hide away. Peasants were an integral part of the economy, and were borrowers and lenders, like townspeople; credit was available to see someone through a bad year. Was it a temptation to borrow more than could be repaid, and was the availability of little luxuries like a brooch or a decorated knife adding to that temptation? But in the countryside wealth and display could not be equated with freedom, which probably mattered more than anything else, including land.[56]

All this expenditure was taking place in the fourteenth century against a background of economic uncertainty and agricultural difficulties, shortage of bullion, wars with France, and from 1348 the Black Death. Before that, bad weather in 1315–22 had caused famine, animal disease, and human mortality from which the population may not have completely recovered before the plague killed nearly half of it in just two years. With subsequent outbreaks preventing regeneration,[57] the shortage of labour that followed led eventually to higher wages, though probably not until the 1370s was the spending power of the surviving majority significantly changed, in a market much reduced in volume but with generally lower prices. Institutions like guilds provided a sense of community and long-term continuity, a contrast to the frequent impermanence of families, now even more threatened by lack of heirs and sudden death. This was worse for townspeople than for rural dwellers, but even they could easily find themselves with no close family to pass their land on to, and with it their memories and traditions.

Isolating the effects of these processes is difficult; there is, for instance, a very marked downturn in the number of decorated pottery jugs, but the trend cannot be shown as an immediate consequence of the Black Death killing off all the more skilled craftworkers or causing higher labour costs that would have made the manual application of dancing figures and the like uneconomic. The trend might have started in 1315–22, which would particularly have affected lower earners' already limited spending capacity, and it may have been influenced by other factors, such as greater availability of metal equivalents. Equally, changes in drinking habits could have caused a reduction in demand for large jugs, though this is not clearly seen until later. In the short term, the Black Death is hard to recognize; building work was interrupted at some churches for lack of masons and carpenters, not necessarily because all were dead but because survivors could get higher wages at secular building sites. No immediate upsurge in apotropaic jewellery can be seen; paternoster beads, ring-brooches with IHS and other formulae, or small silver crosses like one in the Dumfries hoard with AGLA, were all current long before 1348.[58]

Although it was not openly stated, the 1363 sumptuary law was probably in part a reaction to the population reduction of the Black Death and attempts to keep things as they were, or at least as they should have been; if the poor could not spend their money on clothes, jewels, and expensive foodstuffs, they would not seek higher wages to acquire them. Certainly attitudes to the poor were changing, from thirteenth-century sentiments that all should receive largesse, whatever their condition, to the fourteenth-century belief that this merely encouraged idleness, and that the poor should be made to work for their living, only getting alms if they were physically incapable. The 1377 Poll Tax targeted 'idle peasants' by making them pay their 4d. even if poverty had exempted them from the Lay Subsidies. From 1379 the tax was meant to be graded, so that the higher ranks paid more—but the fixed sums made no concession to income disparity. After the 1381 Peasants' Revolt, this was reviewed, and movables were brought back into consideration, thereby confirming the importance of possessions, although very few assessments seem to survive.[59]

By 1381 the wars in France had ceased to be a source of profit to the English. High taxation is likely to have had a substantial effect on disposable incomes, though as with the Black Death the direct consequence is incalculable. As higher wages began to be available for the poor, however, the need to give physical expression to differences between ranks was probably further increased, and no downturn in expenditure on clothes or jewellery is discernible.[60] The peasants' main complaint was taxation, but resentment of lords' power over them led to the burning of estate and court records, mainly to destroy evidence of servility, but also because of their awareness of the documents as physical symbols of their oppression. In the same way, the abbot of St Albans set his tenants' quernstones into a pavement over which they had to walk when paying rents and court fines, a physical affirmation of their status so much resented that, when they rioted in 1381, they pulled up the stones, broke them, and handed them round in an echo of the Eucharist.[61]

Social unrest could have led to different conclusions; the aristocracy might have been able to re-establish their feudal means of control by their defeat of the rebels. One reason that England followed a different trajectory from that of France in this matter was that new ways of defining social relations had become deeply ingrained.[62] People had become too accustomed to defining their place by what they owned and what they could be seen to own, the results of their own achievements rather than of their inheritance.

8

The Wars and the Posies
The Fifteenth Century and the First Half of the Sixteenth

The problems of the second half of the fourteenth century continued to affect the fifteenth. Sudden death remained a constant threat, and population levels probably did not begin to recover much, if at all, until the 1540s. Instability in England was briefly restrained by the century's first two Henries, but thereafter losses in France soon began to prove expensive, the Wars of the Roses were resumed, and uprisings in Wales added to the uncertainty. Nor did the new Stewart dynasty bring internal peace to Scotland. Commercial profits could still be made, especially in the cloth trade, but exports rose and fell with alarming rapidity. Population reduction led to much restructuring, not least in widespread abandonment or shrinkage of rural sites and of urban back areas and suburbs. For archaeology there are some compensations; stone-lined rubbish-pits were one response to fears of smell-spread disease, and their final fills are less often mixed up with residual material than those left unlined. But in London the establishment of the stone waterfront means that the dump deposits peter out, so that the place of the capital in setting standards for the rest of the country becomes even more difficult to assess.[1]

Although there was enough bullion to sustain a silver currency in England and Scotland and to allow at least intermittent minting of gold coins, sometimes in quite large numbers, the site-find record is an indicator of decreased overall usage. Both silver and gold became available from new sources after 1460, some compensation for the fall of Constantinople in 1453 and the consequent extra difficulty of trading with the Near East, but the maritime route that opened up for bringing gold from West Africa may not have increased the quantity coming into Europe as a whole, as trans-Sahara caravans were fewer. Use of the sea, however, put first Portugal and later England in the middle of commercial flow-lines, rather than at their ends. After the fifteenth century gems began to come round the Cape to enter Europe by the same western route, and emeralds even crossed the Atlantic, to be followed by new supplies of gold.[2]

Higher wages did not necessarily mean increased spending by labourers and artisans, one of whose social goals emphasized leisure, not self-improvement; once they had earned enough for their basic upkeep, they often preferred to stop work rather than to accumulate a financial surplus. Nevertheless, an increase in the quantity of copper-alloy cauldrons and other vessels and utensils is one indication of greater spending on commodities. The thirteenth-century assessments recorded such things in quite a small minority of households, and fragments are not usually found in contemporary contexts; they are much more frequent in later medieval levels, just as vessels are more often mentioned in documents. Because they could be melted down for recasting, fragments are not especially plentiful, except on sites where founding took place, such as Pottergate, Norwich, where a fire recorded in 1507 provides a closing date for the range of feet, rims, handles, and patches that were recovered. Another, earlier workshop was the foundry at York's Bedern.[3]

Unlike cauldrons and another increasingly used metal cooking vessel, the tripod skillet with a projecting handle, some copper-alloy vessels were probably not confined to the kitchen but were used at table; the number of tripod ewers with long, narrow spouts suggests that they were an alternative to aquamaniles for washing hands before a meal or between courses. A tripod ewer with a pouring lip rather than a spout found in the Gower peninsula has an inscription that declares it to be a 'laver', so its washing function is not in doubt (Fig. 8.1, left). Another form of ewer is jug-shaped with a flat base and a pouring lip, more likely to have been used for serving drink. One looted by British troops from the royal palace of the Ashanti in Ghana has heraldic badges that associate it with the Yorkist kings, so it was made at the end of the fourteenth century. It may have reached the 'Gold Coast' in the fifteenth as part of an early attempt either to trade commodities or to exchange gifts in return for precious metal. A very similar one was found in a Norfolk manor-house, a context that suggests the sort of hall in which such vessels appeared. Furthermore, long inscriptions in English or French cast around the bellies can be taken to imply users who could be expected to be literate or who at least needed to be flattered by the presumption that they would be.[4]

Pewter vessels also enhanced domestic settings; none merited an inscription, so far as is known, only makers' marks. Few whole ones survive, although the range was extended from saucers to drinking flagons known mostly from their lids, for example in Exeter and London, the former close to the source of tin for the metal, the latter the main manufacturing centre. York was a minor competitor, yet apart from a few fragments at the Bedern, pewter has not been found there, though it occurs increasingly in urban wills and inventories, as it does in those of better-off peasants. It was not necessary to be very much better-off, however; an ounce of silver would have bought twelve pounds of pewter in an average year, and valuations put it as low as 2*d.* per pound, though a single pewter pot might have cost 6*d.*, enough to pay for twelve pots in clay.[5]

Fig. 8.1. Two fourteenth-/fifteenth-century copper-alloy vessels, both from Wales. Shown at approximately one-third of their actual sizes, for comparison of capacities.
Left: copper-alloy tripod ewer, found in the Gower peninsula. The inscription is in French, cast in individual letters, a bell-founder's technique, and reads IE SUI LAWR GILEBERT/KI MEMBLERA MAL I DEDERT, 'I am the laver Gilbert; who carries me off, may he obtain evil from it'. The curse formula sounds rather like the Order of the Garter's *Honi soit* . . . , and the personification of the object suggests its status. (Photograph reproduced by courtesy of the City & County of Swansea: Swansea Museum Collection. Actual height 260 mm.)
Right: tankard from Caerphilly Castle, its lid missing. The absence of a pouring-spout shows that it was used to drink from, as were an increasing number of vessels in pewter and clay of similar sizes. (Photograph reproduced by courtesy of the National Museums and Art Galleries of Wales. Actual height 135 mm.)

Pewter spoons are more often recovered, some having makers' marks. Many have decorative end-knops like silver ones, including one or two with figures which at first glance can be taken as apostles, but on second could be seen differently.[6] Pewter may here have been overtaking wood as a material, but greater use of table cutlery in general may be another factor; more table knives occur in later fourteenth-century wills, at the same time as does a new form of handle, in which two strips of horn, bone, wood, or metal were riveted to a flat tang. These may not all have been for table knives, but the change is suggestive; a Suffolk chaplain who had a pair of table knives worth 12*d*. in 1370 may provide an early example of the trend. Forks, on the other hand, do not seem to have been used except for picking exotica like green-ginger out of their syrup; they do not appear in the archaeological record, at least recognizably.[7]

A glass goblet typically cost twice as much as a pewter pot, and the finest were still imported. A few beakers with small projecting prunts were brought from the Low Countries into London, and some opaque white glass achieved by adding tin as a colourant was coming from Venice. Finds of broken glass in towns and villages do not generally increase in the fifteenth century, however, so wine drinking was not spreading down to a new market. Indeed, a temporary decrease in its consumption within aristocratic households may be recognizable, as finds of glass are fewer at fifteenth-century castles and manor-houses, and some vessels were already a hundred or more years old when broken.[8]

Even if wine was not descending the social scale, changes in taste stimulated by higher wages are probably identifiable. Small vessels, usually with handles, seem a more appropriate size for use as beakers to drink from than as jugs to pour from (Fig. 8.1). Metal was now being challenged by pottery; in London in particular a bright green glaze in the second half of the fourteenth century perhaps made clay mugs acceptable on a table if the gloss was seen as no less showy than the gleam of pewter, and if whatever was served from them was not demeaned by the association, as wine would have been in the past. English-made beakers were already in competition with stoneware imported from the Rhineland. By 1400 it was as cheap to ship even low-cost bulk goods across the Channel and the North Sea as to make them in eastern England and Scotland, especially if they had to be transported any distance by land.[9]

Similar cost factors affected cooking ware, both pot and metal, usually entered in customs records as *baterie*, without identifying individual components of the cargoes. Short-handled pottery pipkins, with or without feet, were equivalent to the copper-alloy skillets. Dripping-pans and small bottle-like 'measures' also suggest new cooking methods, with roasts and sauces becoming more often eaten, probably a reflection of higher incomes as well as of new tastes.[10] Cooking-pots were still made, however, some with handles as though to imitate metal equivalents, so stews and pottages were still important foods.

The drinking-mugs seem to have been made in fairly standard sizes, so may have been measures for a new introduction, beer, which is ale brewed with hops that make it stronger. A taste for its distinctive flavour had to be acquired, but the number of mugs and beakers suggest that many people were quite happy to make the necessary effort. It was probably the preferred drink of immigrants from the Low Countries, small numbers of whom had begun to arrive in Edward III's reign, and who by 1440 made up over 5 per cent of

London's population, enough to be worth specially taxing. They seem to have had a disproportionate influence on the brewing trade, though few went into cooking and victualling, so their effect on what people ate was probably a lot less than on what they drank.[11]

Although the Flemings concentrated in London, they were not confined to it; nor were imports of German stoneware, Dutch redwares, and so on. The new drinking-vessels were also well represented in York, so if they really were associated with beer, that too was getting popular outside the capital. Norwich, which had strong connections with the Low Countries, seems to have had rather less of its pottery, however. Imports from France and further afield continued also to arrive in England, but not as commercial rivals to the Low Countries cargoes, though some were containers for ginger and other exotica. They are more often found in southern ports, as geography would dictate, but only in small numbers; the stonewares and redwares hardly reached Southampton or Exeter until the end of the fifteenth century, so that for the first time since the Norman Conquest a significant difference between regions can be seen in portable material culture.

Rather different are small, wide-mouthed lobed cups, usually with two handles, very thin-walled and with glossy green or yellow glaze inside and outside. What they were used for has not been established, but a potent loving-cup for passing from hand to hand is one possibility. Some have moulded figures inside, such as birds that would seem to be drinking as the level of the contents was lowered. They are the only clay vessels for which direct metal equivalents have not been recognized, though there are wooden mazers with similarly internal jests.[12]

The Flemings were not only brewers; many were goldsmiths,[13] but if any of their products survive, they have not been distinguished from those made by indigenous craftsmen, or from French imports, as standards were international. At the end of the fifteenth century the Venetian ambassador reported that England had very large stocks of plate, fine pewter, and gems, in its churches as well as in its houses. He said that there were more goldsmiths in the St Paul's area in London than in the four leading Italian cities put together, which suggests that considerable allowance for hyperbole should be made, but he had no reason to exaggerate beyond all measure. Turning gold and silver into plate 'immobilized' it by preventing its use in currency, a problem for servicing cash transactions when metal supplies were limited; people could turn their wealth back into coin if they needed to, but status display was a higher priority. Plate and jewels were no less portable than coins in times of trouble, although also vulnerable to theft. One recourse was to deposit them in a church, in the hope that fear of sacrilege would make it immune from attack by conflicting armies, and more secure against the breakdown of law and order. Something of the problems involved are shown in an agreement drawn up in

1471 between a knight's widow and the abbot of Glastonbury for the return of the husband's 'cup of gold, salt cellar . . . and a locked casket stuffed with jewels etc.', the abbot to be 'satisfied' for 'all costs and damages', a kind of storage charge.[14]

The alternative was to bury valuables. This was hardly practical for plate, because the size of the hole would make it more difficult to disguise, but a purse of coins and jewels could quickly be hidden. Hoards are not only deposited when there is a national crisis, but two which had jewellery are both dated by the coins in them to the particularly troubled 1460s. One, found in the bank of the River Thame in Oxfordshire, had rings of various sorts with silver coins that take it up to 1460; the other, from Fishpool in Nottinghamshire, is notably richer, with a more varied range of jewels and over 1,200 gold coins, the latest datable to 1464 (Figs. 8.2–6).[15]

The Thame and Fishpool hoards each has one large gold ring that would not have looked out of place in the thirteenth century. Both have claw settings, Thame's holding a toadstone, Fishpool's a domed turquoise. Thame has a smaller turquoise in a stirrup-shaped ring of the type that had appeared by the first half of the thirteenth century. None of these three rings looks much worn, so either they had been kept unused in chests or caskets, or the designs had a long currency, which shows how difficult dating by style can be. A third ring in the Thame hoard shows more evidence of recent fashions, with leaves and flowers engraved on its hoop, and in its bezel a peridot that had been cut, not just polished and otherwise left in its natural state; behind the stone, however, is a small hole to bring it into direct contact with the wearer's finger, so traditional beliefs about the properties of gems were being maintained. Indeed, the cutting of inscriptions and even of images of saints inside the hoops of rings suggests that direct physical contact was more rather than less important than before.[16]

All three of the other Fishpool rings have short inscriptions, as has one in the Thame hoard, which has a gold hoop without a bezel of any sort, engraved with sprays of flowers and a 'posy' text in Gothic lettering, *tout pour vous* ('all for you'). Some earlier rings had had amatory texts, but they became much commoner in the fifteenth century; flowers and leaves seem to place them within a garden of love. A new technique was to inlay them with enamel, usually white, to lighten the ring's appearance (Col. pls. H.1–3). The texts were nearly always still in conventional French, another common one being *Sans partier* ('Never to depart') or a rarer variant *Sans repentir* ('Without changing'/'Without unfaithfulness') on a ring excavated recently on the waterfront at Poole, Dorset, a site used by shipwrights, which does not suggest particularly well-to-do owners.[17]

Rings with inscriptions like these may have been love-tokens, given as gestures of affection to partners or hoped-for partners, but the same sentiments of good faith could usually apply equally well in other social relationships. A

Fig. 8.2. The gold finger-rings in the Thame, Oxfordshire, hoard, deposited after c.1457. Upper photograph: the large ring on the left can be opened—see lower photograph. The others have a peridot held in a claw setting, the hoop engraved on the shoulders with leaves and flowers; a toadstone, also in a claw setting; a turquoise in a stirrup-shaped setting; and the fourth ring is a band with enamelled flowers and an inscription.
Lower photograph: the large ring opens by turning the quatrefoils on the ends of the frame. The openwork top has letters, MEMANTO, 'Remember' (MEI DOMINE, 'Me, O Lord', is completed round the sides), and two Marian fleurs-de-lys; the large amethyst held in place by the top is cut in a Byzantine-style double-armed 'Lorraine' cross, and suggests that a relic of the Cross would have been held between the separate gold plate and the back-plate, with their elegant trailing enamelled flowers (see also Fig. 8.4). (Photographs reproduced by courtesy of the Ashmolean Museum, Oxford. Actual sizes.)

Fig. 8.3. The four gold finger-rings from the Fishpool, Nottinghamshire, hoard, coin-dated to c.1464. Top left is a turquoise in a claw setting. Top right is a very worn iconographic ring, with the figure of a saint or a bishop. Lower left is the seal-ring of an unidentified owner. Lower right has a hoop cut to look like beaded cabling and an inscription inside, *uphaf ye entier*, with a heart between the last two words. (Photograph by courtesy of the British Museum, London. Actual sizes.)

Fig. 8.4. Enlarged view of the reverse of the largest ring in the Thame hoard, showing the Crucifixion against a red enamel background, and some of the sapphires cut to fit the curve of the hoop. On Christ's right side (viewer's left) is the Virgin Mary, on his left St John, holding a book to symbolize how he recorded Christ's last words in his gospel. Above the arms of the Cross are the sun and moon, witnessing the Crucifixion and about to plunge the world into darkness. (Photograph reproduced by courtesy of the Ashmolean Museum, Oxford. Enlarged.)

gold ring inscribed *tout le vostre* ('[I am] all yours') between leaves inlaid with white enamel was excavated in a late fifteenth-/sixteenth-century context, at a Yorkshire castle, Sandal, much visited by King Richard III (1483–5); 'all yours' is the sort of expression of loyalty that a king likes to hear. A ring like that would have been a reminder of their place to a household member, appropriate for giving at New Year, a practice still continued—*en bon an* ('for a good year') was a favourite text. The hint of a loving relationship in many of these inscriptions would show that the household was not entirely governed by self-interest. A different sort of gift was of rings from newly appointed serjeants-at-law to the king, the lord chancellor, and other dignitaries 'in token of their duties', with inscriptions such as *Vivat Rex et Lex*, 'Long live the king and the law', explicitly and flatteringly linking the sovereign and justice.[18]

One of the Fishpool rings had a device cut into its bezel so that it could be used as a seal, though its owner is not identifiable from the hawk that is shown, a rather generalized reference to an aristocratic sport (Fig. 8.3). Although used earlier, seal-rings without gems were much commoner in the fifteenth century than before, partly in response to increased communication by private letters, such as those made famous by the survival of so many of the Paston family's. The usual range of devices was heraldic, pseudo-heraldic, a play on the owner's name, a merchant's mark, or, at least from later in the fifteenth century, a single letter. A seal from a matrix usually worn on the finger may have been seen as a better guarantee of confidentiality than a seal-die dangling on a chain or thong. Sometimes, just as they may have been in the Saxon period, a ring was dispatched as an authentication of a message, and a seal-ring with a recognizable motif would have been appropriate; the Fishpool ring has *de bon coer*, 'of good heart', inside the hoop (Fig. 8.6)—the text is very common on other rings and jewels, and is quite apposite for an authenticating ring, carrying a hint of good faith from the sender.[19]

Seal-rings, especially in silver or base metal, may have been used by a lord's steward or other officer on his lord's business; one with the device of a Yorkshireman, Sir Brian de Stapleton, was found on the Isle of Man, where he had an estate. A heavy gold seal-ring from Raglan, Monmouthshire (Col. pl. H.6), has the initials 'WA'; whoever 'WA' was, he owned a seal not unworthy of someone in a senior position under Lord Herbert, who in the 1460s was in effect governing Wales from Raglan Castle. Much more routine are those probably owned by merchants, found in some number in London and many other towns.[20]

Another of the Fishpool rings was engraved with the figure of a saint or bishop with a staff. It also had an inscription, probably *en bon cuer*, but the whole ring is very indistinct and shows how quickly motifs would get rubbed away if a ring was much worn, though in this case the lettering is fifteenth-century, and the ring is of the type known as iconographic, with figures of Christ, the Virgin and Child, saints, or symbols of the Passion (Col. pls.

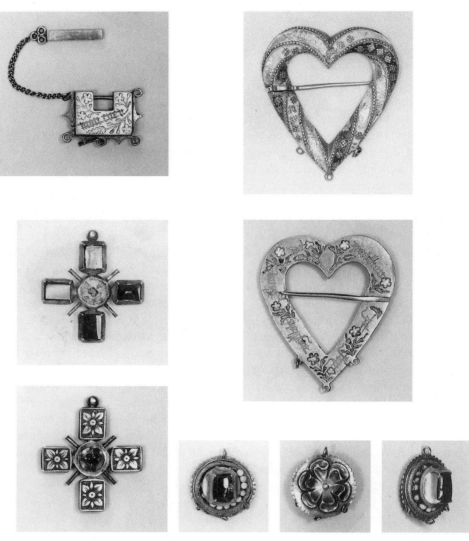

Fig. 8.5. Gold jewels from the Fishpool hoard. Top left: a miniature padlock, its key attached by a short chain; it has enamelled flowers and *mon cuer*—an inscription completed on its other side. The little loops along its edges probably held dangling pearls. Top right: two views of a heart-shaped brooch, the front with blue and white enamel, with grains of gold in small groups all over it, the sprays on the back picked out in white enamel and inscribed *Je suy vostre sans de partier*, 'I am yours constantly'. It too has loops for pearls. Lower left: two views of a pendant cross, with four amethysts on the arms (and a missing central stone) on one side, and a ruby in the centre of the other. The four pegs would have held drilled pearls. Lower right: three views of a pendant roundel with a large sapphire surrounded by small pearls and a very fine gold cable on one side, and a six-petalled flower on the other. (Photographs reproduced by courtesy of the British Museum, London. Actual sizes.)

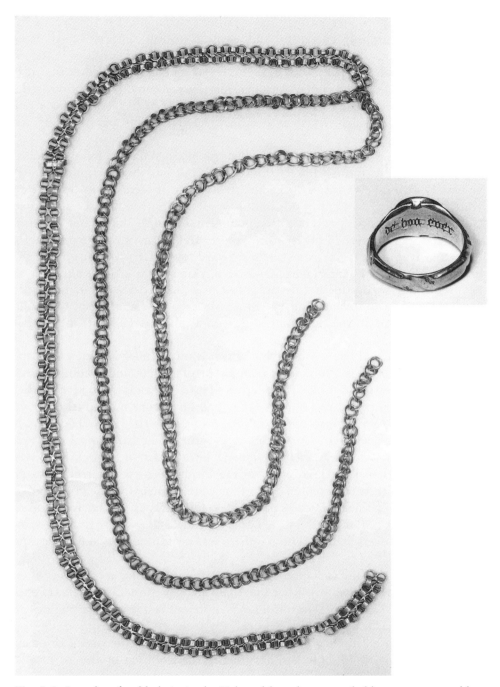

Fig. 8.6. Lengths of gold chain in the Fishpool hoard were probably worn as a necklace from which some of the jewels were suspended; rings too were sometimes carried round the neck on chains. Also shown here is the inside of the hoop of the Fishpool seal-ring, showing its black-letter inscription *de bon cuer*. (Photographs reproduced by courtesy of the British Museum, London. Actual sizes.)

H.4–5). Like seal-rings they may have earlier precedents, but the very great majority are certainly fifteenth- and early sixteenth-century. Many have inscriptions, which unlike the posy-rings are increasingly likely to be in English—the Fishpool ring is an exception, but its condition shows that it is an early example in the series. Another, relatively common, exception is the inscription *Honour et joie*, for purity and the bliss of heaven. At least one iconographic ring also served as a rosary, having knobs on the hoop for repetition of the *Ave*.[21]

The fourth ring in the Fishpool hoard has no bezel, and is cabled and beaded on the exterior, as though purely ornamental, but has the inscription 'uphaf ye entier' with a heart between the last two words. It seems to mean 'Lift up your whole heart', an English translation of a Latin prayer. Phrases like 'As in God' are more clear-cut and not usually hidden within the hoop, but 'Most in mynd and in myn hert / Lothest from you fer to depart' is on the inside of a hoop and would be taken as a straightforward love-token were it not for the findspot, Godstow Nunnery near Oxford, a context that at least allows it to be a nun's ring expressing her devotion to Christ. In any case, contemporaries may have made no distinction; the young Margery Paston referred to a 'ring with the image of St Margaret that I sent you as a keepsake' in a letter to her husband.[22]

The Thame hoard has a fourth ring which is much more complex than the other three. Its bezel is a miniature reliquary, rectangular, and holding a large amethyst cut into a double-armed cross (Figs. 8.2 and 8.4). Seven other amethysts are set round its hoop—so they had to be cut on a curve, and two were shaped to expand into the hoop's junctions with the bezel. The bezel is gold openwork with two fleurs-de-lys and letters that form the Latin text *Memanto mei Domine*, 'Remember me, O Lord', part of a popular prayer beginning *Mater mei*, an invocation to the Virgin Mary to intercede for the supplicant's soul. At each end are two four-leaved flowers that can be turned to unlock the container for access to the relic. On the back is a finely engraved crucifixion with red enamel, and inside is a loose plate which is also enamelled and has flowers engraved on it—there was no trace of any relic when the ring was opened.

Mechanisms like the locks on the Thame reliquary ring were more often used on small pendants; an earlier one that opens to reveal enamelled scenes held part of the Crown of Thorns. Slightly different is a miniature padlock in the Fishpool hoard, with its key held to it by a chain. An inscription, *de tout mon cuer*, 'with all my heart', suggests a lover locked to the object of devotion (Fig. 8.5). It could, however, have been a badge, used by the Yorkists—'fetterlocks' are in several inventories (Fig. 7.4). A gold seal-ring from London has the same device, with the lock surrounded by a chain such as was probably meant to be attached to the Fishpool piece, with a black-letter inscription inside the hoop, *ma souvereigne*, possibly a reference to a queen, or to the

Queen of Heaven, but perhaps a sign that the device had simply become overused, the sovereign being the ruler of the owner's heart. Another object in the Fishpool hoard makes a different reference to the centre of love, a brooch with a heart-shaped frame, enamelled in white and blue (Fig. 8.5). The padlock, cross, and small roundel do not have pins and were probably meant to hang from necklaces like the gold chains found with them (Fig. 8.6).[23]

The Thame and Fishpool hoards may have been deposited because of the Wars of the Roses, and there are other things that may directly reflect the period's instability. Finds in the grounds of, or close to, Middleham Castle in Yorkshire include a gold finger-ring with 'Sovereynty' engraved inside and with an SS chain on the outside. As the SS collar was practically an official royal symbol as well as a Lancastrian badge in the first half of the fifteenth century, the ring could well have been a gift from Henry VI to the Nevill family who owned the castle until they were dispossessed by the Yorkist faction in 1472. A gilt copper-alloy badge of a boar may be associated with Richard III, whose device was a white boar, as may be a plaque with 'R' and 'A', perhaps for Richard and his wife, Anne (cf. Col. pl. H.7). The biggest of the Middleham objects is a lozenge-shaped gold pendant with a large, but imperfect and probably reused, sapphire set on the front above an engraved crucifixion, framed by a Latin text of the Mass prayer *Ecce Agnus Dei* . . . ('Behold the Lamb of God . . .'), ending in two 'charm' words. On the back are the Nativity and the Lamb surrounded by saints; details of the Nativity scene link it to the popular cult of St Brigit. Ironically, this most splendid of the Middleham series is the only one not obviously with political significance, although its probable dating in the 1420s–50s would put it in the thick of the wars. It could be unlocked to reveal a small cavity for relics; silk and gold thread fragments were found inside it.[24]

Pendants that were eye-catching reliquaries were not new, but they were more colourful and probably more frequent in the fourteenth and fifteenth centuries. One that can be dated by its lettering to the early fifteenth is the gold and enamelled Clare cross, which opens in the centre to reveal a relic, presumably part of the True Cross or a piece of stone from Calvary. In the angles between the arms of the cross are pearls on gold rods, pearls being used like enamel to lighten the tones of much of the jewellery of the period. A simpler cross in silver was excavated at Threave Castle, Galloway, where another type of reliquary, a locket, might have been taken as a love-token but for the IHC engraved on it (Fig. 8.7). Most pendants were not also reliquaries, though they might be devotional, like the equal-armed cross with four amethysts and originally four pearls in the angles, which was in the Fishpool hoard (Fig. 8.5). To have a crucifix to gaze upon in the hour of death was important, so to have one always about the person was a prudent measure. Some pendants were not overtly religious, such as a gold heart-shaped one from Rocklea Sands, near Poole, engraved with an ivy-leaf—perhaps chosen for its fidelity in

Fig. 8.7. Two silver-gilt fifteenth-century devotional objects excavated at Threave Castle, Galloway. Both are reliquaries with small compartments that can be opened, the locket, left, by sliding the lid upwards, the cross by pulling out a rivet at the back. The locket's Sacred Monogram IHS was a common late medieval defence against sudden death. The cross is engraved with quatrefoil and trefoil leaves, and had pegs (now filed nearly flat) for holding pierced pearls to the ends of the cross arms, and there are holes in the centre where dangling pearls could have been attached. (Photograph reproduced by courtesy of the Trustees of the National Museum of Scotland, Edinburgh. Actual sizes.)

attachment—and a French posy, *Tristes en plesire*, 'Sadness in pleasure', probably referring to the lovers' delight in their devotion to each other and their sadness that it could not be requited. From the heart dangle short wires, probably to suspend pearls.[25]

Pendants were favoured partly because they went well with later medieval costume—tailored clothes move with the body, and a swinging pendant would emphasize a gesture; open-necked costume tantalized all the more when shown off by a necklace with something dangling from its centrepiece. Some pendants' motifs seem bizarre choices—miniature knives, ear-scoops, and toothpicks, for example, but such things could be disguising subtle messages; bitterns' claws were favoured as toothpicks, so a theme of 'catching' someone could be insinuated. For the discreet or pious, by contrast, a high-necked robe would hide a reliquary pendant or a small crucifix from view and make its wearing close to the heart a private act of devotion.[26] Gold chains in the Fishpool hoard may have been necklaces, which became fashionable again in the late fourteenth century. Margery Paston asked her husband for one in 1453, having borrowed a cousin's when the queen visited Norwich, 'because I was ashamed to appear in beads among so many pretty ladies'. The little Fishpool padlock may have been meant as a pendant to be fitted on one, and a small roundel also in the hoard was another, a complex construction of enamel beads and a sapphire, with a gold flower on the back.[27]

Formal collars were widely worn; a silver one of SS was found on the Thames foreshore in 1983, and has as its centrepiece a trefoil loop from which dangles a cabled and beaded ring. 'S' was not the only letter used; a collar of 'P's for the Percy family, major contenders for power in the north, is engraved on a silver crescent-moon badge that was one of the Percy devices—as well as the Virgin Mary's. SS collars can be seen on many funeral effigies, but one is also shown on one of the first portraits of anyone other than a king, a panel painting of Edward Grimston, an ambassador, who commissioned it from a Dutch painter while on a royal diplomatic mission in Bruges in 1446. He had himself shown with the SS collar in his hand, to display his trusted status, a heavy gold chain around his neck, but no other jewellery, even on his hat. The close ties between England and the Low Countries led to a few such portraits, such as one of Sir John and Lady Donne, owners of Kidwelly Castle, Carmarthenshire, showing them at prayer flanked by St Catherine and St Barbara; Sir John and his wife are both wearing Yorkist livery-collars with enamelled white lion pendants, the badge of Edward IV. Other paintings are of members of the royal family, but in general they lack the subtlety of colours and perspective, until Henry VIII employed Holbein.[28]

Silver SS collars like that found on the London foreshore were for esquires to wear, gilded if they were for knights, and were not intrinsically valuable, only worth a few shillings. Others were in base metal, presumably for servants. Someone keen to show their service to a Lancastrian king wore an SS collar gladly even if it was not gold; when John Baret, a leading citizen of Bury St Edmunds, Suffolk, died in 1463, among his bequests were 'my colors of silver of the king's livery'. Baret's will went into great detail and gave interminable instructions about his funeral. His tomb survives in Bury St Edmunds Abbey, to whose monks he left individual items—jet paternoster beads, amber beads, a silver ring, even a girdle with a silver pendant and buckle inscribed 'Grace me governe', his personal motto.[29]

Baret was using the beads and other objects to ensure that he would be remembered individually in the monks' prayers, so that he might spend less time in Purgatory. To the shrine of St Edmund he gave what sounds like a heart-framed brooch—'my best herte of gold with aungellys and a ruby with four labels [inscriptions] of white innamyt [enamelled] . . . to be hanged, nailed and fastened to the shrine'; the object was to be in direct contact with the sacred structure, so that the blessing of the saint could pass to the soul of its former owner. This was a frequent request in wills, which must have left many altars and shrines festooned with rings and brooches. Like many testators, Baret also gave the shrine a gold coin, rather than its cash equivalent, probably because of the coins' fine appearance and the religious inscriptions struck on them. Another example of devotional use of gold coins is shown by one mounted as a pendant which has on it the text from St Luke's Gospel about Christ passing unscathed through his enemies, a charm for a journey safe from robbery. Edward IV introduced a half-mark coin that showed St Michael the Archangel skewering a monster on one side, so the type became known as 'angels'. Because Michael drove Satan out of heaven, they became icons for driving out disease, made particularly potent if blessed by royalty; many were adapted for suspension by having holes drilled through them.[30]

Baret owned several rings, including an iconographic one with the Trinity that was to go to his wife, and a double one with a ruby, a turquoise, and a 'scripture' written inside the hoop. He also had a cramp ring with 'black enamel', which suggests that the custom of Good Friday blessing by the king or queen was as strong as ever; it was later discontinued by Henry VIII as old-fashioned and backward-looking.[31] Another of Baret's jewels which may have had a royal connection was a 'little fetirlock of gold with a lace of pearls and small beads therto of black', which sounds as though it might have been like the padlock in the Fishpool hoard, which had loops from which pearls might have dangled on short chains.

Baret's tomb at Bury shows him on the side, below a 'cadaver' originally staring up into mirrors set in the ceiling of his chantry; the mirror-image of life is death. The 'stinking carrion' cadaver represented the torment of the body in Purgatory; the Dance of Death was a more widespread image. In general these expressions of mortality had little effect on the designs on iconographic or devotional jewellery in the fifteenth century, but there is a gilt-silver ring with a heart between two deaths' heads, inscribed 'Ioh'es Godefray', that seems to be of this period. *Memento mori* may, however, be recognizable in texts like 'If this you see, remember me', which are valid even after a donor's death, and which would have been appropriate on the memorial rings occasionally recorded in fifteenth-century wills.[32]

Whether jewellery can be seen as expressing very specific ideas and beliefs is problematic, as is whether it can be seen as expressing ideas and beliefs particular to particular social groups. Iconographic rings and charm-words were clearly very widely used, and can be seen as analogous to various recorded cleansing and apotropaic rituals. They were certainly not confined to 'ignorant' peasants and artisans, however, as the valuable Middleham pendant clearly shows. What is less clear is whether 'learned' senior churchmen shared in or merely tolerated the underlying ideas, but a Hereford bishop buried in 1516 with a ring holding a 'rough ruby' with a Tau cross and bell engraved and enamelled on each shoulder, and *Ave Maria* inside the hoop, provides a strong hint that Christian charms were important even at his level. The material culture seems to show a wide range of belief and practice that united rather than divided fifteenth-century society.[33]

Baret's will did not state the values of the objects bequeathed, but as an upper to middling man of business he could have owned the sorts of things that are in the hoards. The Pastons owned some jewels, but as Margery aged she seems to have lost interest in necklaces, though not in her family's gowns and other clothes. When her husband drew up Sir John Fastolf's inventory at Caister Castle, he revealed something of what might be owned by people on the next social rung, including three jewels to the value of 600 marks held as a pledge from the duke of Norfolk, clearly articles like some recorded in royal and ducal treasuries that were in a different league from what is in the hoards; a single gold collar in Henry VI's inventory was worth £2,800, so no wonder it was described as 'riche'. That inventory also included a great 'ouch' (brooch) of St George worth £200, and two other brooches with gold chains and pearls that had been bought from the executors of Lord Fanhope for a combined total of £540. Valuables can sometimes be tracked in more than one inventory, their values changing if they were remodelled; the 'Icklington collar' appears several times in the inventories, with a lower valuation after stones were removed from it.[34]

The Yorkist, Lancastrian, and Tudor kings all used their jewellery as their predecessors had done—to wear as a display of their magnificence, to give as presents, and to use as pledges for loans, as plate continued to be; the Icklington collar's value before it was remodelled is known because it was stated when being redeemed. It was still important for everyone to show themselves in full finery at occasions such as royal tournaments.[35] Henry VII's reputation for meanness takes on a different complexion when he is found giving away rings with diamonds, emeralds, and other stones, and maintaining the New Year gift tradition, even though in general the practice of making such gifts to senior household members may have been becoming less the norm; they were more likely to be paid in money, and the lower ones to get lengths of cloth rather than robes. Gifts, however, were still used at various levels to smooth paths and open doors; the Pastons seem to have used money, but others were more subtle, such as the prior of Worcester who paid £5 for a gold brooch set with gems with which to gain the favour of Lady Margaret Beauchamp in 1444–5.[36]

An alternative to leaving money or gifts to an abbey or parish church so that the testator's soul would be prayed for was to make gifts to the new late medieval foundations, colleges. As more people received education at them, many of whom did not then go on to take holy orders, so the gifts from old members increased. One jewel which looks as though it could have held its own in a royal treasury is a silver-gilt brooch in the shape of a letter M, with a ruby at its centre cut and polished to form a vase, from which emerge lilies (Fig. 8.8). In the arches of the letter are modelled gold figures of the Virgin and the Angel Gabriel, partly enamelled, and the frame is set with various stones and pearls. The cutting of the ruby is a technical triumph, as is that of the amethyst in the Thame ring. In this case, the history of the jewel is known, as it was given to New College, Oxford, in 1455 by a Winchester citizen and his wife with their son Thomas, who was a fellow of the college, which is dedicated to St Mary. Gifts of plate were also made by generous benefactors,

Fig. 8.8. Silver-gilt brooch in the shape of a crowned letter M, for Mary, Queen of Heaven. In the arches is the Visitation, with the Archangel Gabriel on the left and the Virgin on the right, standing on bases as in sculptures such as rood-screens. A finely carved ruby vase in the middle holds a flowering lily. The other stones are emeralds, pearls and more rubies. The brooch was given to New College, Oxford, in 1455. (Photograph reproduced by courtesy of the Warden and Fellows of New College, Oxford. Actual size.)

particularly wooden mazers set with gold or silver-gilt mounts that would ornament the high table, as they did also in many guildhalls. Passing vessels from hand to hand for each member to drink from was a bonding ritual.[37]

The Suffolk chaplain who had a pair of table knives in 1370 also had a belt with a purse and knife worth 5s., a prominent and unsubtle combination often seen in illustrations of people out of doors, and criticized by moralists, as in an early fifteenth-century poem which derided the 'long knife astrout [sticking out]' of men who strutted round in fashionably slit costume. The sexual overtone of such knives and daggers was obvious, made more so by the vogue for a hilt known to modern sensibility as the 'kidney' type. A comparable fashion was for a 'ballock' purse, that seems to have been one with two compartments.[38]

A symptom of the importance of fittings dangling from belts is that metal hangers survive in some number; the rich had elaborate ones studded with gems, but most were copper-alloy, swivelling on bars riveted to the belt (Fig. 8.9). The belt might receive more emphasis by having a large chape fitted to its dangling end, much larger than was needed just to prevent fraying. Again, precious metal was available to those who could afford it, but several lyre-shaped copper-alloy chapes were mercury-silvered, a well-recorded illegal deception. Various other shapes and decoration occur, such as St Christopher figures at Kidwelly Castle and Snargate, Kent, which were icons for a safe journey and against sudden death. Others had personal names on their plates (Fig. 8.9); although the names may not now be identifiable, they show the sense of self-awareness, or self-importance, earlier shown by kings like Richard

II. Another copper-alloy dress fitting that may imitate late medieval designs in gold or silver is the cloak clasp, an example recently excavated in Southampton comprising an openwork disc encircling two standing figures.[39]

Another example of base metal following precious is a copper-alloy pendant from Norwich that has small glass beads dangling on the ends of chains, comparable to the fittings on the gold Rocklea Sands pendant or the Fishpool hoard jewels (Fig. 8.10). They are attached to a wire frame round a pair of copper-alloy pilgrims' badges set back-to-back—which are unlikely to post-date the 1530s; some pieces of wire-work may have been misidentified as post-medieval when not found in such an association or in a closed archaeological context.[40]

The two Norwich pilgrims' badges in the pendant are of a type that was new in the later fifteenth century, when thin 'bracteate' embossed discs to be sewn to a cap or other garment, or even into a book, partly replaced the large openwork pewter badges and ampullae. Some were probably guild badges, with a religious theme because of the dedication of the fraternity to a particular saint—indeed, both the Norwich badges might be examples; one shows St George, the other the Virgin and Child, both frequent guild dedications as well as having shrines in England—St George's cult was promoted by royal association and his heart was at Windsor; the Virgin and Child could have come from Walsingham.[41] These thin metal badges were made in gold or silver as well as in copper alloy, and tend to be better made and therefore more likely to have contemporary stylistic detailing than those in pewter. They were not necessarily round; datable examples include a lozenge shape, one having *Ave* in a script attributable to the early sixteenth century, others coming from the shrine of the murdered Lancastrian Henry VI, which was first at Chertsey Abbey and then after 1484 at Windsor Castle, so that the Yorkist Richard III could control the cult as a reconciliation gesture (Fig. 8.10). It was subsequently encouraged by the Lancastrian and first Tudor, Henry VII (1485–1509). At least Henry VI had had more earthly sanctity than that other Lancastrian martyr, Thomas of Lancaster. More orthodox new devotion found expression in other badges, such as a crescent moon to emphasize Mary's steadfastness in a constantly changing world, but they are not ideas which suggest fundamental changes in popular devotion away from medieval symbolism to new Renaissance thinking. The late fifteenth-century popularity of St Barbara was because of her promise of protection from sudden death, not some new theology; one of her copper-alloy badges was excavated in Exeter, no less elaborately executed than one that survives in silver gilt.[42]

Another pendant from Norwich, found at the same site as the other but in a medieval context, is a heart-shaped piece of bone, rather crudely incised with lines to represent Christ's blood (Fig. 8.10). Clearly devotional, it provides a hint that other heart-shaped pieces, even the Fishpool brooch, that seem amatory on the surface could have carried a hidden meaning. One of the surviving iconographic rings with *honnour et joie* inside its hoop is also from

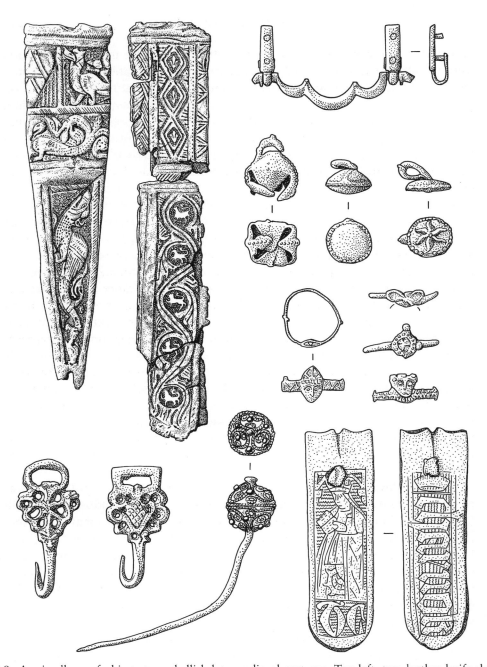

Fig. 8.9. A miscellany of objects to embellish late medieval costume. Top left: two leather knife-sheaths embossed with dragons, heraldic devices and shields. Top right: a swivel fitting that was riveted to belt, from which a purse dangled. Centre: a bell, typical of small items that were sewn on dress, as wer the buttons next to it. Below are examples of pewter finger-rings, some perhaps devotional, like th mitred head that may be Thomas Becket, others just decorative. Bottom right is a copper-alloy chape of belt-end, inscribed on one side 'TC' below a St Catherine with her wheel, and on the other 'Charnok presumably for T[homas] Charnock, who is otherwise unknown. Next to it is a silver pin with a glo bular head, mercury-gilded and with filigree-wire decoration. Bottom left are two hooked tags, used a cloak-fasteners. (Drawn by Nick Griffiths from the collections of the Museum of London, the Cit of Winchester Museum and the Norfolk Museums and Archaeology Service Actual sizes, except the tw scabbards, half actual sizes.)

Norwich.⁴³ Another late medieval Norwich object is a buckle with four quatrefoils on its rectangular plate, not particularly remarkable except that it is almost identical—including a casting fault in one corner—to one found amongst a large heap of buckle frames and plates, and strap-ends, found in a well near Cheapside in London, the debris of a maker continuing the tradition of cheap mass production. A new technique was the application of a lacquer-like finish, now black but thought originally to have been reddish brown—enough at least to take off the shine which formerly would have been a desired effect.⁴⁴

Norwich also exemplifies another later fifteenth-century development, the use of metal for purse-frames, especially straight copper-alloy bars from which the bag was suspended, attached to a swivel-loop to dangle from a belt. These would have made the purse wider at the mouth, and more prominent than one closed by drawstrings, perhaps more vulnerable to pickpockets but less so to cutpurses—metal loops may also have been sewn on to deter the latter. Some purse-bars have very conventional religious formulae on them, the Marian 'Angelic Salutation' *Ave Maria*, an IHC, or a Tau cross, the last more frequent in the fifteenth century, and an invocation to St Anthony against madness associated with ergotism resulting from eating flour made from diseased grain. One found in Denham, Buckinghamshire, invoked that other new cult, St Barbara, together with the names of Christ and Mary. A concession to the times is the purses' frequent use of black niello inlay, regarded as more devotional; another is that one has a form of Tudor rose on it. A Tau cross is also the shape of a later fifteenth-century reliquary pendant from Matlaske, Norfolk, which has black enamel rather than the vivid colours of earlier work like the Thorn reliquary.⁴⁵

Rose-like flowers occurred in various guises in the fifteenth century, such as the one on the back of the Fishpool pendant that has enamel beads and a sapphire on the front (Fig. 8.5). Another with a sapphire at its centre was found recently at Farnham, Surrey, forming the head of an S-shaped pin that may have been designed to hold together folds of overlapping drapery, perhaps on the centre of a hat. These flowers may not be specifically Yorkist or Lancastrian, or subsequently Tudor, referents,⁴⁶ but livery badges were as important in Richard III's reign as they had been in Richard II's, with similar allusive doggerel written about them. The king's badge was a boar, so he was derided as a hog (Col. pl. H.7 and Fig. 8.10). Thereafter, however, badges attributable to the great families seem almost to disappear, leaving Tudor roses, sunbursts, knots, and portcullises as the only safe emblems to wear. One of the few exceptions is attributed to the Gainsfords, a family of insufficient standing to offer any threat to the monarchy; it is in parcel gilt and enamel, dates to the second quarter of the sixteenth century, shows a female figure in contemporary costume with long flowing hair, and is quite unlike anything from the previous century (Fig. 8.11). More typical are silver-gilt hooks, which are difficult

Fig. 8.10. Many pilgrims' and secular badges continued the mass-produced pewter tradition, like the heraldic creature on the right which is a yale, an animal associated in the fifteenth century with both the Beaufort and the Bedford families. Smaller, more finely made embossed badges were a late medieval innovation, such as, top left, the copper-alloy lozenge-shaped frame containing an image of Henry VI, who became a cult figure after his murder in 1472. The circular copper-alloy badge with wire border, pendants and beads shows Mary and Jesus, with two letters, one indistinct and the other 'R', for robe, which is shown below; it may have originated at Aachen in Germany, where Mary's nightdress was preserved. Bottom left is a bone pendant, for Christ's heart, shedding blood from the wound made by the Roman soldier's spear at the Crucifixion. (Drawn by Nick Griffiths from the collections of the Museum of London, the Salisbury and South Wiltshire Museum and the Norfolk Museums and Archaeology Service. Actual sizes.)

Fig. 8.11. Silver-gilt and enamelled livery badge associated with the Gainsford family, c.1525–50, found at Chelsham, Surrey. The maiden is wearing contemporary dress and has long flowing hair unlike any medieval representation other than of mermaids. She is holding a garland of flowers, however, which is more traditional, carried by brides on their wedding-days—cf. also the Mayday milkmaid, Fig. 7.4. One of the Gainsfords, Sir John, served King Henry VIII, and may have felt secure enough in royal favour for his household to be seen with these badges. (Photograph by the British Museum, reproduced by courtesy of the owner. Actual size.)

to date precisely, but seem to develop more complex technology towards the end of the fifteenth century than straightforward casting, as used for some time on simpler versions (Fig. 8.9). A few of these hooks have an IHS or other religious motif, and there are cap-hooks with Tudor roses—but none in the sixteenth century can be shown to have displayed any other allegiance, and most of the decoration is filigree spirals, flowers, and lozenges.[47]

The rose was favoured as a badge because of its ambiguity, symbolizing both the Yorkist and Lancastrian factions, and one that could be read in hope as bringing the two together for national unity and prosperity, in which colleges and guilds might provide fraternity and 'peaceful union of the worthier and lesser commons'.[48] Guild or official town badges seem to have remained tolerated; in 1521 the lord mayor of London led a great pageant in which he was followed in procession by men wearing the badges of the city offices, a continuation of the way in which oligarchies manipulated public occasions to display and maintain their grip on power. Chains and regalia were worn whenever a mayoral feast or other civic ceremony provided an opportunity.[49] The badges suggested that the city was like a household, united in its own defence. The responsibility of burgesses to arm themselves to protect their towns from attack was always fairly nominal; in Perth a mace-head has been identified as something owned by a baker wealthy enough to have to perform watch and ward duty. As any practical value in citizens having arms passed, so the duty to bear them became a valued right. Having weapons on display in his hall thus became an affirmation of a burgess's social position, and a reason for maintaining the traditional space that the open hall involved.[50]

Tradition also meant that guild feasts remained an important social bonding experience, and large sums were still spent on them, with more detail of what was involved surviving. In 1507 London's mayor hired more than 9,000 pewter dishes and other vessels to make sure of an adequate display. Wood, pottery, and stoneware were also acceptable as drinking-vessels on such occasions, even for wine; small 'Tudor green' cups are thought to have supplied this need, and their near-copying in much darker red clay 'Cistercian ware' further north suggests the spread of ideas; rather larger vessels were probably for drinking ale and beer. Also new at the end of the fifteenth century may have been ideas about the temperature at which food should be eaten; at least that may be the implication of the metal chafing-dishes best known archaeologically for their triangular or heart-shaped handles, several of which were found in Norwich, others in Winchester, Exeter, and London. They too were copied in pottery. Plates may have been heated on them, but they may also have warmed water for hand-washing, and been fuming-pots in which dried herbs were warmed to scent the air and drive out the plague.[51]

New practices are also seen in recognizable imports. Stoneware vessels continued to arrive, almost certainly in increasing numbers, their fabrics unchallenged by native potters, probably from inability to discover the formula rather than sentiment that it would be inappropriate to attempt to reproduce them, as their shapes were sometimes imitated. The stoneware was highly enough regarded for some examples to be fitted with pewter lids, makers' marks showing that these were often imported as well. New imports included occasional tin-glazed lustrewares from Iberia and Italy, and from the end of the fifteenth century white maiolica from Italy and the Low Countries. The last included vases with the Sacred Monogram painted on them in blue, a type which features in Dutch still-life paintings holding Mary's lilies on altars; others have the English royal arms, so were produced specifically for export.[52]

A valuable collection of lustreware and maiolica pottery and Venetian *cristallo* glass was broken in Southampton around 1500, either an importer's tragedy or the property of a citizen known to have been a royal ambassador, who may have acquired it for his own use. *Cristallo* is not as crystal clear as its name suggests, because impurities could not be avoided; some of it was decorated with gold leaf. A rare complete example of this relatively clear glass is a small beaker said to have been found bricked up in a house in Culross, Scotland.[53] Another very rare complete survival is a beaker in white glass with narrow vertical clear bands, almost certainly made in Venice but so valuable in England that its lid, rim and base were embellished with silver-gilt lids and mounts by a London goldsmith in the 1540s. The ultimate aim of the glass-makers was to create a white rival to the tin-glazed maiolica pottery, which was itself partly a response to the eastern porcelain that was beginning to enter the European market; rare enough in the Mediterranean, it cannot have been part of the north European experience at least until the sixteenth century, so the white glass achieved a distinction of its own. Fragments of deep blue have been found in York and Leicester, and of green of various kinds in Exeter, where various other fragments show glass's spreading use in the first half of the sixteenth century.[54]

Despite national economic and political problems, more household items were clearly being bought in the fifteenth century, and the large number of surviving gold and silver finger-rings is another indication of expenditure, albeit one that involved no great cost for a single item. Taxation that may have made people more aware of social stratification in the thirteenth and fourteenth centuries by assessing individuals' ownership of goods was ceasing to be a restraint on possessions in the fifteenth. Although the socially graded poll taxes of 1379 and 1381 were not repeated and subsidies based on tenths and fifteenths continued intermittently, the levies do not seem to have been accompanied by assessment of individuals' property; furthermore, other methods of taxation were being applied, such as forced loans and, from 1411, payments based on lands and rents, a shift of emphasis to tax on income rather than on goods. Much less concern was expressed about social restraint.[55]

More important were 'mercantilist' protection measures and closing of national ranks by attempts to restrict imports and exports, as in the 1440s when the 'aliens' were taxed partly on the pretext of stopping them from slipping their supposed wealth out of the country back to their homelands, and in a 1463 statute by restrictions on exports and imports of various sorts, including a long list of manufactured goods that could be made just as well in England as abroad. Even wire-headed pins, used in large numbers in the later fourteenth and fifteenth centuries to facilitate sewing and tailoring, were included. Protectionism of this sort underlay the renewal of sumptuary legislation in 1483, which inveighed against the lack of 'restraint of the excessive apparel of the people', so that 'the realm was fallen into great misery and poverty' from imports of cloth, furs, and silk. These were duly restricted, though only as far down the social scale as to those 'under the estate of lord', with no attempt at control of other forms of expenditure such as jewellery, and no suggestion of a need to ordain what knights, burgesses, or labourers should or should not wear.[56]

Changes can be seen to have been taking place in the popularity and function of jewellery. Recent finds of silver-gilt hooks imply that dress fastenings involving precious metal were more widely worn than had been realized, but they were worn in ways that did not emulate the aristocracy. Long-tested favourites such as ring- and frame-brooches died out, affected by costume that did not need central fitting, but also probably by seeming old-fashioned and inadequate. Two with hexagonal frames, one set with garnets, were both quite worn when deposited with gold and silver coins in Edward IV's reign at Holbrook, Suffolk; they may have been as much as a hundred years old when buried, stored for their intrinsic value rather than because they were still sought after for themselves. They had no successors.[57] They were things that had not been hugely expensive; bourgeois and yeoman incomes were sufficient for a few pins and hooks, but not for the elaborate jewels seen in the Fishpool hoard, let alone the three-dimensional Georges and other royal and aristocratic clasps and brooches. Their elaboration and colouring could not be copied cheaply with any conviction. A division had opened up, in which emulation of the upper social echelons was no longer possible, and therefore their influence on everyday outlooks on life was diminished.

A few iconographic rings are specifically attributed to the end of the fifteenth century or the beginning of the sixteenth, such as a particularly large gold one from Coventry which has an English text 'Well of Mercy, Well of Comfort . . .' on the outside, and the Latin Five Wounds invocation on the inside, ending very traditionally with the names of the Three Kings and two 'charm' words. The lettering allows some sort of dating in these cases, and there may be a trend away from such devotional rings, a trend that is not seen so much in signet- and posy-rings; the former seem to cease to have iconographic images on their shoulders, and the latter begin to switch to the use of English, which may be nationalistic, or a trace of new ideas of expression. In a very few cases, 'Renaissance' inspiration can be recognized in such finds, like the Gainsfords' badge. Three rings found together at Wragby, Lincolnshire, were unfortunately not accompanied by coins, but a silver one with a classical cornelian of Minerva is ascribed to the mid-sixteenth century stylistically and could be taken as indicative of renewed interest in the ancient world; one of the others is distinctively Italian in style. A few rings with scalloped settings, like two from Wiltshire with toadstones, are likely to be sixteenth-century also; new thinking did not reject belief in the virtues of stones.[58]

Some traditional practices survived; an abbot of St Augustine's, Canterbury, was buried in his vestments in 1510, with things made specially for the grave such as a lead mitre and a gilt copper-alloy ring with a two-part rock crystal cemented together, and glass imitation rings, the sorts of things that had been placed with such burials since at least the thirteenth century. Not many pilgrims' badges can be positively assigned to the early sixteenth century, however, a possible sign of some decline in interest in saint's shrines and their cures. This is not necessarily a sign of fundamental new concepts about salvation, although pendant reliquaries and crucifixes that can be given a specific date seem to disappear from the record. On the other hand, paternoster beads probably remained no less popular, as they continued to be frequently mentioned in wills, such as those that belonged to Dame Alice Clere of Ormsby in 1538, who also had a 'harte of gold with a large diamond in it', which sounds like a traditional heart-shaped brooch. Otherwise, there would seem to be a case for saying that traditional devotional objects were already falling out of use well before Henry VIII's break with Rome.[59]

The interests of kings Henry VII and VIII, and even apparently of the boy-king Edward VI and his sister Mary, in jewellery are well chronicled by inventories and portraits, and Holbein's paintings include new settings and designs. The SS collar returned to favour after the brief Yorkist interlude ended in 1487; one bequeathed to the lord mayors of London in 1545 to be worn as testimony of the city's loyalty is still used. It has white and red enamelled roses, gold openwork knots, and a portcullis, as well as S letters. A different version is shown in a painting of Sir Thomas More. Otherwise, it was safer to be shown in rich but sober garb. Archbishop Warham was even painted without finger-rings, although he still had a gem-encrusted mitre and a gold processional cross in the background. His successor Cranmer wore a signet-ring, but eschewed the mitre and cross. The great city merchant Thomas Gresham was painted in 1544 with two rings and two very small pendants, but without even a jewel on his hat. His wedding-ring survives, a gimmel with a ruby and a diamond, the use of two stones traditional enough, but in a complex *memento mori* setting, and with two hoops that fit together and can be unlocked, not a single hoop that divides to create two bezels.[60]

A few new trends can be seen, such as miniature enamelled girdle-books, some with texts from English Bibles on the cover, showing the new concept of personal salvation through contemplative reading and prayer rather than the mechanical recitation of *Aves* and *Paters*. *Memento mori* finger-rings were also beginning to appear, and even miniature coffins; one pendant with black and other enamel that opens to reveal a skeleton was found at Tor Abbey, Devon, so probably pre-dates its dissolution in 1539. The costs of these things, and therefore how widely they were used and worn, is not known, but they do not seem common.[61]

Even in the early 1530s people may have been reluctant to express Catholic traditional sentiments too openly, but appear to have been very conservative; between 1532 and 1534 several Lincolnshire testators left bequests to shrines like Walsingham, and three to Henry VI's. Only thirteen of 585 surviving Lincolnshire wills mentioned jewellery, thirty-four beads. A lot of these wills were made by farmers of various sorts, however, many of whom were not very well off, so that only twelve specified silver plate, forty-five silver spoons—and none any gold, though they had quantities of kitchenware of various sorts. Somerset wills of 1544 and 1545 include bequests of a girdle garnished with silver, another with a silver buckle and chape ('mordle'), a silver and gilt pendant, and a brooch; several have beads and five have rings, often a wedding ring left to a church—though not to specific shrines or altars. Those, however, are from a total of a couple of hundred.[62]

It is at gentry, bourgeois, and yeoman level rather than at the royal court that change seems most observable in the century before 1550. The readiness to accept new types of pottery had already shown a flexibility that may not be discernible in many other sources. The vanities of the court mattered little to those who needed to work and to keep up with rising costs and lower real wages. New ideas were not only about the development of 'Renaissance' artistic styles, but more fundamentally were about the purpose of material culture and what it expressed, and which made social and religious change more acceptable.[63]

Envoi

The significance of material culture, and the portable objects that are part of it, is dictated by people's economic and social power, and their need to give physical expression to their status and aspirations. As in any society, the ability and wish to acquire, display, and use metals, glass, gems, or pots depended in the Middle Ages upon the supply of raw materials and finished products, and the demand that their availability might meet or create.

The island of Britain had never been united by the Romans, and different reactions to their army's withdrawal were only to be expected. Generally, however, power-seeking leaders establishing petty and impermanent fiefdoms relied largely upon being able to demonstrate their success by the acquisition of booty that could be profligately consumed, shown off, or distributed to families and supporters. Swords, brooches, or drinking-vessels symbolize how these social affinities were created and maintained, whether recorded in graves, hoards, and other deliberate deposits, or in accidental loss or intentional jettisoning of what was beyond reuse. The precise meanings that were given to gold and silver, glass and garnets, changed according to their contexts; some gave physical expression to an ambition to inherit the prestigious authority of Rome, others gave credence to stories of descent from far-travelling heroes, while others stressed a person's place within their own immediate society. Yet artefacts such as pottery show that even people whose priority was subsistence were part of a wider network of contact.

External factors influenced behaviour: no leader of a group in Britain could negotiate directly with the Byzantine emperor for the subsidies that brought gold into western Europe, so none could take action to ensure its continuing availability during the seventh century. Its relative value changed as it became rarer, so that it had to be used sparingly if at all; consequently, for some people the display of access to it became even more important. Contemporaneously, however, Christianity's infiltration changed beliefs about what happened after death, and how people should use and dispose of their worldly goods. In bigger political units, using symbols to show origins and allegiances mattered less, but the large numbers of artefacts now known show that prosperity was not confined in the eighth and ninth centuries to the royal families. Similarly, both the types of artefact and the motifs upon them show increasing cultural uniformity.

A major role in changing perceptions of the importance of material culture was again played by external factors, as viking raids and settlements led to renewed emphasis upon treasure in its most bulky and least sophisticated forms. Those who successfully resisted the Scandinavians in warfare expressed themselves in the deep Christian meaning of many of the objects that they used. In the later ninth and tenth centuries others for a while used petty artefacts to show their different origins, but personal display increasingly mattered less as social systems dependent upon landholding and urban markets developed. The latter spread the use of small and cheap goods, while ownership of estates and residences at their centres began to focus more attention upon households, which developed into the main social unit for family, work, and ambition.

Because demand for jewellery with which to express allegiances fell away, its absence in the eleventh and twelfth centuries was not a factor of availability and supply of materials to the rich and powerful. At lower social levels, however, ability to acquire disposable goods of any sort was restricted by the heavy tax demands of Norman kings. Uniformity spread into Scotland and much of Wales. Only towards the end of the twelfth century can a loosening be seen, with an urban market feeding commodities into the countryside. Beliefs about protection against death, disease, and physical harm, allied to concepts of what was proper for the settings of the prophylactics whose efficacy was widely credited, brought gem-set finger-rings into vogue, closely followed by brooches that were expressions of wealth and sophistication. At the same time, new systems of taxation, now based upon people's goods, brought new importance to the status that ownership bestowed. Awareness of possessions led also to awareness of group expression, seen in badges that came to undermine the political system as its leaders encouraged physical demonstration of factional allegiance amongst their followers, but which gave cohesiveness to social groups that defined their places in relation to their peers as much as to those in different bands of wealth and occupational acceptability.

With gold again easily available in western Europe, and eastern gems obtainable at prices that were not prohibitive, the fourteenth century saw an increase in the importance of the elaboration of the settings that skilled craftsmen could produce. Passable imitations of plain gold rings and brooches could be made in cheaper materials, but the increasing complexity of enamelwork could not be emulated. During the fifteenth century the aspirations of different classes grew apart. Although conventional piety was a common factor, use of different physical tokens and different patterns of behaviour created a gulf of interests in which different religious beliefs could find expression, and a flexibility of approach fostered new belief in the worth of the individual. Use of material culture had always been fundamental to medieval society; now it was promoting the changes that were to lead to its end.

Notes

INTRODUCTION

1. 'Middle Ages' and 'medieval' are sometimes used in England to denote the period after the Norman Conquest. I follow the ruling of the Society for Medieval Archaeology that the terms should be used for the whole of the post-Roman period, up to the Renaissance and the sixteenth century. Of course, to understand the early Middle Ages it is necessary to go back into their classical background, and 'the Renaissance' is only a term for a set of developments that had antecedents in the later Middle Ages, but I am a traditionalist, and books have word limits.

2. The new *Journal of Material Culture* expresses this as research into ways in which 'artefacts are implicated in the construction, maintenance and transformation of social identities', which is a useful portmanteau.

3. 'Mainland Britain' is distinct from 'Great Britain' or 'United Kingdom'. I have not reviewed any part of Ireland, though a couple of times I have referred to objects found on that island, and similarly the Isle of Man and the Channel Islands have not been directly included. No one will be equally familiar with all parts of the geography of Britain, so I have tried when first mentioning a place also to state its county; similarly, an object referred to for the first time ought to be 'a gold ring from Nateley Scures, Hampshire', and thereafter 'the Nateley Scures gold ring'; in the only too likely event of a reader having forgotten what was said previously about the ring, it should be traceable through the index.

4. For these and the other major developments, including intellectual ones, of the last thirty years of later medieval archaeology, see Gerrard 2003, 133–231.

5. Like most archaeologists, I have had bad experiences with a few metal-detectorists, but I have also had many good ones. For a summary of some of the problems, now ameliorated by the Portable Antiquities Scheme, see Dobinson and Denison 1995. I would personally prefer that all antiquities should belong to the state, with perhaps a small reward for their prompt reporting, but that is a socialist concept unacceptable to the present government.

6. Many are cited in this book, though not the caricatures; I was surprised to discover that such things existed, but only know of those that show Jews, and I have not found a general compilation: Roth 1962 for those of Jews. See Chs. 7 and 8 for late medieval developments towards more personal representation.

7. The names of individuals can be found in the references. Much of this book was written during a financial crisis at the British Museum which has led to redundancies and early retirements that are a grave threat to the cultural leadership that the museum has always given. The Victoria and Albert Museum has not recovered from its similar problems in the previous decade. Scholarship depends

upon such pools of expertise, and catalogues of museum collections are the backbone of studies like this book.

8. I confess that my delight was slightly tempered by discovering on the museum's website that one of the exhibits is to be the tomb of Sir John Baret, as I have cited Sir John frequently on the basis that I thought that the coincidence of the survival of both his tomb and his will deserved to be better known.

9. Courtney's thought-provoking 'One wonders to what extent our perception of history would be altered if the birth of Jesus Christ was forty or fifty years earlier and the progression of centuries so displaced' (1997, 10–1) underlines how our thinking has been shaped; even concepts such as 'the long thirteenth century' do not break down the barriers. Although I have tried to be even-handed, sometimes balance has been lost, for instance in the seventh century. I have given the same ratio of chapters to the period after the Norman Conquest as to the period before it, but the greater volume of evidence is reflected in generally longer endnotes.

10. Japan is often cited as an example of a 'feudal' society and therefore analogous, which may well be true in some respects. But its differences seem to me such that it can only be used as an analogue for motivation and change in the medieval West with extreme caution, if at all, even though similarities at a particular point in time can be discerned. The best overall review for someone wanting to explore further this sort of question about historical archaeology, with international coverage, is Andrén 1998.

11. A lord giving a present to a servant or other member of their household might receive a token gift in exchange to show that the servant owed the lord a 'boon'. So far as gifts to households are concerned, I do not know of a precedent before the second half of the sixteenth century for Queen Elizabeth's canny reversal of the procedure, so that what her courtiers gave her was worth more than what she gave them.

12. Johnson 1997, 147.

13. Astill 2000*a*, 225. The most helpful explanation of *habitus* that I have read is Giles 2000, 9–11, not least because she proceeds to demonstrate its applicability to the rest of her work. Also useful is Lilley's definition that *habitus* 'conditions the way that things are done, and makes things the way they are': 2002, 14.

14. Goetz 2003, 44–5. Isidore used '*discolores* (different) *habitu*' of the Germanic peoples; he also picked on their weapons as characteristics. He referred in the same passage to origins, but the Latin text seems to be specifically about the origins of the Germanic languages being unknown, rather than that of the peoples. Isidore's general principle was 'Gens est multitudino ab uno principio orta', 'A *gens* is a people sprung from a single/common origin'.

15. Hastings 1997, 17, citing Davies, R. R. 1994, 10, a paper which examines national identity in Britain both in the twelfth and the fourteenth centuries. The bishop's words were 'lingue, legibus et moribus, judiciis et consuetudinibus': Davies, W. O. (ed.) 1920, 141–2. Because it was not a single *regnum*, it is wrong to refer to 'Wales' in the Middle Ages as though it was a unitary authority, rather than a land area; terminological problems create many difficulties in a book like

this one, and I have attempted to avoid using such labels inappropriately. 'Welsh' seems to be acceptable as a synonym for 'British', and can be used of people living in the west generally as well as in Wales specifically, at least until their political absorption in 'Anglo-Saxon' kingdoms during the seventh and eighth centuries, but it causes confusion to do so. 'Anglo-Saxon' can be used fairly vaguely, as it is a modern conglomerate word, and I have tried not to use 'Saxon' when I mean anything other than those people who lived in Essex or counties south of the River Thames at a time when they were at least in some ways different from the 'Anglians' to the north. 'English' may not be appropriate until the tenth century and political unification; but linguists call the language spoken before then 'Old English'—'Anglian' and 'West Saxon' being identifiable dialects. Lewis Carroll would have explained it better. For recent discussions, see Hines 2000, 87–8; James 2001, 5–6; and Pohl 2003.

16. I was introduced to this Marxist-functionalist approach by Rigby 1995; see Hinton 1999 for an attempt to relate it to archaeology.
17. The title of this book is not merely alliterative—as *Guardian* readers will realize from that newspaper's frequent (but entirely creditable) corrections, 'gilt' is a homophone.
18. Although some of the formal doctrines of the Church may never have made much impact—only a few people eschewed gold because of its temptations—the decrees of Lateran Councils were generally put into effect, so that some of the changes in medieval cultural perception originated outside the society in which they were promulgated—it was not because of existing belief in Britain that the Eucharist was developed in the thirteenth century, with the concomitant remodelling of many churches that were an important part of everyone's perceptions of space. This is one reason why I am chary of a too ready acceptance of the validity of anthropological analogues, as few societies have been so affected by extraneous control.
19. Some archaeologists may regard this attempt to understand change as disciplinarily flawed, as it is inevitably sequential and therefore has become geared to a chronology dictated by history. I do not see this as a reason for not essaying a task that other disciplines have also set out to achieve. I also believe that archaeology will not take its place in explanation until more work on sequences is done; there are still historians who can write such blindingly obvious but dismissive things as 'our information on buildings and housing is often drawn from what has survived, which may or may not be typical' (Bolton, J. 1996, 55), as though that applies no less to court rolls, customs accounts, or any other form of documentary source. Archaeological evidence is often more concerned with long-term trends than the short timescales that interest many historians, but even that is changing with better sequences and new dating methods, notably for the Middle Ages the precision of dendrochronology for wooden structures.
20. This question is raised by Rigby 1999, 24.
21. Hatcher and Bailey 2001, who end up advocating Chaos Theory. Admittedly they are specifically addressing economic rather than social development, but I am not sure that there is a difference at this level of generalizing. It is also disappointing

that on the only occasion that the authors give any thought to material culture, it is to propose an absurd model with the sole idea of destroying it: 220–1.

1. ADAPTING TO LIFE WITHOUT THE LEGIONS

1. The literature on the fourth and fifth centuries is voluminous, with Dark, K. R. 2000 and Esmonde Cleary 1989 providing summaries of different viewpoints. Raiders came with various tribal names: James, E. 2001, 91. Gildas described the Britons looting each other, as well as suffering enemy assaults: Winterbottom, M. (ed.) 1978, 23. For hoards, Archer 1979; Abdy 2002; Johns 1996, including colour pls. 1–2 for Thetford, 6–7 and 11 for Hoxne, and 54 for the first Amesbury—Burnett, A. 1996 for the second. Both the contents and the nature of the hoards are very different from those in contemporary Scandinavia, where deposits were votive offerings, though some of those in Britain might be from temples rather than from households: see below. Canterbury and Whorlton both have silver ingots, and suggest something more than private owners panicking: Johns and Potter 1965.

2. Imperial restrictions: Reece 1999, 113; Ireland (where there was little or no gold): Ryan 2002, 1–15; Dolaucothi: Arnold and Davies 2000, 97–100; Hoxne: summary in *Current Archaeology*, 136 (1993), 152–7.

3. Discussions include Esmonde Cleary 1989, 99; Henig 1995, 171–3. For Water Eaton, Painter 1999.

4. Johns 1996, 165–6, for enamels; Dark, K. R. 2000, 20–1, for the tutulus-brooches (the different classifications used for brooches are explained succinctly by Lucy 2000, 25–40; the Ashmolean Museum collection catalogue is also a very useful and well-illustrated source: MacGregor and Bolick 1993; Hills and Hurst 1989 for the Gloucester Goth—where they place him back into the pre-410 Roman army, rather than into the early fifth-century sub-Roman period in which I, among others, had wrongly positioned him: Hinton 1990a, 7.

5. Crossbow-brooches: Johns 1996, 168–9; Janes 1996; Swift 2000, 3; Wroxeter's example: White, R. and Barker 1998, 105 and 117; Leahy 1993, 30, for a useful discussion of the belt-buckles. Swift 2000, 228–30, suggests that late Roman jewellery was strongly gendered, which may have affected people's ideas about what was suitable to hoard.

6. Curle 1923—the mouthwatering inventory on pp. 11–12 of fifty silver bowls, twenty-two circular dishes, and so on is worth reading on its own; p. 91 for the coins—the latest two are of Honorius (395–423), but the issue dates are probably no later than *c*.411; see also Esmonde Cleary 1989, 99; Proudfoot and Aliaga-Kelly 1996, 7–8. A suggestion that, as at Thetford, the treasure could have been the concealed property of a native shrine seems less convincing than the traditional explanation, which accounts for the objects' condition. Curle 1923, 84–6, anticipated discussions about the recognition of Germanic troops when he identified the Traprain belt-mounts, etc. as 'Teutonic'.

7. Casey 1989, 320–9.

8. White, S. 1998; White, S. *et al.* 1999. The hoard contains a single much older silver *denarius* of the first century BC.
9. Orna-Ornstein 1999; Abdy 2002, 64–6.
10. Manley and White 1999, 313.
11. The weights and alloys are given by Johns 1999 and the silver weight-units by Manley and White 1999. The larger gold ring is four times the weight of the lightest gold coin, that of the smaller over twice two of the heaviest, so that added together they would have weighed the equivalent of six of the average coins, but the difference in the alloys suggests that that is probably not very significant. As Johns notes, the smaller ring bears comparison with one in the Wieuweerd hoard deposited in the early seventh century, though containing a few coins of the early sixth: Mazo Carras 1985, 161, where the possibility of sword-pommel rings (see below) is mooted, but Patching's do not look like any that I know.
12. Grierson 1991, 22; Spufford 1988, 12.
13. Webster 1999.
14. Knight, J. K. 1999, 152; note, however, Mediterranean glass, below.
15. Place-names allow the idea that 'he' might have been the Paecc(a) whose name occurs not only in Patching, *Paeccingas*, '(settlement of) the followers or family of Paecc(i)', in a document of 960, but also in Patcham, 15 miles away in East Sussex, 'homestead (*ham*) of a man called Paecca', near which Patchway suggests that a *weoh*, 'temple' or 'shrine', was owned by or dedicated to him: Mills, A. D. 1991, 254 and Meaney 1995, 40, n. 68. These names may not have existed in the fifth century, however, and Paecca may not have been a real person, but a mythical founder-figure invoked to create a cohesive identity for people in the area. Fluidity of any such identity felt by these 'people of Paecca' is shown by the failure of the area to become a recognizable administrative district in the eleventh century, either as a rape or as a hundred, unlike Hastings, Malling, or Steyning: Haselgrove 1978, 198–200. The dating of Aelle of Sussex to the 470s–490s by the *Anglo-Saxon Chronicle* may 'fit' the hoard, but may also be too early: Yorke 1990, 16.
16. As noted by Manley and White 1999.
17. Amongst the extensive literature are Ager 1990; id. 1996; Harrison 1999; Suzuki 2000 and reviews of it by Welch 2001*a* and by Ager 2001; and Inker 2000.
18. For vicarious transfer, see e.g. Dickinson 1993, 39, and for gender signals, Stoodley 1999, 39 and 104 (note that Stoodley is talking of the dead, Swift 2000 of the living).
19. There are base-metal coins, often pierced to wear on necklaces, in some graves, but they were probably chosen as good-luck tokens, and they are not with quoit-brooches: White, R. 1990, 138–40, and see further below.
20. Winterbottom (ed.) 1978, 26–7 and 97. Gildas did not use the word *foederati*, the late Roman term used for those given land in return for military service, but his use of *foedus* with other formal Latin words such as *epimenia* and *annona* in the same context suggests knowledge of late Roman practice: Higham 1994, 40–2; use of late Roman types of gear is thus perfectly likely. Gildas's knowledge

might have resulted from his education, however, not from actual British experience.

21. Henig 1995, 172. See also Whitfield, 1995, 90–3. Inker 2000 shows that the technology used in making these pieces derives from late Roman practices.
22. Exemplified by the visits of Bishop Germanus to St Albans: e.g. Knight, J. K. 1999, 59–62.
23. Barber, B. *et al.* 1990, 11 and pl. 3. Note Symonds and Tomber 1991, esp. 81–4, for some of the relatively few imported pottery sherds, etc. from London that belong to this transitional period.
24. Evison 1968, 233; the cemetery has yet to be published. There is a Roman site in the area, but the belt-set grave was not in it. The occupation site was in use from the first half of the fifth to the early eighth century: Hamerow 1993, 5–7, but it might not have existed when the 'mercenary' was buried. (That the 'founder' rejoiced in the name Mucca is very unlikely; the place-name is not known to have been an *-ingas* ending, unlike Patching, and may be a much later formation: Gelling 1993*a*.) Another possible 'mercenary' further up the Thames at Dorchester, Oxfordshire, seems to have been with at least one woman, but was not in a late Roman cemetery or close to a known rural settlement; current dating puts him in the 430s/440s, so he could have been an early settler rather than a soldier serving abroad with a partner or two: Hamerow 1999, 24.
25. Brighthampton: MacGregor and Bolick 1993, 235–6; Welch 2001*a*, 437 and Ager 2001, 388 both exclude it from the quoit-brooch corpus, however. The settlement site at Mucking had a number of late Roman/early post-Roman 'military' fittings scattered in its rubbish deposits, but all could have been old when lost or discarded, any 'military' significance long forgotten: Hamerow 1993, 63.
26. Inker 2000, 41–3.
27. Ager 2001, 388–9.
28. Unpublished work by Mark Corney, information from Dark, K. R. 2000, 52 and Swift 2000, 2.
29. Eagles and Mortimer 1993.
30. Ward-Perkins 2001 is a good recent survey, explaining how language can change without large-scale population change; for instance, if the 'British' were disadvantaged by taxation penalties and adopted 'Anglo-Saxon' speech as an avoidance measure. Nevertheless, I still think that I would now be writing in Welsh if the Anglo-Saxon invasion had involved only the same sort of numbers as William the Conqueror's: Gelling 1993*b*. As well as artefacts and burial practice such as cremation (above), comparisons between settlement structures can now be made: Hamerow 2002, 94. DNA, non-metric traits, and other osteological tests seem unlikely to be able to sort out where people came from: Tyrrell 2000. Recent work on isotopes and tooth enamel is more promising, as it may reveal the geological origin of food eaten and water drunk during childhood, and therefore where people were born, thus providing unambiguous differences that can safely be used to differentiate population groups.

31. Welch 2001*b*, 150, on regions and cremations; Dark, K. R. 2000, 48–50, on provinces, but note that Ager 2001 warns against overemphasis; Eagles and Briscoe 1999 on urns and their decoration; Williams, H. 2002, 58–9, on problems of cremation and their labelling as 'Germanic' or 'Anglian', and noting how cremation-only cemeteries are regionally restricted, but not cremation as a rite. His warning that variability cautions against assuming wholesale transfer of large numbers of people is fair (p. 70), but that cremation was practised by groups creating or retaining identity for themselves does not seem quite to explain why there are so many cremation-dominated cemeteries in eastern England if there were not at least large numbers of people who had direct memories of seeing the practice in their homelands. If *Beowulf* is correct in giving women a leading role as keepers of folk memories and in funerals, the introduction of cremation could be taken as evidence that migration was not only of a few over-adventurous males.

32. Suzuki 2000, *passim*.

33. Inker 2000, 41–3; other data from the catalogue in Suzuki 2000, 122–65.

34. Whitelock (ed.) 1961, 9. I have not found an edition that offers a source for this annal, which suggests that its author had heard an old story and thought it credible.

35. Price, J. 2000, 22 and 25 (a small cache of glass vessels at Burgh Castle, Norfolk, originally thought fifth-century is now thought more likely to be late fourth-); Evison 2000, 65—she points out that the vessels are round-bottomed and could not have been placed upright on a flat surface, so should not be called 'tableware'; Bimson and Price 2000.

36. A small number found in a Flintshire lead-mine could have been deposited at any time, but show that they had been available in north Wales: Knight, J. K.1999, 161–2.

37. The largest excavated cemetery, at Cannington, Somerset, had objects in a few graves, but they were either Roman or seventh-/eighth-century; nothing in between was deliberately included: Rahtz *et al.* 2000. Another Somerset cemetery, at Shepton Mallett, produced a silver pendant with beaded arms to create a cross and a central disc punched with the Christian monogram, in a grave radiocarbon-dated to before AD 410: Leach 2001, 96–7 and report by C. Johns, 257–60.

38. 'Potentates' is the preferred term of Professor Leslie Alcock, who has done so much to elucidate these sites and their ownership, e.g. Alcock 1992.

39. One that has been much debated and disputed: Dickinson 1982 succinctly demonstrates the nature of the problems. Some of the 'quoit-brooches' are also penannular, but they have flat hoops on which decoration was punched or engraved; Type G and others have circular-sectioned frames. For a wide range from Ireland as well as Britain, Youngs (ed.) 1989; and for Welsh examples, Redknap 1995.

40. Caerwent: Savory 1956, 41 and pl. V, g; Bifrons: Hawkes, S. C. 2000, 12–13; another zoomorphic penannular has been found as far east as Barham, Suffolk: West 1998, 8 and fig. 8.1.2; red enamel: Youngs 1995, 32, but note doubts

expressed by Graham-Campbell 1991a, 228 on whether enamelling survived as a tradition in Britain, or was reintroduced from Ireland; Dinas Powys: Graham-Campbell 1991a, 224–30, where he argued that because the item had been cut up before its loss, it had not been a 'model' from which moulds were made, but is a failed casting; in that case it would not be evidence specifically of production of zoomorphic penannulars at Dinas Powys, as it could have come to the site as scrap, probably from Ireland. Coatsworth and Pinder 2002, 74–5, however, accept it as a model, noting the roughening of its recesses to bond the enamel better to the finished product. An enamelled penannular from Traprain Law, not from the treasure, is difficult to call 'zoomorphic', but should nevertheless be mentioned: Cree 1923–4, 277–9.

41. Hen Gastell: Lloyd-Morgan 1995, 24; Cadbury Congresbury: Rahtz *et al.* 1992, 128–30; Anglo-Saxon sites: Dickinson 1982, 58–60. Dating is highly problematic, so the discovery of one with hand-worked (not cast) terminals in a context ascribed to a date before the middle of the seventh century at Drim, Dyfed, is especially welcome: Williams, G. and Mytum 1998, report by J. Webster, 88–9.

42. The first appearance of inscriptions on memorial stones is generally taken as being post-Roman and in the fifth century, e.g. Edwards, N. 2001, 17–19, but Handley 2001 has proposed that they originate in the fourth and should be seen initially as part of late Roman culture. They show more than mere ability to form letters and to create simple texts: Thomas, C. 1998 may have pursued this theme a little further than some would wish, but the basic message is secure, and Gildas's work shows that a good Latin education was available. For Roman burials, Philpott 1991.

43. Cadbury Congresbury: Rahtz *et al.*1992, 223; South Cadbury: Northover 1995; Dinas Powys: Graham-Campbell 1991a, 220–1; Longbury Bank: Campbell and Lane 1993a, 30; a gold chain there could possibly be fifth-century—but is more probably nineteenth-!

44. Meols: Philpott 1999, 201 and report by D. Griffiths in *British Archaeology* (2001); Exeter area: Todd 1987, 255; a Byzantine coin converted into a weight, found in Somerset, could be another piece of evidence, though I have not noticed a recent mention of it (it was displayed in the British Library's 'Painted Labyrinth' exhibition in 2003: British Museum acc. no. 1866.12–11.3; it was not included in Smith 1906); Procopius's statement is credited by Wooding 1998, 654. A Valentinian *solidus* of 425–55 said to be from Chichester, Sussex, gains credibility from the Patching hoard, but may have arrived by whatever process brought that hoard, rather than by import to the south-west: Drewett *et al.* 1988, 248.

45. The study of this pottery was put on a firm footing by Thomas, C. 1959. Helpful recent studies include Thomas, C. 1986; Knight, J. K. 1999, 149–58; Dark, K. R. 2000, 125–34. The minimalist position suggested by Thomas, C. 1990, 11–14, is advocated more fully by Wooding, 1998. That the trade was more regular is the preferred view of Campbell, E. 1996a; he makes a useful comparison with the late thirteenth-century polychrome pottery imports from south-west France to show that small numbers of sherds need not mean small-scale wine trading. Spices are justified by dill and coriander found in the waterlogged conditions at

Buiston Crannog, below: Campbell, E. 1996*a*, 80. The emergence of 'kings' by the 470s is allowed by Dumville 1995, 181. Exports are discussed in all these works, but see also Biek 1994 and Fox, A. 1995 for recent tin ingot finds, and Maddicott 2000, 36–7, for a recent summary. The Gildas quotation is from Winterbottom (ed.) 1978, 33.

46. Report by D. Griffiths in *British Archaeology* (2001); Bu'lock 1960, 3–5, 21–3.
47. Anglo-Saxon-style furnished graves are effectively absent from that zone until the seventh century: Dark, K. R. 2000, 99–100. Rather than seeing such patterns as resulting from political enclaves, Roberts and Wrathmell 2002, 75–80, propose that the main factor causing the dearth of cemeteries in, for instance, the London/St Albans area is the amount of woodland, which created a different culture by creating dispersed settlements; they suggest that this also accounts for the relatively few in Essex, compared to Suffolk and Norfolk. This idea needs more discussion, but I am not sure that it explains why no one in the London/St Albans area seems to have been buried in a furnished grave until the seventh century, unlike at least some people in Essex, unless the former was effectively deserted altogether, which such things as Germanus's visit seems to preclude. That material culture does not have to reflect political control is shown by the supposedly British area of Elmet, around modern Leeds, which has furnished graves.
48. Campbell, E. and Lane 1993*a*, 40–9; a glass sherd from Tintagel has a preliminary identification as a Spanish flagon: Morris, C. D. *et al.* 1999, 213. It used to be thought that the glass was arriving at these western sites as broken pieces for recycling into beads, but enough joining pieces have been found at Dinas Powys to show that whole vessels were being broken there: Campbell, E. 2000, 37–8. This militates against the possibility that wine was imported solely for the Mass, though some may indeed have gone to churches. Food was also, of course, an important element in these feasts, with the most tender meat being offered, e.g. at Dinas Powys: Gilchrist 1988.
49. Contrary to popular opinion, the Tintagel slate does not say that Arthur was the father of Old King Cole, but that 'Artognou, the father of a descendant of Col, made [this]': Morris, C. D. *et al.* 1999, 213–14. See Higham 2002, 74–9, for Art-names, and an interesting discussion of Arthurian problems generally. If Handley 2001 is correct in seeing the origin of the memorial stones in the late fourth century, they would not of course be a new phenomenon concurrently introduced with Mediterranean pottery.
50. e.g. a stone mould fragment and other metalworking evidence found at the Cannington cemetery: Rahtz *et al.* 2000, 266–7 and 398.
51. Edwards, N. 1997, 1.
52. Possible reasons include Justinian's reconquest, closely followed by an outbreak of horribly disruptive plague; the effect of a comet's impact; and the damage caused to the Syrian coast by the Persians, the last advocated by Knight, J. K. 1999, 166–7.
53. Campbell, E. 1999, 45–7, for the pottery and id. 2000, 42–3, for the possibility of glass production in south-western France; Wroxeter: Wright, R. and Barker

1999, 128. Arnold 1982, 61, suggested that an Isle of Wight urn could be an import of this period, but that remains unconfirmed.

54. Perry 2000, esp. 312–15; Moloney 2001 for a later report, not adding to the artefactual record. On the basis of the Dunbar radiocarbon, sites such as Clatchard Craig could also have started earlier than the pottery indicates: see Chapter 2.

55. Hill, P. 1997, 24–6, favours the interpretation that there was no continuity at Whithorn of a Christian community established in the fourth century, most of the Roman artefacts found at the site being earlier than that date, and probably therefore brought to it for reuse of various sorts. In addition to the Romanized culture implied by the pottery and glass, Hill also recognizes it in the ploughs used: ibid. 28 and 464. In a later paper he argues that the church could have been for refugee British Pelagian heretics: id. 2001. The glass and pottery were studied by Campbell, E. 1997*a* and 1997*b*.

56. Lane and Campbell 2000, 238–40; Campbell, E. 1999, 11–14.

57. Waterlogging at Buiston Crannog and in Loch Glashan is a warning about the amounts and quality of organic materials that dry sites do not preserve, though the former at least was an aristocratic site: Campbell, E. 1999, 26–8; Foster, S. M. 1996, 58–61. Dating is extremely difficult, and such problems as the Pictish symbols are discussed in the next chapter, though some readers would expect to see their origins discussed in this one.

58. The first detailed study of this sort was Pader 1982, e.g. 'similar objects may be used differently', p. 89; see also Høilund Nielsen 1997, and papers in Hines *et al.* (eds.) 1999, and Lucy and Reynolds (eds.) 2002.

59. Recent summary by Bruns 2003, maps 2 and 3 for distribution.

60. Collingbourne Ducis: Gingell 1975–6, 76–7. Points about the importance of judging connections on the basis of whole assemblages rather than single artefacts have been well made by Catherine Hills at various times, e.g. 1999, 181–4. Another aspect of weapon-burials, discussed by Härke 2000, is that there are many fewer in cremations than in inhumations.

61. Hines 1997, esp. the maps on pp. 101–2. The brooch shown in Fig. 1.8 is from a cemetery to be published by Annable and Eagles, forthcoming. The site is colloquially 'Black Patch', but Blacknall Field is its correct name.

62. There are a couple here and there in Norfolk, etc., but the general picture is valid: Dickinson 1993, fig. 1.

63. Leigh 1984 for Style I; Dickinson 1993, 37–43, for discussions of Style I and saucer-brooches; Richards 1995 for useful discussion of motifs and ideas generally.

64. Cameron 2000, fig. 18, for some of the sword-bands, and fig. 25 for a chape; there are even fewer shield mounts: Dickinson and Härke 1992, 27–30; Malim and Hines 1998, 93–4.

65. Colgrave and Mynors (eds.) 1969, 50–1.

66. Down and Welch 1990, 96, present the alternative and perhaps more likely possibility that she was buried with her husband, having herself come from the Isle

of Wight. Kent–Wight links are shown e.g. by cremation urns that in turn show similarities to some in Denmark, so have been labelled 'Jutish', though Arnold 1982, 61–2 showed that very many like them have been found in the Low Countries and northwards. The absence of bracteates (below) from Wight is also noteworthy; see Lucy 2000, fig. 5.7 (b).

67. Down and Welch 1990, 95–6.
68. With the old certainties must go also the old jokes, so it is no longer apposite to describe someone as 'buried in their Woden's day best'; indeed, it can no longer be assumed that Woden was widely known in fifth-/sixth-century England, perhaps unlike Tiw and Thor: North, J. E. 1997, 16–17 and 231–4.
69. Hines 1997, 132; Welch 2001*b*, 150–1. For costume generally, Owen-Crocker 1986 is the best guide, increasingly augmented by studies such as that by Walton Rogers 1998.
70. Hawkes, S. C. 2000, 12–13, and above.
71. Avent and Evison 1982, figs. 3–11; an exception to the distribution is Mucking, and there are sites in the upper reaches of the Thames valley in which the mask is scarcely recognizable: Class K, fig. 10.
72. e.g. Dickinson 1993, figs. 34b and 44.
73. Parfitt and Brugmann 1997, 110–17; Brugmann 1999; Welch 2002, 122–3.
74. Dickinson 1982, 52–3, and now also Malim and Hines 1998, 204–5. West Heslerton: Haughton and Powlesland 1999, 341–2 and 345–8. The gold-in-glass beads did not necessarily have gold in them, but were made to sparkle as though they did, a tribute to their makers' skill: Hirst 2000, 122.
75. Alternative views, here much simplified, of White, R. 1990; Meaney 1981; and Eckardt and Williams 2003. The last accept (p. 155) that recycling also took place, explaining why Roman coins are found in rubbish deposits as well as purses: see below.
76. Eckardt and Williams 2003, 147–51, argue that the occasional example of a Roman or even Iron Age brooch may result from similar association with an unremembered past—not because there was any direct continuity or 'heirloom' function. This is entirely in line with the non-appearance of coins with quoit-brooches, noted above, and the same holds true for 'antique' brooches. There is, however, one partly contrary case, a ?third-century disc-brooch worn Roman-style on the shoulder of a man at Collingbourne Ducis, Wiltshire, who also had an unusual silver-inlaid buckle, but no weapons: Gingell 1975–6, 78, 97, and fig. 16. The brooch seems too old to have been an heirloom, but the mode of wearing it suggests continuity of practice, as White, R. 1990, 132, accepted; see also Eagles 2001, 218. Again, there may be wide divergence between different areas, and older customs may have survived in Wiltshire even if the artefacts normally found in its burials seem up-to-date.
77. Robinson, F. C. 1991, 147; Bazelmans 2000, 341–2 and 345–8. Robinson's seems to me to be the best short account of the poem and its dating. It survives only in a manuscript written about the year 1000, so arguments continue to rage over when it was composed in the form that we have it, and how far it reflects the

values of periods before the tenth century (and whether it reflects any of the tenth anyway, or was preserved for nostalgic reasons, a reminder of the lost world of heroic behaviour). The structure of its language 'fits' the eighth century, but it was drawing on earlier, oral stories; the descriptions of the objects and the sets of objects that the participants own and use 'fit' the seventh century and England, though the context is Scandinavia. See also, among so many, Brady 1979; Webster 1998; Lapidge 2000; but also Frank 1992.

78. 'A king shall buy a queen with property, with cups and rings. Both must first of all be liberal in gifts': Gnomic verses, Mackie 1934, 39. Similar practice is recorded on the continent: Hardt 1998, 319, and see also Chapter 2, below. Gilchrist 1997, 47, objects to 'exchange of women' being taken to imply that high-status females were not active players in such situations, but the way in which some returned to fathers or brothers when widowed is an indication of their precarious position.

79. Another gender distinction is suggested by Richards 1995, 59–63, that pots were probably used and also made by women, whereas men made but did not wear most of the dress items, so their experience of those would have been different. He notes, however, that there was no obvious divergence, for instance, the stamps on great square-headed brooches being more rather than less similar to those on urns in the sixth century than in the fifth. Hills 1999, 183, considers that long-distance contacts were maintained by sea as well as by land, since similarities between north German and East Anglian cemeteries persisted. Welch 2001b, 148, points out that if pot-making was a female activity it would have been one of the ways in which identity expressed through material culture was spread, if brides travelled. Marriages between people at lower social levels need not have conformed to Beowulfian practice; later in the Middle Ages many men married outside their communities for personal advancement in order to take over a widow's or a sonless couple's tenement or business—but different landholding conditions may have meant that no such opportunities existed in the earlier period.

80. Williams, D. F. and Vince 1997; Blinkhorn 2000, 103.

81. Evison 1975a: hones of course would not break in transit, so might have gone through several owners in a way that pottery is unlikely to have done.

82. Hamerow 2002, 51.

83. Crawford, S. 1993, 85, shows that there are exceptions where children are quite well represented in a cemetery, such as Finglesham, Kent—where, however, infants were not found. Evison 2000, 49, notes three children with glass vessel rim fragments pierced and worn on necklaces. It is a measure of how ideas have become more flexible that when I noticed a fossil in the only child's grave that I have excavated, I at least thought that it might have been a toy, not just an accidental inclusion; but thirty years ago it never occurred to me that it might reflect the concerns of the living about someone who posed a threat to them, rather than a parent's grief: Hinton 1973: 121.

84. Halsall 1998, 31; Lucy 1998, 48–53; Stoodley 1999, 117–18.

85. Lang, J. and Ager 1989, 107; Härke 2000, esp. 387; West Heslerton: Gilmour 1999 for the blade (the sword was from a grave attributed to a date in the first

half of the sixth century: Haughton and Powlesland 1999, 81–7. The grave had two spearheads in it, which is most unusual, and later at least became a mark of special status, cf. Swanton 1973, 15. The sword is the only one from the cemetery, and suggests that an average of 10% sword-graves, except perhaps in Kent, may be an overestimate based on their being more likely to be recognized and kept by non-archaeologists building roads and the like); sword-rings: Evison 1967a; ead. 1975b. The sword and bead illustrated in Fig. 1.11 will be published by Annable and Eagles, forthcoming; see also Cameron 2000, 115. Later, wills show that inheritance of swords was established practice. Removal of the ring rather suggests that it was not a lord's gift, or disposing of it in the recipient's grave might have seemed quite appropriate.

The suggestion by Härke, e.g. 1997, 124–5, that there is a correlation between male height and the numbers or types of weapon with them in the fifth and sixth centuries, and that this is an ethnic indicator, has been challenged e.g. by Lucy 2000, 87–8. It therefore remains only Härke's Height Hypothesis.

86. Malim and Hines 1998, 302.
87. Stoodley 1999, 136–40. Although many cases where people whose biological sex as first identified from their skeletons suggested that they had the 'wrong' grave-goods have subsequently been reconsidered (e.g. a 'female' burial with weapons in a *Time Team* excavation in 2001 at Breamore, Hampshire), a few have been substantiated, raising questions about the role that that person played in life. West Heslerton had two weapon-graves seemingly containing women's skeletons, in a total of 186 inhumations, but one of those is more doubtful than the other because of bone survival: Haughton and Powlesland 1999, 288 and 326. There may be slightly more examples of biological males buried as women, and shamanism and hermaphroditism have been invoked in explanation: Knüsel and Ripley 2000; as they point out, memory of any such practices and conditions would have been obliterated by later Church teaching.
88. There are more tools—and fewer weapons—in cremation graves than inhumation, one of several ways in which the types and styles of objects vary, for reasons that are unexplained: Richards 1995 is an interesting paper on this and on material culture generally.
89. Härke, 1989, 144–18. This has stood the test of time, e.g. Malim and Hines 1998, 217–18, and could be called Härke's Length Law.
90. The myths about Valhalla may have been developing in Scandinavia in reaction to the Christian notion of Heaven. Some literature scholars are objecting to archaeologists' new interpretations about grave-goods having meaning for the living rather than being provided for the use of the dead, arguing that continental sources imply some sort of afterlife belief; animism seems to have dominated beliefs in fifth- and sixth-century England: North, J. E. 1997, 105 and 206–7.
91. Leigh 1984 for Style I's possible meanings.
92. Morris, E. L. and Dickinson 2000; gaming-counters may be symbolic of a rich man's ability to have leisure time, but they seem to occur more in cremation

burials, noticeably in taller urns: Hills 1977, 29. This is an early example of a drinking-horn, considered further in Chapter 2.

93. Morris, E. L. and Dickinson 2000, 94; there is an example in the Hérouvillette cemetery: DeCaens 1971, 91, as well as one in Kent.
94. e.g. at Spong Hill: Hills 1977, 28.
95. A warband, or *comitatus*, involves a constructed friendship rather than a blood relationship: Charles-Edwards 1999, 175–7. 'Territories' here covers a range of different sizes, from multiple estates (perhaps like Paecca's), to dwellers of a river valley, a *provincia*, a shire, and on up to a kingdom: Yorke 2000.
96. Lucy 2000, 27–9; MacGregor and Bolick 1993, 95–111.
97. La Niece 1983, 286–7; Hines 1997, 214–15. The techniques were not new inventions, but existing ones more widely used.
98. Dickinson 1993, 34–6.
99. Hines 1997, 30, 214, and appendix 2, in which it is shown that the alloys of those analysed never rise above one-third pure silver. See also Brownsword and Hines 1993.
100. Evison 1955; ead. 1958.
101. Hines 1993*a*. Axboe 1999 makes a case for seeing deposition of gold and the making of new sorts of protective bracteates in Scandinavia as a reaction to the postulated comet strike and subsequent crop failures; although the two Oxfordshire bracteates could have been some sort of deposit different from the norm, I cannot see a pattern emerging in England, where evidence of climatic deterioration is problematic; acidification of upland soils could have resulted from deposition of volcanic gases, and an asteroid could have created tephra particles: Dark, P. 2000, 22–5 and 152.
102. Hines and Odenstedt 1987, who see the bracteate at Undley as an import from south Scandinavia or Schleswig-Holstein.
103. Gaimster, M. 1998. The Woden images may have given them a protective meaning in Scandinavia, a combination of the emperor's power and the gods': Maguire 1998, 84.
104. Gaimster, M. 1992, whose elegant arguments have in my view gained further strength from the subsequent discovery of the Patching hoard, and its two gold rings.
105. Rigold 1975, 661 and 665, expressed doubt about the validity of the hoard, though Grierson and Blackburn 1986, 159, did not. See also below for a Canterbury coin.
106. Spufford 1988, 15.
107. Hamerow *et al*. 1994, 13–14; it was also made in Frisia, though where it started is not certain. There may be regional variation in the precise sizes of the sunken-featured buildings, but more evidence will be welcome: Marshall and Marshall 1991.
108. Williams, D. F. and Vince 1997.

109. Wade 1983; Russel 1996.
110. Hamerow 1993, 22 and 42.
111. Powlesland 1999.
112. Farley 1976, 169, 173, and 213; Draper 2002, 35–7, for a recent review of the names and their meanings: the overtone of British subservience still has advocates, though Draper, speaking of Wiltshire, suggests a correlation with Romano-British sites.
113. e.g. Slough House Farm: Wallis and Waughman 1998, 125; Wade 1983, 67; McDonnell 1993.
114. e.g. West 1985, 122.
115. Such as the twenty-two in a Mucking sunken-featured building fill: Going 1993, 72–3; also Curnow 1985. See White, R. 1990, 138–40, who points out that those worn on necklaces all seem to pre-date $c.375$, so argue against any 'continuity'.
116. Mortimer 1991.
117. Admittedly the iron scrap collections are a little later in date, e.g. Nazeing, Essex: Morris, C. A. 1983; sword blades: Tylecote and Gilmour 1986, 244–7; wrist-clasps: Brownsword and Hines 1993, 9–10; Linton Heath: ibid. 6–7.
118. White, R. 103; Going 1993, 71–2; West 1985, 84–5. Body sherds were sometimes ground into discs, presumably for the same reasons.
119. Guido and Welch 2000; Bimson and Freestone 2000; Bayley 2000*a*.
120. Wilthew 1991, 46.
121. Hamerow 1993, 60; Evison 1982 for a complete catalogue of a type that is not restricted to the sixth century.
122. Evison 1985; West 1985, 16, 40, and 62.
123. Hamerow 1993, 60; Webster 1993*a*.
124. Mortimer 1994 for the casting technology; Hinton 2003*a* for longer discussion of these two paragraphs.
125. Harris and Griffiths 1999, 46.
126. See e.g. Dickinson 1993, 38; Arnold 1997, 135–9.
127. Hills *et al.* 1995, 26.
128. Blockley *et al.* 1995, 335 and 1068.
129. Evison 2000, 66 and 72; Perkins 2000, 298 and 304–5.

2. EXPRESSIONS OF THE ELITES

1. See Chapter 1.
2. Campbell, E. 2000; Wooding 1996; analyses of E-ware in Scotland have identified traces of Dyer's Madder, so presumably that was one import: Lane and Campbell 2000, 100 and 242; South Cadbury: Alcock 1995, 152.
3. Campbell, E. 2000, 39–43.

4. Ibid., distribution map fig. 6.
5. Alcock 1995, 66–70 and 75–7.
6. Hines 2000a, 95.
7. Rahtz *et al.* 2000, fig. 237, CA 104. There is nothing comparable at the Wells Cathedral site, where glass sherds could be as early as the sixth century, but may be eighth-century, like the earliest coin there; a single, small black sherd is the best immediately post-Roman evidence: Rodwell 2001, 520–33 and report by M. M. Archibald, 516–17.
8. For Somerset, Smith 1906, 373–4 recorded a late fifth-/sixth-century disc-brooch and a small square-headed brooch, both of Anglo-Saxon type, without stating provenances. For both Somerset and Dorset, see also Chapters 1 and 3; two sites on and near Poole Harbour have yielded glass beads, two probably Anglo-Saxon or Frankish, the other less diagnostic but perhaps sixth-century: reports by M. Guido in Woodward 1987, 100–2 and in Hearne and Smith 1991, 92. Bath: Davenport 1999, 60 and 90; Dinas Powys: Graham-Campbell 1991a, 221–3.
9. See Chapter 1.
10. Philpott 1999, 194–5 and 198–202; O'Sullivan 1996.
11. Lane and Campbell 2000, 150–1.
12. Ibid., and Campbell and Lane 1993. They are also different from the earlier zoomorphic terminals mentioned in Chapter 1.
13. Redknap 2000, 71.
14. Lane and Campbell 2000, 211, 238–9, and 245–6.
15. Dunbar: Lowe 1999, 22, for colour plate; Cox 2000, 113–14; Perry 2000, 193; general surveys: Lowe 1999; Proudfoot and Aliaga-Kelly 1996; Cessford 1996a, who stresses that interaction may have been effected by marriage alliances at least as much as by conquest.
16. Longley 2001 for a summary.
17. Woolf 2001.
18. Henderson, I. 1967 is still an excellent extended introduction; see also Thomas, C. 1984; Foster, S. M. 1996, 71–8; and Alcock 1998. The much-discussed 'Pictish beast' could be a beaked whale, fearsome enough but rarely seen—hence its unrecognizability: MacLeod and Wilson 2001.
19. Foster, S. M. 1996, 78, notes that the symbols usually taken as mirrors may actually represent Roman *paterae*, handled silver bowls.
20. Foster, S. M. 1996, 78–9.
21. Close-Brooks 1982, 28. Also incised are some figures with T-shaped axes, for which Lloyd Laing 2000, 93–7, favours a ninth-century or later date, though one is borne by a centaur, noted by Solly 1984, 204 as one of various classical-inspired designs in the art—more likely in an earlier context (and more in line with the Roman bowl suggestion by Foster, above).
22. Carver 2001, 3, notes that the naturalistic human and animal figures on imported Greek pails (below) were not copied. The 'idol' on an urn lid from Spong Hill is

as naturalistic as a pot idol can get, however: Hills, Penn, and Rickett 1987, fig. 82 and pl. 9. There are also the newly found gold seal and the Finglesham buckle, below.

23. The Book of Durrow may have been produced in Iona in the later seventh century, but many other views have been expressed; nor is the similarity of its evangelist symbols to the Pictish animals agreed: e.g. Henderson, G. 1999, 40–53; Stevenson 1993, 19–20; Hicks, C. 1993, and references therein.
24. Breeze 1998; Youngs (ed.) 1989, cat. nos. 7 and 9.
25. Graham-Campbell 1991b; Youngs (ed.) 1989, cat. no. 8. (The significance of these chains, etc. is discussed further below.)
26. Ó Floinn 2001, 2, points out that their origins are probably in 'proto-handpins', from the River Severn area, whence penannular brooches may also have come.
27. Hines 2000a, 100–1, for discussion of the term, pointing out that it need not mean that the objects were made of twisted rods or wires, but may have the sense of 'encircling'—so the poet may not have had actual objects in mind; the same is true of another term in the poem, *kaeawc*, usually translated as 'brooch'; but see also Nieke 1993, 128; Cessford 1996b; further discussion below.
28. Morris, C. D. 1996, 53–7.
29. The first use of ogam in Pictland was probably in the seventh century; its main use seems to have been to record names: Foster, S. M. 1996, 24–5.
30. Illustrated in Youngs (ed.) 1989, no. 38.
31. e.g. ibid., nos. 31–7; Hines 2000a, 91–3; Geake 1999.
32. Lane and Campbell 2000, 154–5.
33. Close-Brooks 1986, 145–7, 156–64, and 168–9.
34. Lane and Campbell 2000, 118–20. The Hunterston brooch has a long bibliography, summarized by Stevenson 1983 and 1993; it is usually dated to *c.*700 because of similarities of silver-gilt panels on its reverse to the Book of Lindisfarne. See also Whitfield 1987 and ead. 1993, 122, for the point about the non-Anglo-Saxon traits in the filigree, and ead. 2001, 233–6, for design similarities to Anglo-Saxon composite disc-brooches. See Youngs (ed.) 1989, no. 92, and nos. 44 and 72 for other examples found in Scotland, some perhaps made in Ireland, as 'closed' frames seem to be found there: ead. 1989, no. 75 is an example, its frame apparently made as a complete circle, but the bridge between the terminals filed away so that it could be attached to a cloak in the traditional way. Although the 'Hiberno-Saxon' manuscripts fuse 'Celtic' and 'Anglo-Saxon', Durrow and others can be seen as deliberately rejecting overt Mediterranean influence, as though to stress independence from Rome. Amber: as beads, Huggett 1988, 64–6; and as settings in the 'Ripon jewel', probably a box- or book-mount, or something of that sort, rather than a personal ornament, Hall, R. A. *et al.* 1996.
35. Nieke 1993, 129; the brooches were probably not restricted to women in Pictland, as there are Irish representations of men wearing them, which is consistent with Irish laws. Nieke points out that the Irish laws spelt out what was appropriate for different social grades to wear; such sumptuary legislation

(recurring in the later Middle Ages, see below), perhaps derived from the Emperor Justinian's. Nieke also discusses the *Y Gododdin* brooch reference, for which see Hines 2000*a* and above. Whatever the reality may have been, stories about matrilineal descent in Pictland were known in England and recounted by Bede, which suggests something special about women in their society: Colgrave and Mynors (eds.), 1969, 19. For Dunadd as a royal *Scotti* centre, see Lane and Campbell 2000, 18–25. The boar symbol carved in the rock there may be a defiant addition made by triumphant Picts after their capture of the site in 736, or it may have royal overtones in being an allusion to pig-roasting at feasts: Forsyth 2000, 272.

36. Gold is occasionally found in Scotland (the *Today* radio programme reported on a small nugget panned from an undisclosed river in Dumfriesshire in June 2002), but such finds are probably too sporadic to have sustained goldsmiths. Amber could have come from the east coast, but is generally reckoned to have come from the Baltic; silver is not known to have been extracted north of Cumberland. For the level of trade, see Wooding 1996 and Campbell, E. 1996, above. Tribute payments are implied by the term *exactores*, 'tax-gatherers, enforcers', used in 729: Alcock 1992, 207. The distinction drawn by Charles-Edwards 1997, 171–5, between tribute paid to a leader who at least offered protection even if he were not actually a relative, and that demanded by a conqueror, is psychologically important but not often archaeologically recognizable.

37. Graham-Campbell 1981, 24–5; see also McCormack 1992.

38. Hill, P. 1997, 16–17, 28: the Dunbar hillfort could have contained an unrecorded church in its Anglo-Saxon phase, accounting for the cross-arm and the potential gold leaf: Cox 2000, 113–14.

39. Barber, J. W. 1981, 318–46.

40. Rigold 1975, 676, no. 125 and 671, no. 71; Metcalf 1993 noted the peripheral provenances of the two northern examples before the publication of that from Carisbrooke. A further example could be Louth, Lincolnshire, but recent finds make that less isolated: Fitzwilliam Museum, Cambridge, Early Medieval Coins Corpus.

41. See Chapter 1.

42. Metcalf 1993, 37–40; Williams, G. 1998*a*, 140; and see Chapter 1.

43. Rigold 1975, 656; Lucy 2000, figs 5.10 and 5.11; and new information from the Cambridge Fitzwilliam Museum Early Medieval Coin Corpus making seven. For Essex, see Tyler, R. 1996. One exception to the 'near-absence' is the cemetery at Prittlewell which produced the dramatic discovery of a wood-lined chamber grave in November 2003, reported after this chapter had been written.

44. Archibald 1991*a*, no. 24. Because the coin might not actually have been struck in the town, to call Canterbury the earliest English mint might be wrong.

45. She was not the daughter of the Frankish king's current wife when she married, however, so her importance should not be overemphasized: Wood 1999, 71.

46. The circumstances of the discovery are unfortunately hazy; the assumption is that the 'medalet' was from a woman's grave, with other pendants: Haith 1991, no.

5; also Werner, M. 1991. Gannon 2003, 25–7, compares some of the busts on these gold coins to some in manuscripts, which could strengthen the argument for a Church involvement in their production.

47. Unfortunately lost, but known from a colour plate in Akerman 1855a, pl. 33. For the hoard, Sutherland 1948; Metcalf 1993, 29–62.
48. As is generally assumed from Kentish laws, e.g. Grierson and Blackburn 1986, 15; but Metcalf 1993, 29, n. 4 is unconvinced that the documentation is explicit enough to justify the connection.
49. Whitelock (ed.) 1979, 392. Other people 'cost' more, or less, according to rank; as there were no half-coins, twelve became the subdivision of twenty-five, an anomaly that may have helped to make the duodecimal system acceptable. Only two gold coins have been reported from the Prittlewell chamber-grave, but others might yet be revealed in soil blocks taken back to the laboratory.
50. In weight they make the total equivalent to sixteen *solidi*, but the purity of the larger is below that of all the coins, and the smaller would only just have been within their tolerance: Bruce-Mitford 1975, 646–7; Stahl 1992, 5–7 and 11. For Merovingian uses, Grierson and Blackburn 1986, 95.
51. Metcalf 1993, 53.
52. Wormald 1999, 94–100. Runic letters were already known by the mid-fifth century, appearing on Spong Hill urns and on various sixth-century brooches, including a cruciform type at West Heslerton: Haughton and Powlesland 1999, 99; however, they became more frequent in the seventh century, in line with writing generally: cf. the Undley bracteate, Chapter 1.
53. Grierson and Blackburn 1986, 15.
54. Scull 1990. Much emphasis is usually placed on the seventh century as a period when tax systems changed, coins making it possible for agricultural surpluses to be converted into a permanent means of payment which did not have to be consumed before the foodstuffs went rotten; although this is indeed an important factor, the weight system evidence suggests that coins facilitated an existing trend. Equivalents for compensations expressed in *solidi* recorded in the *Lex Ribuaria* of the continental Franks, e.g. a horse in lieu of six *solidi*, suggest that 'a major part of distribution of goods was based on barter' to Lebecq 1997, 72, but is not the same as mundane twelve-eggs-for-a-cheese transactions, and seems to be at aristocratic level; see also Lebecq 1998; Campbell, J. 2000, 232–3, for an Anglo-Saxon example; and below. King Ine's late seventh-century Wessex laws seem more down-to-earth and may indicate a well-understood system of market values, even though they are probably compensation payments: Whitelock (ed.) 1979, 405, clauses 55 and 58–9.
55. Metcalf 1993, 38–9.
56. Filmer-Sankey and Pestell 2001, 195–8; their dating is mid- or late sixth century, though Bruce-Mitford 1974, 131, suggested *c*.600; the photographs of the earlier Krefeld-Gellep ring and of the Snape ring show as many differences as similarities in the goldwork, and the lost blue glass fragment, if its colouring was cobalt,

would at least point to a date later than the middle of the sixth century. There are very few Anglo-Saxon rings set with gems, engraved or otherwise, despite the implication in *Maxims II*, *Gim sceal on hringe standan*, 'a gem should stand on a ring': Mackie 1934, 22–3.

57. Preliminary report by L. Webster in *Treasure Annual Report 1998–1999*, 31–2, where she cites a number of Frankish parallels, including one that names what were presumably a betrothed couple. Webster suggests that the object may have been sent as a way of authenticating the origin of a message, with no intention that it was for use in England to produce wax seals. That the bearded male is shown bald-headed could indicate that he at least was not a member of the Merovingian royalty, who were familiarly known as 'the long-haired kings'. The scene seems to show copulation, but with apparently armless figures it is difficult to know. The length of hair on the head on the inscribed side would not preclude a long-haired king's representation, but the name is certainly a woman's, and the stylized lines below the head are more likely intended to be a woman's robe than a man's beard, to judge from the beard on the other side. See also n. 107 below.

58. Campbell, J. 1992, 86; Wood 1992, 237.

59. Arrhenius 1985.

60. Arrhenius 1985, 56, developed the fixed-place theory to argue that water-power was used, and that templates or drawings would have been sent to the very few centres where the requisite technology existed. Bimson 1985, 128, cited modern Persian lapidaries as using the bow-drill. Drawings are advocated by Henderson, G. 1999, 32–7. Wax tablets are another possibility: Coatsworth and Pinder 2002, 168—the study of techniques generally has been much enhanced by this book. Faversham: Chapter 1.

61. Bimson 1985, 128.

62. White inlays: La Niece 1988; shells as beads: Evison 1975*b*, 313 and pl. LXV, e–f. White glass used tin as a colourant, but seems not to have been used for inlays despite being available, except at Sutton Hoo: Bimson and Freestone 2000, 131; also Hook and La Niece 2000, 80. Niello: La Niece 1983.

63. The skills are best appreciated through magnification and experiment: e.g. Duczo 1985; Whitfield 1998; Oddy 1977.

64. If Eusebius was the designer of his coin, however, the die-maker and coiner may have been unfree. Comparable to him as a free agent was the continental bishop-moneyer-smith, Eligius.

65. Hawkes, S. C. 1981.

66. For a range of Kentish pendants and disc-brooches, see MacGregor and Bolick 1993, 156–9 and 70–6; many of the latter have Style I ornament, and go well back into the sixth century: Evison 1987, 39–47 and 138–9—a recent example from outside Kent was excavated at Lechlade: Boyle *et al.* 1998, 60 and 196. Composites: Pinder 1995, who warns against assuming that all were Kentish products, especially some that have copper-alloy rather than gold cloisons. See further discussion below.

67. The *Chronicle* is a Wessex source, however, and may be making the most of a slight skirmish; its date seems suspiciously early if King Aethelberht really was involved; see Yorke 1990, 28.
68. Arnold 1982, 27–8 and 106–7.
69. Bede's phrase about the Church echoes Gildas' about Britain, 'like a chosen bride arrayed in a variety of jewellery': Winterbottom (ed.) 1978, 16–17; see also Chapter 1. Geake 1997, 128–9, makes the point that alliance-forming marriages would have become even more important as political units grew, and that this may be reflected in the larger number of goods placed with a few women like the one at Chessell Down.
70. Filmer-Sankey and Pestell 2001, Graves 4 and 47. The graves also contained a range of textiles, and the authors make a number of important points about the difficulties of making interpretations based only on surviving inorganics in graves, as do Cameron and Fell 2001. Horse-harness makes its first appearance in the second half of the sixth century; see further below.
71. Lawson, G. 2001; Roberts 1992, 186, suggested that the placing of a *hearp* in a grave could have been to symbolize the silenced song and lost happiness—a theme of much of the Old English poetry. Another has now been found at Prittlewell.
72. See Chapter 1. This East Anglian fondness for association with Roman foundation stories may also show in a bone plaque from Larling, and on eighth-century coins. It does not mean that their kings had direct descent from a Roman forebear—a point worth remembering when the Scandinavian links at Sutton Hoo are used to claim that the dead there were directly related to a Swedish dynasty, a point made by Yorke 2000, 80–1.
73. Filmer-Sankey and Pestell 2001, 264–6. The date (above) is crucial in this argument; if the later date stands, there would probably be overlap with Sutton Hoo, rather than a clear sequence. Another factor is the recent discovery of a cemetery at Sutton Hoo slightly separate from the mounds, and whether that is part of a chronological development. At Prittlewell the chamber-grave was either within an existing cemetery or had later burials grouped around it.
74. Burnell and James 1992.
75. e.g. Williams, H. 1997, 17–18. Some of these barrows are isolated, but recent exploration of Taplow suggests that there may have been a few associated graves after all: *Current Archaeology*, 175 (2001), 288. Maddicott 2000 proposed that reversions to paganism could have happened quite late in the seventh century, as a reaction to God's failure to give protection from plagues in the 660s and 680s, which could be a reason for some late rich burials. It would not be possible to detect this, as even a richly furnished burial in a churchyard or recognizably Christian cemetery need not be seen as an attempt to 'conquer' Christianity, though it is very noticeable that apart from the exceptional situation at Taplow, none has been found.
76. The possible one at Coombe is probably late sixth century: Davidson and Webster 1967, 10 and 35–6; the site is close to Woodnesborough, *Wodnesbeorge* or Woden's barrow in the twelfth century: ibid. 6–9. Eighteenth-century records of

barrows there are discussed by Behr 2000, 39–44. These may have been like other barrows within Kentish cemeteries: Evison 1975*b*, 307.

77. Webster 1982; Webster 1991, no. 10.
78. Frere *et al.* 1987, 68–70; no building identifiable as a church or chapel was found with the cemetery during excavation (admittedly in very difficult and restricted circumstances), and there is no record of a later church at the site which could have been its successor; the nearest church, St Dunstan's, is more than 200 metres away.
79. Burnell and James 1999. Carver 2002, 138 summarizes an argument that he has often made, that the rich graves are related to changes in the nature of tax derived from land; those who were important enough could claim exemption from payment, and therefore had the wherewithal to boast of it in their burials, even if they still owed traditional services. This may have been a factor, but a point to be considered is that land sales in the seventh century sometimes reveal very mixed methods of payments, e.g. 500 *solidi* in the form of twelve beds, a slave and a slave girl, a gold brooch, and two horses with two wagons: Campbell, J. 2000, 232–3. This may be a false analogy, but it seems to argue against very fixed ideas about methods of payment.
80. Härke 2000 shows a decline of weapon burial from around 50% down to less than 25%, tailing off further to nil. Women's graves show similar trends, and such customs as bed-burial are another indication that some were specially treated; an example of that was excavated at Edix Hill, used for a young woman who had been well looked after despite her leprosy: Malim and Hines 1998, 67–8 and 268. Hines 2002, 90, shows that practices in the later sixth and early seventh centuries, even between cemeteries only a few miles apart, like Edix Hill and Medbourne, both in Cambridgeshire, might be as varied as they had been earlier; also Pader 1982 and Chapter 1. Precise chronology is made more difficult by the nineteenth- and early twentieth-century records of excavation of many barrow-burials, e.g. Geake 1997, 123–4. Pattern-welding: Tylecote and Gilmour 1986. Necklaces: Hawkes, S. C. 1990, and below.
81. Brenan, J. 1991; Youngs 2001*a*. The possibility of Irish manufacture is diminished by the same absence of evidence as in Wales. One at Prittlewell was found still attached to the nail that it had hung from in the chamber wall. For the example in Fig. 2.13 from Loveden Hill, see further Bruce-Mitford 1993, 8; Geake 1999, 11–12; Lucy 2000, 115–16.
82. Bruce-Mitford 1983, 202–315.
83. e.g. Youngs 1992.
84. Scull 1985.
85. Bimson 1983.
86. Geake 1999, 7.
87. Gilmour 1979; see also Jones, M. J. 1993, 25–7; and Bruce-Mitford 1993, 52.
88. Bruce-Mitford 1983, 240, n.1; the creature in the centre of the last known in England, from the River Witham in Lincolnshire, might possibly represent an evil spirit exorcized by the water of baptism.

89. Fishes appear in sixth-century continental manuscripts, and perhaps more relevantly on a large gold, silver, and garnet buckle from Crundale, Kent, which may have been a reliquary: Haith 1991, no. 6.

90. Werner, J. 1992, 7–8. Werner raised the possibility that the spoons and bowls could have been made in Francia rather than Byzantium, where the great silver dish received its control stamps between 491 and 518. The two gold-foil crosses above the body at Prittlewell are much more specifically Christian, frequently found in Lombard graves in Italy, for instance; the arrangement of the chamber is quite like one in a church at Morken, Belgium.

91. Campbell, E. and Lane 1993*a*, 34–5 and 64. The division of treasure would help to explain why words for coinage, such as *scilling*, have the same connotation: above.

92. Hardt 1998, 321–4; Henderson, G. 1999, 27.

93. There is a strong possibility that Anglo-Saxons accompanied a Frankish embassy to the emperor in the sixth century, so had direct experience of Byzantium, not solely having it mediated for them: Campbell, J. 1992, 86.

94. Dickinson and Speake 1992, 113–15; certainty is impossible in this case because of the condition of the surviving fragments. To be particularly recommended in this paper is the warning on p. 112 about the problems of calling graves like these 'princely' or 'royal'; Høilund Nielsen's 'paramount' avoids some of the problem: 1999, 198.

95. The Wheathampstead ewer's claim to be termed the 'most extraordinary' can now be challenged by the remarkable lidded flagon at Prittlewell, where a large Coptic bowl was also found. Glastonbury: Webster 1991, no. 68. There are also copper-alloy bowls probably cast in the Rhineland, found in Kent, e.g. at Coombe: Davidson and Webster 1967, 32–3.

96. Mungo 1989 for all but the one discovered in 1999 at Shallows Farm, Breamore, Hampshire.

97. The possibility of some survival of British Christianity even in Anglo-Saxon areas notwithstanding: see Meens 1994 for one view, and Stancliffe 1999 for another.

98. Bruce-Mitford 1978, 304–5.

99. Evans, A. C. 1991, no. 31. There is also a cavity within the large fish-bearing buckle from Crundale that could also have been a reliquary: Haith, no. 6, and above. The gold buckle at Prittlewell has rivets projecting beyond its back-plate, which might possibly therefore have had a locking system; that buckle seems unique in being entirely plain, with a back-plate projecting beyond the sides like a flange—was the intention to put garnets along its sides?

100. Wickham-Crowley, 1992, 47; Hawkes, J. 1997, 319; and see Chapter 3. Although usually thought of as Swedish because of the boat-burial rite, a Danish origin has been suggested for the shield fittings and other objects, on the basis of their ornament (rather than because it puts Sutton Hoo closer to the geographical context of Beowulf's deeds): Høilund Nielsen 1999, 186; see also above for a note on the question of a Swedish dynasty.

101. Bruce-Mitford 1978, 350–2; Filmer-Sankey 1996.
102. Carver 1998, 106.
103. Davidson 1992, 30. Compare the apparently ritually deposited one at supposedly Christian-British South Cadbury, above, and the Pictish old man of Barflat. Carver 1998, 128, more prosaically suggested that it was for ship repairs, but despite Vendel parallels, it seems too unwieldy, and the iron shaft too uncomfortable, for such use.
104. A reverse interpretation has been suggested by Lowden 1999, that the idea was to propitiate an offended god by surrendering his rival's symbols, after a defeat had 'shown' which god was false. It is certainly true that Christian clerics seem to have become adept at persuading people that bad fortune was because of their failure to worship the true God, and good fortune was because of His particular concern for their welfare. Perhaps Thor's priests learned to teach a similar message.
105. Grainger and Henig 1983.
106. Stahl and Oddy 1992, 136.
107. The question-mark in the title of Carver 1998 is essential reading. The absence of a finger-ring like that in the Snape boat has often been noted, as a royal seal might have been expected in a king's grave. This has been enhanced by the recent discovery of the Norfolk seal-die (Col. pl. B.5): see above. Wood 1991, 10–11, argued presciently that for political reasons Redwald would have been unlikely to receive coins from Francia after c.613; only subsequently did that year emerge as the possible closure date of the hoard (Stahl and Oddy 1992)—Redwald could, of course, have kept it thereafter untouched until his death, if it were ever his to touch... Note also that there were barrows at Blythburgh in Suffolk, where King Anna was buried: Campbell, J. 2000, 172–3. Was he with his ancestors there?
108. Colgrave and Mynors (eds.) 1969, 193.
109. Raw 1992, 172–3; Arnold 1997, 208–9. The late fifth-century seal of the Frankish king, Childeric, shows a man with a lance, presumably an authority-symbol subsequently forgotten.
110. Colgrave and Mynors (eds.) 1969, 193; Bede tells the story as a sign of Edwin's charity as well as of his authority. Higham 2000, 42–4, warns that there are many aspects of Bede's account of Edwin that are hagiographical, and may therefore be unreliable.
111. Nieke 1993, 128, for penannulars as more than 'elaborate dress appendages'; see above. Wijnaldum: Besteman *et al.* 1999, 191–201, including 196–7 for the Freya brooch—which also occurs in *Beowulf* as the *Brosinga mene*, which might be descriptive, or signify an object associated with a tribal group (there are no Brosings in Scandinavia, but there was a group called the Brondings). The dying Beowulf gave Wiglaf an object usually translated as 'neck-ring' and other things that sound as though they carried inheritance rights, unlike the gifts handed out at feasts. Words like 'neck-rings' sound like necklaces or solid rings, but a brooch worn at the neck could be intended. Other representations are on Scandinavian

gold foils: Magnus 1999, 170. Style II; Høilund Nielsen 1999 for 'Kentish' and 'Anglian' distinctions; dies for impressing Style II patterns seem surprisingly more often found than for other styles; see Speake 1980 for general discussions. It has been called a Frankish symbolic language: Hedeager 2000, but was not only meaningful to Franks.

112. e.g. Speake 1980, figs. 1–3. My statement is deliberately sweeping.
113. Evison 2000, 72. Glass could have been acquired from the continent, but perhaps it was thought to be too Kentish-seeming for comfort. Prittlewell is a contrast: four glass vessels that look Kentish, yet no garnets, unless some are revealed within soil blocks, notably the one containing the sword and its hilt.
114. Carver 1998, 182.
115. Or at least attributed to Kent: see Chapter 1. The first king to have his name on thrymsas was Eadbald, of Kent, but as he did not begin his reign until 616 perhaps his coins were only issued after the Sutton Hoo parcel had been closed: Williams, G. 1998*a*. Henderson, G. 1999, 19, suggested that if Mound 1 contained Redwald, the coins and some other items might have come to him as a bribe from the king of Northumbria to get a potential rival murdered; Bede recorded *auro*, *ornamentis*, *pecuniae*, and *argenti* being sent.
116. Taplow: Webster 2000*a*, 55–6; Alton: Evison 1988, 18–20, 47; La Niece 1988; Speake 1980, 47.
117. Pinder 1995, 26, for the brooches; he cautions that the distribution of these composite disc-brooches that have copper-alloy cloisons rather than gold is a factor against the too-ready assumption that all were made in Kent, but the Faversham parallel makes this a better case than others.
118. Carisbrooke: Morris, E. L. and Dickinson 2000, 90–3; Snape: Filmer-Sankey and Pestell 2001, 27–9; Rainham: Evison 2000; aurochs: Bruce-Mitford and East 1983; Neuman de Vegvar 1993 for general discussion, particularly of Scottish and Irish examples. The words used in Old English literature are not usually specific enough to reveal what sort of vessel was being used, or what it was made of, so do not reveal whether horns had any preferential connotations: e.g. Frank 1997. A relief stone in Pictland at Bullion, Angus, shows a bald-headed rider with a long beard drinking from a horn with a bird's head terminal looking at him quizzically—possibly the earliest known caricature in Britain: Alcock 1998, 532–3; Close-Brooks 1982, 78, where a tenth-century date is hazarded.
119. Carver has suggested that the Sutton Hoo barrows are near the edge of the East Anglian kingdom for this sort of reason, and has argued that the conglomeration of rich graves in the Peak District in Derbyshire are those of the seventh-century pagan Mercian royal family, challenging Christian Northumbria, rather than reflecting the wealth of the rulers of the Peak dwellers caused by new demand for the lead supplies that they controlled: 2002, 139. Those barrows would not have been visible in the same way, however; a better candidate might be a barrow at Caenby, Lincolnshire, perhaps close enough to the disputed territory of Hatfield Chase, material from which has recently been compared to Sutton Hoo: Everson 1993, 94–8; but it seems to have been a single barrow, from which no pattern

can emerge—and its dating may not be tight enough for it to be ascribed to a king of Mercia rather than one of Lindsey; cf. Yorke 1993, 143. Symbolic use of frontier zones—always fluid, not fixed lines—can be seen in some baptism-places, such as Dorchester-on-Thames, Oxfordshire, used when the king of Mercia probably forced his counterpart in Wessex to accept Christianity, an event which welds the traditional and modern meanings of the word 'god-father'. As for the Peak District, a mixed British and Anglo-Saxon local elite under Mercian overlordship seems a stronger case: Loveluck 1995.

120. Compare the gold panels on the Sarre brooch which are quickly recognizable as a cross to the Kingston Down brooch, on which a second cross formed by garnets actually makes both more difficult to see straightaway: Webster 1991, nos. 31 and 32.

121. Coatsworth 1989, 291–5. For examples, the Ixworth and Stanton crosses, illustrated in Webster and Backhouse (eds.) 1991, nos. 11 and 12. The recently reported Holderness cross is less competently done; it may have embellished a bookcover or the like, not been a personal pendant: MacGregor 2000*a*.

122. Evans, A. C. 1991, no. 13.

123. Colgrave and Mynors (eds.) 1969, 410–11. The Latin word used by Bede was *monile*, for which 'necklace' is a fairly secure translation.

124. Ibid. 396–7. Bede used *margarita* for 'pearl'; seventh-century survivals do not include pearls, and Bede was probably following a classical image rather than his own observation, though he knew that high-quality pearls were to be found in British mussels: ibid. 14. They were still fished for in the River Tay in the early twentieth century. He also knew of Whitby jet, which 'when kindled, drives away serpents', an early example of belief in the properties of stones, discussed further below. Lignite, a similar material, was used in the Roundway Down necklace. Amber: Huggett 1988, 64–6; amethyst: ibid. 66–8.

125. Kent has if anything more cemeteries than any other area which continued in use despite conversion, notably that at Buckland near Dover, which continued well into the eighth century, with grave-good deposition only disappearing at the very end: Evison 1987, 136–45.

126. Webster and Backhouse (eds.) 1991, fig. 2; Behr 2000, 33–42. Note also Maddicott 2000, above. See Chapter 1 for earlier bracteates.

127. Davis 1992, 23–6. There is a certain sense of longing in the *Seafarer* poem, about gold strewn on a brother's grave, as though some regretted the practice's passing: Roberts 1992, 187.

128. Davis 1992, 27; Filmer-Sankey and Pestell 2001 note that most of the sex-identifiable horses in graves were male. The founders of Kent were Hengist and Horsa, of course—Hengist seems to mean 'stallion', i.e. they were twin horse-deities. See also Behr 2000, 27–8.

129. Colgrave and Mynors (eds.) 1969, 258–9. The bishop risked upsetting the king, but preferred humility and self-denial. Another example of the significance of horses occurs in Bede's story of the priest Coifi mounting one to show his rejection of paganism; he must have had an aristocratic youth to have known how to ride: ibid. 184–7.

130. Wood 1992, 237; Hardt 1999, 322. The Byzantine *solidus* minted 613–30 set in the Wilton cross could have been one of them, but the garnets that surround it are very similar to some of those at Sutton Hoo: Evans, A. C. 1991, no. 12. The ship could have been buried as late as the 630s, or the garnets could have continued in production for a decade or two after the jewellery in it had been made, but it seems more likely that the coin had no connection with Dagobert's compensation, and shows that *solidi* reached the west at times other than those that happen to be recorded in documents.
131. Blackburn 1994*a*; Booth, J. 2000, 82, adds another to the series.
132. Metcalf 1993, 31–3.
133. Stahl and Oddy 1992, 136.
134. Metcalf 1993, 54.
135. Blackburn 1994*a*, 207: Booth, J. 2000, 93. The size of Northumbria's monasteries, and the splendour of its stone sculpture and manuscripts, certainly suggest exceptional prosperity in the late seventh and early eighth centuries.
136. Pinder 1995, 24 and 22. Pinder warns that these may not be trends reflecting chronologies, but different makers with different assets available to them: 26–7.
137. Hinton 2000, 83–6. Other small collections are reported there, from Ipswich, and Mound 17 at Sutton Hoo—the latter is the grave of a well-heeled young man who was probably not a smith, but it was not beneath his dignity to have garnets and a millefiori piece rather than coins in his pouch; the date of the burial is not fully discussed yet: Carver 1998, 183.
138. Arrhenius 1985, 24–5 and 35–6. A recent chemical analysis showing that differences can be discerned between Far Eastern and Bohemian garnets studied examples from the upper Rhine/upper Danube and demonstrated that the former were fifth-/sixth-century, the latter later seventh-/eighth-century and much smaller: Quast and Schüssler 2000. The source of the English finds therefore remains open—Bohemia may have supplied the influx in the late sixth and early seventh centuries, the numbers dwindling as much because larger ones could not be found thereafter as because of invasions.
139. Coatsworth 1989, 295–6 ('red inlays' because at least one is red glass, not garnet); Kitson 1983, 75–7. The number could also refer to Jerusalem, and to Aaron's breastplate, other Bedan commentaries: Coatsworth and Pinder 2002, 159. Christian thought seems to have been as much concerned about the waste of resources involved in furnished burial as about superfluous pagan provision of goods for future use: e.g. Pohl 1997 for continental views.
140. Huggett 1988, 66–8; Huggett notes without accepting an unlikely theory that they were all taken by the Franks from Roman graves.
141. Bimson and Freestone 2000, 131.
142. Geake 1997, 39–40. Examples include the Desborough necklace and an intaglio from Epsom, Surrey: Webster and Backhouse (eds.), 1991, nos. 13 and 35. These cabochons may have been what Bede had in mind when talking of 'bloodstones', since he had to face a confusion in his texts with sapphire, which is blue: Kitson

1983, 93–4, for the sources, and Arrhenius 1985, 23, for the stone that is 'the colour of burning coal'.

143. Huggett 1988, 72 and fig. 6; Hills 2001. 'Coptic' bowls could also have continued to arrive from the east Mediterranean, but there are too few for certainty—any in late seventh-century graves might not have been new arrivals.

144. The Charms show acculturation, which Jolly has termed 'middle practice', with earlier popular practice merging with Christian belief—the Christian 'world-view' and Germanic folk-view integrating, but under the control of the Church and its priests: Jolly 1996. If it is really Germanic, migration in large numbers is supported, since there was clearly a lot of folk-view about.

145. Meaney 1981, 184–9; Geake 1997, 34–5.

146. Geake 1997, 81–2. Subsequent discoveries include a set of shears and tweezers in a maplewood box in a male grave at Mill Hill: Parfitt and Brugmann 1997, 76–7 and 258; this had a sword with it, so the shears may have some other meaning. The textiles in Mound 1 at Sutton Hoo are examples of their importance; Filmer-Sankey and Pestell were able to recover evidence at Snape of a very wide range of different materials and weaves, which is a reminder of how unusual it is for such inorganic material to survive: Crowfoot 2001.

147. Bidford-on-Avon: Dickinson 1999; Orsett: Webster 1985; and a new example near Eton: Allen 2002; Lechlade: Boyle *et al.* 1998, 95 (crow) and 116 (bell). For the smith at Tattershall Thorpe: Hinton 2000, 113–14; I did not appreciate until after publication that the recognizably continental items that he was carrying have been called amuletic, i.e. a copper-alloy wheel-shaped mount and four scabbard-studs (Gaimster, M. 1998, 84–7), to add to a curious silk-wrapped globule (the studs are discussed again in Chapter 3); bells and children: Maguire 1998, 80. Meaney 1981 for general discussion; also Loveluck 1996, 32.

148. Gale 1989. His sword Nailing having failed him, Beowulf finished off the dragon with a knife designed for stabbing and sharpened for battle, which may indicate something more than an ordinary short blade.

149. e.g. Welch 1992, pl. 4. Geake 1997, 108–15, has argued for a specifically Roman rather than an east Mediterranean origin mediated through then-declining Francia for most of the trends of the middle part of the seventh century, but even if this were so, it was not total imitation—there are no earrings, for instance, as Geake notes.

150. Meaney and Hawkes 1970, 36–7.

151. Penn 2000, 53–4; there is also a silver pair at Lechlade, Gloucestershire: Boyle *et al.* 1998, 112. Roundway Down includes a gold-mounted glass pendant, perhaps a piece of 'British' workmanship, in the same way that another elite female Wiltshire burial, at Swallowcliffe, has 'Celtic' patterns embossed in foils set in a bag mount: Speake 1989, 175–80. A male burial al Lowbury Hill, Berkshire, contained an enamel-decorated spearhead: Härke 1994, 204–6. Such things imply the same fusion of Celtic ideas and the Anglo-Saxon world as penannular brooches and hanging-bowls, perhaps reflecting the fusion of aristocracies—Wessex kings had British-derived names, for instance.

152. Aristocratic speech and behaviour differences from the rest of society are demonstrated by Bede's story of Imma, a nobleman who was unmasked when trying to pose as a *rusticus*, but who was able to converse with his social equals in another kingdom: Colgrave and Mynors (eds.) 1969, 400–5. Discussion e.g. in Gelling 1993*b*, Geake 1997, and Ward-Perkins 2000, who at p. 24 points out that at the end of the seventh century Wessex's King Ine distinguished between British and 'Englisc'—not Angles and Saxons—unless the word is a late ninth-century interpolation. The Church was already writing of the *gens Anglorum* as though some sort of unity existed, but it was in its interests to promote a concept that would buttress the ecclesiastical hierarchy.

153. Hope-Taylor 1977, 57. My suggestion would be much more convincing if the coin had been at the very bottom of the hole.

154. Millett 1983, who points out that this lack of material applies to the whole site, however, not just the large building and its enclosure.

155. Webster 1998, 186 notes that Beowulf's *healwudu dynede*, 'echoing tread', would result from walking on raised floorboards.

156. Hamerow 1993, 22–3.

157. Williams, D. F. and Vince 1997, 219–20; Loveluck 2001, 84–5.

158. Catterick: Wilson, P. R. *et al.* 1996, 29 (though I was surprised when checking this reference to see how few loomweights there were); Bishopstone: Bell 1977 (only part of this site's material was made available to Dr Bell, so its report having only a few scraps of copper alloy and iron, a minor contrast to the sites below, may not be meaningful); Collingbourne Ducis: Pine 2001, 111; Mucking: Hamerow 1993, 64–8.

159. Hamerow 1993, 60–1, 122, and 167; but Dr Hamerow has kindly pointed out to me *in litt.* that many of the valuables were at the very bottom of the sunken features, where they could have been deliberately placed in some sort of abandonment rite. She will be publishing a paper in *Medieval Archaeology* on this very interesting possibility of 'structured deposits'. Mucking and other settlement sites mentioned below confirm the disappearance of gilt copper-alloy brooches noted in graves, so their absence is 'real', not a factor of deposition practice.

160. Matthews, C. L. and Hawkes 1985, 74–5 and 100.

161. Laboratory conservation has made such information available recently, e.g. Watson 2000, 87–92; Cameron and Fell 2001.

162. Matthews, C. L. and Hawkes 1985, 80 and 100; see also above.

163. West 1985, 123–4. The Flixton Park Quarry site in north Suffolk briefly reported in *Current Archaeology*, 187 (2003), 81–5, will be interesting in this context.

164. Addyman and Leigh 1973, pl. VI.

165. In the 1970s, and unfortunately still not published, though noted by Eagles 2001, 222.

166. Hamilton-Dyer and Powell 2001, 109; the object cannot be precisely dated.

167. The most recent discussion is Maddicott 2001, who argues that surpluses from food-rents and tribute in kind could not be turned into profit by kings until there

3. KINGS AND CHRISTIANITY

1. Scull 2000, 58.
2. Cameron 2001, 124–5 and fig. 35.
3. Birbeck and Smith, forthcoming; see also Stoodley 2002.
4. Gale 1989; fig. 16.15.1 shows a scabbard with a line of studs in place, on a continental grave-marker. See also Chapter 2.
5. From an enormous bibliography, see Anderton (ed.), 1999; and Hill, D. and Cowie (eds.) 2001. Other possibilities include Fordwich, outside Canterbury, mentioned in charters from c.675: Rady 1987, 201–4. For a sensible discussion of the inherent problems in distinguishing a fishing village and landing-place from a commercial centre, see Gardiner *et al.* 2001, 270–8. Cf. South Newbald, below; there must have been smaller places to serve such areas as Lincolnshire as well: Maddicott 2001, 51.
6. Kelly, S. 1992. There are various references to *wic-gerefa*, etc., suggesting someone distinct from a *scir-gerefa*, still with us in the guise of sheriff. That Ipswich and Southampton both had men with scabbard-studs from northern France or the Rhineland, and that the latter had graves with at least one Frisian object, raises interesting problems about where the elites were from—drafted in from the continent?
7. Birbeck and Smith, forthcoming; there were cremations at the site as well as inhumations, a reminder that although incidences of that rite had decreased, it was not wholly discontinued, another example being in still-pagan Sussex at Apple Down: Down and Welch 1990, 208–10.
8. See the cover of *London Archaeologist*, 9 (Spring 2001). The brooch is now (March 2003) on display in the Museum of London.
9. Williams, G. 1998*a*, 138–9.
10. The first ring is recorded as found in George Street, near Euston Square: MacGregor 1997, 26–7—there is no George Street in the modern A–Z of the area, but Gordon Street is just the other side of Euston Road, so perhaps someone muddled two Christian names; other finds: Vince 1990, 14–15 and 109. Evison 2000, 68, notes cruciform patterns, perhaps deliberately formed crosses, on the cups' bases. Two Frankish pots and a sixth-century Byzantine seal from Putney should perhaps be added to this list, but there are doubts over when they arrived in England; for the latter, Campbell, J. 1992, 91. The Floral Street brooch could have been from a cemetery associated with St Paul's in the way that the Canterbury pendant perhaps related to churches there; see Chapter 2. There are also records of high-status goods such as a hanging-bowl in and near York, but not close to the probable *wic* in Fishergate: Tweddle *et al.* 1999, 168.

11. Evans, A. C. 1991, no. 33(a).
12. Penn 2000, 45–9. The late date at which these brooches were still in circulation suggests that the gold *fibula* with four gold *massiunculis* recorded at Medeshamstede (Peterborough) Abbey before 692 may have been another, if the second word means 'boss': Campbell, J. 1992, 87.
13. Hines 2000*b*. Runes, including moneyers' names, were already being used on Kentish coins, however: Grierson and Blackburn 1986, 158. Aedan, who made the reliquary now in Mortain, also used runes, though perhaps a little later: Hinton *et al.* 1981, 69.
14. Floral Street objects: London Museum display. Narrow-wire rings are found on various late seventh-century necklaces, e.g. the Brooks, Winchester: Hawkes, S. C. 1990.
15. The late sixth-century Chessell Down woman with the Greek pail is one example: Arnold 1982, 26–8 and fig. 22. Cowrie-shells with a drilled hole at one end would have been worn on the ends of such festoons: Hinton 1996*a*, 96; and see Chapter 2.
16. Lowe 1999, 21–2 and 55; Blackburn 2000. Whithorn has produced three silver coins of the late seventh to early ninth centuries: Pirie 1997. An early eighth-century coin was excavated at a Pictish monastery on the Moray Firth by M. Carver: *British Archaeology*, 48 (Oct. 1999), 5; it is interesting that both it and the one from Dunbar were continental, not Anglo-Saxon, coins.
17. e.g. Foster, S. M. 1992, 233; Laing 2000.
18. The definitive publication is Small *et al.* 1973; see also Youngs (ed.) 1989, 108–12.
19. Spearman 1989, nos. 177–8; Graham-Campbell 2001*a*, 35–6. Analyses: Graham-Campbell and Batey 1998, 228.
20. Okasha 1985.
21. Spearman 1989, no. 102, citing M. P. Brown.
22. The chapes' terminal heads with open jaws, cruel fangs, and protruding tongues are particularly like one on a curved mount found in the River Thames at Westminster: Webster 1991, nos. 178–9. Webster 2001*a* argues that new finds such as a pommel from Beckley, Oxfordshire, make these connections even stronger.
23. Richardson 1993.
24. The hoards were split up and scattered before proper records were made; the one least known was found at Broch of Burgar, Orkney: Small *et al.* 1973, 81–2; Stevenson 1989, nos. 108–12; Graham-Campbell and Batey 1998, 126.
25. Canterbury: Youngs 2001*b*, 215; York: Rogers 1993, 1359—one at Fishergate, the *wic* area, was in dump levels carted to the site.
26. Spearman 1993.
27. Yorke 1995, 60; Bassett 2000, 111–14.
28. Rahtz *et al.* 2000, 96–8, 324, and 414; Graham-Campbell 2000.

29. Rahtz and Watts 1989, 330–71, with a contribution on the glass by V. I. Evison at 341–5.
30. Wedlake 1958, 96; the profits of Mendip lead could account for these acquisitions.
31. Hinton 1998, 40–1.
32. This is argued by Ward-Perkins 2001; note, however, that the names of Ine's predecessors, including that of the Wessex dynasty's reputed founder, Cerdic, were British.
33. Quinnell 1993.
34. Fox, A. 1995; Griffith 1986; further discoveries were made at the latter site in 2001.
35. Charles-Edwards 2001, who points out that the 'Welsh' in Wales and Cornwall were no longer viewed as part of the same generalized community in the eighth century.
36. Pryce 1992. The almost vanished reliquary from Gwytherin is an exception, though if its sheet-metal covering was copper-alloy, it would not have had much intrinsic value: Edwards, N. and Hulse 1992. The Lichfield Gospels were in Wales for a time, and were exchanged for a horse: Backhouse 1991, no. 90; for cattle as wealth, see Chapter 5.
37. For overall summaries, Edwards, N. and Lane (eds.) 1988; Edwards, N. (ed.) 1997; and Arnold and Davies 2000.
38. Dark, K. R. 1994, 221; Graham-Campbell 1991*a*, 223.
39. Campbell, E. and Lane 1993*a*, 45.
40. Wilkinson 1995, 22–3, 34, and 41–3.
41. Knight, J. K. 1996, 50–3. Following Abels 2003, 264, I have used a lower case 'v' to show that the vikings were not a homogeneous group, but a 'historical construct'.
42. Edwards, N. 2001, 36–7, mentions an unsatisfactory record of a 'large piece of silver coin' found in a coffin at the Pillar of Eliseg, but thinks it unlikely that the burial was eighth-century—even if 'piece' actually means a whole coin here, it is difficult to see how the adjective 'large' could ever have applied to an eighth-century coin, let alone a fragment of one.
43. Redknap 2000, 23.
44. The Canterbury coin was from the same extramural cemetery as the gold and garnet pendant discussed in Chapter 2: Frere *et al.* 1987, 56 and 281; it was in a pit, not a grave, but like the pendant had probably derived from one.
45. Boyle *et al.* 1998, 130.
46. Examples include two in the Buckland, Dover, cemetery: Evison 1987, 181. The fall-off is not only a factor of the fall-off in the number of furnished graves, as loop-fitted or pierced eighth-century coins have scarcely been found in rubbish deposits, unlike unadulterated ones.
47. Archibald 1991*a*, no. 52.

48. Grierson and Blackburn 1986, 95–6; a ratio of 10 silver:1 gold can be deduced from later evidence.
49. Metcalf 1993, 45.
50. Ibid. 89, 103, and 115.
51. e.g. Metcalf 1994, 342; Pirie 1997.
52. Saxon Southampton, *Hamwic*, had yielded 150 small-flan silver coins by 1985, and others have been excavated subsequently: Metcalf 1988, 17. Ipswich has over 100: Newman, J. 1999, 38; Wade 2001, 86. *Lundenwic* has about forty: Cowie 2001, 88. The much smaller excavated area at Fishergate, York, has sixteen: Kemp, R. L. 2001, 92. For tolls, see Kelly, S. 1992.
53. South Newbald: Leahy 2000. The use of coins for tax payments may have happened earlier, but silver would have facilitated it: see Chapter 2 for the functions of gold coins.
54. Whitelock (ed.), 1979, 405; the figures are probably still compensation payments, rather than market prices, and could reflect social cachet in cattle ownership (as in Wales: see Chapter 5). Tacitus had long ago said that the German tribes regarded cattle as valuable for their numbers, the only real 'wealth': Hamerow 2002, 129.
55. Kent 1972.
56. The *mancus* and its rare form in gold coins: Grierson and Blackburn 1986, 270 and 328–9; charter references to rings: Birch 1885–9, nos. 245, 353, 370, and 430 (taken from Campbell, J. 2000, 232–4); Birch 1885–9, no. 487 is the latest charter that I know which refers to a payment in physical terms, but it is not clear if it refers to arm-rings—the Latin is 'duas bradiolas fabrefactos quas pensarent xlv/xlviii mancuses', the second word perhaps being originally *bractiolas*, 'sheet', which sounds like a bracteate but was probably an ingot. Campbell, J. 1992, 68, notes that the great gold buckle at Sutton Hoo weighs, at 41 g, about the equivalent of 100 *mancuses*, i.e. 3,000 pennies, see above. Was it worth a large estate? One problem in such matters not considered in the following part of Campbell's discussion is the difference in value likely to have pertained between early seventh- and eighth-century gold values, and different penny reckonings in different kingdoms. (It is hard to believe that Wessex valued a shilling as only five pennies, if real coins were being used: e.g. Grierson and Blackburn 1986, 165.)
57. Arm-rings or bracelets are unproven; a broad gold band with alternate beaded and plain rings, weighing 21 g, found at Coddenham, Suffolk, could be an example, but in the absence of parallels, dating to the seventh century is dependent on its findspot (not a stratified context), and it may prove not to be Anglo-Saxon: Plunkett 2001, 75.
58. Brown, M. P. 2001, 284.
59. Booth, J. 2000. A few Northumbrian coins also had an archbishop's name on them, perhaps indicating that the Church might be involved in the profit of minting, as it still did later at Canterbury, where the bishop's *wic* in an eighth-century charter (S 24) is another sign of trading interests. Nelson 2001 for more explicit continental data, e.g. a bishop supervising trade at Quentovic.

60. See Metcalf 1993, 12–14.
61. Southampton has only one scale-pan and no balance-arms, though it is just possible that some Roman coins were being used as weights: Hinton 1996a, 56–61; Ipswich has rather more evidence, at least in tems of balances: Kruse 1992a, 69 and 73.
62. Nevertheless, Gannon 2003, 128–71, has shown that these can usually be traced back to classical roots, as can similar features on contemporary sculptures.
63. Hadley 2001, 23.
64. Pirie 1987. Church-scot is first mentioned in King Ine's laws, but is not defined: Whitelock (ed.) 1979, p. 399, cl. 4. The more specific payment of a fee for burial (scot is the same word at root as sceat) is not recorded until the late ninth century, though could have been levied earlier: Gittos 2002, 201; decrees banning churchyard trading on Sundays in the early tenth century show that it was taking place, not necessarily only on holy-days.
65. Hadley 2001, 96.
66. *Hamwic*: P. Walton Rogers in Birbeck and Smith, forthcoming; Barking: Webster 1991, no. 67(a) and references therein.
67. Hinton 1996a; the Fishergate site from York has a similar profile: Rogers 1993. Full reports are not yet available from Ipswich or London. On losses at Mucking, however, note the possibility of structured deposits raised by Dr Hamerow, above, p. 290 n. 159.
68. Hunter, J. R. and Heyworth 1998, 53.
69. Stiff 2001, 44.
70. Evison 2000, 86; Perkins 2000; Bayley 2000b. Barking Abbey has become another possibility from recent excavations there.
71. Campbell, E. 2000, 44; there is no evidence that glass from this area was reaching the *wics*, but it must be a possibility.
72. Bayley 2000b for the various sorts of glass-making evidence sometimes recovered.
73. Hinton 2000, 107.
74. Pre-emption rights are attested in a charter: Kelly, S. 1992, 6 and 16.
75. It seems reasonable to use *Beowulf* as evidence of some customs and traditions such as feasting in the eighth century, even if its setting is thought to be in the seventh. After the eighth century the poem is increasingly likely to contain archaisms not part of contemporary memory, but included because they were part of the structure of the poem: see Chapter 1 for bibliography. The words used in poetry rarely show whether the drink was proffered in glass beakers, chalice-like metal, or drinking-horns.
76. Evison 2000, 83; Wormald 1991, 30 and 33; Frank 1997, 21.
77. Whitelock (ed.) 1979, 398.
78. Blackmore 2001 provides a convenient up-to-date summary of a fairly typical, mixed, mid-Saxon coastal group.

79. Stamper and Croft 2000, 68–9 and 119. The term 'Tating' has become misleading, as the pottery is now thought to have been made at more than one centre: Blackmore 2001, 195.
80. Watts, S. 2000, 112, notes that it was still preferred in the sixteenth century.
81. These issues were discussed by my colleague David Peacock, who showed the significance of a Roman background in this interpretation: 1997, 709–15; see also Nelson 2001, 142; Maddicott 2001, 55–6. That some of the lava was brought over in blocks for working into finished querns could, however, allow 'lengths' to be appropriate: Andrews 1997, 240. Nelson stresses the importance of gifts both to and from Charlemagne, it still being necessary for a king to be seen as famous enough to attract appropriate presents and tribute from afar, and rich enough to dispense largesse.
82. Blinkhorn 1999, where he argues that such devices were tolerated because Ipswich's main trading partners were the Frisians, who were still pagan. Stamping had also been used on pots that did not serve as cremation urns, however, and the faces on some of the Ipswich sherds (Fig. 3.7) may be reminiscent of those on the Sutton Hoo whetstone, but are also like heads on coins (Fig. 3.5), and Gannon shows the origin of those to be in Roman busts: 2003, 24–7.
83. Newman, J. 1999, 41.
84. Metcalf 1994, 341–4 for York's series Y, and 502–7 for Ipswich's Series R—though even this may not have been minted exclusively at the *wic*, p. 504: see also Newman, J. 1999, 41–4. Gannon 2003, 190–2, proposes that many were minted at church sites, with royal permission, explaining the sophistication of some of the designs which could have been preaching aids, as well as the frequency of discovery at 'minsters'. If so, the apparent exclusion of some types from some kingdoms is more difficult to understand.
85. Metcalf 1994, 321–32.
86. Grierson and Blackburn 1986, 169, express doubts about the possibility of much precision in this.
87. The type was originally catalogued by Smedley and Owles 1965; York: Rogers 1993, 1354, with references to others. The perimeters very often have twenty-eight moulded beads, a number that it is difficult to see as significant, yet is oddly frequent. Gannon 2003, 148–51, shows that the animal probably derived from coin designs.
88. Thomas, C. 1996, 81–100.
89. Taylor, J. and Webster 1984; Rogers 1993, no. 5319. Strap-ends seem to be a later seventh-/eighth-century introduction in this form, and are current at least until the end of the ninth; they are surprisingly common losses.
90. Hinton 1996*a*, 103; the reader can picture my delight upon seeing the mould illustrated in Blackmore *et al.* 1998, 63. Dr Paul Robinson subsequently drew my attention to one from Upavon, Wiltshire, which at least therefore had the decency to be found in Wessex, and to one that seems to have been a pendant rather than a brooch, from Wandsworth, London: Mitchiner 1988, 71.
91. Hinton 1996*a*, 30.

92. Ramsbury: Haslam 1980 for an iron-smelting site where blacksmiths' tongs and other equipment suggest that things like an iron strap-end were being produced there. York: Rogers 1993 and contributions therein.

93. Roffe 2000*a*. The evidence is of course Domesday Book, when there were three separate units held from the king, which might or might not have all been grouped around the single village site. In Yorkshire disruption in the later ninth century by the viking settlements and land reallocations is particularly likely to have affected land ownership.

94. Stamper and Croft 2000 for the associated features; McDonnell 2000 for discussion; Goodall, I. H. and Clark 2000, esp. 139 for the sword fittings—two of which seem to be seventh-/early eighth-century, two ninth-/tenth-century. They could have been awaiting recycling, of course, and not been made at Wharram Percy, but they must still have had a well-to-do owner to bring them to the smith.

95. Goodall, A. R. and Paterson 2000, 126. Although found on different sites, these may have been worn as a pair; they are attributed to the sixth century, though the number of bow-brooches—admittedly of different types—found at the *wics* could mean that they were worn later in England.

96. Knight, B. and Pirie 2000, 125–6.

97. Bayley 1992*a*; Lang, J. T. 1992*a*.

98. Lang, J. T. 1992*b*.

99. Richards 1999, 89–92, 101–6. The Cottam finds were spread over an area of some 300 m × 150 m, while *Hamwic* is about 1000 m × 600 m. Richards discusses the comparisons and contrasts with other sites; loss of upper levels at the *wics* would reduce their finds totals.

100. Thomas, G. 1996, 92.

101. Leahy 2000; Booth, J. 2000.

102. Loveluck 2001; I am grateful to my former colleague Dr Loveluck for telling me as much as anyone could want to know about this site. There are a few fragments of window-glass at the site as well as the evidence of literacy. The plaque is illustrated and discussed by Brown, M. P. 1991, no. 69(a). A more sinister use of inscribed lead plaques is hinted at in a Hiberno-Latin text, with Ham (Noah's second son) writing magic on them: Cross 1986, 82.

103. Loveluck 2001, 112–13 and 116; Brown, M. P. 1991, no. 69(b). The nature of the Flixborough data changes considerably during the eighth and ninth centuries, with animal bones and glass vessels indicative of feasting in the earlier contexts.

104. Newman, J. 1999, 36–9.

105. e.g. near Carisbrooke on the Isle of Wight: Ulmschneider 1999, 19–44; Bidford-on-Avon, Warwickshire: Wise and Seaby 1995. Such sites have been called 'prolific' or 'productive' because of the quantities of coins and metal finds from them.

106. Tamworth: Rahtz and Meeson 1992 (the mill was some distance from the centre, so paucity of finds could be explained away); Northampton: Williams, F. 1979, 73–4, Williams, J. H. 1979, 243–63, and Williams, J. H. *et al.* 1985, 64–7, all including reports by A. R. Goodall, D. M. Metcalf, G. E. Oakley, and L. E.

Webster; North Elmham: Wade-Martins 1980, 495–516, including reports by A. R. Goodall, I. H. Goodall, S. E. Rigold, and D. M. Wilson. The embossed strip has a parallel not far away at Middle Harling: Margeson 1995, 64–5 (there are other finds from North Elmham that could be either eighth-/early ninth-century, or later Anglo-Saxon); Pennylands: Williams, R. J. 1993; Lot's Hole: Foreman, S. *et al.* 2002, 69–70.

107. Gardiner *et al.*, 2001; there were seventeen coins up to the 820s, but only five copper-alloy pins and a single strap-end there.
108. Webster 1991, no. 174. Frere *et al.*, 1987, for a fairly representative range of mid-Saxon finds in Canterbury—there are bow-brooches, but nothing like Flixborough's range of pins.
109. Painting: e.g. Budny 1999, 243–4; textiles: Maddicott 2001, 56; Coatsworth 1998, 12, cites Aldhelm on 'the red blood of the shell-fish', used by the harlot of the Book of Revelations to set off her jewels, pearls, and gold cup. The dog-whelk that produced the colour was known to Bede. Madder may also have been used, at least for textiles, since it had been taken to Dunadd and elsewhere in E-ware vessels: see Chapter 2.
110. Blair, J. 1996.
111. Speake 1989.
112. Hawkes, S. C. 1990.
113. Maddicott 2000 suggests that Wessex gained little benefit from its expansion westwards, whereas Northumbria's northward movement brought it prosperous cattle-rearing country. (It is necessary not to minimize the Church's contribution, though after Aldhelm's death in 709 there was no author of major consequence in Wessex, and sculptures like Bradford-on-Avon's slab are as likely to be of this period as later, with nothing of sculptural significance until the following century.)
114. Carr *et al.* 1988.
115. Brown, M. P. 1991, no. 66(a); Page 1991, no. 66(b).
116. Page 1991, no 66(o).
117. On a formal level, names on crosses and memorial plaques, perhaps like the lead one from Flixborough, above, were like a book or *Liber Vitae*, memorials to be read in silence: Ó Carragáin 1999, 198–9. Some informal objects with names could have been intended as gifts, to reinforce the importance of the giving, but the longer inscriptions all refer to ownership, commissioning, or making.
118. The allusion is to psalms, such as Ps. 104, '... the fowls of the air have their habitation, which sing among the branches'.
119. Webster 1991, no. 66(c).
120. Webster 1991, no. 66(l). There is also one from York: Tweddle *et al.* 1999, 286. Fevered imaginations used to see naked Mother Earths in attachment plates on a bucket at Hexham, but Bailey, R. N. 1974, 144–5, showed that they are in fact crouching animals.
121. There are almost no others anyway, at least in open country: in a settlement site a hoard may be identifiable but circumstances preclude recognition of anything

deposited with it, as opposed to things that happen to be in the same deposit, as with *Hamwic*'s Kingsland hoard.

122. Brown, M. P. 1991, no. 165; ead. 2001, 272–3.
123. Evison 1991, no. 108(e). The circular gold, garnet, and amber Ripon jewel may be another: Hall, R. A. *et al.* 1996.
124. Webster 1991, no. 107(k); Evison 1991, nos. 107(l)–(n).
125. The man who embellished the Lindisfarne Gospels was Billfrith 'the anchorite', suggesting someone who lived slightly separately from the rest of the community, as though such a wonder-worker was still a cause of unease: Cramp 1986, 193.
126. As befits one of the most interesting of all English objects, there is a huge bibliography on the Casket, and some disagreement over its date and provenance. A good straightforward account is by Neuman de Vegvar 1987, 259–73, in a book which proclaims through its title its author's widely shared belief that the Casket is northern English work. Valuable contributions to its study have been made in the last decade by Webster, e.g. 1991, no. 70 and 1999*b*; and by Henderson, G. 1999, 105–21. Among the reasons for its dating are the animals in the corners of the front panel, one of the very last manifestations of recognizable Style II.
127. Making drinking-vessels from opponents' heads was a favourite practice; for a sixth-century account of a cup made from a king's skull, brought on for special occasions like plate (see Chapter 2), see Wood 1997, 119; and Sturdy 1995, 75, for a Byzantine emperor whose head similarly ended up as a drinking trophy. Gannon 2003, 66–7, suggests that Weland's palm-held offering was deliberately contrasted to the leading Magi's stemmed vessel in the adjacent scene: see next note.
128. Henderson, G. 1999, 108–11. The juxtaposition is comparable to the *Gifts of Men* in the *Exeter Book*: 'Woden wrought idols, the Almighty wrought Glory': Mackie 1934, 41.
129. Seventh-century composite disc-brooches would be appropriate for size, but none is from a male grave. Although the male, perhaps sixth-century, grave at Collingbourne Ducis had a small brooch worn at the shoulder (Gingell 1975–6, 78 and 97, and see Chapter 1), there seems no other evidence of this practice. A Ravenna mosaic has this style worn by the Magi; even if it was alien to eighth-century England, exposure to such images could have led to production of the large ninth-century brooches, see Chapter 4.
130. Webster 1991, no. 133.
131. The Winchester reliquary was found in a rubbish-pit with pottery of the late ninth/early tenth century. There is a cautionary tale here, in that when it was first found it was assumed to date to the late tenth century, and to be part of the famous 'Winchester School' style of that period; so when I published it I was mainly concerned to show that it might be not so late, and to include it as one of the late ninth-century works associated with King Alfred the Great. Consequently I did not fully take into account the possibility that it might be considerably earlier than the pottery, despite citing a number of earlier works as

parallels: contrast Hinton *et al.* 1981, 72–3 with 67–71. General opinion now places it earlier, e.g. to the time of Alfred's father Aethelwulf: Webster 1991, no. 136, and I would not go to the stake even against a date in the second half of the eighth century and Carolingian workmanship. The Tassilo chalice is often called 'Anglo-Carolingian' because the two cannot really be differentiated: Wilson, D. M. 1991, no. 131. English craftsmanship was clearly valued highly on the continent.

132. Webster 1991, no. 134.
133. Bailey, R. N. 1974, 150–5; the findspot is not well recorded, but a provenance within the church seems likely.
134. Bailey, R. N. 1996, 52. The passage is from John 15: 1–8. St John's is the Gospel that starts 'In the beginning was the Word . . .' and stresses the importance of the message in 15: 3, 'Now ye are clean through the Word which I have spoken unto you'.
135. Hinton 1974, no. 36; Webster 1991, no. 180.
136. Thompson, V. 2002, 235.
137. Bailey, R. N. 1996, 38–9.
138. Hinton 1974, 65, tried to be more precise with a comparison to the infilling of a letter in the Book of Cerne, but even if this is indeed the closest analogue, it may not be the closest in date. The *Exeter Book*'s line 'Gold has its fitting place on a man's sword' (Mackie 1934, 41) was not a sentiment confined to the seventh century, though the eighth cannot quite match its gold and garnet pommels.
139. Webster 1991, no. 181.
140. Ibid., no. 179; see also above.
141. Wilson, D. M. 1964, nos. 30 and 80; Sigebereht's knife has acanthus-leaf decoration that puts it into the late ninth or early tenth century.
142. Webster 2001*a*; she notes that the most contorted creatures have a particularly Mercian concentration. A way of showing figures' robes is so distinctive that it has become known as the 'Mercian fold'.
143. Webster 1991, no. 173; its provenance could put it with the rich late seventh-century London graves, above, but its date seems too late for that.
144. Webster 2001*a*, 272–3.
145. Halsall 1998, 3, cites the *Fortunes of Men*'s dictum on hasty words at the mead-bench leading to conflict and the 'sword's edge'. Laws were rulers' attempts to control such violence, particularly in their own presence, presumably for their own safety as well as prestige. Their control over violence would have meant that they could control other things, such as the flow of goods to foreign merchants.
146. Meaney 1992, 112–13 and 116 for eighth-century proscriptions against amulets, though by the end of the century Alcuin was writing specifically against men who wore scraps of parchment round their necks as amulets, suggesting that by then the custom had been thoroughly Christianized.
147. Rogers 1993, 1346–50; Hinton 1996*a*, 7–8. Their paucity seems especially surprising in view of the large number of strap-ends known.

148. Tweddle 1992*a*, with commentary on the inscription by E. Okasha.

149. 'He started from slumber and put on his boar-helm', Cynewulf, *Elene*. As with the Beowulf poem, the date of the earliest known manuscript of texts like these may be considerably later than the time in which the stories were told. Gaimster, M. 1998, 13–17 and 214 for the 'help' that the gods gave humans through animal-crested headgear.

150. Benty Grange, Derbyshire, and the recent find at Wollaston, Northamptonshire. The third complete helmet is Sutton Hoo's, which has boars' heads on the ends of the eyebrow covers.

151. Speake 1980, 78–81; Hawkes, J. 1997, 315–17: see Chapter 2 for her comments on meaning being related to context. For references to wild animals in various sources, Meaney 2000. Hines 2000*a*, 82, notes that the boar came to be associated with Wales, *eofor* meaning both 'boar' in Welsh and 'weaponry' in Old English.

152. It particularly upset St Aldhelm, who in the 680s recalled it being worshipped in 'profane shrines', probably on some sort of stone or wooden pillar: Blair, J. 1995, 2–3. Hawkes, J. 1997, 326–8, suggests that the boar and the stag may have been less 'malleable' than some other creatures for Christian purposes because they were too associated with hunting and aristocratic lifestyles. Goats and rams seem never to have been represented despite their ferocity—a pre-Christian taboo carried forward?

153. Because they were said to suck and consume serpents when feeling unwell, they became an analogue for Christ overcoming the Devil: Yapp 1989, 129. Animal ferocity is also symbolized at Sutton Hoo and Taplow by the aurochs' horns: see Chapter 2.

154. Nelson 1980, 45–6, shows that *beag* was used in early texts, replaced by *cyne-helm*, 'king's helmet', in the tenth century; although that is probably a change of word to produce a more accurate description of the object already in use, the *cyne-helm* may not have been around before the ninth century. See also Gannon 2003, 51–4. Chaney 1970, 126, made the case for helmets as royal insignia.

155. Biddle and Kjølbye-Biddle 1985.

156. Bruce-Mitford 1978, 242–39. For discussion of manufacturing and the time involved, O'Connor, S. A. 1992. The Repton warrior's *seax* unfortunately obscures whether he is wearing a large buckle (see above).

157. When a militaristic bishop was recorded as still wearing his, despite his membership of the clergy.

158. Archibald 1995*a*.

159. Williams, G. 2001*a* for a recent summary generally, pp. 216–17 for the queen's coins specifically. It seems that Offa was not copying a contemporary Byzantine practice, as used to be thought, but took the idea from late Roman issues. Gannon 2003, 31–2, for other aspects of Offa's coin designs, and p. 192 for his re-establishment of any ceded rights over the coinage.

160. Metcalf 1998*a*, 167–9.

161. e.g. Metcalf 1988, 22–3, for *Hamwic*—there are only twenty-two 786–810 pennies, one 810–21, but eight 821–30; these totals include nineteenth-century and perhaps unreliable records, but the 1945–88 excavated numbers are nine, one, and three respectively. See also Metcalf 1998*a*, 172–3.
162. Metcalf and Northover, 1989.
163. Offa's copied an Arabic coin of 773–4; inscriptions on all Arabic coins were routinely 'There is no God but Allah' (the papacy apparently never realized that the paper used in its transactions all came from the Muslim world and was stamped 'Allah is great'): Grierson and Blackburn 1986, 280–1; Williams, G. 2001*a*, 218–19. The word *mancus* is a loan from Arabic.
164. Pagan 1988.
165. Metcalf 1998*a*, 175–7, for details.
166. Booth, J. 2000 for a recent summary.
167. Metcalf 1998*a*, 177–9; Robinson, P. 2001 for a discussion of the southern English finds. The occasional Pictish item, such as the brooch fragment found in Canterbury, raises the same issue: see above.
168. Other poems that include information about social attitudes suggesting concepts current in the eighth century include *The Gifts of Men*, which stresses kings as generous givers of gold—to hoard it away was to court fate and damnation by succumbing to the temptation to the sin of Avarice: Greenfield 1991, 397.
169. The usual assumption is that weapons went 'vertically' from lord to follower, and implied an obligation; some were more 'horizontal', such as the gift by Charlemagne of a sword, with a belt and silk, to Offa—though it was still from an emperor to a king, and may have had different connotations for the one than for the other. The correspondence of Alcuin at the end of the eighth century is full of mentions of gifts: Bolton, W. F. 1979, 115.
170. Campbell, J. 2000 shows how the Church continued to value gifts of treasure as well as of land, but 'gifts' of the latter might actually be sales. Matters are complicated by the duties that landholding seems to have carried, but which might be excused; they could be enforced by threat of confiscation. Gifts of treasure also carried an obligation to serve—the Church in prayer, the warrior in battle—but moral duties could only be enforced by threat to life. Those who have written on these themes include Charles-Edwards 1997.
171. Faith 1997, 89–90, suggests that it was particularly associated with the king, and that the whole 'folk' owed him *feorm* from it. Wormald 2001, 267, distinguishes it from bookland because it was inalienable—but seemingly held by individuals because of their family. There seems to be no sense of communal ownership, anyway.

4. ALFRED *ET AL.*

1. Wilson, D. M. 1964, no. 31 and pp. 22–9; Haith 1984, no. 9; Webster 1991, no. 243. Aethelwulf ruled Kent from 828, so the ring could in theory date from the

decade before 839, though it was found in Wessex, in a cart-rut at Laverstock, near Salisbury, Wiltshire, in 1780. An example of an object being used as a validator may be the *insigle* taken by Helmstan to King Edward in the early tenth century, as it does not sound as though a written document, let alone one with a fixed seal, was involved at that stage in a complex legal dispute: Heslop 1980, 3; Gretsch 1994, 100–2. The Baldehildis matrix (Col. pl. B.5) may have had final use in England in this way: see Chapter 3; the first known Anglo-Saxon seal matrix was cut for Bishop Aethelwald of Dunwich, *c.*845–70, but its precise function is not known: Heslop 1980, 2–3; Wilson, D. M. 1964, no. 18; Webster 1991, no. 205. Earlier English seals have been claimed from time to time, but subsequently discredited, e.g. Tonnochy 1952, pp. xvi–xviii; Heslop 1980, 1.

2. Wilson, D. M. 1964, no. 1; Haith 1984, no. 10; Webster 1991, no. 244. Aethelswith and her husband King Burgred left England for Rome, and she died in Pavia in 888. The ring was not found in their kingdom, but in Northumbrian territory at Aberford, Yorkshire, ploughed up in 1870.

3. Webster 2003, 91; Webster also points out that that both are Carolingian rather than Anglo-Saxon motifs in origin.

4. Graham-Campbell 1982. A 1950s report of one on a finger in a York grave was written long after the discovery and is not to be relied upon: Kemp, R. L. 1996, 4. For 'viking' rings, see below.

5. Bossington: Hinton 1974, no. 4; I was not confident in the dating then, and am no more so now, though the baptismal allusion gains some credence from Webster's suggestion about the royal rings, above. Abingdon: Hinton 1974, no. 1—the gold panel is now lost, but was illustrated in the sword's first publication; Haith 1984, no. 14. Ipsden: MacGregor 1994.

6. If the rings were baptismal, they were presumably given as gifts from royal godparents. King Aethelwulf was a generous giver, at least to the pope: Webster 2003, 91–2.

7. Passage from the description of the battle of Brunanburh in the *Anglo-Saxon Chronicle*, *s.a.* 937: Whitelock (ed.) 1961, 70. Similar beast-head terminals are on a silver pommel, which also has a gold plate set in it, found in the River Seine, perhaps dropped by a viking who won it in England: Wilson, D. M. 1964, no. 66.

8. Wilson, D. M. 1964, no. 153; Webster 1991, no. 257; ead. 2003, 87–9. It has to be admitted that the outer roundels can only be read in the way suggested if fish are ignored, and one of the roundels looks like an abstract pattern rather than a flower. The brooch takes its name for a former owner. Gannon 2003, 167, has noticed that five eighth-century Series K sceattas could make up a set, each representing one of the Senses. The iconography would have had to be extremely well known for it to have been recognizable in such a way. A forthcoming paper by David Pratt will argue for the association of the brooch's iconography with King Alfred. For the Alfred Jewel, see below, and Yorke 1995, 94–5, for Wessex's growth.

9. Webster 2003, 88–9.

10. Wilson, D. M. and Blunt 1961; Pagan 1999.

11. e.g. the 'Tiberius' Bede: Brown, M. P. 1991, no. 170; ead. 2001.
12. Wilson, D. M. 1964, nos. 2 and 3; Brown, M. P. 2001 for the manuscripts.
13. Bruce-Mitford 1974, 311; whether it was hung around a neck or in a church is unknown, but its survival could be because it was kept in a church treasury until the Dissolution in the sixteenth century; it is in such good condition that it may never have been buried, and its iconography would be entirely suited to a church setting. Was it originally donated to be a memorial of its owner, a church benefactor?
14. Wilson, D. M. 1964, no. 152; Webster 1991, no. 189. This brooch is also named after a former owner; although Mrs Strickland had inherited a number of objects from Whitby Abbey, the brooch was not necessarily found there. The beasts may not have any very deep meaning, but the way that they are also used on sculptures shows that they could have some Christian relevance, as reminders of Hell's snares or whatever. Despite the difference in the media and scales, there is considerable likeness between the heads on the brooch and those on cross-shafts such as that at Rowberrow, Somerset: Bailey, R. N. 1996, fig. 9c, and his comparisons on fig. 8; I thought that the figure-of-eight complex of two creatures eating each other on the Abingdon sword, panel 24, was unique until I saw a drawing of a Bedford sculpture: Plunkett 1998, pl. 11, no. 5.
15. Webster 1991, no. 187; ead. 2001, 275–7.
16. Alcuin is better known for blaming the raids on storytelling monks who should have been at their prayers, but 'consider the dress, the way of wearing the hair, the luxurious habits of the princes and people . . .', 793 letter: Whitelock (ed.) 1979, 776–7; and 'It is a confusion of your life to decorate your fingers with gold, or to ornament your neck with silken clothing': Bolton, W. F. (ed.) 1979, 116.
17. Webster 1991, nos. 250 and 251 for swords, nos. 191–200 for strap-ends and hooked tags.
18. Youngs 2000.
19. Metcalf 1998a, 171–4.
20. Metcalf and Northover 1985; eid. 1989.
21. Blair, J., forthcoming, argues for losses to predatory Anglo-Saxons. The *Anglo-Saxon Chronicle*'s 'ravages of heathen men miserably destroyed God's church on Lindisfarne', s.a. 793, Whitelock (ed.) 1961, 36, sounds terminal, yet treasures such as St Cuthbert's cross (Chapter 2) escaped the pillaging.
22. e.g. the Croydon hoard: Brooks and Graham-Campbell 1986, 99; see further below. Occasional finds of small portable Irish objects, such as a harness fitting recently reported from Cruxton on the River Medway in Kent, are best attributed to viking redistribution: Youngs 2001b.
23. Metcalf and Northover 1985, 159–60, argued that debasement was not a reflection of shortages of silver, but a means for English kings to increase their revenues, by forcing their subjects to accept the same number of debased pennies in exchange for their old ones. That argument assumes that the kings maintained sufficient control to ensure that enough old pennies were brought in for remint-

ing to make the exercise worthwhile, and redirection of silver into other channels is an alternative explanation for the currency's problems.

24. For examples in use, Backhouse *et al.* (eds.) 1984, no. 42, admittedly a much later picture, has a particularly good selection. The figure on the cross-shaft at Codford, Wiltshire, has what might be a T-headed pin fastening his cloak in the middle, but the representation is more probably of a short seax hung round the neck: Webster and Backhouse (eds.) 1991, no. 208. For the Franks Casket, see Chapter 3.

25. Webster 1991, no. 187, p. 231, for this suggestion. The Upper Poppleton hoard could be another, as its six strap-ends look very much as though they came from the same workshop; but several have rivets (to hold them to straps) in place, which suggests that they had had some use: Youngs 2000.

26. Wilson, D. M. 1964, nos. 72–8. Coins in the hoard show that it was deposited *c.*850: Booth, J. 1998, 80.

27. Webster 1991, no. 248; Graham-Campbell and Batey 1998, 109.

28. Blinkhorn 1999, 9.

29. Armstrong *et al.* 1991, 243–4. Ninth-century objects from Beverley include a fork-spatula of uncertain use, reported by A. R. Goodall in ibid. 148 and 151, which is like one in the Sevington hoard: Wilson, D. M. 1964, no. 68.

30. Cowie 2000, 197.

31. A hoard in their homeland in Beverley may be less surprising, but also shows that they were worth keeping: Pirie 1991.

32. King, A. 1978; further north, however, Upper Teesdale may have been beyond the coin-using area: Coggins *et al.* 1983, 25.

33. Pirie 1999, 80–1; O'Sullivan and Young 1991, 84. The decline of the 'prolific' site at South Newbald can be traced through the decline in its styca numbers in the mid-850s: Booth, J. 2000, 92–3; a lead weight there could be because of need to weigh rather than merely to count them, and could be a record of a viking visit.

34. Metcalf and Northover 1985, 165; Booth, J. 1998; Blackburn 1998, 108–20.

35. Wilson, D. M. and Blunt 1961, 117–19.

36. Wilson, D. M. and Blunt 1961, 98 and pl. 28b; Dickinson 1982, no. 52 and p. 44: Dickinson classifies it as a 'G.3', otherwise found in northern Ireland and north-west Scotland, with one example now from Wales: Redknap 1995, 60.

37. A missing gold pendant could have been Scandinavian: Wilson, D. M. and Blunt 1961, 94–5.

38. Webster 1991, no. 246, for identification problems. I do not see the chalice as necessarily ecclesiastical, as it has no specifically Christian iconography, and the Franks Casket illustrates one in a curious but hardly Christian context on a side panel, and 'That woman offering the lethal drink of the brothel in a golden chalice (Latin *calice*)' was no religious: Frank 1997, 21. The only real parallel for the 'scourge' was found in a Norse grave at Ballinaby in the Hebrides; that does not preclude its being ecclesiastical, as it could have been looted from a, probably

Irish, church: Ritchie 1993, fig. 74. Hart 1999, 145–8, shows the development of the scourge in manuscript illuminations.

39. Brooks 1996, 140–1, shows that Cornwall was expected to perform shire service for the West Saxon kings by the end of the ninth century, but that its men could not be trusted not to support the vikings; they, 'the west Welsh', are recorded as doing so in 838: Whitelock (ed.) 1961, 41. The argument that the Trewhiddle hoard indicates cultural integration depends, of course, upon the assumption that it was assembled locally; its deposition in a mining area (the coins are distinctively stained by copper residues: Pagan 1999) suggests local rather than seafarers' knowledge.

40. That they represent the Last Judgement does not make their image less striking. 'There shall be wars and rumours of wars': Hawkes 1996, 108–9.

41. Biddle *et al.* 1986*a*, 16–18; Biddle and Kjølbye-Biddle 2001, 66–74. The ring was beside the man's head, not on a finger.

42. Pagan 1999; Brooks and Graham-Campbell 1986, 109.

43. Brooks and Graham-Campbell 1986, 91–106.

44. Graham-Campbell 2001*b*, 54; Wilson, D. M. 1964, no. 20. The glass stud is described as surrounded by a twisted filigree setting of gilt copper-alloy wire, which seems unique and must have been difficult to achieve. Both *Hamwic* and York have yielded glass bosses, though not marbled, and with silver-wire circumferences: Hinton 1996*a*, 54.

45. Brooks and Graham-Campbell 1986, 101.

46. Wormald 1982, 132.

47. Kruse 1992*a* for a general review, and ead. 1988 for hack-silver and ingots.

48. Williams, G. 1999, 29–30.

49. Examples include the set from Colonsay: Ritchie 1993, fig. 65. The one from Talnotrie, Webster 1991, no. 248e, has interlace that could be either Anglo-Saxon or Celtic, and one from Llanbedrgoch used a brooch terminal: Redknap 2000, fig. 82. An exception to the general rule that 'Celtic' examples are not found in coinage areas is one from Ixworth, Suffolk, with an eye-catching gilt copper-alloy male head, quite probably from an Irish shrine or reliquary: West 1998, 69 and fig. 100.4.

50. Wilson, D. M. 1964, no. 5; Webster 1991, no. 245. Cf. the Patching hoard rings, Chapter 1, and one in the Wieuwerd hoard: Mazo Carras 1985, fig. 4.1. The Beeston Tor hoard was with coins that are no later than *c*.875.

51. The reappearance of furnished burial is of course evidence in itself of some new source of ideas, as are the cremations at Ingleby, Derbyshire: Richards 1991, 111–16; Richards *et al.* 1995; Richards 2002.

52. Hadley 2002, 223. The same point has been made by Halsall, 2000. The number of known burials of this type has increased, e.g. one from Middle Harling, Norfolk: Rogerson 1995, 24–5 and 79–80, and a possible one from Meols, Cheshire: *British Archaeology*, 62 (2001), but they remain very few, and apparently less overtly 'viking' than on the Isle of Man, despite its proximity. Other

churchyard burials that may be 'viking' include York: Hall, R. A. 1998, and below; a woman in Heysham, Lancashire, with a bone comb who may have been a 'wavering pagan': Cook, A. and Batey 1994; and much more doubtfully at Addingham, Yorkshire, where a bone plate was not from a grave: MacGregor 1996. Recent summaries include Graham-Campbell 2001c; swords, often broken, and axes found without further context in various churchyards may also be from disturbed viking graves. A new discovery made in Yorkshire was reported in February 2004, with the claim that nails with it indicate a ship-burial.

53. Repton: Biddle and Kjølbye-Biddle 2001, 67. Reading: East 1986; Brooks and Graham-Campbell 1986, 107; Astill 1978, 77.

54. Santon Downham: Webster 1992, no. 365; oval brooches must (alas) no longer be called 'tortoises'. A whalebone smoothing-board reported as from Ely by Shetelig 1940, 67 and fig. 69, is probably not an English find: Owen, O. and Dalland 1999, 81; Shetelig 1940, 67 and fig. 69.

55. Claughton Hall: Richards 1991, 115; Edwards, B. J. N. 1992, 46. A pot containing a cremation was also recorded, but the find was made in 1822, and the pot is lost, so whether it contained a man, a woman, a man and a woman, or possibly even neither cannot be known, though the weapons at least make the first possibility the most likely. The Santon Downham brooches were poorly recorded, but were said to be with a skeleton and a sword. Historical sources occasionally mention women with the raiders, but do not reveal their antecedents. A female burial with a pair of oval brooches was reported from Yorkshire in the autumn of 2003. (In *Laxdaela Saga* (ch. 20), set in the c.950s, a norseman does dress a slave girl he has purchased and voyage to the Baltic with 'fine clothing' from his ship; but he is not on a raiding expedition. Reference supplied by Jeff New.)

56. Biddle and Kjølbye-Biddle 2001, 60–5.

57. Webster 1991, no. 134; Edwards 1992, 51; Webster 2001a, 271. Although found in a churchyard, the Pentney brooches do not seem a likely loot assemblage. If a churchyard is available it makes a good place to bury a hoard, as it has plenty of markers for finding the right spot again; somewhere close to the edge seems to have been preferred, at any rate later: Robinson, P. 1984, 200.

58. Watkin, J. and Mann 1981; Haith 1991, no. 249.

59. Webster 1991, nos. 250 and 251.

60. Watkin, J. R. 1986, 98. These weapons, and other Trewhiddle ornamented sword fittings such as a pommel found outside York (Tweddle *et al.* 1999, 287–8), may of course have been deposited or lost by their first owners!

61. Graham-Campbell 1992a, 10.

62. Archibald 1992, 15 and 20. The term 'Norse' is used of vikings thought to have been of Norwegian rather than Danish origin. The eastern coins are called kufic because of their Arab inscriptions; they could be minted anywhere in the Arab world, 'from Spain to the Hindu Kush': Archibald 1992, 18, but can be assumed to have crossed Russia to reach the Baltic and a Scandinavian welcome.

63. Graham-Campbell 1992b, 114.

64. Graham-Campbell 1992a, 10–11.
65. Kruse 1992b, 79–82.
66. Graham-Campbell 1992b, 112–13; id. 2001d for the most recent summary; also Richards 1991, 18; Blackburn and Bonser 1990. Although now in Scotland, Berwickshire should probably be considered as part of the political sphere of northern England, accounting for the Gordon hoard: Graham-Campbell 1995, 27–8.
67. The term should strictly be used of the plain penannular rings found in later tenth-century Scotland, but the other types should be considered in the same discussions. See Graham-Campbell 1995, 59; Kruse 1988; ead. 1992b; ead. 1995.
68. Graham-Campbell 1992b, 109–10.
69. Repton: Biddle et al. 1986a, 16–18; Biddle and Kjølbye-Biddle 2001, 66–7. In situ finds were on a woman's wrist at Unst, Shetland: Graham-Campbell 1995, 13; and on an unsexed arm in York: Wenham et al. 1987, 80. There are documentary references to arm-rings, however, suggesting that they were worn at least on some occasions.
70. Fuglesang 1992.
71. Graham-Campbell 1992b, 109–10; Edwards, B. J. N. 2002, 50.
72. The Goldsbrough hoard included an intact 'thistle-brooch', and part of at least one other; their name derives from their globular terminals which are 'brambled', i.e. covered with raised dots so that they look a little like the plant: Graham-Campbell 1983, 319; id. 1992b, 112–13 for the hoard.
73. Knight, J. K. 1996, 56; Arnold and Davies 2000, 187; and Redknap 2000, 53–4, for this and other possible examples. The Caerwent burial was on the edge of the known cemetery area, but this liminality may be an illusion of incomplete excavation: see Redknap 2000, fig. 150, for plan.
74. Hiberno-Norse is the term used to signify something made in Ireland or the Norse areas of Britain. In this case the pin is very distinctive, being a ring with four protruding cross-shaped knobs on which a shaft swivelled: Knight, J. K. 1996, 51; Redknap 2000, fig. 32. The pin was in the cemetery that produced the Anglo-Saxon pins, above.
75. Redknap 2000, fig. 154.
76. The authenticity of Asser's Vita has been impugned recently by Smyth 1995, but by no one else.
77. Redknap 2000, fig. 29. A sword with silver mounts reported as from Builth Wells could be another example: Arnold and Davies 2000, 177.
78. Redknap 1995, 60–4; the brooches were reportedly found 400 m apart, so a brooch-hoard like Pentney seems unlikely.
79. Dykes 1976, 21; cf. Talnotrie and Llanbedrgoch.
80. Redknap 2000, 61–84, for a well-illustrated summary of this important site.
81. There is a similar hoard from a cave in south Wales, on the Gower peninsula: Redknap 2000, fig. 30. A single coin from the south of France found at Caernar-

fon could argue for direct trade, but is as likely to be a viking loss as evidence of a direct link: Metcalf 1998*a*, 176. The same can be said of a Northumbrian styca found there: Dykes 1976, 27.

82. It could symbolize a prince as his people's 'sword-polisher', but analogy with Sutton Hoo should not be taken too far: Redknap 2000, 53, is careful not to pursue this line.
83. Kruse 1992*b*, 80–2, citing Northover 1986; illustrated in Redknap 2000, figs. 15 and 56.
84. Illustrated in Redknap 2000, fig. 83; see also Dykes 1976, 19.
85. Campbell, E. and Lane 1989; Llangors is Wales's only known crannog, and is further evidence of Irish connections. More of them were probably precluded because most of the Welsh lakes are too deep for artificial islands to be constructed in them.
86. Granger-Taylor and Pritchard 2000; the stitching details are paralleled in the Cuthbert Stole (below), though textiles are such rare survivals that such a detail cannot be called exclusively 'Anglo-Saxon'. It has been shown that the minute decorative detail could alternatively have been carried out in soumac weave: H. Prosser, pers. comm.
87. Keynes and Lapidge 1983, 97.
88. Redknap 1995, 65–7.
89. Edwards, N. 1997; Arnold and Davies 2000, 162–4; Redknap 2000, 81–2. For ringed pins, Fanning 1994.
90. Davies, W. 1990, 83.
91. Davies, W. 1977, 36, 59 and 60. The charters may reflect pre-viking conditions, but a reversion in the tenth century after ninth-century gestures towards using coins seems possible.
92. Dykes 1976, 12–4, considered that the coin might have been for a later Howell, struck from old, recut dies.
93. Dykes 1976, 20.
94. Graham-Campbell 1973; Webster 1991, no. 247. Coins of King Alfred were found nearby, but as they were pierced they were certainly not being used in the usual way: Graham-Campbell 1995, 86. The elderly tippler with his bird-headed horn on the Bullion, Invergowrie, stone may be of this period: see Chapter 3. Other Anglo-Saxon objects include a gold Trewhiddle-style ring said to be from Selkirk: Webster 1991, no. 203; strap-ends, e.g. a copper-alloy pair from Tain, Sutherland, not recorded as found with anything else and perhaps made in the eighth century, though they need not have travelled until the ninth: Hinton 1974, nos. 33–4; and less certainly a silver ring set with gold wires and foil, and green glass, perhaps tenth-century: Webster 1995.
95. See above. The hoard also had a globular-headed pin which seems neither Anglo-Saxon nor Scandinavian in type: Graham-Campbell 1983, 315.
96. Graham-Campbell and Batey 1998, 151, argue that recent discoveries have shown that there was little cultural difference between the Western and the Northern Isles.

97. Graham-Campbell and Batey 1998, 8 and 150.
98. A single grave at Broch of Gurness, Orkney: ibid. 128; the grave was sketched in 1939, reproduced in Ritchie 1993, fig. 43. If the hammer is shown, it must be the object near the woman's left arm, and probably therefore dangled on a festoon. Graham-Campbell and Batey note other amulets with her, and suggest that they dangled from her necklet.
99. Owen, O. and Dalland 1999, 73–88 (the plaque is shown in colour on the front cover); Ritchie 1993, 44–7 (the plaque is shown in colour on the back cover); Graham-Campbell and Batey 1998, 138–40.
100. Owen, O. and Dalland 1999, 160–73 for the brooch, 52–9 (by D. H. Lorimer) for the people's ages, 157–65 for the dating. Their proposal, 875–950, is a compromise, one not inappropriate for an elderly woman, but the results from the three skeletons varied quite widely and show that radiocarbon is not without problems: cf. Hinton 1990*a*, 44–6; id. 1992.
101. e.g. Graham-Campbell 2001*a*, 33. The phrase is from *Beowulf*, see Chapter 2.
102. Paired burials include Ballinaby, below.
103. Scar is again an example; Owen, O. and Dalland 1999, 89–91.
104. Ritchie 1993, 27, points out that there could be exceptions, but the matter remains controversial: see also ibid. 32.
105. Ibid. 77.
106. Owen, O. and Dalland 1999, 103–36.
107. Graham-Campbell and Batey 1998, 122–5; as they point out, there are several male graves in Norway which have both swords and tool-sets, indicative of a chief supplying the needs of his people. There were other burials at Ballinaby, some probably as well furnished.
108. Especially in the photograph in Ritchie 1993, pl. 65. See also ibid. 79–84; Graham-Campbell and Batey 1998, 90.
109. Metcalf 1995, 16.
110. Youngs (ed.) 1989, no. 70; Crawford, B. E. 1987, fig. 33; Graham-Campbell and Batey 1998, 136. Strictly, the brooch is a 'brooch-pin', the pin swivelling on the hoop.
111. Stevenson 1974, 16. See also above, Chapter 3, and Youngs (ed.) 1989, no. 69.
112. It has to be categorized as a 'stray find', however, as it was found on its own: Graham-Campbell 1995, 5, 88.
113. Graham-Campbell 1995 is the definitive catalogue; see pp. 26–31 for the early evidence. The synthesis in Graham-Campbell and Batey 1998, 232–47, is an invaluable summary. For later developments, see Chapter 5.
114. For the metallurgy, Kruse and Tate 1992; eid., 1995.
115. Graham-Campbell 1995, 59; Graham-Campbell and Batey 1998, 243–4.
116. Kruse 1995, 193–4.
117. Metcalf 1995, 19.

118. Graham-Campbell 1995, 61–2.
119. Ibid. 154–5; Graham-Campbell and Batey 1998, 235. The ring is lost, but other objects in the grave put it in the ninth century.
120. Graham-Campbell and Batey 1998, 128. See also above.
121. Fanning 1983 and 1994. Ringed pins are also in a few graves, and at Birsay.
122. Hunter, J. R. 1986, 188–9; Kaaland 1992, no. 64; Graham-Campbell and Batey 1998, 223. (There is also some in France, but that is a most unlikely source.)
123. Hamilton 1956: there is no entry in the index. Amber is in the Norse graves, but usually only as single beads worn by both genders, perhaps as amulets: Graham-Campbell and Batey 1998, 149–50. The woman at Westness had a single large one on her necklace.
124. Hill, P. 1997, 369–70 and 464, no. 14.
125. Campbell, E. 1997*b*.
126. Graham-Campbell and Batey 1998, 177; Marner 2002, 26–8.
127. At least according to the *Anglo-Saxon Chronicle*: Whitelock (ed.) 1961, 48; a late tenth-century writer associated their oath with a word that in other contexts means 'cup': Frank 1997, 22–3; was he implying a demonic perversion of the Mass chalice?
128. Whitelock (ed.) 1961, 48. The vikings were at Wareham at the time, and it may have been one of their scouting parties that lost the two weights, above. A rather fine gilt-silver Carolingian mount with acanthus-leaf ornament found just outside the defences may be another bit of their carelessness then: Webster 1991, no. 256.
129. Brooks and Graham-Campbell 1986, 101, n. 56, and see above. A letter from the pope to the archbishop of Canterbury in 877–8 also refers to the harsh tributes levied by the king, who attained a bad reputation at Abingdon Abbey because of his demands. It seems likely that these fell primarily upon the Church, because the king needed the support of his ealdormen and others, and could not risk antagonizing them by heavy taxation.
130. Blackburn 1998, 106–7.
131. Maddicott 1992, 165–6. A king needs 'tools and resources', i.e. to be able to offer his men 'land to live on, gifts, weapons, food, ale, clothing . . .'. The high priority of gifts is interesting.
132. Charles-Edwards 1998, 48–50 and 55–7.
133. Keynes and Lapidge 1983, 97. Both gifts were special, as incense, like silk, had to be imported. The Llangors garment, above, may give an idea of what the robe was like.
134. Keynes and Lapidge 1983, 188. The date of the letter is unknown but after 879, so by then perhaps Alfred was making fewer demands on his churches.
135. Keynes and Lapidge 1983, 126; Webster 2003, 83, suggests that the word *aestel* may be rare because it related specifically to objects that Alfred's enquiring mind devised as an educational aid. The *mancus* was notionally worth 30 silver pennies:

Grierson and Blackburn 1986, 270; Chapter 3; also Nelson 1992, 152–4, for discussion of *mancuses* in Alfredian contexts (she says that if one of the rare gold coins was a *mancus*, it would only have been worth one-third of 30 pennies, but I think that that overlooks that the known gold coins weighed about three times as much as a normal silver penny; in any case, the bishops were in no position to send the gifts back in protest at their size).

136. For fuller discussions, and opposing views, cf. Kornbluth 1998 and Webster 2001*b*. See also Hinton 1974, no. 23; Webster 1991, no. 260. It would not altogether surprise me to learn that it had once held a chain, in view of the animal heads through which chains pass, held in place by rivets, on the seventh-century Roundway Down pins: Youngs (ed.) 1989, no. 40; Webster 2003, 82, suggests that it would not cause her great surprise to learn that it was the head of some sort of staff of office.

137. Keynes and Lapidge 1983, 187.

138. Although no other metalwork has 'to be worked' except a silver ring that may very well not be genuine: Okasha 1971, 8 and no. 156. The king's own phrase about Weland the smith and other heroes, 'what is there left of them but a meagre fame and a name writ with a few letters' (Booth, P. A. 1997, 42–3 and 63) might conceivably have been written with such inscriptions in mind. Sturdy 1995, 179, has made the interesting suggestion that the beast's head on the Jewel could be a reference to Aethelwulf—which would push it back into Alfred's father's reign, since it is not very likely that Alfred would have had his father remembered in that way.

139. Wilson, D. M. 1964, no. 80; Okasha 1971, no. 109.

140. Brown, M. P. 1991, no. 154; Brooks and Graham-Campbell 1986, 103–5. A further implication is that the ealdorman and his wife had a personal interest in the book, which could have been because they had been shown it at some time—an indication that a church's treasures were displayed to privileged visitors: see Gameson, R. 1995, 57–8 and 248–60, for lay interest in religious art in the tenth and eleventh centuries. Another Alfred was 'a foolish man' who 'libidinously committed debauchery' of various sorts, according to the bishop of Winchester, though that did not stop him becoming an ealdorman: Rumble 2002, 117–18; Sturdy 1995, 157.

141. The vernacular might have been chosen rather than Latin for the inscription because the book distributed to the bishops was itself in Old English, and in his accompanying letter Alfred did not call himself *Aelfred cyning*, though he said he was 'honoured with the dignity of kingship'. He did use his title in the preface, and in other vernacular texts, however, such as his will: Keynes and Lapidge 1983, 123, 124, and 174.

142. Asser: ibid. 106.

143. Evidenced by the royal rings, above; the Abingdon sword and Fuller brooch both have features that would allow them to be dated within Alfred's reign, but in my view could equally well go in his father's, with the Aethelwulf ring.

144. Howlett 1974 for Wisdom. Enamelling on penannular brooches and hanging-bowls involved melting into cast work, not into cloisons.

145. Kornbluth 1989. There is a tantalising mention by William of Malmesbury of a shrine donated by King Aethelwulf with a crystal lid on which Aldhelm's (or its: *nomen eius* could be taken either way) name could be read in gold letters: Hinton *et al.* 1981, 71–2. Charlemagne's search for *spolia* may account for the 'black stones' that King Offa wanted, above.

146. Whitelock (ed.) 1961, 50 and 52. The book sent out to his bishops with the *aestels* was Alfred's translation of Gregory's *Cura Pastoralis*. Webster 2003, 99–101, points to Francia as the source of crystal *spolia*.

147. Blackburn 1998, 112–14; id. 2003, 207. Sturdy 1995, 48, notes a similarity between the 'London monogram' coin and ninth-century papal bulls, which may well have been another, though not necessarily alternative, source. Both Sturdy 1995, 48–52, and Hill, D. 2003, 226–8, note how Rome may have affected Alfred in his fort-building as well as in other ways.

148. Hinton 1974, no. 22; Webster 1991, no. 259. Minster Lovell is just north of the River Thames, so would fall in Mercia, but Alfred's control of Oxford implies that for a time its shire would have been part of his kingdom.

149. Reported as having been found on the beach at Bowleaze Cove: Webster 1991, no. 258.

150. Webster 2003, 83–5. A gold object found at Cherry Burton, North Yorkshire, has also been called an *aestel*, but it is not quite the same as the four in Wessex; a beast's head holds a suspension loop, not a nozzle, and in lieu of ears has two splayed tubes, apparently unpierced for rivets: *Portable Antiquities Annual Report 2000–2001*, 55.

151. La Rocca and Provero 2000, 251–3.

152. Le Jan 2000, 285; Yorke 2001, 29.

153. Keynes and Lapidge 1983, 132; cf. Le Jan 2000, 303, and Godden 2003, 144. Alfred made an explicit contrast between fighting men and working men.

154. See Chapter 3.

155. Coatsworth 2001, 292–3 and 302–5.

156. The Anglo-Saxon word is *belt*: Gretsch 1994, 98. This leaves less room for doubt about the correct translation than usual, but does not specify what sort of belt was involved. Smyth 1995, 397–8, assumed that it was an heirloom because of the dearth of known contemporary belt-fittings, but that can be revised in the light of the St Cuthbert 'girdle'. See also the Winchester pieces, below. The dispute goes on to be about a five-hide estate, a valuable property, but there is no suggestion that the value of the belt was equivalent to that of the land; the theft provided an opportunity, and if the belt had actually belonged to the land-taker, he would have claimed reparation for the insult as well as for the material cost of the belt.

157. Keynes 2001, 48; a late tenth-century writer says that there was a royal crown—*stemate royale*—but that may be an anachronism: Campbell, A. (ed.) 1962, 51.

158. Archibald 1984a, no. 181. A crown is also shown worn by a king in a contemporary manuscript usually assumed to represent King Athelstan and St Cuthbert: Backhouse 1984, no. 6; Rollason 1989, 421–4.

159. Dolley 1965; Blackburn 2001. A Thor's hammer paired with a bow and arrow might be another conquest allusion. Innovative designs such as a reliquary or tower were produced in north-west English mints, but they ceased when the king's aunt died and Edward took over direct rule: Lyon 2001. Other surveys include Blackburn *et al.* 1983, 14–15. For viking reasons to convert to Christianity—not necessarily the same thing as accepting baptism—see Abrams 2001*a*.

160. The most recent discussion is Coatsworth 2001; see also Granger-Taylor 1989. An Aelfflaed was recorded as the king's *amicabilis femina* in a 928 charter: Dumville 1992, 87, n. 153. The absence of *Regina* from the inscriptions can, as with the Alfred Jewel, be explained away.

161. Wormald 2001, esp. 275. Peter's Pence was probably still sent to Rome, however, and the brooch set with the imitative Edward coin found there might have accompanied one such payment: Blunt 1986, 166; Wilson, D. M. 1964, no. 64; Rumble 2001, 243. The Forum hoard probably represents another, from the 940s: Graham-Campbell and Okasha 1991.

162. Hinton 1996*b* for full references. This is not to say that Winchester had a monopoly of the 'Winchester style', even in metalwork production. For the origin of the style in the back of the Alfred Jewel and other artefacts, see Cramp 1975, esp. fig. 19, and Wilson, D. M. 1975, esp. figs. 22–3.

163. Biddle 1983 and James, T. B. 1997 for summaries. For other work in the Brooks, Scobie and Zant 1991, including p. 37 for an extraordinary collection of glass, mainly window, from a hearth close to a pit dendrochronologically dated to *c*.880.

164. Kilmurry 1980.

165. Bayley 2000*a*, 139.

166. MacGregor *et al.* 1999, 1919–22.

167. Bayley 1992*b*; Ottaway 1992. Small cast ingots of copper alloy are increasingly being reported at various places, e.g. Dawson 2002, 256–7.

168. Pirie 1986, 33–41.

169. Ottaway 1992, 525; an earlier suggestion that this was where the dies were being cut for use elsewhere remains possible but much diminished by the repair evidence: Hinton 1990*a*, 89.

170. Archibald 1991*b*, 331–46, argues this on the evidence of London, where there are many more, though none found with dies. A punch-stamped lead fragment at Llanbedrgoch is difficult to explain as a record, but equally it is difficult to see why arm-ring punches needed to be tested in such profusion: Redknap 2000, 84.

171. Wenham *et al.* 1987, 80–1, and 83 for other burials; Hall, R. A. 1998 for a new possibility at the same cemetery, St Mary Bishophill Senior, based on the discovery of a plaited knot of silver wires, which has parallels in graves of the first half of the tenth century on the Isle of Man and elsewhere. He refers to another at Carlisle, which may indicate a viking-style burial there as well. The strap-end (Fig. 4.12) also came from St Mary Senior.

172. MacGregor 1982, 85–6.

173. Rogers 1993, 1973–5; Tweddle *et al.* 1999, 284–5.
174. Waterman 1959, 94; Tweddle 1992, 334; Mainman and Rogers 2000, 2591. It has no obvious Romano-British parallels, e.g. Allason-Jones 1996.
175. Rogers 1993, 1375.
176. Waterman 1959, 72; a second English find of a chape of this sort was made recently in Chatburn, Lancashire: Edwards, B. J. N. 2002.
177. Thompson, V. 2003, 216–17, is the most recent discussion.
178. Mainman and Rogers 2000, 2541–4. In the same way, but from different areas, much of the imported pottery had reached the eighth- and ninth-century *wics*.
179. Walton 1989, 341–5.
180. Walton Rogers 1997, 1821–2. Stamford pottery, below, makes immigrants from the Rhineland/north France another possible ingredient.
181. Mainman and Rogers 2000, 2500–1.
182. Huggett 1988, 64–6.
183. See above; its appearance in Norse graves appears to have been only as single beads: Graham-Campbell and Batey 1998, 149–50.
184. Mainman and Rogers 2000, 2484–98, with a section on the geology by G. D. Gaunt; the phyllite cannot be tied down, but is probably Norwegian.
185. Mainman and Rogers 2000, 2501–8, with analyses by I. Panter.
186. Mainman and Rogers 2000, 2593, 2596, and 2641–2, for the two gold-foil covered beads, found together but in a residual context, which limits discussion of whether the manufacturing technique was introduced by a first- or second-generation Scandinavian immigrant, or whether the beads were imported.
187. Phillips *et al.* 1995, 522–3; cf. Fanning 1994, 16; Mainman and Rogers 2000, 2580–2. The phrase used in the first of these by Martin Carver, 'colonial viking', is a good rendering of the cultural mix.
188. See above for the Near East contacts.
189. Walton 1989, 374–9.
190. Hall, R. A. 1994, 87.
191. Pirie 1986, 29; there is a genuine one from Winchester, which shows that such things could get into the English-controlled areas: ibid. 29.
192. MacGregor 1982, 87–9; Thomas, G. 2001a, 42.
193. Mainman and Rogers 2000, 2569–70.
194. Tweddle *et al.* 1999, 258–61. Most objects from Coppergate postdate *c.*850 and they become prolific from *c.*900. There is, however, a significant number of things that seem earlier; although there are no eighth-century sceattas, there are at least ten stycas, unlikely to have been minted any later than the mid-860s: Pirie 1986, 51–3. The spiral-headed pins in particular seem unlikely to be so late, none having been reported elsewhere at sites where there is no likelihood of residuality. There is some Ipswich ware, now thought to have ceased production in the mid-ninth

century, and 'Anglian' glass: Stiff 2000, 2540 (though in that case I cannot see why it should not have been cullet for the glassworking hearth, above). The helmet pit has its own problems, see Chapter 3.

195. MacGregor *et al.* 1999, 1942–3, 1962–3, and D. Tweddle therein, 1961. A much more intricate Trewhiddle motif-piece was found elsewhere in York: Tweddle *et al.* 1999, 277–8. London has also produced bone motif-pieces, with Trewhiddle but apparently not Jellinge or Borre features: Pritchard 1991, 178–93, but the latter style has turned up in Canterbury: Wilson, D. M. 1965a. The extent to which these styles are Scandinavian rather than insular derivations remains problematic, however, e.g. Lang. J. T. 1986; Bailey, R. N. 1996, 14–16.

196. Mainman and Rogers 2000, 2571–2.

197. Mainman and Rogers 2000, 2569, and 2475–7. Moulds include one for which Borre-style work is a possibility, but it is too broken for certainty: Roesdahl *et al.* (eds.) 1981, no. YMW 14; Hall, R. A. 1994, 110. The Borre-style strap-ends exemplify near-duplication. An iron mould from Coppergate is evidence of mass production, but only one end survives: Ottaway 1992, 523–4.

198. Hattat 1987, 316, no. 1312. The brooch imitates the 'Hand of Providence' type, itself following the contemporary West Mercian series. See Gannon 2003, 63–5, for earlier hands on coins.

199. Hadley 2000a, 329; Abrams 2001b, 128–34; Holman 2001; and Hadley 1997, 84–6, for comments on the use of the term 'Danelaw'.

200. Graham-Campbell 2001b, 55–7; Atkin and Evans 2002, 237. Margeson 1997, 13–24, for a scatter of artefacts around Norwich.

201. Wilson, D. M. 1985; Mason 1985, 64–5; Carrington 1994, 60–1; Matthews, K. 1995, 63–4.

202. Whitelock (ed.) 1961, 48.

203. They have been found in context only at Repton, Cuerdale, and Goldsbrough, but are being reported by metal-detectorists: Webster 2000b. Only one was listed on the Portable Antiquities Scheme website in August 2002, but Graham-Campbell 2001c, 57, reports knowing of eight. As Repton shows that they were worn by men, they cannot be taken as evidence of Scandinavian women, though the Broch of Gurness grave, above, shows that they were not exclusive to either sex.

204. There is one oval brooch not provenly from a burial, in Norfolk, on the Scheme's website; see also Santon Downham, above.

205. My statement that there was a paucity of metalwork in the Danelaw (1990, 71) has been disproved, and Margeson (1996, 47) and Paterson (Leahy and Paterson 2001, 191) have both cited it in order to refute it. I accept that there is much more than I could have known of; but I am still not convinced of their corollary, that there must have been many Scandinavian settlers. I favour the view that the objects show that the Danelaw countryside was part of Anglo-Scandinavian culture, like the towns, not that there were large numbers of immigrants in it; for a range of opinions, see Leahy 2001; Thomas, G. 2000; Hadley 2000a, 325–30. Coin evidence may reflect political rather than population factors, e.g. in north-west Essex: Blackburn 1998, 110.

206. Richards 1999, 94–7; no steatite is recorded from the site, but it is rather friable, so its absence may not be significant. West Heslerton also probably shifted at this time, so dislocation of settlement is something else to be taken into account when considering the 'viking impact'.
207. Goodall, A. R. and Paterson 2000, 128–31; Goodall, I. H. and Clark 2000, 139; Richards 2000, 197.

5. AN EPOCH OF NEW DYNASTIES

1. Administrative systems are clearly recognizable from much earlier, as in coins, charters, and laws, but state 'bureaucracy' is not quite appropriate, even to Domesday Book: Clanchy 1993, 31–2. The book was a record of land and the people who held it, however, first the king and then his tenants-in-chief (not Domesday's term), for they were the wielders of power: e.g Roffe 2000b, 224–6. For a summary of the 'nation-state' and 'people' concepts, see Chibnall 1999, 7 and 125–9, but also Harvey, B. 2001, 54–5, for the continuing importance of rulers with dispersed territories.
2. Hare, M. 1999.
3. See Chapter 4.
4. Archibald 1984a, nos. 203 and 214. The first representation of heavenly crowns are of the latter type: Deshman 1976. The lily, or fleur-de-lys, was originally a classical symbol of sovereignty, only later acquiring Marian associations: Pipponier and Mane 1997, 124; when Mary is shown with a short plant-stem or a flowering plant in Anglo-Saxon art, it was a reference to the stem of Jesse, and Christ's human descent, with Christ himself as the flower: Clayton 1990, 151 and 171.
5. Archibald 1984a, no. 214; see e.g. both English and Normans in the Bayeux Tapestry: Stenton (ed.) 1965. It may have had deliberate overtones of a bishop's mitre: Holmes, M. 1959, 219.
6. Turner 1984, nos. 26 and 62; Dodwell 1982, 211. The earlier representation that may be King Athelstan has a crown with three projecting ball-shaped finials, not lilies: Turner 1984, no. 6. Other sources indicate the significance to Cnut of the sceptre: Tyler, E. M. 1999, 255–7.
7. Edward did not use the title *Imperator*, as his predecessor Athelstan had occasionally done. For Athelstan it had also been a proclamation of his independence, though perhaps also an allusion to his own successes over the Welsh, Scots, and Norse: Rose 1992, 7. King Edgar had been shown bearded as well as crowned in the Winchester manuscript (Turner 1984, no. 26), possibly an allusion to his maturity at the canonical age of 33. A staff, ring, and crown that might have been taken from the Confessor's grave in the thirteenth century survived until the seventeenth: Holmes, M. 1959, 214–16.
8. North, J. J. 1963, pl. XII, nos. 33–40 and pl. XIII, nos. 1–14. There were variations within Harold's coinage, however, and the obverse legend 'PAX' had not

been used in that form before; it was more probably seen as a promise that Harold would supply peace, rather than as an appeal for it: Pagan 1990. Ciggaar 1987, 60–1, noted that the sword-type coins have similarities to a full-length emperor's pose on coins of 1057–9.

9. Dodwell 1982, 65; Talvio 1990.
10. Heslop 1984, no. 328. Keynes 1988, 216–8, proposed that Regenbald, the German or French *cancellarius*, might have suggested the idea. See also Ciggaar 1987, 53–63, for Byzantine elements influencing William.
11. Rose 1992, 26. Evans, J. and Serjeantson 1933, 1 and 13–15, and Ciggaar 1987, 55, 58–9 and 61 for early lapidaries in the west, and the twelve gemstones of the Apocalypse, as well as the twelve on Aaron's breastplate (and cf. Bede, Chapter 2).
12. Holmes, M. 1959, 219; the 'Hungarian Crown' is contemporary with these, and includes enamels as well as gems, as does the Holy Roman Emperor's, but that does not have the dangling bits: Swarzenski 1974, pl. 31.
13. Chibnall 1999, 90. This classic chivalric image continued to resonate throughout the Middle Ages.
14. Stenton (ed.) 1965, pls. 1, 33, and 36. The sword of state represented justice. The Bayeux Tapestry bears the weight of a myriad of interpretations, the traditional poetic theme of a man bringing his own fate upon himself by the unforeseen consequences of his actions being one of them: cf. the Weland story, Chapter 3; vernacular French can be recognized in the language, however: Short 2001, 275–6.
15. There are a few earlier base-metal examples, such as a Jellinge-style one from West Stow Heath, Suffolk: Hinton 1974, no. 35. The clasps are shown in Stenton (ed.) 1965, pls. 11, 14, 31 and 34. The cloaks could be swung to one side, cf. ibid., frontispiece. Edward's finery included elaborate embroideries and other trappings, not necessarily his own choice, but forced on him by an image-building wife: Tyler, E. M. 2000, 100.
16. Named after the donors: Wilson, D. M. 1964, no. 10; Haith 1984, no. 16. It was found in 'Palace court', presumably part of the archbishops' complex adjacent to the south-west corner of the present cathedral; I have not been able to discover whether this was within the Anglo-Saxon cathedral's cemetery, and therefore whether the brooch could originally have been in a grave. The manufacturing technique had been used earlier on the Ormside bowl: Coatsworth and Pinder 2002, 175.
17. Okasha 1971, no. 19; Hinton 1974, no. 6.
18. Tweddle *et al.* 1999, 268, where it is suggested that a ninth-century date may be more appropriate.
19. There is a large cast lead brooch from York of the same sort, also thought to be tenth-century (Mainman and Rogers 2000, 2572–3), but so far as I know, no others; if there were any base-metal examples with imitations of later coins, they would suggest that the precious-metal brooches continued to be made.

20. Evans, J. 1922, 130. The formula was also used on sword-blades, though none has been found in Britain: Roesdahl *et al.* (eds.) 1992, 284.

21. Wilson, D. M. 1964, no. 83; Okasha 1971, no. 114; Haith 1984, no. 105; Blackburn and Pagan 1986, 299, no. 276. Found in 1694, the hoard was in a lead container and also had five 'heavy gold rings', not otherwise described, and lost long ago. The curse may sound like a pagan survival, and there are Old English charms that have pre-Christian antecedents, but Eadwynn's formula contains nothing that would have been out of place in a contemporary charter, all of which were written by people trained in the Church. The most recent survey of the Urnes style is Owen, O. 2001: it takes its name from the carved wooden doors in the church of the Norwegian village of that name, but was very widely used outside Scandinavia.

22. Blackburn 1991*a*, 165, and West 1998, 9. The weight of tenth-century pennies varied, but if 1.3 g is taken as a rough average, a 30 penny *mancus* would be 39 g; the Barsham brooch weighs 48.4 g. A gold coin that may have been meant as a *mancus* weighs 3.34 g (Metcalf 1998*b*, 84), slightly less than three average pennies, which would take the brooch's value up a bit. Another large disc-brooch that may well be Anglo-Saxon was found with English and other coins of *c*.1025 in Sweden, but from its decoration was at least fifty years old when buried: Haith 1984, no. 17.

23. They were more vulnerable than men to deprivation of estates, for instance: Crick 2000, 27–8.

24. Whitelock (ed. and trans.) 1930, is the main source; see also Whitelock (ed.) 1968; Crick 2000 considers the possibility that women's wills reflect a 'homemaker' sentiment, for which she finds the evidence insufficient. Whether these ladies chose to live in seclusion or were forced into it by their relatives to prevent land from passing outside the family is debated, as is the extent to which phrases such as *feminae religiosae* or *ancilla dei* really mean that they committed themselves to a contemplative, perhaps even cloistered, life: e.g. Foot 2000, vol. 1, pp. 134–6.

25. Owen, G. 1979, 198, n. 4 and 213 for discussion of these terms; *preon* might mean brooch, clasp, or even pin ('preen' is still a Scottish word for pin). Owen pointed out that *agrafen* could be taken to mean 'inscribed'.

26. Whitelock (ed. and trans.) 1930, 14–15; Coatsworth and Pinder 2002, 213. Taking 1.3 g as the average penny again, six 30 penny *mancuses* would make 180 pennies weighing around 234 g, considerably more than known silver brooches, so unless Wynflaed was inflating its value, her old brooch must have had a gold component like the King's School, Canterbury, brooch. Precision is implied by the reference to the value of a cup, below. Heirlooms were important as one way to preserve family memory, see e.g. Foot 1999, though instability of such families as can be partly reconstructed has to be noted: Stafford 1989, 152–8. Van Houts 2001, 7 asks whether a woman was supposed to pass on her own or her husband's family's traditions. In another will it was stipulated that the *bule*, 'ornament/brooch', that a girl was to receive had been her grandmother's, but does not say whether it came from her maternal or paternal side: Whitelock (ed. and

trans.) 1930, 50–1. Later Wulfwaru left two *preonas* to her daughter: ibid. 64–5. This was not invariable practice, as Ramsey Abbey received a brooch as a bequest from Scheldwara: Gameson 1995, 253. In Wynflaed's case, her granddaughter was also to receive her best tunic and better cloak, which also sound like rather intimate things (I think Crick 2000 underestimates such feelings; she does not discuss jewellery bequests). Wareham 2001, 381–2, uses Wynflaed's bequests as evidence of a tenth-century change to a more restricted sense of family and inheritance by children and grandchildren rather than by cousins or a wider kin.

27. Whitelock (ed. and trans.) 1930, 12–13; Whitelock's translation 'has been put on it' has subsequently acquired unfortunate overtones of modern valuations, as though Wynflaed had called in Sotheby's. Morris, C. A. 2000, 2136, suggests that the two *gesplottude* wooden cups were made of burr-wood like many later mazers, which creates a 'spotted' effect when turned and polished. A less plausible explanation is offered below.

28. Whitelock (ed. and trans.) 1930, 12–3. Whitelock translated *wesen* as 'buffalo', which is possible but unlikely in northen Europe; 'wild ox' is probably better, implying that the horns were trophies from the hunting of wild cattle, perhaps in Wales or Northumbria; aurochs, as at Sutton Hoo, from northern Europe, are just possible: Bruce-Mitford 1983, 408 (see Chapter 3). For horns, see also the Devil's offering, below. The Bayeux Tapestry pictures are in Stenton (ed.) 1965, ills. 4 and 49. Morris, C. A. 2000, 2183–5, points out that other vessels shown there are likely to be turned wood, particularly those with foot-rings and girth-grooves.

29. Whitelock (ed. and trans.) 1930, 57. If pictorial evidence is reliable, the use of drinking-horns declined rapidly after the eleventh century, perhaps getting a revival for ceremonial use in the fourteenth and fifteenth centuries; like hunting horns, they could be symbols of land-tenure: Cherry 1989, 114–15; Campbell, M. 1987, nos. 545–6.

30. Clanchy 1993, 739, 156–7, and 288–9. Material objects could receive Christian blessing and be used for less formal purposes, such as curing a horse struck by elf-shot by using a knife with a horn handle held in place by three brass nails and on which a Christian prayer had been incised; this is presumably a pre-Christian practice given a Church gloss: Jolly 1996, 152–3.

31. Webster 1984, no. 112; the design of the bust on Godwin's side of the seal is close to coins of *c*.1040, so it could have belonged to the earl who played such a prominent part in the Confessor's reign, and who fathered Harold, but if for his personal use *dux* or *comes* might have been used. A Godwin who might have called himself a thegn and who was active in the Wallingford area at the right time was the 'port reeve' of Oxford: Baxter 2001, 26; there were various grades of thegn, from a 'king's thegn' downward: Williams, A. 1995, 72–3.

32. The word used for Godgythe's profession is *monache*, which could suggest a cloistered nun rather than a 'vowess', a *nunna*, which is what a widow living in religious seclusion may have been called: Foot 2000, vol. 1, pp. 134–6, but see also above. If Godgythe was a nun in the modern sense, even if a widow, she should

not have needed a seal as she should not have been owning personal property. Foot does not discuss this seal, and I have not found another use of the phrase *deo data*. Earl Godwin's widow is recorded in Domesday Book as refusing to live off the income of an estate that had belonged to a nunnery, Berkeley, dissolved by her husband (Foot 2000, vol. 1, 157 and vol. 2, 40). Was it his intention that she should have become its abbess, or abbess of a replacement? If so, she ignored the idea, and led an uprising against William I: Stafford 1997, 276–7. (Her name was Gytha . . . Had Godwin wanted to add 'God'? Probably not.)

33. Webster 1984, nos. 111–13; Heslop 1980.
34. Whitelock (ed. and trans.) 1930, 118.
35. Ibid. 20–1. Whitelock translated these as 'armlets' and 'necklace', but 'rings' is less specific and does not exclude disc-brooches; and 'neck-ring' avoids overtones of the seventh-century necklaces with pendants. Such necklaces remained potent images nevertheless: Aelfric's life of St Agnes of *c*.1000 has her neck 'encircled with precious stones and with shining gems' (cited by Dodwell 1982, 31), though these were heavenly not earthly gifts. There is an early mention of a wedding-ring in the same text.
36. Hinton 1978, table 2. A third woman, Wulfwaru, whose will dates to King Ethelred's reign (984–1016), also left *preon* to her daughter not her sons. She gave rings of 60, 30, and 20 *mancuses*, as well as cups and textiles. I have not found any references to rings, *armillae*, in tenth- or eleventh-century charters (see Chapter 3), only to '*mancuses* of pure gold'. Gold arm-rings were presented to St Cuthbert's shrine in 945: Higgins 1989, 333; see also Chapter 4.
37. Hinton 1978, 140–1. Because of the variation in coin weights, there is a wide bracket into which these rings can fit. Allowing for the posibility that a real *mancus* might have weighed a little less than three average silver pennies (above), the figures may underestimate the rings' values a little.
38. Hinton 1990*b*, no. 2066.
39. Graham-Campbell 1988; said to have been found in a stone coffin, but Professor Graham-Campbell has told me (pers. comm.) that the first report of its nineteenth-century discovery suggests that this is incorrect: see further below for burials. Rings are also in silver and copper alloy; Thetford has several: Goodall, A. R. 1984*a*, 68–9. York even has them in lead alloy and iron: Mainman and Rogers 2000, 2583–5.
40. e.g. the two in London: Pritchard 1991, 150–1.
41. Hinton 1975, 177–8, and 1978, 141. I have not been able to recognize such rings being worn in the Bayeux Tapestry and other illustrations, but gold-embroidered sleeves make one or two ambivalent. Writing in the early twelfth century, William of Malmesbury described how golden rings could safely be left at crossroads in King Alfred's reign: Wormald 1999, 137; he may have had in mind Bede's account of the drinking-cups hung up in similar places by Northumbria's King Edwin, and converted them to an image familiar to him from other sources.
42. The Attleborough ring (Okasha 1971, no. 5) is a plain silver band. Only three ornamented finger-sized rings were attributed to the tenth century in the British

Museum 1984 exhibition, and at least one of those, from Ebbesbourne Wake, Wiltshire, is as likely to be of the ninth: Haith 1984, nos. 88–90.

43. Whitelock (ed. and trans.) 1930, 13. The display of such valuables in battle may seem foolhardy and recklessly bold, but there could be a motive beyond boastfulness. By drawing attention to himself, a leader like Byrtnoth created a challenge to an enemy to come to win booty—which would draw him towards the best-defended part of the host.

44. Colour reproduction in Coatsworth and Pinder 2002, pl. VIIIb. The manuscript has usually been taken to be mid-eleventh-century, but a post-Conquest date has been proposed: Heslop 1992.

45. To be undone if the peace broke and the sword had to be used. For wedge-shaped ends, Coatsworth 2001, 302–4. What I have taken to be a shield has had various other interpretations suggested. The bowl looks like beaten metal rather than wood, but is shown with dots all round it which could be meant for rivets to hold metal sheets to a wooden core, providing another reading of *gesplottude* in Wynflaed's will (see above).

46. This sword has been less discussed than many, probably because of uncertainty over its provenance; the London dealer who sold it said that it had come from the Temple Church, but its condition suggests that it came from a river. Also, it may have been made in Scandinavia. Its very worn ornament has been called Jellinge-style, but I cannot see why it should not be Urnes-, although that fits my argument, below, less well. Publications include Read 1888; Shetelig 1940, 77–8 and fig. 45; Müller-Wille 1972, 85, 102 and figs. 31 and 33. The quantity of weapons of all sorts from the Thames at London, and from other rivers nearby, was noticed by Wheeler 1927, 18–42; as a former soldier, Sir Mortimer naturally saw them as testimonies of battles, and his interpretation (p. 18) of one group from near London Bridge as coming from a viking ship sunk in Cnut's fight for the city still seems perfectly credible, not least if a vicious iron implement is correctly identified as a grappling-iron.

47. See Wilson, D. M. 1965 and Evison 1967b for representative selections of swords; there have been several subsequent discoveries, such as in Bath, Hereford, and at Crowmarsh. MacGregor *et al.* 1999, 1945, for the whalebone pommel.

48. Haith 1984, no. 106; Owen, O. 2001, 212–13.

49. Whitelock (ed. and trans.) 1930, 7. Loyn 1962, 105, drew attention to a *sicam unam optime insignatam auro et argenteo*, 'a sword/weapon very highly distinguished with gold and silver', in a late tenth- or early eleventh-century legal dispute: Blake (ed.) 1962, 106. The 'gift' of King Edmund is one of the very few direct English references to gift-giving in tenth- or eleventh-century England, although continental sources suggest its ongoing importance: Leyser 1994, 73–104 and Charles-Edwards 1998, but see below.

50. Tylecote and Gilmour 1986, 247–8; Lang, J. and Ager 1989, 101–2.

51. Okasha 1971, no. 37; Wilson, D. M. 1964, no. 17. The inscription is *Eofr me f*, where the 'f' is presumably an abbreviation for *fecit*.

52. Hinton and Okasha 1977; Okasha 1983, no. 179. The 'th' is rendered as the runic thorn, and those who like to think runes magical will take comfort from knowing that it was not the Latin letters that first caught my eye when I noticed the inscription, but the rune. Princes like Aethelstan were known as *aethelings*.
53. Evison 1967b, 167 and fig. 7. The symbolic value of weapons generally was still considerable, implying free status: Brooks 1978, 83. The well-known statement that a *ceorl* was still a *ceorl* even if he owned body-armour, a helmet, and a gold-plated sword—he had to have at least five hides of land to become a thegn—takes on even more meaning when it is realized how few swords had that sort of embellishment: Stafford 1989, 152, for the irony in the concept.
54. Graham-Campbell 1995, 34–48 and 108–27.
55. Graham-Campbell 1995, 41–6.
56. Halton Moor, Lancashire, has the only precious-metal one that I know (illustrated in Thompson, J. D. A. 1956, pl. 15), and Barsham, Suffolk, has one in copper alloy: West 1998, fig. 3.17.
57. Kruse 1995, 193–4.
58. Graham-Campbell 1995, 28 and 59; Graham-Campbell and Batey 1998, 243–4.
59. There is an isolated single example from Gulberswick, Shetland, similar to one in Cumbria: Graham-Campbell 1995, 35–6 and 160–1.
60. Metcalf 1995, 21–4.
61. There are no recent reports of stray finds: Bateson and Holmes 1997; there are a few hoards: Metcalf 1995, 18–24.
62. Webster 1995; Metcalf 1995, 22. The ring is one of the very few attributable to the tenth century, but the loss of its hoop is one reason for suggesting that it was far from new by 986. There are no close parallels for its decoration. Despite the coins, it may not be Anglo-Saxon, but is more likely to be continental than Irish or Scandinavian.
63. Pirie 1997, 335–6.
64. Nicholson, A. 1997, 398.
65. Hill, P. 1997, 55–6.
66. Ritchie 1993, 75; Blackburn and Pagan 1986, nos. 209 and 216—see also no. 302; the Lindores hoard cannot bear much interpretative weight.
67. e.g. Spearman 1989, 101–3; a form of urbanism may have begun to emerge before 1100, e.g. at Perth: Yeoman 1995, 54, but written evidence is shadowy: Dennison and Simpson 2000, 718–20.
68. Redknap 2000, 14 (this is a second Bangor hoard; see Chapter 4).
69. Boon 1986: the Bryn Maelgwyn and Pant-Yr-Eglwys hoards.
70. In 927 King Athelstan supposedly took 20 pounds of gold, 200 of silver, and 25,000 oxen as well as hawks and hounds from north Wales: Arnold and Davies 2000, 178–9, but the source of this is William of Malmesbury, writing in the early

twelfth century, leading Boon 1986, 14, to cite one of Sir Frank Stenton's most judicious statements, that the amount is 'not quite . . . incredible'. In the 950s and 960s tribute was being paid to vikings from Ireland.

71. Arnold 1998, 101; the coin was a rare one, though that may not have been realized at the time by whoever carried out the burial. Hoards on the coast in the north continue to reflect the Chester–Meols–Dublin links, as do some single finds: Blackburn 1996, 1–2 and 10–12.
72. Redknap 2000, 44, 50, and 75; Quinnell and Blockley 1994, 169: Rhuddlan was probably an English 'burh' from 921.
73. Campbell 1996*b*, who argues that the object might be considerably earlier.
74. Pryce 2000, 51–3.
75. Exeter evidence was reviewed by Maddicott 1992, 184.
76. There are two Edgar pennies from St Austell now on the Fitzwilliam Museum Early Medieval Coins database. For the Mawgan Porth penny, Bruce-Mitford 1997, 85.
77. Bruce-Mitford 1997. The house walls had cupboard-like 'nooks' built into them, but not necessarily for valuables; wall recesses could have been niches for candles or pottery lamps: ibid. 26–7, 40–1, and 87; also Mercer 1969, 54.
78. Bruce-Mitford 1997, 75, for distribution; see also O'Mahoney 1994.
79. Redknap 2000, 43, 54, 66, and 91; Ellis, B. M. A. 1994; Campbell, E. 1996*b*.
80. One from Pakenham, Suffolk, for instance, has no surviving terminals: West 1998, fig. 120, no. 8; more convincing evidence that spurs were used would be to find a pair in a grave, not a single object, though admittedly the Middle Harling viking grave-find, below, is a singleton.
81. Carver 1998, 183.
82. La Rocca and Provero 2000, 251–3; Ellis, P. 2002, no. 1, is an elaborately cast spur that looks suitable for a count.
83. Webster 1991, no. 264i; Webster suggests that the curved mounts could also have come from spur straps.
84. Hinton 1974, no. 29. There is another with animal-head terminals from Suffolk, at Icklingham: Shortt 1964. Shortt maintained that both were Iron Age or Roman, a view presumably shared by West 1998, who does not include them. Another has recently been found at Lyng, Norfolk, though that one lacks the heads and has even less curved arms: Geake 2001, 242.
85. Boon 1959; this spur might be a Carolingian import, but the animal heads holding the terminals in their mouths are not very diagnostic.
86. Margeson 1995*a*; ead. 1997, 17.
87. Williams, D. 2002. I remain a little unsure about the function of the Pakenham object, despite these new finds. If indeed a spur, it seems on the evidence of the animal heads to be ninth-century (if it is not 'Celtic' after all), so pre-dates them by over a century. The two 'new' ones with flat-backed goads both have longer

and more curved sides. Each of the Pakenham terminals also has only a single, quite insubstantial rivet to hold the spur-strap, or a buckle; when rivets were used on spurs they were either more solid, or in multiples: Ellis, B. M. A. 2002, nos. 1–2, 8–9, etc. But perhaps all these differences can be explained away if it was a ninth-/tenth-century prototype. Figure 6.2 shows a copper-alloy twelfth-century spur, and that metal continued to be used occasionally for spurs thereafter, e.g. Crummy 1988, 70–1.

88. Graham-Campbell 1992c, 79; Edwards, B. J. N. 1992, 43–6.

89. Graham-Campbell 1992c, 81; this paper is an important general overview of riding equipment.

90. Ellis, B. M. A. 2002, 2–7.

91. Seaby and Woodfield 1980, 89; Graham-Campbell 1992c, 78–9—Graham-Campbell notes that they are not shown on the eighth-century equestrian sculpture found in Repton since Seaby and Woodfield's paper was published; Edwards, B. J. N. 1992.

92. Hinton 1974, nos. 25 and 26; Seaby and Woodfield 1980, nos. 23 and 26; Blair, J. and Crawford 1997 suggest that as they were from a site near St Clement's at Magdalen Bridge and were found with a spur, horse and human bones, and other things, they might be from the burial of a viking active between 990 and 1013 in King Aethelred's reign, when Danes were in Oxford and the victims of the Massacre of St Brice's Day in 1002: e.g. Innes 2000, 66–7. But Graham-Campbell 2001c notes that this date may be too early for the stirrups, and that the assemblage would postdate equestrian burials in Denmark, thus casting doubt on the hypothesis that they are grave-goods. (Professor Graham-Campbell's review of the Oxford plaited gold ring takes away another viking burial possibility: see above.) For a colour plate of a very similar stirrup with copper-alloy overlay from Kilverstone, Norfolk, see Margeson 1997, fig. 11.

93. Robinson, P. 1992, correcting e.g. Hinton 1974, no. 19.

94. Williams, D. 1997a. Williams's work was made possible by reports made to him of finds made by metal-detectorists.

95. Williams, D. 1997a, Group A, Type 3, nos. 71–2; Type 11A, no. 202.

96. Williams, D. 1997a, 6–7; id. 1997b: fig. 3 for the inlaid type. See also Worrell 2002.

97. Graham-Campbell 1992c and Margeson 1987 for examples; they have not yet been comprehensively collated.

98. e.g. the *radcnihts* of Domesday: see Gillingham 1995. That the English did not fight on horseback at Hastings in 1066 may have been by choice, based on factors such as the advantage of high ground, rather than because there were as yet no knights equivalent to those of the Normans—note that many of the English are shown fighting on foot with kite-shaped 'cavalry' shields. Strickland 1997, 355 and 359–67, for recent discussion of whether the English chose not to fight on horseback at any time before the Conquest, not just at Hastings. The cost of body armour would have been one factor distinguishing an English elite, however.

99. Fuglesang 1980, 75 and 117–20, for the problems of attributing Ringerike to any particular source; she shows that Anglo-Saxon and Ottonian developments were at least as important to its origin as Scandinavian. Owen, O. 2001 for Urnes.
100. Hinton 1990a, 109, though Ringerike was not in fact only practised on southern sculptures, as it is on a slab at Otley, Yorkshire: Bailey, R. N. 1996, 15. A 'second period' of mass immigration, following Cnut's triumph, seems much less likely than a 'first period' (see Chapter 4); in November 2002 the Portable Antiquities Scheme website had no brooches attributed to the Ringerike or Urnes styles in the four 'eastern counties', though there are two earlier finds from Norfolk: Margeson 1987; ead. 1997, 32–3; there is a new find from London: Thomas, G. 2001b. As Cnut gave his followers estates throughout England, no regional variations would be expected in aristocratic patronage.
101. Williams, D. 1997a, 14–23 for discussion and maps.
102. For a recent summary and references, Astill 2000b, 34–43. The eighth- and ninth-century 'prolific' sites may have been markets and fairs, of course, but operating without an urban system.
103. Gifts and many forms of barter exchange have to be direct, face-to-face transactions; a coin is totally impersonal, and makes indirect exchanges between total strangers separated by long distances possible.
104. Williams, D. 1997a, fig. 15; Metcalf 1998b, 42–4 and maps 2 and 4–8; Metcalf notes variations, such as the north being more self-contained: ibid. 277. Comparison of the mounts and coins shows very similar patterns, numbers of both falling off to the west. The importance of securing even coverage of finds-reporting is also shown by the paucity of both categories in Essex; it is hard to believe that a populous shire adjacent to London was economically backward. For this reason, I am not sure that the evidence is reliable enough to argue that the city was drawing coins out of Essex, or that the north-west of the shire was distinctively more 'viking' and northward-looking than the rest.
105. Williams, D. 1997a, Type 3; if based on the story of Loki, those mounts can be seen as part of the same culture that allowed a story from Scandinavian sagas to be shown on the walls of the Old Minster at Winchester: Tweddle et al. 1995, no. 88.
106. Williams, D. 1997a, fig. 15. Williams rightly notes that the quality of workmanship as well as the basic shape should be taken into consideration.
107. Metcalf 1998b, map 5, for Norwich coins, which bear comparison to the mount subtype; map 6, of Lincoln coins, has more examples. Norwich as a metalworking centre has been graphically demonstrated by the discovery in 1999 of a small but valuable gold ingot with crucibles and other residues: Bradley and Gaimster 2000, 295. The Ringerike-style mount there which has a close parallel in a rural find from Norfolk may be another example of one of Norwich's products: Margeson 1987; see also above.
108. Blackburn 1996, 5.
109. The complexities of the coinage of this period are clarified by Metcalf 1998b. It is even possible that coins for issue from one mint were actually made at another

and sent there; the carriage of large numbers of new coins is shown by the recent Appledore, Kent, hoard, about half of which was made up of 1050 × 53 Canterbury coins, and by the smaller Bramdean Common, Hampshire, hoard of London coins that had come straight from the mint. It is assumed that they were carried by merchants: Williams, G. 1998b; id. 1998c.

110. Williams, G. 1999.
111. Mainman and Rogers 2000, 2561–4, who note many Scandinavian and Dublin parallels for the cased weights; Margeson 1995b, 68–9, and ead. 1997, 40, for an example from Middle Harling, Norfolk, and others in the county. See also Nightingale 1987, 560–1; Kruse 1992a, esp. 82–9; other references include an early eleventh-century charter that mentions 30 *mancuses* measured by the lead weight. See Chapter 4 for earlier weights.
112. Mainman and Rogers 2000, 2572–3.
113. Clark 1989, 22.
114. Moulds: MacGregor 1980; Newman, J. 1993; West 1998, fig. 97, 7; brooches: Webster 1984; Goodall, A. R. 1984a, 68: Mills, J. M. 1995, 358–9; Reynolds, A. 1994; Mainman and Rogers 2000, 2572–4. One was also found in Dublin, another example of close links across the Irish Sea. There may be a link with the casting of bells in the production of these things, and the use of tin in their alloy.
115. O'Hara 1994, 239.
116. e.g. two pennies of c.865–75 riveted together, one Mercian and one East Anglian, but found in Winchester: Dolley and Mays 1990, no. 2006.
117. The group was first recognized and published by Robinson, P. 1990. A list has now been published of eighteen made from English coins, only four of which are said to be from north of the Thames: Williams, G. 2001b. A subsequent report is of one from Abbot's Worthy, near Winchester, Hampshire: Geake 2002, 131. The pendant from Mildenhall, Suffolk, made from a coin of Sven Estridsen of Denmark (1047–75), can be noted in the context of the brooch series, though its cross is much less obvious at first glance: West 1998, 84 and fig. 116, no. 6. An oddity that probably has no direct connection to the series is a copper-alloy copy of a penny of Henry I with a pin on the back: Archibald 1984b, no. 468.
118. The group was recognized and published by Buckton, 1986 and 1989. These were presumably made in England, but may derive from the Carolingian 'saint-brooches', of which several English finds are known: Buckton 1991. Other prototypes may include a large enamel disc from Oxford, and a brooch from East Anglia: Evison 1977. Like the penny-brooches, their talismanic virtues should probably not be seen as amuletic remnants of pagan belief, but as manifestations of new secular concerns to ward off the Devil and the spirits of the dead, although concern over 'revenants' and the like is better attested on the continent, e.g. Caciola 1996; Innes 2001, 27–8; cf. the Canterbury inscribed brooch, above. An individual problem is whether the Towneley brooch should be included in this discussion; it is a fine object, but may not have been in Britain in the Middle Ages: Buckton 1986, 16.

119. Mainman and Rogers 2000, 2591–7; see also Chapter 4.
120. A few have simple cut decoration, but normally their only appeal is that they shine, a polished finish being necessary for their efficient use, The transition from double- to single-ended pin-beaters is thought to be associated with the decline of the vertical loom using clay weights in favour of the two-beam vertical loom: Riddler 2001, 240–1.
121. This case is argued in depth by MacGregor *et al.* 1999, 1921–2 and 2005–6.
122. Kilmurry 1979 remains the authoritative study.
123. Hassall *et al.* 1989, 208. For a colour plate of a Stamford-ware pitcher, Mellor, M. 1997, fig. 25.
124. These two paragraphs attempt to summarize a complex pattern; there are no known kilns in York, for instance, although there is 'York ware'; similarly, 'Winchester ware', which is glazed, may have been made in that southern town, although there are wasters in Southampton. Sources include Kilmurry 1979, Leah 1994, and Brown, D. H. 1995. Astill 1989 remains an excellent summary. Profitability and costs can only be inferred from the shift to rural production, and the rents payable by three groups of potters in southern England recorded in Domesday Book. If only it could be known whether the nine pennies lost or concealed at a pot-making site in Norwich soon after 1066 had belonged to a potter, or to someone who knew that a kiln would be a safe hiding-place because it had fallen into disuse: Clough 1973, 142!
125. Vince 2000 for London; Brown, D. H. 1995 for Southampton, where the ratios are higher.
126. Morris, C. A. 2000, esp. 2182–6 and 2213–15. Street names begin to suggest craft zoning in larger towns.
127. Bayley and Doonan 2000 for references.
128. For jet and shale in York, Mainman and Rogers 2000, 2587–8; and in London, Pritchard 1991, 154–6.
129. Kjølbye-Biddle 1990, 830.
130. Pritchard 1984; Walton 1989; Walton Rogers 1997. Furs are also evidenced, e.g. from a Domesday Book entry for Chester, but they probably were only for the really wealthy: Owen-Crocker 1998, 77–9. Although Fleming, R. 2001, 10, suggests that cat-skins reached a wider market, the bone record does not reveal enough cats in sufficiently good condition to yield usable furs, e.g. O'Connor, T. P. 1982, 38–40; id. 1989, 186. Black cat-fur was permitted to nuns in the early twelfth century, however: Sawyer 1986, 191.
131. Pritchard 1991, 173.
132. Pritchard 1984, 70; Granger-Taylor 1989. A few Byzantine seals and coins are further evidence of these contacts, but the spices and peppers recorded in a London toll-list as valuable imports, and perhaps already used in lieu of cash payments, are archaeologically invisible: Biddle (ed.) 1976, 462 and 478; Leyser 1994, 100–2; Nightingale 1995, 106. Royal and aristocratic clothing: Fleming, R. 2001, 9–11.

133. Pritchard 1991, 218–19 and 232; Reid 2001; but see below for the court and diatribes against its follies. 'Fashion' is here taken to mean the deliberate choice of a style, rather than unthinking acceptance of current *habitus*.
134. Cameron 2000, 57–69, esp. figs. 43–52; the most elaborate example is in the treasury at Aachen: Okasha 1995, no. 185. Again, there is a good example in Dublin: Okasha 1983, no. 163.
135. e.g. Hinton 1990*b*, 160.
136. Loveluck 2000, 102–3.
137. Crockett 1996, 30–2 and 39–40. Cottam was out of use by the eleventh century, so cannot be used as an example.
138. Archibald 1995*a*, 50; Margeson 1995*b*, 60–1; and note the weight, above. Other finds, such as rings and a few hooked tags, may be later than the early tenth century, but are not closely datable.
139. Sites like Steyning, Sussex, are associated with minster churches and are not directly comparable, though similar fall-off patterns might be claimed: Gardiner 1993; Gardiner and Greatorex 1997. *Sandtun* seems to have had a hiatus until the middle of the eleventh century, when finds include two pennies of Harold I (1037–40): Gardiner *et al.* 2001, 270. Two iron spurs are said to be of an earlier type, however: Riddler 2001, 247.
140. Whitelock (ed. and trans.) 1930, 10–11.
141. Fairbrother 1990, 244–72, including specialist reports by L. E. Webster *et al.*; see also Haith 1984, nos. 85–7.
142. For a recent discussion, Coatsworth and Pinder 2002, 213–14; also Dodwell 1982, 74–8.
143. Rahtz 1979, including specialist reports by L. Biek and D. M. Wilson.
144. Whitelock (ed. and trans.) 1930, 56–7 and 60–1. Household smiths were sometimes bequeathed their freedom; but other goldsmiths were landowners, and therefore freemen: Coatsworth and Pinder 2002, 213–14.
145. Webster 1984, no. 76; Dodwell 1982, 80–1. Porphyry occurs at pre- and post-Conquest sites, recently at Whithorn: Hill, P. 1997, 239 and 467.
146. Mannig of Evesham and Bishop Spearhafoc both seem to have been practising craftsmen, but the reputations of Dunstan, Aethelwold, and others are probably only posthumous: Dodwell 1982, 48–50 and 53–5.
147. Illustrated in the *Liber Vitae*: Turner 1984, no. 62. The picture, presumably by a monk who knew the altar, shows it as plain apart from expanded ends, a marked contrast to twelfth-century descriptions of it as 'having a likeness of the crucified Lord, with a great mass of gold and silver, also precious stones'; if the picture was lifelike, either these were exaggerations, or much embellishment was added in its hundred years of existence, after which it was said to have had 'more than 500 marks of silver and thirty of gold': King, E. (ed.) and Potter (trans.) 1998, 105.
148. Bailey, R. N. 1996, 5–9; Gameson 1995, 82–3 and 245–50. Descriptions of materials and values were quite probably often exaggerated, but can be shown to have been substantial nevertheless: Dodwell 1973–4.

149. Haith 1984, no. 77.
150. Sandford reliquary: Hinton 1974, no. 30. A much simpler pendant cross-reliquary, thought to be eleventh-century Scandinavian, has recently been reported from Thwaite, Suffolk: J. P. Robinson in *Treasure Annual Report 1998-9*, no. 176.
151. St Augustine's: Sherlock and Woods 1988, 203–4; Oxford: Hinton 1974, no. 27; Castle Acre: Hinton 1982*a*, found in an early context at the post-Conquest site; Lewes: Lyne 1997, 17, from levels underlying the late eleventh-century priory; Rhuddlan: Boon 1994, 164 (the crystal is not further described).
152. Biddle (ed.) 1976, 200 and 427–9; Rumble 2002, 29.
153. Ottaway 1992, 716–18. The pieces could have come from old blades, awaiting recycling, but they would even so show that York smiths were in contact with people who had swords to dispose of. York in 1065 served as a weapon-store for Earl Tostig—see next note: Whitelock (ed.) 1961, 138.
154. Keene 1998, 95–7; Lawson, M. K. 2000, 83–4; Gillingham 1995, 136–7, but note that a good sword still took a long time to make: Peirce 1986, 155–6. Tyler, E. M. 1999, 266, n. 67, rightly points out that Hinton 1975 attempted to make too much of a distinction between the aristocracy and the towns. I am not sure, even so, that a landowner would have been very interested in the knick-knacks available in the town streets, even though the role of merchants as suppliers of commodities to the rich and powerful made them part of the social fabric: Godden 1990.
155. The last that can be dated by inclusion in coin hoards are a pair in Rome inscribed for donation to Pope Marinus (942–6), and a plain pair from Tetney, Lincolnshire, with coins of *c*.963: Graham-Campbell and Okasha 1991; Wilson, D. M. 1964, nos. 86–7; Blackburn and Pagan 1986, 296, no. 141. Both may have been purse-fittings.
156. Robinson, P. 1979/80 for a summary not substantially affected by later finds, though Margeson 1995*b*, 55 saw them as eighth-/ninth-century. They are disturbingly similar to some much later medieval pins (Fig. 8.9).
157. See n. 167 below.
158. Hinton 1990*b*, 496–500.
159. Illustrated in Thompson, J. D. A. 1956, pl. 15.
160. Ibid., no. 86 and pl. 10a; Blackburn and Pagan 1986, no. 144. It was found in a 'Chester-type' ware pot.
161. Unless the Oxford, Magdalen Bridge, finds are from one, above. Another practice that could be seen as deviant may have been to add a couple of coins to a grave: Robinson, P. 1984; the instances that Robinson cites as possibilities include as many from the south of England as the north, including now Trowbridge, so it was not a 'viking' practice, if it took place. The two Rhuddlan coins with the leather bag and crystal suggest that coins may have been placed rather than surreptitiously thrown in when the priest was not looking. The coin in the skeleton's mouth on Bardsey Island is very odd: Arnold 1998, 101; and see above. A copper-

alloy circular buckle with a skeleton in Oxford is probably not very meaningful: Boyle 2001, 341 and fig. 6.

162. Stories that seem to stress the New Vikings' appalling paganism, such as their murder of the archbishop of Canterbury, may be prompted by hagiographical tradition, not historical reality: McDougall 1993. Brooks 1978, 90–1, suggested that the description of the laying-out of a dead warrior with his weapons in an early twelfth-century text might refer to actual past practice—but when and where?

163. Hadley 2000*b*, 125–6, makes the point that a new leadership would seek 'to adapt to existing forms of lordship', and would have no reason to associate itself with a peasantry, even if in the Danelaw it claimed Danishness for itself. This would have been still more true for the eleventh century than the tenth. Differences between Danish and English lords remained a factor in politics, however: Nightingale 1987, 577.

164. Unfortunately, the wills which were such a valuable source of information for the tenth and early eleventh centuries change character, and those that survive for the rest of the eleventh century are much shorter, and come from less rich people. Family and memory change can probably be seen in the near-disappearance of women's wills as well, so that brooches and the like vanish from the record. Artefacts ceased to carry dynastic meaning.

165. Thompson, J. D. A. 1956, no. 334.

166. Thompson, J. D. A. 1956, no. 250. A gold ring found with the Oulton, Staffordshire, hoard on 7 March 1795 had apparently become 'a number of gold rings and bracelets' by 9 March, but by 1798 had reverted to being a single ring, with a 'lump of pure gold': Robinson, P. 1969, 24–6.

167. Report by L. Webster in *Treasure Annual Report 2001*, 32–3; note also a slightly earlier gold and enamel ring from Warwick and one attributed to the tenth or eleventh century, from Rotherby, Leicestershire, both reported in the same issue by S. M. Youngs, 34–6.

168. Jessup 1950, pl. 32. Another possible import is the Towneley brooch, above.

169. Pitney: Haith 1984, no. 109—its calibre can be judged by the magnified colour picture on the back cover.

170. A ring from Attleborough, Norfolk, has *Ethelric on Lund*, 'Ethelric of London', and is one exception, but the letters are crudely incised, a contrast to the neat niello of earlier years: Okasha 1971, no. 5.

171. Okasha 1983, no. 163; Okasha 1993, nos. 185 and 207. Wider survival of organic materials might of course give a different picture from the one presented in this paragraph.

172. Okasha 1995 and Bredehoft 1996 for the extent to which such 'speaking texts' may imply widespread literacy or merely recognition of letters.

173. Boddington 1996, 104–8 (Fleming, R. 2001, 12, n. 77, points out that their smashing can be seen as a very overt statement of usurpation by a new Norman owner after 1066). Daniell 2002, 242, cites Butler 1964 on the east Midlands as

evidence that the Conquest made no discernible difference to production of grave covers; studies in other areas would be useful.

174. Nightingale 1987, 573–5, argues that London's wealth oscillated violently; the hoards may reflect a temporary boom after the mid-eleventh century.

175. Whitelock (ed.) 1961, 132.

176. Bartlett 2000, 573–4. William's prominent moustache on the coin shown in Fig. 5.13 may be a misrendering; at any rate, photographs of this coin type show him clean-shaven.

177. Williams, A. 1995, 188–90. Long hair was also attributed to Danes, for instance. The mincing young men at William II's court, with their 'close-fitting robes'—what could actually be done without buttons was probably limited, even with lacing—gain some credence from the London discoveries of long-pointed shoes, showing that extremes of dress really did exist: Harriss, J. 1998 and Reid 2001.

178. Tyler, E. M. 1999, 260. Note also the pennant above Christ in the Harrowing of Hell scene in the manuscript that also shows His temptation: Backhouse *et al.* 1984, pl. 20, or an earlier picture of angels: ibid., no. 65. The absence of evidence of Norman settlement in the surviving material culture in Norwich is noted by Atkin and Evans 2002, 238.

179. It is worth stressing that ornamented, probably ninth-/tenth-century, rings continue to be found in excavations, one coming from Steyning in the last decade: Webster 1993*b*; there are none from the much more prolific, later, urban sites.

180. Stafford 2000, 78; Tyler, E. M. 2000, 84.

181. Tyler, E. M. 2000, 87–92. Tyler suggests that all this colour and display appealed more to those of Scandinavian than of English affiliation: pp. 98–9 and 103; ead. 1999, 264–5 and 268. See Leyser 1994, 81–3, for some Carolingian- and Ottonian-period royal gifts to churches and the need for rulers to be seen to be receiving 'costly and rare objects from abroad' as recognition of lordship and their ability to exercise the 'royal function of patronage and largesse', but as part of diplomacy 'between rulers'—he does not cite instances of gifts from kings to their subjects. In the twelfth century a reason for Edward the Confessor's eligibility for canonization was that he had once given a ring to a beggar, who turned out to be St John the Baptist; the ring was returned to the king and was subsequently said to have been found in his coffin: Barlow 1970, 133, 274, and 282. Whether this could be evidence of a memory of the real Edward as a ring-giver seems unlikely, not least because it sounds a bit like a favourite story of St Martin dividing his cloak with a beggar, which subsequently came to be worn by Christ.

182. A useful model is propounded by Ormrod 2000, 198–200, which has the late Saxon system changing from a 'tribute state' to a 'domain state', with kings drawing their income principally from estates, profits of justice, and other rights of lordship, making tax like 'Danegeld' and tolls less important—note that Edward the Confessor managed for some years before the Conquest without the Danegeld, though William restored it.

6. FEUDAL MODES

1. The chapter heading disguises recent work on the reality of feudalism, e.g. Reynolds, S. 1994, and of its mode of production. For social relationships and gifts to (and of) churches in the twelfth century, see Green 1997, 218, 392–3, and 414–20; Newman, C. A. 1988, 77–8. For oaths of fealty and the difficulties of knowing whether household knights, unlike stipendiary knights and some other soldiers, received cash fees before the thirteenth century, Chibnall 1986, 15; Church 1999, 16 and 74–81. Knights were 'girded' by the late eleventh century, but full-scale 'belting' with a sword is not recorded at their level before 1189: Crouch 1992, 73. Population growth is hard to quantify, but the ability of new towns such as Battle, Sussex, to draw in settlers shows that the countryside had surplus people to dispose of, many into occupations linked to agriculture, making them a poorer element than that of the continental immigrants: Clark, C. 1979. Another example is the Shaftesbury Abbey record of the 1120s for Corfe, Dorset, from which seven *fugitivi* had been licensed to move from the estate, five of them into the nearest town, Wareham: Hinton 2002, 90.

2. Summary in Kenyon 1990, 171–8; subsequent publications include Ludgershall, where a box lid formed of bone strips gives a good example of a widespread type: MacGregor 2000*b*, 161–2, and Carisbrooke, where two coins of the 1080s and two of 1117–19 were found, and nine gaming-pieces: Robinson, P. 2000, 132; Cleal 2000, 174–6. Leather caskets also begin to survive: Cherry 1982*a*; locked jewellery caskets and their keys took on overtones of lovers, control, and containment: Camille 1998*a*, 65–71. For chess, see Eales 1986; Stratford, N. 1997, 31–5; Hall, M. A. 2001*a*. For the Castle Acre pins, Margeson 1982, 248–52. Despite its name, the precise nature of Castle Acre's first period is debated, though the character of the finds has not been part of the discussion. (The site also had several coins, including eleven of King Stephen, so many that the accidental dispersal of a hoard has to be considered a possibility: Archibald 1982.) Similar pins have been found in Beverley, Winchester, and other sites, but in much smaller numbers: Foreman, M. 1991, 183–4 and 190–1; Biddle 1990, 55.

3. It is notable that Henry I faced down many rebellions, but rarely went so far as to disinherit anyone, let alone to execute them: Chibnall 1986, 63. It is unlikely but just possible that the introduction of the ring-brooch occurred much earlier than any representation of it, in which case there are one or two which might belong in the first half of the twelfth century: see below. 'Norman' here is shorthand for 'Anglo-Norman', as there was fusion through marriage even directly after the Conquest.

4. Hudson 2000, 115. King, E. (ed.) and Potter (trans.) 1998, 11–3, for William of Malmesbury—who also said that some courtiers went so far as to have hairpieces.

5. Kaufmann 1984, nos. 33 and 76, for particularly good examples.

6. Caviness 1984, 135.

7. Rose 1992, 50; Crouch 1992, 178–9. Pilbrow 2002, 195–6, notes how the corollary for a false knight was to have his spurs cut off, another physical reminder.

8. An exception is the highest-quality woollen cloth such as 'Lincoln Green' ('Grain'), which is actually scarlet, achieved by using imported kermes, beetles that looked like grain when packed into barrels: Munro 1999. Nightingale 1995, 33–5, for early twelfth-century high-level trade and its difficulties. One rich merchant is recorded as being robbed of a purse that included jewels as well as gold and coins, to the value of £10: ibid. 30. Even if accurate, this story would still be the only direct evidence of jewellery being traded in the first half of the twelfth century.
9. Archibald 1984*b*, no. 468; Pritchard 1991, 152–3; Egan and Pritchard 1991, 78–82 and 96–7.
10. Mainman and Ottaway 2002; Goodall, A. R. 1984*b*; Clarke and Carter 1977.
11. Winchester: Hinton 1990*b*, no. 1110, and Norwich: Margeson 1993, 24–7, from a late eleventh-/early twelfth-century context. A very fine, probably slightly later, example came from the River Witham: Stratford, N. 1984, no. 256. An interesting recent addition is a small buckle with two birds in relief, found in north Lincolnshire: *Portable Antiquities Annual Report 2000–1*, 65.
12. Stratford, N. 1984, no. 246; Hinton 1990*b*, no. 2323. There is disagreement on its dating as well as its function; Stratford thought it late eleventh-/early twelfth-century, whereas I saw it as second or third quarter of the twelfth century, on the basis of initials in manuscripts of *c*.1130. The Gloucester candlestick has a good claim to have been made in England, but that there should be disagreement is symptomatic of the problem of attribution, even of the many small items found in England.
13. Stratford, N. 1984, nos. 247–56. The needles may have been 'couching needles' for use with fabrics that might include gold thread, i.e. they were not ordinary domestic implements; the identification is not uniformly accepted, but the 'eye' being near the point, not the head, seems to preclude any use with dress or as hairpins (for which see above): Biddle and Elmhirst 1990, 807–9. Another example of the difficulty of knowing the use of some of these Romanesque objects is provided by a hollow-cast head holding a bird recently found at Edmondsham, Dorset; it appears to have a rivet-hole in the open socket, as though it was the head of a staff, or dangled on a chain or ribbon, but that leaves two other holes unexplained: Geake 2002, 130–1. Another Winchester piece that shows some of the problems of making positive attributions is a flat rectangle with a struggling man in relief, probably originally enamelled, that may be either a casket mount, as Stratford, N. 1984, no. 286, or a buckle-plate, as Hinton 1990*b*, no. 1201. It comes from the second half of the twelfth century or the early thirteenth, by which time metal artefacts were coming back into more general use, as the ring-brooches show, below. The date is more or less agreed, but not the design, which Stratford took as foliage, but which I saw as a man struggling with a dragon. I cannot now remember whether Nick Griffiths's drawing (ibid., fig. 132) created my view or confirmed what I already thought, but the point is worth making because it shows that a drawing is as much interpretative as is a written description.
14. London: Vince 1985*a*, 34–43; id. 2000, 246–8; Nenk and Pearce 1994; Lincoln: Adams Gilmour 1988, 66–7 and 113; York: Mainman 1990, 513. East Anglia:

Rogerson and Dallas 1984, 125–6; Andrews and Penn 1999, 8. See also Chapter 5.

15. The only evidence for the former is still a pottery costrel from Winchester which appears to imitate leather; pottery imitations of jugs are a much later development. The London evidence of surviving leather boots and shoes is probably enough to suggest that if vessels were being produced in any quantity, some fragments would have been recognized: Pritchard 1991, 211–40 and Egan 1998, 238–40.

16. Winchester: Keene 1990; London: Pritchard 1991; Keys 1998; York: Morris, C. A. 2000, 2220; Lincoln pottery: Adams Gilmour 1988; Miles et al. 1989.

17. Brown, D. H. 1995, 140; id. 2002, 152 and 161.

18. Allan 1984, 15. The impact of the Conquest took longer to have an effect than was allowed for by one of the pioneers of pottery studies, Dr G. C. Dunning, whose well-known distribution maps had arrows notably broad in relation to the volumes that they represented, e.g. 1956, 220. The twelfth century did see an increase in Normandy Gritty ware, but, as its (modern) name suggests, this would have had no qualities to make it a viable competitor to English unglazed pottery; it was getting as far west as Exeter in the eleventh century: Allan 1984, 14, and at least as far north as Norwich: Jennings 1981, 33.

19. e.g. Thetford, which has about a dozen sherds: Rogerson and Dallas 1984, 124. Norwich has slightly more, as would be expected from its more flourishing condition: Jennings 1981, 26–33. Coastal Yarmouth has only a few sherds of Pingsdorf-type ware, however, despite its growing population—it had seventy burgesses by Domesday Book, although scarcely existing before the middle of the eleventh century; an Edward the Confessor coin, a hooked tag, and Thetford-type pottery attest its origins, the last being replaced in the twelfth century by more locally made pots: Rogerson 1976.

20. Vince 1985a, 39–41; three of Thetford's imports are of this type: Rogerson and Dallas 1984, 124.

21. Loughor tripod: Lewis, J. M. 1978, 6. Colour photograph of Oxford examples in Mellor, M. 1997, fig. 28. They were made as far west as the Malverns, a little later in Herefordshire: Vince 1985b, 36–43 and 48–9. Their use is sometimes said to be for wine, but they would be in the richer east if so, and wine would normally be associated with higher-status materials. Another regional contrast is that the east used many more pottery bowls and dishes. A reconstruction of a London kitchen on the front cover of Vince (ed.) 1991 shows one reason why many vessels were round-bottomed, for use on hearths or rush-strewn floors.

22. Morris, E. L. 1980, 224.

23. Mellor, M. 1994, 51–2, 57–60, 65–6, and 71; ead. 1997, 25–6.

24. Coppack 1987, 158 and 167 for jugs (there are not many well-dated groups, so this one is worth emphasizing), and 140–1 for the imported vessel: in the report this is compared to 'Islamic' sherds in Lincoln, which have subsequently been shown to be debris from industrial processes. It is said to have come from the late Saxon 'weaving shed', but also that much of it came from 'later deposits in which

it was residual'; I have interpreted it here as broken after that building's demolition, with some sherds intrusive; the argument would fall if the pieces were sealed by the Norman earthworks. Fragments of exotica are sometimes found unexpectedly, such as a fragment of glass from a Greek scent bottle at the deserted village of Seacourt, Oxfordshire, and a sherd of raqqa-type pottery, more appropriately at the Templars site, South Witham, Lincolnshire, perhaps the remains of a jar brought back filled with green-ginger or some sugary confection: Hurst 2002.

25. Kaufmann 1984, no. 33. This drawing, dated 1130–40, seems more lifelike than other representations, such as plough scenes, perhaps because the artist had no obvious sources to draw upon for his peasantry. Other illustrations are less obviously rural, e.g. bystanders at the arrest of Christ, their mocking faces a contrast to their elegant gestures, who are not shown wearing any metal objects despite the careful depictions of cross-gartering, red hose, or embroidered sleeves: ibid., no. 76. To be a peasant was to belong to a different 'order' altogether; they smelt, were stupid, and were to be kept at a distance, e.g. Crouch 1992, 17–19; Lachaud 2002, 111, notes how the dream of Henry I used depictions of dress to emphasize group distinctions.

26. Ivens *et al.* 1995, 331, 307, and 243–5.

27. Newman, C. A. 1988, 21. Contrary evidence can be cited, such as William of Malmesbury's eulogy of Gloucestershire as the producer of excellent wines: Clanchy 1998, 9.

28. Chibnall 1986, 98–9; perhaps the most obscure to do so was Henry de Neuborg, lord of Gower, who issued a few coins at the Swansea mint: Boon 1986, 53–4. William of Malmesbury criticized King Stephen for being 'a generous giver and, most inappropriately for a prince, a spendthrift', so prodigal generosity was no longer a good quality: King, E. (ed.) and Potter (trans.) 1998, 31–3.

29. Blackburn 1991*b*; Fitzwilliam Museum, Cambridge website, Check List of Coin Hoards, Nov. 2002: eleven from 1100 to 1135, eighteen from 1135 to 1154. The first twelfth-century hoard with objects as well as coins is that from Lark Hill, Worcester, below.

30. This view is an attempt to counter the suggestion that it is mere chance that so little survives, expressed e.g. by Lightbown 1992, 7. Hoards with objects would not suffice alone—there is a long gap in the thirteenth century, for instance—but they add to the overall picture.

31. Graham-Campbell 1995, 55–6 and 165–6. Various objects not found with coins could be twelfth-century losses, e.g. an Iona hoard: ibid. 166–7. See further below.

32. Seal and writ: Harvey, P. D. A. and McGuinness 1996, 3; coins: Metcalf 1977, 8; id. 1995, 16: Metcalf stresses that introducing Scottish coins was not the same as introducing coinage for the first time as a medium of exchange rather than as a means of wealth storage; Stewart 1977, 67. Mayhew 1977, 94–6, made the point that although the quantity of medieval Scottish coinage was never great, it was high in relation to what can be ascertained of the total population in the thirteenth century. Spufford 1988, 124, n. 2, played down the possible value of the Alston Moor mines, but Blanchard 1996, 25–33, has output reaching and

surpassing three-quarters of a tonne annually, a very large amount in Europe at that time. A subsequent record that the sheriff owed £145 in rent arrears from the mines could indicate that quite large amounts had continued to be extracted, even if the claim that they were now unproductive was true: Warren 1977, 271. Spufford 1988, 112, for 1160s discoveries on the continent.

33. Cant 1991 for a summary of St Andrews, Rains and Hall 1997 for excavation report, including pp. 56–8 for the pottery sources, p. 44 for the aquamanile spout. Two other examples are recorded by Caldwell *et al*. 1998, 58; see Lewis, J. M. 1987 for a general review, and Yeoman 1995 on Scottish developments. The courtesy of offering to wash a guest's hands—and even his feet—had overtones of Christian humility.

34. Bogdan and Wordsworth 1978, 8, 21, 22, and 23; Macaskill 1987; Cox 1997, 741–4, and 768 for another merchant's seal. Hall, M. A., and Owen 1998, 159–60, for Perth's culture generally; see also Chapter 8, and for seals and ring-brooches, see further below.

35. Murray, J. C. 1982, 123; Murray, H. K. and Murray 1993.

36. McCarthy and Brooks 1988, 208–10.

37. Stratford, N. 1997; some of the pieces may be whale tooth, see ibid., appendix B.

38. Holmes, N. 1997, 345; Hill, P. 1997, 239 and 423–4 (the pierced bar in the seventh-century Tattershall Thorpe collection could have been one, but its use is disputed: Hinton 2000, 26–31; the Whithorn draw-plate may be a testimony to harder iron being available, better able to withstand the pressures of the drawing process).

39. Higgitt 1995, 83.

40. Goodall, A. R. 1993, 191–2.

41. Pollexfen 1862–4; Curle 1924; Lightbown 1992, 109–10. Lightbown favours the hair-ornament interpretation, but notes that twelfth-century texts which speak of hairbands tend to imply nests of textile braids. He takes *ligaturae* in Queen Matilda's will as possible examples, but the word need not mean more than bindings generally. For the Iona spoons, Stratford, N. 1984, no. 298. He ascribed the gold strips to the thirteenth century, but the coin-dating of the Bute hoard supports Lightbown's ascription, which I follow here.

42. Metcalf 1977, 35, and references. One of the rings was reported to be gold, the other gilt-iron, which sounds doubtful. Presumably the stones were blue, but the setting in the iron ring could have been a glass paste. See below for this type of ring generally.

43. Walker 1990, 16–17 and 21–8.

44. Davies, R. R. 1987, 115; see e.g. Emanuel 1967, 119; payments in pennies and shillings (*solidi*) both occur frequently. As the texts are based on Latin and Greek grammars, a long list of metals should be read as a school text, not as setting out what was actually available in Wales: ibid. 2. For clothing, Charles-Edwards 2000, 328–9 and 335; Stacey 2000, 340–5. For buildings, Butler 1987.

45. Courtenay 1998, 164; Thorpe (trans.) 1978, 236–7: as Giraldus also cited the use of bread as trenchers, which so far as is known was normal practice in England, his view is probably derogatory only of the princes; Johnstone 1997 for a Welsh princely *llys* site with thirteenth-century pottery. Nant Col aquamanile: Lewis, J. M. 1978, 27.

46. Lewis, J. M. 1970.

47. Arnold and Davies 2000, 97–8, but see above, Chapter 5. Giraldus Cambrensis mentioned a 'rich vein' and successful deep mines, so there was earlier production even if he exaggerated the depth of the mines: Thorpe (trans.) 1978, 196. At times, quite large amounts have been extracted from north Wales, enough in the seventeenth century to make it worth opening a mint at Aberystwyth, but Spufford 1988, 124, n. 2, considered 'Carreghofa' to have been a very small vein.

48. Walker 1990, 59. The profits that the Anglo-Norman lords took from Wales are hard to estimate, but were clearly considerable: ibid. 60; Davies, R. R. 1987, 122. On attitudes to coin as *delu*, 'wealth', see Boon 1986, 60–2. Giraldus, however, put the emphasis on landowning, not specifically on cattle: Thorpe (trans.) 1978, 260–1.

49. Insley 2000, 181–4; Maund 2000, pls. 14–16.

50. As well as English and French, there were substantial numbers of Flemings in Pembrokeshire, whose culture included fortune-telling with rams' shoulder-blades: Toorians 1990; Thorpe (trans.) 1978, 145–7.

51. Brenan, D. F. M. 1994; in the late fourteenth and fifteenth centuries there was production inside the walls, but earlier kilns may have been outside. The larger market town at Cowbridge, south Glamorgan, would have provided another south Welsh example, had most of the pottery from excavations there not been destroyed by a warehouse fire: Parkhouse and Evans 1996, 2!

52. Courtenay 1998, 164.

53. Davies, R. R. 1987, 166–7; Griffiths, R. A. 2000, 683 and 704–5; James, H. 1999, 161.

54. Lewis, J. M. 1982*a*.

55. Daston and Park 1998. Becket's biographer writing in the 1170s mentioned gems from the Nile: Nightingale 1995, 58. This could mean that merchants from Alexandria were involved in the trade, rather than that he believed the Nile to be in the Far East. The context is a list of what could be bought in London, purportedly in the future archbishop's boyhood, but the details cannot be taken as reflecting conditions that early. See Chapters 3 and 5 for Bede and William I, and gems. To be effective as cures, etc., some stones had to be ground up so that they could be swallowed and their properties digested.

56. Studer and Evans 1924, pp. xiii–xvii, for commentary; Evans, J. and Serjeantson 1933, 20–1 for a text on sapphires—they were in the Old English texts, but in those texts were merely said to be like the sun with golden stars in it: ibid. 15.

57. Ascriptions in e.g. Hinton 1982*b*, 14, rightly had cold water poured upon them by Stratford, N. 1984, nos. 311–14. The locations of the graves do, however,

indicate that some at least are likely to be twelfth-century. For a recent list of bishops' rings, Bird 1996, 4. Abbots were also buried with rings: Oman 1930, 32–3, e.g. one in front of the high altar at Hulton Abbey, a sapphire in a claw setting in a neatly engraved hoop: Cherry 1985c.

58. The earliest record of the shape seems to be a mid-thirteenth-century drawing by Matthew Paris, which shows a ring then at St Albans which Queen Eleanor of Aquitaine had given to 'Richard the Animal', who had presented it to the abbey: Stratford, N. 1984, no. 318, 3. Paris also illustrated one that looks vaguely stirrup-shaped to symbolize a marriage: Vaughan (ed. and trans.) 1983, 60.

59. Campbell, M. 1991, 135–16; Lightbown 1992, 12–6. Faceting, as in the ring once attributed to Bishop William de St Barbe at Durham, was a step towards more intricate cutting: Stratford, N. 1984, no. 313. The large intaglio gem set in the ring buried with the archbishop of York in 1255 (an undoubted attribution) seems to have had one face ground bare to remove marks that could not be given a Christian interpretation, so some working was possible: Henig 1983, 58–9. Henig suggests that one of the Chichester gems might be a medieval copy, but even if it did not belong to Bishop Seffrid (d. 1151), it would still seem too early for copying to have been undertaken: ibid. 159.

60. Dalton 1912, pp. xxi–xxiv; Oman 1930, 17; the second finger was the *digitus infamus* to the Romans, but is sometimes shown with a ring on it, e.g. on the effigy of King John.

61. Rumble, 1981, 163. A carbuncle would normally have meant a ruby by this time (unlike earlier when it may have been garnet that was thought of): Lightbown 1992, 29.

62. Henig and Heslop 1986; Stratford, N. 1984, no. 318; Campbell, M. 1991, 138.

63. One of the earliest known is an impression taken from one owned by Thomas Becket's father, a London businessman: Tonnochy 1952, pp. xix–xxi; see also Clanchy 1993, 316–17. Campbell, M. 1991, 198; Henig 2000. Some gems may have been collected from Romano-British sites; some of those at St Albans could have come from Verulamium. Others were newly imported, though it is not usually possible to say which was which. The supply in western Europe may have increased after the sack of Constantinople in 1204. King Richard's ring: Harvey, P. D. A. and McGuinness 1996, 9, 14, and 35. A recently published pendant seal from Ludgershall Castle is a cornelian intaglio with a lion that would have looked heraldic and therefore more meaningful than most gems to a medieval owner: Cherry and Henig 2000.

64. Stratford, N. 1984, no. 318; Evans, J. and Serjeantson 1933, 76.

65. Stratford, N. 1984, nos. 320, e and f; both of these seem to be the earliest of their types known in Europe, and gold predecessors have not been claimed. Nevertheless, there is no reason to doubt the integrity of the hoard, which was reported as found 'all in a lump together', probably in a bag sealed with wax: Akerman 1855b, 200. A broken silver ring with crosses in panels like 320f has recently come from Boteler's Castle, Warwickshire, a site abandoned in the early thirteenth century: Jones, C. *et al.* 1997, 51–2 and 54–5. There is one in copper alloy from an early twelfth-century context in York: Ottaway and Rogers 2002,

3070–1. For *fede* rings, Tait 1976, 256; clasped hands had been used as a Roman-derived idiom before, on seventh-century gold coins: Gannon 2003, 63–5. The Matthew Paris illustration in Vaughan (ed. and trans.) 1983, 60, not only shows that rings were used to seal a marriage, and that they were not necessarily plain bands, but also has two clasped hands making the *fede* gesture above. The date of the introduction of the wedding-ring custom into England is not recorded, but was known to Aelfric in the early eleventh century: see Chapter 5. Nuns might be given a ring to show their espousal to the Church when they took their vows, and since in 1138 they were forbidden to 'put on gold rings' (Sawyer 1986, 191), the practice may have been well established by then. The ban had no long-term effect, since later decrees were that nuns' rings should be plain, but those distributed by Edward I included sapphires, proving that their coldness could promote chastity in both sexes: Lightbown 1992, 91.

The Sarum Missal and others prescribed that the wedding-ring should be placed first on the thumb by the priest ('in the name of the Father'), then on the index finger ('and of the Son'), next on the middle finger ('and of the Holy Ghost'), and left in place on the third finger ('Amen'), because it was believed to have a vein in it that ran directly to the heart: *Notes & Queries*, 5th series 12 (1879), 408 and 474; Fleming, P. 2001, 44–5, shows that this was done at the door of the church, because the ring confirmed the secular contract involving dowry settlement that a marriage necessitated. Oman 1930, 15–17, suggested that the ring was put on the right, not the left, hand, where it is shown on effigies and in other representations, but I have been unable to substantiate this.

66. Ayers 1987, 79. Rings were often worn on the upper digits, however, so small diameters are not always evidence that they were intended for children, or for women.

67. Illustrated in the original publication, Akerman 1855*b*, pl. 17, but subsequently lost, or at least never mentioned in discussions. For sculpture, Cherry 1969*a*, 225.

68. York: Ottaway and Rogers 2002, 2911–2; London: Egan and Pritchard 1991, 253–4.

69. Norwich: Margeson 1993, 14–16; Benington: Cherry 1987*a*, no. 641; also the gold Kames brooch, unprovenanced: Lightbown 1992, pl. 30. Although usually ascribed to the thirteenth century, I think that the type could have been current a bit earlier.

70. Deevey 1998, 121 and pl. 17; Egan 1999, 440. It probably reached Ireland after Henry II's invasion, so can be said to show English trends—which also allows English taste to be seen in the extraordinary text on a brooch found in Kerry, *ieo:eim:mun:potage*, or 'I like my soup': Dalton 1912, no. 918. Could that have been amatory?

71. Musty *et al.* 1969, 147; the brooch was dated *c.*1220 at the time of publication, but an earlier date is tenable. Although its filigree is different, I suspect that a finger-ring found at Meaux Abbey, Yorkshire, may be of the same date; even if the report of its discovery in the abbey moat is incorrect, it is still an unlikely find on the site of a house not established until well into the twelfth century: Dalton 1912, pp. xxxiii and 112–14; Oman 1930, no. 226.

72. The misericord is presumably a self-image by the carver himself, and therefore a representation of how someone at that social level thought it appropriate for himself to appear: Grössinger 1997, 28. York pottery: Jennings 1992, 15; splash-glazed wares were going out of use by the early thirteenth century.

73. Deevey 1998, 5; application of such principles has been recognized even in such matters as town planning: Lilley 2002, 158–67. One brooch type used on the continent but not known from Britain is the 'cluster brooch', a disc with stones set all over it in geometrical patterns: Lightbown 1992, 140.

74. Some are beyond understanding, if the craftsman did not copy a text properly, e.g. a ring from Hill Deverill, Wiltshire, with *Honor vous urull*, in which the last word may be a misrendered *veille*, making 'May honour watch over you': Cherry 1984*a*. The inscription on a brooch found at Offham, Sussex, seems even more of a mishmash: Poole 1996.

75. Lightbown 1992, 138; Deevey 1998, 69–70. 'Courtly love' derives from lyric poetry that became popular during the twelfth century; it implies a man's excessive amorous passion, usually unrequited, constant devotion, and unquestioning obedience to the adored one's demands, but it also commodified women by elevating them to a pedestal: see Sklar 1998 for a summary. Cherry 1987*a*, no. 644, for the Writtle brooch; a silver-gilt brooch with an inscription that seems to say 'I hold closed . . .' may have a similar innuendo: Murdoch 1991, no. 303.

76. Presumably at all social levels it was enough to know that AGLA was a protective formula; one brooch in silver gilt has reversed letters, so it was not only craftsmen in base metals who could go wrong: Saunders 1982. Other 'charm' words were nonsense, though were charms because they could be read in both directions, such as 'ansoganagosna': Evans, J. 1922, 122–8. Ring-brooches with clasped hands are widespread: see Deevey 1998, 123–6, for a range of examples. Sir Gawain received a silk girdle as a love-token, which he wore next to his skin for protection. He was a man who appreciated an exposed white throat and bosom: Barron, W. R. J. (ed.) 1974, 31 and 79.

77. Coatsworth and Pinder 2002, 12–13.

78. Lightbown 1992, 24, 49: because they made plate, goldsmiths were also jewellers, a term that only became used for makers later in the Middle Ages (a *joaillier* was a mercer, a dealer in rich goods generally).

79. Lilley 2002, 218–19.

80. Brown, R. A. *et al.* 1963, 65; Henry's expenditure on palaces and houses was usually a little less: ibid. 81; at Orford between 1165 and 1173, just over £1,400 was spent on the new castle with its stone keep, perimeter wall, and projecting towers: ibid. 769–70.

81. Entries in the *Pipe Rolls*, vol. 5, p. 2; vol. 8, p. 43; vol. 23, pp. 81 and 197; vol. 33, p. 19.

82. Otway-Ruthven 1980, 47.

83. Cherry and Goodall 1985.

84. Hastiludes and display: Hanawalt and Reyerson 1994, p. x. Griffiths, N. 1989 cites only two other examples of shield-shaped brooches.

85. A 'device' was the heraldic term for a figure on a coloured background; the creation and recognition of a knight's 'arms' became increasingly arcane (as it still is, as anyone having to overhear conversations in the Society of Antiquaries library knows only too well), requiring specialist knowledge reserved to a few heralds: Crouch 1992, 178–88 and 228–9; Boulton 1998; Piponnier and Mane 1997, 60; Crouch 2002; Ailes 2002, 83–4. The knights shown in Henry I's dream may have specifically heraldic devices on their shields: Green 1997, 344–5. Another example of specialist knowledge developing in the twelfth century was caused by the increased flow and accounting of money, and the use of the abacus and checked cloth; Hollister 1985, 128–30; Chibnall 1986, 124–5.

86. Stratford, N. 1984, no. 295; Griffiths, N. 1995 for an assessment based on the London finds; Ashley 2002 for Norfolk examples, and pp. 27–9 for their introduction at the beginning of the twelfth century.

87. Tonnochy 1952, pp. xxiv–xxviii and lviii–lxiii; Rigold 1977; Heslop 1987; Goodall, J. 1993; Clanchy 1993, 308–17, who called such things 'harbingers of literacy'; Harvey, P. D. A. and McGuinness 1996, 77–88. Matrixes might be round, like de Brun's (Fig. 6.5), but were more often either oval, or smaller and conical-handled. The squirrel could signify the penis in French *fabliaux*, and was often shown as a lady's pet, so the inscription boasted of sexual conquest: Camille 1998a, 103–4.

88. Spencer 1998 for a general introduction and for the quantities found in London, and id. 1990a for Salisbury, where a smaller number is in not dissimilar proportions in relation to population size. Their preservation and recovery is affected by their alloy, however, as lead is less stable than most metals. See also Lightbown 1992, 188–90, for the badges' introduction in Europe generally. Pierced scallop-shells presumably from Compostela have been found in Winchester: Spencer 1990b, and Norwich: Margeson 1993, 8. See also Chapter 7.

89. Mitchiner 1986, 38 for the Plantagenet badge; Spencer 1998, 311–13; Koldeweij 1999. For cockney badges and others, Mitchiner 1986, 127 and 212. The cock's egg (*ei*) badges had inscriptions like 'Koc ne/lok on me'. Jones, M. 2001, 205 suggests that some of the secular badges may have been worn hidden under clothing, like some amatory brooches, but not so much to conceal a covert love as to be a good-luck token for sexual success. Dating badges can be problematic: 'affinity' badges are discussed below in Chapters 7 and 8.

90. Stott 1991 is the best discussion, though I do not agree with his conclusion that they were cheap jewellery items. Admittedly my own does not explain their disappearance at the end of the thirteenth century or a little later, unless they were replaced—after an interval?—by the small bifacial seals that were known by the end of the fourteenth century: Egan 1994. If a cord was passed through the holes, it could have been tied round a bale and the device would hang flat against the side. Bales of English cloth might have been landed at Perth, or the Scots may have followed English customs practice—one of the two spangles from there has a four-pointed star, reminiscent of the design on de Brun's seal (Fig. 6.5): Moloney and Coleman 1997, 747–8; for the other from Perth, Yeoman 1995, 81; for one found in Monmouth: Marvell (ed.) 2001, 69, report by M. Redknap; for other uses and tokens generally, Mitchiner and Skinner 1983; Mitchiner 1988.

91. Hinton 2003*b*, 109–10. Because Jews were distinctive in religious and other cultural practices, it was easier to enforce regulations upon them than upon other groups. The *tabula* was a device specific to England; on the continent a wheel, the *rota*, was used instead. I am unsure why this was so, but it serves as a reminder that things may have different meanings in different but contemporary and interconnecting societies. Lepers were treated slightly differently, in that they were supposed to carry a horn—later, wooden clappers—to warn of their presence. See Mellinkoff 1993 for the complexities of meaning attributable to dress and colours generally, as well as to badges, and Moore, R. I. 1987 for measures against lepers and Jews as 'heretics', and the means employed to recognize them so as to avoid contact with their 'pollution'. One way that emblems were worn is shown in a drawing by Matthew Paris of a French torturer whose cloak is 'powdered' with red hammers like those depicted as one of the instruments of Christ's passion: Vaughan (ed. and trans.) 1993, 28.
92. King, E. 1979, 68–9; most but not quite all the money was collected: Jurkowski *et al.* 1998, 3–4. Spufford 1988, 109–19 for new silver supplies.
93. Fillongley: Wise 1999; Brackley: Cherry 2001; Stratford: Palmer and Seaby 1983–4 (this hoard was not a new discovery, but had not been properly published before).
94. Allowing for gold to be worth ten times as much as silver, and taking a silver penny as weighing 1.4 g (Archibald and Cook 2001, 25), the second ring would only have weighed 0.85 g, so it must have been extremely thin if that was really its value. Comparison may be made with the contemporary value of farm stock—sheep 3*d.* to 9*d.*, cows 3*s.* to 8*s.*, with averages at the lower ends: Cazel and Cazel (eds.) 1976–7, p. ix.
95. *Curia Regis Rolls*, vol. 1, pp. 255 and 230–1; vol. 3, p. 324; vol. 4, p. 37; vol. 8, pp. 35–6; vol. 10, pp. 332 and 214. For other references, see Lightbown 1992, 105 and 109.
96. Southampton: Harvey 1975, 268; Llantrithyd: Lewis 1982*b*.
97. London: Egan and Pritchard 1991, 255 and 327–9; Winchester: Hinton 1990*b*, 641 and 651; York: Ottaway and Rogers 2002, 2911–13 and 2923–7; Canterbury: Frere *et al.* 1987, 305; Carlisle: McCarthy 1990, fig. 166. The gold content in these varies, the Canterbury ring being 65%, one of those in York 80%, London's between 45% and 75%.
98. See previous note for references; Hatcher and Barker 1974, 30–9, for London pewter; Allan 1984 and Bogdan and Wordsworth 1978, 23, for moulds. The ratios have to be viewed against preservation conditions: gold will survive unaffected by most environments, silver and tin may decay, copper alloy more so, and lead worst of all.
99. Cherry 1987*b*; Campbell, M. 1998, 72. They should perhaps also be thought of as cheap imitations of Limoges enamels, occasionally used for buckles: Cherry 1980, and the Winchester item, above; also a buckle from the River Witham, Lincolnshire: Stratford, N. 1984, no. 256.
100. e.g. Boteler's Castle: Jones, C. *et al.*, 1997, 55; Winchester: Hinton 1990*b*, no. 1145; Norwich: Margeson 1993, 24–5; Tetsworth: Robinson, M. *et al.* 1973,

100; London: Egan and Pritchard 1991, no. 500, and Steane 1985, 221; Horndon: Ramsay 1987, no. 434. I am sensitive about these, having mistakenly published one as mid-Anglo-Saxon: 1974, no. 20.

101. Cazel and Cazel (eds.) 1976–7, e.g. on p. 4, Simon of Kyne, who had 18*d*. as well as several lengths of linen cloth, but only three cows, so may have been a small-scale dealer. Animals, cloth, and cash are the only 'chattels' regularly itemized in these, the first surviving Lay Subsidy assessments, with occasional mentions of a beehive or similar equipment; see further below. 'Kyne' is now South and North Kyme, Lincolnshire, where by coincidence a metal-detectorist recently found a gold ring set with a red garnet attributable to the twelfth/thirteenth century (Col. pl. F.4) and a copper-alloy strap-end, thirteenth- or fourteenth-century, with an inlay of mica, not of silver, which is rarely recognized but might have been widely used: *Treasure Annual Report 1998–9*, nos. 107 and 162. Could either of those have belonged to Simon, who seems to have been one of the richer peasants in the community?

102. Ivens *et al.* 1995, 331–3. For more general figures on coin-find increases, Blackburn 1989.

103. Barclay *et al.* 1990, 44–5. Another indication of the increase in objects of all kinds is the statistics of the Portable Antiquities Scheme, which in 2001 recorded forty items attributed to the twelfth century, 153 to the thirteenth: Geake 2002, 128.

104. MacGregor 1991, 367–8.

105. Vince 1985*a*, 43–50; Mellor, M. 1997, 16 and 25–31; Le Patourel 1968, 113–20. In addition to metal aquamaniles, a number of bowls are known, some of which could have served in the same ceremony: Cherry 1984*b*. Some of these have various scenes engraved on them, apparently not imitated in pottery. Others are plain, but may still have been for hand-washing, e.g. one from Faccombe: Goodall, A. R. 1990, 431. Servants are shown in deferential postures in front of tables from the Bayeux Tapestry onwards: Stenton (ed.) 1965, fig. 49.

106. Blinkhorn and Dix 1991; Jennings 1981, 47–8; poem on towns: Rothwell (ed.) 1975, 881–4. One 'potter' and three 'crockers' are in the 1225 assessment survivals, all amongst the poorest to fall into the taxable net, but unfortunately with no values put upon any stocks, so they may not have been active makers at the time: Cazel and Cazel (eds.) 1976–7, 56, 74, 93, and 103.

107. Warren 1986, 139; *Exchequer Roll* 1207–8, p. 120; Evans, J. 1922, 114, for the pears, a story from a late source. Presumably such stones were set in pendants like those shown in the mid-thirteenth-century drawing of the St Albans cameo: Stratford, N. 1984, no. 318; none seems to have survived from Britain.

108. *Pipe Rolls* John, vol. 6, p. 94; vol. 7, p. 82; vol. 13, pp. 107–12. 'Balas' rubies were named after the mines in Balakshan, Afghanistan, whose king restricted their supply, thus enhancing his own position by being sole distributor of the rarities. In practice, many of those in the western European records may have been garnets: Arrhenius 1985, 26. The two merchants were 'Jacob Curcestriu and

Pasiliano Grace ... Placentinis': does this mean that they were Italians from Piacenza, making inroads into London in the early thirteenth century? See Nightingale 1995, 86. For other references, see Lightbown 1992, 105–6.

109. Lachaud 1996, 281–2; Church 1999, 85. The problems that John had with his money are discussed by Barratt 1996; despite his expenditure, he had quite large sums in reserve in 1214. To put £40 on three jewels in some sort of perspective, a knight could be had for 8*d*. per day in 1160, but had gone up to 24*d*. by 1220. For the sword 'Curtana', Rose 1992, 48.

110. Cazel (ed.) 1974–5, 36. A 'gimmel' was probably a ring with a divided hoop so that the stones are held alongside each other.

111. Oman 1930, 27; the first record of conversion of coins into rings is for Edward II. They came to be a safeguard against epilepsy, if that is what the 'falling sickness' was.

112. Cameos continued to be important, one 'with a head in the middle' being part of a pledge to a Florentine merchant; another was to be sewn to the king's chasuble. In 1259 St Edward's shrine received a cameo for which a Cologne merchant was offered 100 marks, though he demanded £100, which he was supposed to be 'paid with all speed', presumably to stop him taking it elsewhere; but he did not get his money with 'speed', only receiving 10 marks the following year, when the king, 'to his vexation, has no money at present'. Some jewels were well-enough known to have names: *la cerise*, 'the cherry', was presumably a particularly large ruby or garnet which the king had on his finger-ring. See *Patent Rolls*, vol. 1, p. 449; vol. 3, p. 5; vol. 4, pp. 314–15, 397, and 400; vol. 5, pp. 135, 206, and 212; *Liberate Rolls*, vol. 1, pp. 167, 276, 279, and 317; vol. 2, p. 83; vol. 3, pp. 103, 109, and 111; vol. 4, pp. 462 and 488; vol. 5, pp. 6 and 13. Also Lachaud 1996, 283.

113. Lachaud 1996, esp. 297–8; Woolgar 1999, 9 and 19; Watts, J. 2002, 265; Coss 1995 for the emergence of the 'gentle man'.

114. It is one thing to establish use of base-metal costume fittings, glazed pottery, and coins at thirteenth-century rural sites, another to know whether any of it was accessible to the labourers as well as to those with small landholdings. The latter, men like Simon of Kyne, above, are only a little more identifiable in documentary sources, making occasional appearances in manorial court records and estate surveys, but little else.

115. Rubin 1992; Hilton 1998, 13; Golding 2001, 144–8; Gurevich 1988 for discussion of popular or 'vernacular' dichotomy.

116. Jurkowski *et al.* 1998, pp. xiii, xvi–xvii, xxvi–xxviii, 3, and 8. Cazel and Cazel (eds.) 1976–7 for the earliest survivals, as above. Women were assessed if they were heads of households, e.g. as widows. The late twelfth- and thirteenth-century transition to new tax arrangements was to take England in the fourteenth century from a 'domain' to a 'tax' state on Ormrod's model: 2000, 198–9.

117. Hicks, M. 1995, 104 and 121–4, summarizes discussions and debates. Tied in with this seems to be the increasing difficulty that knights had in maintaining independence, because of the rising costs of maintaining their position: Faulkner

1996. Hilton 1998 distinguishes the rural 'class' from urban 'estates', towns putting even more emphasis on economic standing, but the Lay Subsidies applied to all.

118. Swanson, R. N. 1999, 142. Dirt was not the only pollutant; gold and silver, if used for credit which made a profit by unnatural use of God's time, also became pollutants, e.g. Barber, M. 1992, 60.

7. MATERIAL CULTURE AND SOCIAL DISPLAY

1. 'Social display' is deliberately borrowed from the title of the recent book edited by P. R. Coss and M. Keen (2002), in which all the contributors emphasize the importance of 'visual culture' in the later Middle Ages.

2. Gold supply: Spufford 1988, 267–4; Henry's coins: Eaglen 1992 (and see Chapter 5 for the Edward coin); Henry's seal: Heslop 1987, no. 276; Binski 1999, 76–8, who shows that the renunciation of the claim to Normandy in 1259 necessitated a change to the inscription, and may have made the king more aware of the need to stress a different image of kingship; the mounted warrior image was retained on the seal's reverse, however.

3. Capel Maelog: Courtney 1990, 59–60; Coventry: Thompson, J. D. A. 1956, no. 103 and pl. 10b; Telford 1956; Wright 1982, 87; Perth: unpublished information from Dr Mark Hall; York: Ottaway and Rogers 2002, 2923–5; Dumfries: Callander 1923–4, 160–3; Thompson, J. D. A. 1956, no. 139; Metcalf 1977, no. 43; Hambleden: Babb 1997. For pedlars or 'bagmen' retailing trinkets, haberdashery, and the like, Nightingale 1995, 365–6. Lightbown 1992, 53–5, cites examples of goldsmiths at fairs, despite their guild regulations; the pedlars were 'mercers', unconstrained dealers in petty finery of all kinds—a French poem has 'brooches of gilt brass and of silvered latten; and so fond are folk of latten that often it is valued as silver'. An alternative term for 'cabled' is 'wrythen', but both suggest physical twisting, whereas the brooches were in fact cast. The 'ring-brooch' is a version of the 'frame-brooch', which may have a flat band or intertwined creatures and the like, and may be circular, square, hexagonal, etc.

4. Callander 1923–4 for a general review of all the Scottish examples as then known; Canonbie: Thompson, J. D. A. 1956, no. 70 and pl. 9; Langhope: ibid., no. 229 and pl. 16b; Metcalf 1977, no. 127. The coins no longer survive, and the hoard's county of origin seems uncertain—it was recorded as Roxburghshire, but may be Selkirkshire; Perth: Bogdan and Wordsworth 1978, front cover and 23; Hereford: Cherry 1985a, who notes one now in Devizes Museum, though not certainly of Wiltshire origin; Boxley: Kelly, D. B. 1989, 405; Aberdeen: Murray, J. C. 1982, 186; Rattray: Goodall, A. R. 1993, 189–90; Norwich: Atkin *et al.* 1985, 204–5; Leicester: Mellor, J. E. and Pearce 1981, 137.

5. Canonbie: Thompson, J. D. A. 1956, pl. 9, 2; Lightbown 1992, 342–3, for the use and introduction of paternoster beads, which he suggests had become commonplace by the mid-thirteenth century; London: ibid. 349; Egan and Pritchard 1991, 305–17; York: Ottaway and Rogers 2002, 2745 and 2948; Winchester:

Hinton 1990*b*, 644–5. Spanish jet is said to be softer and better for finer work than Whitby; for its various uses, Stalley 1989, 411–12, and for analyses, Hunter, F. 1999: fourteenth- and fifteenth-century material from Fast Castle, Berwickshire, was found to be all Spanish, earlier material from Perth to be Whitby. Even fishbones were used for rosary beads: Stallibrass 2002. A knotted cord could also be used for counting off the prayers. The word 'bead' seems to derive from the Old English *beod*, 'prayer', so was not used on the continent, or much in British wills and inventories before the fifteenth century, an interesting example of the power of the vernacular to resurge.

6. Schorn: Spencer 1998, 8–9 and 192–5; Lightbown 1992, 188–94, for some continental examples. For the Compostela journey, Stalley 1989; Childs 1999. Spencer 1998, 199–203, for the politics of the Thomas of Lancaster shrine at Pontefract; also Steane 1993, 19.

7. Spencer 1998, 24–5; Duffy 1992, 183–6; Merrifield 1987, 108–12; Stalley 1989, 411. Papal bulls were also used as pilgrim symbols in graves: Daniell 1997, 172. Candles were like bells, in having both functional and symbolic meanings. Occasional finds, such as a gold ring found in a post-hole at Chichester, Sussex, could have been placed for good luck, or merely show that someone had had a careless moment of bad luck: Youngs *et al.* 1985, 202.

8. Spencer 1998, 17–18; Bayley *et al.* 1984; Egan and Pritchard 1991, 358–64; Camille 1993, 284–90; id. 1998, 44–6 and 347–8; Melchior-Bonnet 2001, 189–90 and 192–5. For the Perth mirror, Hall, M. A., and Owen 1998, who stress how it shows Scotland's place in European culture, not just Anglo-Norman. The cased mirrors were so small that using them while combing the hair would seem impractical, but vanity should never be underestimated, and they were presumably cheap enough to be widely accessible. This cannot be tested against an increase in the use of combs, as most were organic and few have survived; some of those from London were decorated, and one had an amatory text: Egan and Pritchard 1991, 366–76. Chaucer's Squire was a 'popinjay' and all his campaigns had been against fellow-Christians, whereas his father the Knight had only fought infidels: Rigby 1996, 30, 32–3, and 120.

9. Deevey 1998, 51 cites a gold brooch from Waterford, Eire, that had pastes; it is one of the earliest, however, perhaps late twelfth-century and before rules had been formulated; Winchester: Hinton 1990*b*, no. 2086; Lynn: Clarke and Carter 1977, 287–8; London: Murdoch 1991, no. 409; false settings, etc.: Lightbown 1992, 17–22; Deevey 1998, 50; 'doublettas': Newton 1980, 22 and 36. The Lark Hill hoard's rings, discussed in Chapter 6, include such techniques, but again may pre-date regulations.

10. Tutbury: Hawkins 1832, 167—the ring appears now to be lost, and the inscription may have been misrendered; I am grateful to my colleague Christopher Woolgar for recognizing *spreta* as the past participle plural of *sperno*; though 'rejected things live' is not an obvious text in the circumstances. Seal-rings: Rigold 1977, 328–9; Cherry 1983.

11. Davies, R. T. (ed.) 1963, 21 and 25; Evans, J. 1922, 111; Goodridge (trans.) 1959, 76. In Chaucer's *Romance of the Rose* a stone was worn against toothache.

Poets are not always reliable witnesses; one who included earrings among his strictures was unlikely to have seen any being worn in Britain: quoted by Prestwich 1980, but see Lightbown 1992, 293–4; earrings were bought in 1351 by the French dauphin—but for his fool: Nevinson 1980, 80. Spencer 1998, 14, for the fraudulent pilgrim. Pounds 1994, 135 for *deodand*.

12. Jurkowski *et al.* 1998, 20–1; Gaydon (ed.) 1959—p. 109 for the rural peasants with pots; Brown, W. (ed.) 1894, pp. xx–xxiii, noted a knight's inventory of goods that would have been excluded from taxation; Millar 1932, 54–6, for Sir Geoffrey Luttrell's will of 1345: his bequests included silver vessels and jewellery, not individually itemized, but jewels 'of the weight of twenty shillings' were left to various shrines, 'to remain there in perpetuity'. The stress on 'perpetuity' reflects the suspicion that such things were frequently removed by the clergy: 'that men offren to nowe Hongen | broches, ouches, and rynges. | The preest purchaseth the offrynges': Dean (ed.) 1991, 87.

13. Lynn: Owen, D. M. (ed.) 1984, 235–49; Isaacson and Ingleby 1919–22, vol. 1, pp. 149–51 and vol. 2, pp. 88–90; Shrewsbury: Cromarty and Cromarty 1993—pp. 38–40 for jewellery and plate; Colchester: Hadwin 1977, who at pp. 151–2 noted that the values seem very low, which is certainly true in relation to royal, inventory, and crime records, but perhaps not always; among East Anglian early fourteenth-century thefts were rings valued at 1*s*. each, twelve silver spoons at 10*s*. in total, and three rings at only 2*s*.—presumably they were silver: Hanawalt 1976, nos. 87, 175, and 418.

14. Lynn: Isaacson and Ingleby 1919–22, vol. 1, pp. 2–5: Peter of Thornden, burgess (d. 1309–10), bequeathed various tenements but otherwise only *bonis meis*, 'my goods'. John of Spalding made charitable bequests which included two silver cups, one *pictum cum tribus leonibus*, presumably 'engraved/enamelled with three lions'. Bridport: Bartelot 1907, 100–1; Derby: *Cal. Inq. Misc.* vol. I, no. 737; Bishop of London: Hale and Ellacombe (eds.) 1874.

15. Campbell, M. 1987, no. 209; ead. 1988, 312–13. For pewter, Brownsword and Pitt 1987; Hatcher and Barker 1974. Pewter seems to have had primarily ecclesiastical use until the late thirteenth century. Hatcher and Barker found no entries for pewter in the Lay Subsidy assessments, but three entries in the subsequently published Lynn record are for tin *in vasis*, which seems to mean that it was in plate, 'vessels', and presumably was pewter, not pure tin; if so, at only 2*d*. per pound, it was cheap stuff, but the value is consistent with later references: Owen, D. M. (ed.) 1984, 240 and 243; and see below.

16. Polychrome: Brown, D. H. 1997. Even when found in inland towns, the polychrome tends to be on tenements known to have had owners who were involved in the wine trade, e.g. John de Tyting in Winchester and John of Colehill in Oxford. Laverstock: Musty *et al.* 1969; seals: Jennings 1992, 19 and 41; dancers: Cherry 1985*b*, 17–18, suggests that dancing figures may represent feast-day music; face-jugs e.g. Rackham 1947, 19 and Pearce and Vince 1988, 38–42, 49, and 60. Rackham 1947, 23, identified a dignified, elderly head as that of Edward II, but Pearce and Vince 1988, 14 and 84, date it to the 1270s, so if anyone it would be Henry III. An occasional buckle has a crowned head which would not

have flattered a king who noticed it, but they are too few and too obscure to be taken as serious expressions of discontent: Goodall, I. H. 2002, 104–6, for an example. Jettons and tokens were also cheap and mass-produced, but many were produced from official coin dies, so must have been issued by authority, and would not express inflammatory ideas; the commonplace of an ape incomprehendingly following human behaviour seems as extreme as they get, even when produced by or for merchants and guilds: Mitchiner and Skinner 1983, pl. 71, nos. 34–6; Mitchiner 1988, 24–5.

17. The jug has been quite heavily restored, only one of the musicians being original: Dunning 1933, 130–2; Dunning suggested that it might be a French potter's *chef d'oeuvre*, made as annual tribute to a landlord, but that would not explain its being in Exeter. For conflicts in Exeter between citizens and cathedral, see Rigby and Ewan 2000, 292. For the jug, Allan and Timms 1996, 34–5. The two bishops inside the tower certainly have mitres and croziers, but apparently nothing else—no robes, let alone vestments. That the sentiment was anti-episcopal gets further support from the details of the spout, on the end of which is an animal's head clearly shown with a bridle, the reins represented by thin clay straps back to the jug. The animal's long ears suggest a donkey, a much lowlier creature than a horse despite its presence at Christ's birth and its role in carrying Him into Jerusalem. That a bishop should be riding or otherwise associated with a donkey would be derogatory, therefore. The vessel may be a little too early for its musicians to be subtle referents to the angel-minstrels carved in the cathedral, but building work would certainly have been going on there.

18. Three men were lucky to escape Dicoun's fate when arrested in a brewhouse with stolen goods that included three silver clasps. Jewellery was usually grouped with clothes and plate at a composite value in such cases: *Calendar of London Trailbaston Trials under the Commissions of 1305 and 1306*, 252, 254, 259, 267, 269, and 322.

19. Tyson 2000, 128, makes the points about distribution and contexts of use, and the analogy with polychrome pottery. See also Clark, J. 1983 for the London beakers, and Tait 1968 for complete examples. Eleanor of Castile was paying for glass that may have been of this sort; it was sold by a merchant of Palestine, but described as Venetian: Lightbown 1992, 59. Ludgershall: Henderson, J. 2000, 169–72; Old Sarum: Tyson 2001, 27–30; Rattray: Graves 1993.

20. Statute of Winchester: Brown, A. L. 1989, 93–4; wealth assessments in various towns (which did not take urban tenements and rentals into account): Cromarty and Cromarty 1993, 53 and 68–73; in 1327 only two Shrewsbury citizens would have met the criterion. Barron, C. M. 2002, 226–8, for London paying for knights rather than expecting its own citizens to fight, even though the implication of an early thirteenth-century custumal is that aldermen would lead the city in self-defence, and the fourteenth-century Midsummer Watch Ritual gave the same impression. Perhaps it is not mere coincidence that one of the objects found in the rubbish-pit that contained so much of the property of a wealthy Southampton citizen (e.g. Fig. 7.6) was a sword in perfectly serviceable condition: Harvey 1975, 79. See also Chapter 8.

21. Sumptuary legislation: Myers (ed.) 1969, 1153, no. 681, translated from the original French; Crouch 1992, 249–50; references in Hinton 1999; Lachaud 2002. Fear of 'impoverishment' was expressed e.g. in 1369: *Close Rolls 1369–74*, 34 and 114–16. The threat posed by imitation was expressed by Sir Henry Knighton in 1350, quoted by Hatcher and Barker 1974, 53.
22. For processions and pageants, Rubin 1992; Hanawalt and Reyerson 1994; Lindenbaum 1994; McRee 1994. Kermode 1998, 14, cites people who attended church 'three times a year and mock the priest'. Piers Plowman also sneered at gilt knives and sheaths, but as carried by priests. Saul 1986, 170, notes the ermine-lined robes owned by a Sussex knight seven years after the 1363 Act restricted ermine to royalty. Spectacular social rises in the fourteenth century show that sumptuary laws were not a barrier. The extreme case is the de la Poles, whose Hull origins were probably in the Rottenherring family, but that is the only example of quite such stinking fish. Army service was one route: Robert Salle was a Norfolk bondman when recruited in the 1340s, but died a knight, a wealthy landowner, and the captain of Norwich Castle when killed there in 1381 by a peasant mob, some of whose members may have known his origins: Fowler 1971, 10. For guilds, Rubin 1991; Giles 2000.
23. Jurkowski *et al.* 1998, 58–9, for the 1379 ranks.
24. State and status: Harding, A. 1993, 321; for discussion of whether sumptuary legislation is part of 'closure theory', Hinton 1999—anyone who has read Bourdieu will presumably appreciate the involvement of 'symbolic objects' in the concept.
25. Lewis, J. M. 1982*c*: the findspot may not reflect the status of the brooch's first owner, as the castle was not built until the fifteenth century, by the Mansel family. See also Lightbown 1992, 24–5 and 148; Cherry 1987*a*, no. 653, where it is suggested that the cameos are mid-thirteenth-century, reset into an early fourteenth-century brooch that they do not fit very well, which suggests a very mixed history.
26. Manchester brooch: Cherry 1987*a*, no. 651; Lightbown 1992, 148.
27. Plantagenet name and badges: Lightbown 1992, 268–70. Swan knights and the 1306 feast: Crouch 2002, 60–2. The swan as an allusion to both gluttony and pride can be seen in Chaucer's Monk's love of them: Biebel 1998, 17. Swans were both semi-domesticated and wild, one reason for their exclusiveness being that 'swanneries' for the former were seigneurial privileges, though catching the birds in them could be hazardous, and the latter could be hunted with falcons: Digby 1971, 50–1 and pl. 15. Edward I was already elderly in 1306, but unlike his predecessor Henry III remained militarily active and promoted a very different, martial image of himself: Binski 1999, 91–2.
28. Dunstable swan: Cherry 1969*b*; Cherry 1987*a*, no. 659; Lightbown 1992, 166; Steane 1993, 73. Gaimster, D. and Goodall 1999, 396, note a swan badge on a woman's brass and suggest that the Dunstable swan could have been a gift for a lady; the delicacy of its pin fitting certainly indicates that it was intended for light use. The Bohun swan was chained, Henry IV's was free: Mitchiner 1986, 201, and 122–5 for aristocratic badges generally. Parisian merchants: *Patent Rolls*, vol. 6, p. 218. The mark was a sum of 13*s.* 4*d*.

29. Even William II may have died by accident. One chronicler called de Montfort's death murder, not a battle wound: Carpenter 2003, 380. Faukes de Bréauté's brother was hanged in 1224, effectively a judicial murder, but for the 'crime' of breaking the convention that a castle should be surrendered when clearly unable to withstand a siege, to avoid the cost of undermining it and subsequently having to rebuild it; but the man was an alien mercenary, with no stake in the country.

30. *Records of the Household and Wardrobe, 1285–6*, 203; Parsons 1977, 11–12 and 81–6 (the queen was buying perfume, showing a sensitivity to odour that caused her well-known aversion to sea-coal, and may help to explain her purchases of earthen pots and urinals); Lightbown 1992, 59; Parsons 1995, 50–3 and 67; her table knives are important in showing that such things were getting known before the fourteenth century and a surge in Italian production: Good, D. F. 1983. For the coronet episode, Lightbown 1992, 123: the repair was effected in the year that the king's daughter was married, so she may even have been wearing it on her wedding-day when the event occurred. Edward I also spent lavishly on shrines, e.g. St Thomas's at Canterbury at a cost of £347. 1s. 1d., including many gemstones: Taylor, A. J. 1979.

31. Roberts (ed.) 1929; unfortunately the jewels were not described or valued in the treaty of 1312–13. Palgrave (ed.) 1836, vol. 3, p. 123 for some of Edward II's possessions.

32. Blackley and Hermansen (eds.) 1971, 149, 223, and 227.

33. *Patent Rolls s. a. 1348–50*, 202, and *1350–4*, 122; Brush 1984; *Memoranda Rolls 1326–7*, 27, no. 142. The royal treasure had been kept at Westminster, but in Edward I's time some of the clerics had purloined it.

34. Coins: Cook, B. 1987, 490–2; the Garter: Lightbown 1992, 245, 251, and 253–4; titles and ceremonies: Crouch 1992, 73 and 98. Crouch shows how 'symbolism of exclusiveness' developed a 'new language of power': ibid. 345; also id. 2002, 60–2 for the less formal Swan knights. Pilbrow 2002 for the similarly less formal Bath. Edward III seems particularly to have liked to see himself in animal allusions, principally the leopard, but also other brave creatures such as the bull and the lion: Shenton 2002. The domination phrase is Braudel's, cited by Burnett, J. 1990, 299.

35. *Black Prince's Register*, vol. 4, pp. 40–1, 66–70, 284, 297, 301–2, 333, 389, 402–3, 427, and 475. For his badges, Mitchiner 1986, 116–21. As ruler of Aquitaine, the Black Prince also issued gold coins, showing him uncrowned: Cook, B. 1987, nos. 619–20. Part and parcel of aristocratic hierarchy was the replacement of the free-for-all hastilude by the individuals' joust at tournaments, in which heralds could ensure that the adversaries were of appropriate status.

36. *Issues of the Exchequer, Henry III to Henry VI*, 170; Lodge and Somerville (eds.) 1937, nos. 90, 327, 463, 556, 557, and 715; Crouch 1992, 301–2; Goodman 1992, 49. Emery 2000, 399, cites some of Gaunt's building expenses, including £276 just for timbers for the Kenilworth hall roof; Johnson 2002, 139–42, considers the impact that the sight of the building would have had upon a visitor, but not the impact of the sight of its owner: see Steane 1993, 134–6; Woolgar 1999, 22 and 148–51. Gaunt is shown in a painting done approximately a century

after his death, but still expressive of the importance of dining in state: Hammond 1993, pl. 11. Tapestries, notably French ones, were especially sought-after because of new techniques and designs: Emery 2000, 440; Crowfoot et al. 2001, 69–72, for London fourteenth-century finds and other references; Digby 1971 for the Devonshire Hunting Tapestries of the 1430s/40s. Cantor 2001, 22–3, states that tapestry production was greatly increased because of belief that curtains prevented the entry of plague-bearing air through open windows, but he gives no reference, and window-glass and waxed linen cloth were in use at the wealth level that could afford textile hangings: Salzman 1952, 173–86. The SS collar may have been the first livery collar in Europe; the 'S' may have stood for 'Souvereigne', but perhaps not until Gaunt's son had become Henry IV: Lightbown 1992, 245–8; see also Chapter 8. Letters had been used in constructing brooches since at least the 1240s: ibid. 39, and cf. Henry III's messengers, Chapter 6. 'Plate' would not only have been in the hall, but in the chapel as altars, chalices, and the like. The east end of a chapel or church became the setting for the main altar in the thirteenth century, where the priest raised the chalice during the Eucharist; the dais end of a hall mirrored this physical setting, with the lord's cup as equivalent to the cleric's chalice—made visually explicit in the Luttrell Psalter: Camille 1998*b*, 89.

37. Dillon and Hope 1897.
38. London gifts: Nightingale 1995, 333—it is not stated whether these things were made by London goldsmiths, or were imports; 1396 gifts: Lightbown 1992, 69–70; New Year gifts: cf. Henry II, Chapter 6 above. The quotation is from *Sir Gawain and the Green Knight*: Barron, W. R. J. (ed.) 1974, 31. Rubin 1991, 138, notes gift-exchange as creating open-ended debts; wearing the gift could presumably imply an ongoing obligation, but there is a difference between a gift that is a bribe, one that shows largesse, and one that is so routine that it becomes part of someone's wages. An example of the last is provided by the household expenditure of the bishop of Salisbury in 1406–7, when he bought twelve gold rings at 3$s.$ each, twelve at 23$d.$, twenty-four at 17$\frac{1}{2}d.$, with nine silver-gilt at 9$d.$ and twenty-three at 8$d.$; he also bought some brooches and beads: Woolgar 1992, 422.
39. Richard's own badge was the hart, a word-play on 'rich-hart', which is shown together with the broom-pod on the diptych; his under-robe in the Westminster panel has the more formal rose with the letter 'R': Tudor-Craig 1987, no. 713; Gordon et al. 1997. The Westminster painting was full-size, and was meant to be left in place so that the king was 'present' even when absent: Binski 1999, 80–3; this may not have been an entirely new concept, as there is a record of Henry III having his seat in Windsor Castle hall painted with the figure of a king—but not therefore a representation of Henry himself—holding a sceptre, which suggests that the back of the chair would have carried a reminder of him when he was away: Mercer 1969, 45. Richard did not realize that alliances and badges could be used against him by the treacherous—'Ye were deceived through your double h[e]arts'; 'For one hart were lost a dozen hearts'. The sad story of the countess of Oxford's distribution of silver-gilt harts to rally support for Richard in 1399, not knowing that he was already dead, shows that not everyone deserted

him: Ailes 2002, 96. The hart could also have a religious meaning, hunting it being an analogy for the soul's pursuit of Christ. Richard's 'secret' visit is in *Issues of the Exchequer, Henry III to Henry VI*, 265.

Piers's image of the peacock is made despite the supposedly unputrefying flesh of the peacock being an analogue for the everlasting incorruptibility of Christ; he also said that the peacock has a harsh cry and tastes disgusting: Goodrich (trans.) 1959, 186–7. A peacock's feather was excavated in a fourteenth-century London waterfront deposit, with precious silks and other items for a rich household, quite possibly the royal Great Wardrobe: Egan 1998, 12 (and cf. the Black Prince's ostrich feather, above).

40. Campbell, M. 1987, no. 541.
41. Lightbown 1992, 129. While abroad and on pilgrimage, Henry Bolingbroke had been a buyer of jewellery in Germany, Italy, and Prague, which suggests personal interest: ibid. 41.
42. *Cal. Inq. Misc.*, vol. 7, no. 431.
43. Woolgar 1999, 171–5: Woolgar 1992 has no entries for the thirteenth century.
44. Nightingale 1995, 69–70; Keene 1999, 70.
45. Woolgar 1999, 95. Swabey 1999 shows the intricacies of social and economic intertwining of one widow's household, in which the primary boons were livery cloths and furs.
46. Given-Wilson 1991; *Cal. Inq. Misc.*, vol. 7, no. 41.
47. Hughes 1993, 82–8. One stone, oritis, or corinth, was believed to stop a woman from conceiving and to cause abortion, but was not forbidden despite Church teaching on such matters generally. The hawkstone was supposed to make a man attractive to a woman. Lucre: Goodrich (trans.) 1959, 76.
48. Deevey 1998, 13–14, for examples of the *Ave Maria* formula on brooches; Lightbown 1992, 342–3, for the possible Marian association with women. It was used e.g. by an archbishop of Canterbury on two of his rings, one of which he wore and one which he presented to a statue of Mary to symbolize his 'espousal' to her through his celibacy: Camille 1989, 239. For *Amor vincit omnia*, Clanchy 1983, 48–9. The phrase was well-enough known to appear in relief letters on a pottery jug from Strixton, Northamptonshire: Hall, D. N. 1974, 46–9; like 'Adam and Eve', it may have had no sinister implication in that context. Note the suggestion above that the Dunstable swan brooch may have been intended for a lady. The glass beakers from Italy have *Magister Alexandrinus me fecit*, where *magister* may imply a commissioner: Tait 1968, 150. Whereas the inscription on the Offham brooch, Chapter 6, seems like mere incompetence, the Cliffe Hill brooch is probably a deliberate mixing of French and Latin: Cherry 1981a; this occurs elsewhere in Sussex at Etchingham, for it was a conceit used on some late fourteenth-century memorial brasses to knights and others: Saul 1996, 155–6. If the analogy is valid, it is a pointer to the social level at which the inscribed ring-brooches were aimed.

The religious women in the *Canterbury Tales* were superficially devout, but their use of rosaries was as much to catch the eye as to aid concentration; one on the Prioress's arm was of coral, with green mounts; this sounds much like the way that St Apollonia wore hers in the Luttrell Psalter—the beads are her teeth wrenched out in torturing her, and her mouth is blood-red to show her suffering: Camille 1998b, 336; colour illustration: Backhouse 1989, pl. 16 (I had always 'read' this picture superficially, as mockery like Chaucer's of a nun's false coyness).

49. Lightbown 1992, 66–7, for behaviour; in more commercially minded Italy girls were encouraged to wear as much jewellery as they could, to attract a rich suitor. Thompson, M. W. 1995, 132–3 and 152–5, for French and English aristocratic halls, with John of Gaunt's Kenilworth one of the few first-floor English halls not contained within a tower-keep. Guildhalls, by contrast, were much more likely to be raised: Giles 2000, 59–60. Backhouse 1989, pl. 48, for the Luttrell Psalter scene—in which unfortunately any fastening in the centre of Sir Geoffrey's robe is obscured by his arm. Proper behaviour in the hall was encouraged by the many etiquette books of the period.

50. Egan and Pritchard 1991, 336–42. Misogynous attitudes were stated in fifteenth-century Italy, but whether they were more, or more extreme, than those in the rest of Europe, and whether extremes of male dress were an expression of them, is less clear: Hunt 1996, 219–23. Particoloured dress is well shown in a picture of four Irish mayors: Nolan and Simms (eds.) 1998, 73. What seems an early reference to bells is in a knight's 'reputed wife's' inventory of 1378, whose jewellery included a gilt collar with the letter 'N' repeated, hung with twenty-three 'coke-bells' as well as gilt buttons with the letter 'S' and gold buttons; as her name was Alice, and the knight's William de Windsor, the choice of letters seems random: *Cal. Inquisitions Misc.*, vol. 4, no. 17; cf. Lightbown 1992, 282–3. An eloquent rat was heard by Piers Plowman to advocate fitting bells to the gold chains and collars of London aldermen, to warn people that they were coming, which may be an allusion to an existing conceit: Goodridge (trans.) 1959, 67–8. Tin bells were also a Canterbury pilgrims' device, but usually had inscriptions round their bases: Mitchiner 1986, 72–4 and 131–2. In 'The Miller's Tale' Alison's purse picks up a common medieval allusion to its open mouth as a vagina: Camille 1998a, 64–5. This was occasionally made totally explicit by men who wore one with a knife thrust through it: Scott, M. 1986, pls. 13 and 24; she cites a mid-fourteenth-century moralist complaining of dissolute women following this practice when dressing as men at tournaments. See also Chapter 8.

51. Nelson 1980, 9 and *passim*; Piponnier and Mane 1997, 63–8; Egan and Pritchard 1991, 272–90; Ottaway and Rogers 2002, 2918–20; Biddle and Cook 1990, 571–80. 'Points' were also used to hold men's doublets to their hose: Crummy 1988, 12–13, where she shows that they begin to appear in Colchester towards the end of the fourteenth century. Silk and other laces worn round the neck are the origin of the word 'necklace'.

52. Norwich: Margeson 1993, 20–4 and 38–41; York: Ottaway and Rogers 2002, 28–31; York artisans: Swanson, H. 1989, 163: Swanson estimates that 20% of them made wills, and that 30% of those mention at least one piece of silver; Carlisle: Ferguson (ed.) 1893, 123–4; what was to happen to the rest of the goldsmith's tools is not stated, but it may have been axiomatic that they should go to his widow, or a partner.

53. Keene 1999 and Barron, C. M. 2000, 438–40, for summaries of magnates in London; Keene 2000, 201, for shops and 'selds' or bazaars in Cheapside; for the finds, Egan and Pritchard 1991, esp. 162–219 for all the mounts, including some heraldic ones and others that may be badges; Crowfoot *et al.* 2001; Cowgill *et al.* 1987; Grew and de Neergard 1988—heraldry also features prominently on the fourteenth-century scabbards. The Perth knife-handle may have local links to May festivities: Hall, M. A. 2001*b*, 182–7, who shows that the face is not obviously a 'green man', as plants are not sprouting from him; at least one leather sheath with embossed emblems from Perth is very similar to London pieces: Bogdan and Wordsworth 1978, 28. For purses and knives, see further Chapter 8.

54. The bone handles are discussed by Hall, M. A. 2001*b*, 176–7; see also MacGregor 2000*b*, 163, for one from Ludgershall Castle. Cowgill *et al.* 1987, 40–50, for London scabbard decoration.

55. Egan 1996 for 'shoddy' London goods and Keene 1996 for marks and Cheapside. Morris, C. A. 2000, 2261, makes the point that a mark might not be a maker's on many items, but an owner's, and might even be protective, to prevent the contents of something quite ordinary like a barrel from going off; see also Barber, J. 1981, 117, for wooden vessels at Threave Castle with a heart cut into them, a device adopted by the Douglas family—whereas a 'J' might be the maker's mark. Cloth was also marked, with a seal. Norwich jetton-brooch: Margeson 1993, 16; a number of brooches made from pennies are also known. Toys: Egan 1998, 281–3; id. 2001, 105–6; Lightbown 1992, 90–1, for elite playthings such as a gold windmill; Orme 1995 for children's culture.

The argument in this paragraph might seem partly to contradict what has been said above about earlier Londoners' range of choice, but then the aristocratic market was probably not so prominent.

56. For good-quality rural building at what seems likely to be a socially modest level, Grenville 1997, 129–33 and 151–2, and for a recent example, a late thirteenth-century aisled hall on an ordinary plot in Barrington, Cambridgeshire, see Oosthuizen 2002, 113; in reverse, moated sites might be separate but peasant-owned, not manorial. Wharram finds: Goodall, A. R. 1989; Westbury (also Tattenhoe): Mills, J. M. 1995. In general, Dyer 1989 and 1998*a*; Massschaele 1997, 38–60: peasant spending as a whole is reckoned to have been two-thirds of the Gross Domestic Product. Coins: Blackburn 1989. For lending, Postles 1996 and Bailey, M. 1998—the latter suggests that various factors after 1315 may have reduced capital availability and particularly affected richer peasants. Peasant values are extremely difficult; leisure was one, even though lords' complaints about peasant idleness may be exaggerated: Whittle 1998; Hatcher 1998. One man who lost a court case over whether he was a villein committed suicide, which shows depth of feeling about legal servility. Kitsikopoulos 2000, 248, has a 'model' which proposes that a relatively well-to-do peasant might have an annual surplus of only 7*s*. 7*d*. for expenditure on fripperies or extra food; most would have had far less. Inventories are few, but a particular custom applied to Wenlock Priory estates in Shropshire has led to records revealing very meagre fourteenth-century holdings: Mumford 1965.

57. Figures are irrecoverable, but Goldberg 1996 considers that 45% mortality is quite possible (including those who would have died in those years even without the Black Death); on its own, the 1348–50 outbreak might not have had such a long-lasting effect—there had been high mortality in 1315–22, but numbers seem to have been more or less made up by the 1340s. The later outbreaks may have reduced the population even further. For other summaries, see Hatcher 1994; Ormrod 1986.

58. Dumfries: Callander 1923–4, 160–1. Lindley 1996 and Platt 1996, 137–75, for summaries on art and church architecture; 'austere' Perpendicular architecture, like ideas such as the 'macabre' Dance of Death or the Three Living and the Three Dead had begun to appear before the Black Death's impact on labour and costs: Caciola 1996, 41–3. Magnate building would have been less affected if lords were prepared to pay higher rates to secure such labour as could be found: James, T. B. 1990, 110–24, for building in the 1350s at the Kennington, Savoy, Westminster, and Windsor palaces, largely financed by success in war. Their owners were not prepared to bide their time for things to improve, and, as shown above, their expenditure on jewellery grew rather than diminished. The latest results from dendrochronology show rural aristocratic and gentry housing falling off markedly after the first third of the fourteenth century, beginning to recover only after 1400; peasant and yeoman building, however, merely remained static over the second third of the century, resuming its increase in the final third; urban building actually increased over the Black Death years, possibly because of investment to attract tenants: Pearson 2002; Pearson's earlier study of Kent, 1994, 58, suggested a rural hiatus in the 1340s–1370s, which suggests exactly the sort of differences between regions that help to make overall wage and price fluctuations so difficult to establish. Donations to a variety of shrines is sometimes cited as evidence of Black Death concerns, but Sir Geoffrey Luttrell missed it by three years, yet spread his risks: see above.

59. Rushton 2002, 69–70, for a summary of poverty attitudes; Piers Plowman stressed the need only to help the genuinely needy. Dyer 1996 on the resentment felt to those who did not contribute to taxation, for which see Jurkowski *et al.* 1998, pp. xxxiv–xxxviii and 56–8; Goldberg 1996.

60. For magnate expenditure, see above. War in France had been profitable for individuals because of contracts, ransoms, and plunder, but when fortune swung the other way, expenditure of £1,100,00 between 1369 and 1381 had to be met by taxation: Sherborne 1977, Prestwich 1980, 194 and 200–4. In London, group expression was not only in relation to rank: the 1381 Revolt provided Londoners with an opportunity to set upon and kill immigrant Flemings, who were seen as aliens and outsiders: Pearsall 1997, 54–9; and see Chapter 8.

61. Thompson, M. W. 1998, 111, notes an increase in gate towers that could be used for muniment storage as well to improve a façade; for Bury, Aston 1994*a*, 27–32.

62. The 'Brenner debate', as it has become known, has been joined with almost no regard to the significance of physical evidence.

8. THE WARS AND THE POSIES

1. Hatcher 1996 for a synopsis, and for towns, Astill 2000*a*. On the changes in London deposits, Egan and Forsyth 1997, 215–16.
2. Spufford 1988, 321, 328–37, and 367–70; Nightingale 1995, 365–6. Scottish coins diverged for the first time from the English, being progressively debased, something that parliament prevented the king from practising regularly in England: Nicholson, R. 1977, 109–11. Blackburn 1989, 19, shows a decrease in coin finds of about two-thirds from 1351 to 1412, then to about four-fifths before a slight recovery after the mid-1460s. Subsequent records from e.g. South Ferriby: Cook, B. J. 1998, and Westbury: Ivens *et al.* 1995, 325–34, are broadly comparable. Numbers of coins may not reflect the numbers of transactions, i.e. a population reduced by half would in theory lead to a 50% reduction in coin loss if the same per-capita volume was maintained. The number of base-metal Venetian *soldini*, 'galley halfpence', suggests low-value trading in coin substitutes taking place; furthermore, adroit use of credit could maintain trade: Childs 1991.
3. 'Task orientation': Blanchard 1985; vessels: Lewis, J. M. 1978, 26–33. Norwich: Margeson 1993, 90–3; York: Ottaway and Rogers 2002, 2809–12; London has a few fragments: Egan 1998, 158–74, but fewer than Winchester, where they do not seem to appear before the fourteenth century: Biddle 1990, 947–59. A dump of clay moulds and waste has also been reported from Chester: *Past Uncovered* (Feb. 2003). The total value of commodities may have been quite low, however, reflecting low profit margins: Dyer 1991, 15–20.
4. Cherry 1987*a*, nos. 726–7; Lewis, J. M. 1978, no. 31, for the Gower jug. At manor-house level, metal vessels of all sorts were owned, even more in a castle: contrast the Pastons' Hellesdon with Fastolf's Caister: Bennett 1951, 98–9.
5. Exeter: Goodall, A. R. 1984*b*, 345; York: Ottaway and Rogers 2002, 2812; London: Egan 1998, 183–93. The poor survival of lead would be a big factor in these recovery rates, but the spoons, below, show that pewter can be preserved in the right conditions. Hatcher and Barker 1974, 42–59, and Homer 1991, 68–79, for summaries; the former cite inventories showing a range of vessel types separately itemized from the late fourteenth century onwards; again, the Pastons' holdings at Hellesdon are a case in point—two-dozen vessels, two basins and ewers, and two salts: Bennett 1951, 98–9.
6. e.g. London: Egan 1998, 244–52—fig. 194 has a figure with arms akimbo who might be making an obscene gesture—and Salisbury: id. 2001, 104–5. A stone mould for producing spoons is illustrated in Homer 1991, fig. 21. Further examples of pewter spoons were published recently from Ludgershall: Ashworth and Ellis 2000, 157–8. The London pewterers' guild used spoons in a dish as a badge: Mitchiner 1986, 211.
7. Cowgill *et al.* 1987, 26–32 and 51–2; Tymms (ed.) 1850, 1–2; Woolgar 1999, 157.
8. Tyson 2000; ead. 2002, 2828–9, for York; London: Keys 1998—at p. 219 she cites 'London glassez' at 4*d.* for six in 1444, but points out that these need not refer to drinking glasses; p. 225 for opaque white glass.

9. For this and the following paragraph, Pearce and Vince 1988 for London supplies generally and pp. 68–72 and 85–6 for Cheam whiteware biconical and small rounded beakers specifically; also Pearce 1992, 88–90. Stoneware: Gaimster, D. 1997, 84–9. Shipping: Harding, V. 1995, 160.

10. 'Sauce' bottles were being used in the fourteenth century, a few ending up as containers for coin hoards; a cook is clearly shown pouring from one in the Luttrell Psalter: Backhouse 1989, pl. 47. As with mortars used for pounding foodstuffs and flavourings, it is difficult to be sure how far down the social scale they were used: Hinton 2002, 99–100.

11. Beer: Harding, V. 1995, 156 and 158 for late fourteenth-century imports; Galloway 1998, 90, for London production after *c*.1400. The Venetian ambassador in *c*.1500 reported that beer and ale had to be experienced four or six times before they would be thought 'agreeable to the palate': Sneyd (ed.) 1848, 10. (Because beer could be stored, it was worth making in larger quantities, making its production more commercial and more likely to be a male activity than the domestic brewing of ale.) 'Measures' were to be served in London ale-houses in pewter pots to ensure fair practice: Hatcher and Barker (eds.) 1974, 68—it is more difficult to ensure a precise capacity in a ceramic pot without complex control of clay and kiln. Harding, V. 1995, 166, n. 28, hazards that the 'bakestones' in many cargoes were bricks or tiles for ovens or stoves, which might imply new cooking methods, but surviving examples of those are a bit later, which supports her favoured interpretation of them as flat pieces of terracotta or stoneware—perhaps like griddle flatstones. Barron, C. M. 1995, 11–17, for a brief summary of the Flemings' impact on other aspects of material culture. They were, of course, the first 'alien' group since the Jews, and suffered badly in 1381: Chapter 7; they seem to have been more acceptable in the fifteenth century, partly because of the religious factor: Bolton, J. L. (ed.) 1998, 8, 21, and 35–9; Barron, C. M. 1995. Jurkowski *et al.* 1998, 94–6, and 106 and 120–1 for acts in 1442, 1453, 1483, and 1487.

12. York: Jennings 1992, 29, for drinking vessels and alternative uses, 30–1 for the Yorkshire lobed cups, the equivalent of southern 'Tudor green', now known to be a misnomer, and other lobed cups, for which see Pearce and Vince 1988, 61 and 81; Vince 1985*a*, 72. Norwich: Jennings 1981, 32 and 109. Imports in southern England: Guttiérrez 2000, chapters 3 and 4; Exeter: Allan 1994, 20–3; Southampton: Brown, D. H. 2002, 34–40. Other aspects of material culture showed different sorts of regional difference, e.g. in buildings the 'cruck' frontier: Alcock 2002.

13. Bolton, J. L. (ed.) 1998, 20–1.

14. Sneyd (ed.) 1848, 11, 28–9, and 42–3; Oman 1979, 93; Cherry 1992, 68–70; *Calendar of Ancient Deeds*, vol. 3, D. 1278. The losses suffered by the Pastons when driven out of one of their manor-houses—an example of how violence was used to back a fairly spurious legal claim—are instructive in showing a knightly family's movable property: beds and bedding, kitchen equipment, a diamond ring owned by a friend, 'an unce of gold of Venice', 'a close glasse of yvery, a grete combe of yvery', and many clothes; they had stored things also in the church,

mainly arms and armour in the steeple, but also a purse and three gold rings, 'a coler of silver of the king's livery' (presumably an SS collar, like Baret's (below), though the Pastons had not done royal service for it, unless being in the royal law-courts a lot counted), and a gold coin, presumably in a chest in the body of the church: Gairdner (ed.) 1904, vol. 4, pp. 201–3.

15. Thame: Evans, J. *et al.* 1941; Cherry 1987*a*, no. 657. Fishpool: Cherry 1973; the number of gold coins in Fishpool is probably related to the numbers being minted, which at times in the 1460s was greater than those of silver: Mayhew 1995, 245. Cherry 2000 points to other hoard peaks in the equally difficult 1320s and 1390s.

16. Another long-lived type was the *fede* ring with clasped hands, first seen in the Lark Hill hoard, but to judge from examples in datable contexts still current in the fifteenth century, e.g. in gilt copper alloy from Norwich: Margeson 1993, 5. Murdoch 1991, no. 78, is a good example of a ring with hidden decoration. A Norwich manuscript of *c.*1400 shows a wedding ring worn over a glove, recorded as a standard practice: Swabey 1999, col. pl. 1; The ring is being placed on the lady's finger by her husband, not a priest, on the right hand, as Oman 1930, 15–17, contended: see Chapter 6. Lightbown 1992, 124, cites an early fifteenth-century English text on a bride having a ring on her finger for true love, a brooch on her breast for purity of heart and chastity, and a garland on her head for gladness and the dignity of the marriage sacrament.

17. The Poole ring actually has *Cans* for *Sans*: Cherry 1994*a*. See also the Fishpool heart-shaped brooch, below. As Col. pl. H shows, the known number of rings of all types is being greatly increased by reports to the Portable Antiquities Scheme (cf. also Col. pls. F.4–6).

18 For these and other inscriptions, Evans, J. 1931; Sandal: Goodall, A. R. 1983, 231: the excavation also yielded a pair of high-quality spurs with unusual hinged sides from a slightly earlier context: ibid. 252; *en bon an* is even on a ring found in the grave of a bishop of Hereford who died in 1474: Merewether 1846, 252, and on iconographic rings as well, i.e. it was not confined to secular circles, e.g. Murphy 1991, nos. 74–5. Myers 1959, 114, noted how Queen Margaret's gifts in 1452 were still 'nicely related to the precise rank and importance of the recipient'; she was giving gold bracelets as well as rings, silver collars, etc. Myers also pointed out that it was important for her to maintain her gifts to her dependants despite being strapped for cash, but she cut back on what she gave to her aristocratic 'friends' compared to her 1440s expenditure. Serjeants' rings: Evans, J. 1892, 11; Watts, J. 2002, 256–7, notes that their dress had become distinctive—a kind of uniform.

19. e.g. London, where the earliest is attributed to the fourteenth century: Murdoch 1991, 318–20. A single-letter seal was one of a group of three rings found recently at Wragby, Lincolnshire: Cherry 1981*b*. Seal-rings were often worn on the thumb, less often on the first finger: Dalton 1912, p. xxi. For the apparent disappearance of fob-like seals and their replacement by signet-rings towards the end of the fourteenth century, Tonnochy 1952, p. xxi; Rigold 1977, 324–5.

20. White, R. H. 1986, fig. 12, for the Stapleton ring; the Raglan ring was published by M. Redknap in *Treasure Annual Report for 1998–9*, no. 136. Johnson 2002,

87–8, is the most recent summary of the castle; he sees its design as 'facing two ways' in proclaiming its owner's identity as both Welsh and English—I can detect no such ambiguity in the ring; for an array of London gold rings, including a seal-ring, Platt 1978, colour pl. U, and others from e.g. Exeter: Goodall, A. R. 1984*b*, M 64.

21. Cherry 1973, 310, suggested that lack of French examples may mean that the iconographic type is specifically English. The use of English for Latin texts raises the question of Lollardy and the problems of Wyclif's translation of the Bible. 'As in God' is on a recent discovery at Fladbury, Worcestershire: Wise 1994. For *honour et joie*, see Cherry 1982*b*, including one from the tomb of an archbishop of York (d. 1423), and two on iconographic rings.

22. Godstow ring: Dalton 1912, no. 962; cynicism would allow it to be the sort of thing that a clerk like Absolon would have used to tempt a novice (see Chapter 7). See Dalton 1912, p. xvi, for the difficulties of rigid categorization. Paston letter: Barber, R. (ed.) 1993, 19; sending a ring as a token of affection during absence was commonplace, e.g. from a husband to his young wife in the Stonor letters, 1476: Myers (ed.) 1969, no. 708. For 'decade' rings, Oman 1930, 23 and no. 723, and another from Netley Abbey, Hampshire (a context that might seem to indicate a pre-Dissolution date, except that the monastery was converted into a mansion: Hare, J. 1993, 216–20): Dalton 1912, no. 788. There are a few fifteenth-century posy-rings with English inscriptions, e.g. Oman 1930, no. 631.

23. The Thorn reliquary was probably part of the French crown jewels: Lightbown 1992, 224–5. For locks as jewels and the London ring, Cherry 1973, 312–13; Murphy 1991, no. 116, and cf. no. 118 and the quotation of *c*.1530 that has 'my sovereign' as queen of the heart. For padlocks as a Lovell badge and fetterlocks as a Yorkist, Spencer 1990*a*, no. 183; Ailes 2002, 97; see Baret's will, below, for an inventory record. The gold 'lok' purchased for the earl of March with a gold brooch for £3. 6*s*. 8*d*. may have been another: Woolgar 1992, 597. March spent considerably more, £32, on a gold ring with a ruby and four diamonds, ibid. The term 'black letter' is used of late fourteenth- and fifteenth-century inscriptions which have letters so squeezed together as to be all but unreadable: Tonnochy 1952, p. xxix—unfortunately, it can be thought to refer to niello or black enamel inlay, which some inscriptions indeed have.

24. Cherry 1994*b*; Lightbown 1992, 216–17, and 185–6 for heart-brooches, which could even have witchcraft associations: Cherry 1973, 315; and see below, the Rocklea Sands and Norwich pendants. It is not always possible to tell from the inventories whether a phrase like 'harte of gold' means heart, or hart, like Richard II's, but will usually have been the former, and were often used as *ex votos*, e.g. at Archbishop Scrope's tomb, which was hung with seven silver legs and feet, four teeth and hearts, eight eyes and two hands: Richmond 1994, 187. For Richard III's boar, see below. The continuing importance of badge symbolism is shown in other media, such as the Devonshire Hunting Tapestries: Claxton 1988.

25. Clare cross: Tait 1976, no. 366; Lightbown 1992, 203—Lightbown's three chapters on pendants are fundamental; Fishpool cross: Cherry 1973, 313–14; Threave:

Caldwell 1981, 106–7; Rocklea Sands: Cherry 1983–4. The wearing of reliquaries by aristocrats was a noted late medieval trend, probably emphasizing personal devotion but also pride of possession: Richmond 1994, 198; for the 'good death', Aston 1994b, 207–9.

26. An early fifteenth-century manuscript shows the poet reading his work to a well-dressed audience, including some ladies with very high-necked collars and some with quite low-cut dresses. One of the men wears a hat like Grimston's (below), but with a brooch or badge in the middle, and other ornaments, and another has dangling pendants all across his shoulders with others dangling from his belt: Scott, K. L. 1996, no. 58; Scott, M. 1986, colour pl. 45. For toothpicks, etc., Lightbown 1992, 236–7; Campbell, M. 1990.

27. Paston letters: Barber, R. (ed.) 1993, 61–2. Fishpool: Cherry 1973, 311–16. Lightbown 1992, 198–9, for the Percy badge. Lightbown points out that the padlock could have been hung from a bracelet, of which a few mentions are made in fifteenth-century inventories: 1992, 297. They had been introduced into the coronation regalia in the twelfth century, presumably too long ago to have been the immediate influence: Rose 1992, 52.

28. Spencer 1985, 449–51, for the collar. Lightbown 1992, 198–9, for the Percy badge, and 243–4 for Grimston, whose hat was dark but had a very long 'bourrelet' for greater effect; his tunic was also fairly sombre, in keeping with fifteenth-century trends, but his shirt was light and embroidered. See Lightbown 1992, colour pls. 2, 40, and 82–9 for European examples; there are royal portraits of Edward IV, his queen, and Henry VII, colour pls. 43–4 and 71. The Donne portrait was painted by Hans Memling before 1482: McFarlane 1971, 2–11, and black-and-white illustrations; colour illustrations in Scott, M. 1986, pls. 114 and 115, and in Kenyon 2002, 19; see also National Gallery, London, website, Donne triptych; see below for the two virgin-martyrs.

29. A gold SS collar weighing $2\frac{1}{2}$ ounces cost £15. 6s. 8d. in 1452, but another weighing $1\frac{3}{4}$ ounces cost only £2. 8s. 7d., yet one weighing only 1 ounce cost the same amount; one of silver and 'tissewe', presumably silk, was only worth 6s. 8d., which is in line with one in silver-gilt valued at 10s. 10d. when Henry VI's regalia were itemized for the incoming Edward IV: Myers 1959, 118, 123, and 127; Palgrave (ed.) 1836, vol. 2, p. 252. Copper-alloy examples were excavated at a hospital site at Ospringe, Kent, in a fourteenth-century context: Goodall, A. R. 1979, no. 154. Baret's will is printed in Tymms (ed.) 1850, 15–44. Lightbown 1992, 381, also uses this source, and cites other examples. For a study of Bury wills and funeral instructions, Dinn 1992, and for some aspects of Baret's property and local metalwork, Campbell, M. 1998. Baret's motto was not inappropriate in a religious context, but individual monks should not have been owning personal property such as a girdle.

30. Tait (ed.) 1976, no. 373. Highway robbery was a constant problem, especially in times of weak government, but travel could not be avoided, as the need to attend in person to business in London and on estates was constant, as the Pastons show; hence the popularity of St Christopher. See also Sir Geoffrey Luttrell, Chapter 7. For 'angels', see Seaby 1985, 76; unlike cramp rings, which Henry VIII ceased to

bless because it seemed an out-of-date custom (Dalton 1912, p. xliv), royalty continued to bless 'angels' well into the seventeenth century.

31. It has no known connection with Baret, but a silver-gilt ring, Dalton 1912, no. 701, with a heart in relief, *IHC*, and other details was found in Bury—an interesting example of Suffolk willingness to embrace new ideas, the relief heart, whilst retaining traditional formulae; cf. Bury houses, below. Specification for Baret's tomb and chantry were very precise: Tymms (ed.) 1850, 19–21; he showed a good mix of ambition and care—the shrine's cross was to be 'as at Eye or else better' but 'at no greater cost than necessary'. For his tomb, James, M. R. 1930, 41, Duffy 1992, 307–8, and Aston 1994*b*, 224–7; for 'cadaver' tombs and their possible Lancastrian associations, Kemp, B. 1994, 210; they seem to be specifically English, perhaps symptomatic of a move away from some aspects of continental culture. They are also known as *transi* tombs because they mark the passage of life from earthly display to physical decay: Duffy 1992, 306–8. Lightbown 1992, 77, 218, and 381, for other 'fetirlock' references. The 'double' ring may mean that it was a 'gimmel'; Baret did not bequeath his to his widow, but to Dame Margaret Spurdance 'for a remembrance of old love virtuously [lest anyone should suspect otherwise] set at all times to the pleasure of God': Tymms (ed.), 1850, 36. Another of his bequests was 'my best gay cup of earth covered', which sounds as though it might be an example of stoneware mounted with a lid. He also left 'a great earthen pot that was my mother's', an act of filial piety that may not have much impressed the recipient.

32. Dalton 1912, no. 928, a gold ring from the Thames at Westminster, could be a case in point, since the Crown of Thorns has been identified on the exterior. 'John Godfrey' has not been traced in documents: Oman 1930, no. 218; ibid. 38 for memorial rings, and Dalton 1912, pp. li–lii for other bequests.

33. Duffy 1992, 266–98, for discussion of evidence from prayer-books and the like; Merewether 1846, 249–50, for the Hereford Tau and bell, symbols of St Anthony: Spencer 1990*a*, 45.

34. Fastolf had held the duke of Norfolk's pledge since 1452; he also owned some jewels of his own, but unfortunately John Paston could not value them, or Fastolf's two gold cups and ewers; he valued the silver plate at £1,615 on its weight in ounces, without regard to embellishment by gilding, enamelling, or other ornamentation, although he described it. Fastolf had another £382 worth of plate at his house at Bermondsey in London, and he had £2,643 in ready money, mostly deposited at Hulme Abbey, with some of the plate: Barber, R. (ed.) 1993, 98–9; inventories in Amyot 1827; 1452 record in Gairdner 1908, vol. 2, pp. 280–1. Palgrave 1836, vol. 2, pp. 31–2, 208, and 257 for Henry VI. Another very high price is the £160 which the king paid to the duke of Suffolk for a single item: Thompson, J. A. F. 1979, 535. For examples of Margery Paston's concerns about clothes, Barber, R. (ed.) 1993, 73, 123, and 166.

35. Devon 1837 (ed.), 403 and 451 for the George, and pp. 341, 386, 397, and 411 for other such pledges. John Paston's letter in 1467 about the gold, pearls, jewels, cloth of gold, silk, and 'a procession of lords and ladies better arrayed than anyone I ever saw or heard of' shows how a joust was an occasion for a display

of opulence—and of loyalty: Barber, R. (ed.) 1993, 140; Scott, K. L. 1996, colour pl. 14, for a particularly good illustration of what John Paston meant, and see also the Dunstable swan (Fig. 7.8).

36. Palgrave (ed.) 1836, vol. 1, pp. 393–9; one hopes for their sakes that the king was magnanimous to 'my lord Prince' and others who were reported for losing various pieces, 'and the King knowith it'; no wonder there are things for metal-detectorists to find. The Society of Antiquaries of London owns a portrait of Henry VII showing him with a jewel in his hat, clasps on his clothes, and rings on his fingers. Textile gifts: Piponnier and Mane 1997, 133; the prior of Worcester: Dyer 1998*b*, 59; a typical Paston example is a letter of 1450: 'Spend something of your own now, and get influence and friends "for on that hangs all the law and the prophets"': Barber, R. (ed.) 1993, 53. Similar Suffolk cynicism is expressed on a ring from Sudbury, *Amour fait moulte argent fait tout*, 'Love achieves much, money achieves the lot': Dalton 1912, no. 564.

37. Campbell, M. 2002; for the New College jewel, Cherry 1987*a*, no. 640: it has often been misidentified as the Founder's Jewel, not least by me: Hinton 1982*b*, 35, where I got the metal wrong as well; a fine example of a college mazer is Campbell, M. 1987, no. 722, one of several All Soul's College pieces recently loaned for display in the Ashmolean Museum. Drinking-horns also returned to fashion in these sorts of table display, e.g. ead. 1987, nos. 515–16. Two-handled pottery lobed cups may be loving-cups used similarly for communal drinking, see above. College founders often bequeathed their gloves or shoes to act as tangible, personal memorials.

38. Davies, R. T. (ed.) 1963, no. 63, for the poem—no. 64 is about a cock, some of whose attributes are compared to coral, jet, and stones. Note also Chaucer on burgesses, Chapter 7. For purses, see also Chapter 7. 'Ballock' is a male sexual referent: McDonald 2000; this inverts the normal allusion to a female vagina from a purse's open mouth: Hall, M. A. 2001*a*, 177–8. The word is entirely comprehensible in English, but wordplay jesting in French, e.g. *anel* (ring) being hilariously close to *agnel* (young lamb) and to *asniel* (young ass), as well as to anus, would have been lost on an Englishman, who thus became a butt for continental subtlety: Hines 1993*b*, 38–9. 'Kidney daggers': Ward Perkins 1940, 47–8 and pl. 9. Hines 1993*b*, 134–5, notes how Chaucer's Miller's weapons make inverted phallic reference to his (the Miller's) impotence.

39. Lightbown 1992, 320 and 336, for valuable suspension bars, Margeson 1993, no. 484, for a good example of one in base metal still on its fittings, from Norwich: I once identified these as drawer-handles, a plausible guess which I would not like to defend, though casket handles remain a possibility for some: 1990*b*, no. 2393; for others, from London: Egan and Pritchard 1991, 222–4; York: Ottaway and Rogers 2002, 2904–5; Guildford: Poulton and Woods 1984, fig. 42, 1. Chapes: Lightbown 1992, 333–4; mercury gilding was recognized by Hook *et al.* 1988; Kidwelly: Kenyon 2002, 17; Snargate: Kelly, D. B. 1987, 366. A copper-alloy example from Winchester has 'TC', 'Charnok', and a St Catherine figure, but Charnock is not a name known in the city until later than the chape's fifteenth-century date: Hinton 1990*b*, no. 1082, and p. 503 for references

to others from Guildford and Oxford; the former has a number of belt-ends identified as coming from book-straps thought to be from a friary library: Poulton and Woods 1984, 79. Scott, K. L. 1996, pls. 36 and 333, for illuminations. The Southampton clasp was shown to me by Dr Andrew Russel; for comparanda, Lightbown 1992, 299 and 302.

40. Spencer 1993, 8; Margeson 1993, 19, for other short lengths of chain from Norwich, one from a late medieval context; some London pieces are very hard to date closely: Egan and Forsyth 1997, 226–9. Increased production of gold wire with a draw-bar presumably underlay this sort of wirework: Campbell, M. 1991, 134, and cf. the draw-bar from Whithorn, Chapter 5.

41. Spencer 1993; 8, where he shows, however, that two letters on the Virgin and Child badge may indicate that it came from a continental shrine.

42. Mitchiner 1986, 229; id. 1988, 89–94 (sewing was a reversion to an earlier practice, before pins had become standard) and 227–9; Spencer 1998, 3–7, 20–1, 137, 142–5, 151, and 188–92; id. in Goodall 1984*a*, 337–9, for the Exeter Barbara; and id. in Williams, J. H. 1979 for a Henry VI badge from Northampton (Lincolnshire wills show bequests still being made to foster the cult in the 1530s: Hickman (ed.) 2001, p. xxvi). Duffy 1992, 3–4, sets out the terminological problems of 'popular' and 'traditional', the former falsely implying class divisions in beliefs, the latter seeming to preclude new ideas and practices such as are evidenced by the popularity of the cults of virgin-martyrs like Barbara: ibid. 169–74. See also Hutton 1994, 72–3, on popular and elite culture as a false dichotomy, and Richmond 1994, 190; 'formal' and 'informal' would probably be no better; similarly, Deetz's distinction (1996, 65) between folk—regional, conservative, rural—and popular—faddish, urban—is not really applicable to a society more integrated than America's in the seventeenth and eighteenth centuries.

43. Margeson 1993, 8; Dalton 1912, no. 757; Cherry 1982.

44. Margeson 1993, 24–8, no. 147; Egan and Forsyth 1997, 216–17; Murdoch 1991, 11; another fragment is from Northampton, identified as a button blank, but the cabled border shows that it is actually from a buckle-plate: Williams, J. H. 1979, 257–8, no. 88.

45. Evans, J. 1922, 129–30; Margeson 1993, 40–5; Ward Perkins 1940, 162–71; Egan and Forsyth 1997, 233. Purse-shaped badges, some with coins inside, were probably a way of wishing someone good fortune: Spencer 1998, 312–17. Spencer 1990, 45, for the Tau cross, the symbol of St Anthony, usually with a bell, on badges; also the Hereford bishop's ring, above. Denham: Greep 1982, 179. Matlaske pendant: Lightbown 1992, 204. Black enamel was noted on his cramp-ring by Baret, above.

46. Cherry 1997; Ailes 2002, 101. References include a rose of pure gold worth 40*s*. given by Queen Margaret to a knight of her household at New Year in 1452: Myers 1959, 127. Some 'roses' may be rosary references, however.

47. Richard III had 13,000 white boar badges made in 1483, to distribute in the north to create an affinity: Harriss, G. L. 1994, 21, and Spencer 1998, 278–99, who suggests that Richard's boar may have been wordplay, an anagram of the Latin *Ebor* for York, one of his strongholds: ibid. 289. The Gainsford badge was

found in 1996 at Chelsham, Surrey, near property which the family owned: Gaimster, D. and Goodall 1999. One of the very few extant livery badges in precious metal is the Percy family's, above; significantly it is still owned by the duke of Northumberland—there had come a time when it was better not to let such a thing out of the house. The portcullis had originally been a Beaufort badge, absorbed by marriage: Ailes 2002, 101. The royal pomegranate was Katherine of Aragon's device, and for a while there were badges that showed half a fruit and half a rose, to show her marriage to Henry VIII, e.g. in lead from London: Murdoch 1991, no. 265; presumably it would have been unwise to wear one after 1529 and the divorce proceedings. My colleague Jon Adams has noted a similar trend in the naming of royal ships, from the religious dedications such as *Grace Dieu*, in the early fifteenth century to the Tudors' secular *Peter Pomegranate* and *Mary Rose*: 2003, 97. Cap- and dress-hooks have been found in some numbers recently by metal-detectorists: Gaimster *et al.* 2002.

48. Lindenbaum 1994, 177–8; Attreed 1994, 223–4. Tolerance had its limits: in 1472 the king ordered the citizens of Coventry not to have 'retainers, liveries, signs or tokens of clothing', as potential symbols of disloyalty: Myers (ed.) 1969, no. 666.

49. A good example is provided by the surviving four sets of silver chains worn by the Exeter waits, musicians paid to play to those doing guard duty, during elections, festivals, and presumably also Guildhall feasts. They are made of links of openwork letters, 'X' and 'R', and have the city's badge in a miniature shield as a dangling centrepiece. Brownsword 1992, fig. 142: Allan and Timms 1996, 38–9.

50. A few London halberd badges are known: Mitchiner 1986, 244–5. My colleague Roger Leech has noted weapons in halls in Bristol: 2000, 3 and 7, and it is interesting that a late fifteenth-century picture of the city's sheriff shows him with a supporter bearing a pole-axe: Scott, K. L. 1996, no. 134 and ill. 484; furthermore, Bristol has two surviving ceremonial swords; one may be the earliest civic sword known, probably acquired in or soon after 1373, when the city was given its royal charter, and has the city's and the royal arms on its silver-gilt pommel: Blair, C. 1987, no. 15; the other has a silver-gilt hilt inlaid with the the city's and Richard II's arms, but is inscribed 'John Wells of London, Grocer and Mayor, to Bristol, gave this sword . . .': Oakeshott 1991, 168. (Wells was mayor of London in 1431–2. I do not know why a Londoner who came from Norfolk should have made a gift to Bristol.) For Perth, L. M. Blanchard in Holdsworth (ed.) 1987, 45; Yeoman 1995, 60–1; note also the late thirteenth-century Southampton sword, Chapter 7. Barron, C. M. 2002, 239–41, shows that in the late fifteenth-century London merchants were much more likely to be knighted than before, because artillery was making mounted men with shield and lance militarily redundant, though chivalry was still symbolically important. (Was any gentleman pictured with a pistol in the fifteenth century? Henry VIII owned elaborate hand-guns, but the earliest suggestion that it was a socially acceptable weapon seems to be the instruction manual of 1570, 'to teach noble men and gentlemen . . . to skirmish on horseback with pistolles': *OED*.)

The practice of storing weapons as a status symbol in halls did not prevent the space's gradually diminishing social importance; Leech notes how inventories show Bristol halls becoming anterooms rather than a house's social centre: 2000,

1 and 6–7, a process noted slightly earlier at Bury St Edmunds, perhaps because weapon storage for defence was less necessary in smaller, unwalled towns: Dymond 1998, esp. 281 (and note that John Baret left detailed instructions for the division of his house, showing no great concern for tradition), and in yeomen/lesser gentry houses in Kent: Pearson 1994, 95–6 134–6.

51. Hatcher and Barker 1974, 52, 54–9, 60, 63, and 80 for pewter and the feast; McCarthy and Brooks 1988, 450 for later Tudor Green and 388 for 'Cistercian', also Gaimster, D. and Nenk 1997, 177–8; for London cups and drinking-jugs: Pearce 1992, 24–5 and 88–90. Metal chafing-dishes: Lewis, J. M. 1973; id. 1978, 35; Margeson 1993, 78–9, where it is pointed out that some handles could be from cupboards, and Gaimster, D. and Nenk 1997, 177, for other pottery examples. The earliest British reference specific about usage that I have come across is in a priest's will of 1546, 'a chafron to heat water in': Lang, S. and McGregor (eds.) 1993, 2.

52. Gaimster, D. and Nenk 1997, 173–6, and see above; Egan 1998, 189–93, for London's pewter lids. Stoneware was more widespread by the late fifteenth century, with some found in Portsmouth: Fox, R. and Barton 1986, 82–3; Southampton: Brown, D. H. 2002, 35–6; Exeter: Allan 1984, 23; but still not necessarily in Bristol: Good, G. L. 1987, 36–7. Maiolica: Rackham 1939; Lewis, J. M. 1978, no. 26; Gaimster, D. (ed.) 1997; Brown, D. H. 2002, 33–4; some are shown containing a peacock's feather, cf. Chapter 7.

53. Holdsworth n.d.; Brown, D. H. 2002, 104–6 and 166–7; Tait 1968, no. 172—see nos. 173–5 for other complete examples.

54. Willmott 2002, 6, advises against assuming clear differentiation between the new soda-glass and potash-glass; the earlier use of lead seems to have ceased, until revival in the seventeenth century: Tait 1968, 133 and 142; York: Tyson 2002, 2822–3; Exeter: Charleston 1984, 259–60; Norwich: Haslam 1993, 97. For other new decoration and forms, and the beginnings of potash-glass in England, see Willmott 2002, 17, 22, 25, and 28. The earliest piece of porcelain in England seems to be a celadon bowl owned by Archbishop Warham, according to metal mounts on it which date it to before his death in 1532: Campbell, M. 2002, 138.

55. Finger-rings are being reported in large numbers by metal-detectorists, confirming the evidence of old finds that they were being worn by very many people. Their attribution to the fifteenth century depends on the relatively few that have come from coin-dated hoards or on which inscriptions allow some dating by letter form. Taxation: Jurkowski *et al.* 1998, 78–9, 84–5, 91–2, 94–6, 106, 115, and 120–1. Ownership taxes came to be expressed in terms of knights' fees and fractions of them, which may have sounded more acceptably traditional, like calling imposed levies 'benevolences'. As late as 1549, movable goods were taxable, but only when worth over £10: ibid. 148–9.

56. Statutes: Myers (ed.) 1969, nos. 602 and 692. Aliens: Bolton, J. L. (ed.) 1998, 38–9; even resident 'aliens' were accused of spending the money that they earned in England overseas. Bolton notes that, despite such feelings, resentment of the 'outsider' did not go further than violence; lives were not taken this time, though

Italians' houses were looted, as were the Flemings' again in 1517. Many continued to be goldsmiths and 'stone-slypers'. Pins: Caple 1991; British and continental products cannot be told apart, and the metals used are indistinguishable. Being very light and small, they often work their way down into layers underlying those in which they were originally deposited, so increases in quantities can be a little misleading; some of Winchester's dozen examples in the thirteenth century could be intrusive, as indeed could some of its eighteen in the fourteenth, but the number nevertheless more than doubles to thirty-nine in the fifteenth: Biddle and Barclay 1990. Also supposedly protected by legislation were purses, girdles, chafing-dishes, and other things already discussed above.

57. Newman, J. 1994; the hoard was found and dispersed in the 1940s, not fully recorded, so its precise date is unknown. Another hexagonal-frame brooch is the 'Glenlyon', which may have been in Scotland in the fifteenth century, but its origins are not known: Tait 1976, no. 369c. Lightbown 1992, 151–3, has the last high-status reference to the type in an early fifteenth-century inventory. Divergence of upper- and middling-class practice can also be seen in housing, above, and in the introduction of beer, which was provided in some aristocratic households but was not a taste promoted in them: above, and Woolgar 1999, 128.

58. Dalton 1912, no. 718 and Tait 1976, no. 371 for the Coventry ring; the 'Five Wounds' theme was another relatively new, fourteenth-century, cult of the later Middle Ages, stressing devotion to Christ, though with the Three Kings' names as an insurance: Evans, J. 1922, 127; Richmond 1994, 190. It was used on at least one memorial ring, in 1487: Oman 1930, 38. Cherry 1981*b* for the Wragby rings, one of which is the gold seal-ring mentioned above; Cherry 1991, nos. 9–10, for the Wiltshire toadstones. One recently published cap-hook has a cameo: Gaimster, D. *et al.* 2002, 169–73. 'New thinking' might also be shown if Oman was right that wedding-rings were worn on the right, not the left, hand until 1549, a change that he ascribed to rereading of classical texts rather than reliance upon commentaries: Oman 1930, 17; if correct, this seemingly small switch would in fact have been a profound break with long-held tradition. Later there was a switch to the thumb: Evans, J. 1892, 8. I have the impression that there was a trend away from iconography on seal-rings: Dalton 1912, no. 545 with Becket and the Virgin may be the last, but cf. Oman 1930, nos. 484–5. Evans, J. 1892, 18–19, for posy-ring texts.

59. St Augustine's: Thorn 1981, 76–80—other such rings from St Augustine's lack contexts: Sherlock and Woods 1988, 190–1. The maiolica altar vases ceased to be imported, and it is just possible that those found discarded in late 1540s/50s contexts at Southampton: Platt and Coleman Smith 1975, nos. 1173–4, and in Coventry: Woodfield 1981, 113 could indicate that Marian devotion was no longer openly declared after 1547. Decline in pilgrims' badges is hard to assess—note Henry VI's shrine, above.

60. The City's SS: Somers Cocks 1980, 52–3; Scarisbrick 1995, 36. More: Somers Cocks 1980, no. P3; Warham and Cranmer: Scarisbrick 1995, 24–5—Oman 1930, 2, noted that the latter's followed a sixteenth-century trend to heavier signet-rings, worn on the index finger; Gresham: Scarisbrick 1995, 32–3: the skull

at his feet took up the same *memento mori* theme. Edmund Lee of Bury St Edmunds recorded in 1535 that he wore a 'two wrethed ring of gold on my thumb', which could possibly have been such a two-hooped gimmel: Tymms (ed.) 1850, 125–6. Henry VIII's illegitimate son's jewellery was thick with Tudor royal insignia: *Camden Miscellany 3* (1855), 5.

61. Girdle-books: Tait 1976, 174–6; Somers Cocks 1980, 48–50; Scarisbrick 1995, 48. Tor Abbey coffin: Somers Cocks 1980, no. 13; Scarisbrick 1995, 51 (unlike Netley, above, Tor Abbey was left to decay, apart from adaptation of its gatehouse at the end of the sixteenth century). The *memento mori* trend may be a revival unconnected to the fifteenth-century 'cadaver' tombs, though underlying thoughts of mortality seem the same. Dame Alice sticks in the mind for having left an annuity to 'Mother Hubbarde': *Calendar of Ancient Deeds*, vol. 4, A.12173.

62. It is difficult to use many of the published wills as they are not well indexed: Hickman (ed.) 2001 is a very honourable exception. Somerset wills: Weaver (ed.) 1901–5; Shilton and Holworthy (eds.), 1925. Fourteenth-century wills do not refer much to jewellery, girdles about as often, and spoons and other plate a great deal more; fifteenth-century wills seem to have more jewellery bequests, with more description given; French 2001, 105–6, suggests differences between town and country, and between men and women, in Somerset, and notes the preponderance of wedding rings. The problems of the 1530s are well shown in the Bury St Edmunds wills; Edmund Lee had not sniffed the wind and sought burial in his namesake's abbey, with his parents, but two years later William Shepard dated his will by the years since the accession of Henry VIII as 'the supreme head' of the Church in England, forsaking 'the Bysshope of Romes usurped power'. Rosaries were still bequeathed, however, as by Alyce Harvey in 1538—though not by a former prioress who died in the same year: Tymms (ed.) 1850, 125–6, 132, and 136.

63. One difference between the old and new worlds is perceptively summarized in Lightbown's final two sentences: 'Perhaps the distinction between the two epochs is most suggestively conveyed by the uncut or simply faceted stones of the Middle Ages . . . [which] suggest the mysterious heavenly virtues that medieval man thought God had implanted in them for his protection or cure. Although belief in those stones survived . . . it is man who seems in Renaissance jewels to dominate the stones he has cut and set so skilfully': 1992, 385. Beyond this, the material culture of the whole of Britain concerned ideas about property and behaviour as well as about physical appearance.

Bibliography

ABDY, R. 2002, *Romano-British Coin Hoards*, Shire Archaeology 82, Princes Risborough: Shire Publications.
ABELS, R. 2003, 'Alfred the Great, the *micel hæthen here* and the viking threat', in Reuter (ed.): 265–79.
ABRAMS, L. 2001a, 'The conversion of the Danelaw', in Graham-Campbell *et al.* (eds.): 31–44.
—— 2001b, 'Edward the Elder's Danelaw', in Higham and Hill (eds.): 128–43.
ABULAFIA, D., M. FRANKLIN, and M. RUBIN 1992 (eds.), *Church and City 1000–1500*, Cambridge: Cambridge University Press.
ADAMS, J. 2003, *Ships, Innovation and Social Change. Aspects of Carvel Shipbuilding in Northern Europe 1450–1850*, Stockholm: Stockholm Studies in Archaeology 24/Stockholm Marine Archaeology Reports 3.
ADAMS, M. 1996, 'Excavation of a pre-Conquest cemetery at Addingham, West Yorkshire', *Medieval Archaeology*, 40: 151–91.
ADAMS GILMOUR, L. 1988, *Early Medieval Pottery from Flaxengate, Lincoln*, Archaeology of Lincoln 17-2, London: Council for British Archaeology.
ADDYMAN, P. V. and D. LEIGH 1973, 'The Anglo-Saxon village at Chalton, Hampshire: second interim report', *Medieval Archaeology*, 17: 1–25.
AGER, B. M. 1990, 'The alternative quoit brooch: an update', in Southworth (ed.): 153–61.
—— 1996, 'A late Roman buckle- or belt-plate in the British Museum, said to be from northern France', *Medieval Archaeology*, 40: 206–11.
—— 2001, review of Suzuki 2000, *Medieval Archaeology*, 45: 387–9.
AILES, A. 2002, 'Heraldry in medieval England: symbols of politics and propaganda', in Coss and Keen (eds.): 83–104.
AKEHURST, F. R. P. and S. C. VAN D'ELDEN 1997 (eds.), *The Stranger in Medieval Society*, Medieval Cultures Vol. 12, Minneapolis: University of Minnesota Press.
AKERMAN, J. Y. 1855a, *Remains of Pagan Saxondom*, London: J. R. Smith.
—— 1855b, 'Account of silver rings and coins discovered near Worcester', *Archaeologia*, 36: 200–2.
ALCOCK, L. 1992, 'From the dark side of the moon: western and northern Britain in the age of Sutton Hoo', in Carver (ed.): 205–15.
—— 1995, with S. J. Stevenson and C. R. Musson, *Cadbury Castle, Somerset. The Early Medieval Archaeology*, Cardiff: University of Wales Press.
—— 1998, 'From realism to caricature: reflections on Insular depictions of animals and people', *Proceedings of the Society of Antiquaries of Scotland*, 128: 515–36.
ALEXANDER, J. and P. BINSKI 1987 (eds.), *Age of Chivalry: Art in Plantagenet England 1200–1400*, London: Royal Academy of Arts/Weidenfeld & Nicolson.
ALLAN, J. P. 1984, *Medieval and Post-Medieval Finds from Exeter, 1971–1980*, Exeter Archaeological Reports Vol. 3, Exeter: Exeter City Council/University of Exeter.

ALLAN, J. P. 1994, 'Imported pottery in south-west England, c.1350–1550', *Medieval Ceramics*, 18: 45–50.
—— and S. TIMMS, 1996, *Treasures of Ancient Devon*, Tiverton: Devon Books.
ALLASON-JONES, L. 1996, *Roman Jet in the Yorkshire Museum*, York: Yorkshire Museum.
AMYOT, T. 1827, 'Letter . . . and a transcript of two rolls, containing an inventory of the effects belonging to Sir John Fastolf', *Archaeologia*, 21: 232–80.
ANDERTON, M. 1999 (ed.), *Anglo-Saxon Trading Centres: Beyond the Emporia*, Glasgow: Cruithne Press.
ANDRÉN, A. 1998, *Between Artefacts and Texts. Historical Archaeology in Global Perspective*, New York and London: Plenum Press.
ANDREWS, P. 1998 (ed.), *The Coins and Pottery from Hamwic*, Southampton Finds Vol. 1, Southampton: Southampton City Museums.
—— and K. PENN 1999, *Excavations in Thetford, North of the River, 1989–90*, East Anglian Archaeology Report 87.
ARCHER, S. 1979, 'Late Roman gold and silver hoards in Britain', in Casey (ed.): 29–65.
ARCHIBALD, M. M. 1982, 'Coins', in Coad and Streeten: 266–73.
—— 1984a, catalogue entries in Backhouse *et al.* (eds.).
—— 1984b, catalogue entries in Zarnecki *et al.* (eds.).
—— 1991a, catalogue entries in Webster and Backhouse (eds.).
—— 1991b, 'Anglo-Saxon and Norman lead objects', in Vince (ed.): 326–46.
—— 1992, 'Dating Cuerdale: the evidence of the coins', in Graham-Campbell (ed.): 15–20.
—— 1995a, 'The Middle Harling hoard', in Rogerson: 46–8.
—— 1995b, 'The medieval coins', in Blockley *et al.*: 950–1.
—— and B. J. COOK 2001, *English Medieval Coin Hoards: I, Cross and Crosslets, Short Cross and Long Cross Hoards*, London: British Museum Occasional Paper 187.
ARMSTRONG, P., D. TOMLINSON, and D. H. EVANS 1991, *Excavations at Lurk Lane, Beverley, 1979–82*, Sheffield Excavation Reports 1.
ARNOLD, C. J. 1982, *The Anglo-Saxon Cemeteries of the Isle of Wight*, London: British Museum Publications.
—— 1997, *An Archaeology of the Anglo-Saxon Kingdoms*, 2nd edn., London: Routledge.
—— 1998, 'Excavations at "Ty Newydd", Ynys Enlli (Bardsey Island), Gwynneth', *Archaeologia Cambrensis*, 147: 96–132.
—— and J. L. DAVIES 2000, *Roman and Early Medieval Wales*, Stroud: Sutton Publishing.
ARRHENIUS, B. 1985, *Merovingian Garnet Jewellery: Emergence and Social Implications*, Stockholm: Almqvist and Wiksell International.
ASHWORTH, M. and P. ELLIS 2000, 'Objects of lead, silver and pewter', in Ellis (ed.): 157–60.
ASTILL, G. G. 1978, *Historic Towns in Berkshire: An Archaeological Appraisal*, Reading: Berkshire Archaeological Committee Publication 2.
—— 1989, 'Medieval ceramics and urban development: a review', *Archaeological Journal*, 146: 559–70.

—— 2000a, 'Archaeology and the late medieval urban decline', in Slater (ed.): 214–34.
—— 2000b, 'General survey', in Palliser (ed.): 27–50.
ASTON, M. 1994a, 'Corpus Christi and Corpus Regni: heresy and the Peasants' Revolt', *Past and Present*, 143: 3–47.
—— 1994b, 'Death', in Horrox (ed.): 202–28.
ATKIN, M. and D. H. EVANS 2002, *Excavations in Norwich 1971–1978, Part III*, Gressenhall: East Anglian Archaeology Report 100.
—— A. CARTER, and D. H. EVANS 1985, *Excavations in Norwich 1971–1978, Part II*, Gressenhall: East Anglian Archaeology Report 26.
ATKIN, S., S. MARGESON, and S. JENNINGS 1985, 'The artefacts', in Atkin, M. *et al.*: 105–13, 130–9, and 179–218.
ATTREED, L. 1994, 'The politics of welcome: ceremonies and constitutional development in later medieval towns', in Hanawalt and Reyerson (eds.): 208–31.
AUSENDA, G. 1995 (ed.), *After Empire. Towards an Ethnology of Europe's Barbarians*, Woodbridge: Boydell Press.
AVENT, R. and V. I. EVISON 1982, 'Anglo-Saxon button brooches', *Archaeologia*, 107: 77–124.
AXBOE, M. 1999a, 'The year 536 and the Scandinavian gold hoards', *Medieval Archaeology*, 43: 183–5.
—— 1999b, 'Towards the Kingdom of Denmark', *Anglo-Saxon Studies in Archaeology and History*, 10: 109–18.
AYERS, B. 1987, *Excavations at St Martin-at-Palace Plain, Norwich, 1981*, Gressenhall: East Anglian Archaeology Report 37.
BABB, L. 1997, 'A thirteenth-century brooch hoard from Hambleden, Buckinghamshire', *Medieval Archaeology*, 41: 233–6.
BACKHOUSE, J. 1984, catalogue entries in ead. *et al.* (eds.).
—— 1989, *The Luttrell Psalter*, London: British Library.
—— 1991, catalogue entries in Webster and ead. (eds.).
—— D. H. TURNER, and L. WEBSTER 1984 (eds.), *The Golden Age of Anglo-Saxon Art 966–1066*, London: British Museum Publications.
BAILEY, M. 1998, 'Peasant welfare in England, 1290–1348', *Economic History Review*, 51: 223–51.
BAILEY, R. N. 1974, 'The Anglo-Saxon metalwork from Hexham', in Kirby (ed.): 141–68.
—— 1996, *England's Earliest Sculptors*, Publications of the Dictionary of Old English 5, Toronto: Pontifical Institute of Mediaeval Studies.
BAKER, P. *et al.* 1999 (eds.), *Theoretical Roman Archaeological Congress 98*, Oxford: Oxbow Books.
BARBER, B., D. BOWSHER, and K. WHITAKER 1990, 'Recent excavations of a cemetery of *Londinium*', *Britannia*, 21: 1–12.
BARBER, J. 1981, 'Wooden objects', in Good and Tabraham: 116–23.
BARBER, J. W. 1981, 'Excavations on Iona, 1979', *Proceedings of the Society of Antiquaries of Scotland*, 111: 282–380.
BARBER, M. 1992, *The Two Cities*, London: Routledge.
BARBER, R. 1993 (ed.), *The Pastons. A Family in the Wars of the Roses*, Woodbridge: Boydell Press.

BARCLAY, K., M. BIDDLE, and C. ORTON 1990, 'The chronological and spatial distributions of the objects' in Biddle (ed.): 42–74.
BARLOW, F. 1970, *Edward the Confessor*, London: Eyre & Spottiswoode.
—— 1986, *Thomas Becket*, London: Weidenfeld & Nicolson.
BARRATT, N. 1996, 'The revenue of King John', *English History Review*, 101: 835–55.
BARRON, C. M. 1995, 'Introduction: England and the Low Countries 1327–1477', in ead. and Saul (eds.): 1–28.
—— 2000, 'London 1300–1540', in Palliser (ed.): 395–440.
—— 2002, 'Chivalry, pageant and merchant culture in medieval London', in Coss and Keen (eds.): 219–41.
—— and N. SAUL 1995 (eds.), *England and the Low Countries in the Late Middle Ages*, Stroud: Sutton.
BARRON, W. R. J. 1974 (ed.), *Sir Gawain and the Green Knight*, Manchester: Manchester University Press.
BARTELOT, R. G. 1907, 'Fourteenth-century life in Dorset', *Proceedings of the Dorset Natural History and Archaeological Society*, 28: 96–106.
BARTLETT, R. 2000, *England under the Norman and Angevin Kings 1075–1225*, Oxford: Clarendon Press.
BASSETT, S. 1992 (ed.), *Death in Towns: Urban Responses to the Dying and the Dead, 100–1600*, Leicester/London: Leicester University Press.
—— 2000, 'How the West was won; the Anglo-Saxon take-over of the West Midlands', *Anglo-Saxon Studies in Archaeology and History*, 11: 107–18.
BATESON, J. D. and N. N. McQ. HOLMES 1997, 'Roman and medieval coins found in Scotland, 1988–95', *Proceedings of the Society of Antiquaries of Scotland*, 127: 527–61.
BATEY, C. E., J. JESCH, and C. D. MORRIS 1995 (eds.), *The Viking Age in Caithness, Orkney and the North Atlantic*, Edinburgh: Edinburgh University Press, paperback edn.
BAXTER, S. 2001, 'The earls of Mercia and their commended men in the mid eleventh century', in Gillingham (ed.): 23–46.
BAYLEY, J. 1992*a*, 'The metalworking evidence', in Milne and Richards: 59–66.
—— 1992*b*, *Anglo-Scandinavian Non-Ferrous Metalworking from Coppergate*, Archaeology of York 17/7, London: Council for British Archaeology.
—— 2000*a*, 'Glassworking in early medieval England', in Price (ed.): 137–42.
—— 2000*b*, 'Saxon glass working at Glastonbury Abbey', in Price (ed.): 161–88.
—— and R. DOONAN 2000, 'Glass manufacturing evidence', in Mainman and Rogers: 2519–28.
—— P. DRURY, and B. SPENCER 1984, 'A medieval mirror from Heybridge, Essex', *Antiquaries Journal*, 64: 399–402.
BAZELMANS, J. 2000, 'Beyond power. Ceremonial exchanges in *Beowulf*', in Theuws and Nelson (eds.): 311–75.
BEDWIN, O. 1996 (ed.), *The Archaeology of Essex: Proceedings of the Writtle Conference*, Chelmsford: Essex County Council.
BEHR, C. 2000, 'The origins of kingship in early medieval Kent', *Early Medieval Europe*, 9: 25–52.

BELL, M. 1977, 'Excavations at Bishopstone,' *Sussex Archaeological Collections*, 115: 1–299.

BENNETT, H. S. 1951, *The Pastons and Their England*, Cambridge: Cambridge University Press.

BERESFORD, G. 1987, *Goltho. The Development of an Early Medieval Manor*, London: English Heritage Archaeological Report 14.

BERESFORD, M. 1994, 'Old Lanyon, Madron: a deserted medieval settlement. The late E. Marie Minter's excavations of 1964', *Cornish Archaeology*, 31: 130–69.

BESLEY, K. 1993, 'Recent coin hoards from Wales', *British Numismatic Journal*, 63: 84–90.

BESTEMAN, J. C., J. M. BOS, D. A. GERRETS, H. A. HEIDINGA, and J. DE KONIG 1999, *The Excavations at Wijnaldum. Reports on Frisia in Roman and Medieval Times, Volume 1*, Rotterdam: Balkema.

BEUNINGEN, H. J. E. VAN, A. M. KOLDEWEIJ, and D. KICKEN 2001 (eds.), *Rotterdam Papers 12: A Contribution to Medieval Archaeology. Heilig en Proffan*, Cothen: Uitgever.

BIDDLE, M. 1961–2, 'The deserted medieval village of Seacourt, Berkshire', *Oxoniensia*, 26–7: 70–201.

——1983, 'The study of Winchester: archaeology and history in a British town, 1961–1983', *Proceedings of the British Academy*, 69: 93–136.

——1990, *Object and Economy in Medieval Winchester*, Winchester Studies 7, ii, Oxford: Clarendon Press.

——1976 (ed.), *Winchester in the Early Middle Ages: An Edition and Discussion of the Winton Domesday*, Winchester Studies 1, Oxford: Clarendon Press.

——and B. KJØLBYE-BIDDLE 1985, 'The Repton stone', *Antiquity*, 14: 233–92.

————2001, 'Repton and the "great heathen army", 873–4', in Graham-Campbell et al. (eds.): 45–96.

——and K. BARCLAY 1990, '"Sewing pins" and "wire"', in Biddle: 560–71.

——and L. ELMHIRST 1990, 'Sewing equipment', in Biddle: 804–17.

——B. KJØLBYE-BIDDLE, J. P. NORTHOVER, and H. PAGAN 1986a, 'Coins of the Anglo-Saxon period from Repton, Derbyshire: II', *British Numismatic Journal*, 56: 16–34.

——————1986b, 'Coins of the Anglo-Saxon period from Repton, Derbyshire: 1, a parcel of pennies from a mass-burial associated with the Viking wintering at Repton in 873–4', in Blackburn (ed.): 111–23.

BIEBEL, E. M. 1998, 'Pilgrims to table: food consumption in Chaucer's Canterbury Tales', in Carlin and Rosenthal (eds.): 15–26.

BIEK, L. 1994, 'Tin ingots found at Praa Sands, Breage, in 1974', *Cornish Archaeology*, 33: 57–70.

BIMSON, M. 1983, 'Coloured glass and millefiori in the Sutton Hoo grave deposit', in Bruce-Mitford: 924–44.

——1985, 'Dark-Age garnet cutting', *Anglo-Saxon Studies in Archaeology and History*, 4: 125–8.

——and I. C. FREESTONE 2000, 'Analysis of some glass from Anglo-Saxon jewellery', in Price (ed.): 131–5.

BINSKI, P. 1999, 'Hierarchies and orders in English royal images of power', in Denton (ed.): 74–93.
BINSKI, P. and W. NOEL 2001 (eds.), *New Offerings, Ancient Treasures: Studies in Medieval Art for George Henderson*, Stroud: Sutton Publishing.
BINTLIFF, J. and H. HAMEROW 1995 (eds.), *Europe Between Late Antiquity and the Middle Ages*, Oxford: British Archaeological Reports International Series 617.
BIRBECK, V. and R. J. C. SMITH, forthcoming, *The Origins of Mid Saxon Southampton: Excavations at the Friends Provident St Mary's Stadium, 1998–2000*, Salisbury: Wessex Archaeology.
BIRCH, W. DE G. 1885–99, *Cartularium Saxonicum*, 3 vols., London: Whiting.
BIRD, N. DU Q. 1996, 'Medieval episcopal rings from Somerset and Dorset', *Somerset and Dorset Notes and Queries*, 34: 3–9.
BLACKBURN, M. A. S. 1989, 'What factors govern the number of finds found on an archaeological site?', in Clarke and Schia (eds.): 15–24.
—— 1991a, 'Aethelred's coinage and the payment of tribute', in Scragg (ed.): 156–69.
—— 1991b, 'Coinage and currency under Henry I: a review', *Anglo-Norman Studies*, 13: 49–81.
—— 1994a, 'A variant of the seventh-century "York" group of shillings found in Lincolnshire', *Numismatic Chronicle*, 154: 204–8.
—— 1994b, 'Coinage and currency', in King (ed.): 145–205.
—— 1996, 'Hiberno-Norse and Irish Sea imitations of Cnut's *Quatrefoil* type', *British Numismatic Journal*, 66: 1–20.
—— 1998, 'The London mint in the reign of Alfred', in Blackburn and Dumville (eds.): 105–23.
—— 2000, 'Danish silver penny ("sceat")', in Perry: 168–9.
—— 2001, 'Expansion and control: aspects of Anglo-Scandinavian minting south of the Humber', in Graham-Campbell *et al.* (eds.): 125–42.
—— 2003, 'Alfred's coinage in context', in Reuter (ed.): 199–217.
—— 1986 (ed.), *Anglo-Saxon Monetary History: Essays in Memory of Michael Dolley*, Leicester University Press.
—— and M. J. BONSER 1990, 'A Viking-Age silver ingot from near Easingwold, Yorkshire', *Medieval Archaeology*, 34: 149–50.
—— C. COLYER, and M. DOLLEY 1983, *Early Medieval Coins from Lincoln and its Shire*, Archaeology of Lincoln 6-1, London: Council for British Archaeology.
—— and H. PAGAN 1986, 'A revised check-list of coin hoards from the British Isles, c.500–1100', in Blackburn (ed.): 291–314.
—— and D. N. DUMVILLE 1998 (eds.), *Kings, Currency and Alliances: History and Coinage of Southern England in the Ninth Century*, Woodbridge: Boydell Press.
BLACKLEY, F. D. and G. HERMANSON 1971 (eds.), *The Household Book of Queen Isabella of England, 1311–12*, Edmonton: University of Alberta Classical and Historical Studies Vol. I.
BLACKMORE, L. 2001, 'The imported and non-local Saxon pottery', in Gardiner: 192–207.
—— D. BOWSHER, R. COWIE, and G. MALCOLM 1998, 'Royal Opera House', *Current Archaeology*, 158: 60–3.
BLAIR, C. 1987, catalogue entry in Alexander and Binski (eds.).

BLAIR, J. 1995, 'Anglo-Saxon pagan shrines and their prototypes', *Anglo-Saxon Studies in Archaeology and History*, 8: 1–28.

—— 1996, 'The minsters of the Thames', in id. and Golding (eds.): 5–28.

—— and B. E. CRAWFORD 1997, 'A late-Viking burial at Magdalen Bridge, Oxford?', *Oxoniensia*, 62: 135–43.

—— and B. GOLDING 1996 (eds.), *The Cloister and the World: Essays in Medieval History in Honour of Barbara Harvey*, Oxford: Clarendon Press.

—— and N. RAMSAY 1991 (eds.), *English Medieval Industries. Craftsmen, Techniques, Products*, London and Rio Grande: Hambledon Press.

BLAKE, E. O. 1962 (ed.), *Liber Eliensis*, London: Royal Historical Society.

BLANCHARD, I. 1985, 'Industrial employment and the rural land market', in Smith (ed.): 227–75.

—— 1996, 'Lothian and beyond: the economy of the "English empire" of David I', in Britnell and Hatcher (eds.): 23–45.

BLINKHORN, P. 1999, 'Of cabbages and kings: production, trade, and consumption in middle-Saxon England', in Anderton (ed.): 4–23.

—— 2000, 'The pottery', in Cooper: 98–104.

—— and B. DIX 1991, 'A sherd of medieval pottery with a roller-stamped inscription from Flore, Northamptonshire', *Northamptonshire Archaeology*, 23: 107–9.

BLOCKLEY, K., M. BLOCKLEY, P. BLOCKLEY, S. S. FRERE, and S. STOW 1995, *Excavations in the Marlowe Car Park and Surrounding Areas*, Archaeology of Canterbury 5, Canterbury: Canterbury Archaeological Trust.

BLUNT, C. E. 1986, 'Anglo-Saxon coins found in Italy', in Blackburn (ed.): 159–69.

BODDINGTON, A. 1996, *Raunds Furnells: The Anglo-Saxon Church and Churchyard*, London: English Heritage Archaeological Reports 7.

BOGDAN, N. Q. and J. W. WORDSWORTH 1978, *The Mediaeval Excavations at the High Street, Perth, 1975–76*, Perth: Perth High Street Archaeological Committee.

BOLTON, J. L. 1996, '"The world upside down": plague as an agent of economic and social change', in Ormrod and Lindley (eds.): 17–78.

—— 1998 (ed.), *The Alien Communities of London in the Fifteenth Century. The Subsidy Rolls of 1440 and 1483–4*, Stamford: Paul Watkins/Richard III and Yorkist History Trust.

BOLTON, W. F. 1979, *Alcuin and Beowulf*, London: Edward Arnold.

BONNER, G., D. ROLLASON, and C. STANCLIFFE 1989 (eds.), *St Cuthbert, His Cult and His Community to A.D. 1200*, Woodbridge: Boydell Press.

BOON, G. C. 1959, 'A bronze spur from the Thames at Kingston', *Antiquaries Journal*, 39: 95.

—— 1986, *Welsh Hoards 1979–1981*, Cardiff: National Museums and Galleries of Wales.

—— 1994, 'The coins', in Quinnell and Blockley: 164–5.

BOOTH, J. 1998, 'Monetary alliance or technical co-operation? The coinage of Berhtwulf of Mercia (840–852)', in Blackburn and Dumville (eds.): 63–103.

—— 2000, 'Northumbrian coinage and the productive site at South Newbald ("Sancton")', in Geake and Kenny (eds.): 83–97.

BOOTH, P. A. 1997, 'King Alfred versus Beowulf: the re-education of the Anglo-Saxon aristocracy', *Bulletin of the John Rylands University Library*, 79: 41–66.

BOSSY, J. 1983 (ed.), *Disputes and Settlements. Law and Human Relations in the West*, Cambridge: Cambridge University Press.
BOULTON, D'A. J. D. 1998, 'Heralds and heraldry', in Szarmach et al. (eds.): 354.
BOURKE, C. 1995 (ed.), *From the Isles of the North: Early Medieval Art in Ireland and Britain*, Belfast: Her Majesty's Stationery Office.
BOYLE, A. 2001, 'Excavations in Christ Church Cathedral graveyard', *Oxoniensia*, 66: 337–68.
——D. JENNINGS, and S. PALMER 1998, *The Anglo-Saxon Cemetery at Butler's Field, Lechlade, Gloucestershire. Volume 1: Prehistoric and Roman Activity and Anglo-Saxon Grave Catalogue*, Thames Valley Landscapes, Vol. 10: Oxford Archaeological Unit.
BRADLEY, J. 1988 (ed.), *Settlement and Society in Medieval Ireland. Studies Presented to F. X. Martin, o.s.a.*, Kilkenny: Boethius Press.
——and M. GAIMSTER 2000, 'Medieval Britain and Ireland in 1999', *Medieval Archaeology*, 44: 235–54.
BRADY, C. 1979, '"Weapons" in *Beowulf*: an analysis of the nominal compounds', *Anglo-Saxon England*, 8: 79–141.
BRANDON, P. 1978 (ed.), *The South Saxons*, Chichester: Phillimore.
BREDEHOFT, T. A. 1996, 'First-person inscriptions and literacy in Anglo-Saxon England', *Anglo-Saxon Archaeology and History*, 9: 103–10.
BREEZE, A. 1998, 'Pictish chains and Welsh forgeries', *Proceedings of the Society of Antiquaries of Scotland*, 128: 481–4.
BRENAN, D. F. M. 1994, 'Medieval pottery', in Murphy: 75–6.
BRENAN, J. 1991, *Hanging Bowls and Their Contexts*, Oxford: British Archaeological Reports British Series 220.
BRITNELL, R. and J. HATCHER 1996 (eds.), *Progress and Problems in Medieval England: Essays in Honour of Edward Miller*, Cambridge: Cambridge University Press.
BRITNELL, W. J. 1990, 'Capel Maelog, Llandrindod Wells, Powys: excavations 1984–87', *Medieval Archaeology*, 34: 27–96.
BROOKS, N. P. 1978, 'Arms, status and warfare in late Saxon England', in Hill (ed.): 81–104.
——1996, 'The administrative background to the Burghal Hidage', in Hill and Rumble (eds.): 128–50.
——and J. A. GRAHAM-CAMPBELL 1986, 'Reflections on the Viking-Age silver hoard from Croydon, Surrey', in Blackburn (ed.): 91–110.
BROWN, A. L. 1989, *The Governance of Late Medieval England 1272–1461*, London: Edward Arnold.
BROWN, D. H. 1995, 'Pottery and late Saxon Southampton', *Proceedings of the Hampshire Field Club and Archaeological Society*, 50: 127–52.
——1997, 'The social importance of imported medieval pottery', in Cumberpatch and Blinkhorn (eds.): 95–112.
——2002, *Pottery in Medieval Southampton c.1066–1510*, York: Council for British Archaeology Research Report 133.
BROWN, M. P. 1991, catalogue entries in Webster and Backhouse (eds.).
——2001, 'Mercian manuscripts? The "Tiberius" group and its historical context', in ead. and Farr (eds.): 279–90.
——and C. A. FARR 2001 (eds.), *Mercia. An Anglo-Saxon Kingdom in Europe*, London and New York: Leicester University Press.

BROWN, R. A. 1988 (ed.), *Anglo-Norman Studies X, Proceedings of the Battle Conference 1987*, Woodbridge: Boydell Press.
—— H. M. COLVIN, and A. J. TAYLOR 1963, *The History of the King's Works: The Middle Ages*, 2 vols., London: HMSO.
BROWN, W. 1894 (ed.), *Yorkshire Lay Subsidies*, Yorkshire Archaeological Society Record Series 16.
BROWNSWORD, R. and J. HINES 1993, 'The alloys of a sample of Anglo-Saxon great square-headed brooches', *Antiquaries Journal*, 73: 1–10.
—— and E. E. H. PITT 1985, 'Some examples of medieval domestic flatware', *Medieval Archaeology*, 29: 15–25.
BRUCE-MITFORD, R. 1974, *Aspects of Anglo-Saxon Archaeology: Sutton Hoo and Other Discoveries*, London: Victor Gollancz.
—— 1975, *The Sutton Hoo Ship-Burial, Volume 1, Excavations. Background, the Ship, Dating and Inventory*, London: British Museum.
—— 1978, *The Sutton Hoo Ship-Burial, Volume 2, Arms, Armour and Regalia*, London: British Museum.
—— 1983, ed. A. Care Evans, *The Sutton Hoo Ship-Burial, Volume 3, Late Roman and Byzantine Silver, Hanging-Bowls, Drinking Vessels, Cauldrons and Other Containers, Textiles, the Lyre, Pottery Bottle and Other Items*, London: British Museum.
—— 1993, 'Late Celtic hanging-bowls in Lincolnshire and South Humberside', in Vince (ed.): 45–70.
—— 1997, ed. R. J. Taylor, *Mawgan Porth: A Settlement of the Late Saxon Period on the North Cornish Coast*, London: English Heritage Archaeological Report 13.
—— and K. EAST 1983, 'Drinking-horns, maplewood bottles and burr-wood cups', in Bruce-Mitford: 316–47.
BRUGMANN, B. 1997, 'The role of continental artefact-types in sixth-century Kentish chronology', in Hines *et al.* (eds.): 37–50.
BRUNS, D. 2003, *Germanic Equal Arm Brooches of the Migration Period*, Oxford: British Archaeological Reports International Series 1113.
BRUSH, K. 1984, 'The *Recepta Jocalium* in the wardrobe book of William de Norwelle, 12 July 1338 to 27 May 1340', *Journal of Medieval History*, 10: 249–70.
BUCKTON, D. 1986, 'Late tenth- and eleventh-century cloisonné enamel brooches', *Medieval Archaeology*, 30: 8–18.
—— 1989, 'Further examples of late tenth- and eleventh-century cloisonné enamel brooches', *Medieval Archaeology*, 33: 153–6.
—— 1991, 'Enamelled disc brooch', in Vince (ed.): 144–5.
—— and T. A. HESLOP 1999 (eds.), *Studies in Medieval Art and Architecture Presented to Peter Lasko*, Stroud: Alan Sutton Publishing.
BUDNY, M. 1999, 'The *Biblia Gregoriana*', in Gameson (ed.): 237–84.
BU'LOCK, J. D. 1960, 'The Celtic, Saxon and Scandinavian Settlement at Meols in Wirral', *Transactions of the Historic Society of Lancashire and Cheshire*, 112: 1–28.
BURNELL, S. and E. JAMES 1999, 'The archaeology of Conversion on the continent in the sixth and seventh centuries', in Gameson (ed.): 83–106.
BURNETT, A. 1996, 'The Roman gold hoard', in Rawlings and FitzPatrick: 19.
BURNETT, J. 1990, review, *Economic History Review*, 43: 298–9.
BUTLER, L. A. S. 1964, 'Minor medieval monumental sculpture in the East Midlands', *Archaeological Journal*, 121: 111–53.

BUTLER, L. A. S. 1987, 'Domestic building in Wales and the evidence of the Welsh laws', *Medieval Archaeology*, 31: 47–58.
CACIOLA, N. 1996, 'Wraiths, revenants and ritual in medieval culture', *Past and Present*, 152: 5–45.
CALDWELL, D. H., G. EWART, and J. TRISCOTT 1998, 'Auldhill, Portencross', *Archaeological Journal*, 155: 22–81.
CALLANDER, J. G. 1923–4, 'Fourteenth-century brooches and other ornaments in the National Museum of Antiquities of Scotland', *Proceedings of the Society of Antiquaries of Scotland*, 58: 160–84.
CAMERON, E. A. 2000, *Sheaths and Scabbards in England A.D. 400–1100*, Oxford: British Archaeological Reports British Series 301.
CAMERON, E. A. 1998 (ed.), *Leather and Fur: Aspects of Early Medieval Trade and Technology*, London: Archetype Publications.
—— and V. FELL 2001, 'The remarkable survival of organic remains', in Filmer-Sankey and Pestell: 204–7.
CAMILLE, M. 1989, *The Gothic Idol: Ideology and Image Making in Medieval Art*, Cambridge: Cambridge University Press.
—— 1992, *Image on the Edge: The Margins of Medieval Art*, London: Reaktion Books.
—— 1998a, *The Medieval Art of Love. Objects and Subjects of Desire*, London: Laurence King Publishing.
—— 1998b, *Mirror in Parchment. The Luttrell Psalter and the Making of Medieval England*, London: Reaktion Books.
CAMPBELL, A. 1962 (ed.), *The Chronicle of Aethelweard*, Nelson's Medieval Texts, London: Nelson.
CAMPBELL, E. 1996a, 'Trade in the Dark-Age West; a peripheral activity?', in Crawford (ed.): 79–91.
—— 1996b, 'Copper-alloy ornamental fitting', in Schlesinger and Walls: 136–8.
—— 1997, 'The hand-built Dark Age pottery', in Hill: 358.
—— 1997a, 'The early medieval glass', in Hill: 297–314.
—— 1997b, 'The Dark Age ceramics', in Hill: 315–22.
—— 1999, *Saints and Sea-Kings: The First Kingdom of the Scots*, Edinburgh: Canongate.
—— 2000, 'A review of glass vessels in western Britain and Ireland A.D. 400–800', in Price (ed.): 33–46.
—— and A. LANE 1989, 'Llangors: a tenth-century royal crannog in Wales', *Antiquity*, 63: 675–81.
—— —— 1993a, 'Excavations at Longbury Bank, Dyfed, and early medieval settlement in south Wales', *Medieval Archaeology*, 37: 15–77.
—— —— 1993b, 'Celtic and Germanic interaction in Dalriada: the seventh-century metalworking site at Dunadd', in Spearman and Higgitt (eds): 52–63.
CAMPBELL, J. 1992, 'The impact of the Sutton Hoo discovery on the study of Anglo-Saxon history', in Kendall and Wells (eds.): 79–101.
—— 2000, 'Some agents and agencies of the late Anglo-Saxon state', in id. (ed.): 201–26.
—— 2000 (ed.), *The Anglo-Saxon State*, London/New York: Hambledon and London.
CAMPBELL, M. 1987, catalogue entries in Alexander and Binski (eds.).

—— 1988, 'The Shrewsbury bowl and an escutcheon of John, Duke of Bedford', *Antiquaries Journal*, 68: 312–4.
—— 1990, 'A small knife-shaped toiletry implement', *Antiquaries Journal*, 70: 467.
—— 1991, 'Gold, silver and precious stones', in Blair and Ramsay (eds.): 107–66.
—— 1998, 'Medieval metalworking and Bury St Edmunds', in Gransden (ed.): 69–80.
—— 2002, 'Medieval founders' relics: royal and episcopal patronage at Oxford and Cambridge colleges', in Coss and Keen (eds.): 125–42.
CANT, R. 1991, 'The medieval city of St Andrews', supplement to *Archaeological Journal*, 148: 7–12.
CANTOR, N. F. 2001, *In the Wake of the Plague. The Black Death and the World It Made*, London: Simon & Schuster UK (Pocket Book 2002 edn.).
CARLIN, M. and J. T. ROSENTHAL 1998 (eds.), *Food and Eating in Early Medieval Europe*, London and New York: Hambledon Press.
CARPENTER, D. A. 2003, *The Struggle for Mastery: Britain 1066–1284*, London: Penguin Books.
CARR, R. D., A. TESTER, and P. MURPHY 1988, 'The mid Saxon settlement at Staunch Meadow, Brandon', *Antiquity*, 62: 371–7.
CARRINGTON, P. 1994, *Chester*, London: Batsford/English Heritage.
CARSON, R. A. G. and C. M. KRAAY 1978 (eds.), Scripta Nummaria Romana: *Essays Presented to Humphey Sutherland*, London: Spink.
CARVER, M. O. H. 1980, 'Medieval Worcester. An archaeological framework', *Transactions of the Worcestershire Archaeological Society*, 3rd series 7.
—— 1998, *Sutton Hoo: Burial Ground of Kings?*, London: British Museum.
—— 2001, 'Why that? Why there? Why then? The politics of early monumentality', in Hamerow and MacGregor (eds.): 1–22.
—— 1992 (ed.), *The Age of Sutton Hoo*, Woodbridge: Boydell Press.
CASEY, P. J. 1979 (ed.), *The End of Roman Britain*, Oxford: British Archaeological Reports British Series 71.
—— 1989, 'Coin evidence and the end of Roman Wales', *Archaeological Journal*, 146: 88–93.
CAVINESS, M. H. 1984, 'Stained glass', in Zarnecki *et al.* (eds.): 135–45.
CAZEL, F. A. 1974–5 (ed.), *Roll of Divers Accounts for the Early Years of the Reign of Henry III . . .* , London: Pipe Roll Society, NS 44.
—— and A. P. CAZEL 1976–7 (eds.), *Rolls of the Fifteenth of the Ninth Year of the Reign of Henry III . . .* , London: Pipe Roll Society, NS 45.
CESSFORD, C. 1996*a*, 'Exogamous marriages between Anglo-Saxons and Britons in seventh-century northern Britain', *Anglo-Saxon Studies in Archaeology and History*, 9: 49–52.
—— 1996*b*, 'Jewellery and the Gododdin poem', *Jewellery Studies*, 7: 57–62.
CHALLIS, C. E. 1977, 'Debasement: the Scottish experience in the fifteenth and sixteenth centuries', in Metcalf (ed.): 171–96.
CHANEY, W. A. 1970, *The Cult of Kingship in Anglo-Saxon England*, Manchester: Manchester University Press.
CHARLES-EDWARDS, T. M. 1998, 'Alliances, godfathers, treaties and boundaries', in Blackburn and Dumville (eds.): 47–62.
—— 1999, 'Anglo-Saxon kinship revisited', in Hines (ed.): 171–204.

CHARLES-EDWARDS, T. M. 2000, 'Food, drink and clothing in the Laws of Court', in id. *et al.* (eds.): 319–37.
—— 2001, 'Wales and Mercia, 613–918', in Brown and Farr (eds.): 89–105.
—— M. E. OWEN, and P. RUSSELL 2000 (eds.), *The Welsh King and his Court*, Cardiff: University of Wales Press.
CHARLESTON, R. J. 1984, 'The glass', in Allan: 258–78.
CHERRY, J. 1969*a*, 'A ring-brooch from Waterlooville, Hampshire', *Medieval Archaeology*, 13: 224–6.
—— 1969*b*, 'The Dunstable swan jewel', *Journal of the British Archaeological Association*, 32: 38–53.
—— 1973, 'The medieval jewellery from the Fishpool, Nottinghamshire, hoard', *Archaeologia*, 104: 307–22.
—— 1980, 'A thirteenth-century bronze buckle from Stow, Buckinghamshire', *Records of Buckinghamshire*, 22: 137.
—— 1981*a*, 'A silver ring-brooch from Cliffe Hill, Lewes', *Sussex Archaeological Collections*, 119: 221–2.
—— 1981*b*, 'A hoard of rings found at Wragby', *Lincolnshire Archaeology and History*, 16: 82–3.
—— 1982*a*, 'The Talbot casket and related late medieval leather caskets', *Archaeologia*, 107: 131–40.
—— 1982*b*, 'A medieval gold ring from Horncastle, Lincolnshire', *Lincolnshire Archaeology and History*, 17: 83.
—— 1983, 'A medieval gold ring found at Hart, County Durham', *Archaeologia Aeliana*, 11: 315–6.
—— 1983–4, 'A late medieval love jewel', *Jewellery Studies*, 1: 45–7.
—— 1984*a*, 'A medieval gold ring from High Deverill, near Warminster', *Wiltshire Archaeological and Natural History Magazine*, 79: 238.
—— 1984*b*, 'A Romanesque bronze bowl from Fotheringhay, Northamptonshire', *Antiquaries Journal*, 67: 367–8.
—— 1985*a*, 'Comment: the medieval brooches', in Shoesmith (ed.): 21–4.
—— 1985*b*, 'Sex, magic and Dr Gerald Dunning', *Medieval Ceramics*, 9: 5–20.
—— 1985*c*, 'The ring grave', in Wise: 4–5.
—— 1987*a*, catalogue entries in Alexander and Binski (eds.).
—— 1987*b*, 'Recent medieval finds from Lincoln; a Romanesque cast copper-alloy buckle with figural scenes and a bronze buckle', *Antiquaries Journal*, 67: 367–8.
—— 1989, 'Symbolism and survival: medieval horns of tenure', *Antiquaries Journal*, 69: 111–18.
—— 1991, 'Rings', in Saunders and Saunders (eds.): 40–6.
—— 1992, *Medieval Craftsmen. Goldsmiths*, London: British Museum Press.
—— 1994*a*, 'The inscribed ring', in Watkins: 69.
—— 1994*b*, *The Middleham Jewel and Ring*, York: Yorkshire Museum.
—— 1997, 'The Farnham pin', *Antiquaries Journal*, 77: 388–90.
—— 2000, ' "Treasure in earthen vessels": jewellery and plate in late medieval hoards', in Tyler (ed.): 157–74.
—— 2001, 'The ring', in Archibald and Cook: 8.
—— and J. GOODALL 1985, 'A twelfth-century gold brooch from Folkingham Castle, Lincolnshire', *Antiquaries Journal*, 65: 471–2.

——and M. HENIG 2000, 'Seals', in Ellis (ed.): 157–9.
CHIBNALL, M. 1986, *Anglo-Norman England 1066–1166*, Oxford: Blackwell.
——1999, *The Debate on the Norman Conquest*, Manchester: Manchester University Press.
CHILDS, W. R. 1991, ' "To oure losse and hindrance": English credit to alien merchants in the mid fifteenth century', in Kermode (ed.): 68–98.
——1999, 'The perils, or otherwise, of maritime pilgrimage to Santiago de Compostela', in Stopford (ed.): 123–43.
CHURCH, S. D. 1999, *The Household Knights of King John*, Cambridge: Cambridge University Press.
CIGGAAR, K. 1987, 'Byzantine marginalia to the Norman Conquest', *Anglo-Norman Studies*, 9: 43–63.
CLANCHY, M. T. 1983, 'Law and love in the Middle Ages', in Bossy (ed.): 47–68.
——1993, *From Memory to Written Record. England 1066–1307* (2nd edn.), Oxford: Blackwell Publishers.
——1998, *England and its Rulers, 1066–1272*, Oxford: Blackwell Publishers.
CLARK, C. 1979, 'Battle c.1110: an anthroponymist looks at an Anglo-Norman New Town', *Proceedings of the Battle Conference II*: 21–41.
CLARK, J. 1983, 'Medieval enamelled glasses from London', *Medieval Archaeology*, 27: 152–6.
——1995 (ed.), *Medieval Finds from Excavations in London: 5. The Medieval Horse and its Equipment, c.1150–c.1450*, London: HMSO.
——1989, *From* Londinium *to* Lundenwic, London: Museum of London.
CLARKE, H. and A. CARTER 1977, *Excavations in King's Lynn 1963–1970*, Society for Medieval Archaeology Monograph Series 7.
——and E. SCHIA, 1989 (eds.), *Coins and Archaeology*, Oxford: British Archaeological Reports International Series 556.
CLAXTON, A. 1988, 'The sign of the dog: an examination of the Devonshire Hunting Tapestries', *Journal of Medieval History*, 14: 127–79.
CLAYTON, M. 1990, *The Cult of the Virgin Mary in Anglo-Saxon England*, Cambridge Studies in Anglo-Saxon England 2, Cambridge: Cambridge University Press.
CLEAL, R. M. J. 2000, 'Worked skeletal material', in Young: 173–6.
CLOSE-BROOKS, J. 1982, *Dark Age Sculpture*, Edinburgh: National Museum of Antiquities of Scotland.
——1986, 'Excavations at Clatchard Craig, Fife', *Proceedings of the Society of Antiquaries of Scotland*, 116: 117–84.
CLOUGH, T. H. McK. 1973, 'A small hoard of William I type I pennies from Norwich', *British Numismatic Journal*, 43: 142–3.
COAD, J. G. and A. D. F. STREETEN 1982, 'Excavations at Castle Acre Castle, Norfolk, 1972–1977: country house and castle of the Norman earls of Surrey', *Archaeological Journal*, 139: 138–301.
COATSWORTH, E. 1989, 'The pectoral cross and portable altar from the tomb of St Cuthbert', in Bonner *et al.* (eds.): 287–300.
——1998, 'Cloth-making and the Virgin Mary in Anglo-Saxon literature and art', in Owen-Crocker and Graham (eds.): 8–25.
——2001, 'The embroideries from the tomb of St Cuthbert', in Higham and Hill (eds.): 292–306.

COATSWORTH, E. and M. PINDER 2002, *The Art of the Anglo-Saxon Goldsmith*, Woodbridge: Boydell Press.

COGGINS, D., K. J. FAIRLESS, and C. E. BATEY 1983, 'Simy Folds: an early medieval settlement site in Upper Teesdale, Co. Durham', *Medieval Archaeology*, 27: 1–26.

COLGRAVE, B. and R. A. B. MYNORS 1969 (eds.), *Bede's Ecclesiastical History of the English People*, Oxford: Clarendon Press.

COOK, A. and C. E. BATEY 1994, 'The bone comb', in Potter and Andrews: 122–4.

COOK, B. 1987, catalogue entries in Alexander and Binski (eds.).

COOK, B. J. with R. CAREY and K. LEAHY, 1998, 'Medieval and early modern coin finds from South Ferriby, Humberside,', *British Numismatic Journal*, 68: 95–118.

COOPER, N. J. 2000, *The Archaeology of Rutland Water*, Leicester: Leicester Archaeology Monograph 6.

COPPACK, G. 1987, 'Saxon and early medieval pottery', in Beresford: 134–69.

CORRADINI, R., M. DIESENBURGER, and H. REIMITZ 2003 (eds.), *The Construction of Communities in the Early Middle Ages. Texts, Resources and Artefacts*, Leiden/Boston: Brill.

COSS, P. R. 1995, 'The formation of the English gentry', *Past and Present*, 147: 38–64.

—— 2002, 'Knighthood, heraldry and social exclusion in Edwardian England', in Coss and Keen (eds.): 39–68.

—— and M. KEEN 2002 (eds.), *Heraldry, Pageantry and Social Display in Medieval England*, Woodbridge: Boydell Press.

—— and S. D. LLOYD 1992 (eds.), *Thirteenth-Century England IV*, Woodbridge: Boydell Press.

COURTNEY, P. 1990, 'Medieval coinage', in Britnell: 59–60.

—— 1997, 'The tyranny of constructs: some thoughts on periodisation and change', in Gaimster and Stamper (eds.): 9–24.

—— 1998, 'Pottery and metalwork', in Jones: 163–80.

COWGILL, J., M. DE NEERGARD, and N. GRIFFITHS 1987, *Medieval Finds from Excavations in London: 1. Knives and Scabbards*, London: HMSO.

COWIE, R. 2000, '*Londinium* to *Lundenwic*: early and middle Saxon archaeology in the London region', in Haynes *et al*. (eds.): 174–205.

—— 2001, 'London', in Hill and Cowie (eds.): 87–9.

COX, A. 1997, 'The artefacts' in Moloney and Coleman: 740–67.

—— 2000, 'The artefacts', in Perry: 113–49.

CRAMP, R. 1975, 'Anglo-Saxon sculpture of the Reform period', in Parsons (ed.): 184–99.

—— 1986, 'Northumbria and Ireland', in Szarmach (ed.): 185–201.

CRAWFORD, B. E. 1987, *Scandinavian Scotland*, Leicester: Leicester University Press.

—— 1996 (ed.), *Scotland in Dark Age Britain*, St John's House Papers 6, Aberdeen: Scottish Cultural Press.

CRAWFORD, S. 1993, 'Children, death and the afterlife in Anglo-Saxon England', *Anglo-Saxon Studies in Archaeology and History*, 6: 83–91.

CRICK, J. 2000, 'Women, wills and moveable wealth in pre-Conquest England', in Donald and Hurcombe (eds.): 17–37.

CROCKETT, A. 1996, 'Excavations at Montefiore New Halls of Residence, Swaythling, Southampton, 1992', *Proceedings of the Hampshire Field Club and Archaeological Society*, 51: 5–58.

CROMARTY, D. and R. CROMARTY 1993, *The Wealth of Shrewsbury in the Early Fourteenth Century. Six Local Subsidy Rolls 1297 to 1322: Text and Commentary*, Shrewsbury: Shropshire Archaeological and Historical Society.

CROSS, J. E. 1986, 'Towards the identification of Old English literary ideas—old workings and new seams', in Szarmach (ed.): 77–89.

CROUCH, D. 1992, *The Image of Aristocracy in Britain, 1000–1300*, London: Routledge.

—— 2002, 'The historian, lineage and heraldry', in Coss and Keen (eds.): 39–68.

CROWFOOT, E. 2001, 'The textiles', in Filmer-Sankey and Pestell: 207–12.

—— F. PRITCHARD, and K. STANILAND 2001, *Medieval Finds from Excavations in London: 4. Textiles and Clothing c.1150–c.1450*, Woodbridge: Boydell Press.

CRUMMY, N. 1988, *Colchester Archaeological Report 5: The Post-Roman Small Finds From Excavations in Colchester 1971–85*, Colchester: Colchester Archaeological Trust.

CUMBERPATCH, C. G. and P. W. BLINKHORN 1993 (eds.), *Not so Much a Pot, More a Way of Life*, Oxford: Oxbow Monographs 83.

CURLE, A. O. 1923, *The Treasure of Traprain. A Scottish Hoard of Roman Silver Plate*, Glasgow: Maclehose, Jackson.

—— 1924, 'A note on four silver spoons and a fillet of gold found in the nunnery at Iona, etc.', *Proceedings of the Society of Antiquaries of Scotland*, 58: 102–11.

CURNOW, P. 1985, 'The Roman coins', in West: 76–81.

DALTON, O. M. 1912, *Franks Bequest Catalogue of the Finger Rings Early Christian, Byzantine, Teutonic, Medieval and Later . . .* , London: British Museum.

DANIELL, C. 1997, *Death and Burial in Medieval England, 1066–1550*, London: Routledge.

—— 2002, 'Conquest, crime and theology in the burial record: 1066–1200', in Lucy and Reynolds (eds.): 241–54.

DARK, K. R. 1994, *Civitas to Kingdom: British Political Continuity 300–800*, Leicester: Leicester University Press.

—— 2000, *Britain and the End of the Roman Empire*, Stroud: Tempus Publishing.

DARK, P. 2000, *The Environment of Britain in the First Millennium A.D.*, London: Duckworth.

DASTON, L. and K. PARK 1998, *Wonders and the Order of Nature, 1150–1750*, New York: Zone Books.

DAVENPORT, P. 1999, *Archaeology in Bath. Excavations 1984–1989*, Oxford: British Archaeological Reports British Series 284.

DAVIDSON, H. R. E. 1992, 'Royal graves as religious symbols', *Anglo-Saxon Studies in Archaeology and History*, 5: 25–32.

—— and L. WEBSTER 1967, 'The Anglo-Saxon burial at Coombe (Woodnesborough), Kent', *Medieval Archaeology*, 11: 1–41.

DAVIES, R. R. 1987, *Conquest, Coexistence and Change: Wales 1063–1415*, Oxford: Clarendon Press.

—— 1994, 'The peoples of Britain and Ireland 1100–1400; I. Identities', *Transactions of the Royal Historical Society*, 6th series, 4: 1–20.

DAVIES, R. T. 1963 (ed.), *Medieval English Lyrics: A Critical Anthology*, London: Faber & Faber.

DAVIES, W. 1977, *An Early Welsh Microcosm. Studies in the Llandaff Charters*, London: Royal Historical Society, 36.

——1990, *Patterns of Power in Early Wales*, Oxford: Clarendon Press.

DAVIES, W. S. 1920 (ed.), *De Invictionibus*, London: Y Cymmrodor 30.

DAVIS, C. R. 1992, 'Cultural assimilation in the Anglo-Saxon royal genealogies', *Anglo-Saxon England*, 21: 23–36.

DAWSON, M. 2002, 'The copper-alloy objects', in Sparey-Green: 254–9.

DEAN, J. M. 1991 (ed.), *Six Ecclesiastical Satires*, Kalamazoo: Medieval Institute Publications.

DECAENS, J. 1971, 'Un nouveau cimitière du haut moyen âge en Normandie, Hérouvillette (Calvados)', *Archéologie Médiévale*, 1: 1–187.

DEETZ, J. 1996, *In Small Things Forgotten. An Archaeology of Early American Life*, New York: Anchor.

DEEVEY, M. B. 1998, *Medieval Ring Brooches in Ireland. A Study of Jewellery, Dress and Society*, Bray: Wordwell, Monograph Series 1.

DENNISON, E. P. 1999 (ed.), *Conservation and Change in Historic Towns: Research Directions for the Future*, York: Council for British Archaeology Research Report 122.

——and G. G. SIMPSON 2000, 'Scotland', in Palliser (ed.): 715–37.

DENTON, J. 1999 (ed.), *Orders and Hierarchies in Late Medieval and Renaissance Europe*, Basingstoke: Macmillan.

DESHMAN, R. 1976, '*Christus rex et magi regis*; kingship and christology in Ottonian and Anglo-Saxon art', *Frühmittelalterliche Studien*, 10: 367–405.

DETSICAS, A. 1981 (ed.), Collectanea Historica. *Essays in Memory of Stuart Rigold*, Maidstone: Kent Archaeological Society.

DEVON, F. 1837 (ed.), *Issues of the Exchequer . . . Henry III to Henry VI Inclusive*, London: John Murray.

DICKINSON, T. M. 1982, 'Fowler's Type G penannular brooches reconsidered', *Medieval Archaeology*, 26: 41–68.

——1993, 'Early Saxon saucer brooches: a preliminary overview', *Anglo-Saxon Studies in Archaeology and History*, 6: 11–44.

——1999, 'An Anglo-Saxon "cunning woman" from Bidford-on-Avon', in Karkov (ed.): 359–64.

——and H. HÄRKE 1992, *Early Anglo-Saxon Shields*. London: Society of Antiquaries *Archaeologia* 110.

——and G. SPEAKE 1992, 'The seventh-century cremation burial in Asthall Barrow, Oxfordshire', in Carver (ed.): 95–130.

DIGBY, G. W. 1971, *The Devonshire Hunting Tapestries*, London: Her Majetly's. Stationery Office.

DILLON, VISCOUNT and W. H. ST J. HOPE 1897, 'Inventory of the goods and chattels belonging to Thomas, Duke of Gloucester, and seized in his castle at Pleshey . . .', *Archaeological Journal*, 54: 275–308.

DINN, R. 1992, 'Death and reburial in late medieval Bury St Edmunds', in Bassett (ed.): 151–69.

DOBINSON, C. S. and S. DENISON 1995, *Metal Detecting and Archaeology in England*, London and York: English Heritage/Council for British Archaeology.

DODWELL, C. R. 1973–4, 'Losses of art in the Middle Ages', *Bulletin of the John Rylands Library of Manchester*, 56: 74–92.
——1982, *Anglo-Saxon Art: A New Perspective*, Manchester: Manchester University Press.
DOLLEY, M. 1965, *Viking Coins of the Danelaw and Dublin*, London: British Museum.
——and M. MAYS 1990, 'Nummular brooches', in Biddle (ed.): 632–9.
DONALD, M. and L. HURCOMBE 2000 (eds.), *Gender and Material Culture in Historical Perspective*, Basingstoke: Macmillan Press.
DOWN, A. and M. WELCH 1990, *Chichester Excavations VII. Apple Down and the Mardens*, Chichester: Chichester District Council.
DRAPER, S. 2002, 'Old English *wīc* and *walh*; Britons and Saxons in post-Roman Wiltshire', *Landscape History*: 29–43.
DRINKALL, G. and M. FOREMAN 1998, *The Anglo-Saxon Cemetery at Castledyke South, Barton-on-Humber*, Sheffield Excavation Reports 6.
DRISCOLL, S. T. and M. R. NIEKE 1988 (eds.), *Power and Politics in Early Medieval Britain and Ireland*, Edinburgh: Edinburgh University Press.
DUCZO, W. 1985, *Birka V: The Filigree and Granulation Work of the Viking Period*, Stockholm: Almqvist and Wiksell International.
DUFFY, E. 1992, *The Stripping of the Altars. Traditional Religion in England 1400–1580*, New Haven and London: Yale University Press.
DUMVILLE, D. N. 1992, *Wessex and England from Alfred to Edgar*, Woodbridge: Boydell Press.
——1995, 'The idea of governance in sub-Roman Britain', in Ausenda (ed.): 177–204.
DUNNING, G. C. 1933, 'Inventory of the medieval polychrome jugs found in England and Scotland', *Archaeologia*, 83: 126–34.
——1956, 'Trade relations between England the continent in the late Anglo-Saxon period', in Harden (ed.): 218–33.
DYER, C. 1989, *Standards of Living in the Later Middle Ages*, Cambridge: Cambridge University Press.
——1991, 'Were there any capitalists in fifteenth-century England?', in Kermode (ed.): 1–24.
——1996, 'Taxation and communities in late medieval England', in Britnell and Hatcher (eds.): 168–90.
——1998a, 'Did the peasants really starve in medieval England?', in Carlin and Rosenthal (eds.): 53–71.
——1998b, 'Trade and the Church: ecclesiastical consumers and the urban economy', in Slater and Rosser (eds.): 55–75.
DYKES, D. W. 1976, *Anglo-Saxon Coins in the National Museum of Wales*, Cardiff: National Museum of Wales.
DYMOND, D. 1998, 'Five building contracts from fifteenth-century Suffolk', *Antiquaries Journal*, 78: 269–87.
EAGLEN, R. J. 1992, 'The evolution of coinage in thirteenth-century England', in Coss and Loyd (eds.): 15–24.
EAGLES, B. 2001, 'Anglo-Saxon presence and culture in Wiltshire, *c*.A.D. 450–*c*.675', in Ellis, P. (ed.): 199–233.

Eagles, B. and D. Briscoe 1999, 'Animal and bird stamps on early Anglo-Saxon pottery in England', *Studien zur Sachsen-Forschung*, 13: 99–111.
—— and C. Mortimer 1993, 'Early Anglo-Saxon artefacts from Hod Hill, Dorset', *Antiquaries Journal*, 73: 132–40.
Eales, R. 1986, 'The game of chess: an aspect of medieval knightly culture', in Harper-Bill and Harvey (eds.): 12–34.
East, K. 1986, 'A lead model and a rediscovered sword, both with Gripping Beast decoration', *Medieval Archaeology*, 30: 1–7.
Eckardt, H. and H. Williams 2003, 'Objects without a past? The use of Roman objects in early Anglo-Saxon graves', in Williams, H. (ed.): 141–70.
Edwards, B. J. N. 1992, 'The Vikings in north-west England: the archaeological evidence', in Graham-Campbell (ed.): 43–62.
—— 2002, 'A Viking scabbard chape from Chatburn, Lancashire', *Antiquaries Journal*, 82: 321–8.
Edwards, N. 1997, 'Introduction', in ead. (ed.): 1–12.
—— 2001, 'Early medieval inscribed stones and stone sculpture in Wales: context and function', *Medieval Archaeology*, 45: 15–40.
—— 1997 (ed.), *Landscape and Settlement in Medieval Wales*, Oxford: Oxbow Books 81.
—— and T. G. Hulse 1992, 'A fragment of a reliquary casket from Gwytherin, north Wales', *Antiquaries Journal*, 72: 91–101.
—— and A. Lane 1988 (eds.), *Early Medieval Settlements in Wales, A.D. 400–1100*, Early Medieval Wales Archaeological Research Group.
—— —— 1992 (eds.), *The Early Church in Wales and the West*, Oxford: Oxbow Books.
Egan, G. 1994, *Lead Cloth Seals and Related Items in the British Museum*, London: British Museum Occasional Paper 93.
—— 1996, 'Some archaeological evidence for metalworking in London *c*.1050–*c*.1700', *Journal of the Historical Metallurgy Society*, 30: 83–94.
—— 1998, *Medieval Finds from Excavations in London: 6. The Medieval Household: Daily Living c.1150–c.1450*, London: HMSO.
—— 1999, review of Deevey 1998, *Archaeological Journal*, 156: 440–1.
—— 2001, 'Lead/tin alloy metalwork', in Saunders (ed.): 92–118.
—— and H. Forsyth 1997, 'Wound wire and silver gilt: changing fashions in dress accessories, *c*.1400–*c*.1600', in Gaimster and Stamper (eds.): 215–38.
—— and F. Pritchard, 1991, *Medieval Finds from Excavations in London: 3. Dress Accessories c.1150–c.1450*, London: HMSO.
Ellis, B. M. A. 1994, 'Spurs', in Quinnell and Blockley: 187–8.
—— 2002, 'Prick spurs 700–1700', *Datasheet 30*, Finds Research Group A.D. 700–1700.
Ellis, P. 2000 (ed.), *Ludgershall Castle. Excavations by Peter Addyman 1964–1972*, Wiltshire Archaeological and Natural History Society Monograph Series 2.
—— (ed.) 2001, *Roman Wiltshire and After: Papers in Honour of Ken Annable*, Devizes: Wiltshire Archaeological and Natural History Society.
Emanuel, H. D. 1967 (ed.), *The Latin Texts of the Welsh Laws*, Cardiff: Board of Celtic Studies, University of Wales History and Law Series 22.
Emery, A. 2000, *Greater Medieval Houses of England and Wales. Volume II: East Anglia, Central England and Wales*, Cambridge: Cambridge University Press.

ESMONDE CLEARY, A. S. 1989, *The Ending of Roman Britain*, London: Batsford.
EVANS, A. C. 1991, catalogue entries in Webster and Backhouse (eds.).
EVANS, J. 1892, *Posy-Rings*, London: Longmans, Green.
——1922, *Magical Jewels of the Middle Ages and the Renaissance, Particularly in England*, Oxford: Clarendon Press.
——1931, *English Posies and Posy Rings*, Oxford: Oxford University Press.
——and M. J. SERJEANTSON 1933, *English Mediaeval Lapidaries*, London: Early English Text Society 190.
——E. T. LEEDS and J. D. A. THOMPSON 1941, 'A hoard of gold rings and silver groats found near Thame, Oxfordshire', *Antiquaries Journal*, 21: 197–202.
EVERSON, P. 1993, 'Pre-Viking settlement in Lindsey', in Vince (ed.): 91–100.
EVISON, V. I. 1955, 'Early Anglo-Saxon inlaid metalwork', *Antiquaries Journal*, 35: 20–47.
——1958, 'Further Anglo-Saxon inlay', *Antiquaries Journal*, 38: 240–4.
——1967*a*, 'The Dover ring-sword and other sword-rings and beads', *Archaeologia*, 101: 63–118.
——1967*b*, 'A sword from the Thames at Wallingford Bridge', *Archaeological Journal*, 124: 160–89.
——1968, 'Quoit brooch style buckles', *Antiquaries Journal*, 48: 231–49.
——1975*a*, 'Pagan Saxon whetstones', *Antiquaries Journal*, 55: 70–85.
——1975*b*, 'Sword rings and beads', *Archaeologia*, 105: 303–16.
——1977, 'An enamelled disc from Great Saxham', *Proceedings of the Suffolk Institute of Archaeology*, 34i: 1–13.
——1982, 'Anglo-Saxon glass claw-beakers', *Archaeologia*, 107: 43–76.
——1985, 'The glass' in West: 75–6.
——1987, *Dover: Buckland Anglo-Saxon Cemetery*, London: Historic Buildings and Monuments Commission for England Archaeological Report 3.
——1989, 'The glass vessel', in Rahtz and Watts: 341–5.
——1991, catalogue entries in Webster and Backhouse (eds.).
——2000, 'Glass vessels in England A.D. 400–1100', in Price (ed.): 47–104.
FAIRBROTHER, J. R. 1990, *Faccombe Netherton: Excavations of a Saxon and Medieval Manorial Complex*, London: British Museum Occasional Paper 74.
FAITH, R. 1997, *The English Peasantry and the Growth of Lordship*, London: Leicester University Press.
FANNING, T. 1983, 'Some aspects of the bronze ringed-pin in Scotland', in O'Connor and Clarke (eds.): 324–42.
——1994, *Viking Age Ringed Pins from Dublin*, Medieval Dublin Excavations 1962–81, Series B, 4, Dublin: Royal Irish Academy.
FARLEY, M. 1976, 'Saxon and medieval Walton, Aylesbury: excavations 1973–4', *Records of Buckinghamshire*, 20: 153–290.
FARRELL, R. T. 1982 (ed.), *The Vikings*, Chichester: Phillimore.
——and C. NEUMAN DE VEGVAR 1992 (eds.), *Sutton Hoo: Fifty Years After*, Oxford, Ohio: American Early Medieval Studies 3.
FASHAM, P. J. and R. B. WHINNEY 1991, *Archaeology and the M3*, Hampshire Field Club and Archaeological Society Monograph 7.
FAULKNER, K. 1996, 'The transformation of knighthood in early thirteenth-century England', *English Historical Review*, 111: 1–23.

FERGUSON, R. S. 1893 (ed.), *Testamenta Karleonsia*, Cumberland and Westmorland Antiquarian and Archaeological Society Extra Series 9.

FILMER-SANKEY, W. 1996, 'The "Roman Emperor" in the Sutton Hoo ship-burial', *Journal of the British Archaeological Association*, 149: 1–9.

—— and T. PESTELL 2001, *Snape Anglo-Saxon Cemetery: Excavations and Surveys 1824–1992*, Gressenhall: East Anglian Archaeology Report 95.

FLEMING, P. 2001, *Family and Household in Medieval England*, Basingstoke: Palgrave.

FLEMING, R. 2001, 'The new wealth, the new rich and the new political style in late Anglo-Saxon England', in Gillingham (ed.): 1–22.

FOOT, S. 1999, 'Remembering, forgetting and inventing: attitudes to the past in England at the end of the Viking age', *Transactions of the Royal Historical Society*, 9: 185–200.

FOOT, S. 2000, *Veiled Women*, 2 vols., Aldershot: Ashgate.

FOREMAN, M. 1991, 'The bone and antler', in Armstrong *et al.* (eds.): 183–96.

FOREMAN, S., J. HILLER, and D. PETTS 2002, *Gathering the People, Settling the Land. The Archaeology of a Middle Thames Landscape, Anglo-Saxon to Post-Medieval*, Thames Valley Landscapes Monograph 14, Oxford: Oxford Archaeology.

FORSYTH, K. 2000, 'Appendix One: the Ogham inscription at Dunadd', in Lane and Campbell (eds.): 264–72.

FOSTER, B. 1963 (ed.), *The Local Port Book of Southampton, 1435–36*, Southampton Record Series 7.

FOSTER, S. M. 1992, 'The state of Pictland in the age of Sutton Hoo', in Carver (ed.): 217–34.

—— 1996, *Picts, Gaels and Scots: Early Historic Scotland*, London: Batsford.

FOWLER, K. 1971, 'Introduction', in id. (ed.): 1–27.

—— 1971 (ed.), *The Hundred Years' War*, London and Basingstoke: Macmillan Press.

FOX, A. 1995, 'Tin ingots from Bigbury Bay, south Devon', *Devon Archaeological Society Proceedings*, 53: 11–24.

FOX, R. and K. J. BARTON 1986, 'Excavations at Oyster Street, Portsmouth, Hampshire', *Post-Medieval Archaeology*, 20: 31–256.

FRANK, R. 1992, '*Beowulf* and Sutton Hoo: the odd couple', in Kendall and Wells (eds.): 47–64.

—— 1997, 'Old English *orc* 'cup, goblet': a Latin loanword with attitude', in Roberts and Nelson (eds.): 15–24.

FRANKLIN, J. A. 1998, 'Pottery', in Caldwell *et al.*: 53–9.

FRAZER, W. O. and A. TYRRELL 2000 (eds.), *Social Identity in Early Medieval Britain*, Studies in the Early History of Britain, London and New York: Leicester University Press.

FRENCH, K. L. 2001, *The People of the Parish. Community Life in a Late Medieval English Diocese*, Philadelphia: University of Pennsylvania Press.

FRERE, S. S., P. BENNETT, J. RADY, and S. STOW 1987, *Canterbury Excavations: Intra- and Extra-Mural Sites, 1949–55 and 1980–84*, Archaeology of Canterbury Vol. 8, Maidstone: Kent Archaeological Society.

FRIELL, J. G. P. and W. G. WATSON 1984 (eds.), *Pictish Studies: Settlement, Burial and Art in Dark Age Northern Britain*, Oxford: British Archaeological Reports British Series 125.

FUGLESANG, S. H. 1980, *Some Aspects of the Ringerike Style. A Phase of Eleventh-Century Scandinavian Art*, Odense: Odense University Press.

—— 1992, 'Mass production in the Viking Age', in Roesdahl and Wilson (eds.): 198–9.

FULFORD, M. G. and S. J. RIPPON 1994, 'Lowbury Hill, Oxon.: a re-assessment of the probable Romano-Celtic temple and the Anglo-Saxon barrow', *Archaeological Journal*, 151: 158–211.

GAIMSTER, D. 1997, *German Stoneware 1200–1900. Archaeology and Cultural History*, London: British Museum Press.

—— (ed.) 1999, *Maiolica in the North: The Archaeology of Tin-Glazed Earthenware in North-West Europe, c.1500–1600*, London: British Museum Occasional Paper 122.

—— and J. A. GOODALL 1999, 'A Tudor parcel-gilt livery badge from Chelsham, Surrey', *Antiquaries Journal*, 79: 392–9.

—— and B. NENK 1997, 'English households in transition c.1450–1550: the ceramic evidence', in id. and Stamper (eds.): 171–96.

—— and P. STAMPER 1997 (eds.), *The Age of Transition. The Archaeology of English Culture 1400–1600*, Society for Medieval Archaeology Monograph 15/Oxbow Monograph 98.

—— M. HAYWARD, D. MITCHELL, and K. PARKER 2002, 'Tudor silver-gilt dress-hooks: a new class of treasure find in England', *Antiquaries Journal*, 82: 157–96.

GAIMSTER, M. 1992, 'Scandinavian gold bracteates in Britain: Money and media in the Dark Ages', *Medieval Archaeology*, 36: 1–28.

—— 1998, *Vendel Period Bracteates on Gotland: On the Significance of Germanic Art*, Acta Archaeologia Lundensis 27.

GAIRDNER, J. 1904 (ed.), *The Paston Letters A.D. 1422–1509*, London and Exeter: Chatto & Windus/James G. Commin.

GALE, D. 1989, 'The seax', in Hawkes (ed.): 71–84.

GALLOWAY, J. A. 1998, 'Driven by drink? Ale consumption and the agrarian economy of the London region', in Carlin and Rosenthal (eds.): 73–86.

GAMESON, R. 1995, *The Role of Art in the Late Anglo-Saxon Church*, Oxford: Clarendon Press.

—— 1999 (ed.), *St Augustine and the Conversion of England*, Stroud: Sutton Publishing.

GANNON, A. 2003, *The Iconography of Anglo-Saxon Coinage: Sixth to Eighth Centuries*, Oxford: Oxford University Press.

GARDINER, M. 1993, 'The excavation of a late Anglo-Saxon settlement at Market Field, Steyning, 1988–89', *Sussex Archaeological Collections*, 131: 21–67.

—— 2001, 'Continental trade and non-urban ports in mid-Saxon England. Excavations at Sandtun, West Hythe, Kent', *Archaeological Journal*, 158: 161–290.

—— and C. GREATOREX 1997, 'Archaeological excavations in Steyning, 1992–5', *Sussex Archaeological Collections*, 135: 143–71.

GAYDON, A. T. 1958 (ed.), *The Taxation of 1297*, Publications of the Bedfordshire Historical Record Society 39.

GEAKE, H. 1997, *The Use of Grave-Goods in Conversion-Period England, c.600–c.850*, Oxford: British Archaeological Reports British Series 261.

GEAKE, H. 1999, 'When were hanging-bowls deposited in Anglo-Saxon graves?', *Medieval Archaeology*, 43: 1–18.
—— 2001, 'Portable Antiquities Scheme', *Medieval Archaeology*, 45: 236–51.
—— 2002, 'Portable Antiquities Scheme', *Medieval Archaeology*, 46: 128–45.
—— and J. KENNY 2000 (eds.), *Early Deira. Archaeological Studies of the East Riding in the Fourth to Ninth Centuries*, Oxford: Oxbow Books.
GEARY, P. 1999, 'Land, language and memory in Europe, 700–1100', *Transactions of the Royal Historical Society*, 9: 169–84.
GELLING, M. 1993a, 'The place-name Mucking', in Hamerow: 96.
—— 1993b, 'Why aren't we speaking Welsh?' *Anglo-Saxon Studies in Archaeology and History*, 6: 51–6.
GERRARD, C. 2003, *Medieval Archaeology. Understanding Traditions and Contemporary Approaches*, London: Routledge.
GILCHRIST, R. 1988, 'A reappraisal of Dinas Powys: local exchange and specialized livestock in fifth- to seventh-century Wales', *Medieval Archaeology*, 32: 50–62.
—— 1997, 'Ambivalent bodies: gender and medieval archaeology', in Moore and Scott (eds.): 42–58.
GILES, K. 2000, *An Archaeology of Social Identity. Guildhalls in York, c.1360–1630*, Oxford: British Archaeological Reports British Series 315.
GILLINGHAM, J. 1995, 'Thegns and knights in eleventh-century England: who was then the gentleman?', *Transactions of the Royal Historical Society*, 5 (6th series): 129–53.
—— 2001 (ed.), *Anglo-Norman Studies 23. Proceedings of the Battle Conference 2000*, Woodbridge: Boydell Press.
GILMOUR, B. 1979, 'The Anglo-Saxon church at St Paul-in-the-Bail', *Medieval Archaeology*, 23: 214–18.
—— 1999, 'A sword from grave C74', in Haughton and Powlesland: 120–3.
GINGELL, C. J. 1975–6, 'The excavation of an early Anglo-Saxon cemetery at Collingbourne Ducis', *Wiltshire Archaeological Magazine*, 70/1: 61–98.
GITTOS, H. 2002, 'Creating the sacred: Anglo-Saxon rites for consecrating cemeteries', in Lucy and Reynolds (eds.): 195–208.
GIVEN-WILSON, C. 1991, 'Wealth and credit, public and private: the earls of Arundel 1306–1397', *English History Review*, 218: 1–26.
GODDEN, M. 1990, 'Money, power and morality in late Anglo-Saxon England', *Anglo-Saxon England*, 19: 41–65.
—— 2003, 'The player king: identification and self-representation in King Alfred's writings', in Reuter (ed.): 137–50.
—— and M. LAPIDGE 1991 (eds.), *The Cambridge Companion to Old English Literature*, Cambridge: Cambridge University Press.
GOETZ, H.-W. 2003, '*Gens*: Terminology and perception of the "Germanic" peoples from late Antiquity to the early Middle Ages', in Corradini *et al.* (eds.): 39–64.
GOING, C. 1993, 'Roman pottery [and] Roman coins from Anglo-Saxon contexts', in Hamerow: 71–3.
GOLDBERG, J. 1996, 'Introduction', in Ormrod and Lindley (eds.): 1–15.
GOLDING, B. J. 2001, 'The Church and Christian life', in Harvey (ed.): 135–66.
GOOD, D. F. 1983, 'Medieval monetary problems: bimetallism and bullionism', *Journal of Economic History*, 249–301.

GOOD, G. L. 1987, 'The excavation of two docks at Narrow Quay, Bristol, 1978–9,' *Post-Medieval Archaeology*, 21: 25–124.
—— and C. J. TABRAHAM 1981, 'Excavations at Threave Castle, Galloway, 1974–78', *Medieval Archaeology*, 25: 90–140.
GOODALL, A. R. 1979, 'Copper-alloy objects', in Smith: 137–45.
—— 1983, 'Non-ferrous metal objects', in Mayes and Butler: 231–9.
—— 1984*a*, 'Non-ferrous metal objects', in Rogerson and Dallas: 68–76.
—— 1984*b*, 'Objects of non-ferrous metal', in Allan: 337–48.
—— 1989, 'Copper-alloy objects', in Wrathmell: 46–9.
—— 1990, 'Objects of copper alloy and lead', in Fairbrother: 425–36.
—— 1993, 'Copper-alloy objects', in Murray and Murray: 188–94.
—— and C. PATERSON 2000, 'Non-ferrous metal objects', in Stamper and Croft: 126–32.
GOODALL, I. H. 2002, 'The metalwork', in Mayes: 96–112.
—— and E. A. CLARK 2000, 'Iron objects', in Stamper and Croft: 132–47.
GOODALL, J. 1993, 'The earliest imprese, a study of some medieval seals and devices', *Antiquaries Journal*, 73: 152–7.
GOODMAN, A. 1992, *John of Gaunt: The Exercise of Princely Power in Fourteenth-Century Europe*, Harlow: Longman.
GOODRIDGE, J. F. 1959 (trans.), *Piers the Plowman [by] William Langland*, Harmondsworth: Penguin Books.
GORDON, D., L. MOUNAS, and C. ELAM 1997 (eds.), *The Regal Image of Richard II and the Wilton Diptych*, London: Harvey Miller.
GRAHAM, A. and S. M. DAVIES 1993, *Excavations in Trowbridge, Wiltshire, 1977 and 1986–1988*, Salisbury: Wessex Archaeology Report 2.
GRAHAM-CAMPBELL, J. 1973, 'The ninth-century Anglo-Saxon horn-mount from Burghead, Morayshire, Scotland', *Medieval Archaeology*, 17: 43–51.
—— 1980, *The Viking World*, London: Frances Lincoln.
—— 1981, 'The bell and the mould', in Reece: 23–5.
—— 1982, 'A middle Saxon gold finger-ring from the Cathedral Close, Exeter', *Antiquaries Journal*, 52: 366–7.
—— 1983, 'Some Viking-Age penannular brooches from Scotland and the origins of the "thistle-brooch"', in O'Connor and Clarke (eds.): 310–23.
—— 1988, 'The gold finger-ring from a burial in St Aldate's Street, Oxford', *Oxoniensia*, 53: 263–6.
—— 1991*a*, 'Dinas Powys metalwork and the dating of enamelled zoomorphic penannular brooches', *Bulletin of the Board of Celtic Studies*, 38: 220–32.
—— 1991*b*, 'Norrie's Law, Fife: on the nature and dating of the silver hoard', *Proceedings of the Society of Antiquaries of Scotland*, 121: 241–59.
—— 1992*a*, 'The Cuerdale hoard: a Viking and Victorian treasure', in id. (ed.): 1–14.
—— 1992*b*, 'The Cuerdale hoard: comparisons and context', in id. (ed.): 107–15.
—— 1992*c*, 'Anglo-Scandinavian equestrian equipment in eleventh-century England', *Anglo-Norman Studies*, 14: 77–89.
—— 1995, *The Viking-Age Gold and Silver of Scotland (AD 850–1100)*, Edinburgh: National Museums of Scotland.
—— 2000, 'A penannular brooch with trefoil-lobed terminals', in Rahtz *et al.*: 352–4.

GRAHAM-CAMPBELL, J. 2001a, 'National and regional identities; the "glittering prizes"', in Redknap *et al.* (eds.): 28–38.
——2001b, 'The dual economy of the Danelaw. The Howard Linecar memorial Lecture 2001', *British Numismatic Journal*, 71: 49–59.
——2001c, 'Pagan Scandinavian burial in the central and southern Danelaw', in id. *et al.* (eds.): 105–24.
——2001d, 'The northern hoards: from Cuerdale to Bossall/Flaxton', in Higham and Hill (eds.): 212–29.
——1992 (ed.), *Viking Treasure from the North West. The Cuerdale Hoard in its Context*, Liverpool: National Museums and Galleries on Merseyside.
——and C. E. BATEY 1998, *Vikings in Scotland. An Archaeological Survey*, Edinburgh: Edinburgh University Press.
——and E. OKASHA 1991, 'A pair of inscribed hooked tags from the Rome (Forum) 1883 hoard', *Anglo-Saxon England*, 20: 221–9.
——and J. SHEEHAN 1995, 'A hoard of Hiberno-Viking arm-rings, probably from Scotland', *Proceedings of the Society of Antiquaries of Scotland*, 125: 771–8.
——R. HALL, J. JESCH, and D. N. PARSONS 2001 (eds.), *Vikings and the Danelaw. Select papers from the Proceedings of the Thirteenth Viking Congress, Nottingham and York, 21–30 August 1997*, Oxford: Oxbow Books.
GRAINGER, G. and M. HENIG 1983, 'A bone casket and a relief plaque from Mound 3 at Sutton Hoo', *Medieval Archaeology*, 27: 136–41.
GRANGER-TAYLOR, H. 1989, 'Weft-patterned silks and their braid: the remains of an Anglo-Saxon dalmatic of *c.*800?', in Bonner *et al.* (eds.): 303–27.
——and F. PRITCHARD 2000, 'A fine quality Insular embroidery from Langors crannog, near Brecon', in Redknap *et al.* (eds.): 91–9.
GRANSDEN, A. 1998 (ed.), *Bury St Edmunds*, British Archaeological Association Conference Transactions 20.
GRÄSLAND, A.-S. 1992, 'Thor's hammers, pendant crosses and other amulets', in Roesdahl and Wilson (eds.): 190–1.
GRAVES, C. P. 1993, 'Vessel fragment', in Murray and Murray: 199–200.
GREEN, J. A. 1997, *The Aristocracy of Norman England*, Cambridge: Cambridge University Press.
GREENFIELD, B. 1991, 'Beowulf and the judgement of the righteous', in Lapidge and Gneuss (eds.): 393–408.
GREEP, S. 1982, 'A late medieval bronze purse mount from Denham, Bucks.', *Records of Buckinghamshire*, 24: 179–80.
GRENVILLE, J. 1997, *Medieval Housing*, London and Washington: Leicester University Press.
GRETSCH, M. 1994, 'The language of the "Fonthill Letter"', *Anglo-Saxon England*, 23: 57–102.
GREW, F. and NEERGARD, M. DE 1988, *Shoes and Patens. Medieval Finds from Excavations in London: 2*, London: HMSO.
GRIERSON, P. and M. A. S. BLACKBURN 1986, *Medieval European Coinage, I: The Early Middle Ages (5th–10th Centuries)*, Cambridge: Cambridge University Press.
GRIFFITH, F. M. 1986, 'Salvage operations at the Dark Age site at Bantham Ham, Thurlestone, 1982', *Devon Archaeological Society Proceedings*, 44: 29–58.

GRIFFITHS, N. 1989, 'Shield-Shaped Mounts', *Datasheet 12*, Finds Research Group 700–1700.
—— 1995, 'Harness pendants and associated fittings', in Clarke (ed.): 61–71.
GRIFFITHS, R. A. 2000, 'Wales and the Marches', in Palliser (ed.): 681–714.
GRÖSSINGER, C. 1997, *The World Upside-Down*, London: Harvey Miller.
GUIDO, M. and M. WELCH 2000, 'Indirect evidence for glass bead manufacture in early Anglo-Saxon England', in Price (ed.): 115–19.
GUREVICH, A. 1988 (trans. J. M. Bak and P. A. Hollingsworth), *Medieval Popular Culture: Problems of Belief and Perception*, Cambridge: Cambridge University Press.
GUTIÉRREZ, A. 2000, *Mediterranean Pottery in Wessex Households (Thirteenth to Seventeenth Centuries)*, Oxford: British Archaeological Reports British Series 306.
HADLEY, D. M. 1997, ' "And they proceeded to plough and to support themselves": the Scandinavian settlement of England', *Anglo-Norman Studies*, 19: 69–96.
—— 2000*a*, *The Northern Danelaw. Its Social Structure, c.800–1100*, London: Leicester University Press.
—— 2000*b*, ' "Hamlet and the Princes of Denmark", *c*.860–954', in ead. and Richards (eds.): 107–32.
—— 2001, *Death in Medieval England: An Archaeology*, Stroud: Tempus Publishing.
—— 2002, 'Burial practices in northern England in the later Anglo-Saxon period', in Lucy and Reynolds (eds.): 209–28.
—— and J. D. RICHARDS 2000 (eds.), *Cultures in Contact. Scandinavian Settlement in England in the Ninth and Tenth Centuries*, Turnhout: Brepols.
HADWIN, J. F. 1977, 'Evidence on the possession of "treasure" from the Lay Subsidy rolls', in Mayhew (ed.): 147–66.
HAITH, C. 1984, catalogue entries in Backhouse *et al.* (eds.).
—— 1991, catalogue entries in Webster and Backhouse (eds.).
HALE, W. H. and H. T. ELLACOMBE 1874 (eds.), *Accounts of the Executors of Richard, Bishop of London 1303, and of the Executors of Thomas, Bishop of Exeter 1310*, Camden Society Publications, NS 10.
HALL, D. N. 1974, 'Medieval pottery from the Higham Ferrers hundred', *Journal of the Northamptonshire Museum*, 10: 38–58.
HALL, M. A. 2001*a*, 'Gaming-board badges', in van Beuningen *et al.* (eds.): 173–8.
—— 2001*b*, 'An ivory knife handle from the High Street, Perth, Scotland: consuming ritual in a medieval burgh', *Medieval Archaeology*, 45: 169–88.
—— and D. D. R. OWEN 1998, 'A Tristram and Iseult mirror-case from Perth: reflections on the production and consumption of romance culture', *Tayside and Fife Archaeological Journal*, 4: 150–65.
HALL, R. A. 1994, *Viking Age York*, London: Batsford/English Heritage.
—— 1998, 'A silver appliqué from St Mary Bishophill Senior, York', *Yorkshire Archaeological Journal*, 70: 61–6.
—— 1978 (ed.), *Viking Age York and the North*, London: Council for British Archaeology Research Report 27.
—— and M. WHYMAN 1996, 'Settlement and monasticism at Ripon, North Yorkshire, from the seventh to the eleventh centuries A.D.', *Medieval Archaeology*, 40: 62–150.
—— E. PATERSON, and C. MORTIMER 1996, 'The Ripon jewel', in Hall and Whyman: 134–6.

HALSALL, G. 1998, 'Violence and society: an introductory essay', in id. (ed.): 1–45.
—— 2000, 'The Viking presence in England? The burial evidence reconsidered', in Hadley and Richards (eds.): 259–76.
—— 1998 (ed.), *Violence and Society in the Early Medieval West*, Woodbridge: Boydell Press.
HAMEROW, H. 1993, *Excavations at Mucking. Volume 2: The Anglo-Saxon Settlement Excavations by M. U. Jones and W. T. Jones*, London: English Heritage Archaeological Report 21.
—— 1999, 'Anglo-Saxon Oxfordshire', *Oxoniensia*, 64: 23–38.
—— 2002, *Early Medieval Settlements. The Archaeology of Rural Communities in North-West Europe 400–900*, Oxford: Oxford University Press.
—— and A. MACGREGOR 2001 (eds.), *Image and Power in the Archaeology of Early Medieval Britain. Essays in Honour of Rosemary Cramp*, Oxford: Oxbow Books.
—— Y. HOLLEVOET, and A. VINCE 1994, 'Migration period settlements and "Anglo-Saxon" pottery from Flanders', *Medieval Archaeology*, 38: 1–18.
HAMILTON, J. R. C. 1956, *Excavations at Jarlshof, Shetland*, Edinburgh: HMSO.
HAMILTON-DYER, S. and N. POWELL 2001, 'Worked bone', in Pile: 109–11.
HAMMOND, P. W. 1993, *Food and Feast in Medieval England*, Stroud: Alan Sutton Publishing.
HANAWALT, B. A. 1976, *Crimes in East Anglia in the Fourteenth Century: Norfolk Gaol Delivery Rolls, 1307–1316*, Norfolk Record Society.
HANAWALT, B. A. and K. L. REYERSON 1994, 'Introduction', in eaed. (eds.), pp. ix–xx.
—— —— 1994 (eds.), *City and Spectacle in Medieval Europe*, Minneapolis: Medieval Studies at Minnesota 6.
HANDLEY, M. A. 2001, 'The origins of Christian commemoration in late antique Britain', *Early Medieval Europe*, 10: 177–99.
HARDEN, D. B. 1956 (ed.), *Dark Age Britain: Studies Presented to E. T. Leeds*, London: Methuen.
—— 1961–2, 'Objects of glass' in Biddle: 185–6.
—— K. S. PAINTER, R. H. PINDER-WILSON, and H. TAIT 1968 (comp.), *Masterpieces of Glass*, London: British Museum.
HARDING, A. 1993, *England in the Thirteenth Century*, Cambridge: Cambridge University Press.
HARDING, V. 1995, 'Cross-Channel trade and cultural contacts: London and the Low Countries in the Later Fourteenth Centuries', in Barron and Saul (eds.): 153–68.
HARDT, M. 1998, 'Silverware in early medieval gift exchange: *Imitatio Imperii* and objects of memory', in Wood (ed.): 317–31.
HARE, J. 1993, 'Netley Abbey: monastery, mansion and ruin', *Proceedings of the Hampshire Field Club and Archaeological Society*, 49: 207–28.
HARE, M. 1999, 'Kings, crowns and festivals: the origins of Gloucester as a royal ceremonial centre', *Transactions of the Bristol and Gloucestershire Archaeological Society*, 115: 41–78.
HÄRKE, H. 1989, 'Knives in early Saxon burials; blade lengths and age at death', *Medieval Archaeology*, 33: 144–8.
—— 1994, 'A context for the Saxon barrow', in Fulford and Rippon: 202–6.
—— 1997, 'Material culture as myth; weapons in Anglo-Saxon graves', in Jensen and Høilund Nielsen (eds.): 119–27.

—— 2000, 'The circulation of weapons in Anglo-Saxon society', in Theuws and Nelson (eds.): 377–99.

HARPER-BILL, C. and R. HARVEY 1986 (eds.), *The Ideals and Practice of Medieval Knighthood*, Woodbridge: Boydell Press.

HARRIS, E. J. and D. R. GRIFFITHS 1999, 'Mercury plating on some early English coins', *British Numismatic Journal*, 69: 37–46.

HARRISON, G. 1999, 'Quoit-brooches and the Roman-medieval transition', in Baker *et al.* (eds.): 108–20.

HARRISS, G. L. 1994, 'The king and his subjects', in Horrox (ed.): 13–28.

HARRISS, J. 1998, ' "*Estroit vestu et menu costu*": evidence for construction of twelfth-century dress', in Owen-Crocker and Graham (eds.): 89–103.

HART, C. R. 1999, 'The Bayeux Tapestry and schools of illumination at Canterbury', *Anglo-Norman Studies*, 22: 117–68.

HARVEY, B. 2001, 'Conclusion', in ead. (ed.): 243–64.

—— 2001 (ed.), *The Twelfth and Thirteenth Centuries*, Oxford: Oxford University Press.

HARVEY, P. D. A. and A. MCGUINNESS 1996, *A Guide to British Medieval Seals*, London: British Library and Public Record Office.

HARVEY, Y. 1975, 'The small finds: catalogue', in Platt and Coleman-Smith: 254–95.

HASELGROVE, D. 1978, 'The Domesday record of Sussex', in Brandon (ed.): 190–220.

HASLAM, J. 1993, 'Glass vessels', in Margeson: 97–117.

HASSALL, T. G., C. E. HALPIN, and M. MELLOR 1989, 'Excavations in St Ebbe's, Oxford, 1967–76: part I', *Oxoniensia*, 54: 71–277.

HASTINGS, A. 1997, *The Construction of Nationhood: Ethnicity, Religion and Nationalism*, Cambridge: Cambridge University Press.

HATCHER, J. 1994, 'England in the aftermath of the Black Death', *Past and Present*, 144: 3–35.

—— 1996, 'The great slump of the mid-fifteenth century', in Britnell and id. (eds.): 237–72.

—— 1998, 'Labour, leisure and economic thought before the nineteenth century', *Past and Present*, 160: 64–115.

—— and M. BAILEY 2001, *Modelling the Middle Ages: The History and Theory of England's Economic Development*, Oxford: Oxford University Press.

—— and T. C. BARKER 1974, *A History of British Pewter*, London: Longman.

HATTAT, R. 1987, *Brooches of Antiquity. A Third Selection of Brooches from the Author's Collection*, Oxford: Oxbow Books.

HAUGHTON, C. and D. POWLESLAND 1999, *West Heslerton. The Anglian Cemetery. Volume i. The Excavation and Discussion of the Evidence*, Yedringham: The Landscape Research Centre Archaeology Monograph Series 1, Vol. 1.

HAWKES, J. 1996, *The Golden Age of Northumbria*, Newcastle: Tyne and Wear Museums.

—— 1997, 'Symbolic lives: the visual evidence', in Hines (ed.): 311–38.

—— and S. MILLS 1999 (eds.), *Northumbria's Golden Age*, Stroud: Sutton Publishing.

HAWKES, S. C. 1981, 'Recent finds of inlaid iron buckles and belt-plates from seventh-century Kent', *Anglo-Saxon Studies in Archaeology and History*, 2: 49–70.

—— 1990, 'The Anglo-Saxon necklace from Lower Brook Street', in Biddle: 621–31.

HAWKES, S. C. 2000, 'The Anglo-Saxon cemetery at Bifrons, in the parish of Patrixbourne, East Kent', *Anglo-Saxon Studies in Archaeology and History*, 11: 1–94.
—— 1989 (ed.), *Weapons and Warfare in Anglo-Saxon England*, Oxford: Oxford University Committee for Archaeology 21.
—— and G. C. DUNNING 1961, 'Soldiers and settlers in Britain, fourth to fifth century; with a catalogue of animal-ornamented buckles and related belt-fittings', *Medieval Archaeology*, 5: 1–70.
HAWKINS, E. 1832, 'Remarks upon the gold coins discovered in the bed of the River Dove, near Tutbury, Staffordshire', *Archaeologia*, 24: 148–67.
HAYNES, I., H. SHELDON, and L. HANNIGAN 2000 (eds.), *London Under Ground. The Archaeology of a City*, Oxford: Oxbow Books.
HEDEAGER, L. 2000, 'Migration period Europe: the formation of a political mentality', in Theuws and Nelson (eds.), 15–58.
HEDGES, J. D. and D. G. BUCKLEY 1985, 'Anglo-Saxon burials and later features excavated at Orsett, Essex', *Medieval Archaeology*, 29: 1–24.
HENDERSON, G. 1999, *Vision and Image in Early Christian England*, Cambridge: Cambridge University Press.
HENDERSON, I. 1967, *The Picts*, London: Thames & Hudson.
HENDERSON, J. 2000, 'The vessel glass', in Ellis (ed.): 168–76.
HENIG, M. 1983, 'Archbishop Hubert Walter's gems', *Journal of the British Archaeological Association*, 136: 56–61.
—— 1995, *The Art of Roman Britain*, London: Batsford.
—— 2000, 'English Gem-Set Seals', *Datasheet 27*, Finds Research Group 700–1700.
—— and T. A. HESLOP 1986, 'The great cameo of St Albans', *Journal of the British Archaeological Association*, 139: 148–53.
HESLOP, T. A. 1980, 'English seals from the mid ninth century to 1100', *Journal of the British Archaeological Association*, 133: 1–16.
—— 1984, 'Seals', in Zarnecki *et al.* (eds.): 298–329.
—— 1987, 'Seals of merchants, citizens and freemen' and catalogue entries in Alexander and Binski (eds.): 274–7.
—— 1992, 'English manuscript art in the mid-eleventh century: the decorative tradition', *Antiquaries Journal*, 72: 171–4.
HICKMAN, D. 2001 (ed.), *Lincolnshire Wills 1532–1534*, Lincoln Record Society 89.
HICKS, C. 1993, 'The Pictish Class I animals', in Spearman and Higgitt (eds.): 196–202.
HICKS, M. 1995, *Bastard Feudalism*, London and New York: Longman.
HIGGINS, C. 1989, 'Some thoughts on the Nature Goddess silk', in Bonner *et al.* (eds.): 329–37.
HIGGITT, J. 1995, 'Comb, pendant and buckle', in Lewis and Ewart: 83–4.
HIGHAM, N. J. 1994, *The English Conquest: Gildas and Britain in the Fifth Century*, Manchester and New York: Manchester University Press.
—— 2000, 'King Edwin of the Deiri: rhetoric and the reality of power in early England', in Geake and Kenny (eds.): 41–9.
—— 2002, *King Arthur: Myth-making and History*, London and New York: Routledge.
—— and D. H. HILL 2001 (eds.), *Edward the Elder 899–924*, London: Routledge.
HILL, D. 1978 (ed.), *Ethelred the Unready*, Oxford: British Archaeological Reports British Series 59.

——2003, 'The origin of Alfred's urban policies' in Reuter (ed.): 220–33.

——and R. COWIE 2001 (eds.), *Wics: The Early Mediaeval Trading Centres of Northern Europe*, Sheffield: Sheffield Academic Press.

——and A. R. RUMBLE 1996 (eds.), *The Defence of Wessex. The Burghal Hidage and Anglo-Saxon Fortifications*, Manchester: Manchester University Press.

HILL, P. 1997, *Whithorn and St Ninian. The Excavation of a Monastic Town, 1984–91*, Stroud: Sutton/Whithorn Trust.

——2001, 'Whithorn, Latinus and the origins of Christianity in northern Britain', in Hamerow and MacGregor (eds.): 23–32.

HILLS, C. 1977, *The Anglo-Saxon Cemetery at Spong Hill, North Elmham, Part I. Catalogue of Cremations, Nos. 20–64 and 1000–1690*, Gressenhall: East Anglian Archaeology Report 6.

——1999, 'Early Historic Britain', in Hunter and Ralston (eds.): 176–93.

——2001, 'From Isidore to isotopes: ivory rings in early medieval graves', in Hamerow and MacGregor (eds.): 131–46.

——and H. HURST 1989, 'A Goth at Gloucester?', *Antiquaries Journal*, 69: 154–8.

——K. PENN, and R. RICKETT 1987, *The Anglo-Saxon Cemetery at Spong Hill, North Elmham Part IV: Catalogue of Cremations (Nos. 30–2, 42, 44A, 46, 65–6, 2286–799, 2224 and 3325*, Gressenhall: East Anglian Archaeology Report 34.

——R. RICKETT, and K. PENN 1995, 'Early Saxon objects of copper alloy', in Rickett (ed.): 74–6.

HILTON, R. 1998, 'Status and class in the medieval town', in Slater and Rosser (eds.): 9–19.

HINES, J. 1993*a*, 'A gold bracteate from Kingston Bagpuize, Oxfordshire', *Medieval Archaeology*, 37: 219–22.

——1993*b*, *The* Fabliau *in English*, London: Longman.

——1997, *A New Corpus of Anglo-Saxon Great Square-Headed Brooches*, Woodbridge: Boydell Press.

——2000*a*, 'Welsh and English: mutual origins in post-Roman Britain?', *Studia Celtica*, 34: 81–104.

——2000*b*, 'The runic inscription on the composite disc brooch from Grave 11', in Penn: 81–2.

——2002, 'Lies, damned lies, and a *curriculum vitae*: reflections on statistics and the populations of early Anglo-Saxon inhumation cemeteries', in Lucy and Reynolds (eds.): 88–102.

——1997 (ed.), *The Anglo-Saxons from the Migration Period to the Eighth Century: an Ethnographic Perspective*, Woodbridge: Boydell Press.

——and B. ODENSTEDT 1987, 'The Undley bracteate and its runic inscription', *Studien für Sachsenforschung*, 6: 73–94.

——K. HØILUND NIELSEN, and F. SIEGMUND 1999 (eds.), *The Pace of Change*, Oxford: Oxbow Books.

HINTON, D. A. 1973, 'Anglo-Saxon burials at Postcombe, Lewknor', *Oxoniensia*, 36: 120–3.

——1974, *A Catalogue of the Anglo-Saxon Ornamental Metalwork 700–1100 in the Department of Antiquities, Ashmolean Museum*, Oxford: Clarendon Press.

——1975, 'Later Anglo-Saxon metal-work: an assessment', *Anglo-Saxon England*, 4: 171–80.

HINTON, D. A. 1978, 'Late Saxon treasure and bullion', in Hill (ed.): 135–58.
——1982a, 'Gemstone', in Coad and Streeten: 263–4.
——1982b, *Medieval Jewellery*, Princes Risborough: Shire Archaeology.
——1990a, *Archaeology, Economy and Society. England from the Fifth to the Fifteenth Century*, London: Seaby.
——1990b, entries in Biddle.
——1992, 'Revised dating of the Worgret structure', *Proceedings of the Dorset Natural History and Archaeological Society*, 114: 258–9.
——1996a, *The Gold, Silver and Other Non-Ferrous Alloy Objects from Hamwic, and the Non-Ferrous Metalworking Evidence*, Southampton Finds Vol. 2, Stroud: Alan Sutton Publishing.
——1996b, 'A "Winchester-style" mount from near Winchester', *Medieval Archaeology*, 40: 214–7.
——1998, *Discover Dorset: Saxons and Vikings*, Wimborne: Dovecote Press.
——1999, '"Closing" and the later Middle Ages', *Medieval Archaeology*, 43: 172–82.
——2000, *A Smith in Lindsey. The Anglo-Saxon Grave at Tattershall Thorpe, Lincolnshire*, Society for Medieval Archaeology Monograph Series 16.
——2002, 'A "marginal economy"? The Isle of Purbeck from the Norman Conquest to the Black Death', in id. (ed.): 84–117.
——2003a, 'Anglo-Saxon smiths and myths', in Scragg (ed.): 261–82.
——2003b, 'Medieval Anglo-Jewry: the archaeological evidence', in Skinner (ed.): 97–112.
——and R. HODGES 1977, 'Excavations in Wareham, 1974–5', *Proceedings of the Dorset Natural History and Archaeological Society*, 99: 42–83.
——2002 (ed.), *Purbeck Papers*, Oxford: Oxbow Books, University of Southampton Department of Archaeology Monograph 4.
——and E. OKASHA 1977, 'Appendix Two: the Wareham sword', in Hinton and Hodges: 80–1.
——S. KEENE, and K. E. QUALMANN 1981, 'The Winchester Reliquary', *Medieval Archaeology*, 25: 45–77.
HIRST, S. M. 2000, 'An approach to the study of Anglo-Saxon beads', in Price (ed.): 121–9.
HODGES, R. and W. BOWDEN 1998 (eds.), *The Sixth Century: Production, Distribution and Demand*, Leiden and Boston: Brill.
HØILUND NIELSEN, K. 1997, 'The schism of Anglo-Saxon chronology', in Jensen and Høilund Nielsen (eds.): 71–99.
HØILUND NIELSEN, K. 1999, 'Style II and the Anglo-Saxon elite', *Anglo-Saxon Studies in Archaeology and History*, 10: 185–201.
HOLDSWORTH, P. [n.d.], *Luxury Goods in a Medieval Household*, Southampton: Southampton Archaeological Research Committee.
——1987 (ed.), *Excavations in the Medieval Burgh of Perth 1979–81*, Society of Antiquaries of Scotland Monograph Series 5.
HOLLISTER, C. W. 1985, 'Henry I and the invisible transformation of medieval England', in Mayr-Harting and Moore (eds.): 119–32.
HOLMAN, K. 2001, 'Defining the Danelaw', in Graham-Campbell *et al.* (eds.): 1–12.

HOLMES, M. 1959, 'New light on St Edward's crown', *Archaeologia*, 97: 213–23.
HOLMES, N. 1997, 'The late medieval and post-medieval coins', in Hill: 345–51.
HOMER, R. F. 1991, 'Tin, lead and pewter' in Blair and Ramsay (eds.): 57–80.
HOOK, D. R. and S. LA NIECE 2000, 'The composite disc brooch from Grave 11 and other precious metal grave-goods', in Penn: 76–81.
——— and J. CHERRY 1988, 'A fifteenth-century mercury-silvered buckle from Hillington, Norfolk', *Antiquaries Journal*, 68: 301–3.
HOPE-TAYLOR, B. 1977, *Yeavering: An Anglo-British Centre of Early Northumbria*, London: HMSO.
HORDH, B. and L. LARSSON 2002 (eds.), *Central Places in the Migration and Merovingian Periods*, Acta Archaeologia Lundensia 39, Stockholm: Almqvist & Wiksel.
HORROX, R. (ed.) 1994, *Fifteenth-Century Attitudes*, Cambridge: Cambridge University Press.
HOURIHANE, C. (ed.) 2001, *From Ireland Coming. Irish Art from the Early Christian to the Late Gothic Period and its European Context*, Index of Christian Art Occasional Paper 4, Princeton: Department of Art and Archaeology, University of Princeton.
HOUTS, E. van 2001, 'Introduction: medieval memories', in ead. (ed.): 1–16.
——— 2001 (ed.), *Medieval Memories. Men, Women and the Past, 700–1300*, Harlow: Pearson Education.
HOWLETT, D. R. 1974, 'The iconography of the Alfred Jewel', *Oxoniensia*, 39: 44–52.
HUDSON, J. 2000, 'Henry I and counsel', in Maddicott and Palliser (eds.): 109–26.
HUGGETT, J. W. 1988, 'Imported grave goods and the early Anglo-Saxon economy', *Medieval Archaeology*, 32: 63–96.
HUGHES, D. O. 1993, 'Sumptuary law and social relations in renaissance Italy', in Bossy (ed.): 69–99.
HUNT, A. 1996, *Governance of Consuming Passions. A History of Sumptuary Law*, New York: St Martin's Press.
HUNTER, F. 1999, 'The National Museums of Scotland jet project', *Datasheet 26*, Finds Research Group 700–1700.
HUNTER, J. R. 1986, *Rescue Excavations on the Brough of Birsay*, Society of Antiquaries of Scotland Monograph Series 4.
——— and M. P. HEYWORTH 1998, *The Hamwic Glass*, York: Council for British Archaeology Research Report 116.
——— and I. RALSTON 1999 (eds.), *The Archaeology of Britain. An Introduction from the Upper Palaeolithic to the Industrial Revolution*, London: Routledge.
HURST, J. G. 2002, 'Raqqa-type ware', in Mayes: 128–30.
——— and P. RAHTZ 1987, *Wharram: A Study of Settlement on the Yorkshire Wolds. Volume III, Wharram Percy: The Church of St Martin*, Society for Medieval Archaeology Monograph Series 11.
HUTTON, R. 1994, *The Rise and Fall of Merry England. The Ritual Year 1400–1700*, Oxford and New York: Oxford University Press.
INKER, P. 2000, 'Technology as active material culture', *Medieval Archaeology*, 44: 25–52.
INNES, M. 2000, 'Danelaw identities: ethnicity, regionalism and political allegiance', in Hadley and Richards (eds.): 65–88.

INNES, M. 2001, 'Keeping it in the family: women and aristocratic memory', in van Houts (ed.): 17–35.
INSLEY, C. 2000, 'From *Rex Walliae* to *Princeps Walliae*: charters and state formation in thirteenth-century Wales', in Maddicott and Palliser (eds.): 179–96.
ISAACSON, R. F. (transcr.) and H. INGLEBY (ed.) 1919–22, *The Red Register of King's Lynn*, 2 vols., King's Lynn: Thew & Son.
IVENS, R., P. BUSBY, and N. SHEPHERD 1994, *Tattenhoe and Westbury: Two Deserted Medieval Settlements in Milton Keynes*, Buckinghamshire Archaeological Society Monograph Series 8.
JACKSON, R. P. J. and T. W. POTTER 1996, *Excavations at Stonea, Cambridgeshire, 1980–85*, London: British Museum.
JAMES, E. 2001, *Britain in the First Millennium*, London: Arnold.
JAMES, H. 1999, 'Carmarthen', in Dennison (ed.): 158–68.
JAMES, M. R. 1930, *Suffolk and Norfolk*, London: Dent.
JAMES, T. B. 1990, *The Palaces of Medieval England*, London: Seaby.
—— 1997, *Winchester*, London: Batsford/English Heritage.
JANES, D. 1996, 'The golden clasp of the late Roman state', *Early Medieval Europe*, 5: 127–53.
JENNINGS, S. 1981, *Eighteen Centuries of Pottery from Norwich*, Norwich: Norwich Survey, East Anglian Archaeology Report 13.
—— 1992, *Medieval Pottery in the Yorkshire Museum*, York: Yorkshire Museum.
JENSEN, C. K. and K. HØILUND NIELSEN 1997 (eds.), *Burial and Society. The Chronological and Social Analysis of Archaeological Burial Practice*, Aarhus: Aarhus University Press.
JESSUP, R. 1950, *Anglo-Saxon Jewellery*, London: Faber & Faber.
JOHNS, C. M. 1996, *The Jewellery of Roman Britain*, London: UCL Press.
—— 1999, 'Rings and silver bullion', in White *et al.*: 310–12.
—— and T. W. POTTER 1965, 'The Canterbury late Roman treasure', *Antiquaries Journal*, 65: 312–52.
JOHNSON, M. 1997, 'Rethinking houses, rethinking transitions: of vernacular architecture, ordinary people and everyday culture', in Gaimster and Stamper (eds.): 145–55.
—— 2002, *Behind the Castle Gate: From Medieval to Renaissance*, London: Routledge.
JOHNSTONE, N. 1997, 'An investigation into the location of the royal courts of thirteenth-century Gwynned', in Edwards (ed.): 55–69.
JOLLY, K. L. 1996, *Popular Religion in Late Saxon England. Elf Charms in Context*, Chapel Hill and London: University of North Carolina Press.
JONES, C., G. EYRE-MORGAN, S. PALMER, and N. PALMER 1997, 'Excavations in the outer enclosure of Boteler's Castle, Oversley, Alcester, 1992–3', *Transactions of the Birmingham and Warwickshire Archaeological Society*, 101: 3–98.
JONES, M. 2001, 'The sexual and the secular badges', in van Beuningen (ed.): 196–206.
JONES, M. J. 1993, 'The latter days of Roman Lincoln', in Vince (ed.): 14–28.
JONES, N. W. 1998, 'Excavations within the walled town at New Radnor, Powys, 1991–92', *Archaeological Journal*, 155: 134–206.
JONSSON, K. and B. MALMER 1990 (eds.), *Sigtuna Papers: Proceedings of the Sigtuna Conference on Viking-Age Coinage*, London: Spink.

JURKOWSKI, M., C. L. SMITH, and D. CROOK 1998, *Lay Taxes in England and Wales 1168–1688*, Public Record Office Handbook 31, Richmond: PRO Publications.

KARKOV, C. E. 1999 (ed.), *The Archaeology of Anglo-Saxon England: Basic Readings*, Basic Readings in Anglo-Saxon England Vol. 7, New York and London: Garland Publishing.

KAUFMANN, C. M. 1984, catalogue entries in Zarnecki *et al.* (eds.).

KEEN, M. 2002, 'Introduction', in Coss and Keen (eds.): 1–16.

KEENE, D. 1990, 'Wooden vessels', in Biddle (ed.): 959–67.

——1996, 'Metalworking in medieval London: an historical survey', *Journal of Historical Metallurgy*, 30: 95–102.

——1999, 'Wardrobes in the City: houses of consumption, finance and power', in Prestwich *et al.* (eds.): 61–79.

——2000, 'London from the post-Roman period to 1300', in Palliser (ed.): 187–216.

KELLY, D. B. 1987, 'Archaeological notes from Maidstone Museum', *Archaeologia Cantiana*, 104: 350–67.

——1989, 'Archaeological notes from Maidstone Museum', *Archaeologia Cantiana*, 107: 395–409.

KELLY, R. S. 1982, 'The excavation of a medieval farmstead at Cefn Graenog, Clynnog, Gwynned', *Bulletin of the Board of Celtic Studies*, 24: 859–908.

KELLY, S. 1992, 'Trading privileges from eighth-century England', *Early Medieval Europe*, 1: 3–28.

KEMP, B. 1980, *English Church Monuments*, London: Batsford.

KEMP, R. L. 1996, *Anglian Settlement at 46–54 Fishergate*, Archaeology of York 7/1, York: Council for British Archaeology.

——2001, 'York', in Hill and Cowie (eds.): 92–4.

KENDALL, C. B. and P. S. WELLS 1992 (eds.), *Voyage to the Other World. The Legacy of Sutton Hoo*, Minneapolis: University of Minnesota Press, Medieval Studies at Minnesota 5.

KENT, J. P. C. 1972, 'The Aston Rowant Treasure Trove', *Oxoniensia*, 37: 243–4.

KENYON, J. R. 1990, *Medieval Fortifications*, Leicester: Leicester University Press.

——2002, *Kidwelly Castle*, Cardiff: Cadw, Welsh Historic Monuments.

KERMODE, J. 1998, *Medieval Merchants: York, Beverley and Hull in the Later Middle Ages*, Cambridge: Cambridge University Press.

——1991 (ed.), *Enterprise and Individuals in Fifteenth-Century England*, Stroud: Sutton.

KEYNES, S. 1988, 'Regenbald the Chancellor (*sic*)', in Brown, R. A. (ed.): 185–222.

——2001, 'Edward, king of the Anglo-Saxons', in Higham and Hill (eds.): 40–66.

——and M. LAPIDGE 1983, *Alfred the Great*, Harmondsworth: Penguin Books.

KEYS L. 1998, ' Wooden vessels' and 'Glass vessels' in Egan: 196–238.

KILMURRY, K. 1980, *The Pottery Industry of Stamford, Lincolnshire, A.D. 850–1250*, Oxford: British Archaeological Reports British Series 84.

KING, A. 1978, 'Gauber high pasture, Ribblehead—an interim report', in Hall (ed.): 21–5.

KING, E. 1994 (ed.), *The Anarchy of King Stephen's Reign*, Oxford: Clarendon Press.

——(ed.) and K. R. POTTER (trans.) 1998, *William of Malmesbury* Historia Novella: *The Contemporary History*, Oxford: Clarendon Press.

KIRBY, D. P. 1974, *Saint Wilfrid at Hexham*, Newcastle upon Tyne: Oriel Press.

KITSIKOPOULOS, H. 2000, 'Standards of living and capital formation in preplague England: a peasant budget model', *Economic History Review*, 53: 237–61.

KITSON, P. 1978, 'Lapidary traditions in Anglo-Saxon England: Part I, the background; the Old English lapidary', *Anglo-Saxon England*, 7: 9–60.

—— 1983, 'Lapidary traditions in Anglo-Saxon England: Part II, Bede's *Explanatio Apocalypsis* and related works', *Anglo-Saxon England*, 12: 73–127.

KJØLBYE-BIDDLE, B. 1990, 'Early medieval spoons', in Biddle (ed.): 828–31.

KNIGHT, B. and E. J. E. PIRIE 2000, 'Coins', in Stamper and Croft: 124–6.

KNIGHT, J. K. 1996, 'Late and Post-Roman Caerwent: some evidence from metalwork', *Archaeologia Cambrensis*, 45: 35–56.

—— 1999, *The End of Antiquity: Archaeology, Society and Religion A.D. 235–700*, Stroud: Tempus Publishing.

KNÜSEL, C. and K. RIPLEY 2000, 'The *Berdache* or man-woman in Anglo-Saxon England and early medieval Europe', in Frazer and Tyrrell (eds.): 157–91.

KOLDEWEIJ, A. M. 1999, 'Lifting the veil on pilgrim badges', in Stopford (ed.): 161–88.

KORNBLUTH, G. A. 1989, 'The Alfred Jewel: reuse of Roman *spolia*', *Medieval Archaeology*, 33: 32–7.

—— 1998, 'Alfred and Minster Lovell jewels', in Szarmach *et al.* (eds.): 17–8.

KRUSE, S. E. 1988, 'Ingots and weight units in Viking Age silver hoards', *World Archaeology*, 20: 285–301.

—— 1992a, 'Late Saxon balances and weights from England', *Medieval Archaeology*, 36: 67–95.

—— 1992b, 'Metallurgical evidence of silver sources in the Irish Sea province', in Graham-Campbell (ed.): 73–88.

—— 1995, 'Silver storage and circulation in Viking-Age Scotland: the evidence of silver ingots', in Batey *et al.* (eds.): 187–203.

—— and J. TATE 1992, 'XRF analyses of Viking Age silver ingots', *Proceedings of the Society of Antiquaries of Scotland*, 122: 295–328.

—— —— 1995, 'XRF analyses of Viking age silver from Scotland', in Graham-Campbell: 73–82.

LA NIECE, S. 1983, 'Niello: an historical and technical survey', *Antiquaries Journal*, 63: 279–97.

—— 1988, 'White inlays in Anglo-Saxon jewellery', in Slater and Tate (eds.): 235–46.

LA ROCCA, C. and L. PROVERO 2000, 'The dead and their gifts: The will of Eberhard, Count of Friuli, and his wife, Gisela, daughter of Louis the Pious (863–864)', in Theuws and Nelson (eds.): 25–80.

LACHAUD, F. 1996, 'Liveries of robes in England, *c*.1200–*c*.1330,' *English Historical Review*, 111: 279–98.

—— 2002, 'Dress and social status in England before the sumptuary laws', in Coss and Keen (eds.): 105–24.

LAING, L. 2000, 'The chronology and context of Pictish relief sculpture', *Medieval Archaeology*, 44: 81–114.

LANE, A. and E. CAMPBELL 2000, *Dunadd. An Early Dalriadic Capital*, Oxford: Oxbow Books.

LANG, J. and B. AGER 1989, 'Swords of the Anglo-Saxon and Viking periods in the British Museum: a radiographic study', in Hawkes (ed.): 85–122.

LANG, J. T. 1992a, 'The stylistic evidence of the moulds', in Bayley: 65–6.
—— 1992b, 'Fragment of a cross-head', in Milne and Richards: 43.
—— 1986, 'The distinctiveness of Viking colonial art', in Szarmach (ed.): 243–60.
LANG, S. and M. McGREGOR 1993 (eds.), *Tudor Wills Proved in Bristol 1546–1603*, Bristol Record Society 44.
LAPIDGE, M. 2000, 'The archetype of *Beowulf*', *Anglo-Saxon England*, 29: 5–42.
—— and H. GNEUSS 1991 (eds.), *Learning and Literature in Anglo-Saxon England: Studies Presented to Peter Clemoes on the Occasion of his Sixty-Fifth Birthday*, Cambridge: Cambridge University Press.
—— J. BLAIR, S. KEYNES, and D. SCRAGG 2001 (eds.), *The Blackwell Encyclopaedia of Anglo-Saxon England*, Oxford: Blackwell Publishers (pbk ed.).
LAWSON, A. 1983, *The Archaeology of Witton*, Gressenhall: East Anglian Archaeology Report 18.
LAWSON, G. 2001, 'The lyre remains from Grave 32', in Filmer-Sankey and Pestell: 215–23.
LAWSON, M. K. 2000, 'Observations upon a scene in the Bayeux Tapestry, the Battle of Hastings and the military system of the late Anglo-Saxon state', in Maddicott and Palliser (eds.): 73–91.
LE JAN, R. 2000, 'Frankish giving of arms and rituals of power: continuity and change in the Carolingian period', in Theuws and Nelson (eds.): 281–309.
LE PATOUREL, H. E. J. 1968, 'Documentary evidence and the medieval pottery industry', *Medieval Archaeology*, 12: 101–26.
LEACH, P. E. with C. J. Evans 2001, *Fosse Lane, Shepton Mallett: Excavations of a Romano-British Roadside Settlement in Somerset*, Society for the Promotion of Roman Studies Britannia Monograph Series 18.
—— 1984 (ed.), *The Archaeology of Taunton*, Stroud: Western Archaeological Trust Monograph Series 8.
LEAH, M. 1994, *The Late Saxon and Medieval Pottery Industry of Grimston, Norfolk, Excavations 1962–92*, Gressenhall: East Anglian Archaeology Report 64.
LEAHY, K. 1993, 'The Anglo-Saxon settlement of Lindsey', in Vince (ed.): 29–44.
—— 2000, 'Middle Anglo-Saxon metalwork from South Newbald and the "productive site" phenomenon in Yorkshire', in Geake and Kenny (eds.): 51–82.
—— 2001, 'South Humberside and Lincolnshire', *Medieval Archaeology*, 45: 247–50.
—— and C. PATERSON 2001, 'New light on the Viking presence in Lincolnshire: the artefactual evidence', in Graham-Campbell *et al.* (eds.): 181–202.
LEBECQ, S. 1997, 'Routes of change: production and distribution in the West (fifth to eighth century)', in Webster and Brown (eds.): 67–78.
—— 1998, 'Les Échanges dans la Gaule du Nord au sixième siècle', in Hodges and Bowden (eds.): 185–202.
—— 1999, 'England and the continent in the sixth and seventh centuries: the question of logistics', in Gameson (ed.): 50–67.
LEECH, R. H. 2000, 'The symbolic hall: historical context and merchant culture in the early modern city', *Vernacular Architecture*, 31: 1–10.
LEIGH, D. 1984, 'Ambiguity in Anglo-Saxon Style I', *Antiquaries Journal*, 44: 34–42.
LEWIS, J. and G. EWART 1995, *Jedburgh Abbey: The Archaeology and Architecture of a Border Abbey*, Society of Antiquaries of Scotland Monograph Series 10.

LEWIS, J. M. 1970, 'A short cross hoard from Wrexham', *British Numismatic Journal*, 39: 19–23.
—— 1973, 'Some types of metal chafing-dish', *Antiquaries Journal*, 53: 59–70.
—— 1978, *Medieval Pottery and Metal-ware in Wales*, Cardiff: National Museum of Wales.
—— 1982*a*, 'The finds' in Kelly: 889–95.
—— 1982*b*, 'A medieval gold finger-ring from Llantrithyd, South Glamorgan', *Antiquaries Journal*, 62: 129.
—— 1982*c*, 'A medieval ring-brooch from Oxwich Castle, West Glamorgan', *Antiquaries Journal*, 62: 126–9.
—— 1987, 'Bronze aquamaniles and ewers', *Datasheet 7* Finds Research Group 700–1700.
LEYSER, K. 1994, ed. T. Reuter, *Communications and Power in Medieval Europe. The Carolingian and Ottonian Centuries*, London and Rio Grande: Hambledon Press.
LIGHTBOWN, R. W. 1992, *Mediaeval European Jewellery, with a Catalogue of the Collection in the Victoria and Albert Museum*, London: Victoria and Albert Museum.
LILLEY, K. D. 2002, *Urban Life in the Middle Ages, 1000–1450*, Basingstoke: Palgrave.
LINDENBAUM, S. 1994, 'Ceremony and oligarchy: the London Midsummer Watch', in Hanawalt and Reyerson (eds.), 171–88.
LINDLEY, P. 1996, 'The Black Death and English art: a debate and some assumptions', in Ormrod and id. (eds.): 125–46.
LLOYD-MORGAN, G. 1995, 'Objects of copper alloy', in Wilkinson: 24.
LODGE, E. C. and R. SOMERVILLE 1937 (eds.), *John of Gaunt's Register, 1379–1383*, 2 vols., Camden Society 3rd series 57.
LONGLEY, D. 2001, 'The Mote of Mark: the archaeological context of the decorated metalwork', in Redknap *et al.* (eds.): 75–88.
LOVELUCK, C. P. 1995, 'Acculturation, migration and exchange: the formation of an Anglo-Saxon society in the Peak District, 400–700 A.D.', in Bintliff and Hamerow (eds.): 84–98.
—— 1996, 'The development of the Anglo-Saxon landscape: economy and society "on Driffield", East Yorkshire, A.D. 400–750', *Anglo-Saxon Studies in Archaeology and History*, 9: 25–48.
—— 2001, 'Wealth, waste and conspicuous consumption. Flixborough and its importance for mid and late Saxon settlement studies', in Hamerow and MacGregor (eds.): 78–130.
LOWDEN, J. 1999, 'On the purpose of the Sutton Hoo ship-burials', in Buckton and Heslop (eds.): 91–101.
LOWE, C. 1999, *Angels, Fools and Tyrants. Britons and Anglo-Saxons in Southern Scotland*, Edinburgh: Canongate Books.
LOYN, H. R. 1962, *Anglo-Saxon England and the Norman Conquest*, London: Longmans.
LUCY, S. 1998, *The Early Anglo-Saxon Cemeteries of East Yorkshire, An Analysis and Reinterpretation*, Oxford: British Archaeological Reports British Series 272.
—— 2000, *The Anglo-Saxon Way of Death*, Stroud: Sutton Publishing.
—— and A. REYNOLDS 2002 (eds.), *Burial in Early Medieval England and Wales*, Leeds: Society for Medieval Archaeology Monograph 17.

LYNE, M. 1997, *Lewes Priory: Excavations by Richard Lewis 1969–82*, Lewes: Lewes Priory Trust.
LYON, S. 2001, 'The coinage of Edward the Elder', in Higham and Hill (eds.): 67–88.
MACASKILL, M. 1987, 'The pottery', in Holdsworth (ed.): 89–112.
MCCARTHY, M. R. 1990, *A Roman, Anglian and Medieval Site at Blackfriars Street, Carlisle*, Cumberland and Westmorland Antiquarian and Archaeological Society Research Series 4.
—— and C. M. BROOKS 1988, *Medieval Pottery in Britain A.D. 900–1600*, Leicester; Leicester University Press.
MCCORMICK, F. 1992, 'Early Christian metalworking on Iona: excavations under the "infirmary"', *Proceedings of the Society of Antiquaries of Scotland*, 122: 207–14.
MCDONALD, N. F. 2000, '"Lusti tresor"; avarice and the economics of the erotic in Gower's *Confessio Amantis*', in Tyler (ed.): 135–56.
MCDONNELL, G. 2000, 'The ironworking evidence', in Stamper and Croft: 155–66.
MCDOUGALL, I. 1993, 'Serious entertainments; an examination of a peculiar type of Viking atrocity', *Anglo-Saxon England*, 22: 201–25.
MCFARLANE, K. B. 1971, *Hans Memling*, Oxford: Clarendon Press.
MACGREGOR, A. 1978, 'Industry and commerce in Anglo-Scandinavian York', in Hall (ed.): 37–57.
—— 1980, 'A pre-Conquest mould of antler from medieval Southampton', *Medieval Archaeology*, 24: 203–5.
—— 1982, *Anglo-Scandinavian Finds from Lloyds Bank, Pavement and Other Sites*, Archaeology of York 17/3, London: Council for British Archaeology.
—— 1991, 'Antler, bone and horn', in Blair and Ramsay (eds.): 355–78.
—— 1994, 'A pair of late Saxon strap-ends from Ipsden Heath, Oxfordshire', *Journal of the British Archaeological Association*, 147: 122–7.
—— 1996, 'The bone plate from Layer 4', in Adams, M.: 158–60.
—— 1997, *A Summary Catalogue of the Continental Archaeological Collections (Roman Iron Age, Migration Period, Early Medieval)*, Oxford: British Archaeological Reports International Series 674.
—— 2000a, 'A seventh-century pectoral cross from Holderness, East Yorkshire', *Medieval Archaeology*, 44: 217–22.
—— 2000b, 'Objects of bone, antler and ivory' in Ellis, P. (ed.): 160–8.
—— and E. BOLICK 1993, *Ashmolean Museum, Oxford: A Summary Catalogue of the Anglo-Saxon Collections (Non-Ferrous Metals)*, Oxford: British Archaeological Reports British Series 230.
—— A. J. MAINMAN, and N. S. H. ROGERS 1999, *Craft, Industry and Everyday Life: Bone, Antler, Ivory and Horn from Anglo-Scandinavian and Medieval York*, Archaeology of York 17/12, York: Council for British Archaeology.
MACK, K. 1984, 'Changing thegns: Cnut's conquest and the English aristocracy', *Albion*, 16: 375–87.
MACKIE, W. S. 1934 (ed.), *The Exeter Book. Part II: Poems IX–XXXII*, London: Early English Texts Society.
MACLEOD, C. D. and B. WILSON 2001, 'Did a beaked whale inspire the "Pictish beast"?', *Tayside and Fife Archaeological Journal*, 7: 45–7.
MCREE, B. R. 1994, 'Unity or division? The social meaning of guild ceremony in urban communities', in Hanawalt and Reyerson (eds.): 189–207.

MADDICOTT, J. R. 1992, 'Reply', *Past and Present*, 135: 164–88.
—— 2000, 'Two frontier states: Northumbria and Wessex, *c*.650–750', in id. and Palliser (eds.): 25–45.
—— 2001, 'Prosperity and power in the age of Bede and Beowulf', *Proceedings of the British Academy*, 117: 49–71.
—— and D. M. PALLISER 2000 (eds.), *The Medieval State. Essays Presented to James Campbell*, London and Rio Grande: Hambledon Press.
MAGNUS, B. 1999, 'Monsters and birds of prey', *Anglo-Saxon Studies in Archaeology and History*, 10: 161–72.
MAGUIRE, H. 1998, 'Magic and money in the early Middle Ages', in Nees (ed.): 79–96.
MAINMAN, A. J. 1990, *Anglo-Scandinavian Pottery from Coppergate*, Archaeology of York 16/5, London: Council for British Archaeology.
—— and N. S. H. ROGERS 2000, *Craft, Industry and Everyday Life: Finds from Anglo-Scandinavian York*, Archaeology of York 17/14, York: Council for British Archaeology.
MALIM, T. and J. HINES 1998, *The Anglo-Saxon Cemetery at Edix Hill (Barrington A), Cambridgeshire*, York: Council for British Archaeology Research Reports 112.
MANLEY, J. and S. WHITE 1999, 'Discussion', in White *et al.*: 313.
MARGESON, S. 1982, 'Worked bone', in Coad and Streeten: 241–55.
—— 1987, 'A Ringerike-style mount from Stoke Holy Cross', *Norfolk Archaeology*, 40: 126–7.
—— 1993, *Norwich Households. Medieval and Post-Medieval Finds from Norwich Survey Excavations 1971–78*, Norwich Survey, Gressenhall: East Anglian Archaeology Report 58.
—— 1995a, 'Objects from Burial *451*', in Rogerson: 79–80.
—— 1995b, 'The non-ferrous metal objects', in Rogerson: 53–68.
—— 1996, 'Viking settlement in Norfolk: a study of new evidence', in ead. *et al.* (eds.): 47–57.
—— 1997, *The Vikings in Norfolk*, Norwich: Norfolk Museums Service.
—— B. AYERS, and S. HEYWOOD 1996 (eds.), *A Festival of Norfolk Archaeology, in Celebration of the 150th Anniversary of the Norfolk and Norwich Archaeological Society*, Norwich: Norfolk and Norwich Archaeological Society.
MARNER, D. 2002, 'The sword, the spirit, the Word of God and the Book of Deer', *Medieval Archaeology*, 46: 1–28.
MARSHALL, A. and G. MARSHALL 1991, 'A survey and analysis of the buildings of early and middle Anglo-Saxon England', *Medieval Archaeology*, 35: 29–43.
MARVELL, A. G. 2001 (ed.), *Investigations along Monnow Street, Monmouth*, Oxford: British Archaeological Reports British Series 320.
MASON, D. J. P. 1985, *Excavations at Chester: 26–42 Lower Bridge Street 1974–6: The Dark Age and Saxon Periods*, Chester: Chester City Council Archaeological Service Excavation and Survey Report 3.
MASSCHAELE, J. 1997, *Peasants, Merchants and Markets: Inland Trade in Medieval England 1150–1350*, Basingstoke: Macmillan.
MATTHEWS, C. L. and S. C. HAWKES 1985, 'Early Saxon settlements and burials on Puddlehill, near Dunstable, Bedfordshire', *Anglo-Saxon Studies in Archaeology and History*, 4: 59–116.

MATTHEWS, K. 1995, *Excavations at Chester: The Evolution of the Heart of the City. Investigations at 3–15 Eastgate Street 1990/1*, Chester: Chester City Council Archaeological Service Excavation and Survey Report 8.

MAUND, K. 2000, *The Welsh Kings. The Medieval Rulers of Wales*, Stroud: Tempus.

MAYES, P. 2002, *Excavations at a Templar Preceptory. South Witham, Lincolnshire, 1965–67*, Society for Medieval Archaeology Monograph 19.

—— and L. A. S. BUTLER 1983, *Sandal Castle Excavations 1966–1973*, Wakefield: Wakefield Historical Society Publications.

MAYHEW, N. J. 1977, 'Money in Scotland in the thirteenth century', in Metcalf (ed.): 85–102.

—— 1995, 'Population, money supply, and the velocity of circulation in England', *Economic History Review*, 48: 238–57.

—— 1977 (ed.), *Edwardian Monetary Affairs (1279–1344)*, Oxford: British Archaeological Reports British Series, 36.

MAYR-HARTING, H. and R. I. MOORE 1985 (eds.), *Studies in Medieval History Presented to R. H. C. Davis*, London and Roncevert: Hambledon Press.

MAZO CARRAS, M. 1985, 'Seventh-century jewellery from Frisia', *Anglo-Saxon Studies in Archaeology and History*, 4: 159–77.

MEANEY, A. L. 1981, *Anglo-Saxon Amulets and Curing Stones*, Oxford: British Archaeological Reports British Series 96.

—— 1992, 'Anglo-Saxon idolators and ecclesiastics from Theodore to Alcuin: a source study', *Anglo-Saxon Studies in Archaeology and History*, 5: 103–26.

—— 1995, 'Pagan English sanctuaries, place-names and hundred meeting-places', *Anglo-Saxon Studies in Archaeology and History*, 8: 29–42.

—— 2000, 'The hunted and the hunters: British mammals in Old English poetry', *Anglo-Saxon Studies in Archaeology and History*, 11: 95–105.

—— and S. C. HAWKES 1970, *Two Anglo-Saxon Cemeteries at Winnall*, Society for Medieval Archaeology Monograph Series 4.

MEENS, R. 1994, 'A background to Augustine's mission to Anglo-Saxon England', *Anglo-Saxon England*, 23: 5–17.

MELCHIOR-BONNET, S. 2001 (trans. K. H. Jewett), *The Mirror: A History*, New York and London: Routledge.

MELLINKOFF, R. 1993, *Outcasts. Signs of Otherness in Northern European Art of the Late Middle Ages*, Berkeley: University of California Press.

MELLOR, J. E. and T. PEARCE 1981, *The Austin Friars, Leicester*, London: Council for British Archaeology Research Report 35.

MELLOR, M. 1994, 'A synthesis of middle and late Saxon, medieval and early post-medieval pottery in the Oxford region', *Oxoniensia*, 59: 17–218.

—— 1997, *Pots and People That Have Shaped the Heritage of Medieval and Later England*, Oxford: University of Oxford, Ashmolean Museum.

MERCER, E. 1969, *Furniture 700–1700*, London: Weidenfeld & Nicolson.

MEREWETHER, J. 1846, 'Account of the discovery of the episcopal rings . . . at Hereford Cathedral', *Archaeologia*, 31: 249–53.

MERRIFIELD, R. 1987, *The Archaeology of Religion and Magic*, London: Batsford.

METCALF, D. M. 1977, 'The evidence of Scottish coin hoards for monetary history, 1100–1600', in id. (ed.): 1–60.

METCALF, D. M. 1988, 'The coins', in Andrews (ed.): 17–59.
—— 1992, 'The monetary economy of the Irish Sea province', in Graham-Campbell (ed.): 89–106.
—— 1993, *Thrymsas and Sceattas in the Ashmolean Museum, Oxford, Volume 1*, London: Royal Numismatic Society/Ashmolean Museum.
—— 1994, *Thrymsas and Sceattas in the Ashmolean Museum, Oxford, Volume 3*, London: Royal Numismatic Society/Ashmolean Museum.
—— 1995, 'The monetary significance of Scottish Viking-Age coin hoards, with a short commentary', in Graham-Campbell: 16–25.
—— 1998a, 'The monetary economy of ninth-century England south of the Humber: a topographical analysis', in Blackburn and Dumville (eds.): 167–97.
—— 1998b, *An Atlas of Anglo-Saxon and Norman Coin Finds 973–1086*, London: Royal Numismatic Society/Ashmolean Museum.
—— 1977 (ed.), *Coinage in Medieval Scotland (1100–1400)*, Oxford: British Archaeological Reports British Series 45.
—— and J. P. NORTHOVER 1985, 'Debasement of the coinage in southern England in the age of King Alfred', *Numismatic Chronicle*, 145: 150–76.
—— —— 1989, 'Coinage alloys from the time of Offa and Charlemagne to *c.*864', *Numismatic Chronicle*, 149: 101–20.
MILLAR, E. G. 1932, *The Luttrell Psalter*, London: Trustees of the British Museum.
MILLETT, M. 1983, 'Excavations at Cowdery's Down, Basingstoke, Hampshire, 1978–81', *Archaeological Journal*, 140: 151–279.
MILLS, A. D. 1991, *A Dictionary of English Place-Names*, Oxford: Oxford University Press.
MILLS, J. M. 1994, 'The finds', in Ivens *et al.*: 305–96.
MILNE, G. and J. D. RICHARDS 1992, *Wharram: A Study of Settlement on the Yorkshire Wolds, VII: Two Anglo-Saxon Buildings and Associated Finds*, York: York University Archaeological Publications 9.
MITCHELL, B. and F. C. ROBINSON 1998, *Beowulf: An Edition*, Oxford: Oxford University Press.
MITCHINER, M. 1986, *Medieval Pilgrim and Secular Badges*, Sanderstead: Hawkins Publications.
—— 1988, *Jetons, Medalets and Tokens; Volume 1: The Medieval Period and Nuremberg*, London: Seaby.
—— and A. SKINNER 1983, 'English tokens *c.*1200 to 1425', *British Numismatic Journal*, 53: 29–77.
MOLONEY, C. 2001, 'New evidence for the origins and evolution of Dunbar: excavations at the Captain's Cabin, Castle Park, Dunbar, East Lothian', *Proceedings of the Society of Antiquaries of Scotland*, 131: 283–317.
—— and R. COLEMAN 1997, 'The development of a medieval street frontage: the evidence from excavations at 80–86 High Street, Perth', *Proceedings of the Society of Antiquaries of Scotland*, 127: 707–82.
MOORE, J. and E. SCOTT 1997 (eds.), *Invisible People and Processes: Writing Gender and Childhood into European Archaeology*, Leicester: Leicester University Press.
MOORE, R. I. 1987, *The Formation of a Persecuting Society*, Oxford: Blackwell.
MORRIS, C. A. 1983, 'A late Saxon hoard of iron and copper-alloy artefacts from Nazeing, Essex', *Medieval Archaeology*, 27: 27–39.

—— 2000, *Wood and Woodworking in Anglo-Scandinavian and Medieval York*, Archaeology of York 17/13, York: Council for British Archaeology.

MORRIS, C. D. 1996, 'From Birsay to Tintagel: a personal view', in Crawford (ed.): 53–7.

—— et al. 1999, 'Recent work at Tintagel', *Medieval Archaeology*, 43: 206–15.

MORRIS, E. L. 1980, 'Medieval and post-medieval pottery in Worcester—a type series', in Carver: 221–54.

—— and T. M. DICKINSON 2000, 'Early Saxon graves and grave goods', in Young: 89–96.

MORTIMER, C. 1991, 'A descriptive classification of early Anglo-Saxon copper-alloy compositions: towards a general typology of early medieval copper alloys', *Medieval Archaeology*, 35: 104–7.

—— 1994, 'Lead-alloy models for three early Anglo-Saxon brooches', *Anglo-Saxon Studies in Archaeology and History*, 7: 27–33.

MÜLLER-WILLE, M. 1972, 'Zwei wikingerzeitliche Prachtschwerter aus der Umgebung von Haithabu', *Offa*, 29: 50–112.

MUMFORD, W. F. 1965, 'Terciars on the estates of Wenlock Priory', *Transactions of the Shropshire Archaeological Society*, 58: 68–76.

MUNGO, M. M. 1989, 'A sixth-century Mediterranean bucket from Bromeswell Parish, Suffolk', *Antiquity* 63: 295–311.

MUNRO, J. H. 1999, 'The "industrial crisis" of the English textile towns, c.1290–c.1330', in Prestwich *et al.* (eds.): 103–42.

MURDOCH, T. 1991 (comp.), *Treasure and Trinkets. Jewellery in London from pre-Roman Times to the 1930s*, London: Museum of London.

MURPHY, K. 1994, 'Excavations in three burgage plots in the medieval town of Newport, Dyfed, 1991', *Medieval Archaeology*, 38: 55–82.

MURRAY, H. K. and J. C. MURRAY 1993, 'Excavations at Rattray, Aberdeenshire. A Scottish Deserted Burgh', *Medieval Archaeology*, 37: 109–218.

MURRAY, J. C. 1982, 'The pottery', in id. (ed.): 116–76.

—— (ed.), *Excavations in the Medieval Burgh of Aberdeen, 1973–81*, Society of Antiquaries of Scotland Monograph Series 2.

MURRAY, J. E. L. 1977, 'The organisation and work of the Scottish mint, 1358–1603', in Metcalf (ed.): 155–76.

MUSTY, J., D. J. ALGAR, and P. F. EWENCE 1969, 'The medieval pottery kilns at Laverstock, near Salisbury, Wiltshire', *Archaeologia*, 102: 83–150.

MUTHESIUS, A. 1989, 'Silks and saints: the Rider and Peacock silks from the relics of St Cuthbert', in Bonner (ed.): 343–66.

MYERS, A. R. 1959, 'The jewels of Queen Margaret of Anjou', *Bulletin of the John Rylands University Library of Manchester*, 42: 113–31.

MYERS, A. R. 1969 (ed.), *English Historical Documents IV, 1327–1485*, London: Eyre & Spottiswoode.

NEES, L. 1998 (ed.), *Approaches to Early Medieval Art*, Cambridge, Massachusetts: Medieval Academy of America.

NELSON, J. L. 1980, 'The earliest surviving royal *Ordo*: some liturgical and historical aspects', in Tierney and Linehan (eds.): 29–48.

—— 1992, 'Comment 2', *Past and Present*, 135: 151–63.

—— 2001, 'Carolingian contacts', in Brown and Farr (eds.): 126–43.

NENK, B. and J. PEARCE 1994, 'Two Stamford ware modelled birds from London', *Medieval Ceramics*, 18: 77–80.
NEUMAN DE VEGVAR, C. 1987, *The Northumbrian Renaissance: A Study in the Transmission of Style*, Selinsgrove: Susquehanna University Press.
—— 1995, 'Drinking horns in Ireland and Wales: documentary sources', in Cormac (ed.): 81–7.
NEWMAN, C. 1995, 'The Iron Age to Early Christian transition: the evidence from dress fasteners', in Bourke (ed.): 17–25.
NEWMAN, C. A. 1988, *The Anglo-Norman Nobility in the Reign of Henry I: The Second Generation*, Philadelphia: University of Pennsylvania Press.
NEWMAN, J. 1993, 'Three Antler Moulds from Ipswich', *Datasheet 17*, Finds Research Group 700–1700.
—— 1994, 'A late medieval jewellery and coin hoard from Holbrook, Suffolk', *Proceedings of the Suffolk Institute of Archaeology and History*, 38: 193–5.
—— 1999, 'Wics, trade and the hinterlands—the Ipswich region', in Anderton (ed.): 32–47.
NEWTON, S. M. 1980, *Fashion in the Age of the Black Prince*, Woodbridge: Boydell Press.
NICHOLSON, A. 1997, 'The gold and silver', in Hill: 397–400.
NICHOLSON, R. 1977, 'Scottish monetary problems in the fourteenth and fifteenth centuries', in Metcalf (ed.): 103–14.
NIEKE, M. R. 1993, 'Penannular and related brooches', in Spearman and Higgitt (eds.): 128–34.
NIGHTINGALE, P. 1987, 'The origin of the Court of Husting and Danish influence on London's development into a Capital City', *English Historical Review*, 102: 559–78.
—— 1995, *A Medieval Mercantile Community. The Grocers' Company and the Politics and Trade of London 1000–1485*, London and New Haven: Yale University Press.
NOLAN, W. and A. SIMMS, 1998 (eds.), *Irish Towns: A Guide to Sources*, Dublin: Geography Publications.
NORTH, J. E. 1997, *The Heathen Gods in Old English Literature*, Cambridge Studies in Anglo-Saxon England, Cambridge: Cambridge University Press.
NORTH, J. J. 1963, *English Hammered Coinage, Volume I, Early Anglo-Saxon to Henry III, c.650–1272*, London: Spink and Son.
NORTHOVER, J. P. 1986, 'Analyses of five Hiberno-Viking armlets', in Boon (ed.): 101.
NORTHOVER, P. 1995, 'Analyses of early metalwork from Cadbury Castle', in Alcock: 73–4.
Ó CARRAGÁIN, E. 1999, 'The necessary distance: *Imitatio Romae* and the Ruthwell cross', in Hawkes and Mills (eds.): 191–203.
Ó FLOINN, R. 2001, 'Patrons and politics: art, artefact and methodology', in Redknap et al. (eds.): 1–14.
O'CONNOR, A. and D. V. CLARKE 1983 (eds.), *From the Stone Age to the 'Forty-Five. Studies Presented to R. B. K. Stevenson*, Edinburgh: John Donald.
O'CONNOR, S. A. 1992, 'Technology and dating of the mail', in Tweddle: 1057–82.
O'CONNOR, T. P. 1982, *Animal Bones from Flaxengate, Lincoln, c.870–1500*, Archaeology of Lincoln 17-2, London: Council for British Archaeology.

—— 1989, *Bones from Anglo-Scandinavian levels at 16–22 Coppergate*, Archaeology of York 15/3, London: Council for British Archaeology.

O'HARA, M. D. 1994, 'An iron reverse die of the reign of Cnut', in Rumble (ed.): 231–82.

O'MAHONEY, C. 1994, 'Pottery', in Beresford: 152–66.

O'SULLIVAN, D. M. 1996, 'Six pagan burials from Cumbria', *Anglo-Saxon Studies in Archaeology and History*, 9: 15–24.

—— and R. YOUNG 1991, *English Heritage Book of Lindisfarne Holy Island*, London: Batsford/English Heritage.

OAKESHOTT, E. 1991, *Records of the Medieval Sword*, Woodbridge: Boydell Press.

ODDY, W. A. 1977, 'Gilding and tinning in Anglo-Saxon England', in id. (ed.): 129–34.

—— 1977 (ed.), *Aspects of Early Metallurgy*, London: British Museum Occasional Paper 17.

OKASHA, E. 1971, *Hand-List of Anglo-Saxon Non-Runic Inscriptions*, Cambridge: Cambridge University Press.

—— 1983, 'A supplement to *Hand-List of Anglo-Saxon Non-Runic Inscriptions*', *Anglo-Saxon England*, 11: 83–116.

—— 1985, 'The non-ogam inscriptions of Pictland', *Cambridge Medieval Studies*, 9: 43–69.

—— 1993, 'A second supplement to *Hand-List of Non-Runic Inscriptions*', *Anglo-Saxon England*, 21: 37–85.

—— 1995, 'Literacy in Anglo-Saxon England', *Anglo-Saxon Studies in Archaeology and History*, 8: 69–74.

OMAN, C. 1930, *Catalogue of Rings in the Victoria and Albert Museum*, London: Victoria and Albert Museum, repr. Ipswich: Anglia Publishing, 1993.

—— 1979, 'Security in English churches, A.D. 1000–1548', *Archaeological Journal*, 136: 90–8.

OOSTHUIZEN, S. 2002, 'Ancient greens in "Midlands" landscapes: Barrington, south Cambridgeshire', *Medieval Archaeology*, 46: 110–5.

ORME, N. 1995, 'The culture of children in medieval England', *Past and Present*, 148: 48–88.

ORMROD, W. M. 1986, 'The English government and the Black Death of 1348–49', in id. (ed.): 175–89.

—— 2000, 'The English state and the Plantagenet Empire 1259–1360: a fiscal perspective', in Maddicott and Palliser (eds.): 197–214.

—— 1986 (ed.), *England in the Fourteenth Century: Proceedings of the Harlaxton Symposium*, Woodbridge: Boydell Press.

—— and P. LINDLEY 1996 (eds.), *The Black Death in England*, Stamford: Paul Watkins.

ORNA-ORNSTEIN, J. 1999, 'Coin catalogue and numismatic discussion', in White *et al.*: 304–10.

OTTAWAY, P. 1992, *Anglo-Scandinavian Ironwork from Coppergate*, Archaeology of York 17/6, London: Council for British Archaeology.

—— and N. S. H. ROGERS, 2002, *Craft, Industry and Everyday Life: Finds from Medieval York*, Archaeology of York 17/15, York: Council for British Archaeology.

OTWAY-RUTHVEN, A. J. 1980, *A History of Medieval Ireland*, London: E. Benn.

OWEN, D. M. 1984 (ed.), *The Making of King's Lynn: A Documentary Survey*, London: British Academy Records of Social and Economic History, NS 9.

OWEN, G. 1979, 'Wynflaed's wardrobe', *Anglo-Saxon England*, 8: 195–222.

OWEN, O. 2001, 'The strange beast that is the English Urnes style', in Graham-Campbell *et al.* (eds.): 203–22.

—— and M. DALLAND 1999, *Scar: A Viking Boat Burial on Sanday, Orkney*, East Linton: Tuckwell Press/Historic Scotland.

OWEN-CROCKER, G. 1986, *Dress in Anglo-Saxon England*, Manchester: Manchester University Press.

—— 1998, 'The search for Anglo-Saxon skin garments and the documentary evidence', in Cameron (ed.): 27–43.

—— and T. GRAHAM 1998 (eds.), *Medieval Art: Recent Perspectives*, Manchester: Manchester University Press.

PADER, E.-J. 1982, *Symbolism, Social Relations and the Interpretation of Mortuary Remains*, Oxford: British Archaeological Reports International Series 130.

PAGAN, H. E. 1988, 'The imitative Louis the Pious *solidus* from Southampton', in Andrews: 71–2.

—— 1999, 'A missing coin of Aelfred rediscovered', *British Numismatic Journal*, 69: 199–200.

—— 1990, 'The coinage of Harold II', in Jonsson and Malmer (eds.): 179–205.

PAGE, R. I. 1991, catalogue entries in Webster and Backhouse (eds.).

PAINTER, K. S. 1999, 'The Water Newton silver: votive or liturgical?', *Journal of the British Archaeological Association*, 152: 1–23.

PALGRAVE, F. 1836 (ed.), *The Antient Kalendars and Inventories of the Treasury of His Majesty's Exchequer*, 3 vols., Record Commission Publications 23, London: Record Commission.

PALLISER, D. M. 2000 (ed.), *The Cambridge Urban History of Britain. Volume I, 600–1540*, Cambridge: Cambridge University Press.

PALMER, N. and W. A. SEABY 1983–4, 'An early thirteenth-century hoard from Cross on the Hill, near Stratford-on-Avon', *Transactions of the Birmingham and Warwickshire Archaeological Society*, 93: 105–10.

PARFITT, K. and B. BRUGMANN 1997, *The Anglo-Saxon Cemetery at Mill Hill, Deal, Kent*, Society for Medieval Archaeology Monograph 14.

PARKES, M. B. and E. SALTER 1978, *Troilus and Criseyde: A Facsimile of Corpus Christi College, Cambridge MS. 61*, Cambridge: D. S. Brewer.

PARKHOUSE, J. and E. EVANS 1996, *Excavations in Cowbridge, South Glamorgan, 1977–88*, Oxford: British Archaeological Reports British Series 245.

PARSONS, D. 1975 (ed.), *Tenth-Century Studies. Essays in Commemoration of the Council of Winchester and the* Regularis Concordia, Chichester: Phillimore.

PARSONS, J. C. 1977, *The Court and Household of Eleanor of Castile in 1290*, Toronto: Pontifical Institute.

—— 1995, *Eleanor of Castile: Queen and Society in Thirteenth-Century England*, Basingstoke: Macmillan.

PEACOCK, D. P. S. 1997, 'Charlemagne's black stones: the re-use of Roman columns in early medieval Europe', *Antiquity*, 71: 709–15.

PEARCE, J. 1992, *Border Ware*, London: HMSO.

—— and A. Vince 1988, *A Dated Type-Series of London Medieval Pottery. Part 4: Surrey Whitewares*, London and Middlesex Archaeological Society Special Paper 10.

Pearsall, D. 1997, 'Strangers in late fourteenth-century London', in Akehurst and Van D'Elden (eds.): 46–62.

Pearson, S. 1994, *The Medieval Houses of Kent*, London: Royal Commission on Historical Monuments for England.

—— 2002, 'The chronological distribution of tree-ring dates, 1980–2001', *Vernacular Architecture*, 32: 68–9.

Peirce, I. 1986, 'The knight, his arms and armour in the eleventh and twelfth centuries', in Harper-Bill and Harvey (eds.): 152–64.

Penn, K. 2000, *Norwich Southern Bypass, Part II: Anglo-Saxon Cemetery at Harford Farm, Caistor St Edmund*, Gressenhall: East Anglian Archaeology Report 92.

Perkins, D. R. 2000, 'Jutish glass production in Kent: and the problem of the base cups', *Archaeologia Cantiana*, 120: 297–310.

Perry, D. R. 2000, *Castle Park, Dunbar. Two Thousand Years on a Fortified Headland*, Society of Antiquaries of Scotland Monograph Series 16.

Phillips, D. and B. Heywood 1995, ed. M. O. H. Carver, *Excavations at York Minster, Volume 1: From Roman Fortress to Norman Cathedral*, London: HMSO/Royal Commission on Historical Monuments for England.

Philpott, R. 1991, *Burial Practices in Roman Britain. A Survey of Grave Treatment and Furnishing A.D. 43–410*, Oxford: British Archaeological Reports British Series 219.

Philpott, R. A. 1999, 'Recent Anglo-Saxon finds from Merseyside and Cheshire and their archaeological significance', *Medieval Archaeology*, 43: 194–202.

Pilbrow, F. 2002, 'The Knights of the Bath: dubbing to knighthood in Lancastrian and Yorkist England', in Coss and Keen (eds.): 195–218.

Pinder, M. 1995, 'Anglo-Saxon garnet cloisonné composite disc-brooches', *Journal of the British Archaeological Association*, 148: 6–28.

Pine, J. 2001, 'The excavation of a Saxon settlement at Cadley Road, Collingbourne Ducis, Wiltshire', *Wiltshire Archaeology and Natural History Magazine*, 94: 88–117.

Piponnier, F. and P. Mane 1997 (trans. C. Beamish), *Dress in the Middle Ages*, New Haven and London: Yale University Press.

Pirie, E. J. E. 1986, *Post-Roman Coins from York Excavations 1971–1981*, Archaeology of York 18/1, London: Council for British Archaeology.

—— 1987, 'Early Northumbrian coins', in Hurst and Rahtz (eds.): 174–5.

—— 1991, 'The Northumbrian coins: single finds and the purse hoard', in Armstrong et al. (eds.).

—— 1997, 'The early medieval coins', in Hill: 332–45.

—— 1999, 'Post-Roman coins', in Richards: 79–81.

Platt, C. 1978, *Medieval England. A Social History and Archaeology from the Conquest to 1600 A.D.*, London and Henley: Routledge and Kegan Paul.

—— 1996, *King Death. The Black Death and its Aftermath in Late-Medieval England*, London: University College London Press.

—— and R. Coleman-Smith 1975, *Excavations in Medieval Southampton 1953–1969*, Leicester: Leicester University Press.

PLUNKETT, S. J. 1998, 'Appendix: Anglo-Saxon Stone Sculpture and Architecture', in West: 324–57.
——2001, 'Some recent metalwork discoveries from the area of the Gipping Valley, and their local contexts', in Binski and Noel (eds.): 61–87.
POHL, W. 1997, 'Discussion', in Hines (ed.): 407–8.
——2003, 'The construction of communities and the persistence of paradox', in Corradini *et al.* (eds.): 1–15.
POLLEXFEN, J. H. 1862–4, 'Notice of the coins of David I of Scotland, Henry I and Stephen of England, found with gold ornaments etc. at Plan, in the Island of Bute, in June 1863', *Proceedings of the Society of Antiquaries of Scotland*, 5: 372–84.
POOLE, H. 1996, 'The Offham brooch', *Sussex Archaeological Collections*, 134: 232–3.
POSTLES, D. 1996, 'Personal pledging: medieval reciprocity" or "symbolic capital"', *Journal of Interdisciplinary History*, 26: 419–35.
POTTER, T. W. and R. D. ANDREWS 1994, 'Excavation and survey at St Patrick's Chapel and St Peter's Church, Heysham, Lancashire, 1977–8', *Antiquaries Journal*, 74: 55–134.
POULTON, R. and H. WOODS 1984, *Excavations on the Site of the Dominican Friary at Guildford in 1974 and 1978*, Guildford: Surrey Archaeological Society Research Vol. 9.
POUNDS, N. J. G. 1994, *The Culture of the English People*, Cambridge: Cambridge University Press.
POWLESLAND, D. 1999, 'The Anglo-Saxon settlement at West Heslerton, North Yorkshire', in Hawkes and Mills (eds.): 55–65.
PRESTON-JONES, A. and P. ROSE 1986, 'Medieval Cornwall', *Cornish Archaeology*, 25: 85–135.
PRESTWICH, M. 1980, *The First Three Edwards*, London: Weidenfeld & Nicolson.
——1999, 'The "wonderful life" of the thirteenth century', in id. *et al.* (eds.): 161–71.
——R. BRITNELL, and R. FRAME 1999 (eds.), *Thirteenth-Century England VII: Proceedings of the Durham Conference 1997*, Woodbridge: Boydell Press.
PRICE, J. 2000, 'Late Roman glass vessels in Britain and Ireland from A.D. 350 to 410 and beyond', in ead. (ed.): 1–31.
——2000 (ed.), *Glass in Britain and Ireland A.D. 350–1100*, London: British Museum Occasional Paper 127.
PRICE, R. with M. PONSFORD 1998, *St Bartholomew's Hospital, Bristol: The Excavation of a Medieval Hospital, 1976–8*, York: Council for British Archaeology Research Report 110.
PRITCHARD, F. 1984, 'Late Saxon textiles from the City of London', *Medieval Archaeology*, 28: 46–76.
——1991, 'Small finds', in Vince (ed.): 120–278.
PROUDFOOT, E. and C. ALIAGA-KELLY 1996, 'Towards an interpretation of anomalous finds and place-names of Anglo-Saxon origin in Scotland', *Anglo-Saxon Studies in Archaeology and History*, 9: 7–8.
PRYCE, H. 1992, 'Ecclesiastical wealth in early Wales', in Edwards and Lane (eds.): 22–32.
——2000, 'The context and purpose of the earliest Welsh lawbooks', *Cambrian Medieval Studies*, 39: 39–63.

QUINNELL, H. 1993, 'A sense of identity: distinctive Cornish stone artefacts in the Roman and post-Roman periods', *Cornish Archaeology*, 32: 29–46.

——and M. R. BLOCKLEY 1994, *Excavations at Rhuddlan, Clwyd 1969–73: Mesolithic to Medieval*, London: Council for British Archaeology Research Report 95.

RACKHAM, B. 1939, 'A Netherlands maiolica vase from the Tower of London', *Antiquaries Journal*, 19: 287–90.

——1947, *Medieval English Pottery*, London: Faber & Faber.

RADY, J. 1987, 'Excavations at St Martin's Hill, Canterbury, 1984–85', *Archaeologia Cantiana*, 114: 123–218.

RAHTZ, P. 1979, *The Saxon and Medieval Palaces at Cheddar*, Oxford: British Archaeological Reports British Series 65.

——and R. MEESON 1992, *An Anglo-Saxon Watermill at Tamworth*, London: Council for British Archaeology Research Report 83.

——and L. WATTS 1989, 'Pagan's Hill revisited', *Archaeological Journal*, 146: 330–71.

——S. HIRST, and S. M. WRIGHT 2000, *Cannington Cemetery*, Society for the Promotion of Roman Studies Britannia Monograph Series 17.

——*et al.* 1992, *Cadbury Congresbury 1968–73: a Late/Post-Roman Hilltop Settlement in Somerset*, Oxford: British Archaeological Reports British Series 223.

RAINS, M. J. and D. W. HALL 1997 (eds.), *Excavations in St Andrews 1980–1989*, Glenrothes: Tayside and Fife Archaeological Committee Monograph 1.

RAMSAY, N. 1987, catalogue entry in Alexander and Binski (eds.).

RAW, B. 1992, 'Royal power and royal symbols in *Beowulf*', in Carver (ed.): 167–74.

RAWLINGS, M. and A. FITZPATRICK 1996, 'Prehistoric sites and a Romano-British settlement at Butterfield Down, Amesbury', *Wiltshire Archaeological and Natural History Society Magazine*, 89: 1–43.

READ, C. H. 1887, 'On an iron sword of Scandinavian type . . .', *Archaeologia*, 50: 530–3.

REDKNAP, M. 1995, 'Insular non-ferrous metalwork from Wales of the eighth to the tenth centuries', in Bourke (ed.): 59–74.

——2000, *Vikings in Wales: An Archaeological Quest*, Cardiff: National Museums and Art Galleries of Wales.

——N. EDWARDS, S. YOUNGS, A. LANE, and J. KNIGHT 2001 (eds.), *Pattern and Purpose in Insular Art*, Oxford: Oxbow.

REECE, R. 1981, *Excavations in Iona 1964 to 1975*, University of London Institute of Archaeology Occasional Publication 5.

——1999, *The Later Roman Empire: An Archaeology*, Stroud: Sutton Publishing.

REID, P. 2001, 'Knowing people through their feet', *London Archaeologist*, 9: 228–30.

REUTER, T. 2003 (ed.), *Alfred the Great*, Aldershot: Ashgate Publishing.

REYNOLDS, A. 1994, 'A late Anglo-Saxon disc-brooch from Steyning, West Sussex', *Medieval Archaeology*, 38: 169–71.

REYNOLDS, S. 1994, *Fiefs and Vassals: The Medieval Evidence Reinterpreted*, Oxford: Oxford University Press.

RICHARDS, J. D. 1991, *Viking Age England*, London: Batsford/English Heritage.

——1992, 'Anglo-Saxon symbolism', in Carver (ed.): 131–48.

——1995, 'An archaeology of Anglo-Saxon England', in Ausenda (ed.): 51–66.

RICHARDS, J. D. 1999, 'Cottam: an Anglo-Scandinavian settlement on the Yorkshire Wolds', *Archaeological Journal*, 156: 1–111.
——2000, 'The Anglo-Saxon and Anglo-Scandinavian evidence', in Stamper and Croft: 128–31.
——2002, 'The case of the missing Vikings: Scandinavian burial in the Danelaw', in Lucy and Reynolds (eds.): 156–70.
——M. JECOCK, L. RICHMOND, and C. TUCK 1995, 'The Viking barrow cemetery at Heath Wood, Ingleby, Derbyshire', *Medieval Archaeology*, 39: 51–70.
RICHARDSON, H. 1993, 'Remarks on the liturgical fan, flabellum or rhipidion', in Spearman and Higgitt (eds.): 27–34.
RICHMOND, C. 1994, 'Religion', in Horrox (ed.): 183–201.
RICKETT, R. 1995 (ed.), *The Anglo-Saxon Cemetery at Spong Hill, North Elmham, Part VII: The Iron Age and Early Saxon Settlement*, Gressenhall: East Anglian Archaeology Report 73.
RIDDLER, I. 2001, 'The small finds', in Gardiner *et al.*: 228–52.
RIGBY, S. H. 1996, *Chaucer in Context*, Manchester: Manchester University Press.
——1999, 'Approaches to pre-industrial social structure', in Denton (ed.): 6–25.
——and G. EWAN 2000, 'Government, power and authority', in Palliser (ed.): 291–313.
RIGOLD, S. E. 1975, 'The Sutton Hoo coins in the light of the contemporary background of coinage in England', in Bruce-Mitford: 653–77.
——1977, 'Two common species of medieval seal-matrix', *Antiquaries Journal*, 57: 324–9.
RITCHIE, A. 1993, *Viking Scotland*, London: Batsford/Historic Scotland.
ROBERTS, B. K. and S. WRATHMELL 2002, *Region and Place. A Study of English Rural Settlement*, London: English Heritage.
ROBERTS, J. 1992, 'Anglo-Saxon vocabulary as a reflection of material culture', in Carver (ed.): 185–204.
——and J. L. NELSON with M. GODDEN 1997 (eds.), *Alfred the Wise. Studies in Honour of Janet Bateley on the Occasion of her Sixty-Fifth Birthday*, Cambridge: D. S. Brewer.
ROBERTS, R. A. 1929 (ed.), *The Lords Ordainers and Piers Gaveston's Jewels and Horses (1312–1313)*, Camden Miscellany 15.
ROBINSON, F. C. 1991, 'Beowulf', in Godden and Lapidge (eds.): 142–59.
ROBINSON, M. 1973, 'Site 4: excavations at Copt Hay, Tetsworth', *Oxoniensia*, 38: 41–115.
ROBINSON, P. 1969, 'The Stafford (1800) and Oulton (1795) hoards', *British Numismatic Journal*, 38: 22–30.
——1979/80, 'A pin of the later Saxon period from Marlborough and some related pins', *Wiltshire Archaeological and Natural History Society Magazine*, 74/5: 57–60.
——1984, 'Saxon coins of Edward the Elder from St. Mary's churchyard, Amesbury', *Numismatic Chronicle*, 144: 198–201.
——1990, 'Two medieval coin brooches from Wiltshire', *Wiltshire Archaeological and Natural History Society Magazine*, 83: 208–9.
——1992, 'Some late Saxon mounts from Wiltshire', *Wiltshire Archaeological and Natural History Magazine*, 85: 63–9.

—— 1993, 'Coins, jetons and tokens', in Graham and Davies: 78–81.

—— 2000, 'Catalogue of coins, jetons and tokens', in Young: 132–4.

—— 2001, 'A Northumbrian "styca" from Wiltshire: the problem with southern provenances of "stycas"', *British Numismatic Journal*, 71: 160–1.

RODWELL, W. 2001, *Wells Cathedral. Excavations and Structural Studies, 1978–93*, 2 vols., London: English Heritage.

ROESDAHL, E. and D. M. WILSON 1992 (eds.), *From Viking to Crusader: The Scandinavians and Europe 800–1200*, New York: Rizzoli.

—— J. GRAHAM-CAMPBELL, P. CONNOR, and K. PEARSON 1981 (eds.), *The Vikings in England*, London: Anglo-Danish Viking Project.

ROFFE, D. 2000a. 'The early history of Wharram Percy', in Stamper and Croft: 1–16.

—— 2000b, *Domesday: The Inquest and the Book*, Oxford: Oxford University Press.

ROGERS, N. S. H. 1993, *Anglian and Other Finds from Fishergate*, Archaeology of York 17/9, London, Council for British Archaeology.

ROGERSON, A. 1976, 'Excavations on Fuller's Hill, Great Yarmouth', *East Anglian Archaeology Report*, 2: 131–245.

—— 1995, *A Late Neolithic, Saxon and Medieval Site at Middle Harling, Norfolk*, Gressenhall: East Anglian Archaeology Report 74.

—— and C. DALLAS 1984, *Excavations in Thetford 1948–59 and 1973–80*, Gressenhall: East Anglian Archaeology Report 22.

ROLLASON, D. 1989, 'St Cuthbert and Wessex: the evidence of Cambridge, Corpus Christi College MS 183', in Bonner (ed.): 413–24.

ROSE, T. 1992, *The Coronation Ceremony and the Crown Jewels*, London: HMSO.

ROTH, C. 1962, 'Portraits and caricatures of medieval English Jews', in id. (ed.): 26–45.

—— 1962 (ed.), *Essays and Portraits in Anglo-Jewish History*, Philadelphia: Jewish Publication Society of America.

ROTHWELL, H. 1975 (ed.), *English Historical Documents Volume IV: 1189–1327*, London: Eyre & Spottiswoode.

RUBIN, M. 1991, 'Small groups: identity and solidarity in the late Middle Ages', in Kermode (ed.): 132–50.

—— 1992, 'Religious culture in town and country: reflections on a great divide', in Abulafia *et al.* (eds.): 3–22.

RUMBLE, A. R. 1981, 'The purposes of the Codex Wintoniensis', *Proceedings of the Battle Conference on Anglo-Norman Studies*, 4: 153–66.

—— 2001, 'Edward the Elder and the churches of Winchester and Wessex', in Higham and Hill (eds.): 230–47.

—— 2002, *Property and Piety in Early Medieval Winchester*, Winchester Studies 4iii, Oxford: Clarendon Press.

—— 1991 (ed.), *The Reign of Cnut*, Leicester: Leicester University Press.

RUSHTON, N. S. 2002, 'Spatial aspects of the almonry site and the changing priorities of poor relief at Westminster Abbey c.1290–1540', *Architectural History*, 45: 66–91.

RUSSEL, A. 1996, 'Anglo-Saxon pottery', in Jackson and Potter: 654–7.

SALZMAN, L. F. 1952, *Building in England Down To 1540: A Documentary History*, Oxford: Clarendon Press.

SAUL, N. 1986, *Scenes from Provincial Life: Knightly Families in Sussex, 1280–1400*, Oxford: Clarendon Press.

SAUNDERS, P. R. 1982, 'An inscribed medieval brooch from Amesbury', *Wiltshire Archaeological and Natural History Magazine*, 77: 146–7.
—— (ed.) 2001, *Salisbury and South Wiltshire Museum Medieval Catalogue, Part 3*, Salisbury: Salisbury and South Wiltshire Museum.
—— and E. SAUNDERS 1991 (eds.), *Salisbury and South Wiltshire Museum Medieval Catalogue, Part 1*, Salisbury: Salisbury and South Wiltshire Museum.
SAVORY, H. N. 1956, 'Some sub-Roman British brooches from south Wales', in Harden (ed.): 40–58.
SAWYER, P. H. 1968, *Anglo-Saxon Charters. An Annotated List and Bibliography*, London: Royal Historical Society.
—— 1986, 'Anglo-Scandinavian trade in the Viking Age and after', in Blackburn (ed.): 185–99.
SCARISBRICK, D. 1995, *Tudor and Jacobean Jewellery*, London: Tate Publishing.
SCHLESINGER, A. and C. WALLS 1996, 'An early church and farmstead site: excavations at Llanelen, Gower', *Archaeological Journal*, 153: 104–47.
SCOBIE, G. D., J. M. ZANT, and R. WHINNEY, *The Brooks, Winchester. A Preliminary Report on the Excavations, 1987–88*, Winchester: Winchester Museums Service, Archaeology Report 1.
SCOTT, K. L. 1996, *Late Gothic Manuscripts 1390–1490*, 2 vols., London: Harvey Miller Publishers.
SCOTT, M. 1986, *A Visual History of Costume: The Fourteenth and Fifteenth Centuries*, London: B. T. Batsford.
SCRAGG, D. 1991 (ed.), *The Battle of Maldon A.D. 991*, Oxford: Oxford University Press.
—— 2003 (ed.), *Textual and Material Culture in Anglo-Saxon England. Thomas Northcote Toller Memorial Lectures*, Cambridge: D. S. Brewer.
SCULL, C. 1985, 'Further evidence from East Anglia for enamelling on early Anglo-Saxon metalwork', *Anglo-Saxon Studies in Archaeology and History*, 4: 117–24.
—— 1990, 'Scales and weights in early Anglo-Saxon England', *Archaeological Journal*, 147: 183–215.
SEABY, W. A. and P. WOODFIELD, 'Viking stirrups from England and their background', *Medieval Archaeology*, 24: 87–122.
SHENTON, C. 2002, 'Edward III and the symbol of the leopard', in Coss and Keen (eds.): 69–81.
SHERBORNE, J. W. 1977, 'The cost of English warfare with France in the later fourteenth century', *British Institute of Historical Research*, 122: 135–50.
SHERLOCK, D. and H. WOODS 1988, *St Augustine's Abbey: Report on Excavations 1960–78*, Maidstone: Kent Archaeological Society Monograph 4.
SHETELIG, H. 1940 (ed.), *Viking Antiquities in Great Britain and Ireland. Part IV: Viking Antiquities in England*, Oslo: Haschehoug.
SHILTON, D. O. and R. HOLWORTHY 1925 (eds.), *Medieval Wills from Wells*, Somerset Record Society 40.
SHOESMITH, R. 1985, *Hereford City Excavations Volume 3*, London: Council for British Archaeology Research Report 56.
SHORT, I. 2001, 'The language of the Bayeux Tapestry', in Gillingham (ed.): 267–80.
SHORTT, H. DE S. 1964, 'Another spur of the first century A.D. from Suffolk', *Antiquaries Journal*, 44: 60–1.

SKINNER, P. 2003 (ed.), *Jews in Medieval Britain*, Woodbridge: Boydell & Brewer.
SKLAR, E. S. 1998, 'Courtly love', in Szarmach *et al.* (eds.): 214–16.
SLATER, E. A. and J. O. TATE 1988 (eds.), *Science and Archaeology, Glasgow 1987*, Oxford: British Archaeological Reports British Series 196.
SLATER, T. R. 2000 (ed.), *Towns in Decline, A.D. 100–1600*, Aldershot: Ashgate.
——and G. ROSSER 1998 (eds.), *The Church in the Medieval Town*, Aldershot: Ashgate.
SMALL, A., C. THOMAS, and D. M. WILSON 1973, *St Ninian's Isle and its Treasure*, Oxford: Oxford University Press.
SMITH, G. H. 1979, 'Excavation of the Hospital of St Mary of Ospringe', *Archaeologia Cantiana*, 95: 81–184.
SMITH, R. A. 1906, 'Anglo-Saxon remains', *Victoria County History of Somerset, Volume 1*, London: James Street: 373–81.
SMITH, R. M. 1985 (ed.), *Land, Kinship and Life-Cycle*, Cambridge: Cambridge University Press.
SMYTH, A. P. 1995, *King Alfred the Great*, Oxford: Oxford University Press.
SNEYD, C. A. 1848 (ed.), *A Relation of the Island of England c.1500*, Camden Society 37.
SNYDER, C. A. 1996, *Sub-Roman Britain (A.D. 400–600): A Gazetteer of Sites*, Oxford: British Archaeological Reports British Series 247.
SOLLY, M. C. 1984, 'Zoomorphic design: a new look at Pictish art?', in Friell and Watson (eds.): 189–210.
SOMERS COCKS, A. 1980, *Princely Magnificence. Court Jewels of the Renaissance, 1500–1630*, London: Debrett's Peerage.
SOUTHWORTH, E. 1990 (ed.), *Anglo-Saxon Cemeteries: A Reappraisal*, Stroud: Alan Sutton Publishing.
SPAREY-GREEN, C. 2002, 'Excavations on the south-eastern defences and extra-mural settlement of Little Chester, Derby, 1971–2', *Derbyshire Archaeological Journal*, 122: 1–328.
SPEAKE, G. 1989, *A Saxon Bed Burial on Swallowcliffe Down. Excavations by F. de M. Vatcher*, London: English Heritage Archaeological Report 10.
SPEARMAN, R. M. 1988, 'Early Scottish towns: their origins and economy', in Driscoll and Nieke (eds.): 96–110.
——and J. HIGGITT 1993 (eds.), *The Age of Migrating Ideas, Early Medieval Art in Northern Britain and Ireland*, Edinburgh: National Museums of Scotland/Stroud: Alan Sutton Publishing.
SPENCER, B. 1985, 'Fifteenth-century collar of SS and hoard of false dice with their container, from the Museum of London', *Antiquaries Journal*, 65: 449–53.
——1990a, *Salisbury and South Wiltshire Museum Medieval Catalogue Part 2: Pilgrim Souvenirs and Secular Badges*, Salisbury: Salisbury and South Wiltshire Museum.
——1990b, 'Pilgrims' badges', in Biddle (ed.): 799–803.
——1993, 'Copper alloy pilgrim badges', in Margeson: 7–8.
——1998, *Pilgrim Souvenirs and Secular Badges*, London: HMSO.
SPUFFORD, P. 1988, *Money and its Use in Medieval Europe*, Cambridge: Cambridge University Press.
STACEY, R. C. 2000, 'Clothes talk from medieval Wales', in Charles-Edwards *et al.* (eds.): 338–46.

STAFFORD, P. 1989, *Unification and Conquest. A Political and Social History of England in the Tenth and Eleventh Centuries*, London: Edward Arnold.
—— 1997, *Queen Emma and Queen Edith*, Oxford: Blackwell Publishing.
—— 2000, 'Queens and treasure in the early Middle Ages', in Tyler (ed.): 61–82.
STAHL, A. M. 1992, 'The nature of the Sutton Hoo coin parcel', in Kendall and Wells (eds.): 3–14.
—— and W. A. ODDY 1992, 'The date of the Sutton Hoo coins', in Farrell and Neuman de Vegvar 1992 (eds.): 129–48.
STALLEY, R. 1988, 'Sailing to Santiago: medieval pilgrimage to Santiago de Compostela and its artistic influence in Ireland', in Bradley (ed.): 397–420.
STALLIBRASS, S. 2002, 'The Possible Use of Fish and Cattle Bones as Rosary Beads', *Datasheet 29* Finds Research Group 700–1700.
STAMPER, P. A. and R. A. CROFT 2000, *Wharram: A Study of Settlement on the Yorkshire Wolds, VIII: The South Manor Area*, York: York University Archaeological Publications 10.
STANCLIFFE, C. 1999, 'The British church and the mission of Augustine', in Gameson (ed.): 107–51.
STEANE, J. 1984, *The Archaeology of Medieval England and Wales*, London and Sydney: Croom Helm.
—— 1993, *The Archaeology of the English Medieval Monarchy*, London: Batsford.
STENTON, F. 1965 (ed.), *The Bayeux Tapestry* (2nd edn.), London: Phaidon.
STEVENSON, R. B. K. 1983, 'Further notes on the Hunterston and "Tara" brooches, Moneymusk reliquary and Blackness bracelet', *Proceedings of the Society of Antiquaries of Scotland*, 113: 469–77.
—— 1989, catalogue entries in Youngs (ed.).
—— 1993, 'Further thoughts on some well-known problems', in Spearman and Higgitt (eds.): 16–26.
STEWART, I. 1977, 'The volume of early Scottish coinage', in Metcalf (ed.): 65–72.
—— 1978, 'Anglo-Saxon gold coins', in Carson and Kraay (eds.): 143–72.
STIFF, M. 2000, 'Glass vessels', in Mainman and Rogers: 2537–41.
—— 2001, 'Typology and trade: a study of the vessel glass from *wics* and emporia in north-west Europe', in Hill and Cowie (eds.): 43–53.
STOODLEY, N. 1999, *The Spindle and the Spear. A Critical Enquiry into the Construction and Meaning of Gender in the Early Anglo-Saxon Burial Rite*, Oxford: British Archaeological Reports British Series 288.
—— 2002, 'The origins of Hamwic and its central role in the seventh century as revealed by recent archaeological discoveries', in Hordh and Larsson (eds.): 317–31.
STOPFORD, J. 1999 (ed.), *Pilgrimage Explored*, York: York Medieval Press.
STOTT, P. 1991, 'Spangles', in Egan and Pritchard: 235–8.
STRATFORD, J. 2000, 'The Goldenes Rössl and the French royal collections', in Tyler (ed.): 109–33.
STRATFORD, N. 1984, catalogue entries in Zarnecki *et al.* (eds.).
—— 1997, *The Lewis Chessmen and the Enigma of the Hoard*, London: British Museum Press.
STRICKLAND, M. 1997, 'Military technology and conquest: the anomaly of Anglo-Saxon England', *Anglo-Norman Studies*, 14: 353–82.

STUDER, P. and J. EVANS 1924, *Anglo-Norman Lapidaries*, Paris: Edouard Champion.
STURDY, D. 1995, *Alfred the Great*, London: Constable.
SUTHERLAND, C. H. V. 1948, *Anglo-Saxon Gold Coinage in the Light of the Crondall Hoard*, Oxford: Oxford University Press.
SUZUKI, S. 2000, *The Quoit Brooch Style and Anglo-Saxon Settlement*, Woodbridge: Boydell Press.
SWABEY, FF. 1999, *Medieval Gentlewoman. Life in a Widow's Household in the Later Middle Ages*, Stroud: Sutton.
SWANSON, H. 1989, *Medieval Artisans. An Urban Class in Late Medieval England*, Oxford: Blackwell.
SWANSON, R. N. 1999, *The Twelfth-Century Renaissance*, Manchester: Manchester University Press.
SWANTON, M. J. 1973, *The Spearheads of the Anglo-Saxon Settlements*, Royal Archaeological Institute.
SWARZENSKI, H. 1974, *Monuments of Romanesque Art. The Art of Church Treasures in North-West Europe* (2nd edn.), London: Faber & Faber.
SWIFT, E. 2000, *Regionality in Dress Accessories in the Late Roman West*, Montignac: éditions monique mergoil.
SYMONDS, R. P. and TOMBER, R. S. 1991, 'Late Roman London: an assessment of the ceramic evidence from the City of London', *Transactions of the London and Middlesex Archaeological Society*, 42: 59–99.
SZARMACH, P. 1986 (ed.), *Sources of Anglo-Saxon Culture*, Studies in Medieval Culture 20, Kalamazoo: Medieval Institute Publications.
——M. T. TAVORMINA, and J. T. ROSENTHAL 1998 (eds.), *Medieval England: An Encyclopedia*, New York: Garland.
TAIT, H. 1968, 'European: High Middle Ages to 1862', in Harden *et al.* (comps.): 127–92.
——1976, *Jewellery Through 7000 Years*, London: British Museum Publications.
TALVIO, T. 1990, 'The designs of Edward the Confessor's coins', in Jonsson and Malmer (eds.): 489–99.
TAYLOR, A. J. 1979, 'Edward I and the shrine of St Thomas at Canterbury', *Journal of the British Archaeological Association*, 132: 22–8.
TAYLOR, J. and L. WEBSTER 1984, 'A late Saxon strap-end mould from Carlisle', *Medieval Archaeology*, 28: 178–81.
TELFORD, P. J. 1956, 'Medieval stone moulds from the Herbert Art Gallery and Museum Site, Coventry', *Proceedings of the Coventry and District Natural History and Scientific Society*, 2: 3–8.
THEUWS, F. and J. L. NELSON 2000 (eds.), *Rituals of Power: From Late Antiquity to the Early Middle Ages*, Leiden: Brill.
THOMAS, C. 1959, 'Imported pottery in Dark-Age western Britain', *Medieval Archaeology*, 3: 89–111.
——1984, 'The Pictish Class I symbol stones', in Friell and Watson (eds.): 169–87.
——1986, *Celtic Britain*, London: Thames & Hudson.
——1990, '"Gallici Nautae de Galliarum Provinciis"—a sixth-/seventh-century trade with Gaul, reconsidered', *Medieval Archaeology*, 24: 1–26.
——1998, *Christian Celts: Messages and Images*, Stroud: Tempus Publishing.

THOMAS, G. 1996, 'Silver wire strap-ends from East Anglia', *Anglo-Saxon Studies in Archaeology and History*, 9: 81–100.

—— 2000, 'Anglo-Scandinavian metalwork from the Danelaw', in Hadley and Richards (eds.): 237–55.

—— 2001a, 'Strap-ends and the identification of regional patterns in the production and circulation of ornamental metalwork in later Anglo-Saxon and Viking age Britain', in Redknap *et al.* (eds.): 39–48.

—— 2001b, 'A Ringerike brooch', *London Archaeologist*, 9: 228–30.

THOMPSON, J. A. F. 1979, 'John de la Pole, Duke of Suffolk', *Speculum*, 54: 528–42.

THOMPSON, J. D. A. 1956, *Inventory of British Coin Hoards A.D. 600–1500*, London: Royal Numismatic Society Special Publications 1.

THOMPSON, M. W. 1995, *The Medieval Hall*, Aldershot: Scolar Press.

—— 1998, *Medieval Bishops' Houses in England and Wales*, Aldershot: Ashgate.

THOMPSON, V. 2002, 'Constructing salvation: a homiletic and penitential context for late Anglo-Saxon burial practice', in Lucy and Reynolds (eds.): 229–39.

—— 2003, 'Memory, salvation and ambiguity', in Williams (ed.): 215–26.

THORN, J. C. 1981, 'The burial of John Dygon, abbot of St Augustine's', in Detsicas (ed.): 74–84.

THORPE, L. 1978 (trans.), *Gerald of Wales: The Journey Through Wales and the Description of Wales*, Harmondsworth: Penguin Books.

TIERNEY, B. and P. LINEHAN 1980 (eds.), *Authority and Power: Studies on Medieval Law and Government Presented to Walter Ullman on his Seventieth Birthday*, Cambridge: Cambridge University Press.

TODD, M. 1987, *The South-West to A.D. 1000*, London: Longman.

TONNOCHY, A. B. 1952, *Catalogue of British Seal-Dies in the British Museum*, London: Trustees of the British Museum.

TOORIANS, L. 1990, 'Wizo Flandrensis and the Flemish settlement in Pembrokeshire', *Cambridge Medieval Celtic Studies*, 20: 99–118.

TUDOR-CRAIG, P. 1987, catalogue entries in Alexander and Binski (eds.).

TURNER, D. H. 1984, catalogue entries in Backhouse *et al.* (eds.).

TWEDDLE, D. 1992a, *The Anglian Helmet from Coppergate*, Archaeology of York 17/8, London: Council for British Archaeology.

—— 1992b, catalogue entry in Roesdahl and Wilson (eds).

—— M. BIDDLE, and B. KJØLBYE-BIDDLE 1995, *Corpus of Anglo-Saxon Stone Sculpture Volume IV: South-East England*, Oxford: Oxford University Press.

—— J. MOULDEN, and E. LOGAN 1999, *Anglian York: A Survey of the Evidence*, Archaeology of York 7/2, York: Council for British Archaeology.

TYLECOTE, R. F. and B. J. J. GILMOUR 1986, *The Metallography of Early Ferrous Edge Tools and Edged Weapons*, Oxford: British Archaeological Reports British Series 155.

TYLER, E. M. 1999, ' "The eyes of the beholder were dazzled": treasure and artifice in *Encomium Emmae Reginae*', *Early Medieval Europe*, 8: 247–70.

—— 2000, ' "When Wings Incarnadine with Gold are Spread": the *Vita Aedwardi Regis* and the display of treasure at the court of Edward the Confessor', in ead. (ed.): 83–108.

—— 2000 (ed.), *Treasure in the Medieval West*, York: York Medieval Press.

TYLER, R. 1996, 'Early Saxon Essex A.D. 400–700', in Bedwin (ed.): 108–16.
TYMMS, S. 1850 (ed.), *Wills and Inventories from the Registers of the Commissary of Bury St Edmunds and the Archdeacon of Sudbury*, Camden Society.
TYRRELL, A. 2000, '*Corpus Saxonum*: early medieval bodies and corporeal identity', in Frazer and Tyrrell (eds.): 137–55.
TYSON, R. 2000, *Medieval Glass vessels Found in England c.A.D. 1200–1500*, York: Council for British Archaeology Research Report 121.
—— 2001, 'Glass vessels', in Saunders (ed.): 26–38.
—— 2002, 'Glass vessels', in Ottaway and Rogers: 2814–27.
ULMSCHNEIDER, K. 1999, 'Archaeology, history and the Isle of Wight in the middle Saxon period', *Medieval Archaeology*, 43: 19–44.
VAUGHAN, R. 1993 (ed. and trans.), *The Illustrated Chronicles of Matthew Paris: Observations of Thirteenth-Century Life*, Stroud: Alan Sutton Publishing.
VINCE, A. 1985a, 'The Saxon and medieval pottery of London: a review', *Medieval Archaeology*, 29: 25–93.
—— 1985b, 'Part 2: the ceramic finds', in Shoesmith: 34–82.
—— 1990, *Saxon London*, London: Seaby.
—— 2000, 'The study of medieval pottery in London', in Haynes *et al.* (eds.): 239–51.
—— 1991 (ed.), *Aspects of Saxo-Norman London: 2, Finds and Environmental Evidence*, London and Middlesex Archaeological Society Special Paper 12.
—— 1993 (ed.), *Pre-Viking Lindsey*, Lincoln: City of Lincoln Archaeological Unit.
WADE, K. 1983, 'The early Anglo-Saxon period', in Lawson: 66–7.
—— 2001, 'Ipswich', in Hill and Cowie (eds.): 86–7.
WADE-MARTINS, P. 1980, *Excavations in North Elmham Park, 1967–1972*, 2 vols., Gressenhall: East Anglian Archaeology Report 9.
WALKER, D. 1990, *Medieval Wales*, Cambridge: Cambridge University Press.
WALLIS, S. and M. WAUGHMAN 1998, *Archaeology and the Landscape in the Lower Blackwater Valley*, Gressenhall: East Anglian Archaeology Report 82.
WALTON, P. 1989, *Textiles, Cordage and Raw Fibre from 16–22 Coppergate*, Archaeology of York 17/5, London, Council for British Archaeology.
WALTON ROGERS, P. 1997, *Textile Production at 16–22 Coppergate*, Archaeology of York 17/11, York: Council for British Archaeology.
—— 1998, 'Textiles', in Drinkall and Foreman: 242.
WARD PERKINS, J. B. 1940, *London Museum: Medieval Catalogue*, London: HMSO.
—— 2000, 'Why did the Anglo-Saxons not become more British?', *English Historical Review*, 115: 513–33.
WAREHAM, A. 2001, 'The transformation of kinship and the family in late Anglo-Saxon England', *Early Medieval Europe*, 10: 375–99.
WARNER, R. 1975–6, 'Scottish silver arm-rings; an analysis of weights', *Proceedings of the Society of Antiquaries of Scotland*, 107: 136–43.
WARREN, W. L. 1977, *Henry II*, Berkeley and Los Angeles: University of California Press.
WATERMAN, D. M. 1959, 'Late Saxon, Viking, and early medieval finds from York', *Archaeologia*, 97: 59–106.
WATKIN, J. and F. MANN 1981, 'Some late Saxon finds from Lilla Howe and their context', *Medieval Archaeology*, 25: 153–7.

WATKIN, J. R. 1986, 'A late Anglo-Saxon sword from Gilling West, North Yorkshire', *Medieval Archaeology*, 30: 93–9.

WATKINS, D. R. 1994, *The Foundry Excavations on Poole Waterfront 1986/7*, Dorset Natural History and Archaeological Society Monograph Series 14.

WATSON, J. 2000, 'Wood', in Hinton: 86–93.

WATTS, J. 2002, 'Looking for the state in later medieval England', in Coss and Keen (eds.): 243–67.

WATTS, S. 2000, 'Grinding stones', in Stamper and Croft: 111–15.

WEAVER, F. W. 1901–5 (ed.), *Somerset Medieval Wills*, 3 vols., Somerset Record Society 16, 19, and 21.

WEBSTER, L. 1982, 'The Canterbury pendant', *Antiquity*, 56: 203–4.

—— 1984, 'A late Saxon circular brooch', in Leach (ed.): 133–4.

—— 1985, 'The grave goods', in Hedges and Buckley: 9–14.

—— 1991, catalogue entries in ead. and Backhouse (eds.).

—— 1992, catalogue entries in Roesdahl and Wilson (eds.).

—— 1993a, 'The brooch mould', in Hamerow: 62–3.

—— with E. OKASHA 1993b, 'Gold ring', in Gardiner: 47–50.

—— 1995, 'The Iona Abbey ring bezel', in Graham-Campbell: 49–50.

—— 1998, 'Archaeology and *Beowulf*', in Mitchell and Robinson: 183–94.

—— 1999a, 'The chape-fitting' in White *et al.*: 312–13.

—— 1999b, 'The iconographic programme of the Franks Casket', in Hawkes and Mills (eds.): 227–48.

—— 2000a, 'Ideal and reality: versions of treasure in the early Anglo-Saxon world', in Tyler (ed.): 49–59.

—— 2000b, no. 88 in *Treasure Annual Report 1998–1999*, London: Portable Antiquities Scheme.

—— 2001a, 'Metalwork of the Mercian supremacy', in Brown and Farr (eds.): 263–76.

—— 2001b, 'Alfred Jewel', in Lapidge *et al.* (eds.): 28–9.

—— 2003, '*Aedificia nova*: treasures of Alfred's reign', in Reuter (ed.): 79–103.

—— and J. BACKHOUSE 1991 (eds.), *The Making of England: Anglo-Saxon Art and Culture A.D. 600–900*, London: British Museum Press.

—— and M. P. BROWN 1997 (eds.), *The Transformation of the Roman World A.D. 400–900*, London: British Museum Press.

WEDLAKE, W. J. 1958, *Excavations at Camerton, Somerset*, Camerton Excavation Club.

WELCH, M. 1992, *Anglo-Saxon England*, London: Batsford/English Heritage.

—— 2001a, review of Suzuki 2000, *Antiquaries Journal*, 81: 436–7.

—— 2001b, 'The archaeology of Mercia', in Brown and Farr (eds.): 147–59.

—— 2002, 'Cross-Channel contacts between Anglo-Saxon England and Merovingian Francia', in Lucy and Reynolds (eds.): 122–31.

WENHAM, P., R. A. HALL, C. M. BRIDEN, and D. A. STOCKER 1987, *St Mary Bishophill Junior and St Mary Castlegate*, Archaeology of York 8/2, London: Council for British Archaeology.

WERNER, J. 1992, 'A review of [Bruce-Mitford 1983]', *Anglo-Saxon Studies in Archaeology and History*, 5: 1–24.

WERNER, M. 1991, 'The Liudhard medalet', *Anglo-Saxon England*, 20: 27–41.

WEST, S. 1985, *West Stow. The Anglo-Saxon Village*, Gressenhall: East Anglian Archaeology Report 24.

—— 1998, *A Corpus of Anglo-Saxon Material from Suffolk*, Gressenhall: East Anglian Archaeology Report 84.

WHEELER, R. E. M. 1927, *London Museum Catalogues: No. 1. London and the Vikings*, London: Lancaster House.

WHITE, R. 1990, 'Scrap or substitute? Roman material in Anglo-Saxon graves', in Southworth (ed.): 125–52.

—— and P. BARKER 1998, *Death of a Roman City*, Stroud: Sutton Publishing.

WHITE, R. H. 1986, *Peel Castle Excavations Final Report (1)*, Isle of Man: St Patrick's Isle Archaeological Trust.

WHITE, S. 1998, 'The Patching hoard', *Medieval Archaeology*, 42: 88–93.

—— *et al*. 1999, 'A mid fifth-century hoard of Roman and pseudo-Roman material from Patching, West Sussex', *Britannia*, 30: 301–15.

WHITELOCK, D. 1930 (ed. and trans.), *Anglo-Saxon Wills*, Cambridge: Cambridge University Press.

—— 1961 (ed.), *The Anglo-Saxon Chronicle. A Revised Translation*, London: Eyre & Spottiswoode.

—— 1968 (ed.), *The Will of Aethelgifu*, London: Roxburghe Club Publication 216.

—— 1979 (ed.), *English Historical Documents c.500–1042*, revised edn., London: Eyre Methuen.

WHITFIELD, N. 1995, 'Formal conventions in the depiction of animals on Celtic metalwork', in Bourke (ed.): 89–104.

—— 1998, 'The manufacture of ancient beaded wire: experiments and observations', *Jewellery Studies*, 8: 57–86.

—— 2001, 'The "Tara" brooch: an Irish emblem of status in its European context', in Hourihane (ed.): 211–47.

WHITTLE, J. 1998, 'Individualism and the family-land bond; a reassessment of land transfer among the English peasantry c.1270–1580', *Past and Present*, 160: 25–63.

WICKHAM-CROWLEY, K. 1992, 'The birds on the Sutton Hoo instrument', in Farrell and Neuman de Vegvar (eds.): 43–62.

WILKINSON, P. F. 1995, 'Excavations at Hen Gastell, Briton Ferry, West Glamorgan', *Medieval Archaeology*, 39: 1–50.

WILLIAMS, A. 1995, *The English and the Norman Conquest*, Woodbridge: Boydell Press.

WILLIAMS, D. 1997*a*, *Late Saxon Stirrup-Strap Mounts: A Classification and Catalogue*, York: Council for British Archaeology Research Report 111.

—— 1997*b*, 'Stirrup Terminals', *Datasheet 24* Finds Research Group 700–1700.

—— 2002, 'Two late Saxon spur fragments from Sussex and Hampshire', *Medieval Archaeology*, 46: 115–8.

WILLIAMS, D. F. and A. VINCE 1997, 'The characterization and interpretation of early to middle Saxon granitic tempered pottery in England', *Medieval Archaeology*, 41: 214–40.

WILLIAMS, F. 1979, 'Excavations on Marefair, Northampton, 1977', *Northamptonshire Archaeology*, 14: 38–79.

WILLIAMS, G. 1998a, 'The gold coinage of Eadbald, King of Kent (A.D. 616–40)', *British Numismatic Journal*, 68: 137–40.
—— 1998b, 'A further parcel from the Appledore hoard' *British Numismatic Journal*, 68: 141.
—— 1998c, 'A hoard of Aethelraed II Long Cross', *British Numismatic Journal*, 68: 143–4.
—— 1999, 'Anglo-Saxon and Viking coin weights', *British Numismatic Journal*, 69: 19–36.
—— 2001a, 'Mercian coinage and authority', in Brown and Farr (eds.): 211–28.
—— 2001b, 'Coin-brooches of Edward the Confessor and William I', *British Numismatic Journal*, 71: 60–70.
—— and H. MYTUM 1998 (ed. K. Blockley), *Llawhaden, Dyfed: Excavations on a Group of Small Defended Enclosures, 1980–4*, Oxford: British Archaeological Reports British Series 275.
WILLIAMS, H. 1997, 'Ancient landscapes and the dead; the reuse of prehistoric and Roman monuments as early Anglo-Saxon burial sites', *Medieval Archaeology*, 41: 1–32.
—— 2002, '"Remains of pagan Saxondom"?—the study of Anglo-Saxon cremation rites', in Lucy and Reynolds (eds.): 47–71.
—— 2003 (ed.), *Archaeologies of Remembrance. Death and Memory in Past Societies*, New York: Kleuwer Academic/Plenum Publishers.
WILLIAMS, J. H. 1979, *St Peter's Street, Northampton Excavations 1973–1976*, Archaeological Monograph 2, Northampton: Northampton Development Corporation.
—— M. SHAW, and V. DENHAM 1985, *Middle Saxon Palaces at Northampton*, Archaeological Monograph 4, Northampton: Northampton Development Corporation.
WILLIAMS, R. J. 1993, *Pennylands Hartigans. Two Iron Age and Saxon Sites in Milton Keynes*, Buckinghamshire Archaeological Society Monograph 4.
WILLMOTT, H. 2002, *Early Post-Medieval Vessel Glass in England, c.1500–1670*, York: Council for British Archaeology Research Report 132.
WILSON, D. M. 1957, 'An unpublished fragment from the Goldsbrough hoard', *Antiquaries Journal*, 37: 72–3.
—— 1964, *Anglo-Saxon Ornamental Metalwork 700–1100 in the British Museum*, London: Trustees of the British Museum.
—— 1965, 'Some neglected Anglo-Saxon swords', *Medieval Archaeology*, 9: 32–54.
—— 1975, 'Tenth-century metalwork', in Parsons (ed.): 200–7.
—— 1985, 'The silver brooch', in Mason: 61.
—— 1991, catalogue entries in Webster and Backhouse (eds.).
—— and C. E. BLUNT 1961, 'The Trewhiddle hoard', *Archaeologia*, 98: 75–122.
WILSON, P. R. et al. 1996, 'Early Anglian Catterick and *Catraeth*', *Medieval Archaeology*, 40: 1–61.
WILTHEW, P. 1991, 'Technological material', in Fasham and Whinney: 45–6.
WINTERBOTTOM, M. 1978 (ed.), *Gildas. The Ruin of Britain and Other Works*, Chichester: Phillimore.
WISE, P. J. 1985, 'Hulton Abbey: a century of excavations', *Staffordshire Archaeological Studies*, 2: 1–142.

——1994, 'A medieval gold ring from Fladbury', *Transactions of the Worcestershire Archaeological Society*, 14: 233–4.

——1997, 'The Fillongley hoard—a medieval coin and jewellery hoard from Warwickshire', *British Numismatic Journal*, 69: 201–4.

——and W. A. SEABY 1995, 'Finds from a new "productive site" at Bidford-on-Avon, Warwickshire', *Transactions of the Birmingham and Warwickshire Archaeological Society*, 99: 57–64.

WOOD, I. 1991, 'The Franks and Sutton Hoo', in Wood and Lund (eds.): 1–14.

——1992, 'Frankish hegemony in England', in Carver (ed.): 235–41.

——1997, 'The transmission of ideas', in Webster and Brown (eds.): 111–27.

——1999, 'Augustine and Gaul', in Gameson (ed.): 68–82.

——1998 (ed.), *Franks and Alamanni in the Migration Period*, Woodbridge: Boydell Press.

——and N. LUND 1992 (eds.), *People and Places in Northern Europe 500–1600. Essays in Honour of Peter Hayes Sawyer*, Woodbridge: Boydell Press.

WOODFIELD, C. 1981, 'Finds from the Free Grammar School at the Whitefriars, Coventry, c.1545–c.1557/58', *Post-Medieval Archaeology*, 15: 81–160.

WOODING, C. A. 1998, *Communications and Commerce Along the Western Sealanes, A.D. 400–800*, Oxford: British Archaeological Reports International Series 654.

WOOLF, A. 2001, 'The Verturian hegemony: a mirror in the north', in Brown and Farr (eds): 106–12.

WOOLGAR, C. M. 1992, *Household Accounts from Medieval England*, Records of Social and Economic History, NS 17 and 18, Oxford: Oxford University Press.

——1999, *The Great Household in Late Medieval England*, New Haven and London: Yale University Press.

WORMALD, P. 1982, 'Viking studies: whence and whither?', in Farrell (ed.): 128–53.

——1991, 'In search of King Offa's "law-code"', in Wood and Lund (eds.): 25–46.

——1999, *The Making of English Law: King Alfred to the Twelfth Century, Volume I: Legislation and its Limits*, Oxford: Blackwell Publishers.

——2001, '*On tha waepnedhealfe*: kingship and royal property from Aethelwulf to Edward the Elder', in Higham and Hill (eds.): 262–79.

WORRELL, S. 2002, 'Cheriton', in Geake: 132.

WRATHMELL, S. 1998, *Wharram. A Study of Settlement on the Yorkshire Wolds, VI. Domestic Settlement 2: Medieval Peasant Farmsteads*, York; York University Archaeological Publications 8.

WRIGHT, S. M. 1982, 'Much Park Street, Coventry: the development of a medieval street. Excavations 1970–74', *Transactions of the Birmingham and Warwickshire Archaeological Society*, 92: 1–133.

YAPP, W. B. 1989, 'The font at Melbury Bubb: an interpretation', *Proceedings of the Dorset Natural History and Archaeological Society*, 111: 128–9.

YEOMAN, P. 1995, *Medieval Scotland*, London: Batsford/Historic Scotland.

YORKE, B. 1990, *Kings and Kingdoms of Early Anglo-Saxon England*, London: B. A. Seaby.

——1993, 'Lindsey: the lost kingdom found?', in Vince (ed.): 141–50.

——1995, *Wessex in the Early Middle Ages*, London and New York: Leicester University Press.

YORKE, B. 2000, 'Political and ethnic identity: a case study of Anglo-Saxon practice', in Frazer and Tyrrell (eds.): 69–89.
—— 2001, 'Edward as Aetheling', in Higham and Hill (eds.): 25–39.
YOUNG, C. J. 2000, *Excavations at Carisbrooke Castle, Isle of Wight, 1921–1996*, Salisbury: Wessex Archaeological Report 18.
YOUNGS, S. 1989, catalogue entries in ead. (ed.).
—— 1992, 'A medieval Irish enamel', *Antiquaries Journal*, 72: 188–91.
—— 1993, 'The Steeple Bumstead boss', in Spearman and Higgitt (eds.): 143–50.
—— 1995, 'Medium and motif: polychrome enamelling and early manuscript decoration in Insular art', in Bourke (ed.): 37–47.
—— 2000, nos. 76–7 in *Treasure Annual Report 1998–1999*, London: Portable Antiquities Scheme.
—— 2001*a*, '"From Ireland coming"; fine Irish metalwork from the Medway, Kent, England', in Hourihane (ed.): 249–60.
—— 2001*b*, 'Insular metalwork from Flixborough, Lincolnshire', *Medieval Archaeology*, 45: 210–20.
—— 1989 (ed.), *'The Work of Angels': Masterpieces of Celtic Metalwork, 6th–9th Centuries AD*, London: British Museum Publications.
—— J. CLARK, and T. BARRY 1985 (comps.), 'Medieval Britain and Ireland in 1984', *Medieval Archaeology*, 29: 158–230.
ZARNECKI, G., J. HOLT, and T. HOLLAND 1984 (eds.), *English Romanesque Art 1066–1200*, London: Weidenfeld & Nicolson/Arts Council of Great Britain.

Index

Note: Bold-face denotes references to illustrations

Aberdeen 181
Aberford, ring from **4.1**
Aberlady 78
Abingdon sword 109–14, 128, 131, 148, 169, **4.2**
Aedred 102
Aelfflaed 133
Aelfgar 148
Aelfnoth 149, 165
Aelfric's *Colloquy* 155
aestels 129–31, **4.10**
Aethelberht, King 50–1, 54–5, 57, 64–5, 185
Aethelstan, the aetheling 145, 147–9, 165–6
Aethelswyth, Queen 108, 110
  ring of **4.1**
Aethelwulf, King 108, 111, 117, 147
  ring of **4.1**
Ahlstan 120
Aidan, Bishop 66
Alcuin 114
Aldbrough, pommel from **B.3**
Aldclune 82
Aldfrith, King 87
Aldhelm, Saint 88, 97
Aldred 97
ale 216, 236, 255
Alfred Jewel 129–31, **4.10**
Alfred, Ealdorman 129
Alfred, King 120, 123, 128–34
Alkmonkton, ring from **H.2**
altars 62, 85, 96, 100, 145–6, 165, 191, 259
Alton 63, 132
  buckle from **2.14**
amber 28, 33, 45, 65, 84, 128, 137, 162, 209, 226
Amesbury 7, 13
amethyst, amethysts 65, 68, 74, 188, 213, 244
amulets 28–9, 31, 70, 74, 103, 136, 138
Anglesey 121–2
Anglo-Saxon Chronicle 12, 16, 55, 128, 139
antler 135, 160, 162
Apple Down 26, 28–9
aquamaniles 180, 185, 200, 234, **6.9**
Arthurian legends 200, 222
Arundel, earls of 226
Asser, Bishop 120, 123, 129
Asthall 60, 63, 97
Aston Rowant 85, 87, 98
Athelney 131
Athelstan, King 132–3, 136, 141
Augustine, Archbishop 5, 57, 93

aurochs 63
axe-hammers 40, 42–3, 61, 117

badges 139, 193–6, 199, 201, 220–3, 244–5, 247, 253–5, 258, **7.4**, **7.8**, **8.10**, **8.11**, **H.7**
  pilgrims' 136, 193–6, 209–11, 220, 230, 251, 258, **6.14**, **7.14**, **8.10**
bags 28, 83, 166
Ballinaby 124
  grave assemblage from **4.8**
Bangor 122, 152
Bantham Bay 20, 83
Banwell 83
Bardsey Island 152
Baret, John 247–8
Barflat 42–3
Barham 96–7
Barking Abbey 88
barrows 57, 60, 65, 70, 100–1, 116, 118
bars, metal 11
Barsham 145, 167
Bath 40
Battle of Maldon 147
Bayeux Tapestry 142–3, 145, 155, 169
beach-markets 20, 78
beads 28, 31, 33, 36, 43, 53, 65, 68, 74, 84, 88, 93, 103, 115, 117, 120, 123, 131, 137–8, 158, 160, 209, 212, 230, 246–7, 259, **1.11**, **7.2**
  paternoster 209, 215, 223, 231, 247, 258
beag, beah, baeg 103, 145, 147–8
Beauchamp, Lady Margaret 249
Becket, Thomas 193–5
Beckley 102
Bede 22, 26–7, 29, 39, 56, 60, 62, 65, 68, 93, 187
beer 236–7, 255
Beeston Tor 113, 116–17
bells 70, 140, 142, 211, 227
belts 13, 16, 102, 132, 165–7, 172, 191, 197, 200, 213, 218, 223, 227, 229, 247, 253, 259
belt-fittings 12, 228, 250–1, **1.4**, **8.9**
  see also buckles, strap-ends
Benington 189
Beonna, King 106
Beowulf 31, 57, 65, 89, 100, 107
Bernwood Forest 200
beryls 213–14
Bestiaries 103
Beverley 115, 139

Bidford-on-Avon 70
Bifrons 18, 27
Bigbury Bay 83
Biorhtelm 129, 163
Birsay 21, 43, 80
bishops 216
Bishopstone 74
bismuth 119, 127
bitterns' claws 246
Black Death 231–3
Black Prince 222
black stones, *see* lava
Bladon 178
Blois, Bishop Henry de 128
books, *see* manuscripts
boots 162–3, **5.11**
Boss Hall 77–8, 84
Bossall/Flaxton 119
Bossington 109
Bowleaze Cove jewel 131, **4.10**
boxes 62, 69, 74, 78, 82
Boxley 208
bracelets, *see* rings
Brackley 197
bracteates 33–4, 55, 65
Brandon 97–8, 101
brass 107
bribes 51, 63, 201, 224
bridle fittings, *see* harness
Bridport 214
Brighthampton 13, 16
Brightlingsea 147
Bristol 185
Broadstairs 33
Broch of Gurness 127
brooches 16, 27
   annular 84
   button-, 28, 40, **1.10**
   coin-, coin-imitative 132, 139, 143–4, 159–60, 166, 172, **5.1**
   composite disc- 55, 63, 65, 67, 74–8, 114, **3.3, B.1–2**
   cross-bow 8, 13
   cruciform 15–16, 22, 33
   disc- 33, 58, 92, 100, 110–14, 143, 158, 167, **3.5, 5.1**
   enamel 159
   equal-arm 22, 33, **1.7, A.2**
   equal-armed 124
   filigree 167
   Frisian bow- 93
   great square-headed 22, 26, 33, 35–6, 40, 58, **1.8–9**
   heart-framed 245, 247, 258, **8.5**
   jetton- 229
   letter-shaped 249–50, **8.8**
   oval 117, 120, 123–5, 136, 139, **4.5**
   penannular 17–18, 20, 27–8, 36, 41, 45, 62, 80–3, 115–16, 120, 125, 149, **1.5–6, 2.1–2, 2.5, 3.4, 4.6**
   quatrefoil 209, **7.3**
   quoit- 12–13, 15–16, 22, 33, 35, **A.1**
   ring- 180, 188–93, 197–9, 207–8, 212, 215, 219–20, 224, 230, 258, **6.11, 7.1, 7.7**
   saucer- 22, 26–8, 33, 36, 58, **1.10**
   shield-shaped 192–3, **6.13**
   small-long 35
   square-headed disc-on-bow 62
   square-headed (Kentish) 26, 28
   thistle- 149, 151
   tutulus 8, 13
buckle fittings 74, 136, 172, 198–9
buckles, buckle-frames 7, 63, 103, 132, 140, 152, 154–5, 162, 164, 172, 178, 214, 228, 247, 253, 259, **3.1**
   inlaid iron 33, 71–2, **2.12**
   late Roman 8–9, 12–13, 35, **1.1**
   Kentish triangular 55, 63, 65, **2.14–15**
   Sutton Hoo great gold 53, 61–3, 132, **2.11**
   see also clasps
Buiston Crannog 49
bullion economy 119, 122, 127, 179
Burghead 123
Bury St Edmunds 139, 232, 247
   stud from near **B.4**
Bute 179, 183
buttons 223, 228–9

Cadbury Congresbury 18
Cade, William 192, 196
Caerphilly, vessel from **8.1**
Caerwent 17–18, 84, 92, 120
   brooch from **1.5**
Caister 249
Caistor St Edmund, *see* Harford Farm
cameos 62, 188, 219
Camerton 83
candlesticks 172
Cannington 40, 82–3
Canonbie 208, 219
   hoard **7.2**
Canterbury 7, 36, 49–50, 57, 65, 82, 84, 93, 96, 106, 129, 165, 193–5, 198, 209, 218, 258
   brooch from **5.1**
   King's School brooch 143, 145
Canterbury Tales, see Chaucer, Geoffrey
caps 141
Capel Maelog 206
carborundum 53
carbuncles 188
Carisbrooke 31, 49, 63
   ring from **H.4**
Carlisle 92, 198, 228
Carlus, sword of 132
Carreghofa 185
caskets 171
Castle Acre 166
castles 171, 178, 180, 185, 192, 197–8, 200, 215–16, 236
Catterick 74
cattle 47, 84, 123, 185

Cefn Graenog 186–7
censers 60
Cerne, Book of 98, 113
chafing-dishes 255
chains 7, 43, 115, 124, 151, 245, 247, **2.3**, **8.6**
chalices 89, 100–1, 115, 148
chalk 53
Chalton 74
chapes 10, 12–13, 80, 102–3, 136, 228, **1.3**
Charlemagne, Emperor 89
charms 190–1, 245, 247–8
Charms 68
Charnwood, Forest of 29
Charon's obol 32
charters 85, 87, 107, 123, 128, 145, 147, 185
Chaucer, Geoffrey 211, 213, 218, 227–9
Cheddar 165
Chelsham, badge from **8.11**
Chertsey Abbey 251
chess, chess-board, chess-pieces 171, 181, 224
Chessell Down 55, 61
Chester 123, 139, 152, 167
Cheviot Hills 41
Chew Stoke 83
Chiddingly, badge from **H.7**
children 29, 70, 83, 99, 124, 188, 226, 229
Chilperic 34
Chiswick 102
Christianity, Christian symbolism 6, 8, 13, 21, 45, 47, 51, 57, 59–62, 65, 68, 70, 74, 82, 97–8, 100–3, 108–13, 118, 128–9, 133, 141–3, 146, 165, 170, 187, 190–1, 193–6, 199, 209–11, 231, 238–59
Church, the 47, 54, 56, 141–2, 165, 178, 203–4, 211
churches, churchyards 21, 47, 50, 57, 59–60, 75, 80, 82, 84–5, 87, 92, 96–7, 100, 103, 107, 114–18, 124, 127, 131, 133, 136, 142, 145–6, 165–7, 169, 171–2, 200, 211, 237–8
cider 216
Clare cross 245
Clare, Bogo de 226
Clarendon Palace 189, 220
clasps 63, 143, 145, 178, 197, 200, 213–14, 251, 257
Clatchard Craig 45
Claughton Hall 117
Cliffe Hill 227
Cnut, King 141–2, 151, 157–8, 166–7
cobalt 88
Coddenham 97
Codex Aureus 129
coins 7, 10, 12, 19, 28, 31–5, 49–54, 57, 52–3, 66–7, 71, 77, 80, 83–5, 91, 93–4, 96–8, 103, 106, 108, 114–17, 119, 121–3, 127–8, 131–2, 140–5, 147, 151–3, 157–60, 163–4, 166–70, 178–81, 183, 196–202, 206–8, 211, 237–8, 257
 dinars 107
 dirhams 138–9, 149
 farthings 158, 178, 199
 halfpennies 158, 178, 185, 199
 kufic 116, 119, 123, 127
 late medieval gold 206, 222, 231, 233, 238, 247–8
 pennies 85, 106–7, 115, 136, 149, 152, 157, 180, 185, 199, 231
 sceattas 85, 87, 92–3, 96, 106, **3.5**
 siliquae 9, 11
 solidi 8–9, 11, 34, 49, 66, 77, 106, 131, 163
 stycas 107, 115, 125
 thrymsas (*trientes*, tremisses) 34, 36, 49, 51, 66–7, 77, 84
 see also mounts; weights
Colchester 214
collars 223, 244, 247, 249, 258
Collingbourne Ducis 22, 74
 brooch from **1.7**, **A.2**
columns 89
combs 32, 87, 96, 123, 135, 151, 160, 182
compensation 49, 51
cones 82
containers, *see* bags; boxes; caskets; purses
copper alloy 16, 18, 234–6
 see also vessels
Coptic 60
coral 187, 209, 213
cornelian 258
Cornwall, as kingdom 83, 116, 152
coronations 103, 141–3
coronets 221
costrels 175
Cottam 94, 96–7, 115, 140
Coventry 207, 215
 brooches from **7.1**
Cowdery's Down 72, 74
cowrie-shells 68, 74, 138
craftworkers 92, 94, 98–9, 103, 110, 129, 133, 145, 155, 160–5, 172, 195, 199, 218, 229, 231, 233–4
 see also smiths
Craig Phadrig 43, 58
Cranborne 113
 strap-end from **4.4**
crannog 122–3
cremations 15, 26, 32, 34–6, 62–3, 90
Crieff 82
cristobalite 53
Crondall 51, 67
cross patterns 57, 63, 68, 82, 98, 101, 113, 119, 132, 159
crosses, jet 215
 metal 42, 57, 65, 67, 98, 116, 141, 165, 197, 199, 231, 245, 253, 258, **2.16**, **8.5**, **8.7**
Crossmichael 127
crowns 43, 103, 132, 141–2, 170, 190, 192, 200, 226
Croydon 116, 119
crucibles 18, 47, 88, 93, 135, 160, 165
Crundale 63

crusades, crusaders 178, 193, 196, 204, 217
crystal 33, 78, 96, 129–31, 166, 188, 197, 213, 258
Cuddesdon 60, 97
Cuerdale 119
Culross 256
cupel dishes 135
cups 62–3, 99, 145, 147–8, 161–2, 166, 175, 191, 214, 216, 226, 237
Cura Pastoralis 129
curses 143
Cuthbert, Saint 67, 132
   cross of **2.16**
cylinders 68, 70
Cynethrith, Queen 106

Dagobert, King 66
Dàl Riata 43, 80, 82
Danegeld 128
Danelaw, the 139–40, 157
David I, King 179–8
Denham 253
deodand 213
Derby 214
Desborough 65
diamonds 213–14, 224, 249, 258
dies 97, 135, 138, 158, 199
Dinas Powys 18, 20, 40, 84
discs 43, 77, 118, 165, 167, 228, 251
Dolaucothi 8, 19
Domesday Book 157, 178
Donne family 247
draw-plate 182
Dublin 119, 122–3, 127–8, 138–9, 151, 158, 169, 185
Dumfries 207, 231
Dumnonia 83
Dunadd 18, 21, 41, 43, 45, 47, 58, 80
   objects from **1.6, 2.1, 2.5**
Dunbar 21, 42, 67, 78
Duncan II, King 179
Dunkeld 82
Dunstable 220, 224
   swan jewel **7.8**
Durrow, Book of 43, 45, 47
dyes 35, 97, 217

Eadbald, King 77
Eadwynn 143–5
Eanred 102
East Anglia, kingdom 57–8, 62, 74, 91–2, 106, 128, 132
Edmund, king of East Anglia 132
Edmund, king of England 132, 148
Edgar, King 141, 143
Edward I, King 206, 221
Edward II, King 210, 222
Edward III, King 211, 236
Edward IV, King 247–8, 257
Edward the Confessor, King 142–3, 159, 162, 170, 200, 206

Edward the Elder, King 132–3
Edward VI, King 258
Edwin, King 60, 62
Eigg 124
Eleanor of Castile, Queen 221, 226, 229
Ely 65
emeralds 68, 187, 189, 192, 201, 222, 233, 249
enamel 18, 33, 58, 93, 121, 129, 165, 193, 219–20, 223, 226, 238, 248
Eoba 106
Eofric 149
Essex, kingdom 49, 70, 91
Etheldreda, Saint 65
Ethelred, King 141, 145, 149
Eusebius 49, 54, 63
Exeter 19, 109, 116, 152, 172, 198, 215–16, 234, 237, 251, 255–6
   jug from **G**

Faccombe 165
Fairford, brooches from **1.10**
fairs 96, 157, 160, 166, 172, 178
Fanhope, Lord 249
Farnham 253
Fastolf, Sir John 249
fasteners, *see* clasps
Faunus 8–9
Faversham 36, 53–4, 63
   pendants from **2.7**
feasts, feasting 5, 7, 9, 20, 39, 60–1, 72, 84, 89, 107, 141, 201, 227, 250, 255
   see also halls
female/male, *see* gender
feuds, feuding 28, 51
Fillongley 196–7
Finglesham buckle 65, **2.15**
Fishpool hoard 238–46, 248, 251, 253, **8.3, 8.5–6**
Fiskerton 118
flabellum 82
flax 124
Flemings, Flemish 169, 180, 236–7
Flixborough 74, 94–7, 163–4
   objects from **3.8–9**
foederati 13
Folkingham 192–3
   brooch from **6.13**
forks 82, 226, 236
fortune-telling 28, 68, 70
Franks Casket 99–101, 114, **3.10**
French language 188, 190, 203, 238
Freya/Freyja 62, 124
Frithestan, Bishop 133
   vestments of **F.1–2**
Fuller brooch 110–3, 129, **4.3**
furs 192, 217, 221, 226, 257

Gainsford family 253, 258
   badge of **8.11**
gaming-counters, -pieces 31, 35, 124, 171

garnet, garnets 33, 53–5, 61–2, 67–8, 77, 129, 197, 212, 258, **2.10**
Gauber 115
Gaulcross 43
Gaveston, Piers 222
gems 51, 58, 98, 100, 142, 166, 187–92, 197, 200–3, 206, 212–14, 219–24, 226, 233, 238–44, 249
gender 12, 26, 28–9, 31, 45, 57, 94, 100, 117, 123–4, 136–7, 139, 145–7, 169, 171, 188–90, 192, 211, 213, 226–7, 244–8, 258
Gewissae, see Wessex
gifts, giving 12, 28, 31–2, 34, 45, 47, 55, 60, 63, 66, 84, 90, 100, 107–10, 125, 128–9, 131–3, 157, 165, 170–1, 185, 192, 200–1, 222, 224, 226, 234, 238–41
Gildas 12, 18, 39
gilding 16
ginger 226, 236–7
girdle-books 259
glass 16, 28, 35–6, 53, 57–8, 78, 84, 98, 101, 115–16, 131, 162, 172, 188–9, 199, 209, 212, 217, 219
  window- 101
  -working, -houses 39, 153
  see also vessels
Glastonbury 60, 88, 238
Gloucester 8, 13, 141, 160, 162, 185
Gloucester Abbey candlestick 172
Godgythe 147
  seal of **5.2**
Godstow 244
Godwin 146–7
  seal of **5.2**
gold 7, 12, 16, 18, 21, 33, 66, 68, 84–5, 97, 100, 107, 109, 135, 148, 169, 203, 206, 233
  leaf 97
  thread 87–8, 133, 245
Goldsbrough 119–20
Goltho 178
Gomeldon 230–1
Gower peninsula, vessel from **8.1**
Gravesend 116
Great Chesterford claw-beaker **1.12**
Greek language 61, 133, 191
Green Shiel 115
green-ginger, *see* ginger
Gregory, Pope 100, 129, 131
Grimston 161, 175
Grimston, Edward 247
Grosseteste, Bishop 201, 205
guilds, guild-halls 195, 199, 231, 250–1, 255
Guthrum, King 128

hack-silver 9, 16, 116, 119, 121–2, 127, 151–2, 167
haematite 135
hair 32, 106, 131, 142, 169, 172, 253
  -ornaments 171, 183, 226–7

halls 72, 100, 145, 185, 200, 224, 227, 234, 255
Halton Moor 167
Hambleden 207–8
hanging-bowls 43, 45, 58–61, 70, 74, 80, 102, **2.13**
Harford Farm 70, 77–8, 84, 98
  brooch from **3.3**
harness 57, 66, 120, 153–4
  pendants 193, 201, 230, **6.17**
Harold, King 142–3, 169
Hartlepool 65, 93
hats 227, 247, 253, 258
headdresses 56, 65, 88, 138
healing 28, 68, 70, 211
hearp 57
Hebrew language 191
heirlooms 16, 27, 62–3, 108, 131, 145, 167
helmets 61, 103, 141, 223
Hen Gastell 18, 84
Henry I, King 172, 178–9, 193, 204
Henry II, King 191–2
Henry III, King 200, 206, 220
Henry IV, King 220, 226
Henry VI, King 245, 249, 251, 259
Henry VII, King 249, 251, 258
Henry VIII, King 247–8, 258
heraldry, heraldic designs 192–3, 198, 216, 222, 234, 241, 256
Hereford 208–9
Hereford, bishop of 248
Hexham Abbey 101
hides 20, 139
Highdown 12, 16–17
Hild, Saint 65, 93
hoards, hoarding 7–9, 34, 43, 51, 62, 67, 80–2, 85, 87, 98, 108, 113–17, 119–24, 126–8, 145, 149–52, 158, 166–7, 169, 179, 183, 185, 187–9, 196–7, 206–9, 213, 219, 231, 238–46, 248, 257, **1.2–3, 2.4, 3.4, 4.7, 5.5, 5.9, 5.13, 6.10, 7.2, 8.3–6**
Holbein 247, 258
Holberrow Green 167
  disc from **F.3**
Holbrook 257
hones 29, 91, 138, 140
Honorius, Emperor 11
hooked tags 114, 166, **3.5**
hooks 253–4, 257
horn, horns 85, 89, 149, 161, 235
  blast- 89, 123
  drinking- 31, 57, 63, 145, 147–8, 165–6, 169
Horndon-on-the-Hill 199
horses 57, 66, 84, 117, 124–5, 145, 153, 155–7, 166, 172, 204, 213, 217
  see also harness
Hoxne 7–8, 11
Hunterston brooch 45, 47, 82, 126, **2.6**
hunting 45, 63, 70, 75
  -dogs 20
Hywel Dda 123

Icklingham, brooch from **3.5**
Icklington collar 249
identity 5, 15, 18, 27–8, 32, 39, 42, 83, 117, 124, 136–40, 151–2, 169
inaugurations 132, 141
 see also coronations
incense 100, 128
Ine, King 83–5
Ingelrii 149
ingots:
 gold 47, 51, 116–17, 139
 silver 116, 119, 126–7, 150, 163, 167, 179, 183, 185
 tin 20
inns, inn-keepers 214, 216, 218
inscriptions 18, 20, 51, 94, 97–9, 100, 102–3, 106, 108–9, 120, 126, 129, 133, 143, 146–7, 149, 158, 165, 167, 188–9, 197, 199, 200, 213, 224, 226–8, 231, 234, 238–48, 250–3, 257–8
inventories 216–17, 224, 228, 234, 249, 258
Iona 21, 47, 151, 183
 objects from **6.8**
Ipsden 110
Ipswich 75–7, 88–9, 92, 106, 115, 158
 sherd from **3.7**
iron 20, 31, 33, 35, 47, 55, 135, 154
Isabella, Queen 222
ivory 53, 68, 74, 100, 129

Jarlshof 127
Jarrow 93
Jedburgh 151
jet 138, 143, 162, 209
jewellery 7–8, 57–8, 65, 67, 88, 179, 213–15, 218, 221, 226, 257, 259
Jews, Jewish 187, 191, 196
John of Gaunt 223
John of Sicily 205
John, King 197, 200–1, 204
Julius Caesar 57
Justinian, Emperor 19
Jutes, Jutish 26–8, 33

Kells, Book of 82
Kenilworth 225
Kennington 222
Kent, earl of 226
Kent, kingdom of 26–7, 32–3, 36, 49, 53, 55, 57, 62–5, 70
keys 164–5, **3.5**
Kidwelly 247, 250
Kiloran Bay 125
King's Lynn, *see* Lynn
Kingston-on-Thames 34, 153–4
Kirk Deighton, ring from **H.1**
Kirkwall 181
Knaresborough 217
knighthood, knights 155, 172, 179, 181–2, 193, 200–1, 203–4, 213–14, 217, 221–2, 238, 247

knives, knife fittings 22, 31–2, 70, 83, 93, 102, 129, 136, 146, 163, 217–18, 226, 228–9, 231, 235–6, 250, **7.10**
knots, gold 222

laces, lace-ends 228–9
ladles 124
land 85, 93, 107–8, 124, 129, 139, 145, 167, 169, 171, 179, 200, 204, 217–18, 224, 231, 256
landing-places 20, 78
 see also beach-markets
Langhale 161
Langhope 208
Langland, William 211, 213
 see also Piers Plowman
lapidaries 187, 191, 209, 226
Lark Hill, Worcester, hoard 188, 196–7, **6.10**
Latin language 20, 33, 43, 80, 97–9, 100, 188, 190–1
lava 89, 91, 93, 96
Laverstock 189, 200, 216
 ring from **4.1**
laws, lawcodes 29, 51, 54, 70, 83, 85, 89, 183–5, 217–19, 226, 231, 256–7
Lay Subsidies 204, 213–15, 217–18, 232, 234, 256
lead 7, 20–1, 35, 135, 139, 200
leather 20, 49, 162–3, 175, 228–9
 see also hides; tanning
Lechlade 70, 84
 grave and pendant from **2.17**
Leicester 209, 256
Lewes 166
Lewis 181
Lichfield 106
Lilla Howe 92, 118
Lincoln 59, 138–9, 148, 160, 167, 174–5, 178
 mount from **5.4**
Lindisfarne 67, 115–16
Lindores 151
Lindsey, kingdom 97
Linton Heath 35
Liudhard, Bishop 50
liveries 201, 205
Llanbedrgoch 41, 121–3
 brooch from **2.2**
Llanelen 152
Llangors 122–3
Llantrithyd 197–8
 ring from **6.16**
Llywelen, Gruffyd ap 183
lockets 245, **8.7**
log-boats 57, 63, 66
Lombard letters 190
London 13, 20, 75, 85, 88, 90, 92, 102, 115–16, 128, 131, 133, 158, 161–3, 167, 169, 172, 174–5, 189, 192, 195, 198–9, 209, 211–12, 216, 219, 221, 224, 226,

228–9, 233–4, 236–7, 241, 244, 247, 253, 255–6, 258
  objects from **3.2**, **5.9**, **5.11–13**
London, bishop of 142, 214–15, 221
Longbury Bank 18, 20, 60, 84
Lot's Hole 96–7
Louis the Pious, Emperor 106
Loveden Hill hanging-bowl **2.13**
Luda 77
Ludgershall 217
Luttrell Psalter 211, 214, 227
Lydford 152
Lynn 172, 212, 214, 216, 226
lyres 57, 61

magic, magical power 203
  see also charms
magnesite 53
Maiden Castle 83
male/female, *see* gender
Man, Isle of 122, 127, 241
Manchester brooch 219–20, **7.7**
mancuses 87, 107, 129, 131, 145, 147–8, 158
manuscripts 43, 45, 65, 97–8, 100, 102, 113, 129, 133, 136, 141, 148, 154, 157, 162, 165, 171–3, 211
Marbode, Bishop 187, 203
marriage 12, 27–8, 47, 55–6
  see also rings
Marshall, William 201
Mary, Queen 258
Matlaske 253
Mawgan Porth 152, 164
mazers 214, 250
mead 89
men, *see* gender
Meols 19–20, 122
Mercia, Mercians 82–3, 89, 97–8, 102, 106, 108, 115, 118, 120, 129
mercury 36
metal-detecting, -detectorists 2–3, 94, 139–40, 166, 198, 230
metalworking 17–18, 20–1, 35–6, 40–3, 45, 47, 58, 80, 88, 92–3, 97, 120, 123, 135, 139, 157–8, 160, 164–5, 180, 182, 195, 198, 207–9
  see also smiths
Middle Harling 154, 164
Middleham 245, 248
Milton 63, 68
Milton Keynes 158
Minster Lovell jewel 131, **4.10**
mints, minting, moneyers 8, 11, 49, 51, 66–7, 77, 91–2, 106–7, 123, 132, 135–6, 152, 157–8, 167, 199, 206, 233
mirrors 211–12, 225, 230, 248, **7.5**
money, moneyers, *see* mints
Monk Sherborne buckle **2.12**
Monkton brooch 67, **B.2**
Monkwearmouth 93, 102
Montfort, Simon de 220

mortars 83
mosaics 100
Mote of Mark 42
motif-pieces 65, 80, 138, 152, **2.5**
moulds 18, 21, 36, 41, 43, 45, 58, 80, 92–3, 139, 157–8, 180, 195, 198, 207–9, **1.6**, **2.1**, **6.6**
mounts 40, 71, 74, 82, 98, 115, 117, 120, 123, 165, 167, 227
Mucking 13, 16, 36, 73–4, 88
  belt-set from **1.4**
murex 97

Nant Col, aquamanile from **6.9**
Neckham, Alexander 191, 204
necklaces, necklets 28, 49, 58, 65, 125, 131, 209, 245–6
  see also rings
needles 174, **6.3**
New College, Oxford, brooch 49–50, **8.8**
New Radnor 185
Newcastle-upon-Tyne 197
Newport, Dyfed 185
Newton Moor 120
niello 33, 53, 113, 143, 207, 253
Norrie's Law hoard 43, **2.4**
North Elmham 96
North Marston 209
North Warnborough, ring from **H.3**
Northampton 96, 160
Northumbria, Northumbrians 60, 62, 66–7, 82–3, 92, 107, 115
Norwich 53, 139, 157, 160–1, 169, 172, 188–9, 200, 209, 228–9, 234, 237, 246, 251–3, 255
  objects from **8.9**
  seal-ring from near **B.5**
Nottingham 178

Odin 128
Offa, King 89, 106–7, 149
ogam 43
Old Sarum 193, 217
olive oil 20, 39
orbs 142–3, 170, 206
Orkney islands 43
Ormside bowl 101, 118
Orsett 70
Orton Scar brooch 120, **4.6**
Oshere 103
ostrich feathers 223
Oswine, King 66
Oving 167
Oxford 147, 154, 160, 165, 178, 249
  objects from **5.3**, **5.7**, **5.10**
Oxwich brooch 219–20, **7.7**

Paecca 29
pails 57, 61
Pakenham 153–4
Paris, Matthew 201

Paston family 241, 244, 246, 248–9
Patching 10–12, 16, 19, 51
  objects from **1.3**
paternosters, *see* beads
peacocks 13, 226
pearl, pearls 65, 209, 220, 222–3, 227, 245, 248–9
pendants 16, 33–4, 50, 55, 57–8, 65, 67, 70, 75, 77–8, 96, 113, 116–18, 136, 138, 165, 167, 209, 244–6, 251–3, 258–9, **2.7**, **2.17**, **8.5**, **8.7**, **C.2**
Penhallam 217
Pennylands 96
Pentney brooches 113–15, **D, E**
Percy, Henry 226
perfumes 16
peridots 238
Perth 180–1, 195, 198, 204, 207–8, 211, 229, 255
  objects from **6.2**, **6.5–6**, **6.15**, **7.1**, **7.5**, **7.10**
Pewsey 24, 30
  objects from **1.8**, **1.11**
pewter 16, 35, 93, 158, 215, 228–9, 234–7, 255–6
phyllite 138
Picts, Pictish, Pictland 7, 42–5, 62, 80–2, 102, 119, 123, 128
Piers Plowman 211, 213, 224, 226
pilgrims, pilgrimages 20, 209–11, 213, 218
pilgrims' badges, *see* badges
pins 94–6, 115–16, 172, 180, 253, **3.5**
  ball-headed 124
  disc-headed 75, 97–8, 101, **3.9**
  garnet-headed 74
  globular-headed 166
  hair- 171
  hand- 43, **2.4**
  Irish 84
  knobbed 120
  linked 70, 87–8, 102
  ringed 123, 127–8, 138–9, 149, 151
  spiral-headed 92, **3.5**
  stick- 151
  wire-headed 257
Pitney 167
Plantagenet 195, 220
plaques 43, 94, 97–8, 100, 123, 136, **3.8**
plate:
  gold and silver 7, 9, 16, 43, 60, 80, 85, 101, 167, 200, 213–15, 221, 223–6, 229, 237–8, 249, 259, **1.2**, **3.4**
  pewter 16, 216–17, **7.6**
pledges, pledging 8, 201, 206, 222, 249
Pleshey 223
Plymouth 209
poll taxes 232, 256
pommels 63, 80, 101–2, 131, 148–9, 152, 166, 169, **3.4**, **3.11**
Poole 238
popes 131, 192, 200–1
  see also Gregory

porphyry 89, 169
porpoises 82
portraits 224, 247, 258
pots, pottery 20, 49, 72–3, 87, 96, 133, 140, 160–1, 169, 174–8, 180–1, 185–7, 191, 199–200, 231, 234, 236, 255–6, 259, **6.4**
  British: bar-lug 152; Charnwood Forest ware 34–6, 73, 91; Cistercian ware 255; grass-marked 83, 152, 181; Ham green ware 185; Ipswich ware 90, 93–4, 96, 115, **3.6**, **3.7**; Maxey-type ware 74; organic-tempered 34–5, 73, 93; Rattray ware 151; Romano-British 35, 100; sandy 152; shell-filled 93, 133; Souterrain ware 128; sparsely glazed 174–8, 190, 199; Stamford glazed 160, 174–5, 180, **5.10**; Stamford red-painted 133, 160; Tudor green 255
  imports: amphoras 59; blue-grey 175; Dutch redware 237; E-ware 39–40, 45, 49, 78, 83; French post-Norman Conquest 175, 185, 199, 237; Low Countries 175, 180, 236; lustreware 256; maiolica 256; Mediterranean 19–21, 39–40, 61, 178; porcelain 256; Saintonge polychrome 216–17, **G**; stoneware 236–7, 255–6; Tating ware 89, 93; wheel-made 73, 89
pouches, *see* purses
prolific sites 97, 107
Puddlehill 74
punch-marks 15, 26, 33
purses 28, 51, 70, 78, 83, 218, 227, 229, 250
  -frames 253

quernstones 89, 93, 115, 232

Raglan 241; ring from **H.6**
Ragnald 136, 139
raids, raiding 7, 9, 12, 20, 28, 43, 55, 57, 64, 82, 107, 116, 138, 151, 154, 167
Rainham 63
Ramsbury 92, 97
ransoms 129, 196
Rattray 181–2, 209, 217
  objects from **6.7**, **7.3**
Raunds 169
Raven banner 128
Reading 117, 124, 167
Red Wharf Bay 122
  rings from **4.7**
Redwald, King 62
reeves 75, 83
relics, reliquaries 45, 61, 68, 96, 100, 165, 244–6, 253, 258, **8.7**
renders, rents 20, 54, 85, 157, 161, 169, 200, 232, 256
Repton 87, 103, 116–17, 119, 136
  sculpture from **3.13**
Rhuddlan 152, 166, 183
Richard I, King 185, 188, 196
Richard II, King 206, 220, 223–6, 250–1, 253
Richard III, King 241, 245, 251, 253

rings 10–11, 53, 70–1, 87, 94, 103, 116–17, 119, 122, 126–9, 136, 145, 147–51, 158, 165, 167, 171, 179, 183, 185, **1.3**, **4.7**, **5.3**
  arm- 7, 18, 27, 87, 120, 127, 133, 136, 147, 151
  ear 77, 147
  finger- 7, 18, 51, 77, 87, 102, 108–10, 116–17, 120–1, 136, 147, 151, 167, 169, 172, 183, 187–92, 197–203, 207, 213–15, 222–6, 230–1, 238–49, 256–9, **2.9**, **3.2**, **4.1**, **6.10**, **6.16**, **7.1–2**, **8.2–4**, **8.6**
  gimmel 201, 258
  glass 162
  marriage- 188, 203, 227–8, 258–9
  Odin's 128
  seal- 51, 53, 188, 197, 213, 241, 244–5, **2.9**, **8.3**, **8.6**, **B.5**, **H.5**
  wire 78
ring-money 51, 119, 151, 179, 185
robbery, *see* theft
Rocklea Sands 245, 251
rods 116, 167
Rogart 82
rosaries, *see* beads, paternoster
Roundway Down 70, 97
rubies 200–1, 213, 219, 221–4, 247–9
runes, runic 33, 61, 97–9, 102, 126
Rupertus Cross 100

S, SS, *see* collars
saddles 138
St Alban's 20, 188
St Andrews 180
St David's 120
St Ninian's 47, 80–2
  hoard from **3.4**
Sandal 241
Sandford 165
Sandtun 89, 96
Santon Downham 117
  brooches from **4.5**
sapphires 68, 183, 187, 189, 197–8, 200–1, 212–13, 246, 253
sardonyx 188
Sarre 67
  brooches from **A.1**, **B.1**
scabbard-bosses, -studs 61, 75, 84, **2.18**
scabbards 10, 13, 75, 162–3, 169, 229, **5.12**, **8.9**
Scar 124
Scarborough 200
sceptres 61, 132, 142, 206
schist 138
Scilly, Isles of 152
Scone 229
Scotland, kingdom of 58, 62, 124, 128, 141, 149–53, 179–83, 200, 206–9, 229, 233
Scotti 21
Scotton, ring from **H.5**
scourge 115, 124
scrap 28, 35, 40, 70, 107, 115

sculptures 80, 102–3, 116, 136, 138, 165, 188
seals, seal-dies 51, 53, 108, 142, 146–8, 169, 179–80, 185, 188, 193, 197, 199, 206, 213, 216, 230, 241–5, **5.2**, **6.5**, **B.5**, **H.6**
seax knives 70, 75, 106, 163
Sevington 114, 116
Sewerby 41
shale 162
sharks' teeth 214, 221
sheets, metal 40
shells 53
  see also cowrie-
Shetland Islands 123, 128
shield-pendants 74
shields, shield-makers 26, 29, 61, 124–5, 148, 166, 169, 193
ship-burials 51, 56–7, 61–2, 124–5
shoes 162–3, 229, **5.11**
shoulder-clasps 61–2
Shrewsbury 214–15
shrine fittings 123–4, 154, 165, 183, 188
shrouds 87, 92
Sigebereht 102, 129, 163
Sigurd 68
Sihtric, King 119
silk 70, 85, 122, 129, 133, 138, 162, 172, 181, 227–9, 257
silver 7, 12, 16, 18, 20–1, 33, 43, 67, 80, 84–5, 97, 106, 114, 128, 135, 152, 167, 179, 185, 196, 203, 233–4
Sittingbourne 102, 129
Skaill hoard 149–51, **5.5**
slate 20
slaves 12, 20, 31, 57, 78, 117, 124
slick-stones 123, 162
smiths 15, 28–9, 34–6, 41, 47, 53–4, 58, 61, 67, 77, 93, 99–100, 102, 112–15, 129, 142–3, 149, 157, 165–7, 183, 191, 212, 216, 220, 227–8, 238, 253, 256
Snape 51, 53, 56–7, 63, 66
  ring from **2.9**
Snargate 250
Snorri the tax-gatherer 193
soapstone 127, 136, 138
Soberton 167
sock 136
South Cadbury 18, 39, 40, 42
South Newbald 85, 94
Southampton 75, 78, 84, 87–8, 90, 92, 94, 97, 103, 106, 115, 158, 164, 175, 197, 215–16, 237, 251, 256
  objects from **3.1**, **6.16**, **7.6**, **C.2–3**
Southwark 133
spangles 195, **6.15**
Spearhafoc, Bishop 142, 165
spices 16, 20, 172
Spileman 166
Spong Hill 36
spoons 7, 8, 11, 43, 56, 60, 78, 82, 162, 183, 191, 197, 214–16, 228, 259, **4.11**, **6.8**
spurs 153–5, 171–2, 180, **6.2**

Stafford 160
staffs 62, 141–3, 170
Stamford 133, 160, 175
  pot made in **5.10**
Stanwick, buckle from **1.1**
Stephen, King 178–9
Stewarts 233
Steyning 158
stirrups 154–6, **5.7**
  -mounts 154–8, **5.8**
stones, *see* gemstones
Storr Rock 127, 151
strap-distributors 182, **6.7**
strap-ends 8, 15, 82, 88, 92, 94–6, 98, 110, 113–15, 118, 125, 133, 138–40, 144, 153, 162, 165–6, **3.5, 4.4, 4.11**
Stratford-upon-Avon 197
Strickland brooch 113
strips, metal 96, 171, 183, **6.8**
studs 40, 98, 100, 116, 131, 189, 199
Style I 26, 31, 33, 40
Style II 40, 42, 58, 62, 98, 102
styles:
  Borre 140, 152, 157
  gripping beast 117, 124
  Jellinge 138, 143, 152, 157, 166
  Mammen 149, 157
  quoit-brooch 12–16, 18, 26, 33, 35
  Renaissance 258–9
  Ringerike 143, 152, 157, 164
  Romanesque 132–3, 189, 193
  Trewhiddle 113–17, 120, 123–4, 138, 147, 152–3
  Urnes 138, 143, 157
  Winchester 133, 157, 162, 165
styli 94–6, 174, **3.9**
subsidies 9, 12, 34, 43, 47, 51, 53, 64, 66, 116
sumptuary law 217–19, 226, 231, 256–7
sundials 165
Sussex, kingdom 27
Sutton 143–4, 167, 169
Sutton Hoo 51, 53, 57–9, 61–7, 74, 103, 106, 145, 152; buckle from **2.11**
Swallowcliffe 97
swans, Swan Knights 220, 223
  swan jewel **7.8**
Swaythling 164
Swein 166–7
Swindon 74
swords, sword-makers 22, 26, 29, 31, 35, 57–9, 63–4, 93–4, 102–3, 106, 109, 114, 117–18, 120, 124–5, 131, 140, 142–3, 148–9, 154, 165–7, 169–71, 200, 206, 217, **1.11, 4.2**
  see also pommels

tafl 151
tags, *see* hooked tags
Talnotrie 115, 123

Tamworth 96
tanning 97, 135
Taplow 60, 63, 97, 103, 132, 145
Tassilo, Duke 101
Tattershall Thorpe 67–70, 75, 88, 99
  objects from **2.10, 2.18–20, C.1**
Taunton 158
tents 145
textile production 34–5, 69, 74, 96, 123–4, 137, 160, 162, 164, 257
textiles 63, 68, 97–8, 100, 122–3, 132–3, 145, 162, 180–1, 192, 217, 223–9, 249, 257
Thame hoard 238–45, **8.2, 8.4**
theft 7, 70, 132, 143, 197, 247–8
Theodoric 142
Theodosius II, Emperor 77
Theophilus 191
Thetford 7–9, 11, 18, 158, 160–1, 175
Thomas of Lancaster 210–11, 220, 251
Thomas of Woodstock 223–4
Thor 61
Thor's hammers 118, 123, 132, 136, 139
Threave 245; reliquaries from **8.7**
tin 18, 20, 35, 152, 198, 209, 234
tin-lead alloys, *see* pewter
Tintagel 20
toadstones 187, 238, 258
toilet sets 77–8, 246
tokens 211
tolls 75, 85, 91, 195
Tom a'Bhuraich 183, 187
tools 31–2, 69–70, 93, 99–100, 117, 123–4, 145, 187, 213, 228, **2.19–20, C.1**
Tor Abbey 259
torcs 43
Torksey 139
tournaments 192, 223, 249
toys 229
trading-places 85
  see also beach-markets; *wics*
Traprain Law 9, 11, 16, 21, 60
  hoard from **1.2**
treasure 12, 16, 34, 51, 60, 65, 114, 119, 185, 213
Trewhiddle 113, 115–16
tribute 32, 45, 47, 63, 85, 116, 128, 151–2, 170
tufa 62
turquoises 238
tusks 103
Tutbury 213
tweezers 32, 97–8, 164

Ulfberht 149
Undley 33, 57
Unst 127
Upavon, brooch from **3.5**
Upper Poppleton 114
urbanism, urbanisation 133–6, 139, 157, 166, 178, 185, 199

vessels, copper-alloy 16, 60–1, 191, 213, 234, 236, **6.9**, **8.1**
   glass 16, 20–1, 36, 40, 57, 63, 77, 83, 88–9, 93, 162, 216–17, 236, 256, **1.12**
   gold and silver, *see* plate
   tin-lead, *see* pewter
   see also hanging-bowls
vikings, viking 82, 84, 107, 110, 114–40, 147, 152, 154, 158, 167
vittae 88
votives, votive offerings 40, 42, 127
   see also water deposition

Wales 16–17, 20, 43, 58, 83, 120–3, 139, 141, 152–3, 183–7, 206, 233, 241
Wallingford 146
Walsingham 209, 251, 259
Waltham Abbey 188, 197
Walton 35
warbands, *see* raids
Wareham 117, 149, 169–70
Warminster 131
Watchfield 51
   balance-set from **2.8**
water deposition 118, 154, 211
Water Eaton 8
Waterford 189
weapons 29, 32–3, 57, 63, 66, 100, 102, 106–7, 117, 119–20, 124, 127, 143–5, 151, 158, 163, 166
   see also shields; swords
weights 9, 11, 51, 70, 85, 87, 107, 116–17, 120–1, 123–4, 127, 143–5, 151, 158, 163, 166, **2.8**
Weland 99–100, 149
Wellingborough 190
Wendover 147
wergilds 83
Wessex, West Saxons 40, 55, 67, 70, 82, 92, 97, 109–13, 115, 120, 131–2, 141, 193
West Gilling 118
West Heslerton 28, 35
West Lindsey, ring from **F.5**
West Stow 74, 88
Westbury 178–9, 199, 230
Westminster 102, 200, 224, 229
Westness 125
   grave assemblage from **4.9**
Weymouth 131
whales, whale-bone 99–100, 123, 145, 166
Wharram Percy 87, 89–90, 93–7, 140, 164, 229–30
Wheathampstead 60

whetstones 29, 61, 122, 136, 213
Whitby 65, 85, 93, 98, 100, 209
Whitecleugh chain **2.3**
Whithorn 21, 47, 85, 128, 151, 181
Whorlton 7
wic sites 75–8, 85, 88–93, 96, 107, 115, 157
Wight, Isle of, kingdom 27, 57
William I, King 142–3, 159, 169, 179
William II, King 220
wills 145–8, 165, 169–70, 228, 234, 247, 258–9
Wilton diptych 224–6, **7.9**
Winchester 92, 97, 100, 133, 138, 141–2, 145, 147, 158, 162, 164–7, 172–6, 183, 195, 198–200, 209, 212, 228, 249, 255
   objects from **3.5**, **4.11**, **6.3**
Windsor 20, 39, 45, 85, 89, 172, 200, 216–17, 236, 255
   pommel from **3.11**
wine 20, 39, 45, 85, 89, 172, 200, 216–17, 236, 255
Winnall Down 70
wire 16, 33, 45, 53–4, 75, 78, 92, 94, 110, 115, 124, 140, 145, 147–9, 154, 163, 165, 167, 182–3, 188–9, 213, 246, 251
women, *see* gender
Wonston, brooch from **1.10**
wood, wooden objects 21, 49, 63, 74, 82, 100, 161–2, 175, 209, 235, 255
Woodstock Forest 178
Worcester 178
   see also Lark Hill
Worcester, prior of 249
Wragby 258
Wrexham 185
wrist-clasps 27–8, 35
Writtle 190, 226
Wroxeter 8, 18, 21
Wudeman 143–5, 167
   brooch of **5.1**
Wulfric 149, 165–6
Wulfsige, Bishop 129
Wychwood Forest 178
Wynflaed 145–7, 165
wyrms 45, 102

Y Gododdin 43
Yeavering 49, 71, 93
York 66, 75, 82, 92–4, 98, 100, 103, 115, 119, 122, 132–40, 143, 148, 151, 158, 160–2, 166, 172, 174–5, 189–90, 193, 198, 207, 209, 228, 234, 237, 256
   objects from **3.12**, **4.12**, **6.11**, **7.1**